To
Robin
love

Lucinda

10/25/22

Somewhere

Somewhere

In The South Pacific

The story of a young couple separated
by the Second World War,
as told in their letters and journals.

Edited and Compiled by
Leina'ala Jackie de Roxtro

Cover design by the author
Photo by Joey Pistachio from Pexels.com, a free website.

ISBN: 978-0-578-93692-5 (paperback)

Library of Congress Control Number: 2021912626

Table of Contents

Foreword

Somewhere is a multi-faceted endeavor that grips the reader from several angles, all of which provide a fascinating, educational, enlightening, and moving depiction of World War 2 from the perspective of a sailor stationed in the South Pacific, knowing every day might be his last but never missing an opportunity to keep his family both comforted and informed to the extent he could, given extensive censorship.

It is an epistolary epic in which two happily married people forge an even stronger and bonded relationship almost entirely through letters exchanged during a world war. It shows clearly that while the ravages of war can be horrendous, both physically and emotionally, true love indeed has the power to overcome.

Somewhere provides, as well, an illuminating history of the war in the South Pacific as well as the broader historical context of that war. This is accomplished through the masterful "editing" by Leina'ala Jackie de Roxtro. I put "editing" in quotes because the term does not do justice to the totality of the effort that the book represents. It is a truly artful interspersion of personal correspondence and a history of the War, both in the Pacific and elsewhere. (For example, who today is aware that in 1889 Japan's first official constitution named England, Holland, France and the United States as official enemies?)

"Editor" Leina'ala's approach to and treatment of the subject matter capture both the beauty and the frustration that comes from mailed letters and a personal diary. The beauty is having something you can hold in your hands and read over and over again. The frustration comes from waiting possibly long periods of time between correspondences. In wartime, the worlds of both the sender and the receiver could have changed significantly in that lag time.

In today's world of instant communication, it is difficult to imagine a time when letters received and sent were the main ways people kept in touch. During wartime those letters were particularly important, keeping the thread of connection between fighting soldiers and those back home worried for their safety. The exigencies of war dictated that, for the soldier-correspondent, only positivity was permitted. Although free to chronicle such mundane events as torrential rains and insect infestations, he could not report on the progress—or the lack thereof—of the day-in and day-out performance of his duties. This has to have been frustrating in the extreme to his beloved wife, who in turn had to present an almost idyllic picture of home so as not to be a depressant on the sailor's morale.

In a nutshell, Leina'ala's book documents how a marriage can not only continue but also be strengthened during wartime through a courtship in letters. We as readers of Johnny's and Lou's decades-old correspondence are privileged to witness how, even in the face of war, the power of love can be triumphant. We become a part of their ongoing romance, to follow wartime events provided in historical context and, at the same time, mourn the lost art of letter-writing. Johnny's letters epitomize the poignant passion that poured out of servicemen who were shipped off to war, never knowing which correspondence would be their last. Mail was slow and spotty during wartime. But that didn't stop homesick sailors, Johnny included, from penning love letters by the thousands.

In sum, Leina'ala's book provides a welcome reminder that intimacy and connection lived on--indeed thrived--alongside and in spite of the divisiveness of battle.

James B. Craver
President and CEO
James B. Craver & Associates, LLC, (law firm)
Dover, MA

In Remembrance

This book is dedicated to my father
John de Roxtro
February 12, 1912–December 17, 1977

Who fought in the Second World War with the
15th United States Naval Construction Battalion
In the South Pacific
from 1943 to 1945,

And to all of the courageous men and women,
past and present, of the
United States Armed Forces

Preface

In the months after my mother Lucia passed, my husband Michael and I cleaned out her half of the duplex house where I grew up and where she had lived alone for 31 years after my father died, an effort that took many months of sifting through everything my mom ever owned. The only way to walk through the dank cellar of the 100-year-old house was by way of a narrow path that led from the rickety stairs to the furnace, long since converted from coal to gas. Having finally discarded the stacks of deteriorating old newspapers and magazines, I reached the antique, dilapidated dining room chest. It was beautiful albeit badly scratched with intricately carved designs on the drawer fronts and legs and a royal blue velvet-lined silverware drawer musty with age.

As a small child, I was not allowed to venture near the chest. Once when I was four, I could no longer resist and quietly opened the small doors on the bottom. A thrill ran through me as I found the treasure! It was a very large wishbone painted with beautiful, shiny, dark red nail polish, a pretty pink ribbon carefully tied around its neck. The wishbone was most likely a keepsake from a special occasion, perhaps the Thanksgiving of 1941 when my parents became engaged. Mom never said. I had just learned about wishbones, and I experimented with how far apart I could spread the arms. When it inevitably broke, I quietly secreted it back amongst the other things within the chest. When my transgression was discovered, I was duly punished.

After years of languishing in the cellar, the chest was now filled with useless junk. Remnants of the wishbone were gone. I sat on a low stool to clean out the space behind those small doors and noticed that a light blue suitcase of the old cardboard variety had been cached on the floor beneath, pushed back to the wall. I was surprised to find the beautifully written love letters that my father had written to my mother while he was stationed in the South Pacific with the Seabees during WW2. At first I thought that I would merely transcribe all the letters and Mom's daily journal entries so they could all be in one place, but it wasn't long before the idea of a book was born.

It was when my dear friend Nani Michi McCreary told me she had had a dream in which my father appeared and asked her to tell me that he wanted to be remembered, I understood the monumental task that lay before me.

Introduction

The Courtship and Marriage

Upon high school graduation Lucia had secured a clerical position in the offices of The Town of Morristown, New Jersey. John had been working for the Water Department for a number of years. For John it was love at first sight. It took him awhile before he built up the courage to ask her out, but once he did, he was persistent. My mother played hard to get but John pursued her intensely. Mom told me how one day after work while she was walking home he followed her in the Town truck, beeping the horn until, embarrassed, she finally agreed to get in and ride with him. They were married on February 15, 1942, not long after the bombing of Pearl Harbor.

Lucia

At age 23, soon after she and John were married, Lucia became pregnant with their first child and lived, together with her mother and four sisters, in the house built by my grandfather, Raphael Petrone at 219 Speedwell Avenue. "Lou" was the second daughter and fifth sibling in an Italian American family. There were four brothers: Joe, Louis (whom they called Gene), and Mike, who were all older, married, and living elsewhere. Ralph (the youngest at 19), was drafted into the Army. The four sisters were Ann, Lucia, Joan (whom they called "Fanny"), and Grace, age 11, and still in school. Their mother Mary had been widowed three years prior and worked as a seamstress in a local coat factory. My great grandparents, Lucia (pronounced LuGEEa and called Mama G), and Giuseppe Scinto (whom we called Tadone), lived in a rented house on Race Street in the then Italian section of Morristown known as "The Hollow."

When John left for overseas in 1942, Lou began keeping a daily journal. The journals of 1942 and 1943 did not survive; however, the journal entries from 1944 and 1945 together with the letters from my father provide the content of this book. I have kept as closely as possible to the original writings, warts and all.

John

I loved my father dearly, and in my early years we had a very special connection. In his letters he often said that when he came home from the war he would spend as much time with me as he could, and he kept that promise. Almost every night was spent playing with me and my toys, reading to me, or drawing pictures of animals. He constructed wonderful things with my Tinker Toy, and I especially remember the Ferris wheel. As I outgrew my toys and became a teenager, Dad and I became distant even though he continued to engage me in sports like tennis, badminton, or even a 'catch' in the yard. But we didn't talk about things. Mom and I had a difficult relationship, and I felt awkward going to my Dad for solace and support. Instead I withdrew. Dad didn't push the issue, and we never developed a close adult relationship, though I continued to love him dearly.

As outgoing and sociable as he was, Dad was quite inwardly reserved and rarely expressed any feelings. I never realized that he was a whirlwind of passion, love, and emotion. Through his letters I have come to know him in a different way, and I appreciate him even more now. This book is a tribute to my father John de Roxtro, Electrician's Mate First Class (EM1/c), 15th Construction Battalion, United States Naval Reserve and all-around greatest Dad.

The Seabees (CBs-Construction Battalion)

The founding of the Seabees was a part of

unprecedented American military history. The CBs, or Seabees, were an armed construction brigade responsible for creating necessary infrastructure for military support. Prior to January 5, 1942, construction crews were purely civilian, unarmed, and vulnerable to enemy attack. Under international law, civilians are not permitted to resist enemy attack and are, therefore, subject to summary execution as guerrillas. It soon became evident that these civilian construction crews for the first time in our history were to be enlisted, armed, and trained in weaponry and warfare.

The Seabees toiled on amid deplorable conditions on the newly recaptured and thickly jungled Pacific islands to build air strips, water towers, utility lines, communications, and lodgings for the men. The tropical heat, subsistence level food, around the clock exertion in extreme weather, sometimes in blinding monsoon rains and wind and knee-deep mud, disease, and being shot at, all combined to make life miserable. Mosquitoes, an unrelenting enemy, brought their own weapon, malaria which was a common affliction among the men.

Mail was sporadic, arriving in bunches perhaps twice a week if the carriers were lucky enough to get through. The men waited longingly for letters and photographs from home and news of loved ones thousands of miles away. The main thing from which the men suffered was homesickness, an affliction that badly affected my father, as you will read in these pages.

The United States formally declared war on Japan on December 8, 1941. It was apparent that all able-bodied men and women would be called to defend our country. So in early 1942, at age 30, John enlisted in the Naval Construction Battalion, and together with a unit of 1000 volunteers and skilled technicians, he reported to Camp Allen, Virginia, for a 21-day period of orientation. The men were taught military discipline and the use of light arms and were officially commissioned as the 15th U.S.N.C.B. It was a journey that would take them more than 24,000 miles in total secrecy. They bonded together as an unshakable team, made lasting friendships, and gave moral support to one another, as they were separated from families, sweethearts, wives, children, and babies whom they wouldn't see for 2½ years.

The 15th United States Naval Construction Battalion, Southwest Pacific
World War II

That's Johnny in the middle

Everything was a military secret. The men could not write as much as a hint about what island they were on or even about the work they were doing. Common phrases of the day were, "The slip of a lip could sink a ship," or "Loose lips sink ships." Every outgoing letter was read by a censor, and if one did mention operations or location, that information was cut out. My mother once showed me an early letter from my Dad in which every other sentence was cut out and it looked like a piece of lace. Hence, under the date of every letter my father wrote the word *"Somewhere."*

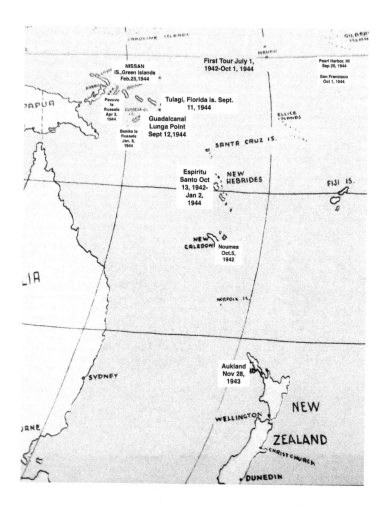

Chapter 1
The War, Marriage, Enlistment, Espiritu Santo

December 7, 1941 Japanese attack Pearl Harbor, Hawaii.

December 8, 1941 - U.S. declares war on Japan. Together with its allies, the U.S. embarked on a strategy to re-capture the islands of the Pacific and to neutralize Japan itself.

Although it was the bombing of Pearl Harbor on December 7, 1941 that forced the United States into declaring war on Japan, Japanese expansion in the Pacific began much earlier in history. Japan had been largely a feudal society before 1900, each island intermittently waging war on the other as well as with neighboring Korea, eastern China, and Manchuria. When trading ships from Europe and the United States appeared in Japanese ports in the 1800's and established trading colonies on Japanese mainland, the Japanese rulers, intimidated by the grand size of the ships and in fear that these foreigners would become established and take control, began to organize into a central governing body. In 1889 the first constitution of Japan was ratified which expressly named England, Holland, France, and the United States as official enemies.

By 1942 Japan had ventured far into the Pacific and conquered the western Aleutian islands in the north, all of southeast Asia as far west as Burma, as far south to parts of New Guinea and the Solomon Islands, and as far east as Wake Island, the Marshall Islands, and the Gilbert Island group. The goal was to seize the natural resources thereby gaining riches for trade. Yet unconquered further south were the New Hebrides, Fiji Islands and Samoa, and to the east, Midway and Hawai'i

January 5, 1942 - Seabees are founded.

January 11, 1942 - Japan invades Dutch East Indies. On December 8, 1941 the Netherlands declared war on Japan. The Dutch ground forces in the Pacific fought valiantly but were unable to stop the Japanese invasion and finally surrendered to the Japanese on March 8, 1942. (National Museum of the US Navy.)

January 24, 1942 - Battle of Makassar Strait. During the Pacific War, several naval actions occurred in Makassar Strait off Borneo. Allied aircraft and U.S. Navy destroyers attacked and bombed the Japanese landing force. It was the first USN surface engagement in Southeast Asia during the Pacific War. (National Museum of the U.S. Navy.)

February 15, 1942 - Singapore surrenders to Japanese forces.

February 15, 1942 - Johnny and Lucia were married in Morristown, N.J.

February 15, 1942

February 19, 1942 - Battle of Badung Strait. When the Imperial Japanese forces invaded Bali on February 18, 1942 the combined Allied forces steamed to attack. The Japanese forces drove off the Allied forces sinking a Royal Netherlands Destroyer and cruiser. The USS Stewart was damaged but returned to port in Surabaya. (Wikipedia)

February 19, 1942 - Japan bombs Darwin, Australia, the first and deadliest of 111 Japanese attacks on Darwin leaving hundreds of people homeless, resulting in the abandonment of Darwin as a major Allied naval base. The Allied forces had sought to use the bases in northern Australia to contest the conquest of the Netherlands East Indies. (Wikipedia.org.)

February 27, 1942 - Battle of Java Sea. The Java Sea lies between Borneo, Java to the south, Sumatra to the west and Sulawesi to the east and is the connecting link between these ports and the Indian Ocean. The Allied forces attempted to intercept the Japanese convoys here but the battle resulted in one of the costliest battles of the entire war and Allied navies suffered a disastrous defeat. (Wikipedia/Battle of Java Sea)

March 9, 1942 - Java surrenders to Japan. Japanese forces invaded Java on February 28, 1942. Unable to withstand the attack, allied commanders signed a formal surrender at Bandung on March 12, 1942. (Wikipedia)

March 8-13, 1942 - Japan lands in the Solomon Islands. The invasion of the Solomon Islands and Bougainville Island by the Imperial Japanese forces was uncontested. Japan occupied these islands and began construction of several naval and air bases. Japanese forces were successful in occupying Salamaua and Lae in New Guinea. (Wikipedia)

April 5, 1942 - Japan raids Ceylon, Indian Ocean. The Imperial Japanese Navy launched an air attack against Colombo, Ceylon (now Sri Lanka), much in the style of the Pearl Harbor attack. The targets were British warships, the harbor, and air bases. Alerted to the attack, Admiral Sir James Somerville retreated with the Royal Fleet and some Royal Netherlands Navy warships to safety at Addu Atoll in the Maldives. The survival of these ships prevented the Japanese from later attempting a major troop landing in Ceylon. (Wikipedia)

April 9, 1942 - Bataan surrenders to Japan. The Japanese invasion of the Philippines began on December 8, 1941. Within a month, the Japanese forces had captured Manila and with no naval or air support, the American and Filipino defenders were forced to retreat to the Bataan Peninsula. Finally on April 9, "with his forces crippled by starvation and disease, U.S. General Edward King Jr. surrendered his approximately 75,000 troops" at Bataan to the Japanese. The surrendered Filipinos and Americans were marched about 65 miles to San Fernando during which many died from the brutal treatment of their captors. They were taken by rail to prisoner-of-war camps, where thousands more died from disease, mistreatment and starvation. (History.com)

April 18, 1942 - Doolittle Raid on Tokyo. As an act of retaliation for Pearl Harbor, Col. Jimmy Doolittle led an air raid on the Japanese capital of Tokyo. It was the first air strike on the Japanese archipelago. (Wikipedia and Navy.mil)

May 7-8, 1942 - Battle of the Coral Sea. This was the first air-sea battle in history between the Imperial Japanese Navy and Allied naval and air forces, thwarting Japanese efforts to control the Coral Sea by invading Port Moresby in southeast New Guinea. (Wikipedia and History Channel)

May 8, 1942 - Corregidor Island in Manila Bay falls, Philippines surrendered to Japan. US forces repelled the Japanese invaders for 27 days until they were forced to surrender.

May 20, 1942 - Japan completes the capture of Burma.

May 1942 - Lucia becomes pregnant.

June 4-6, 1942 - Battle of Midway. US code-breakers had become aware that an attack on Midway was imminent and Admiral Nimitz, the Pacific Fleet Commander, deployed carrier forces to be ready for battle. The USS Enterprise, Hornet, and Yorktown were in place to attack the Japanese fleet and battle ensued for two days resulting in a critical US victory that stopped Japanese expansion in the Pacific. (National WW2 Museum.org, Battle of Midway.)

June 7, 1942 – Japan takes Attu, Aleutians, USA. Japanese naval forces land unopposed in Attu and captured the entire population consisting of 45 Aleuts and two white Americans. They were taken to a prison camp on Hokkaido. The American Charles Jones was killed immediately due to his refusal to fix the radio he had destroyed to prevent the troops from using it.

July 1, 1942 - Johnny reported to Camp Allen, Virginia, one of 1000 men destined to become the Fifteenth U.S. Naval Construction Battalion.

[It is not clear whether or not Johnny knew at this point that Lucia was pregnant.]

July 22, 1942 –The "isolation period" is completed at Camp Allen, Virginia. The battalion held its dress parade and was commissioned as the 15th U.S.N.C.B.

July 23-August 23, 1942 – Battalion moved to Camp Bradford, Virginia, constructed the first one hundred ton pontoon dry dock ever attempted by a construction battalion and launched it successfully.

July 28, 1942 - The following is a letter written on a Navy handkerchief, the first letter written by John to Lucia, from Camp Bradford, Virginia:

July 28, 1942

My Darling Wife:

  All day long, I dream of you. I love you more tonite than words can ever tell. I miss you and love you more each passing second. The sweetness and tenderness of your last caress will be everlastingly etched on my most accepting lips.

Love

Johnny

JdeR

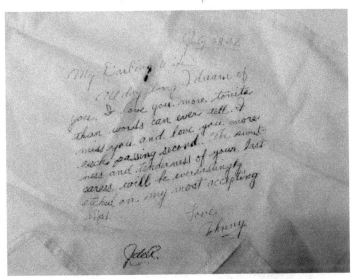

August 7, 1942 - U.S. Marines land at Guadalcanal, Solomon Islands. Codenamed Operation Watchtower, the battle for Guadalcanal lasted from August 7, 1942 to February 1943 and began when US Marines launched a surprise attack and took control of an air base under construction. The Japanese made repeated attempts to recapture the airfield engaging in three major land battles, seven large naval battles, and almost daily aerial battles. The Allied success was a turning point along with Midway that placed the Allied troops on the offensive. (Wikipedia)

August 9, 1942 - Battle of Savo Island. In an attempt to interrupt Allied landings in the eastern Solomon Islands in support of Guadalcanal, the Imperial Japanese Navy mobilized a task force of seven cruisers and one destroyer to attack the Allied amphibious fleet and its screening force. In a night action, the Japanese Navy launched a surprise attack sinking one Australian and three American cruisers. The Allied ships retreated before unloading all supplies on Savo, leaving the ground forces with limited supplies, equipment, and food to hold their beachhead. The battle is cited as the worst defeat in the history of the United States Navy. (Wikipedia)

August 15-19, 1942 – The battalion was granted five days leave from Camp Bradford, Virginia. Johnny wasted no time in heading straight for home.

August 16, 1942 - Home on furlough before being shipped out. The following photos were taken in front of the Speedwell Avenue house: Johnny, Ralph, Grace, and Lou.

August 19, 1942 – Raid on Dieppe, France.

August 20th, 1942 - The 15th Seabee Battalion of over one thousand men boarded trains and headed west, while the Navy band played "Anchors Aweigh."

August 23, 1942 – Battle for Stalingrad starts.

August 24-25, 1942 – Battle of Eastern Solomon Islands, between the Imperial Japanese Navy and the US Navy during the Guadalcanal campaign resulted in a tactical and strategic victory for the US. The final action was an attack on the rescue destroyer Mutsuki, which was bombed and sunk by four US B-17's from *Espiritu Santo,* code name "Island X." (Wikipedia)

August 25, 1942 – The battalion arrived in Port Hueneme, California, 40 miles north of Los Angeles and 410 miles south of San Francisco.

August 25-September 6, 1942 – Liberty at Port Hueneme.

August 26, 1942 – Japanese forces land at Milne Bay, New Guinea in an attempt to capture the airstrip.

September 5, 1942 – Japanese forces were driven out of Milne Bay, New Guinea by Australian and American forces..

September 7, 1942 - The 15th Battalion set out for Treasure Island Naval Base in San Francisco Bay where the men were equipped with firearms and bivouac gear.

Souvenir received by Lucia on September 12, 1942

September 14, 1942 – The battalion boarded a cargo ship the M.S. Island Mail, together with a large contingent of U.S.N. airplane "mechs", the contingent known as ACORN RED TWO, and headed for destination unknown Code name Island "X." **[Espiritu Santo in the New Hebrides Islands.]**

September 25, 1942 - The cargo ship M.S. Island Mail crossed the equator, and in accordance with tradition, the men experienced their "Shellback Initiation" and received their Neptune Certificate:

October 5, 1942- After 22 days at sea, the M.S. Island Mail arrived at Noumea, New Caledonia, and for five days lay anchored a half a mile off shore awaiting orders.

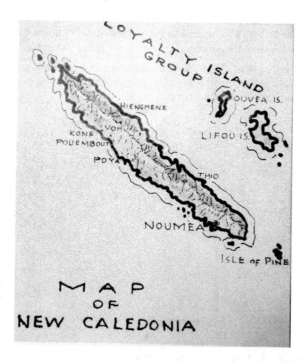

October 11-12, 1942 – Battle of Cape Esperance. US naval forces intercepted a major supply and reinforcement convoy enroute to Guadalcanal forcing the Japanese to abandon their mission. [Wikipedia]

October 11, 1942 – MS Island Mail received orders to proceed northward. The ship arrived at Island "X" and anchored. After dark, a Japanese submarine launched shells at them. The 15ᵗʰ yearbook says, "We could hear them whizz as they passed over the ship and the dull boom as they exploded on the shore."

ESPIRITU·SANTO·ISLAND·
NEW·HEBRIDES·GR.·
OCT. 13,1942 TO NOV.23,1943

October 12, 1942 - At dawn, while the men were unloading cargo and supplies onto the base at Espiritu Santo, they were flashed a warning that a Japanese task force was approaching and moved the ship immediately. During the night, with Johnny aboard, they sailed on evasive maneuvers to avoid being struck.

October 13, 1942 – At dawn, after playing tag with the Japanese submarine most of the night, the M.S. Island Mail **arrived off the Island of Èfatè**, part of the Shefa Province in the New Hebrides, now Vanuatu, an island nation northeast of New Caledonia and southeast of Espiritu Santo. As they were steaming toward the narrow entrance to her harbor, a U.S. plane appeared and repeatedly swiped the bow in an attempt to ward them off. The Skipper brought the Island Mail to a stop at which time a small pilot boat informed them that they were in the middle of a minefield. All were on edge expecting to get blown up, as the Skipper backed out for about two miles. [Map courtesy of Wikipedia.]

October 15, 1942 – The MS Island Mail finally reached Island "X" and completed unloading. They were immediately assigned to the task of supplying fuel and ammunition for U.S. B-17s flying round the clock during the battle of Guadalcanal, as well as building an airstrip. Meanwhile, the Seabees cleared the land to build roads, airstrips, a hospital, bomb shelters, water tanks, towers, piping, airfields, camps, galley and mess hall, laundry, sick bay, and repair of a water tank that was sheared off by a plane crash.

October 25, 1942 – Battle of Santa Cruz. The Japanese Navy again tried to drive the United States' forces from Guadalcanal. During this naval battle, the USS Hornet and USS Porter were lost and the USS Enterprise was badly damaged. It was a tactical victory for the Japanese, however, the U.S. gained time to further strengthen Guadalcanal's defenses. (Wikipedia)

November 8, 1942 – Allied invasion of North Africa.

November 12-15, 1942 – The Naval Battle of Guadalcanal began with Japanese air attacks on U.S. ships bringing reinforcements to the island and involved hard fighting at sea and in air. Japan had severe losses. Two U.S. cruisers Atlanta and Juneau and seven destroyers (Barton, Monssen, Cushing, Laffey, Preston, Benham and Walke) were sunk. All five of the famous Sullivan brothers were lost with the Juneau following the November 13, 1942 battle. (See the 1944 movie, "The Fighting Sullivans.") It was the loss of all five Sullivan brothers that the Sole Survivor Policy was enacted as law in 1948. It is this policy that gave rise to the 1998 movie, "Saving Private Ryan." (Wikipedia)

November 30, 1942 - Battle of Tassafaronga. US Task Force 67, intercepted eight Japanese destroyers bringing reinforcements to Guadalcanal but were crippled by a brilliantly executed Japanese torpedo counter attack. (National Museum of the US Navy, history.navy.mil)

Chapter 2
1943
Ralph is Drafted, Birth of Baby Girl

January 2, 1943 - Japanese defeated at Buna on the north coast of New Guinea. Japanese troops first landed at Buna on July 21, 1942. American troops initially closed on Buna in November 1942. Reinforcements arrived and attacked on the morning of January 1, by nightfall destroyed the Japanese positions, and secured the position by January 22, 1943.

January 31, 1943 – Germany surrenders army at Stalingrad.
February 9, 1943 - Guadalcanal was declared secure.
February 19-25 – Battle of Kasserine Pass, Tunisia.

February 24, 1943 – At 4:50 p.m. Lucia gave birth to a baby girl, 7lbs 6oz, 20". [The story of the name can be confusing. I was named 'Annette' at birth, but was called 'Jackie' from then on. "Why?..," I asked my mother years later. Her answer was that she wanted her first child to be a boy, to be named John, nicknamed Jack, after my father. She wanted her second child to be a girl named 'Jill,' so she could have 'Jack and Jill.' The closest she could get to this was to name me Jackie, but she said the Catholic hospital where I was born insisted that Jackie was not the required Saint's name for a Catholic child. So, at the last minute and under duress, she picked the name Annette. The name Annette had been in the forefront of the daily news for a number of years as it was the name of one of the Dionne quintuplets, a phenomenon of the time. As an adult, and by personal reasons of my own, I changed 'Annette' to the Hawaiian name of Leina'ala.]

March 2-4 – Battle of Bismarck Sea.

Letter postmarked March 23, 1943, stamp upside down. [*The upside down position of the stamp indicated that a kiss was being sent. This was important to both John and Lucia and therefore I have included the notation with every letter.*]

March 22, 1943
Island X

Hello, My Darling:

Just a few lines to let you know I love you, miss you, and am always thinking of you. You are eternally on my mind. I received two airmail letters yesterday, one from my mother, and one from your mother, so I got one from each of our mothers. The one from your mother was most important, though, and was she excited. Anyone would think it was she instead of you that had the baby.

At least, according to the letter from your mother, we have had the distinction of having a pretty baby girl. She weighed seven pounds and was born about four-thirty. That's all I have so far, so it will be up to you to tell me the rest. Was it born the twenty-fourth? From this letter, dated Feb. 25, and postmarked four P.M., I figured that's the day. However, as my wife, it is up to you to inform me of details. Is she dark or light. Dark, I imagine (and hope). I love black haired baby girls. I love you, sweetheart.

In your mother's letter she said "I never saw a nice baby born the first few hours, even if I do say so myself." From that, my love, I gather that we do have a really pretty baby. Gee, sweet, we'll have to take care of her, won't we. Isn't it swell, now that it's all over, and both of us are satisfied. Your mother also said that she hopes I won't be too disappointed because it's a girl. Tell me why anyone and everyone thinks that I would be. Dearest, as long as you and the child are well, what more could I ask. I am not disappointed, sweet. I am proud of us to be able to have anything at all. I'm honestly and truly glad, sweet. Why, I even stole cigars and passed them out this morning, even though it isn't the cigar passing out kind. Are you happy? If only I could be there to hold you in my arms, tenderly kiss you, and tell you how glad I am to be your husband, the father of your children. I don't know why, but words can't seem to describe my feelings about it. Gee, I'd love to see it, even though it is almost a month old. Come to think of it, old Doc. Wade came pretty darn close to picking the day, didn't he. Closer than I thought he would. Tell your mother that I said the next time she won't be able to say she missed me walking the floor with her, because I'll be there, and she won't have to pace at all. She said also that for (I don't know just how many, can't make it out) days you hadn't received any letters, but they came all at once. How many did you get while you were in the hospital? How long did you stay there? Did you have a hard time? Are you glad that it's all over? Did you miss me very much? Do you love me just as much? Or has some of it gone over to our child? I love you more. That's about all I can say about that now, but once again I'll say that I'm not disappointed a bit. I always wanted a girl, anyway, didn't you? Please, sweet, name her Lucia? I like that name.

I will now answer your letter of Feb 9. Ralph had more shots than I did, didn't he. I don't remember just how many we had, but I know it wasn't that many. And that stove in the tent business doesn't sound so hot to me. Maybe we are lucky to be in the tropics after all. I don't blame him for not enjoying the fellows coming and going, but he'll get used to it. You should see our tent. It seems like a neighborhood house. As for the place being a swamp, what do you think this place is. But I wouldn't worry about him if I were you. He will get along alright.

In this letter you ask me not to repeat anything you told me in one of your former letters. It's just a wee bit too late for that because I wrote and gave them both the devil. In a nice way, though, so they wouldn't feel too hurt. In it (your letter) I understood that you were quite angry, and taking into consideration your condition and all, you couldn't be held responsible. So, think nothing more of it. What's done is done. But as long as you didn't want me to repeat any of it, I'm sorry I did. Besides, you were angry with me also, so I had to take it out on someone.

(Tell me, does our baby say dada yet?)That letter you sent via airmail, you know, and I received that about two or three weeks ago, and wrote to them the following Sunday. So, let's hope that they got lost. Are you still angry at me? So far, my mother hasn't said anything to me about it, so I guess she never will now, unless she does get my letter. I'll be sure and let you know if she does, so meanwhile, lets forget it.

So my wife is satisfied with her fruit juices and canned pineapple. Well, sweet, another fellow and I ate about a peck of nice, juicy apples today. Boy, were they good. Moan, dearest one, moan. They don't grow here on the island, though, they were imported from that place called the states. It seems that I've heard of it, but can't place it.

I didn't know that Fran had to quit her job because of her feet, but she did tell me about working on planes. We have quite a few of them here and they do a thorough job. As you say, that is just like Fran. Here today, elsewhere tomorrow. In the letter Fran wrote, Butch wrote also. But I told you all that in another letter. I hope our daughter never goes through what Butch did. But one thing I do know, and that's that if our Jr. is anything like her mother, she'll be a knockout both in beauty and smartness. You see, I do love you.

Tell me, can Lucia Jr. walk yet? Has she any teeth or hair? Don't forget to describe her to me, and by all means, send pictures. Sweetheart I love you and miss you and want you more than ever now, because instead of just one, you are now two, and we are three.

As ever, eternally loving you,

Johnny

J.de Roxtro, EM2/C

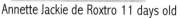

Annette Jackie de Roxtro 11 days old   Jackie 7 months old

March 26, 1943 – Battle of the Komandorski Islands, Alaska.
Orders were to prevent an Imperial Japanese supply convoy from
resupplying their forces on the American Aleutian Islands. The
Japanese fleet retreated and never again sent supplies to these
posts. (Wikipedia, HistoryNet.com, Battle of the Komandorski Islands.)

J.de Roxtro EM2/c U.S.N.R.
Co.C. 15th N.C.B. –c/o F.P.O.
San Francisco, Calif.   *March 28, 1944*
                                                             Island X

Dear Mom Petrone,

*I received your most welcome and unexpected letter, although I was
certainly wishing for it. If you thought that I would be disappointed because
it was a girl, you are way wrong. I really didn't care one way or the other as
long as both Lou and child were alright. As long as we can't have anything to
say about the sex of our children, why should we worry about it. The Lord's
will be done. He decides all that for us, and we should be satisfied that
everything turns out well. I am, and I hope that Lucia is, and everyone else.
Now I am anxious to get home to see my wife and her people, my people and
friends, and most of all to see if my daughter is as pretty as her grandmother
tries to make me believe. But how could she be otherwise, with a beautiful
mother who comes from a family of beautiful mothers.*

*Say, mom, seven pounds is pretty heavy for a baby nowadays, isn't
it? I know that in former years thirteen and fourteen pounds was the average,
but I had an idea that the average now was bout five or five and one half
pounds.*

*I wish that law was changed so that the father had to see the baby.
Then I would have been there. But as long as I wasn't there to see it, I'm glad
that you were able to. By this time, I suppose everyone has seen it but me. Oh,*

16

well, it won't be too long, I hope, before I can see it.

If Lou hasn't already done it, will you keep after her to have some pictures taken to send to me, please? So far, I don't know any more about her than you told me in your letter. From that, I gathered that the date of birth was the twenty-fourth. I guess you forgot to mention it. Anyway, I will keep on expecting to learn all the details in each batch of mail that comes in.

Gee, I bet that was a long three hours you waited there in the hospital. I'm glad you went home, though, because after all, there was nothing you could do while there, and at home you could keep busy and not worry quite as much. Now if I had been at home, you could have had company walking the floor. I think I would have gone out and gotten us a few bottles of beer to while away the time.

I'm sure glad to hear that your daughter at least had some news from me the first day at the hospital anyway. I don't know why, but for some reason my letters seem to cheer her up. Gee, I bet she is real busy these days what with feeding baby Lucia and changing diapers, and dressing her and bathing her. Tell me, does Lou treat her as if she were a doll? I sort of have an idea she does.

Well, I guess that's all about my heiress and as there isn't much more to say, I will have to make this a short one. By the way, your son-in-law even stole cigars and passed them out, even though it wasn't that kind of a child. Does that look as if he was disappointed? Not by a darn sight. Give my regards to all the family and friends, especially Mama G and Tadone.

J. de Roxtro, EM2/c   Love, Johnny

Raphael & Mary Petrone

Maria (Mary) Fidele Scinto Petrone

April 18, 1943 - Yamamoto shot down by P-38's during an air battle over Bougainville in the Solomon Islands. Adm. Isoroku Yamamoto was the architect of the attack on Pearl Harbor. (Wikipedia/Operation Vengeance)

May 11-June 30 - U.S. retakes Attu in the Aleutians.

June 21, 1943 – Battle of New Georgia, Solomon Islands. US forces landed at Segi Point and proceeded westward on foot through intense rain and thick mud to attack Japanese installations at Viru Harbor. The "campaign for New Georgia and other islands in the central Solomon group lasted until the end of September, 1943 and was one of the bloodiest fights in the South Pacific." (Warfarehistorynetwork.com)

July 6-7, 1943 – Battle of Kula Gulf was an inconclusive naval clash between American and Japanese forces, who successfully transported their reinforcement troops onto Kolombangara. (Historyofwar.org Battle of Kula Gulf)

July 12, 1943 – Battle of Kolombangara, in the New Georgia Islands group of the Solomon Islands. Throughout July and August, nightly actions took place during which the US attempted to prevent the Japanese from landing reinforcements on Kolombangara. US efforts failed and the Japanese were successful, however after this series of battles in the Kula Gulf, the Japanese used the Vella Gulf and the Blackett Strait along the other side of the island. (Wikipedia.org)

July 5-17, 1943 – Kursk tank battle, Soviet Union.

July 9, 1943 – Allies invade Sicily.

August 5, 1943 – Germany driven from Kursk, Russia.

August 6, 1943 – Battle of Vella Gulf, Solomon Islands. Having learned their lessons in the Kula Gulf and at Kolombangara, a US Navy task group of six destroyers was dispatched to intercept the Japanese force, which continued to supply reinforcements to Kolombangara via the Vella Gulf and were free to use their own tactics. Hidden in the shadows of Kolombangara Island, the task force successfully sank all four Japanese destroyers.

Pvt. R. Petrone-32760416
3415 Ord. M.M. Co. (Q)
APO 502, c/o Postmaster
San Francisco, Calif.
August 8, 1943

Friday 6.30 A.M.

Hello Lou:

Well another week is nearly gone and still no mail from you or the folks. Gee, I don't know what the matter is. I'm sure the kids do write to me and especially Fanny. She was always good for at least one letter a week. Maybe they are sending them through the regular mail instead of Air Mail.

Gee, I wish they wouldn't because if the boat does come across it will take at least a month. That's quite a long while. It seems to me that I write several letters a week and hardly get any reply. I sure am disappointed in Gene. I haven't heard from him since I left the states and that was in May or June. I forget, but anyway it sure was a long time ago. Well I guess there's no use crying about it, is there. I only hope Johnnie's mail is a lot more than mine. I wrote him about three letters not so long ago and I expect a reply any day now. Well, so much for that. Boy, these darn mosquitos are bad. Well, Lou, how's Jackie? I'll bet she's pretty big now. Let's see, she must be about 6 months or better, is that right? I still look at her picture that you sent me. She sure looks like a nice baby. It won't be long now and we will be coming home. (I hope). I wrote to Ann & Fanny last week and now I'm writing to you and I want to send Joe a letter too. I wrote to mom the other day and told her of some money I was going to send. I haven't had a chance as yet but I'll come around to it in a couple of days. Boy this sure is a sloppy letter isn't it. Before I even started I spilt the ink on my bed and some on the paper. I can't help it though because it's hard as hell to write like this. I am writing on that book you gave me and this is some of the paper that was in it. Well, Lou, I can't think of anything else to say at the moment so I'll have to close now. I'm in good health and I hope that you and Jackie are the same. Give her a big kiss for me and tell her it's from her uncle. Give my love to the kids and best regards to Mrs. De Roxtro whenever you see her. Well, so long for now.

Love,
Ralph

Louis Gene Petrone

Joe Petrone

Ann, baby Judy, Joan "Fanny"

Ralph Petrone

September 9-17, 1943 – battle at Salerno, Italy.

October 1, 1943 – Naples recaptured by Allied forces.

October 13, 1943 – It was at the one-year anniversary celebration of landing on Espiritu Santo that the celebratory variety show featured Ray Bolger and Little Jack Little, the guests of honor. **Actor, singer, dancer, Ray Bolger is best known for his role as the Scarecrow in the Movie "Wizard of Oz" starring Judy Garland.**

Ray Bolger's autograph on a One Dollar silver certificate

November 1, 1943 – Marines land on Bougainville, Solomon Islands. Fierce fighting and dogged determination by the Marines, finally accomplished their mission. On January 9, 1944, The U.S. Marines turned the island over to the army forces who continued the bloody fighting until March 28, 1944 when the Japanese army retreated and began their withdrawal from the island. (warfarehistorynetwork.com "Battling for Bougainville")

November 2, 1943 – Battle of Empress Augusta Bay. US cruisers and destroyers repelled Japanese forces attempting to interrupt US shipping off Bougainville. This marked the end of Japan's advantage in night warfare.

20

November 5, 1943 - Allied air attack on the Japanese cruiser force at Rabaul, an island town in what is now Papua New Guinea. Rabaul, on the island of New Britain in the Territory of New Guinea was the main Japanese naval base for the Solomon Island campaign and heavily defended. Against this seemingly impenetrable force, Admiral William Halsey, with only two carriers under command of Rear-Admiral Sherman, behind cover of an early morning weather front, launched all available 97 aircraft with orders to damage as many warships as possible. At daybreak, Navy bombing was followed an hour later with an Army Air Force raid, causing heavy damage. The strike was a stunning success ending Japanese naval presence in the area.

November 21, 1943 - Battle of Makin and Tarawa, Gilbert Islands. After two days of determined fighting, Japanese resistance was quelled and the island was cleared. On Tarawa, the Japanese defenders opened fire with their four 8-inch guns. Three of the four guns were shortly disabled by fire from two battleships, thus opening the approach to the lagoon whereupon naval bombardment of the island was sustained for three hours. Two minesweepers cleared the shallows of mines and the Marines landed. By the end of the third day the island was declared secure.

November 23, 1943 – The 15th Battalion Boarded the U.S.S. Pinckney, headed for Auckland, New Zealand for some Liberty.

November 28, 1943 – Arrived Auckland New Zealand for ten days' liberty.

December 24-26, 1943 - battle of North Cape (Norway).

December 26, 1943 - Battle of Cape Gloucester, Solomon Islands: 1st Marines invade New Britain continuing "Operation Cartwheel" to isolate Rabaul and after much fighting, on January 16, 1944 the island was secured.

Chapter 3

1944

The Battalion Moves to the Russell Islands and Pavuvu,
Johnny Home on Furlough, Transfer to California

January 2, 1944 – The Battalion boarded the U.S.S. Rixie and headed for the Russell Islands.

January 3, 1944 – Lucia's first journal entry.

Monday, January 3, 1944. Jackie does (V) for Victory.

Tuesday, January 4, 1944. Check of $80.00.

Thursday, January 6, 1944. Jackie's 6th tooth cut thru.

Friday, January 7, 1944. Check of $80.00.

January 8, 1944 – The Battalion arrived on Banika Island in the Russell Islands.

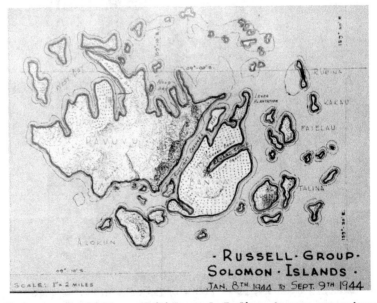

· RUSSELL · GROUP ·
SOLOMON · ISLANDS ·
JAN. 8TH 1944 TO SEPT. 9TH 1944

January 9, 1944 – British and Indian troops recapture Maungdaw, Burma. Ranges of steep hills channeled the Allied advance into three attacks, where the 5th Indian Division along the

23

coast captured the small port of Maungdaw. (Wikipedia.org, Battle of Maungdaw)

Friday, January 21, 1944. Letters of Jan. 9-11. Pictures enclosed in that of the 11th, of South West Pacific.

Espiritu Santo. That's Johnnie on the left.

Vincent Forbes, Carl Blosser, Johnny de Roxtro, Frank Fitzpatrick

January 22, 1944 – Battle of Anzio, Italy.
Monday, January 24, 1944. Letter of Jan. 10. Mom home from work - cold. Tadone came. Judy here. Gift from Ralph. Letters for Ann.

Jackie at 11 months old

Tuesday, January 25, 1944. *Letters of Jan. 12-13-14. Vene came down at 12:00. Had lunch - left both kids here. Brought back ice cream and film. While gone - Jackie walked alone about 10 steps. At night went to show with Mil and Gene, saw "Girl Crazy." (Adieu jusqu'a ce revoir - farewell until we meet again).*

(Vene) de Roxtro Naughton   Mil & Gene

Wednesday, January 26, 1944. *Baby bottles. Washed clothes. Tadone came.*

Thursday, January 27, 1944. *Letter of Jan. 15. Letter from Ralph. Put Jackie out 12:30. Slept until 2:15. Beautiful day. Cooked sauce in morning and went downtown. Went to Post Office - stamps - Sandrian - $3.80-$4.00. $1.50 for copy work, $.40 a print. Made 6 copies of each - $4.00. Stopped in stores on way back. Jackie very good - at Jodo's she was impatient.*

Friday, January 28, 1944. *2 letters of Jan.18. Jackie coughing all day.*

Saturday, January 29, 1944. Ann had half a day. Washed diapers. Ann & I went downtown shopping - (pictures) - movies.

Sunday, January 30, 1944. *Cold. Baby sick with cold. Joe & Angie came. All went down to Mama G's. 7:30 M.D.R.* [Mrs. De Roxtro, Nana] *comes. 9:30 Joe & Angie, Mom comes home. M.D.R. left with them. Jackie sick - cough & cold. (tooth coming).*

Mama "G"   Mrs. Annie Gardiner de Roxtro
                          with Jackie

Joe and   Angie Petrone

January 31, 1944 - U.S. Marines invade and capture Kwajalein and Majuro Atolls in the Marshall Islands. The battle lasted until February 3, 1944. Wikipedia says, "For the US, the battle represented both the next step in its island-hopping march to Japan and a significant morale victory because it was the first time the Americans had penetrated the "outer ring" of the Japanese Pacific sphere."

Monday, January 31, 1944. Joey [Vetere] came to say good bye. Leaves for Navy tomorrow - trying to get into band.

Joe Vetere, Lucia's 1st cousin

Tuesday, February 1, 1944. Letters of Jan. 21-22. Check of $80.00. Vene came down 10:30. Jackie asleep. Vene went out to buy baby food-$2.69. Had lunch. Went down to M.D.R. with Nan [Nancy Naughton]. Came back at 3:00. Stayed until 5:00. Jackie kisses.

26

Wednesday, February 2, 1944. *Letters of Jan. 16-17-20. Went to Post Office. Sent money order to Grolier. Stopped and bought wool - Girls stayed in Newark. Went to show with Mil "Destination Tokyo." Very good. Jackie eats chopped foods 11 ½ mo.*

Thursday, February 3, 1944. *Received gift of shakers. Vene dropped in few min. M.d.R. called. Told her about them.*

Paua shell salt & pepper shakers. Paua is only found in New Zealand.

Friday, February 4, 1944. *No entry.*

Saturday, February 5, 1944. *Letter of Jan. 24th. Fan and I went downtown.*

Sunday, February 6, 1944. *Arkie* [Archangel Bianco, next door neighbor] *on maneuvers - Tennessee. Joe and Angie came. Girls and I went to show. "His Butler's Wife* [Sister].*" Very good.*

Monday, February 7, 1944. *Letters of the 23rd & 25th of Jan. Second snow.*

Tuesday, February 8, 1944. *Took pictures. Kept Jackie down while we ate. Says, "Oh, yeah," plainly.*

Photos taken on February 8

Wednesday, February 9, 1944. *Cat* [Catherine Palmieri Russo] *came over. Joey at Sampson, N.Y.*

Cat

Thursday, February 10, 1944. Letter of Jan 27. Grace .

Grace Petrone, the youngest sister,
at age 11 and at high school graduation.

Friday, February 11, 1944. Snow 6 in. Letter of Jan. 28. Gray home at 2. I went out. Bought rubber pants, wool, scrap book, Castoria. 6:00 Vene .

February 12, 1944 - Menachem Begin, future Israeli Prime Minister and Nobel Prize Winner, declares revolt against the British mandate in Palestine.
(Wikipedia.org/wiki/Menachem_Begin.)

Saturday, February 12, 1944. Cleaned house. Changed living room. Went downtown with girls. Then to show. Very good. Johnnie's birthday.

Sunday, February 13, 1944. Family went to Newark. Started to knit hat, 12:00, red. Jackie hugs and pats back, shakes hand.

Monday, February 14, 1944. Letters of Jan 31, 29, 30, Feb 1, 2, 3, 4. Jackie received val. from Judy, Mil & Gene, Ann, Fan, Grace, Mom, Carol Ann. Received Anniversary card from Mil & Gene. One for me from Jackie. Washed in afternoon. Left when Grace came home to go downtown. Bought wool. Red & blue polo shirt. Finished washing. Cooking. Rained all night. Much

28

snow, gone by morning. Jackie hugs, pats back, blows nose, cleans mouth, shakes hands, winks, & points.

Judy, Mil & Gene's daughter   Carol Ann Russo, Cat's daughter

Tuesday, February 15, 1944. *Vene called 8:15 a.m. Letters of Feb. 5,6, Anniversary cards from Jo & Mike, Martha, Fan, Ann, Mil & Gene, Vene & M.D.R. Vene came 12:00, went to dentist, after lunch M.D.R. came. Vene back - ice cream & candy. V & M.D.R. left kids here. V-5:30 back - left. At supper - blouse from Ann, at night went to show. Fannie's treat to me. Show good. "The North Star."*

Wednesday, February 16, 1944. *Letters of Jan. 26 - Feb 6. Letter from Ralph. Beautiful day. Put Jackie out to sleep - 2hrs. Had her dinner and then went to visit Cat. Had her bottle there: 2:30, stayed until 4:00. Took pictures by Martha's at night, Jackie fell from carriage - injured top teeth and gum. Face all swollen. Gum cut up and bleeding. Called Doctor W. 6:30, came and said everything all right. Tried to push gum into shape. Bathed mouth cold water, didn't undress at all that night. Jackie very restless, couldn't sleep, awake until 3:00. We both were on bed. Slept couple of hours. (can drink bottle)*

February 17-18, 1944 - US carrier-based planes destroy the Japanese naval base at Truk in the Caroline Islands in Operation Hailstone. Truk had been the main base for the Combined Japanese Fleet since the beginning of the war and considered impenetrable. The Americans, however, in two days of raids, destroyed most of the ground facilities and fighter cover, and wiped out almost everything that floated. (combinedfleet.com/battles/destruction of Truk)

Thursday, February 17, 1944. *Jackie's face still swollen considerably. Baby cranky and irritable. Doctor came at 11:00, examined gum and said three teeth were all right. One was dislocated. Might be lost. Said, injury wouldn't affect formation of teeth or permanent teeth. Doctor coming again Sat. Mom called [from work] to find out about baby. So did Ann. She slept a little better at night in my bed, woke several times during the night.*

Friday, February 18, 1944. *Swelling on Jackie's face gone down - able to close mouth - some. Disposition much happier.*

February 17-23, 1944 – Battle of Eniwetok Atoll, Marshall Islands, "Operation Catchpole." After air and naval bombing, the island was taken.

Saturday, February 19, 1944. *Little swelling left. Three teeth and tip of 4th came down from gum. M.d.R. & Vene came in afternoon. 5:00 Doctor came. At night - went downtown with Ann and Fan - finished hat.*

February 15-20, 1944 – Battle of the Green Islands, Territory of New Guinea, "Operation Squarepeg." The focus of the operation was to capture *Nissan*, the main island of the group, continuing the northward push to capture Rabaul, the main Japanese base. Land fighting was brief but sharp with heavier fighting in the air. The Allies declared the island secure on February 20th.

Sunday, February 20, 1944. *M.d.R. came 1:45 Mom & Mama G. went to Newark - ate early.*

[Banika Island, Russell Islands]

Letter postmarked Feb.23, 1944, stamp right side up.   *February 20, 1944*

Somewhere

Hello Mom:

It sure is nice to hear from you. I received your card the day after my birthday so it was just in time. I really appreciate it. Thanks loads. Here's hoping that I am home to stay before the next one rolls around. I think there's a good chance of my being home in the very near future, about six months from now. I know it isn't very near, but it sure would be swell, if true. Now don't depend too much on that because it's only my personal idea.

I am as well as it is possible to be, down here in this heat and continual dampness. It doesn't rain quite as much as it did for our first month here, but it still rains daily. I hope that this finds you feeling better than you were the last I heard from Lou. Take care of yourself, mom, because you have a large family to care for. A darn nice family they are too. Every darned one of them.

There seems to be nothing more I can say from here. I'm still looking at coconut trees. It seems they are all over the place. The flies and mosquitos aren't as bad as they were on Santos though so that's one thing to be thankful for.

I hear from Ralph every once in awhile and he seems to be doing alright. The last letter I received from him was written the second of February, so I should be getting another any day now. I always tell Lou about his letters, but there isn't anything important in them. Don't you worry about him, because he is in a nice, quiet safe place. He is even more safe than I am and we don't have any precautionary measures here. There hasn't even been a black out in quite some time. Well, mom, here's the best to all our friends. I hope I'll be seeing you very soon.

J.De Roxtro EM2/c   *Your son, with love, Johnny*

Monday, February 21, 1944. *Big wash - lovely day. Cat came over couldn't go out. Gracie home for two days. Fuel conservation. She took baby out for airing. Card from Mary. Letters of Feb. 8,9,12. Letter from Gene, Tipp, Ohio.*

Mary Lukawitz (Lucia's friend), became WAC

February 22, 1944 – The Battalion boarded L.S.T.s, headed for Nissan Island in the Green Islands, *which had been secured only two days earlier.*

Tuesday, February 22, 1944. *Vene came 11:30. Lunch, then left with babies. Had to go to dentist. Jackie cranky, fretful. Would not sleep. Vene & M.d.R. - 3:00. Kay here for spaghetti supper. Made cream puffs. White wine. After supper we went to*

31

Community, saw "A Guy Named Joe." Very good. Went to station with Kay. Early so went in Lack. bar for drink. Train at 12:15.

Wednesday, February 23, 1944. *Went to church in morning, got ashes. Went downtown bought stockings and knitting needles. Letter of Feb. 14. Wrote to Ralph.*

February 24, 1944 - Merrill's Marauders begin a ground campaign in northern Burma. Organized as a light infantry assault unit, the offensive was designed to disrupt Japanese offensive operations in Burma. Outnumbered by the Japanese armies, the Marauders harassed supply and communication lines, shot up patrols, assaulted Japanese rear areas and continued throughout the war in Burma, ending in 1945.

Thursday, February 24, 1944. *Went to church. Lovely day - warm. Put Jackie out to sleep - 2 hrs. M.d.R. called - Happy birthday. Cards from Ann, Fan, Grace, Mom, Joe & Angie, Jo & Mike, Vene, Eleanor & Herb, mommy & daddy, Martha. 1:30 Cat & Carol Ann came. Dressed Jackie up. Mama G. came. Took pictures. Tadone came. Went in and had ice cream. Cooked and asked M & T to stay. Ate in dining room. Jackie up 'til 7:50. Big cake - Happy Birthday to Jackie. Gifts from Mom, Gracie, Mama G, Ann, & Fan. Books from us, 2 dresses, cup, comb & brush set. $1.00 Mil, and striped pinafore & blouse.*

February 24, 1943, Jackie's first birthday.

[This letter begins and ends with page 2. All other pages are missing. Letter written on February 24, 1944 aboard the L.S.T.s:]

Today is the first anniversary of Jackie's birth. A whole year ago she was born. Gosh, it seems ages ago, doesn't it. Yet the time has passed so quickly. My daughter's first birthday, and I wasn't even able to send her a little present. Gee, how I would love to be there. I sure would be able to enjoy myself romping on the floor with my two sweethearts. I wonder if she'll like me. I guess I'm a little afraid that she won't. I sure would feel hurt if she was, but even so, she would get used to me. Oh, well, time enough for that later, I hope. Gee, sweet, I hope that she had a pleasant day. Regardless, it surely was better than mine was. Here's hoping that I am there before long.

Sweetheart, I don't feel much like writing, but I will do my best to answer your letter of February third. Thanks loads for the kiss you sent by way of the stamp. I would miss them, if you ever forgot to invert that routine. On the inside of the envelope you have, written out, "Hello Darling", and in initials, "I am yours always – I love you." Them are pretty words, sweet, and are my sentiments prezactly. I love you, miss you and want you.

So you finally received those salt and pepper shakers. I'm glad they weren't broken. The way I packed them they shouldn't have broken, but perhaps the censors didn't do quite as good a job. They are made of a shell supposedly found only on the coast of New Zealand. It is called Pahu, or something similar to that. I'm glad you like them, but then, I was quite certain that you would. Believe it or not, even I thought that they were pretty.

You are a wonderful Mother to be thinking of knitting one hundred per cent wool sweaters for our daughter. You certainly are swell. I love you more than ever. Glad you were able to get to see a show again. So you thought that show, "Destination Tokyo" was good. I missed that one.

You should make your letters more distinct when you send those things on the letters. How did you like my translation of yours of the twenty ninth. Quite original, no?

February 25, 1944 – The Battalion landed on Nissan Island.

Friday, February 25, 1944. *Letters of Feb. 10,11. Lovely day - baby walked again, put baby out - washed - baby woke - fed her - put her out while I hung clothes. Mil called - came back last night - came at 3:00, took walk to Acme, bought baby food and supper. Put baby in basket - Gene came over after supper. Went to church - stations of the cross.*

Saturday, February 26, 1944. *Letter of Feb. 13, 1944, damp out - Vene came 11:30 - snow. Had to go to ration board. Left at 2:30. Went to M.D.R., gave Jackie whole milk for first time. Took 4 oz. only. Washed hair.*

Sunday, February 27, 1944. *Jackie fell in crib. Jackie & I went to Mil's for dinner - her family raved about Jackie. Fan called - 6:30. M.D.R. here - Nora down. Supper. M.D.R. stayed until 9:30.*

Monday, February 28, 1944. *Letters of Feb. 15-16. Lovely day. Trouble with Jackie. Caught cold. Washed diapers.*

February 29, 1944 – U.S. Army lands in the Admiralty Islands,
an archipelago group of 18 islands in the Bismarck Archipelago, to the north of New Guinea in the South Pacific Ocean, sometimes called the Manus Islands.

Tuesday, February 29, 1944. Letters of 17,18. Cards from Tompkins, Anniversary and birthday. Vene dropped in.. Panty and slip.

Wednesday, March 1, 1944. M.D.R. called. Mil & Judy over. Wrote to Mary.

Thursday, March 2, 1944. Letter of Feb. 19-20. Mil called - got letter, also, Mom, Ann. Jackie climbs stairs.

Friday, March 3, 1944. Started to knit blue sweater.

Saturday/Sunday, March 4/5, 1944. Mama G & Tadone came up. M.d.R. & Vene dropped in. Roselle Park. No dog. Joe & Angie came.

Mama G, Jackie, Tadone

March 5, 1944 - General Wingate's troops begin operations behind Japanese lines in Burma.

Monday, March 6, 1944. Letter of Feb. 21. Took pictures, baby slept: 2:15, washed clothes, went downtown - post office - bank - bought cards - cod liver oil, Jackie throws kiss. Jackie's birthday gift from Jo.

Tuesday, March 7, 1944. Went to church - pouring rain, cleared at 12:00, letter of Feb. 25th. MdR called-told about Roselle-Leslie with chicken pox. At night went to movies with Mil & Cat. "Madame Curie." Stopped at Silver Tavern for pizza & beer.

Eddie & Fran de Roxtro Kugler   Lesley Ann Kugler with Jackie

Wednesday, March 8, 1944. *Letter of Feb. 22,23,24. Sent for stroller. Went to movies-double feature - good.*

Thursday, March 9, 1944. *Vene dropped in. Carl, M.d.R. went to Roselle. Jackie sick. No 2:00 bottle.*

Friday, March 10, 1944. *Letters of Feb. 26,27,28,29, March 1.*

Saturday, March 11, 1944. *Went downtown. Sat. night met Joe. Talked.*

Sunday, March 12, 1944. *Was going to show 4:30 - Cat and Carol Ann came over 5:30. Gene & Judy. - Cat went 4:45. Then at 5:15 came M.D.R., Fran, Eddie & Leslie Ann, brought Jackie & me flowers, stayed until six - came up just for M.d.R.'s glasses. Left. Went to show with Joe & Angie & Tadone "The Sullivans" very good. Wrote to Ralph.*

Gene & daughter Judy

Monday, March 13, 1944. *Letters of Mar. 2,3. Letter from Mary. Lovely day. Went to Cat's and then took a walk downtown, bought training pants. Stopped at Acme. Bought baby food. Mil & Aunts.*

Tuesday, March 14, 1944. *Lovely day. Cooked sauce in morning. Put Jackie to sleep. She woke at 1:15. Fed her, dressed her, and we went to the doctor's. waited an hour. Baby very good. Cried when doctor was examining her. Height - 19 ½ in., weight 22 ½ lbs. Will begin injections Sat. for whooping cough. Started to train Jackie for bladder control.*

March 15, 1944 – Japan invades Imphal and Kohima in India.

Wednesday, March 15, 1944. *Letter from Ralph. Jackie climbs*

on furniture. Jackie says, "Oh dear" & "Ah, Gee."

Thursday, March 16, 1944. Cat came in afternoon. Jackie was asleep. When she awoke we all went outside. Talked with H. Pizz. Joey came to visit us. Chain letter.

Friday, March 17, 1944. Letters of Mar. 4,5,6. Fan got a letter too.

Saturday, March 18, 1944. Went to doctor's, did not get injections, bought serum. Bowel trouble. Stopped in stores, present for Bonnie, Jersey cardigan.

Bonnie   Bonnie, Jackie, Nancy Naughton 1945

Sunday, March 19, 1944. St. Josephs. Got up 5 of seven, Mama G & Tadone for dinner. Gene & Judy in, snow at night, gave Tadone a dollar each, 5 from Gene. Started to snow.

Monday, March 20, 1944. Letters of Mar. 7-8. Money order in 8th for seventy-five. Snow all night & day. Snowstorm - 4 inches. Mom home, no work, worked on Jackie's sweater, shoveled snow off walk.

Tuesday, March 21, 1944. Lovely day. Snow melting. Side walks clear. Jackie out in afternoon. Took pictures. Bathed Jackie in tub for first time.

March 22, 1944 - US forces land at Hollandia, Dutch New Guinea.

Wednesday, March 22, 1944. Brought Jackie to doctors for her first injection(whooping cough) met Cat at corner of Sussex and we went down together. Jackie cried as soon as we entered waiting room. No one there. She cried like the devil when injection was administered. Must go next Wed. for 2nd dose. Stopped at P.O. to cash check. Went to Aunts with Cat - stayed half hour.

Thursday, March 23, 1944. Letter of Mar. 15th. Rain - most of snow gone. At night went to movies with Ann & Fan. Saw "Gung Ho." Very good.

Friday, March 24, 1944. Letter of Mar.9th. Lovely day. Washed while baby slept. Catherine came. Went out. Took pictures. Archie came home. Wrote to Ralph.

Saturday, March 25, 1944. Letters of Mar. 11,12,13,14. Cleaned office - lovely day, went to Laraine San. wedding with Fan - Church of The Redeemer, very lovely, shopped around a little *before coming home.*

Sunday, March 26, 1944. *Jackie can say eat & pot, can do a machine gun, Mama G & Tadone up, went to afternoon show and saw "Song of Russia", very good, when we came home, Joe & Angie were here. They brought 5 packs of Charm Lollypops for Jackie, also box. Took pictures.*

Carol Ann Russo

Monday, March 27, 1944. *Letters of Mar. 15. Letter from Mrs. Fitzpatrick, card from Mary. Call from Mil. Thunderstorm. No bottle for Jackie.*

Tuesday, March 28, 1944. *Got home. after church Vene called- coming down. 11:15-washed clothes. Jackie asleep. Vene came while hanging clothes, lunch, brought carriage down, 2:30-Mil & Judy, went down to doctor's. Bonnie Vaccinated. Came back 4:45.*

Wednesday, March 29, 1944. *Letter of 16-20, rain, was going to Newark but didn't. Jackie fell off the bed. Wrote to Mary. Went to movies, saw Uninvited. Good.*

Thursday, March 30, 1944. *Letters of 17,18,19,21,22, Easter V-mail. Greeting from Ralph. Letter from Evelyn Blosser, wrote to Mrs. Fitzpatrick, wrote to Mary.*

Evelyn and Carl Blosser (Seabee buddy)

[On Nissan Island, Green Islands.]
Postmarked Mar 31, 1944, 9c stamp upside down.

March 30, 1944
Somewhere

My Beloved Sweetheart:

I love you, miss you and want you more as each day slowly passes, bringing us more close together, gradually. Honey, I want so much to hold you close to me and kiss you. Just to look into your beautiful eyes will make my blood race through my veins more rapidly. I sure do love you.

Today I received two letters. One was from your mother, and the other was from the most wonderful wife in all the world. You wrote this one on the sixth, and it wasn't postmarked until the twenty-first of March. It made darn good time after it was posted, didn't it. Only nine days. Boy, I wish I could make as good time, when I start home.

I think I'll have to answer your letter of February twenty-ninth, tonight. I now have four of yours to answer now. Enclosed in this envelope were the pictures taken of Jackie; the one of the bambino sitting on the Toidy seat, and the other of her standing in the chair on the sun porch, in case you don't remember. I told you all about them, and they both are really swell.

The "Toidy Seat" photo

On the sun porch

38

Those two stamps usually mean, to me, that there are pictures enclosed. It's darn seldom I'm wrong, either. Thanks for the two kisses, Sweet, I sure intend to collect for them when we meet each other. Inside the envelope you have, "darling, I love you and miss you so much. I want you too.

Forbes has all my pictures out, and he's trying to get the fellows to say that Ann is better looking than you are. He has that old picture of yours in which you three girls are standing on the front steps. Every single one of them pick the one in the center. That's you, in case you don't remember. I agree, naturally.

Well, it's good to know that Charlie Tompkins is better. That man has had the darnedest luck. All his life there has been something wrong with him. That is, ever since I've known him. They are a swell couple and would give you the shirt off their backs. But Cora talks too much. It was darn nice of them to send the cards.

Say, it sounds to me as if N.G., [naughty girl, Nancy Gardener Naughton] Bonnie [Naughton} and Jackie got along well together. Can it be that Bonnie and our little roughneck were together for once without going for each other's hair and eyes. Doesn't seem possible. But I'm sure glad they had a swell time, and were enjoying themselves. And now our Jackinelle is getting whole milk. I suppose that by this time she is drinking it from a glass. Don't worry about her not liking it, either, because when she gets hungry enough, she'll drink it.

Our daughter's sense of equilibrium seems to be slightly screwy, or something. But she may be just a very active child. That would explain all her falls. Don't worry too much about them. She'll get over all the bruises, etc. later on. You may be a nervous wreck before I see you, though. Don't let it get you, sweet.

You know, your mom told me in her letter today that Jackie was up and down the stairs to beat hell. Well, I know darn well that she has taken a few spills there, too. Oh, me, how I wish I were there to comfort you. Many, many times since you became a mother you have really been scared, and you will be that way many more. She'll take a lot more spills yet, so you may as well expect them. Here's hoping none of them are serious.

Gee, sweetest girl in the world, you sure are lucky to have Mil to invite you out to dinner once in awhile. It's a lot more pleasant, eating something you haven't had to prepare yourself, isn't it. And this time you had another opportunity to show off our Annette to your brother's in-laws. How could they be anything but pleased with our little girl? As for her being comparable to a baby doll, I'm not sure, myself, but I know darn well that she is wonderful. Gee, I love you both. How I want to see you and our Jackie. Soon, I hope, we will all three be together.

It's just as well that the Rahms didn't pay you a visit. If they're too darned lazy (or something) to remove their fat asses from the car and wait a few minutes, to hell with them. Personally, I don't care much for either of them, even if Nora is my sister. I would like to see the two kids, though. They get along with the Naughtons, though. Johnny and Carl have similar tastes, or something, and chew the rag about the same things. You probably were better off not seeing them. They are merely casual acquaintances to me.

Sweetest wife in the world, I don't care if you don't write daily, but I do wish you could arrange to get them posted sooner. Can't you make some arrangements with the mailman to pick them up, or something? Gee, it's so darn many days between the time you write, and the day they are mailed. There's something wrong somewhere. Enough of that, I said before that I would never mention it again. I'm sorry, sweet.

How did it ever happen that the two girls didn't go out to one of our many theatres the other night? Hell, I mean the Sunday night when the Rahms were there. It must have been terribly cold, or something.

This letter is the first in which you ever told me that Jackie wakes often, almost every night, especially when she has a cold or is teething. Honey, were you trying to keep me in the dark concerning that? I have my doubts about the every night business, though. Hell, honey, you know darn well that I would rather you didn't write at all than neglect the baby. By all means, my sweetheart, take good care of her.

Say, I just happened to think of something. Are you predating your letters, because you somehow became late in writing? No, that couldn't be possible. That would account for the difference in dates though. Hell, you wouldn't have any reason for doing anything like that, though, because we never did have a schedule to follow, either of us. 'Scuse, please, I mentioned it again, didn't I? Must be preying on my mind. I love you.

Vene certainly must like to sew. I don't see how she finds time to do it, with those two little ones to care for. But then, you do a bit of alright, yourself, knitting all those things for our bambino. Personally, I always did like those home-made slips, dresses and everything else that kiddies wear. They seem to have a sort of difference in them. They don't seem so common as the bought things, or something. I can't explain my feelings about them, but I guess you know what I mean.

You say you had quite a time taking that picture of Jackie on the toidy seat, but it sure did turn out good, didn't it. I'm proud of that one. At least it's different. I'll bet I've shown it to at least fifty different fellows. While we're on the subject, please don't forget to send one to Forbes. That is, of course, if you care to. He missed it when he was looking through my pictures tonight, and asked me about it again.

Again, as always, I must sign off. I am quite tired, the letter is answered, and I have a busy day ahead of me tomorrow. You will have to be satisfied with the brevity of this note of love. Most wonderful wife, sweetheart and companion, another day comes to a close, and I will again retire, with thoughts of you, Jackie and home on my mind. I love you more as each day passes. Honey, I want so much to be able to lie down beside you and kiss you goodnight. Oh, my sweet bundle of love, I am so homesick – I want you – I need you. Every hour brings us closer together.

J.De Roxtro EM 2/c   Yours forever, *Johnny*

Note on flap: "Here's my hug and kiss for Jackie and also your millions. Love and kisses"

Friday, March 31, 1944. *Received Atlas maps - R.H.S. In afternoon, Vene, M.D.R. kids and Dot Conent dropped in, stayed until 3:30. M.d.R. just got back from Trenton.*

[Nissan Island, Green Islands.]
Posted April 1, 1944, 9cent stamp upside down.   March 31, 1944
                                                            Somewhere

My Darling Wife:

I love you, miss you and want you. Each and every day I am thinking of you, and I dream of you each night. I want so much to take you tenderly in my arms and kiss you. To feel the warm softness of your lovely young body as it presses eagerly against me, ah, that will be heavenly. More than anything else, I want to be there with you. Gee, sweet, I want to see you so much. I want to hear you talk, see you smile, and watch you as you do things. Sweetheart, you are the only girl in the world for me, there will never be anyone else. I long to be with you. You are the mother of our child, and I am proud of you. You are taking excellent care of Jackinelle, I know. You may even be neglecting yourself, you are taking such good care of our Annette. Gee, I want to see you both so very much.

Honey, I'm not going to write a long letter tonight, because I intend going to the show. Flying Tigers is playing. I don't know what it's all about, but I will, very soon. It's about time for the show to start, so when it does, I'll save this and finish it later. Then I will probably tell you all about it. Only whether it's good or not, that's all. I may have seen it, I don't remember so well anymore. Isn't it funny how I can't seem to remember some things. Must be this extra long stay in the tropics. It isn't doing me any good, but it's only temporary. I will soon return to normal, after I cast eyes on you again. Boy, that's going to be a swell day. And my hunch seems to be getting more strong as the days slowly pass, gradually turning into months and the months into years. It has been over a year and a half since I've seen you. Gee, I never thought it would be that long, did you.

It doesn't rain quite as much as it did when we first arrived. I guess maybe the rainy season is about over. Boy, I sure hope so. I've had enough of this damp weather. It has been quite hot the past couple of days. I really have done a heck of a lot of sweating lately. But I don't mind that so very much. I work harder than I have to, because it makes the days pass more quickly. Heck, if I was lazy, and didn't work, I'd think of home too much, and then I'd become sick, or something. Boy, I sure am glad I'm so healthy. It sure would be terribly lonesome and tiresome, lying flat on my back. I never want to become ill down here. I'll take my work to keep me from getting too homesick.

Things look pretty good for us getting home in the next two or three months. Some say June, and others July, but I wouldn't care if it turned out to be May, but don't expect me for sure until you see me. You might get a few cases of beer for me, though, and keep a couple on ice. No, don't bother about the ice. I'll let you know in time to chill some for me. You might also get a bottle of gin or whiskey, and then we (you and I) will be able to have a nice highball, or a Tom Collins. I want to try one of your Collins'. They may be even better than I expect. I am quite willing to try one, though. I want to try a little zig-zig, too. Do you think you will be able to satisfy me? Remember when I was home last time, you wouldn't give me any more. I hope the same thing doesn't happen this time. But when I hit the States this time, I expect to have at least thirty days, but it may include my traveling time. Even so, we should be together for at least eighteen days. Gee, that won't be very long, will it. But we will have to make the most of it, and do the best we can until we are finally together for good. How I hope for this war to end soon.

Well, honey-bun, I just went to see the beginning of the picture, but

I've already seen it, back on that other Isle of Hades. It's all about the volunteer air corps in China. Boy, I just returned in time. One of our most sudden showers came up, and believe me, it's really coming down. It's been raining only since I started this page, and already the drainage ditches are running full. I've never seen it rain as hard back home as it does here. Even the smallest showers here are more heavy than your heavy rains. And as it rains daily, you can imagine the traveling conditions aren't any too good. But if one stays on the paths and roads, the going isn't so very bad. In fact, it's fairly decent. It took a heck of a lot of hard work to make things the way they are, though. But then, the sun is so strong, that when it does come out, in a very few hours there is a considerable bit of dust. So you see, it's never too wet or too dry. To prove that, all I have to tell you is that there is abundant grass, and it is nice and green. Not burnt by the sun or drowned.

In the beginning of this letter I told you that this would be a short letter, but it doesn't seem so now, does it. It seems as if I haven't said anything yet and here I am in the sixth page. Well, this will be the last, because there isn't any more to say. I only wish I could do as well every night.

In case you are interested, Lou dearest, I am as well and happy as usual, and I sure do hope that you, Jackie, and the family are also. More than anything else, even getting home, I want you two sweethearts of mine to be well and happy, and remain that way. And you know how much I want to get home to you both. Most adorable darling, I love you more as each day slowly passes, bringing us gradually more close together. Oh, my dear one, if only there were words to tell you just how much I love you, miss you and want you. I will just have to wait and show you. Regards to all, and my daily hug and kiss for Jackie. To you, my Angel, I give my all.

J.De Roxtro EM2/c   You're mine forever, and I am yours *Johnny*

Note on flap: "Gee, Sweet, I love you so very much. Happy Easter, love & kisses."

Saturday, April 1, 1944. *Lovely day. Brought Jackie to doctors for 2nd injection. Waited ½ hour. Stopped in Acme on way back - baby food. Took Prints - 1D.*

[Written while still on Nissan Island, Green Islands.]Posted Pavuvu Island, Russell Islands April 3, 1944, stamp upside down.   April 1, 1944

Somewhere

Most Beloved Darling:

I love you with all my heart. I miss you and want you. I long to put my arms around your lovely young body, draw you close to me and kiss you forever. Sweetheart, if possible, I want you to remain in my arms forever. I desire you. I yearn for you. I want to see you and hear your sweet voice. Angel of mine, to me, you are the only girl in the world for me. How much I miss you, you will never know. Mere words could never describe my true feelings for you. You are mine, and I am yours, forever.

The weather today has been quite damp, but right now it is perfectly adorable. I am well, as usual, and here's hoping that you, Jackie and the rest of the family are in the best of health, always.

The scuttlebutt still sounds good, so maybe it is right this time. Boy, I sure do hope it's right. These months have been plenty long. Let's see, the mailman will deliver this about the tenth, and, if the latest I hear is correct, I'll be seeing you five or six weeks later. That, of course, is strictly rumor, so don't depend on it. I wish I were able to say definitely when I would see you. But I can't, because there is nothing definite from official quarters. Honey, if and when I am sure of anything, I'll let you know.

Say, dear, I've been thinking quite seriously about getting Jackie a puppy when I get home. Do you think it would be alright with your mother? I know darn well it's a hell of a place to keep a puppy, but I want our daughter to have a pup to grow up with. It will be a lot of trouble for you, too, so let me know what you think about it, too. After we are together permanently, and are snugly settled in our own place, may be time enough to think about it. But then again, Jackie may be a lot older. I'm not quite sure what to do about it, so you will have to help me out. Shall I bring it home with me, or shall I wait, and let you help me pick it out? I won't do anything until I hear from you, anyway. Let's hope I never will be here to receive an answer to this letter. Here's hoping I'll be on my way to the most wonderful girl in the world. Gee, sweetheart, I love you so.

I'm going to see "Tales of Manhattan" tonight at our local cinema. I've seen it before, and enjoyed it. See you later. Well, I was wrong about the picture, my love. The picture, as I told you in a letter I wrote back on Santos, wasn't so hot. It was about a swallowtail coat, and wasn't what I thought it was. I must have been mistaken in the name, or something. Sweetheart, my memory is getting worse daily. All I can remember is you, and the good times we used to have, such a long, long time ago.

There doesn't seem to be anything more to tell you, my love. Gee, it's tough, trying to write, when there isn't anything to say. Except at special times, when I'm in the mood, like I was last night. Gee, I wish I were able to do that every night. Honey, I would much rather be there beside you, where I wouldn't have to send kisses by remote control. If I were there I wouldn't have to waste time writing, and you wouldn't have to read my silly drivel. It's going to be a swell day when you are right beside me where I can see you, hear you and feel you.

And our little daughter - how I want to see her and play with her. You never will know how much I've envied you, having her there with you all the time. Sweetheart, I want so much for the three of us to be together. It isn't right for us to be separated for such a long time. We are bound to be reunited soon. I know the good Lord will answer our prayers and let us enjoy each other's company, as we should. I am still hoping and praying that the day will soon come.

Give my fond regards to your mother, Mama G, Tadone and the rest of the family. Here is my daily hug and kiss for Jackie, and millions more for you, my precious angel. I love you, miss you and want you.

J.De Roxtro EM2/c   Everlastingly, your loving   *Johnny*

Note on flap: "Sweet Lucia, I love you. You are the best girl in the world."

Sunday, April 2, 1944. *Invited to Mil's for dinner. Left note for Joe & Angie. Rain - Betty & Joe Vigilante - wonderful meal - left - 5:15. No nap for baby. Fell right to sleep after supper, went to movies.*

[Written on Nissan Island, Green Islands.]
Postmarked April 3, 1944, **Pavuvu**, stamp upside down.   April 2, 1944
                                                                  Somewhere

Hello, my darling:

I love you, miss you and want you. Each and every hour of the day I am thinking of you, and each night I dream of you. You are eternally on my mind, and locked everlastingly in my heart. I want so much to hold you tenderly in my arms and kiss you. I want, more than anything else, to be there with you. Sweetest girl in all the world, you are mine, and I am yours, forever. May the good Lord hear my prayers and reunite us soon. I love you with all my heart.

Today I will answer your letter of March first. It is next in line. I still will have two more to answer after this. Seems as if your letters are finally beginning to arrive, doesn't it. Thanks loads for the two kisses sent by way of the stamps, my angel. Someday, soon, I hope to collect for all these kisses, and charge interest. On the inside flap you have "Hello, darling, I love you." Thanks Lou, I know you do, but I still want to read it. That is, until I can hear you say it. Gee, I love you so very much.

Enclosed in this letter were the pictures you took of our Juanita on the sixteenth and twenty fourth of February. Say, doesn't Juanita mean John, or Jackie? No, well, what does it mean. Or is Joan the feminine for John.

I'm slightly bawled up. I had better stick to Jackie, or Annette. Come to think of it, my love, what is the bambino's middle name, or hasn't she one? I know she is supposed to wait until she is confirmed, or something, and then choose her own, but didn't you give her one? If not, maybe I can persuade her to use your name. I kind of like that name. Gee, it sounds swell to me. Don't you like me to call you by name, Roberta? [Lucia's Confirmation name.]

Let's see, now, is there anything I meant to tell you, and haven't? I might tell you I wrote to your mother, Joan, Ralph and my mother. I received a letter from Ralph yesterday. I don't think I told you that, did I. He expects to be home in another six months and he received a letter from home in seven days. Not bad, huh?

Say, Angel, in my letter to Fan, I'm afraid I began to preach a little. If she says anything about it, tell her I didn't mean anything by it will you? It's only because I think so darn much of your entire family. Gosh, they are a swell bunch, Lou. I like them all. I know darn well I shouldn't write some of the things I do to those girls, but I just can't help it, and then I don't care to rewrite or change them. Here's hoping I never offend them, but if I do, they will have to get over it, because it's me, and I don't intend to change, for anyone. Not unless you ask me to, then I'll try my best.

I mentioned something about these snapshots in another letter, I think. They are really swell, honey, and I like them. Gosh, but our little one is getting big and fat. She sure is a healthy looking youngster, isn't she. How I wish the three of us were together. When we are, it will be for the first time. Here she is over a year old, and I haven't seen her yet. Why, it's over nineteen months since I've seen you. How time can pass so quickly, and yet seem to drag slowly by, beats me. In those two taken on her birthday, her upper lip does look a trifle swollen, doesn't it. But even so, she looks happy. Those things of yours (my things) are sticking right out there. How I wish I could grab ahold of one of them, and fondle it. Soon, I hope, I will be able to. Gee, I love you, Blackie, darling.

It looks to me as if you are becoming a trifle heavy across the hips, sweet, are you? It may be just the picture. You really do look good to me, and you've made me hungry again. My appetite will be appeased soon, tho. That is, if there is any truth in the scuttlebutt.

This is a mighty short letter you wrote this time, so I may not be able to make my answer very long, but I'll do my best. At least I can guarantee three pages, maybe four.

Sunday [pronounced Soondi] having a baby is sure a mistake. Not only on their part, either. Holy cow, why in the devil didn't she get rid of it? It will be more sinful to have it, than to have gotten rid of it. But I am not the one to judge. She may change considerably and quiet down. Who knows, it may be the best thing that ever happened. It may help even Angie and Patty. Those kids sure will be tough ones. By the way, Lou, whatever came of that girl (I forget the name) who seemed to be stuck on Ralph? You know, some relative of Sunday's who used to care for the house, and then went to nursing. Anyway, she sure had it tough. Especially when Madeline wouldn't co-operate. These are my own opinions so if my thinking is wrong, please correct me. Madeline is too darn good to work, she thinks. Oh, well, she'll get over all that in due time.

Boy, I am preaching today. Maybe I had better stop writing for awhile. Gee, I wonder if I carried on like this to everyone I wrote to today? Other people's business seems to interest me today. I wonder what's come over me? Oh well, let's just skip it all! I love you.

Thanks for sending a couple of pictures of Jackie to Mary, sweet. She's a swell girl, and we both know she will appreciate them. It was darn nice of you to write, too. It will be nice if you two are able to remain good friends always. I like you both but my love is centered upon only you. I adore you.

So, Fran had sent me a ring with the Navy insignia on it. No wonder she asked if I had ever received it. Well, I doubt very much now if I ever will. Being in a small box, with the Christmas rush on, it probably became lost, or dropped on a floor littered with paper, and was thrown away. There isn't anything we can do about it, so I guess it's just another ring gone. It may turn up one of these fine days, but I have my doubts. Perhaps I had better write and tell her, just in case she had it insured.

Yes, my sweet, as I told you in a previous letter, I received all five cards you sent. In fact, you probably have the letter long ago. Thanks again, anyway, just in case that letter becomes lost.

You are perfectly right concerning my location. In fact, you told me more about it than I knew before. I wasn't sure about the spelling before, but I thought I was right. Now that you tell me what you do in this letter, I can assure you that you are perfectly correct. Personally, I had never even heard of that name. Or maybe I did, and always thought of this place, never knowing of any other. I worship you.

Don't you worry your pretty little head about me, or the places I am being safe. Hell, this place is more safe now than your street is. The only thing that can possibly happen here is a coconut hitting one in the noggin. Things might not have been so good at first, but we do the best we can to make things safe. Right now, my next move should be home, but as I said, we can always go farther up the line. I think we have done our share, though. I still think we are returning to the states in a couple of months, more or less.

Boy, it seems as if I can be on the watch for more snapshots. You know, I've seen a lot of baby pictures, but none of them can even closely compare with our daughter. She is the best of the bunch, and I love her, even more than I love Lesley Ann, and you know darn well that I really think a lot of her.

Well, sweetheart, your letter is now answered. I have previously mentioned the pictures, so there doesn't seem to be any more to say. So, belated Happy Easter, sweet, and may we be together for the next one. Regards to all the family. Give Mama G a tch tch for me and say hello to Tadone. Here is my daily hug and kiss for our Annette, and to you, the most wonderful wife, sweetheart, and mate in all the world, all my love, hugs and kisses. I adore you. I worship you. You are mine, and I am yours, forever. Now I lay me down to sleep, to dream sweet dreams of you my sweet.

J.De Roxtro EM2/c   Loving you eternally, I am yours devotedly, *Johnny*

Note on flap: "Gee, my sweet, I love you, miss you, and want you so much. How's Mickey?

Lesley Ann & Jackie

April 3, 1944 – Arrived on Pavuvu Island, in the Russell Islands.

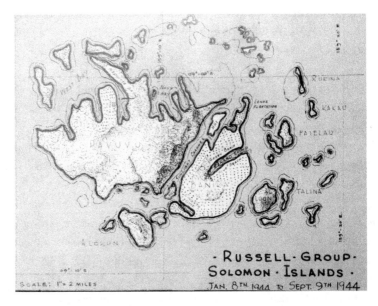

Monday, April 3, 1944. Lovely day. Letters of Mar. 23,24,25,26. Check for $88.00. Letter from Ralph. Jackie cutting lower right molar. Mil came over - went downtown, bought coat & cards. Easter.

[Pavuvu Island in the Russell Islands.]
Postmarked April 6, 1944, stamp upside down.

April 3, 1944

Somewhere

Hello, My Darling:

I love you, want you and miss you. Never an hour passes without thoughts of you passing through my mind. All the love in the world is ours, my sweet. I long to take you tenderly in my arms and kiss you. Adorable Lucia, I'm hungry. I received a letter from my mother today, and, believe it or not, another from you. It was written the thirteenth of March, but wasn't posted until the twenty-fifth.

There seems to be nothing I can say right now, about anything here. I am well, and as happy as I possibly can be away from you. I sincerely hope that you, Jackie and all the family are in the best of health.

Your letter of March second is short, so I guess I'll answer it tonight. I have a feeling I will receive more this week. Thanks for the kiss my turtledove. I intend collecting for them all when I return, which, I hope, will be soon. I love you.

49

Inside the envelope you have the following: "Jackie sends a big hug and kiss, and I send you all the love in the world. L." Thank Jackie for me, will you sweet, and I thank you, for being such a swell wife. Gee, I would like to be there to collect all that love. Glad to hear you liked my long letter of the twentieth of February. Hell, sweet, if I could think of something to say, they would all be long.

Funny, you speak of having the addresses to send those pictures, and Carl received a letter today in which his wife mentioned looking at his picture, which you sent. So, my love, at least one of them reached its destination. Someone was asking about them the other night, and I told him they were already on the way. Say, did you send one to Frosty Zealand who writes to me. Such letters. Would you like me to bring a couple home as an example?

Well, I thought that Silverstein's wouldn't have any ice cream. The sugar rationing, or something, probably caused it to be more inferior in quality. Too bad, sweet, but at least you are able to get some. To tell the truth, I am surprised that they were still able to get it. Of course I remember those butter-pecan cones we used to get during the summer. I, too, wish I were able to have one tonight. We do manage to have some about twice a week. Hell, honey, you got me so I sort of like the stuff. I haven't gone back for seconds yet, but who knows, maybe I will, one of these days. I know darn well that if you want ice cream, we'll have some, even if I have to make it for you. Would you like that, sweetheart?

So, our little one has finally started climbing the stairs. Gee, I wish you could have taken a picture that day, when she first made the landing and called to you. I can imagine the look of pleasure and success written all over her handsome puss. And now she goes all the way up. That's quite an accomplishment for her. But now, sweet, you will have your hands full, trying to keep her downstairs, where you can keep your eye on her. And her spills will be more numerous, I think. She sure is progressing rapidly. Gee, how I wish I had been there to watch her, all through her, as yet short, life. Gee, I want so much to see you both. It wouldn't do much good for you to try to stop her from going up the stairs. It might be even better if you could teach her how to do it properly. I don't know just how you would go about that, though. Time enough when she starts walking up, I guess. She must be a tough little rascal. Boy, oh, boy, I want to get there soon, so I will be able to hold both of you in my arms. I love you both.

That ends your short letter, my honey. I would rather receive a short one daily, with a nice long one once in awhile, than to receive only two or three a week. But you must be too busy to write daily, sweet, so just keep doing as well as you are, and I'll try to make myself satisfied. Like crackerjack, the more I get, the more I want, as I'll never be satisfied.

Well, my angel, there is nothing more to say, except Goodnight, Sweetheart. Give my regards to all. Here is my daily hug and kiss for Jackie, and all my love for you, with millions of hugs and kisses. I love you, miss you and want you, as always.

J.De Roxtro EM2/c   Everlastingly, your loving *Johnny*

Note on flap: "Sweetest girl in the world, I'll be with you in a few months. Love&kisses."

Tuesday, April 4, 1944. Lovely day. No mail. M.d.R. called, said they would not be down. Bonnie has reaction from vaccination. Perhaps would come Sunday. Cooked gravy. Brought baby to doctor for last injection for whooping cough. 2 o'clock, were back before 4:00. Visited Aunt and Carol Ann. Jackie played piano & ball, started to snow.

[Pavuvu Island, Russell Islands.]
Postmarked April 6, 1944, stamp upside down.   April 5, 1944
                                                  Somewhere

Most Adorable Wife:

I love you with all my life (I don't know why that came in there) heart, body and soul. Each and every day I think of you hourly, and each night I dream of you. Thoughts of you are eternally in my mind, and your image is everlastingly locked in my heart. I have reserved a little corner for our future family, though. I love you so much, sweetheart. I don't know how I ever would have managed to keep going out here if I didn't have you to think of. I love everything about you, my darling. I love your hair, your eyes, your nose, your lips, your neck, shoulders, my things, your waist, hips, thighs and your legs. Honey-bunch, I love everything about you, from the tip of your toes to the top of your head. Your personality is very pleasing, your voice is almost perfect, your smile is quite alluring, sweetest wife and companion in the world, to me, you are perfect. Dearest one, I love you more as each day slowly passes, bringing us more close to the day of our reunion. Sweetie-pie, that day can't come too soon to suit me. I miss you, my lovely one, and how I want you. I want so very much to see you, and hold you tenderly in my arms and kiss you. Sweetest girl in the world, I love you. I am hungry, my sweet, and I don't mean for food. One of these days my appetite will be sated, and then I intend to make up for all the time I've lost. I've been away a hell of a long time, so it will take me a long time to catch up. I doubt very much if I'll be able to, but I sure intend to try. Angel of mine, I will be in my heaven on earth when I see you. Gee, those days will be the happiest in my life, I think. I will try my best to do everything you want to do, and go everywhere you want to go. Any and everything you desire will be done if it's at all possible. I love you, miss you and want you more than I've ever loved, missed or wanted anything or anyone in all my life. You are mine forever, and I am more proud of you as each day passes. I am proud to have you for my wife, and I am also proud of you for doing as well as you are for our darling Jackie. Sweetheart, you are the best wife and mother in all the world. I love you more as each day passes.

In a month or two, I feel that I will be leaving here, for home. Boy, no matter how fast the time flies, it will seem ages between the day of my departure and my arrival. But the slowest time will be when I have to take a train across the country. Gee, how I would like to fly from California right to our local airport. Even that would be entirely too slow for me. But I guess that even though I were able to travel from here to your arms with the speed of light, I don't think that I would be satisfied. Can't you just picture me, pacing the deck of the ship, when we are on our way to the states? I surely will be a restless guy, and will probably be a royal pain in the neck to the fellows. I adore you.

Three pages, and I haven't said anything yet. It's too bad, sweetie-pie but there just isn't anything to say. I am quite well, as usual, an am as happy and contented as I possibly can be, away from you. I sincerely hope and pray that you, Jackie and the family are all in the best of health and happy.

You haven't mentioned anything about Jackinella's teeth lately. Are they coming in straight yet? You, being there all the time, probably wouldn't notice it quite as soon as someone else would. But

don't forget to let me know how they're coming in. (or should I say down?) And how is she making out with her spills? Oh, well, she will take a lot more, so don't let them get you down. She'll live through it, and it will make her tough, like me.

Give my regards to all the family and our friends. Especially to Mama Gee and Tadone. Here is my daily hug and kiss for Jackie, and to you, my beloved adorable wife and sweetheart, all my hugs, kisses, love and adoration.

J.DeRoxtro EM2/c   Everlastingly, your loving *Johnny*

Note on flap: "Sweetheart, I love you with all my heart. How's Mickey?"

Wednesday, April 5, 1944. *Snow made everything look lovely. About 2 in.*

[Pavuvu Island, Russell Islands.]
Postmarked April 6, 1944, stamp upside down.   *April 5, 1944*
                                                                    Same place

Most Adorable Lucia:

I love you, miss you and want you more as each day passes, slowly but surely binging us more close together. How I long to hold you tenderly in my arms once again and kiss you. Dearest one, the day we are reunited will really be a happy day for me.

I was lucky today, angel of mine. I received three pieces of mail. One letter from C.H.Nuttle, thanking me for thanking them for the Y bulletin. Now maybe I should write to him, thanking him for thanking me for thanking him. And so it goes, on and on. I also received another bulletin, and a sweet letter from my adorable wife. It was written the fifth of March and postmarked the twentieth. Long time, sweet. However, as this is the oldest letter I have, I will answer it tonight.

I am well and happy as I can be, being away from you. I sincerely hope and pray that all you folks at home are in the best of health. The rains come daily, as yet, but one of these days it may stop. I hope it does, at least if I am here very long. The way the scuttlebutt is running, it seems that we will be together soon. Boy, the day of our next meeting can't possibly come any too soon to suit me. I long to be with you and our sweet darling. Gee, my sweetheart, I love you, miss you and want you, and---.

Thanks for the kiss you so thoughtfully sent by way of the stamp, my lovely one. One of these days we will collect all these little things we've owed each other all these many, many months. Boy, we have a lot to make up for, haven't we. I'll do my best to make you happy, my love.

Inside, on the envelope, you have a sweet message for me. Here it is, "Dearest, I love you with all my heart." As you know, I feel the same about you.

Tell Mama G and Tadone I appreciate them asking for me, and give them my fond regards. I really like them both. Gee, I hope we are as well and able-bodied as they are when we reach their age.

I imagine you were surprised when my mother and Vene walked in, when you thought she (my mom) was in Roselle. But I suppose she had to drop in and see the sweetest little girl in the world before she left. Or perhaps it was because the telephone was most inconvenient. It could be, you know, but I think it was because of Jackie, don't you?

So Vene was making Leslie Ann a red hooded jacket. Well, if she was really interested in her work, she must have done a swell job. And I can almost picture "Butch" all dressed up in it. She really must have looked swell.

53

But then, she looks good in most everything. She is a good-looking kid, but I know a little girl that is, or will be much better looking. We'll have the sweetest little girl in the whole world. And you and I together will do all we possibly can to make her happy, won't we.

Gee, sweet, wasn't it rather peculiar that only such a short while back, you received a letter from me, in which I mentioned about a puppy for our Jackinelle? Must be mental telepathy, or something. But I guess we will be able to wait awhile, at least until I arrive home, to decide that. I want her to have her own dog, too. Gosh, do you know I was actually afraid that she wouldn't like them, or would be frightened by them. It certainly was a relief to receive this letter in which you tell me about her liking dogs. I'm also glad you don't let our daughter get too close to Sandelli's dog. I don't actually know that it is unclean, but I know darn well that there isn't anyone there to have enough ambition to give the poor thing a bath. But that's their business, and I should stick to my own. Too bad that the pup my mother had picked out was stolen, but in a way, I'm glad. I didn't think much of their dog. She was a shaggy, unkempt looking one. As you do, I would like a terrier, or a nice spaniel. If we got a spaniel, I would be able to use her for hunting. Let's get a cocker spaniel, shall we? They don't grow very large. Or maybe we can get a small beagle hound. Or perhaps some sort of a bird dog. Say, am I thinking of my daughter or myself. I am merely killing two birds with one stone. I really don't care what kind of a dog you get, angel. I will be satisfied with any you care for. I love all dogs, so whichever you choose will be alright with me. I love you, miss you and want you. I need you.

Of course you will have a chance to get a puppy for Jackie. But don't worry yourself about it, because after all, she is a trifle young yet. Maybe we will look around and get her a nice one when I get home on leave. We will do our best to make her happy, won't we, and we will start by getting her her own private pup. Maybe we can start with a thoroughbred. What would you think of that?

How nice it will be if and when I am able to see our Annette perform all her tricks. Gee, all the ones that are old to you will be all new to me. But maybe I can teach her a few new ones, like thumbing her nose, or something. But then you wont be liking that very much, and to tell the truth, neither will I. Gee, I used to think those things were cute, but Annette will learn them soon enough.

That's all there is of your letter to answer, my love, as I'm afraid you will have to be satisfied with this brief note. How much I love you, you will never know. Even when I arrive home and tell you, you won't know. There just aren't enough words to describe my love for you.

Give my regards to all the family, and especially to Mama G and Tadone, and your mother. Here is my daily hug and kiss for our darling daughter. How I wish I were there to deliver them in person. Then, if I were there, I could make love to the sweetest, most adorable girl in the world, my wife and sweetheart, Lucia Roberta Petrone de Roxtro. I love you, miss you and want you. I adore you.

J.De Roxtro EM2/c   Everlastingly, your *Johnny*

Note on flap: "Sweetest girl in the world, I'll see you soon, I hope. Love."

Thursday, April 6, 1944. *No mail. Snow melting away. Church, procession, Jackie through shoe in toilet while I washed my hair. Visited church.*

[Pavuvu Island, Russell Islands.]
Posted April 7, 1944, stamp upside down.   *April 6, 1944*
                                                            Same place

Hiyah, Sweetheart:

All the love in the world is ours. You are forever in my heart, and eternally in my thoughts. I am in love with you so much that even when I am absorbed in my work, your image is there before me. Sweetest girl in the world, I love you, miss you and want you, more as each day slowly passes, bringing us more close to the day of our reunion. Mere words could never describe my feelings for you.

One of these days, soon, I hope, you will be before me in person. Then I will be able to hold you close to me, as I've longed to do this past year and a half. Then while I have you close to me, I will be able to kiss you, and tell you of my love and adoration. Sweetheart, more than anything else in the world, I want to be with you. You are the only girl in the world for me. My love for you is greater than ever. I am hungry my sweet, and my hunger can only be appeased by you. You're mine, and I want you. I want to stay with you forever, my lovely one, never more to roam. I hope and pray that when we are together again, I will be able to stay with you always. I love you.

I can't think of a thing to say, honey, simply because there isn't anything. I am as well and happy as I usually am, and I hope you, Jackie and the family are in the best of health, and are happy. Give my regards and tch tch to Mama G and Tadone.

Sweetheart, I received your letter of the twentieth of March today. It was postmarked the twenty-eight. That isn't so bad but I wish they were even better. Gee, if this had been a letter of the day before the posted date, that would mean I would have received it in only nine days. Boy, that really would be something, wouldn't it. Let's see, that would make you receiving an answer to your letter in three weeks or less. That is, of course, if I answered it right away.

Mrs. Blosser received her pictures and was very pleased to get them. She told Carl all about them in a letter he received from her today. She was very grateful, and Carl asked me to thank you very much for sending them. He also said that he will be glad to do something for you sometime. While on the subject, Mrs. Forbes also received hers. Vincent also sends his thanks to you. I haven't seen Fitz in a couple of weeks, so I'm not sure about his mother, but I have an idea that she did also. My darling, you are a really marvelous girl, and I love you for what you are. By the way, if you would like to have an enlargement of that picture, Fitz said to let me know, and he will tell his brother to make one for you. I suppose I should have told him to have one made, but I would rather know for sure that you want one. Anyway, in order to get one, just let me know. I worship you.

I still have your letters of March sixth, thirteenth and twentieth to answer, but I think I will wait for tomorrow to answer one. Say, my lovely one, there is a week between each of them. Can it be that you are writing only once a week, now? I have an idea that you are doing better than that, though. I surely hope so. If you ever stop writing more regularly than that, I think I would do the same. Sweetheart, I love you.

Gee, angel of mine, there doesn't seem to be anything more to say. The scuttlebutt is still running good, so maybe we can depend on it this time. By deducting this and that, and basing my report on common sense, I figure that the latest, absolutely the latest, that I will be home, with you in my arms, is the first of July. Now, sweet, there is absolutely nothing official to base my opinions on, so don't depend too much on me. My prayers will have to be answered one of these days, and when they are, we will be the happiest couple in all the world. Honey, I don't see how I can be there before the first of June, either, so you see, I haven't given myself much leeway. However, don't expect me until you see me or hear from me, and then we'll see just how good I am at figures.

Goodnight, most precious angel. You are my one and only. I send millions of hugs and kisses to you, and my daily to our Jackie. Give my regards to all the family and our mutual friends. I hope we will be able to be alone for most of my stay at home. I want to be with you and Jackie, nothing more.

J. De Roxtro EM2/c   Everlastingly, your adoring *Johnny*

Note on flap: "How is Mickey? I want to kiss her and make love to her. Love and kisses ever.

Friday, April 7, 1944. Good Friday. No mail. Warm out. Cleaned sun porch in afternoon, went down town. Gracie took Jackie for walk. Trouble with Jackie - not well - teeth.

[Pavuvu Island, Russell Islands.]
Posted April 8, 1944, TWO stamps upside down.

April 7, 1944

Somewhere

Hi Beautiful:

I love you, want you and miss you more as each day passes, slowly bringing us more close together. I yearn to hold you in my arms and kiss you. I long to tell you how fond I am of you. I am hungry for love, and being with you is all that can possibly satisfy my hunger. I want you so much, my darling. My thoughts are continuously of you, and believe it or not, I even dream of you, and the more than happy times we've had together. One of these days, soon, I hope we will be reunited, and then our happy days will begin all over again. Gee, it sure will be swell, being there with you and our little Jackie. I want so much to see you both.

This will be an exceptionally short letter, my love, because I don't have time to write more. I had a special job to do tonight, and I have just returned, showered, and prepared for bed. I just had to drop you a few lines, in order to keep my chain of daily epistles of love and adoration to you unbroken. It seems to be a habit, now, but more than that, I know darn well that you, the most magnificent creature in the world, appreciate them very much, even though some of them are very short. Every once in awhile I manage to pen a fairly long one, though, so maybe they make up a little for the short ones. Say, my dearest angel, how would you like to receive a nice long one like I received today? Herb, believe it or not, wrote me a twenty two-page letter, and he didn't say anything, either. All he did was tell me about his short stay in the hospital, while his appendix was removed. He can throw more bull than a toreador. Such a line I never read before. No other mail came for me, not even from you. I don't have many to write this Sunday so far. And unless I get more mail tomorrow, all I have to do is write three letters. One each to Herb, my mother, and my wife, sweetheart, and companion. I will do my best to make yours a nice long (extra long) one then. How I wish that I could demonstrate my true feelings for you, instead of having to write them. This business of writing isn't any fun, and is so much more work than actually being there and being intimate with you. In fact, one could almost call this work.

I don't have a damn thing to write about, sweetheart. News that I can send you is very scarce, and most of it you also get there. Hell, I wish I could tell you everything, just as I would like to. I have to think of something

57

to say, and also what not to say, all at the same time. I guess that every once in awhile I insert something that the censors must remove, though. They must have a hell of a job. I don't envy them at all. Their job is tough.

My younger brother also mentioned his visit to Morristown. He started off telling me how sweet my "prettiest niece" was all during Mother's stay there. He also mentioned the blessed event which is due in August. Maybe I'll be home then, and we may go down to visit them. Would you like that? While we are there, we can go see your relatives. Here's what he said about our "lovely little daughter," "Gee, she's a honey. I'm telling you, brother, I did not think you could make such a swell child. Honestly, she's a picture. Dark hair, fair complexion. What a combination. I'll be honest with you, tho, I don't know what color eyes she has." Coming from him, that's really something. Our little one must be even nicer than I had imagined. I can hardly wait to see her. But as for him thinking I had anything to do with her beauty, he's absolutely nuts. Hell, all I did was sow the seed. All the rest was up to you. You did all the hard work, and I wasn't even there to hold your hand when you were needing me the most. Damn this war. It not only took me away from you, but it's keeping me away. All the health and beauty of our child can be blamed on you. I would like to take a little credit, but I find that I can't. Yes I can. I'll take credit for all her wrong deeds and actions. That will be something, anyway. But then, she will probably be an individualist in them, too. Sweetheart, I am really proud of you. I love you more each time someone else writes about you and Jackie. I am a proud father, but a more proud husband. You two are all I have, and I love you both. When Herb brags about our Annette, she must be tops. But then, she is your daughter, so how could she be anything but the best and prettiest child in the world. How I want to see you both. I adore you.

Well, my love, this has turned out to be quite a fair-sized letter after all, hasn't it. And I didn't even have to answer one of your sweet letters to do it. I've been writing rather rapidly, but I'm afraid that any minute now the lights will go out. In case they do, I want to have the envelope all ready for this epistle of love, and I'll take time out to address it.

There was a little discouraging scuttlebutt today, but I don't think it means anything. I sure am hoping and praying, my little wife, that we will be soon in each other's arms. How I long to be close to you, real close. I yearn for the feel of your luscious red lips against mine. Oh, beloved one, if only I never have to leave you, once we are together again. Sweetheart, I should be there with you, helping to bring Jackie up. And that's the only place in all the world I want to be. All my love is yours.

J.De Roxtro EM2/c   *Hugs & kisses, from your devouted Johnny*

Note on flap: *"Here's Jackie's hug and kiss, and my regards to all. I love you and Mickey.*

Saturday, April 8, 1944. *Rain this morning. Cleared by noon. Cleaned rooms. Went downtown. Bought plant for Mom, azalea, ordered corsage for M.D.R. white carnations. Jackie has fever. Letters of 25 & 27 of Mar.*

[Pavuvu Island, Russell Islands.]
Postmarked April 10, 1944, two stamps upside down.   *April 8, 1944*

Somewhere

My Sweetheart:

I love you, miss you and want you. Thoughts of you are forever running through my mind, and every night I dream of you. I long to take your lovely body in my arms once again and kiss you. Dearest one, you are mine and I am yours, forever. The day of our reunion can't come any too soon to suit me. Darling, more than anything else in the world, I want to be there with you.

Today I received your letter of March ninth. It was postmarked the twenty-third. That's all the mail I have received today. Maybe I'll get some more tomorrow. This evening, I will answer your letter of the sixth, as that is the next I have. There is nothing I am able to tell you from here, as usual. The weather remains about the same, although it doesn't rain quite as often as it used to. Gee, I love you.

It kind of looks as if my pen needs cleaning, doesn't it. Or perhaps you hadn't noticed that it writes fine sometimes, and others it writes heavy, as it is now. It's a wonder it writes at all, the abuse it has had since I've had it. Oh, well, so far it's been a handy one, so if it breaks or anything, I will just send it home and you can have it repaired. While on the subject, I may as well tell you about the mate to my pen. In all the time I've had it, the only time I've used it has been to do a few crossword puzzles. Even then it's not so hot. It's a bit too hard for that, and those leads I bought along for it are too thick. So, when I return to the states, I'll have to get some real thin leads for it. Soft ones, too. I lost that old pencil I had, back on Santos. It came in handy while I was at work, and I missed it. Perhaps someone wanted it more than I did. But no one could ever want anything or anyone half as much as I want you, the most wonderful girl in the world.

You know, sweet, I was bout to throw this paper out several times. Now I'm glad I kept it. It is a bit too heavy for airmail, but maybe the guy in the post office won't notice it. This is still some of that which you sent me a year ago last Christmas. Remember it? Air-mail paper is almost out of the question now, unless one has a chance to go aboard ship, and I haven't had a chance. No place on the island has any. Most places don't have stationery of any kind. I guess I'll have to stock up on some when I return to you.

You say that you could write daily, if I were satisfied with only a couple of pages. Hell, you know darn well that I would never be satisfied. Not even if you wrote a book every day. Are you satisfied with any of my letters, even the real long ones? I know you would never be. Besides, what's the use of writing daily, when it takes up to two weeks to mail them? Just keep going as you are, and I'll be almost satisfied. I adore you.

Say, that wouldn't be a bad idea at that. I mean, you shopping while I remained outside with our Jackie. That way, I wouldn't have to drag you away from the counters. That'll be killing two birds with one stone, won't it? You won't be rushed by me and you will know that Jackie will be alright. Then my lovely one, you may spend all day in one shop if you care to. But if you stay too long, you may come out and find us both gone. Then you might learn not to dawdle. Hell, I didn't ever hear of that happening to Betty Vigilante's baby. No wonder my sweetheart is a bit afraid to leave the baby out while she is shopping. What a heck of a thing to do. But that happens only once in a lifetime, so don't worry too much about it. I'll be home one of these days to help you care for your young one. Here's hoping nothing happens to our little one. Gee, can you imagine having a child that would do a thing like that? I'll bet poor Betty was in a hell of a condition that day.

By this time you must certainly have heard that I received your birthday cards, and our anniversary card, and the Valentines. Altogether I received five cards that day. They were both from you and our lovely daughter.

Gee, sweet, that is about all I am able to answer of your letter. I am well and happy as I possibly can be, being away from you and our beloved daughter. I want so much to hold you tenderly once again. I miss you so much. Here's hoping you, Jackie and all the family are in the best of health also. Here's hoping I'm there to see you real soon. More than anything else in the world, I want to be there with you, to remain forever. I will do my best to make you and our family happy. There won't be anything I will not try to do to make your life more fully complete, and worth living. You are my guiding light. Without you I would be lost. How I ever lived without you, I still can't figure out. Gee, I love you with my all.

A fellow in the tent just told my fortune with cards, twice. It seems that the first time, there was a dark old man and trouble connected, somehow, and a blond woman. In the second attempt, there was the same blond woman and money and I would hear something about it in four days. Now ain't dat sompin'. It's a good thing I don't believe such tripe, else I would be so darn worried, I wouldn't be able to sleep for a week or more. Have you ever had your fortune told, sweet? I never have before. Honestly, that's the first time in my life that it's ever happened.

I went to the show this evening and saw "Always a bridesmaid" with the Andrews sisters. Lousy, like most of our shows. I sat through it though, like a dope.

Goodnight, sweetheart, until we meet tomorrow, in spirit only. How I wish we were able to be in each other's arms again. I love you more than I ever did, my sweet. The more I think of you, the more I want you, so I really want you. Adorable one, I love you truly.

J.De Roxtro, EM2/c   Eternally, your *Johnny*

Note on flap: "Here's Jackie's daily hug and kiss. I love you, my sweet."

Easter Sunday, April 9, 1944. At 7:00 was lovely and warm. 10:00 rain. 11:00 Gene & Mil Judy. 11:15 Jo & Mike & M. Jr. came for dinner. 4:00 took a few pictures. 5:00 Vene & Johnnie - Nan. 5:30 - visited Aunt Santa. Joe & Angie came. 6:30 - home. Jackie got a bunny from Ann, a bunny from Fan. Mom's coat, polo shirt from Mil, money from Mike - $1.

Michael, Jackie, Judy   Judy, Jackie, Michael

Michael (26 months) Jackie (13 months)

Mike, Michael, Tadone   Lou, Jo, Grace, Mike, Tadone, Ann,

[Pavuvu Island, Russell Islands.]
Postmarked April 11, 1944, one stamp upside down.

April 9, 1944

Somewhere

Happy Easter, Darling,

I love you, miss you and want you. Each and every hour of the day and night I am either thinking of, or dreaming of you. Your image is continually before me. Your smiling face leads me wherever I go, in whatever I do. Without you, I would be lost. I long to hold you in my arms and kiss you. I want to tell you of my love and adoration for you. We belong together, sweetheart but there is nothing we can do about being apart. One of these days, we will be reunited for good, then we will be happy once again. I hope and pray that that day will soon come.

This is a beautiful Easter day, out here in this tropical paradise. It hasn't stopped raining all morning, and the breeze is just strong enough to blow a little spray all over everything, inside and out. I sincerely hope that the weather there is nice, and that you and Jackie are able to wear your new outfits. I wish I were there to show you off, but that is impossible, so you will have to be alone again this year. Make the best of everything, my beloved angel, and enjoy yourself. I love you, and want you to be happy.

We are supposed to have a chicken dinner today. I imagine we will have to be satisfied with canned chicken, though, so it will be fairly nice. While I'm eating, I will think of you and the family, and imagine I am there, eating parmigiana.

This afternoon, there is to be a stage show here, sponsored by the red cross. If it stops raining, I may go, but I have my doubts as to that becoming a reality. So far, it's been raining steadily all day. It may stop later, though, and clear up for the show. The weather is quite unpredictable, here, as one never knows what to expect. The show isn't until fourteen hundred, so there is plenty of time. It is now about eleven hundred.

I've already written to my mother and Herb, in answer to their

letters, so this is all I have to answer. I had intended making this a nice long letter, my sweet, but somehow or other, I'm not in the mood to write. Perhaps I'll be in a better mood after dinner. I guess I'll go now to dine. Be back later. Well, here I am, and I don't feel much better. I'm sort of blue today, and don't know why. Maybe as I write, my mood will change. You will be able to tell, as I proceed.

Sweetest girl in all the world, I will now attempt to answer your letter of the ninth of March. This is the last letter I've received from you, but I still have two to answer. Thanks loads for the kiss you sent by way of the stamp. How I wish I were there to collect for all these kisses and all the love you have saved up for me. Someday I will be there, and then will really make love. On the inside flap of the envelope you have merely "Darling, I love you." Those words are simple and short, yet they mean so much. Sweetheart, I too, am in love with you. What more can anyone say. Those three words make the world go round. They mean everything.

Yes, I guess you are lonesome for me. Especially when you are alone. I am never alone, my sweet. Maybe it's a good thing I'm not. I might go crazy, if I were alone much. I sure wish I could be there to keep you company, my love. You wouldn't be very lonesome then. Boy, would we be happy, for a change. But then, all this unhappiness and discontent will make us appreciate each other more, when we do see each other again.

Believe it or not, the sun has finally come out. The actors and actresses have arrived and the band is just coming in. I will go to see the show, and will finish this when I return. Forbes just brought me two letters, one from Grace, and one from Vene. None from my honey, though. I'm a wee bit disappointed, but as I still have a couple to answer, all will be taken care of. It's funny but I'm always that way when I don't get a letter or two from my lovely wife.

I have just returned from the show, and it was pretty good. It was an all service show, and not a red cross show. There were two girls in it, and were they hags. I've seen worse, but I don't know where. Maybe it was in a side show or something. A fellow who used to whistle in Sammy Kaye's orchestra did three or four numbers, a couple of guys (twins) danced (tap), a negro quartet sang a few songs, and a comedian was quite a bit of alright. The band was darn good, too. All the two hags did was sing. The fellow from Sammy Kaye's band whistled Easter Parade, and it made me feel almost as bad as White Christmas used to. That's about all there is to tell you about the show. Taking it all in all, it was rather a good show.

So you didn't recognize Carl when he came to see if Vene was there. One can't very well blame you, because, after all, you have seen very little of him. As far as I'm concerned, you are better off. I don't care a hell of a lot for that guy. But I guess my poor darling was a little embarrassed, were you?

It wasn't very nice of my mother to leave and not let them know she wasn't coming. After all, she must have told them she would pay them a visit. But what the hell, as long as he came for her, (I am really surprised that he did) all he could do was become angry. And I'll really bet he was a bit angry. Ha, ha, I feel for him.

You're getting to be quite a gal, now. Here you go to the show and then stop in for pizza and beer. Heck, gal, don't make a habit of it. I am glad you are able to do such things, my love, while I am away. Hell, you may as well enjoy yourself while you can. Could it be that you are beginning to like beer now? Say, sweetie-pie, have you ever tried that new place on Speedwell Avenue yet? What is it? Club 48, or something, isn't it? Let me know more about it, will you? Who runs it, the sort of people who patronize the joint, whether it's quiet or refined, and anything you think I may be interested in. Maybe we'll try it sometime, when we are reunited. That is, of course, if you care to. Maybe it will be alright. I love you, miss you and want you.

I told you about the gals receiving those pictures, didn't I? In her letter to Carl, Evelyn said she was going to write to you. I hope you do receive a letter from her. You two may get to be real good friends. I wonder if you will ever meet her, or any of the boys? Only time alone can tell, and we will have to wait.

I'm glad to hear you bought a stroller my sweet. It's about time she had one, and it will be a heck of a lot easier on you than pushing the carriage. I'm sure glad to know that you don't take time to write and ask me about those things. Anything you do will suit me fine, so keep up the good work, sweetheart. As long as you think it's okay and you see things clearly, why go right ahead and do whatever you care to do. For all I care, you may even go into debt for whatever you desire. I know you won't do that, though, without consulting me. Let's see, sweet, I can't think of anything else you may need for the care and comfort of our Jackie. If you are wishing for anything, and can see your way clear, well, we will see what we can do about it. If there is anything I can do out here, don't hesitate to let me know.

So our little one now takes only two bottles a day. That's swell, darling. It makes a lot less work for you, doesn't it. And she is now drinking more milk. That's good, too. Maybe if you put a little sugar in it, she would care a little more for her milk. Heck, by this time, our Jackie may be doing without any bottles.

Well, this will be my last page, sweetheart. Your letter is practically answered, and I have nothing more to say. In this letter was enclosed the clipping of Washington's headquarters. I wonder why they are printing them. There must be very little news for them to print. Thanks for the clipping, sweet. I would be glad to see all those familiar places again, even if it's only by pictures. Send them along, my beloved angel, and I will look them over. There will probably be quite a few things I will have never seen before. The same thing happened in a Chamber of Commerce booklet that Charlie Fetzer sent me. Half the places pictured I was unable to recognize.

Grace wrote her letter the thirtieth of March, and it was postmarked the second of April. It made darn good time, didn't it. Cheese, a week ago today she mailed this letter. Boy, that really is something, isn't it. And a day is lost on the way over, too. Boy, that must have come by plane all the way. Gee, I wish your letters came as quickly. Do you realize that it'll be less than three weeks between the day of her writing, and receiving the answer. I guess I'll be dropping her a line tonight before the movie, just to see how long it'll take. You let me know.

Give my regards to all the family and our friends. Here is my daily hug and kiss for Jackie, and to you, my dear one, all the love I can possibly send to you.

J.De Roxtro EM2/c   Everlastingly and eternally, your loving *Johnny*

Monday, April 10, 1944. *Today's Mama G's birthday. Gave money last night. Letters of 28,29,20,31, April 1. Letter from Mary, card from Vene. Washed clothes, mom home for week. Gracie pulled Jackie in wagon, went down to Mama G's.*

Jackie on rocking horse

Gracie, Jackie, wagon

"Panda," Jackie in crib

Jackie, Lou

[Pavuvu Island, Russell Islands.]
Posted April 11, two stamps upside down.

April 10, 1944
Somewhere

Hello, Adorable:

I love you, miss you and want you. Thoughts of you are continually running through my mind. Your image is constantly before me. My one desire is to be with you, hold you close to me and kiss you. Gee, my sweet angel, the day we are reunited will really be a happy one, won't it. Our red-letter day. (Another one, I mean.) If we keep this up, every day will be a day for us to remember.   There is a little disturbance here this evening. The boys are having a friendly little crap game here on the deck. I will get in it, after I finish this letter. That is, of course, if it's still going. I shot last night, so enclosed find a money order for a hundred dollars. If I run this ten dollars up into an amount large enough, I'll send another tomorrow. But don't look forward to it. You may do as you please with this, because it's yours.

Honey, I have a little surprise for you tonight. The Holy Name Society of St. Margaret's
sent me a box containing four packs of cigarettes, chewing gum and several bars of nickel candy. It was a complete surprise to me. Gee, I never expected anything from them. I will now have to write and send my thanks and appreciation. Besides that, I received an Easter card from your mom, a letter from my mother, and two (2) lovely letters from my one and only, the sweetest girl in the world. They were written the twenty-third and twenty-sixth of March, and were postmarked the twenty-ninth and thirty-first of March, respectively. That's a lot better, sweet, thanks a lot. I am pleased to see that you are posting them more rapidly. One of them had the latest pictures in it, and they sure are swell. Say, is that a banana our little one is holding so tightly in her left hand? I didn't think she was eating them quite yet.

The Banana photo   With Rosalinda

With Blackie the dog

I guess you will be receiving an answer to your letter of the thirteenth of March tonight. I may as well, because now I have four letters from you to answer. Gee, I haven't had that many in quite a long time now. I feel that I will receive quite a few more this week, too. Maybe I'll be writing every night this week, in answer to yours.

Thanks loads for the kiss you sent by way of the stamp, my love. One of these days we will be together again, and then I'll collect all those kisses you send that way. Boy, I sure hope it comes soon. Inside the envelope, you have, "Darling, I'm thinking of you always. I love you. L." 'Tis good to know you are, sweetheart, because the same goes for me, too.

Blosser just came in and got angry because the boys were shooting crap. It seems he wanted to write a letter and the noise bothered him. Now isn't that just too bad. He is getting to be more of a pain every day. Can't even let the boys have fun. Hell, all a little game like that does is help them forget, temporarily, the trials and tribulations of being away from home. Maybe it's just as well, though. I might have lost what I have, then I'd be broke again.

You know, sweetie-pie, it makes me feel good to know that you appreciate all the trouble I go through to write all those letters to you. Now you have a slight idea of how I feel when I receive the grand total of two like I did today. I feel swell tonite honey, better than I have in a long time. And the scuttlebutt today was bad, so it must be because I received those letters. The scuttlebutt has us out here at least another eight months. But I still think we'll be back in a couple of months. Gee, I hope so.

The twelfth of March must surely have been a busy day for you. Especially with all that company. Gee, you must have had a house full. No wonder you and Ann weren't able to go to the show.

I would like to see "Butch" myself. I'll bet she really did look swell in that red jacket Vene made for her, especially if it was bright. She is one gal that can wear those gaudy (on most people) colors, and look real sweet in them. She always was a honey, and I have an idea that she always will be. That is, unless she becomes too fat. The poor kid must lead a hell of a life, with both Eddie and Fran working. I wouldn't want our child to have to go through anything like that, would you? It's funny, but every time she goes anywhere there are children, or grown-ups that show a little appreciation and interest in her, she never wants to leave. Remember how she used to beg us to stay there? As I said before, she really is a little sweetheart.

In my mother's letter, she said that Leslie was a little (no, a lot) jealous because Jackie was getting all the attention, and she was put in the background for once. She probably would get over that, tho', if she were around our little one for awhile. Boy, can you picture those two together in a couple of years. Won't they be a couple of knockouts though. But they won't be together. Nature usually puts a good-looking, and an ordinary looking girl together. And there can be no question about the good looks of either of them. Come to think of it, all children on my side of the family are good-looking. That is, of course, except the ones that aren't. Pete is a handsome chap, but I don't know about his brother John, but why should I go into that? You know as much about them as I do, maybe more. I like all kids, don't you? And I think they're all good-looking. But, of course, all must play second fiddle to ours. How I want to see her.

Sweet Lucia, how forgetful of you to forget telling me that your mother's Thursday night club broke up. There were plenty of times I wished they were all blown up. But those were the times when I was anxious to be alone with you. There were no personal feelings involved, except my own. I love you. I am glad, however, that your mom now belongs to another club. The Neighborhood House is the best place to hold the meetings, too, although they would probably have more privacy and comfort at their individual homes. At least your mother has something to interest her. Say, how about getting her a new hat, or something, with some of that hundred?

You, yourself, will have a little surprise coming in a few days. Gee, I love you, sweet.

It is unusual for Tadone to go to the show, isn't it? But I have an idea that he likes it. Joe and Angie are really a swell couple, aren't they. I like them a lot, and if possible, you and I will visit them quite often, after this thing is over. It was darn nice of them to treat you, too. If you knew how swell it makes me feel to know that you are able to, and do, go to the theatre once in awhile, you would go more often. Why don't you, angel, if you can get someone to mind the bambino. I adore you.

Say, that really would be swell for you if Mary were able to spend a few days with you, during May. But I'll be damned if I will stand for her, or any other guest, being there when I come home to you!! But as long as I don't expect to be there in May, I am glad for you that she is coming. Thank her for sending her regards, and send her mine, when you next write. Here's hoping you two really have a good time. Save this hundred, if you want to, and you two can go on a shopping spree in the big city. But you just go ahead and suit yourself.

The pictures that came today must be the ones you mention in this letter. Yes, I just checked the dates on the reverse side of the snapshots and there are two taken the twenty-fourth, and the first of March. This is quite a long letter, my love, so I will not say anything more about the pictures, except thanks again. I'll mention more about them in another letter, at a later date. Maybe tomorrow, if I feel like doing much writing. How I love you.

Well, this is getting to be quite a long letter, isn't it. You aren't any more surprised than I am. I don't know whether I'll be able to fill all these two sheets, but I'll sure try.

Sweetest, when I mention sending my regards to the family I also mean your two aunts, especially the one from Columba St. She is quite a honey, in her own way. The old man isn't so bad, either. My darling, you haven't mentioned anything about Harry lately. How is he making out?

Well, my most magnificent darling, as your sweet letter has been answered, and there seems to be nothing I am able to say, I am afraid I'll have to close. I am quite well and happy as I can possibly be, away from you. Most adorable sweetheart, you are the only girl in the world for me, and there is no one or nothing in this entire world that I could possibly care more for. Here's hoping that you, Jackie, and all the family are well and happy. I want you to be.

The show tonight was (or rather is) "Once upon a Honeymoon," with Ginger Rogers and Gary Grant, at least I think they are the correct names. I saw it back on Santos, so I didn't care to go. Besides, I am not in a mood for writing tonight, hence my attempts at such a short letter. I do hope you won't be too disappointed with the brevity of this. I only wish I were able to continue, but I find myself at a loss for words. I would much rather be there, telling you how much I love you. I yearn to feel the warmth of your luscious lips as they press firmly against mine. My sweetheart, just to be near you would suit me fine, but to hold you in my arms again would seem heavenly. I want so much to hear your sweet voice, and to see you smile. I love you more than life itself. I need you so much. If I have to remain away much longer, I can't depend on my sanity very long. Dearest one, I am depending on you more than you could ever know. Without you, I would be lost. I love you, miss you and want you. I'm hungry.

J.De Roxtro, EM2/c   *Everlastingly, I am yours.*   *Johnny*

Note on flap: "Here's Jackie's daily hug and kiss and all there are for you. Love and kisses."

Tuesday, April 11, 1944. Letter of Mar. 18 (Fire) with weekly news. Ann home with cold. Vene came down 11:00, had lunch then we went out while Vene did shopping. Could use Johnnie's car. Rash on Jackie.

[Pavuvu Island, Russell Islands.]
Postmarked April 12, 1944, two stamps upside down.   *April 11, 1944*

Somewhere

Hello Lovely Lucia:

Your image is before me each and every hour of the day, and at night, when I dream, I dream of you. My Adorable angel, I love you, miss you and want you. I am continually thinking of you. You are guiding me in everything I say or do. More than anything else, I want to be there with you, so that I will be able to hold you close to me and kiss you. My precious, mere words could never tell you how hungry I am, and there is only one way my hunger can be appeased. That, as you know, is by being there with you.

Today I received your letter of March twenty-ninth. It wasn't postmarked until the first of April, but I don't mind that at all. Thanks, honey, for getting them in the post office so soon after writing them. It really is swell to know that you are trying, anyway. I realize also, that you probably didn't realize how long it was taking. Thanks again, my lover. I want so much for your mail to come as soon after you write it as possible. Of course you know the reason why. No? Well I guess I'll have to tell you then.

It's because I love you so very much.

There are two little items I want to comment on in that letter before I go on to answer yours of the twentieth. Yes, I will answer another tonight, because I don't want them to get too far ahead of me. I will answer one each night, as long as I receive any. Naturally, I won't be long in catching up, because you aren't writing daily, as I am.

First of all, in your latest letter, you seemed to be under the impression that I would be there to assist in the celebration of your birthday. Unless I leave here within a month of today, I doubt very much if I can make it in time. Now a month isn't a very long time, so don't expect me on that date, or very much before, if any. I will, I feel sure, be there this summer, but if I'm not, you will just have to wait. Please honey, don't depend or rely on anything I tell you in my letters, because there are absolutely no official reports on it. Everything I tell you is merely all I hear, condensed, and boiled down to what I think. Sooo, as you may depend on this weather out here, you can depend on me. As soon as there is anything official, I will let you know. That is, provided the censors will pass it. Just look for the date, sweetheart.

I may have written two letters in one day, but I doubt it. I probably misdated one of them. The other thing I wished to speak of in your letter was your intended date with Mrs. Fitzpatrick, in New York. If you do go, my lovely one, and need some extra spending money, just let me know. I'll get in another game and either win you some, or else. You may of course, use the ten I sent you enclosed in my letter of yesterday. I am glad to know that you think you like Fitz's mother. I think she is a small person, and from her pictures, she looks to be very likable.

I almost forgot, in the beginning of my letter to mention the insignificant detail of another two letters I received today. One was from your brother, the soldier, and the other, believe it or not, was from Nora. I really was surprised to get that one, because even though Vene said she was going to write, I disbelieved.

In Nora's letter she didn't say much of any importance, except that you looked so cute at Xmas time. Hell, she didn't have to tell me that. I know darn well how cute you are. She mentioned that you sent gifts to John and Peter, and how nice it was of you. She wrote as if she meant it, too. Maybe she did, for a change. She can't be depended on to always say what she thinks. Anyway, it was nice of her to write me.

All Ralph did was tell me how tough they are becoming down there since the two-year rotation thing has gone into affect. That means that he will be out here two years, providing nothing happens to increase his stay. He also said you told him where I was. Thanks, my sweet, you are a swell sweetheart.

Now, my love, I guess I can go ahead and answer your letter. Thanks for the kiss. I appreciate them all. I only wish I could be on the receiving end of one direct from your lovely luscious lips. I think I will be, real soon. Inside your envelope you had "Hello Darling. I love you, miss you, and oh, how I want you." That sounds swell, sweet, and you know how I feel about you. Lucia, I'm hungry!!

Thanks, honey-bunch, for sending those clippings about the snowstorm, and the swans parading up Washington Street. That really must have been something.

I sure am glad to know that you bought yourself and Jackie a new Easter outfit. Hell, if you can't get yourself something nice once in awhile, what's the use of living, no? Here's hoping the pictures you had taken turned out swell. At least as good as all the others. I am quite satisfied with all I have received. In fact, I think every darn one of them turned out swell. Keep 'em coming, my love, I'm expecting them.

I think it's a good idea to give Mama G and Tadone money, whenever the occasion arises. They are becoming rather old, now, and they can make a dollar last quite a long while. Gee, they sure are a swell couple, honey. I hope we are as well and able-bodied when we reach their age. I rather envy them.

That snowstorm on March nineteenth was a freak of nature. Hell, I can't see any connection between the blizzard of '88 and that four inches of the lovely white that you had there. I sure do miss the snow. Gee, I hope I have a chance to see and feel some this year. But I may be back out here before then.

Sweetheart, I am going to leave this for a short while. "The Major and the Minor" is playing tonight, so I will go to see it. I think you told me that it was a good picture, didn't you? Anyway, I will go and see for myself. I will write another couple of pages tomorrow. Wait a minute. How did that get in there. I meant, after the show, of course. I love you, and I want you.

I agree with you, my darling. It was a fairly good picture. I enjoyed it, but I've seen a hell of a lot that I liked better. I would never have seen it the second time, if I had remembered seeing it before. But I did, and I saw the entire thing over again. That's pretty good for me. Usually, when I see a show the second time I have nothing else to do. So that should convince you that I enjoyed it. I have to finish this letter, and I will, if it takes all night.

Oh, my sweet, you are trying to make me moan again. Coasting, snowball fights and snowmen. Boy, you certainly succeeded, if that was your intention, which I doubt. I, too, almost wish I were a kid again. But I said almost. I wouldn't have you if I were, and my complete happiness would be yet to come. I love you, sweetheart, and only wish I could have met you sooner and been able to remain there with you in my arms forever. How come you weren't able to shovel snow in a long time? Sweet, you weren't ill, were you?

You don't want me to come home any more than I want to. Just thinking about the two of us lying there in bed, listening to the hailstones blowing against the window makes me homesick. Not really homesick, though. Honey more than anything else, I want to go home to you.

I am as well as I usually am, and as happy as I possibly can be, away from you and our darling daughter. I hope and pray that you, Jackie and the family are, and remain forever, in the best of health. I love you both. Your letter has been answered my sweet, and there is nothing more I can think of at the moment. So, I will have to close. Goodnight, my sweet. Give my regards to all the family and our friends. Here is my daily hug and kiss for Jackie, and millions more for you. Don't bother explaining what you meant when you said you weren't able to shovel snow. I always knew what you meant. Ha!!

J.De Roxtro EM2/c   Everlastingly, your adoring *Johnny*

Wednesday, April 12, 1944. *No mail. Jackie still has rash. Stroller came. Wrote to Ralph.*

[Pavuvu Island, Russell Islands.]
Postmarked April 13, 1944, stamp upside down.   *April 12, 1944*
                                                          Somewhere

Hello, Lovely Lucia:

Gee, I love you. I miss you and want you, too. You are really swell, my adorable one. Everything about you suits me perfectly. From the tip of your toes, to the top of your head, you are every inch perfect. Your personality is sweet, and your character is beyond reproach. Your voice and your smiles are perfect. Your eyes, ah, those nice eyes, are sparkling eternally, even when you are angry. Thank the Lord that those moments are very seldom, though. Did I ever tell you how much I like your eyes when they seem ablaze with some inner fury? Your figure, my sweet, although you seem to have an idea it is slightly obese, I am delighted with it. Darling, each and every square inch of your four feet eleven and three quarters inches is loved by me. I miss you and want you so much. I want to hold you in my arms and kiss your luscious lips. I long to tell you of my love and adoration. But more than anything else, I want to be there with you, and remain forever. Sweetheart you are mine, and I am yours. I adore you.

I am afraid this will be an exceptionally short letter, my love. There just isn't anything to write about. No mail came today, either.

Forbes was writing to you when I came from chow, to thank you for sending those pictures to his mother. But it seems he became disgusted with his attempt, and tore the paper up. He said, quote—"Hell, Joe, I don't know what to say. You tell your wife that I thank her very much. I can't send that stuff." I told him to go ahead and write tonight. He's one swell kid. Here's hoping you are able to meet him and Fitz some day. Either of them would do damn near anything I asked them to. They are true gentlemen.

I saw Fitz today for the first time in a couple of weeks. He said I must insist that you spend a weekend with his mother. There is plenty of room, he said, and guaranteed you would have a real good time. I explained to him about the lambkins, and he was agreeable. You probably will get a letter telling you to take Jackie along with you. As for myself, I am remaining neutral. You may suit yourself about that. You must consider so many things that I would never even dream of, that you must make your own decisions. So, I can't do any insisting.

Gee, sweetest one, I can't think of a darn thing to write about. It's really tough, isn't it, trying to write a letter and having not a single idea. Isn't it funny that some nights I am able to sit here and write eight or ten pages, and other times, I can hardly fill three. I often wonder how the mind works. I worship you. I guess I will go to the show tonight, simply because there isn't anything else to do. I could find a crap or poker game without very much trouble, but I don't even feel like doing that. Besides, I may not be very lucky. I haven't the slightest idea what is playing at our open-air theatre, so I am unable to tell you. Heck, I will go over, light my cigar, and enjoy it, anyway. I mean I will enjoy my cigar. I'm not sure about the show.

It is very hot and close right now, so I presume we will be getting a little more rain. It hasn't rained all afternoon, so we need it. The clothes might have dried tomorrow, if it didn't rain. What the hell do we care, we can't control that.

Give my fond regards to all the family, and any of our friends. Here is my daily hug and kiss for our darling daughter, and millions more for you, the most wonderful and magnificent wife, mother and sweetheart in the world.

J.De Roxtro EM2/c   I love you, *Johnny*

Note on flap: "Sweetheart, I will see you in a couple of months, I hope. Love & kisses."

Thursday, April 13, 1944. *Letters of 2nd, 3, 5. Notice of allotment - $50. Letter for Fan & Mom. Went downtown with Mom, bought stamps, material.*

[Pavuvu Island, Russell Islands.]
Postmarked April 14, 1944, stamp upside down.

April 13, 1944

Somewhere

Hello, Lucia, my love:

I love you, miss you and want you more as each day passes, slowly bringing you more close to the day of our reunion. I see you daily, because your image is always before me. I am thinking of you eternally. I long to hold you in my arms and kiss you once again. Gee, honey, won't it be swell if we are together again in a couple of months. If my prayers are answered, we will be. I adore you, I worship you.

I hit the jackpot again today, dearest one. There were four pieces of mail here on my cot when I returned from work. There was a letter from Vene, and three others. You, my darling, sent an Easter card, and a letter. Your letter was written the first, and was postmarked the fourth of April. Thanks a lot for posting them more quickly, sweet. Even though you sort of gave me hell for telling you off about it. Honey, do you blame me for becoming a little angry? Say, what's the idea? You put two stamps on this letter, and there were no pictures inside. Hell, I sure was disappointed. But not when I opened the letter and saw how nice and long it was. Gee, it sure was swell, reading that. And darling, will wonders never cease? I received an Easter card from our daughter. Holy cow, I didn't know she could write. I wonder where the past few years flew to. It seems that just the other day she took her first steps. Thanks loads, sweetie-pie. I love you.

I will start to answer your letter of March twenty-third, and in case I don't finish by show time, I will end it afterwards. This one also has two stamps on it, so I'm returning two kisses to you in this answer to yours. Gee, it feels good to be so close to you. I sure does love ya, honey.

The pictures were in this letter, sweet, but I think I will save them to comment on later. I have an idea that this will be quite long, without that. I'll see, and if this turns out to be short, I'll mention them.

You know, sweet, whenever you mention going to the show or having another enjoyable evening, it makes me glad all over. Honey, just knowing that you are able to enjoy yourself makes me feel much better. Keep up the good work, honey. I want you to enjoy yourself all you possibly can. I haven't seen the picture "Gung Ho" yet. It may have been here, though. What makes you cry when you see a war picture? They are made a lot worse than the actual conditions are. Hell, it isn't so very bad out here. Everything is very

75

quiet, my sweet. There never is a blackout or anything like that. In fact, I am more safe here than you are. And I'm not saying that merely to make you feel better. I can prove that statement, too, right here and now. If the above statement isn't true, may the Lord keep me out here, away from my wife and family for another year. There, I guess that's proof enough for you. So now, my angel, please refrain from crying whenever you see a war picture. It makes your nose shiny. I love and adore you.

So the snow has disappeared, at last. Well, it's about time, I guess. The weather must be really nice for you now. Gee, the spring flowers are in bloom, the grass is getting green, and the leaves are beginning to come out on the trees. How I wish I could be there to enjoy it with you. Maybe by this time next year, we will be together again for good. How I wish I could depend on it. Gosh, wouldn't that be swell. Oh, well, there's no use speaking of that now. Naturally, I would much rather be there with you now.

I, too, hope those pictures of Jackie in the snow turn out well. I enjoy receiving them, and only there is one thing wrong. There aren't enough of you in with them. Gee, I have so many pictures of our sweetheart. I feel that through those pictures, and your descriptions, I really know a heck of a lot more about her than I would otherwise. Gee, I want to see you both. So long for awhile my love - the picture just started. I love you. Hello, sweetheart. Here I am again. The show was "Swing Your Partner," with Lulabelle and Scotty. It was pretty fair, but nothing exceptional. A nice pleasant entertainment, light, and not one of those darn war pictures, as most of the ones we have out here are. But then, I suppose you have the same things there. Gee, won't it be swell when we won't even have to think about it (the war) at all. That day can't come any too soon to suit me. How I long for it to end soon, so that you and I will be able to settle down in our own place, and be together happily forever. I adore you.

Isn't it swell that our little one likes the water so much? But it must be tough on you, bathing her in the tub. Gee, sweet, why not get a new bathinette, to save yourself all that bending over? Hell, I'll send you the money tomorrow, if I have a chance to get a money order. I had no idea the other one was so worn out that it leaked. Why didn't you tell me about it sooner? But maybe you did, and I've forgotten it. And there isn't any use in asking where I'm going to get the cash, either. You let me worry about that. I'm not going to steal it, or get it by any other dishonest means. Who knows, I may play poker, or get in another sociable crap game, and win it. Anyway, I'll do the best I can for you. If you think you don't need the bathinette, well, you may use it as you see fit. I know darn well that you won't squander it. Say, angel, if you don't use it for the original purpose, why not buy something nice for yourself; something that you've wanted, and couldn't quite manage to acquire? That new hat, or those shoes, or anything personal. You might even get Ann a birthday present from us. As you see, I really don't care how you spend it. Just enjoy yourself, my love, and keep as happy as you can. Gee, honey, I sure do love you. I kind of strayed from the subject of this paragraph, didn't I. Sweetheart, would you let me bathe the bambino when I come home? That is, of course, if she isn't too old? I don't think she will be, though. She won't be eighteen months old by the time I see her, I hope.

I can't say that I blame Jackie very much for crying when she had the injection. In her mind, every time she has been hurt real badly, she has seen the doctor, so naturally, he, being practically a stranger, she associates her pain with him. I don't think it was the injection that made her cry, as much as it was seeing the doctor. That's the reason she stopped as soon as you left his place. She will get over all that in time, my love, so don't worry about it. I imagine it was rather funny, seeing our darling wave good-by while crying so hard.

As you know by now, Mr. Forbes is completely well, and has recovered from his illness. He and Carl thank you for sending your regards, and return theirs to both you and Jackie.

Sweet, there is a little surprise on the way to you. It should be there by the time you receive this. In fact, it should have been there last Sunday, but I may have figured a little late. Ann has one coming also, from Forbes. Boy, will she be surprised. Anyway, I hope you both like them. That's the only thing we were able to do. I know that you will realize that, so I love you.

Sweetheart, I hope you won't mind, but this will be my last page. I have a slight headache (my first) and I think I'll turn in. Working in the sun today must have done it. It'll be gone tomorrow. Regards to all, and to Jackie, my daily hug and kiss. To you, my sweet, I'll merely say, I wish I could send myself to you.

J.De Roxtro EM2/c   Your loving hubby, *Johnny*

Note on flap: "Sweetheart, I love you, miss you and want you. I will be with you soon to prove it. Love and kisses."

Friday, April 14, 1944. *Weekly paper. M.d.R. called. 5:30-[rosaries?] for me & Ann. Lovely day. Baked 40 cream puffs for mom to take to party, washed clothes. Gracie took Jackie for ride in stroller. Found out Jackie was cutting 3 molars at once, and one tooth on the bottom.*

[Pavuvu Island, Russell Islands.]
Postmarked April 15, 1944, two stamps upside down.
April 14, 1944
Somewhere

Hello, Adorable:

I love you, miss you and want you more each day. You should be seeing me in a couple of months. I am doubtful now, if I will be there to assist in the celebration of your birthday, but I am still hoping and praying. Sweetheart, there isn't anything to base my doubts on, but I have them, anyway. Maybe it's just the mood I happen to be in tonite.

Your smiling face is always before me. I am thinking of you constantly. Adorable one, I want so much to hold you tenderly in my arms and kiss you and ____. You are mine, to have and to hold, but I am not able to do either. Hell, I want to be home so very much. I want to see you, and talk to you. Gee, my sweet, how I miss you. I am hungry for your kisses and your laugh. I am hungry for your mellow voice, and your always ready smile. I am hungry, and you are the only thing that will satisfy me.

Today, there was only one letter for me, and that was from a girlfriend of mine. She's a swell kid, and I like her loads. It was written the seventeenth of March, posted the twenty-fifth, and just arrived here today. This must be one of those that missed the plane and came out by ship. Thanks for the kiss, my love. Gosh, won't it be swell when we are able to collect for them all. By the way, this letter was from you, my sweet, in case you hadn't guessed. I intended answering your letter tonight, but I doubt if I will, now. I am going to the show, and maybe afterwards, I will. The name of the picture is "Moonlight Masque," [Moonlight Masquerade] and as I've never heard of it before, I will go. I guess I'll answer it anyway. A heck of a lot of the fellows are going to the theatre now, so I will wait until later to answer yours. The one that came today is the last that I have, so that will be the one that I'll answer, naturally. Gee, honey, I sure do wish I were there to hold you close to me tonight. I love you so.

Well, honey, here I am again. I went to see the beginning of the picture, but it started raining too hard, and as I was unable to hear it, I decided to leave. I have an idea that it would have been quite good, too. Oh, well, better luck tomorrow. "As Thousands Cheer" is playing then, and all reports consider it quite good.

Boy, Ralph must have been in a writing mood when he used five large sheets of paper. And it was really swell of him to send flowers for Mother's Day and Easter, to your mom. I wish I had been able to do the same for you. But, alas, my love, you will have to be satisfied with those bright red rose buds. Gee, I hope you like them. I am sorry I wasn't able to have them there on time, that's all. As for Mother's Day, well, I must admit that I don't know when it is. But as Ann will take care of that for me, you will receive something special. I hope this doesn't reach you before your surprise, because if it did, there just wouldn't be any, would there.

Your brother and I don't write very often, because there isn't anything to say. But we do answer each other's letters just as soon as is possible. I hear from him about every three weeks, so I guess he does the same from me.

I can well imagine that Joe [Vetere] looks good in his uniform. He is a swell kid, and I like him too. It's funny, but I have seen him but very little, and I think he is much more well-behaved and gentlemanly than either Rodzy or the other kid. What's his name? Gene, I guess, isn't it? Anyway, the life in the Navy will do him a lot of good. He'll be well taken care of, too, and he'll learn a lot.

Waiting an hour for the doctor-heck. I couldn't ever wait that long. I don't see how our Jackie ever remained well behaved for such a long time. Our daughter always looks sweet, I'll bet. And anyone that says she isn't is cracked. How could she be anything but, when she has such a loving, lovable mother. Gee, you must have your hands full, trying to keep all her clothes clean, and her face and hands. You are marvelous.

This is the fourth time I've read this letter so far, and it just came to me what you meant when you spoke of the two sisters dressed in black. Somehow or other, it just never occurred to me. I though you merely meant two girls who were dressed in black for mourning. Silly of me, wasn't it. I'm really glad that Jackie took to the one so readily. It must have made her feel good, especially when she said most children were frightened of the black they wear. And as for being proud that the sister noticed how well cared for Annette is, well, I want you to know that I am proud of you, very proud, and of your daughter. How I wish I could see her soon. Gee I love you both so much. Your description of the clothes our little one was wearing sounds good to me, so she must have looked okay. But then, your daughter would be a delightful looking lassie, no matter what she wore.

So the bambino's teeth are all back, and are strong again. Gee, that sure is swell, isn't it. We sure were lucky, too. Or rather, you were. I would not have been there to go through all that. Once more, you would have had to do it alone. She is getting to be a big girl, isn't she. Two and a half feet tall (minus one half inch) and twenty two and a half pounds. Honey, do you realize that your wee one is almost half as tall as you are? Holy cow, I hope I get there soon or I won't be able to tell my wife from our daughter. Now wouldn't that be something. I'll be there this year, sometime, unless something turns up. Those injections may bother her a little, sweet, and she might even run a temperature, but don't worry about it, because it won't be serious.

I haven't the faintest idea how you intend to train Jackie to control her bladder. It sounds like a lot of foolishness to me, but then there is a lot I don't know about raising little ones. What's the idea of that, my love. You will have to turn the light on, because I am completely in the dark. The only thing I can think of is training her to notify you of the close proximity of the floodgates opening. And it doesn't sound like that.

Gee, by the time I arrive home, our Jackinelle will be a regular athlete. Climbing the stairs, on and off chairs, and all over the place, I guess. Heck, I wanted so much to see her go through all that. But I couldn't, so what's the use crying over spilt milk. I'll be there for the next one, though, I'll bet. You really must be tired, when you finally get her in bed, and asleep. Our little bundle from heaven must be coming right along with her speech, too. Quite a vocabulary she has, too, I imagine. She says "oh dear" and "oh gee," now, so perhaps I can teach her to say "oh nuts." Or probably I can't.

Helen Pizze, that's the girl across the street from you, isn't it. The one you said came from Summit, and whose husband was a Seabee? It doesn't matter, I was just sort of placing her in my mind as I go along. The three little ones must have looked pretty happy and gay, out there together, having a good time. Don't you envy them, at times? They are so carefree and happy?

No, my sweet one, as far as I know, the shakers aren't made of greenstone. They are made of a shell that has only four or five letters in it. Pahu, or something like that. Come to think of it, though, that may be the native name for it. Could be greenstone, at that. We will just call it that, and forget about it. I will probably be able to tell you more about the Maori's of New Zealand when I return and refresh my memory a little. I will have quite a few stories to tell, some to everyone, and some to you, in the privacy of our room.

Hell, honey, if they put all these islands on the map, there would be very little room for water. Look up Green Island for me, will you? I am slightly interested in that, too. Give my fond regards to all the family and our friends. Here is our Jackie's daily hug and kiss. You are the most magnificent woman in all the world. None of the beauties of history can compare with you. You are tops, sweetheart and wife, and I love you, miss you and want you.

J.De Roxtro EM2/   Everlastingly, your *Johnny*

Note on flap: "Dearest one I love you. You are always in my heart. I will see you soon. Love & kisses."

Saturday, April 15, 1944. *Letter of April 6th. Rain all day. Went to movies. Saw "Ali Baba & 40 Thieves."*

[Pavuvu Island, Russell Islands.]

Postmarked April 17, 1944, stamp upside down.   *April 15, 1944*

Somewhere

My Darling:

I love you, miss you and want you. Thoughts of you are continually running through my mind. Your vision is eternally before me. You are mine sweetheart, and I am yours, forever. I long to hold you tenderly in my arms once again and kiss you. To be able to make love to you again would be divine. Boy, I hope we will be together again before very long. I sure do want to see you again, and I also want to see your daughter.

Let's see, Mother's Day is about four weeks from tomorrow, so maybe I'll be able to send something. Say, if I send a money order to you, will you do the honors and purchase something for each of our mothers? I haven't had time to get that other order yet, so maybe fifty will do for all, no? I think I'll get in a little game tonight. Hope you don't mind.

No mail came today, my love, for me, so I guess I will comment on the latest pictures I have, and close this brief note. Two of these were taken the twenty-fourth of Feb., and the other four, the first of March. Jackie looks as if she is just about ready for her nap in this one where she is in the carriage. She doesn't care to remain in it, either. To me, it looks as if she is sort of pleading with you to take her out. She has a nose quite similar to Vene's hasn't she. And her lip is still a little swollen, isn't it.

Jackie, Lou, Judy

My love, I am now going to go to the mess hall and get my third bottle of beer, since I left New Zealand. Now ain't dat sompin!!!! One lousy bottle. A hell of a lot for a guzzler like I am. Oh, well, it's better than none at all, isn't it. I love you, so I will return immediately and finish this epistle of love to the most wonderful girl in the world. How I wish you and I could be together having beer or a Tom Collins. I adore you.

Here I am again. Believe it or not, I had two bottles. One of the fellows here in the tent didn't want any, so he gave me his card. It really tasted good, too.

You know, sweet, in this picture the carriage does look sort of top heavy. Tis no wonder it toppled. Glad it wasn't any worse, though, aren't you. Our little one looks about the same in the other picture, but gee, isn't she getting big. She sure is a honey, too.

That mailman in the background doesn't look like Willard to me. Could it be that he is now a member of the armed forces? This fellow looks more like a guy named Doolan. And the streets look quite dirty. Better get old man Johnson out with his street sweeping machine.

In all the pictures I have of Jackie standing up, she seems to be making sure she'll stay up. Her feet are planted apart, and her arms are out as a sort of balance. Is that actually a banana she has in her left hand? Does she eat a whole one? Doesn't it bother her digestion? Didn't the dog take a smell? Gee, Annette looks so fat and healthy. No wonder you are proud of her. I'm proud of you, too, my love. There doesn't seem to be much more I can say about these pictures of Jackie. The one where you are holding Judy and our little one, is really swell. Judy looks like a little monkey, sort of, when you compare her to ours. She does stand nice and straight, doesn't she. I will sure be glad when I get some pictures of Jackie in just a little light summer outfit. Then I will be able to see just how fat she is.

You know, sweetheart, every time I see a picture of you, I want you more. In this picture, you look exceptionally good to me. You are getting, or have become, a little full in the face, haven't you? Gee, you, too, look healthy, my one and only. I wish I could be there to press my lips upon yours, to run through your hair with my hands and to put my arms around you and hold you real close to me. Oh, my sweetheart, I love and want you so very much. I'll be there in a couple of months, now, and then I'll make love to you as a husband should.

J.DeRoxtro EM2/c   Everlastingly, your *Johnny*

Sunday, April 16, 1944. *Cloudy, rain. Joe & Angie, Gene & Judy. Jackie not well - cold.*

[Pavuvu Island, Russell Islands.]
Postmarked April 17, 1944, two stamps upside down.   April 16, 1944

                                                                    Somewhere

Hello, Adorable:

 All the love in the world is ours. You are eternally on my mind, and everlastingly in my heart. I love you, miss you and want you. To hold you once again in my arms and kiss you would be heavenly. Sweetheart, you are the most wonderful wife, sweetheart, and mother in all the world. Everything I do is guided by you. You, my love, are tops. Without you to guide me, I don't know what I would do. I think I would go nuts if I didn't have you to think of. How I love you. I am real proud of you, sweet, and proud of our little one. I want to be there with you more than I've ever wanted anything. Today, our newssheet came out, and the doctor said we would be home in four months, and when asked to comment on the doctor's statement, the skipper said he (the doc) was rather conservative. That sounds good to me, but gee, four months is a heck of a long time to wait. Maybe you had better cancel that date we have for the sixth of June, or better yet, just keep it open. I still have the opinion that we will be there in June or July, so here's hoping I'm right. Gee, it sure will be swell to be seeing you again. Just imagine all the swell times we will be able to have together. Gee, I can hardly wait for the day to come. Won't it be swell when I am able to assist you in the care of our little darling. Gee, we three will have swell times together. I love you both.

 No mail came again today, so I will have to merely answer yours of the twenty sixth of March. Say, my love, did I ever thank you and our daughter for the Easter cards you sent? I think I did, but thanks again, anyway. I didn't mark the two envelopes answered, as I usually do, that's why I repeated it. Thanks for the kiss you sent by way of the stamp. I'll be home to collect for all of them someday soon. That was a cute little statement you had on the inside of the envelope, too. I, too, darling, love you very much. I adore you.

That cartoon about Aunt Eppie taking her waste fat to the butcher was pretty good. The other boys thought so, also.

Lets see, this letter is only four pages long, so maybe my answer to it will be short, too. Yep, sweet, it's okay with me if you stop in the middle of your letter to me, in order to go to the theatre with Ann and Fan. That is, of course, provided you finish it before you retire. But what the devil do I have to go through all this for? Gee, I'm a dope letting you get me mixed up in a thing like this. I wouldn't care whether you finished it or not, as long as you mailed it.

Your daughter has a heck of a nerve, besmudging my letter like this. Gee, I haven't any idea at all how rapidly she is progressing. I can't quite keep up with her progress. She is getting ahead of me, and I am unable to cope with her progress. I guess I will just have to wait till I see her.

Ha, ha, I'll bet you have a devil of a time, trying to train the wee one when Mama Gee is around. I can imagine the yell she let out when you whacked Annette. The poor old gal means well, but after all, I can imagine that she whacked your mother plenty of times. But then, I guess my mom is the same way. Darn it, why do you always have to have someone telling you what to do, and what not to do. I don't blame you for whacking her little bottom once in awhile. I probably will have to do it too, even though I wouldn't care to. Oh, well, this hurts me more than it does you, said the old man as he sat on a porcupine. How did that get in here.

Why don't you tell me those things? Hell I didn't know Jackie could call Mama G and Tadone by name. But you have told me, now, haven't you. Thanks loads for all the little items of interest you bring out in your letters, sweet. Gee, the bambino must be acquiring quite a vocabulary. I'll bet even you don't remember all the words she uses, without stopping to think about them. By the time I get there, she'll probably be able to hold quite a conversation with me. Gosh, I hope she won't use words that I can't understand. Gee, it's really swell for them to be so crazy for Jackie's company. They are a swell couple. I hope they teach her to speak some Italian. At least enough so that she can understand it. Languages are swell. I wish I knew some.

As long as our daughter is fascinated by smoke, perhaps I will be able to entertain her with that. But she will probably be over that soon, and will have some other interest.

Those two sisters of ours must be as busy as bees on a Sunday afternoon. But then, they have no time during the week, so it becomes a necessity on Sunday. When I return home, I must remember to stay out of their way. We can take care of that when the time comes, though, can't we. Even if we have to lock ourselves in our room.

As long as Jackie enjoys being in a stroller so much, I'm glad you got one. It will be a lot easier on you, too, getting around. Besides, Annette will be a lot cooler in that than in the carriage. Another thing, the stroller will fold up and go into an automobile, won't it? I am not sure about those things, anymore. I will learn, though.

Arkie sure is lucky to be home again. The army is funny that way, keeping some men there, and promoting them often, and sending others out for a year or more, without a single promotion.

Forbes just said that you must need glasses, because you are so sweet and lovely, and said he was cute. But above all, because you couldn't see what you were doing when you managed to become caught by me. P.S. Forbes just said to tell you he was kidding about the glasses. Maybe two pair would be better so you wouldn't become blinded by my brilliancy. He has been back in and out of the sick bay a couple of times, but I think he is just about well now. The dear boy is crazy about Ann, and says that if she is half as sweet as you are, she must be a perfect little angel. I told him that she was, just about half. Gee, I love you. All kidding aside, my sweet, Forbes and all the boys thank you for sending your regards and wishes for a Happy Easter. Forbes is one swell guy, and I tease him by putting everything he says about you in my letters. I will have to quit now and go to supper. I'll be back later, my sweet, pardon me. Love. Hello, sweetie-pie, my love for your increased by leaps and bounds the short while I was gone to chow. And I missed you more, too. Of all things, they had that crappy spaghetti and meatballs. Naturally they had sauce on it, but such sauce. Jackie used to make better in her diapers, and probably has, many times. I ate it, though. I have learned to eat everything since I've been here in the Navy. The cooks and bakers we have are really good, but they just can't get the proper ingredients. In fact, we, the fifteenth Sea bees, have a reputation for having the best food. Heck, it got so bad back on Santos, with visitors, that our own men couldn't even get in to eat, sometimes. In fact, there were so many visitors that they had to stop them from eating with us. I adore my wife.

I always have as happy a day as I can, my love, and refuse to be worried about anything. That is, of course, I try not to worry, but, as you know, one can't help it sometimes. Too bad we weren't together for Easter, my sweet, but as long as we will be in each others arms soon, that's all that matters. I am looking forward to that day, as you are. It sure will be a red-letter day for us, won't it.

I find that I was a little wrong in the first few statements I made concerning my return to the states. Maybe most of my other estimates were, too, but sweetheart, as I told you earlier, unless something unforeseen happens, I will be there in July or August. Please don't depend too much on any of these things, my love, or you may be disappointed. Anything can happen, you know, and as soon as anything official comes out, I will let you know, if it is possible or permissible to do so. So much for that. I am still hoping and praying that we will become reunited and remain together for the remainder of our lives. Gee, I want you so very much.

Say, you gave me an inspiration when you mentioned fainting from shock when you first see me. I think I'll grow a full beard, and have my hair all removed, and wear dark glasses. Then, when you see me, you won't recognize me, and hence, you won't faint. No, that's not so good either. You might brain me for becoming too friendly. Anyway, I intend to surprise you.

Leave it to Fan to start our wee one in on something like the noise of a machine gun. Grace even sounded disgusted when she told me about it in her letter. Jackie must be rather quick on the uptake, to get something like that down in so short a time. She must take after her mother, she is so smart. Say, does it mean anything when she says "pot," or is it just another word to her yet? I have an idea that you probably have her house broken by now. It must be swell, being there to see all the latest tricks break out, and hear her first words, and watch her expressions as things occur out of the ordinary.

"Journey into Fear" is playing at our local theatre this evening, so I guess I will go to see it. It is an Orson Welles thing, so it may be either good or bad. I've never heard of it before. If I think of it, I will tell you all about it tomorrow in my letter. This is my twelfth letter today. I was tired when I wrote the others, and when I started this. But now, if I could find something to write about, I could go on and on. But alas, there is nothing more to say.

Give my fond regards to all the folks, and any of our friends you may happen to meet. Here is our Jackie's daily hug and kiss, and you, well, everything to you that I may ever be able to give you. I love you more than life itself. I want to be there with you, and remain forever. I adore you.

J.De Roxtro EM2/c   *Everlastingly, your loving* *Johnny*

April 17, 1944 - Japan begins its last offensive in China, attacking U.S. air bases.

Monday April 17, 1944. *No mail. Washed clothes. Wrote Mary. Started diet.*

[Pavuvu Island, Russell Islands.]
Postmarked April 18, 1944, stamp upside down.   *April 17, 1944*
                                                        Same Place

Hello, Adorable:

 I love you, miss you and want you. I am always thinking of you, my beloved, and wishing I were there to hold you tenderly in my arms and kiss you. I am hungry, most wonderful one, and only you can satisfy me.

 Three lovely letters came for me today. Two from you and one from Ann. She called me a stinker, too, so you give her the devil for me. Your two letters were written the fourth and sixth of April, and were postmarked the sixth and seventh, respectively. Your new system seems to be getting results, sweet. That is really getting down to when it should be. Now, I am wondering if the girls actually did drop them the morning after, as they said. Funny they should be postmarked Millburn, Orange, East Orange, and other points along the railroad line, when Ann said they always inserted them in the box in front of the Rectory, at Sussex Ave. intersection, isn't it. Anyway, we should worry, as long as the situation is well in hand now. You are a sweetheart, for mailing them yourself. It sure does make a difference. Thanks a million, my precious.

 That piece you enclosed in your letter, about Irwin S. Cobb was really worth reading, wasn't it. He had some darn good ideas, and I certainly do agree with him about not wearing black, and not going around in mourning. He sounded as if he was happy while writing it too, didn't he.

 Tonight, my beloved, I will answer your letter of the twenty-ninth of March. I accept the kiss you sent via the stamp with thanks. It looks as if I am going to break that date I made with you for the sixth of June. Maybe July or August, or later, but probably not in June. I am certainly hoping and praying that we will be together to celebrate your birthday, though. I may be, but don't depend on it.

 So you don't care for after dinner speeches, either. Neither do I, my sweetheart. But I don't mean for the same reason you do. You mean one like the one in the three [faces?], but I mean the other kind. Heck, darn it, I haven't had any experience with the kind you mean. I suppose it does become tiresome, though. I guess you've had your share, too.

 Too bad you weren't able to go to Newark shopping because of the weather. You were quite disappointed, I know. But never mind, my loved one, another time will come. Maybe by this time you have been and had an enjoyable time. I hope you have.

 Yes, it's quite possible that Mary's cousin is in this outfit, but it's also very probable that he is in another outfit. We, in this area, are moved about in the same circles, so he may be in any branch of the service. Let me know, when you find out, and I'll see if I can get in contact with him. There is quite a possibility that he wasn't on Santos, and isn't here, because there are plenty of islands in each group. I may have known, or do know where his outfit is, though.

You sure do have your troubles with the young one falling, don't you. Oh, well, don't worry about it, because she'll get over it, in time. She may hurt herself badly every time, as you say, but she heals quickly. Let's just hope that she never breaks any bones. The wee one really must be active, anyway. That's good enough for me. Let her fall, as long as nothing permanent develops. Those bumps on the head usually recede rapidly, don't they. Gee, she must be a toughie. In a way, I'm really glad she is. That's good.

Fitz's mother is a swell person, from all that he says about her. Let me know what develops, will you? I mean whether you meet her, etc. etc.

When I read in this letter about your first thunderstorm, I had been quite sure that you were finally in the spring season. But upon receiving your letters today, I am beginning to have my doubts. Golly, I'll bet that snowstorm was a surprise to you, wasn't it. I like to see the snow lying on the trees and fences and everything, like you described it. It sure is a pretty sight. Say, does our Jackie like the thunder and lightning, or is she afraid of it? You may have told me before, but I've forgotten, if you did. Gosh, my memory is getting bad. There are lots of things I can't remember, even though I don't want to forget. Gosh, I wonder if I will ever be able to get back in the groove again. Golly, I love you, sweet.

You sure did wean the little cherub early enough. You are really doing a bang-up job, my precious angel, and I must agree that Annette is now a big girl, perhaps a lot bigger than I imagine. But one of these days I will be there to get the surprise of my life. It can't come any too soon to suit me.

I guess we were both bawled up about Bonnie annoying you all the time with her crying. Hell, honey, I knew she wasn't continually that way. I understood you, but I guess I couldn't make myself clear. There will be plenty of times when we misunderstand each other, in our letters. For instance, I was only temporarily angered when I wrote those letters to you about your letters to me being held up. I forgot it as soon as I finished writing about it, and didn't remember until the next one came the same way.

You must remember that Bonnie has not been injured as often or as severely as our Jackie has, and hasn't been in pain whenever she has seen the doctor, so you can't blame our little one for being slightly afraid of the doc. She will get over that, in time, so we won't say any more about it. She may be over it by now, for all I know. Too bad the doctor couldn't make a social call on his patients once in awhile. In that way, his patients would get to know him better, and be less afraid of him. Say, why not invite him up for a nice Italian dinner some time? Maybe Jackie would learn to like him. I think he's a likeable guy, myself.

My sweetheart, I see by your letters that I have led you to believe that I am sure to return home in a couple of months. Sweetheart, I am going to say something now that will hurt you, probably, but it will be fore the best. I am sorry that I have misled you. There is absolutely nothing official to base my opinions on. I will say, here and now, that you shouldn't expect me in less than six or eight months. I will say nothing more about it in any of my letters, unless there is something official. At least I don't intend telling you anything more. Something may slip in, but don't believe it unless I say it is official. You are trying not to get your hopes up, but I can see by your letters that you are. I want so much to be home with you. I've seen too much of these so called tropical paradises.

It still rains daily here, but I am getting so used to it, I only notice it when I am inside. It's raining now, and I am going to the show to see "As Thousands Cheer." It should be good. The one last night was one of the worst I've ever seen.

Sweetheart mine, I want you to give my fond regards to all the family and our friends. Here is my daily hug and kiss for Jackie, and to you, I send my all. I love you, miss you, and want you. You are forever in my thoughts and everlastingly in my heart.

J.De Roxtro EM2/c   Eternal love and kisses, *Johnny*

Note on flap: "The picture was 'One Dangerous Night,' not the other. Quite good for a change. Love & kisses."

Tuesday, April 18, 1944. *Letter of April 7, 1944. Afternoon Vene, M.D.R. & kids dropped in for few minutes. Night went down to Mama G.'s house. painted - upset. Tadone has abscess on sore arm.*

[Pavuvu Island, Russell Islands.]
Postmarked April 19, 1944, stamp upside down.   *April 18, 1944*
                                                        Somewhere

Hello, Lovely Lucia:

Sweetheart, if only I could be there to prove to you just how much I love you and want you. I might even come close to telling you how I have missed you these past long months. It is so long ago that I last held you tenderly in my arms and kissed you. I want to do it again, but not in saying goodbye. I want our next reunion to last the remainder of our lives. Dearest one, more than anything else, I desire to be with you and Jackie. I love you, miss you and want you more as each day passes, slowly but surely bringing us more close together. I am hungry and only you can satisfy me.

Today, there was no mail again, but I don't care so much, as long as I received two yesterday. I will answer your letter of April first tonight, and that leaves me only the two I got yesterday. This week started out very well, so maybe I will receive one most every day again, as I did last week. Gee, isn't it swell getting mail almost daily. And when they are nice long ones, that makes them twice as good. Say, honey, have you been receiving a letter every day? I don't mean it that way. Why can't I express my thoughts more clearly? Can you account for each and every one of my daily letters up to the last one you have received. I've been writing one every day, and I haven't missed yet. Just thought I'd let you know, so you could check up.

Thanks for the two kisses you so kindly sent by way of the stamps. Thanks, again. I'll expect to collect for them all when I next see you. Boy, I sure will be busy, wont I? That statement you wrote on the inside of the envelope sure has my hearty approval. It will be one of the grandest things that ever happened, when you and I are able to forget all about writing letters. Actions speak louder than words, anyway, and when we meet, there will be plenty of action.

It certainly is a shame that Jackie is so scared of the doctor, but then there is nothing you can do about it. Let's say that she is allergic to him, and let it go at that. You know that he doesn't actually hurt her, because she stops crying so soon after leaving him. Too bad you have to be there to witness it, too. I can well imagine that it hurts both you and the doctor to have her cry. It's for her own good, anyway, so that's some consolation, isn't it.

It seems sort of silly to be drafting so many married men, when from all I hear they have so many now they don't know where to put them. The last I heard from Vene, Johnny was put into 1a, so perhaps he will be in with tommy Principal. Johnnie was expected to leave this month some time, I think. That was unless his company got him another deferment. Herb got one, did you know that? You probably know all that, though.

| Johnny Naughton | William Herbert de Roxtro |

So you had a little excitement in the neighborhood again. Well, I'm sure glad it wasn't anything more serious. Those flats of Zams will really go up some day, and I mean good. I hope no one gets hurt, though.

Well, I'm sure glad to learn that the Sandelli's are doing so well with their store. Their prices would be rather high, but why not, as long as they have fruit that's worth it. Hell, I'd be willing to pay more and get my money's worth, wouldn't you? As for their home, well, I think they lost that long ago, and the bank was merely letting them pay rent for it. Now that Tommy and Julia have bought it back, maybe they'll keep it. If my memory serves me correctly, I heard that the bank took that house away back in thirty-eight or nine. But all that is water under the bridge. We aren't interested, anyway. We wouldn't want it, would we.

By the time you receive this letter, you will know that your letters are coming more regularly, and aren't being held up by the girls, or whoever else could have been the cause of it. Your new system is working perfectly, so I hope you keep it up. Thanks again, my love, for figuring a solution to my problem. I will love you eight days next week for that. You seem to have been a little hot under the collar when you wrote this letter, but I'll overlook it. I still love you very much, and will keep on loving you, no matter what you say or do. That's how much I love you, my sweetheart.

Now, about Carl not telling Evelyn anything about those pictures. His reason, that he didn't wish to disappoint her, in case for some reason you couldn't have them made. Even after I told him they were on the way, he didn't say anything because he wanted to surprise her.

The show tonight is "Journey For Margaret." It seems mighty familiar to me, so maybe I've seen it before. However, I intend to go, so I'll let you know about it when I return. The show last night was a bit of alright. Gee, wouldn't it be swell if you and I could be going to a show together again.

I'll take you to every one in town. All, that is, but the Palace. I don't like that place, and never did.

Maybe by this time my mother will have stopped her wandering. She earned a rest, so I hope she enjoyed herself. She bought a few new clothes for herself, and took time to fix herself up. At least, that's what Vene told me. It was quite a long while since our little one saw my mom, so it's no wonder that she didn't recognize her. It wouldn't take them long to become reacquainted though, as they were real good friends before she left. My mother always does look well, after spending a week or two or more travelling around to her different sons and daughters homes. I think she does it more to see if all her grandchildren are well cared for than for any other reason. She sure does like children, but I think she prefers Jackie to the others. Her letters sound that way to me.

I will sign off now for awhile, my beloved angel, and write one more page after the show. I hope you don't mind too much, but if I don't go, I will get too much sleep and feel lousy tomorrow. I love you.

You know something beloved? My letter of yesterday was the one hundredth that I wrote to you since being on this Island. Boy, that's a long time, isn't it. But compared to the length of time we've been separated, that seems like nothing. Dearest one, I adore you. Now, my sweet, I will leave for awhile. But I shall return shortly. I worship you.

Here I am, sweetheart, and I honestly believe that was a swell picture. If you haven't seen it yet, I would suggest you do if it comes to town. But I'm warning you that you will cry. It is a true story about a girl named Margaret, and a boy named Peter. I won't tell you more about it, because you may see it. Those two children really played a wonderful part. I don't know who the players were, but I guess you know all about it.

Sweetheart, the show is over, and the letter of yours is answered, so I have nothing more to say. I am well, as usual, and am as happy as I can be, away from you. I hope that both you and Jackie, and the rest of the family are well and remain in the best of health, and retain your happiness. Give them all my fond regards. Here is my daily hug and kiss for Jackie. Gee, I want to see her, and romp on the floor with her.

Most adorable wife and mother in the world, I love you, miss you and want you. I am hungry for your hugs and kisses. I am hungry for your love. I am hungry, my sweetheart. I am everlastingly hoping and praying for an early reunion with you.

J.De Roxtro EM2/c   Eternally, your loving *Johnny*

Note on flap: "Oh, my darling, how much I love you, you will never know."

Wednesday, April 19, 1944. *Lovely day - received 3rd issue of C. Breeze. Tickets from Father Sheerin, Mil & Gene brought Judy over at 10:00 A.M. Stayed out with Jackie and Judy.*

[Pavuvu Island, Russell Islands.]
Postmarked April 20, 1944, stamp upside down.   *April 19, 1944*

Somewhere

Dearest One:

    I love you with all my heart, body, and soul. I love every inch of you. I adore you, I worship you. How much I miss you and want you, you will never know. Sweetest one, I long to hold you in my arms and kiss you over and over again. Lucia, darling, I want so much to be there with you. You are the most wonderful girl in all the world. I am proud to have you as my life-long mate, and proud of you as the mother of our daughter. May this war end soon, so that you and I will be together forever, to share each other's joys and sorrows. We will laugh together and be serious. We will ponder over the problems of our family, and do all the things that are done, together. We will some day be reunited, and for my part, that day can't come soon enough to suit me. I want the three of us to be together, as we should be.

    I am grateful to two of your brothers for writing letters to me. Ralph sent one, and the other was quite a surprise. It was from Joe, and he wrote a darn nice one. He told me how nice our wonderful little Jackie is, and how proud he is to be her godfather. He sure is a swell guy, and I like both he and Angie a lot. Ralph didn't have much to say, except that he was tired of the monotonous life he was leading down here. He signed off at eight-thirty, and said that was his bedtime. That is quite remarkable for him, don't you think.

    There isn't anything I can tell you from here, except that I am well, and as happy as I can be, away from you, the only one I really and truly love. I sincerely hope that you, our little one, and the family are the same, and remain in good health continually. Give my fond regards to both your Aunts and especially to Mama G and Tadone. I love you.

    I am a little disappointed tonight, sweet. There were some increases in rates posted, and, although I was quite sure of getting one, I didn't. We have to take examinations, but they don't mean a damn thing. I took two, back on Santos and my boss told me I made the highest grade in one. Today, two fellows that took that exam only, and were under me, made the rate. Politics is hell, isn't it. I guess I will have to start sucking, or leave the same as I entered. I'll be damned if I will suck, though. If I can't make a rate on my work, I don't want it.

Hell, honey, I shouldn't be bothering you with my troubles. You have plenty of your own. Just disregard the preceding paragraph, and consider it all sugary phrases of love and adoration from one who loves you more than anything else in the world. Darling you are magnificent.

I've been trying for the last few minutes to find out the name of the show tonight, but no one seems to know. Oh, well, I'll go anyway. There is nothing else to do. Gee, I would have something to do if I were there with you. Boy, that'll be the bloody day. (That's a New Zealand phrase.)

Mr. Forbes is becoming ill again, and he asked me to tell you to tell Ann that the only thing that can cure him is a visit to her. He really means that, too. He sure is having tough luck, isn't he.

The scuttlebutt is about at a standstill now. No one seems to be able to think anything new up. A couple of our higher-ups are building a boat that will last one year. That doesn't mean anything, though. Hell, they don't know any more than we do. I'm sure hoping and praying that we will be together soon. Here is my daily hug and kiss for Jackie, and millions more to you, my wife and sweetheart.

J.De Roxtro, EM2/c   Everlastingly, your *Johnny*

Note on flap: "Keep you chin up, honey, we'll be together one of these days. I love you."

Thursday, April 20, 1944. *Letters of April 8th, 11th. 9:00 decided to go to Newark. Called Mil to ask if she'd care for baby. Took 11:15 train. Arrived 12:00. Could not find suit. Bought bag, polo shirt, and records for Jackie. "Nursery Rhymes." Left 4:28 - pulled in 5:00. Home at 5:30. Went to Mil's to get Jackie. Stayed awhile.*

[Pavuvu Island, Russell Islands.]

Postmarked April 21, 1944, stamp upside down.   April 20, 1944

                  Somewhere

Most Adorable Lucia:

I love you, miss you and want you. My one desire is to be with you, my beloved wife. I long to put my arms around you and hold you close to me, while I kiss you and tell you of my love and adoration. My lovely one, the day we are reunited can't possibly come any too soon to suit me.

As usual, sweetie-pie, I am well and hope that you, Jackie and the family are in the best of health. My happiness will never be complete until I am with you.

Vince just came in, and told us he had to return to the sick bay. Hell, he ought to reside up there. He has been there almost as much as he has here. Nothing serious, tho! I thought he was kidding last night, but I guess he was serious.

There is nothing more to write of from this end, so I will answer your letter of April fourth. That will leave one more, a real short one, for me to answer on Sunday. That is, providing I don't receive any more. I probably will, though. Thanks a lot for the two kisses you sent by way of the stamps. Boy, they were exceptionally good. Darling, each day that passes brings us closer together. I can hardly wait to see you. The two preceding sentences were on the inside of the envelope. They convey my thoughts also. That day will certainly be one of the best in my life. I love you, Lou darling.

Gee, waiting three quarters of an hour for one patient to leave the doctor's office. He (the patient) must have had everything wrong with him. That was quite a wait, wasn't it. And the wee one didn't make any trouble? That's good. I thought she might have become tired of waiting. And she raised Cain when she saw the doctor, huh? Oh, well, she may be over that by the time she pays him another visit. Let's hope so.

It sounds as if our little one has a bit of spunk, doesn't it. I'll bet you were really surprised to see her whack Carol Ann on the head, weren't you. I know darn well that I would be. Sounds as if she were able to understand what you tell her too. Gee, I can't keep up with her progress. I can't seem to get it into my thick skull that she isn't a tiny baby anymore. Gee, won't I be surprised when I do see her. All your letters mention something new that she does, and inform me of her progress in different ways, but I still can't place her there, most of the time. Carol Ann is only three months older than Jackie, and she may be more developed bodily, but I will lay odds that Carol isn't as smart. Then again, sweet, how about a comparison between your smart daughter and Vene's Bonnie. As far as I know, she hasn't even started to walk yet. Oh, well, there is no use trying to make comparisons between children. They are all so different, yet all alike. Darling, I adore you.

It was darn nice of the Sussex Avenue Petrones to invite the family to dinner on Palm Sunday. And of course, the meal would naturally be good. Mil is a fairly good cook, we must say that for her. But I think the girl I married can and will suit me better. I don't think I know Betty and Joe Vigilante, but it is of course very possible that I do. When I see them, I will recognize them, I know, so don't bother trying to describe them to me.

It is only natural for Jackie to be more at home, and her natural self when she is playing with Judy. Heck, they are together so much, they should be as used to each other as sisters. You know, I think that's a swell idea, don't you. It must have been a circus, watching those two with the carriage. Of course I remember it. Didn't I always have to drag Lesley Ann away from it, when I brought her over to your place? Heck, every child seems to be drawn to that carriage. It must have something that is attractive.

When I answer Joe's letter, I will have to give him hell for giving Annette her first sip of beer. Darn it, I thought that I would have been the first to do that. A sip or two will never hurt her, sweet. In fact, it might do her some good. It's just as well that you took her away from him, though. It could get to be a habit with her. I mean that she might expect a couple of sips every time someone has one. I intend to give her some, once in awhile, myself, when I get home. Gee, I sure hope I get there soon. I love my Lucia.

No, Lou dearest, you never did tell me that the bambino's hair is a little curly. If it is, I'll bet it is your fault. Gee, I'll bet you spend hours daily working on it, trying to get it to curl. Tell the truth, don't you?

You mentioning that you and Mil went downtown and bought Easter cards for the kids reminds me of something. The first Easter I am home, and perhaps before our little Jackinelle will have a real Easter, she will have bunnies, chickens, jelly-beans and multi-colored eggs. And for Christmas, well, she will receive so much from us, that all else will be overlooked. Nothing will be too good for our family, sweet, and if possible, she will get everything she wants.

Gee, won't that child ever stop getting teeth? And molars, too. Boy, that must be rather painful. I have an idea what that Anbesol is, but I am unfamiliar with the name. I know what it is used for, though, and the method of application. Here's hoping she doesn't give you too much trouble.

Your letter is answered my sweet, so I think I will end here and get some sleep. I am exceptionally tired tonight, for some reason or other.

Give my regards to all the family. Here is my daily hug and kiss for our little darling, and millions more for my big darling. Gee, sweetheart, if only I could tell you that we will be home in a couple of months, and really mean it. I love you.

J.De Roxtro, EM2/c   Eternally, your *Johnny*

Note on flap: "Sorry this is so short, sweet. I'm not in the mood to write. I love you."

Friday, April 21, 1944. No mail. Rain all morning. Cleared up in afternoon but not very nice. Mil & Judy over for awhile. Washed clothes. Everybody out. Jackie can raise herself to standing position. 14 mos.

[Pavuvu Island, Russell Islands.]
Postmarked April 22, 1944, stamp upside down.

April 21, 1944
Somewhere

My Wonderful Darling:

I love you, miss you and want you. To be with you once again and hold you tenderly in my arms is my one desire. And when you are in my arms, I intend to kiss you and make love to you. Sweetheart, there is nothing I would rather do than to be with you. To take you places and do things with you would be swell. My love, more than anything else, I want to be there with you and make you happy. Dearest one, I love you more than you will ever know, because when I am with you again, I will be too self-conscious to tell you. I want you, sweet, more than mere words can tell. And Lucia, am I hungry. I am my beloved angel, and there is only one person who can satisfy my hunger and that, sweetheart, is you.

I just came back from the show. It was "Hi Diddle Diddle" with Martha Scott and Adolph Menjou. It was a hell of a picture, and I really enjoyed it. But hell, in my condition, anyone would enjoy anything. Most beloved, I have had an exceptional bit of luck this evening. I ran into a little drinkable alcohol, and there is no need to tell you that I really did indulge. I am in the best of spirits tonite, so if there is anything wrong in this short note, you must forgive me.

I have just been arguing on a very intricate subject, and upon figuring the whole thing out, among great mathematicians, I was finally forced to admit defeat. It was quite embarrassing, but I didn't mind so very much. I learned a little more. You must remind me to brush up on my math, my love. The speed of sound and a projectile had a lot to do with the argument. It was a sociable one, so there were no black eyes, etc. Hell, everything we do is educational. How I wish I were home again, so I could lie in bed, get my breakfast served there, and have my loved one beside me most of the time.

I didn't mean to make this more than two pages my sweet, for fear you might become a little angry with me. But so as you will, I still love you. Gee, sweetest wife in the world, won't it be swell when you and I are reunited, and won't have to try and write nice letters to each other. I want so very much to be there with you. I am hungry, my sweet, and only you can satisfy my hunger.

Lucia, dearest, I didn't want to write to you tonight. My conscience made me. I am a little tight, but loving you the way I do, nothing or no one could make me break the chain of daily letters I've been writing since I hit this god-forsaken hellhole. I wanted to write, but I didn't want you to learn of my inebriated plight. Sweetest wife and mother on this universe, I love you, want you and miss you. If you were here, I would not be the way I am. I adore you.

Most precious angel, no mail came again today, from you or anyone else. I love you, though, and am expecting some tomorrow. Here's hoping I get some.

Give my regards to all the family and any of our mutual acquaintances you may happen to meet. Here is my daily hug and kiss from me to our dearest one, Jackie, and millions more to you, my wife. I am more proud of you than words can say. I love you, miss you and want you. Most adorable, you are mine, forever.

J.De Roxtro, EM2/c   Everlastingly, your *Johnny*

April 22, 1944 - Allies invade Aitape and Hollandia in New Guinea. Allied intelligence, lack of Japanese preparedness, changes in command and a lack of troops contributed to the collapse of Japanese resistance at these bases in New Guinea, resulting in unqualified success for the Allied forces. The Japanese withdrew to the west of New Guinea.

Saturday, April 22, 1944. Mom met girls in Hoboken. Went to New York. Shopped and saw a show. Bought socks and stockings.

[No saved letter for Saturday April 22]

Sunday, April 23, 1944. Mama G & Tadone up. Rain. Gene and Judy. Went to movies in afternoon. Saw "Shine on Harvest Moon." Fair. Found out Jackie cut another canine.

[Pavuvu Island, Russell Islands.]
Postmarked April 24, 1944, one stamp upside down.   April 23, 1944

Somewhere

Lucia, Most Loveable:

All day, every day, I am continually thinking of you, and wishing I were there with you. My love for you increases hourly. Mere words aren't ample to tell you just how much I do love you. You will just have to wait until we are together once again. Then, and only then, will I be able to show you. I miss you more, too, as the hours slowly drag by, bringing us more close to the day when I will be able to hold you tenderly in my arms and kiss you. And how I want you. Sweetheart, I've never wanted anything as much as I want to be there with you. The day of our reunion will not come any too soon to suit me. Your smiling face is ever before me. Thoughts of you are continually in my mind. I often find myself riding with you beside me, real close. I am down at the Red Star with you, eating hot dogs and sipping a beer, or just a little farther down the highway, getting ice cream at Howard Johnsons. There are so many of those pleasant things that I often think of. Lucia, my love, one of these days, after the war, you and I will be able to do all those things you have wanted to do, and haven't. You must ask me to take you here and there, though, because I won't know where you would like to go, or what you would like to do. Every once in awhile I might make a suggestion, but I want you to ask me for anything I don't think of. I love you so very much, sweet, that I am willing to sacrifice anything, in order to make you happy. Your slightest wish will be my desire, my lovely one, so don't hesitate to make known your wants. If it is at all possible for me to do so, your wishes shall be granted. May this war soon end, so that you and I will be able to bring up our children as they should be raised.

Just picture a little house, out of the business section, somewhere. There will be a little lawn in front, with flower gardens, and a porch, upon which we can sit and enjoy the beauties of nature. In the rear, there will be another porch, where our kiddies can play, during the rains. In the yard, there will be flowers and vegetables, of course. We must raise a few tomatoes, and a little sweet corn. Maybe a few beets and carrots, and some parsley. For me, there will be a small bed of onions and garlic. Oh, yes, I had almost forgotten radishes. Under the fruit trees, there will be benches, where we will be able to have light snacks with our beer or Tom Collins. Let's see, there will also be a small goldfish pond. And now, most important of all, there will be a large space, just for our children to enjoy themselves and exercise. Swings, seesaws, parallel bars, and everything else will be there. Just a rough picture, sweet, but how does it strike you. As for the inside of the house, that's up to you. You may do anything you care to, inside, above the basement. We will decide what to do there, when the time comes. We may make it a playroom, or a workshop, or maybe both. There are plenty of things we could do with a nice dry basement, aren't there. You know what, my love, I think it will be swell, when you and I and the family are settled in a nice place of our own. We will have such swell times together. I am looking forward to that day, and when I think of it, I become pleasantly excited.

There was no mail for me again today. I haven't received any from you since last Monday, a week ago tomorrow. I do have a very short one to answer. It was written the sixth of April, and postmarked the seventh. Have you noticed that they are more fast since you decided to mail them yourself? It really is a lot better, lovely one, and I will love you eight days a week for it. Gee, it's swell hearing from you in a couple of weeks again. Thanks loads, dear one. I really do appreciate it. Gee, I love you so much. I don't want to write letters, I want to be there to make love to you in person. That day will come soon, though, it has to. And if hoping and praying help any, I've been doing plenty of that. Darling, won't it be swell, when the three of us can be together. Gosh, I can hardly wait to see you and your daughter. From the few pictures I have of you since you brought Jackie into the world, you seem to me to have become even more beautiful. I'll see for sure, though soon. I worship you.

That April snowstorm you had must have been a beautiful sight. Can you imagine me, way out here on a supposedly tropical paradise, hearing about all the snow you had back there this past winter. Hell, I want to see some snow, or at least some weather a little cooler than the fires of hell. It must be at least a hundred fifty today, in the shade, and there isn't the faintest trace of a breeze. Gee, it sure is hot and close. It will probably rain so darn hard in a short while, that we will be in danger of being washed down the hillside into the bay. By the way, in the bay I speak of, are some of the most beautiful fish I've ever seen. All the colors imaginable are there and even some that you can't think of. Most of them are small, and when they are seen in a school, through the bluish water, well, honey, it is simply fascinating. Besides the beautiful small fish, we have some not so pretty, like shark, porpoise and alligators. There is a fish here called the barracuda, and it is extremely dangerous. With ease, it can bite a finger or toe off, and the larger ones can naturally take a bigger bite. Don't worry, we aren't allowed in without our trunks. I never go in anyway. Not because of the danger of the fish, because I believe they are more scared of a human than the person is of them. I remain out because there is a chance of getting a coral infection in the ears. Very few of the fellows go in. I have been in a few times, but I don't make a habit of it. I would rather be sure of my ears than take a swim when there is a shower handy.

Our little one seems to be following the antics of the profession of childhood. It is far beyond my powers of comprehension to figure the reason for children throwing shoes and other things into the toilet bowl. Every child seems to go through that stage. She is a little devil at times, I imagine, but would you have it otherwise? Heck, if she didn't do things like that, she wouldn't be normal. Personally, I'm sure glad you do love her as much, even when she does annoy you. Gee, sweet, I wish so often that I could be there to see her do some of those things. You can bet your boots that I will be, for the next one. That is, of course, if it is at all possible.

I am sorry your mail wasn't coming quite as regularly as it should have been. Lord, I hope it didn't remain delayed for a week or more. That would be terrible. Not only would you be all worked up into thinking I was coming home, but you would naturally stop writing to me. Maybe that's the reason I haven't received any more this week. Honey, I will let you know, somehow, when we are to leave here, so even though the mail should stop, please don't get all excited and expectant. Don't expect me until you see me. That will be the best thing to do. I will give you a warning, though, by telephone or telegram, so you won't be shocked to badly. I wouldn't want you to faint at your first sight of me. I know I'm ugly enough to do that, but I wouldn't want my wife to do it. Remember, sweet, I'll let you know just when to expect me. I love you.

There is nothing definite in regards to our returning to the states out yet, but the skipper did say that we may receive orders tomorrow, or they may come in six months. As you see, that means we may have to stay out on one of these god-forsaken hellholes indefinitely. I doubt very much if we will remain on this one, though, unless we get more work to do, because we are just about caught up here. When we do leave, it may be to do another job, or to return to home and the ones we love and adore. I certainly do hope it is the latter, don't you?

"Mrs. Miniver" is playing tonight, so, as I've seen it twice now, I will read my latest Readers Digest. It came yesterday. I don't think I told you that, did I? That is a swell magazine, and all the fellows enjoy reading it. Maybe I'll do a few crossword puzzles, I don't know. There is not a darn thing to do, other than what I've mentioned.

Your letter is answered my lovely one, and now, I have no letters at all, from anyone, to answer. All my correspondence has been taken care of. It's a swell feeling, knowing that you owe no one anything. I did better with this letter than I thought. It must be love that enables me to write long letters to you, and say nothing, except that I love you, miss you and want you.

Give my regards to all the family and our friends, and here is my daily hug and kiss for your daughter. To you, sweetie, I would like to give my all. Hugs and kisses.

J.De Roxtro EM2/c   Eternal love and happiness,   *Johnny*

Note on flap: "Maybe we'll be seeing each other soon, huh, sweet. I sure hope so. I love you.

[Pavuvu Island, Russell Islands.]
Postmarked April 24, 1944, stamp upside down.   April 23, 1944
Hello, Joe:

Boy, was I pleasantly surprised when I received your letter. I never expected it. Heck, brother, no alibis or excuses are necessary. I know darn well that if the situation was reversed, I would be quite lax in writing. After all, I realize that you have plenty to do, when you aren't working. As long as you enquired about my state of health I will be satisfied. And you seem to be doing a swell job of acting as little Jackie's daddy. From all I hear, you love the bambino as if she were your own. Thanks a million, Joe. As long as I am forced to remain away for such a long time, there is no one I would rather have taking my place than you. Even though you did give the wee one a sip of your beer. But I guess I would have done the same. I'll bet my lovely wife became a little peeved, when she saw Jackie licking her lips and reaching for more. I can almost see Lou taking the baby from your lap and setting her on the floor. And then you laughed, and she couldn't stay angry. She sure is a swell mother, isn't she.

Joe, I don't mind so much if you don't write to me because I get plenty of letters from both our families. But write to Ralph as often as you can. He needs them more than I do. His life here is very monotonous and I know that letters from home help out a devil of a lot.

Yes, there is a possibility that I will be home this summer but as there is nothing definite upon which to base my opinions, it is also possible that I won't. I know that if hopes and prayers have anything to do with it, that I will be. The day of my departure from this so-called tropical paradise cannot come too soon.

No, Joe, I don't know anyone in our outfit by the name of Farrell. It is possible that he is on this island, though, so if you let me know which battalion he is in, I will be pleased to look him up. Give my regards to all the folks there at your home, Joe. Best of everything to you and Angie, hoping to see you soon.

J.De Roxtro EM2/c

As ever, *Johnny*

Monday, April 24, 1944. *Received $50 bond in mail. Rain.*

[Pavuvu Island, Russell Islands.]
Postmarked April 25, 1944, stamp upside down.

April 24, 1944
Somewhere

Lucia Darling:

I love you, miss you and want you. Thoughts of you are forever in my mind, and your image, sweet and lovely, is eternally in my heart. Sweetest wife in the world, I long to hold you tenderly in my arms and kiss you. I want so very much to be there with you. I still have hopes of being with you in June or July, but the scuttlebutt is getting bad again. Honey, the day of our reunion will certainly be a happy one for me. I can hardly wait, but knowing that that day will eventually come, makes me last through the time. Somehow, sometime, my wife and I will be together. And what a day that will be. All I want to do is sit around and talk with you. I have so much to learn from you about everything, and especially about our lovely little daughter. I have plenty to tell you, too, but I want to hear all yours first. Gee you must have plenty stored up. I will make love to you, most of the time, though. Gee, how I love you.

Today, beloved, I received your letter of April eleventh. It was postmarked the twelfth, too. Honey, I will never be able to thank you enough, for making that extra little effort and mailing your letters immediately after writing them. It certainly does help a lot, too, doesn't it. Gee, darling, you make me more proud of you all the time. I sure am lucky to have gotten you as a wife. I still can't see how I ever managed to convince you that I was the one you should marry.

Sweetheart, I finally managed to get that money order this morning. I will enclose it in this letter. It is for fifty dollars, and I want you to get your mother, my mother, and your grandmother each something for Mother's Day. I don't care what it is or how much you pay for it, either. You have my permission to give the cash to Mama G. It is the best thing to do, I guess. But also get her a box of chocolates or something.

For yourself, my love, you have my permission to get yourself anything you want. I know darn well that you won't spend much for those little things for our mothers, and should have about twenty-five bucks left. I, therefore, insist that you spend it all on yourself, to get a little something that you've wanted badly, but thought that you couldn't spare the money for. Please, my love, do all you can for yourself. Oh, I almost forgot – this little Mother's Day gift is from your lovely little daughter. And if I think I am unable to be there with you on your birthday, I will send another one then. (Money order, I mean.) I will keep hoping and praying that I am, though, and until the middle of next month, I will refuse to give up hope. It sure would be wonderful if we were together to celebrate on that day, wouldn't it. But any day that we are united, we will celebrate.

This will be the end of my short note, though, because there isn't anything to say. I am well, and happy as I possibly can be, being away from you. I sincerely hope that you and Jackie, and the rest of the family are in the best of health and remain so, forever. I think I will go to the show now. Maybe I will be able to fill the remainder of this page. I don't know what the name of it is. Who knows, maybe I've seen it already. I intend to save your letter for a later date, to answer. The rest of this week, I will answer a letter every day I receive one, always saving one for Sunday. That's a pretty good idea, don't you think.

Give my fond regards to all the family and our friends. Here is my daily hug and kiss for Jackie, and millions more to you, the sweetest, most adorable wife, sweetheart and mate in all the world. I love you.

J.De Roxtro, EM2/c   Eternally, your adoring *Johnny*

Note on flap: "*The picture was 'Thank Your Lucky Stars.' Pretty good. I love you.*"

Tuesday, April 25, 1944. Letters of 9th, 10th, & 13th. Money order for $100 in 10th. Went to New York to look for suit. Took 4:52 train. Almost missed it. Met Ann in Hoboken 5:45.

[Pavuvu Island, Russell Islands.]
Postmarked April 26, 1944, postmaster stamp.   April 25, 1944
                                                                  Somewhere

Hello, Adorable:

I love you, miss you and want you more as each day slowly passes, bringing us more close to the day when we will be reunited. I long to hold you tenderly in my arms and kiss you. To make love to you is my desire. I want to be there with you and Jackie so very much.

Today I received three letters. One from my mother, and two from my sweetheart. Yours were dated the eighth and twelfth of April. The one of the eighth was postmarked the tenth, but I can't quite see the one on yours of the twelfth. I think it's the thirteenth, though, anyway, it must have been soon after the day you wrote it. I looked close at that one, because it was postmarked in Orange. Thanks again for working your system out, lovely one. Even though we are sure that those other letters were posted the following morning, something sure speeded them up. I will give you all the credit for that. I love you, my sweet, for being so thoughtful. Keep up the good work, sweet, and I'll repay you in kisses.

Your letter of the eighth will be answered by me tonight, as that is the oldest I have. Oh, by the way, thanks a million for the pictures I received today. Your little one sure is growing up, isn't she. It does seem to me that she is inclined to be a thinker, or she takes after her old man. I seldom smile; I need you to make me do that. Thanks for the double kiss on the envelope. I'll return them in person, soon. Boy, you aren't the only one who wishes and hopes that we will be together soon. That is all that is keeping me going. I, too, feel quite sure that we will be reunited soon, but anything can happen, so all we can do is hope and pray.

Now that the weather back there is getting warmer, maybe I can get that picture of you in a sweater. There is, in my case, the same one you asked me to destroy, you know, and until another comes along, I will keep it there, taking it out occasionally to view it with longing. I may keep it, even after the new one arrives. I like it, myself.

It sure was nice of "We Three" to send Easter cards to all the little ones and to my mother. Thanks for everything, angel. I will have to depend on you for carrying on all our social affairs. I never could remember dates or special events. Your memory is so much better than mine. I don't know what I'd do without you.

Gee, in order to go out without a coat on must have been swell to you, wasn't it. I used to welcome the day that I could. Now I am looking forward to the day when I will have to put a coat on. Boy, won't I feel good when I can roll in the snow, make a snowman for Jackie, take her coasting, and all that sort of thing. I'm even going to teach her to make snowballs and throw them. Boy, we three will have plenty of fun. I love you both.

The grass is green, the tulips and other early spring flowers are in bloom, and the robins and other birds are busy building their nests. How I would love to be there. In the spring, a young man's fancy turns to thoughts of love, you know, and although I am no longer a young man, I am in love. I'm afraid it wouldn't have to be spring for me to fall for you again, either. However, as long as Jackie enjoys watching the birds, all is well. She must be a smart little devil. Those blue jays with all the racket they make would even be a treat to me.

It will be nice when your stroller arrives. Not only will it be quite a bit easier on you, but Jackie will get more air, and will be a lot cooler. Now that the weather is beginning to get warm, it really will be swell.

I am sorry to say so, Lou, but I can't seem to remember what the Zalias (spelling incorrect, I believe) look like. Are they those plants which have small red flowers about the size of small daisies. The flowers have four or five petals, too, don't they. That is about the only thing I seem to remember. Anyway, they will be welcomed by our moms, no matter whether I've made a mistake or not. And as for my mother's corsage, well, I will quote what she said about it in this letter. "I got the most wonderful corsage from Lou and Jack. Thanks son." That's all she said, but she seemed to be in a slight rush when she wrote it. She likes flowers so very much.

It's only natural that Jackie would run a fever and feel rather badly while she is cutting a molar. All children do, so you have nothing to worry about. Maybe by this time, she has recovered. I sure hope so. It must be very trying on your nerves, when she is that way. Gee, the wife and mother has a tough job. The wee one must be very fretful and restless. Oh, well, here's hoping for the best. I love you both. I am glad you thought of giving Annette an alcohol rubdown. That surely must have helped quite a bit.

That answers just about everything in your letter, my love. I am well, and have been, all this while, so there is no need for you to worry about me. I am as happy as I possibly can be, away from you, the one I love. Here's hoping that you, Jackie and the family are, have been, and remain to be in the best of health, and are happy.

I have decided to take another examination for an advancement in rate, and if I don't make it this time, I'll give up. Wish me luck, angel.

Goodnight, my love, until I write tomorrow. I will answer another letter then. Who knows, maybe I'll have another good week. Give my regards to all the family and our mutual friends. Here is my daily hug and kiss for Jackie, and millions more to you, the most wonderful, most beautiful wife on earth. Love and kisses.

J.De Roxtro, EM2/c   *Everlastingly, your devoted* *Johnny*

Note on flap: *"Good night my lovely one. I'm yours forever."*

Wednesday, April 26, 1944. 4th issue of C-Breeze. Letters of 12th & 14th of April. Lovely day. Went downtown with Cat and her mother. Bought socks and overalls. Cashed money order.

[Pavuvu Island, Russell Islands.]

Postmarked April 27, 1944, post office stamp.   *April 26, 1944*

Somewhere

Hello, Beautiful:

I love you, miss you and want you. You are forever in my mind, and everlastingly in my heart. I want so much to hold you in my arms and kiss you. Sweetest wife in the world, more than anything else, I want to be there with you. You are mine, and I am yours, my sweet precious angel, and we belong together. That day will soon come, I hope and pray. And when it does, we will be happy once again. I love you, dear one.

No mail came from you today. In fact, none came at all, for me. But I don't care so much, as long as I have one or two to answer. Tonight, I will answer yours of the eleventh of April. You sort of surprised me on this one. You initialed the outside flap with the following: Sealed with a hug and kiss. Honey, all mine are sealed that way, only I am not allowed to put any initials on them. Believe it or not, I am not even allowed to send you a kiss by the usual ex. I'm afraid you will just have to wait for me to keep that date, sweet. Things don't look any too good, right now. I am still hoping and praying, though, and there is still a chance. I certainly would love to be able to keep that date. Maybe if I tell the skipper about it, he will let me keep it. Oh, yes, he will. If he had anything to do with it, he would have had us home long ago. After all, he has to take orders, the same as we do. I am still wishing

106

to be there, so you keep hoping and praying and your loving Johnny will do the same.

I had forgotten all about the Jewish holidays. It's a wonder they ever closed the factory for a week, isn't it. What the hell do we care, though, as long as your mother was able to get a week off. That's swell, and I'll bet she appreciated it. As for the schools being closed, boy, ain't dat somethin'. Wait a minute, I made a mistake. I thought Gracie was home because of the holidays, but I had the wrong ones. I was thinking, and wondering why they ever closed the schools because of the Jewish holidays. They never did that before.

You know all about my Easter day by this time, so I won't bother you any more with it. I had my usual Sunday, and was quite lucky.

Sweetheart, I am very sorry that I wasn't able to furnish you with a corsage for your new Easter finery on that day of days. I did manage to send some flowers, but I see that they didn't arrive on time. You must have received them by this time, however. I hope you liked them. You haven't mentioned anything about you getting yourself and Jackie a new outfit. Did you get one? You must have, because you said you took some snapshots. I am anxious to see them, but don't rush, my adorable one, I will wait patiently.

You must have had a houseful again on Easter Day. By the sound of it, the whole family was there, except Ralph and I. Boy, we would have liked to have been there, too. My mom did like the corsage you sent her, sweetheart. Thanks a million for sending them. It was too bad that she couldn't have gotten down, but as long as she has secured a position, and is happy there, she will be better off. Neither Vene nor my mother has told me even as much as you have, about her newest position. But they will, in time. What you told me really sounds pretty good, doesn't it. I hope she is happy there.

You sure did have quite a time trying to get over to your Aunt's house that day, didn't you. First John and Vene, and then Joe and Angie.

Jackie seems to have had quite a profitable day, too. Your list of things she received sounds pretty good to me. You didn't let her eat those jellybeans and chocolate bar, did you? Or is she old enough now that she can eat those things?

Say, sweet, any time you feel that you want to give Mama G and Tadone a couple of bucks, or anything, go right ahead. I think it's really swell of you and the family to make all gifts cash. As you say, they need it badly, so help them all you want, sweet, I am for it, myself. I like them a lot, and there isn't anything I wouldn't do to help them be happy through the rest of their lives. After all, they have such a short time here, so let's make the best of it for them, and hope they live to be two hundred. I'll be home soon to see them. Gosh, I don't feel much like writing.

So you finally got a break and were able to go to visit your grandparents. It was nice of Ann to get that cold, and volunteer to stay at home with our little one. I'll bet they were glad to see you.

You never will learn to understand what that little mind is thinking, when she is playing. Gee, she must have had a swell time out riding in the red wagon. Grace must have a swell time with her, too. At times, though, she probably becomes a little vexed. I can't blame her, though. I sure am glad that your daughter is a little roughneck. Heck, isn't that the way we want her to be? A toughie, but always a lady. It must be swell to watch the little one trying to tell you something. For instance her walking over to where you were writing, and laying her head on your lap. Hell, I want to go home. I'm tired of being away out here, so many thousands of miles away.

Sweetheart, your letter has now been answered, and as I have no further news to impart, I will have to close. Give my regards to all, my sweet, including your family and our friends, and especially to Mama G and Tadone. Here is my daily hug and kiss for our little Jackie and millions more to you, the sweetest, most wonderful wife and sweetheart in the world. I love you, miss you and want you. I remain,

J.De Roxtro EM2/c   *Everlastingly, your adoring* *Johnny*

Thursday, April 27, 1944. *No mail. Rain. Mil & Betty went to N.Y. I took care of Judy. (letter to Ann with money order of $50).*

Friday, April 28, 1944. *Letter of April 18. Lovely day. M.d.R called-would spend Tuesday night here. Went downtown-bought Q-tips and powder, film. Went to Mils.*

Saturday, April 29, 1944. *Letter from Mary. Lovely day. Cleaned house-put Jackie out front. Sat. nite - went to movies - saw "The Desert Song" Dennis Morgan, Irene Manning.*

[The letters from Johnny for April 27,28 & 29 are missing. They are possibly lost.]

Sunday, April 30, 1944. *Lovely day. Put Jackie out in morning. Talked with Mil & Judy. Mike & Michael came. Took pictures of the three. After nap, dressed her up in pink. Joe & Angie here. Jackie very sociable. Went for ride in car. Rode in wagon with Michael. 7:00 girls went to movies. 7:30 Mike and Michael went home. Joe took them to station. 1:00 Angie, Mom & Mama G went visiting. Joe sent Gracie for ice cream.*

[Pavuvu Island, Russell Islands.]
Postmarked May 1, 1944, two stamps upside down.   *April 30, 1944*
                                                              Somewhere

My Lucia:

I love you with all my heart, body and soul. You are forever on my mind and eternally in my heart. Adorable one, I long to take you in my arms and kiss you once again. I miss you and want you so much.

So far today, no mail has come, so I will start answering your letter of April twelfth. It was postmarked soon after writing, I guess. Gee, sweet, thanks loads for getting them off more soon. I see by the postmark that you are trusting my letters to your sisters again. Here's hoping they aren't held up again. But enough of that. Thanks loads for the four kisses you sent via the stamps. On the inside of the flap you have, "Hi, Sweet, I love you." That means a heck of a lot to me, more than you will ever know.

First, I will comment on the pictures of our little one you enclosed in this envelope. Gosh, she gets larger and fatter every time I receive pictures. She looks so fat and healthy in her snowsuit, doesn't she. But she seems to be tired, or else the glare from the reflected rays of the sun are making her squint. She is a honey, and I am anxious to see her real soon. That doll she has isn't one that Nora sent her, is it. No, it couldn't be. In this one where she is with the sled, she looks as if she wants to go somewhere, but is bogged down. I can't seem to describe her looks in the other one, though. Perhaps she is intently interested in a bird, or something. She is intelligent, too. I can tell that from looking at this picture. Yes, I believe I'm correct. There was a bird of something up on the porch roof, just above the door that was attracting her attention. The way she is biting her lower lip interests me. I wonder just what she was thinking. It looks as if she were afraid that whatever it was she is watching would fall, but there isn't fear on her face. More as if she were wishing she could do the same. Oh, well, maybe I'll learn her facial expressions when I get there. I sure hope it's soon. Thanks a lot for sending the pictures, sweet, I really do enjoy receiving them, almost as much as I appreciate your letters.

The mail just came down, sweet, so if you'll pardon me a minute, I'll go see if there are any for me. Be right back. I received one letter from you, which was written the thirteenth, but wasn't postmarked until the seventeenth. It was mailed in Orange, too. I think you must have been a little peeved at me, for some reason. The stamp was not reversed, and there was no little note of love on the inside flap of the envelope. Honey, you know darn well that neither of your sisters mean anything to me, except as sisters. You are the only one I have ever really and truly loved, and the only one I ever will.

You should know it, even though you don't. Those reversed stamps don't mean anything, either, and if you say so, I will refrain from writing anything except purely brotherly stuff. Sweet, do you think that if they meant anything to me, that I would write them about it? Hell, I know you read those letters, or at least part of them. I thought you would get a kick out of it. But you seemed so cool and distant in this letter. Honey, I love you and only you. I wouldn't care if all the rest of the women in the world were out here. I would still want to be where you are. More than anything else, my desire to be with you is carrying me on. Sweet, I won't write any more letters like those.

Now to continue where I left off. I hope your girlfriend isn't there when I arrive, but if she is, it won't bother me any. I will make love to you, hug you and kiss you, even though she is. And then, when she leaves, we will become more intimate. Gee, honey, my love, I want to be there so much. Holy cow, according to my calculations, she is due to arrive again on your birthday. Well, here's wishing you a happy one. Also, here's wishing, hoping and praying that I will be there to make you happy. Now I'm wondering if I will be able to make you happy. Do you think I will?

I've sent our weekly paper regularly, as I said I would. Last Sunday I inserted one in an airmail envelope, crossed out the words "air-mail" and wrote free in the place of the stamp. Monday I received a note from the post office saying that I couldn't do that anymore. So I told him to put an airmail stamp on and let it go. Today I will try to send it via airmail. Maybe I will be lucky. We aren't supposed to, but what can a fellow do if he has no plain envelopes. I'll do my best to get it to you, but I may have to carry it with me. I'm glad you and the girls enjoyed reading it so much. It's not much, but I guess all the fellows enjoy it too. There must be four more on the way, and today's makes five. Here's hoping they all arrive at their destination. Please remember to save them for me, will you? I may enjoy reading them a few years from now.

Forbes is much better now. He is lying here on the deck of our tent, right now. He just finished writing a letter to Ann. He will have to sleep at the sickbay for about a week yet, though. Your prayers must have helped him, sweetheart. They have kept me safe all these many, many months, so they must have done him some good, too. I agree with you. They should send him back to the states. Heck, he gets it so darn often now. The only thing that can help him is a cooler climate. Even then, he will have it for maybe two years, whenever he becomes warm. Don't you worry about me, angel, because I'm not worth it. Save your worries for our little Jackie. Besides, as long as I haven't taken sick yet, there is little chance that I will, now. The only thing I can complain of is that I tire so very easily. I am still able to put out a good day's work, though. Dearest, if only I could be there with you.

I gave up my study of music, sweetest girl in the world. I didn't have time, and I learned all I could, from the material on hand. Besides, with no instrument, I couldn't go any farther, anyway. I may take it up at a later date, I don't know. I would much rather make love to you, my wife.

I sure am glad that you received that stroller. I'm quite surprised that the frame and everything else is still in it, except the body. That must have been a pre-war model. Or else they are letting some steel out, to manufacturers. You seem to be really excited about it, honey, and I must say that I am pleased that you are glad you got it. As I said before, it will make everything so much more easy for you. Don't forget to let me know how Jackie likes it. I'll bet she really will enjoy riding in it.

I told Forbes about you having the reprint made of Jackie on her toidy, and he seemed quite pleased, and sends his thanks. He thinks you are swell, sweet, but I know you are. I don't know what I would ever do without you. Just thinking of you helps make me feel better, and when I receive a letter, boy, how I love it. Gee, won't it be swell when we are able to talk to each other again, instead of writing these letters. Actions speak louder than words, my sweet. I have always said that, and I am definitely sure that it is true, now. I love you, miss you and want you, my darling.

Your letter of the twelfth is answered, sweetheart mine, so I think I will go right on and answer the one I just received. I will thank you for the kiss you sent via the stamp, just in case it was an accident, but I doubt if it was. Let me know if I am wrong, Lou, will you?

Yes, one of my letters dated the fifth must have been a mistake. I often make mistakes like that. Sometimes it is intentional, but this time it wasn't. I told you quite awhile ago that I was making out an allotment for fifty dollars, didn't I? That is in addition to the eighty you are now receiving, so don't be surprised when you get them both. It sure took a long time to go through, didn't it. Sweetheart mine, I don't know what you mean when you say that Grace doesn't know the half of it. How do you know that the reversed stamp on Fan's letter wasn't a mistake? Or how do you know that I didn't do it just to tease you? Or – oh, nuts! Why should I bother to explain. Honey, you are mine, and I am yours, forever. That suits me fine, does it you? I would like to know what you meant when you said what you did. Maybe I should merely overlook this letter. Yes, I think I will take it with a grain of salt. There isn't any use in both of us getting angry, and as your girlfriend was there, you weren't quite as gay as usual. I'm sorry. Yes, I'll just make light of it. In the entire letter, you have only one descriptive word, and that is in the salutation. I'm sorry if I have made you angry, sweet, but I assure you that it was unintentional. You are the only one that means anything to me, and you know it. Would I be writing daily if you weren't? Would I be sending you these weekly papers of ours, or the money orders, or increase my allotment, or send surprises, through Ann, to you? Hell no, sweet, you are my one and only. I love you more now than I ever did.

That was a swell idea, buying that material for overalls for Jackie. You never will have enough, because when the time comes, Jackie will certainly wear them out fast. And about her shoes, well, I don't know what you will be able to do about that, unless she goes barefooted. That won't be so good, either. Gee, if only I were there, and we had that place of our own. Wouldn't it be swell, having a nice lawn for our family to go around barefoot on? Don't forget to snap some pictures of your lovely daughter in those coveralls. I want to see her in them. I also want to see how you make out with them. I know darn well that they'll turn out swell, though.

As for the printed dress, why don't you get several patterns and different material, and stock up on them? That is, of course, if you have time. Gee, I love you, Lucia.

If you will pardon me now, for a few minutes, I will dress (I'm nude) and go to chow. I will return and finish this letter to my one and only wife. I love you. Well, here I am back, my love. Our supper consisted of Vienna sausage, boiled rice, dried lima beans, pickled beets with onions (raw), fruit salad, (the kind you like) and coffee. That wasn't so bad, was it? We usually have hot coffee about two evenings a week. It is usually pretty good, too. We have hotcakes three mornings each week, too. I may as well complete the day, and tell you of our dinner today. As usual, we had steak, smothered with fried onions, mashed potatoes, peas and carrots, ice cream with chocolate sauce, and iced lemonade. Now, you know better than to worry about the meals I am getting. We often have corn fritters, nice crisp bacon, creamed chicken, all kinds of canned fruits, cake, pie and crullers, and home made bread. All our baked goods are made right here, and I will tell the world that they are really good. Our cooks can prepare this food better than most can, too. They also are good. We are no longer situated in a place, when the news spreads, and we have bunches of visitors. Some fellows will walk many miles just to eat our food. Oh, yes, we also have flake ice machines, so we have cold drinks. They, and the ice cream machines aren't G.I. They belong to the fifteenth, personally.

I must have given you the wrong impressions when I told you about Ralph. He has a minimum of two years to put in out here, so you can't expect him home in six months, as I seem to have led you to believe. Let's see, he has been out here about a year now, so that leaves him another year. I sure am sorry I misled you, sweetheart. The army has a two-year rotation period. The navy is supposed to be a minimum of eighteen months out here.

Sweetheart, I am sorry, but I must return to the subject of my letters to your sisters. You say that you doubt if I would ever change, even for you. Angel of mine, you know darn well that I have changed, in many ways, for you. And those changes were for the better. Lucia, dearest, you have even improved my disposition, and that really is something. Now, if you remember, way back when we were going together, I told you never to believe anything I ever wrote in a letter. Even that has changed, my love, and you can believe anything I have told you in my letters. As for those I wrote to the girls, well, you may discredit most things I write in them. That, most adorable one, is my line. That's the sort of thing that got me engaged before. As for those intimate items I put in, it's only for the education of those two. They are so naïve, and I'm afraid someone will take advantage of them. Take, for instance, the night we were wed. Remember when Eddie was driving us over to get my car? Hell, you sere worried then, and I wasn't. Now it's just the opposite. I am worried, and you seem not to be. I am not worried about you, because you do have brains and you use them. It would be terrible if anything ever happened to either of those girls. Do you remember how close we were, several times, to intimacy? I still don't know whatever stopped me, unless it was true love. Every time I wrote one of those letters telling them what the fellows look at, I did consider your feelings. Honey, honestly, aren't you glad I am interested enough to tell them things. I will refrain from writing such letters, in the future. I had no idea that you would be hurt by them. I am truly sorry, and I never did hurt you intentionally. I love you too much to hurt you in any way. In the future, I promise to merely answer their letters. Will that be satisfactory to you, sweet?

I like all those pictures you send to me, sweet. I have so many pictures, now, that in a way, I seem to be indirectly watching her grow up. But how swell it would be if we had been together all these months, to bring our family up. I wish this damned war would end soon. I am getting more homesick every day. I love you, want you and miss you.

Gee, it sure is a relief to know that Jackie's teeth are coming out straight, and are down fast. That little space between her teeth won't do any harm, in fact, it may actually do some good. The more air space between teeth the better. They are more easy to keep clean, too. Gee, we sure are lucky to have those teeth coming straight. Wouldn't it be terrible if she had crooked teeth?

I thought she would be taking plenty of spills, but I didn't think they would occur daily. Let's hope they are never quite as bad as the last one she had. I could be so much help to you if I were there.

Well, sweetie-pie, this turned out to be quite a letter, although it wasn't very pleasant, was it. Your two letters have been answered, so now I haven't anymore. All my correspondence is taken care of, too. Dearest one, if only I were able to take you tenderly in my arms once again and kiss you. I want to be there with you and kiss you. I want to run my hands over your nice white breasts and your thighs. From your thighs they would travel across your nice tummy. Angel of mine, I want you. I am hungry for you. More than anything else, I want to be with you. Give my regards to all the family and our friends. Here is my daily hug and kiss for Jackie, and millions more to you, the most adorable girl in the world, my wife.

J.De Roxtro, EM2/c   Everlastingly, your adoring *Johnny*

Note on flap: *"Please don't become angry with me anymore. Goodnight, my sweet. Maybe I'm nuts. Sweetheart, I love you more as time slowly passes. Here's a kiss for Mickey."*

Monday, May 1, 1944. *Allotment check - $80. Letter from Ralph. Lovely day-very warm. Jackie out all day. Wore just sweater & tam. Washed windows in office. (playpen) First issue of Good Housekeeping.*

Tuesday, May 2, 1944. *Allotment check of $50. M.d.R came - 9:00. Went to bed 10:15. Sat and talked with girls & myself. Gave $5.00 to me and Jackie as Easter gift.*

[Pavuvu Island, Russell Islands.]
Postmarked May 3, 1944 stamp upside down.

May 2, 1944
Somewhere

Hello, Sweetheart:

I love you with all my heart, body and soul. Each minute of the day and night I am either thinking or dreaming of you. Your image is everlastingly locked in my heart, to remain forever. I long to hold you tenderly in my arms once again and kiss you. To be there with you to remain forever is my one desire. I miss you so very much, and I want you. I'm hungry for love, and only you can satisfy me. Dearest one, you are mine, and I am yours, forever.

Three letters came for me today and all were from you, my sweet. They were written the fourteenth, seventeenth and eighteenth of April and postmarked the eighteenth, ditto, and twentieth, respectively. Thanks, loads, my love. Your system certainly is working. All three of these were posted in town, so you probably mailed them yourself. You didn't send a stamp kiss on the first one, but on the last there were two. Thanks for all four. I consider the first one also.

I guess I will never make that first class rate, sweet. I got orders today to the effect that I would have to take another examination. Hell, I don't know anything about the one I have to take, but I intend to do my best. There seems to be no justice here, so if there is any chance to get a promotion without kissing someone's ass, I'll take it. And it won't hurt me any to study. I am doing it only for you. If it weren't for you, I think I would tell them where to shove their damn rate. Enough of this. I'll let you know what happens. Sweetest, most adorable darling, I will always think of you as mine. Without you, I don't know what I'd do. You are my inspiration. I love you. Give my regards to all the family and our friends. Here is my daily hug and kiss for Jackie. Sweetie-pie, if I were able to give you all the kisses and hugs I desire to, we would be embracing for the rest of our lives. I love you, miss you and want you. You are my dream girl. Dearest one, I want to go home. I adore you.

J.De Roxtro, EM2/c

Everlastingly, your *Johnny*

Note on flap: *"I wish I could send myself home in this. I love you."*

Wednesday, May 3, 1944. *Letters of April 15, 16, 17, 19, 20, 24, 25. Awoke 7:30. M.d.R. said train whistles bothered her. Vene called. Left 9:00 for appointment. 5th issue of C-Breeze. Money*

115

order of $50.00. let. of 24th. Vene and I went downtown, took picture of three kids. Dropped camera. Met M.D.R. uptown-ice cream when home. Wrote to Ralph.

Bonnie, Nancy, Jackie

[Pavuvu Island, Russell Islands.]
Postmarked May 4, 1944, stamp upside down.

May 3, 1944
Same Place

Most Adorable Lucia:

I love you with my whole heart. I miss you and want you. Thoughts of you are eternally in
my heart, and your image is everlastingly in my vision. No matter what I look at, your lovely face and figure is there. I want so much to hold you tenderly in my arms once again and kiss you. I want to see you so much. I want to be there with you. The day will soon come, I hope, when we will be together again. I adore you. You are mine, and I am yours, forever.

I am quite well, as usual, and I am as happy as I possibly can be, away from you, the one I love best. I sincerely hope and pray that you, Jackie and the family are in the best of health and are happy.

No mail came today, but I don't care much, as long as I have those three of yesterday to answer. I will answer yours of the fourteenth tonight. This wasn't posted until the eighteenth, but that is quite alright. I realize that you can't always do everything you want to do. Say, honey, please don't go out to mail my letters if it is raining, or the weather is in any other way inclement. I wouldn't want you to catch cold or anything, just to be good to me. Thanks again for doing all you are to get my mail here faster. You are the most thoughtful wife and sweetheart in the world. I love you so very much. To be there with you is my one desire. Gee, sweet, I wonder how much longer we'll have to wait.

Remember that Edgeworth tobacco you sent me, over a year ago? Well, I am now using it. And boy, does it ever taste good. For a few days, we weren't able to get cigarettes, so I am really glad I saved this can. Blosser and another fellow are helping me use it up before it becomes moldy. It doesn't take long, out in this climate. Thanks, again for sending it. I will love you eight days a week when I come home. You are adorable, Lou, and you are mine. How proud I am of you, you will never know. Gee, you're swell. How did I ever manage to get you for a wife. I still can't figure what you saw in me. But you can be sure I will do my best for you. After all, you are worth working and fighting for. I'm the luckiest guy in all the world. With you beside me, working with me, I will be able to do anything.

The stamp wasn't reversed on this one, but I will take it as an error, so thanks a million for it. Here's hoping I am there soon to collect for it in person. We do have quite a few to exchange, haven't we. I will answer your postscript first, as it was the first thing I saw, upon opening this letter. Forbes is feeling much better, although he is still up on the hill, in our sick bay. I think he'll pull through okay this time. I sure hope so. He is one of the swellest guys I know. I hope you are able to meet him, after this damned war is over. He may come home with me, just to see Ann. I have been telling him he may, but also that he should see his mother first, and then come up. I was thinking more of myself than him, though I'm afraid. Wouldn't it be hell if we had to be socially entertaining the first few days that we are together again. I want to be alone with you for awhile. Do you think it could be arranged? I would like to have our little one, too, though, and that wouldn't be so very convenient. Maybe we will be able to be secluded there at home. Let me know what you think about it, will you?

Gee, honey, it takes quite awhile to make three and a half dozen cream puffs, doesn't it? I have an idea it does. It was really swell of you to make them for your mother's club. I know darn well that they (the women) enjoyed them. I think I'll have to let you know when I'm arriving, so that you can make a few for me. I like them. Did you, yourself, manage to get any of this batch. If I remember correctly you missed out the last time. Maybe you learned, and had yours while you were making them.

You will have to pardon my writing sweet. I've been studying so as to pass the exam, and I am quite tired. Besides that, all the boys are at the show, so I was able to use the table, for a change. I usually sit on my cot, with a board across my knees, and write that way. I seem to have become used to it, because this writing looks none too good to me. I will have to do a little more practicing, I guess, here on the table. Position means a lot, doesn't it, when one is endeavoring to write. Gee, I worship you, angel.

As long as the flowers finally arrived, I guess I can tell you about them. They were supposed to be there in time for Easter, but I was afraid they wouldn't, so I sent the roses instead of a corsage. I hope you don't mind. Did you think I had forgotten you, sweet? As for Forbes sending Ann some, well, I was broke, so I asked him to loan me some money so that I could send you some flowers, and he asked if I would mind if he sent some to Ann. Naturally I couldn't refuse, so both were sent, on the same order. Those roses may have been a surprise, but you have a bigger one coming. Two, in fact. Gee, I hope I haven't spoiled them. I like to surprise you, because you appreciate it so much. There are so many admirable qualities which you possess. And I love you for all of them. Darling, you are my angel.

Holy Moses, Jackie must have been in a heck of a state, cutting four teeth at once. It's no wonder she was running a temperature and rash. I'll bet her disposition wasn't any too good, either. The poor kid must have been in agony. I sure hope she is better by this time. And you, my poor wife, have to go through all that without me there to help you. I probably wouldn't be able to assist much, but at least I could comfort you. The fresh air and sunshine probably did even more good than even you and I think. Let her get all of it she can, my angel. You get plenty, too. I love you.

So our weekly paper is coming to you quite regularly, now. I am glad that you like them. There probably is quite a lot in them that you can't understand, but I will explain all that to you when I get time. I don't think I can, in a letter, though. Yes, the name of that paper is pretty good. There was a contest held, and that name was picked as the best. The thinker-upper of that name received a half dozen bottles of beer. Quite a prize, eh, what? Your beloved husband didn't even enter the contest. I wouldn't even have had a chance, though.

Well, my lovely one, this ends the answer to your letter. I am sorry I am not able to make it any longer, but I just can't. Maybe I will be able to do better tomorrow. We will have to wait until then to see.

Give my regards to all the family and our mutual friends. Here is my daily hug and kiss for our wee one, your daughter, Jackie. For the most adorable, most wonderful, most lovely wife, sweetheart and mate in the world, all my hugs and kisses, until I am there to prove to you that you are the only girl in the world that I can ever love. I miss you more than I've ever wanted anything. To be there with you in my arms kissing you and telling you of my love is my one desire.

J.De Roxtro, EM2/c   Everlastingly, your adoring *Johnny*

Thursday, May 4, 1944. Letters of 21,16 of April. Took rest of pictures and brought camera to Sandrian - ready in two weeks. Film Wed. lovely day - warm. Took 4:52 train. Met Ann *in Hoboken 5:45. Went to 33rd St. Shopped in Gimbel's and Saks 34th Street. Bought blue suit. Ann bought brown . Home at 10:30. Navy coat for Jackie.*

[Pavuvu Island, Russell Islands.]
Postmarked May 5, 1944, stamp upside down.

May 4, 1944
Somewhere

Hello, Sweetheart:

I love you, miss you and want you. I am always thinking of you. Your lovely vision is eternally before me. How I long to hold you tenderly in my arms once again and kiss you. You are my one and only, my sweetheart. No one will be able to take your place, ever. I am yours forever, too. Gee, my darling, I want so much to be home with you.

I had one heck of a dirty job this afternoon, and it lasted quite awhile. In fact, we didn't even come in for chow tonight. This job had to be done, so we did it. Boy, such a stink. You have never smelled such an odor. But it's finished, and I'm all cleaned up. I had to put shaving lotion on my hands, even after my bath, to kill the aroma.

Three pieces of mail came for your loving husband today. One official one was a ballot, which enables me to vote in the primaries, (That's in the waste can), a letter from Charlie Fitzer, and one from my mother. As yours of the seventeenth is next for me to answer, I will do it now. At least as much of it as I have time for. The show is over, and all the fellows are in bed, resting comfortably. All, that is, but Forbes. He is still up on the hill, but he expects to be let out tomorrow. I will let you know any further developments. He really does appreciate that picture. He said to thank you.

Thanks for the kiss you sent by way of the stamp on this letter. Boy, I have a lot of them to collect in person when next I see you. Inside, on the flap, you have "Dearest, I love you." Those words mean more to me than anything else in the world. I love you.

This is a very short letter, Sweety, and for once, I'm not sorry, but only because I am almost too tired to write. But as long as I am able to write, I will keep up my daily correspondence.

I wouldn't know whether Charlene Clere received her picture of us boys or not, because I haven't seen Frosty, her father, in a couple of months. I expect to see him soon, though, and I will ask him about it. His daughter doesn't write him very often, I'm afraid. I will let you know as soon as I find out. It was quite alright for you to send only one picture to her. After all, she doesn't know any of us, except possibly through her father's letters, so it probably won't mean anything to her. Those originals may fade, sweet, so it was a good idea to save one of the reprints. You are a smart gal, and I adore you.

Now, about those enlargements. I haven't seen Fitz in a couple of months, either, so you will have to wait for any results about that. I will tell him that you would like one, of that one picture, and I am quite certain he will make all the arrangements with his brother. He is also a good kid, and I know darn well that you will meet him. He'll come to see us.

We never seem to have any of those first run pictures here. Every once in awhile we do get a good one, but I can tell you that it doesn't occur very often. But if Ali Baba and the Forty Thieves does come, I will see it, if it's at all possible. I would much rather see Lucia in a nice bedroom scene, though.

Is this molar you mention another one, making five, that Jackie is cutting? The poor kid must be in agony. And you can't be getting much sleep, either. I wish I were there to help you. Even though I would probably be useless, I would do the best I could. At least I could get up in the night and do whatever may be necessary, and let you sleep.

That answers your letter, my most adorable darling. I am well and as happy as I possibly can be, away from you. I must admit that I don't miss your daughter, though it's only because I've never seen her. But gee, how I would like to be able to make her acquaintance. She must be a honey. Here's hoping that you, Jackie and all the family are in the best of health and are happy. I want to see you so very much. Give my fond regards to the family and our friends. Here is my daily hug and kiss for Jackie. Millions of hugs and kisses I send to the most wonderful wife in the world, the mother of our lovely daughter, my most precious angelic sweetheart, Lucia. I love you, miss you and want you.

J.De Roxtro, EM2/c   Everlastingly, your adoring   *Johnny*

Note on flap: "Here's hoping I will be able to keep that date June 6th. Love and kisses."

Friday, May 5, 1944. *Letter from Mrs. Forbes. Mom not working. We washed clothes. Went downtown when Jackie awoke. Greenbergers - girls raved about Jackie. Epstein - bought dress - $5.98. Cranes. Very warm out. Hottest day we had yet. (Jackie goes up and down front stairs.)*

[Pavuvu Island, Russell Islands.]
Postmarked May 6, 1944, stamp upside down.   May 5, 1944

                                           Somewhere

Hello, Sweetheart:

I love you, miss you and want you. You are forever in my mind, and everlastingly locked in my heart. You are my guiding light, sweet one, and everything I do, I do for you. Your sweet face is beside me always. How I wish we could be beside each other in person, instead of separated by so many thousands of miles. I long to hold you tenderly in my arms and kiss you. Lovely one, I am tired of being away from you. I love you so very much. May the day soon come when I will be able to make love to you again. Gee, we will be so happy when that time comes, won't we. It can't come too soon to suit me. The sooner the quicker, and the quicker the better. There is still nothing definite about our next move. News had better come soon, or I am afraid that many of us will crack under the strain. Everyone is on edge, wondering what the next move will be. They all hope it is for the states and home. This waiting is worse than knowing we were going up farther. We are half afraid to hope for a home leave, but most of us are. Things are so bad here that even the scuttlebutt has died down. Every once in awhile some breaks out, but it isn't spread like it used to. Gee, I want to get out of the tropics. The weather is bad, and I am anxious to be with my lovely wife.

Three letters came for me today. One from Ralph, one from Fan, and one from the most adorable girl in the world, my sweet adorable you. Yours, the only one I really care about, was written the twenty-fourth and postmarked the twenty-fifth. Gee, honey, it's swell, receiving them so soon after you write them. Your new system is working so wonderful well, that I am led to believe the delay was somewhere between you and the mailbox.

That fellow with the long nose, the big ears, who is pointing to my name and address is a stranger to me. He is standing on something or other, in which is written the word pyro. What is the significance of that thing, would you mind telling me.

I will answer your letter of the eighteenth tonight. On this one you placed two stamps. Thanks loads for the kisses. Here's hoping I am there soon to collect for all these I have. On the inside of the flap you have, "Lots of luck, Darling, I love you." Thanks loads for those wishes, dearest, I sure will need them. As for the I love you, well, I wish I could be as sure I am coming home to you, as I am of that. You know, Lou, whenever I hear a fellow talking about himself or a buddie of his having trouble with his wife, I think of you, and it makes me feel swell, knowing as I do that I can depend on you to wait for me, as I am for you.

Gee, that's too bad about Tadone having that abscess on his lame arm. I sure do wish him the best of luck. You know, there is a possibility that his arm may turn out to be well again, after the abscess has been removed. Wouldn't it be swell if he were able to use it again as he used to? That Doctor

121

Rice would attempt to operate, using ether as the anesthetic, without testing his heart (Tadone's). I wouldn't trust that guy with a dog. But he does have a good practice, so he must be alright. I don't like him, myself. Give Tadone my best wishes for a speedy recovery.

You seem to be getting quite a few breaks lately. It sure is swell of Ann to have something to do when you have a chance to go out. Too bad it doesn't happen more frequently, isn't it. I wonder who will take care of the little one while you and I go dining, dancing and drinking, or to a movie, or on a trip to the big city. We will be able to take care of all that later, though. It's a little too far ahead of us to make any definite plans. Gee, won't it be swell when we are able to go out stepping again.

It sure was swell of you folks to pitch in and assist in the housecleaning while at Mama G's. It sure did help her out a lot, and she appreciated it. With all you there, it couldn't have taken very long to fix everything up. That home of theirs must look a bit of alright, now that it has been painted. Wish her the best for me too. Gee, I would like to see them again. They are swell people.

I'm glad to hear that my mother was finally able to get down to see you. It's good to learn that she likes it there. In her letter to me, she said that she was getting fat in the face. From what she told me, her job sounds swell, to me, also. I'm glad she likes it there, because she will be more happy if she is satisfied in her work. I suppose when I get home, I will have to find some way to get up there to see her. Maybe I will have to walk. I never would take time to do that, though.

Gee, you say my mom was wearing the corsage she received from you. She must have been keeping it in the refrigerator all this time. That proves that it was satisfactory to her. It was swell of you to send it. She appreciates things like that.

Sweetheart, even if I have to make it a brief line or two, just to say hello and goodbye, I intend writing nightly to you. I know you like to receive lots of mail, and as my record since arriving here has been so good, I will keep it up. I've written over a hundred letters to you since arriving here. Wait a minute, and I'll figure it up. This makes the hundred eighteenth letter. Gee, it doesn't seem that long, at times, and at others, it seems much longer than that. Sunday will make it one third of a year since we arrived on this tropical hellhole. It can't be long now, sweet, it just can't. Gee I want you.

You're damned right. How could Herb, or anyone else, do anything but say that they like your Jackie. Heck, she is the most lovable bambino in the world. How could she be otherwise, having the most wonderful mother in the universe? I still can't think of any reason why Herb should write such a letter. But there wasn't anything to it, except a detailed description of the removal.

The fresh air and sunshine will do the little one the world of good, but I don't know whether it will help that tooth or not. It certainly won't do her any harm. It should help cure her cold, though. I would like to be there to take her for a nice short walk with you by my side. Won't it be swell when we three can go around together? I will feel more like a real father then. I'm too far away to realize, even with your descriptions and snapshots, just how Jackie is growing. I want to see her, and play with her, but more than that, I want to be there with you in my arms.

Forbes came back to reside here in our tent again today. It was a little sooner than we expected, but they needed his bed up there. He feels quite well, but he is still weak. I don't think he is over it yet, though. He said to thank you for your regards, and sends his best wishes to both you and Jackie.

Give my regards to all the family. Here is my daily hug and kiss for Jackie. Darling, you are mine, and I am yours forever. May the day soon come when I will be able to talk to you, eat and sleep with you and love you.

J.De Roxtro, EM2/c   Everlastingly, your loving *Johnny*

Note on flap: "Here's hoping I am able to keep that date. How I love you, miss & want you. Love and kisses & hugs."

Saturday, May 6, 1944. Sat. went downtown. Movies. "The Purple Heart." Letter from Johnnie - Dec. 13.

[Pavuvu Island, Russell Islands.]
Postmarked May 9, 1944, stamp upside down.   May 6, 1944
Somewhere

Hello, Angel:

I love you, miss you and want you more as each day passes, slowly bringing us to the day of our reunion. I hope and pray that that day will soon come, so that I can be there with you in my arms. When I am holding you that way, I will kiss you over and over again, and tell you I love you. Sweetest wife and daughter, I miss you both. I see your lovely face before me always, Lucia, my love. It seems more lovely than ever. How I want to see you. I want to talk to you and hear your pleasant voice. I want to look at you and see the smiles and other features on your beautiful face. If I could reach out now and gently run my hands through your silken black hair. To touch your ears, nose, chin, arms, legs, and every other part of your sweet body. Oh, dear one, more than anything else, I want to be there, making love to you. I want to do all I can to make up for all you've been missing since I left you that day, many, many months ago. Almost two years ago, that was. Gee, how

123

I wish I never had left you. You are too good for me, sweet, but I promise to always do my best to make you happy. Everything possible will be done to keep you happy. I love you.

No mail came today, sweet, so I have only the one letter to answer, and I will do that tomorrow. I only have four to write tomorrow, in answer to letters I've received. It seems funny, having so few to write. It will give me time to study for my next examination, though, so I don't mind. Maybe I'll receive one or more tomorrow.

Forbes is still out, but I think he will be back very soon. His temperature is a little high tonight, but it may be because he took a little boat ride. I hope for his sake that that is the only cause for it. Enough for Forbes, all we can do is wish him the best of luck.

The last couple of days the weather has been fairly decent. In fact, it has only rained during the night, with a few sprinkles during the day. It sure looks and feels like rain tonight, though.

Gee, sweet, wouldn't it be swell if you and I were able to walk downtown, go into Thodes and sip a sundae, or you could go shopping, or we could go to the show. I want to do all those things with you, Angel. Will you get a nice canary yellow dress to wear? I don't care whether it's a street dress or not, just as long as you wear it once in awhile.

Give my regards to all the family and our friends. Here's a hug and kiss for Jackie, and to you, most precious, I send my all. I want you, my sweet. I am hungry.

J.De Roxtro, EM2/c   Everlastingly, your loving *Johnny*

Note on flap: "Here's all my love, sweet. How is Mickey. Hope I see you very soon."

Sunday, May 7, 1944. *Rain. Mama G & Tadone up. Afternoon Joe & Angie came and took Jackie for a ride. At night saw "Cover Girl" Rita Hayworth. Very good. Walk backwards. 4th bottom molar broke through. Luciano.*

[Pavuvu Island, Russel Islands.]
Postmarked May 9, 1944, stamp upside down.   May 7, 1944

                                                                Somewhere

My Darling Lucia:

All the love in the world is ours. I miss you and want you more than words can say. Each and every moment, day or night, I am thinking of you. How I long to hold you tenderly in my arms and kiss you. Sweetheart, the day will come, soon, I hope, when we will be together again, and then my happiness will be complete. I want to do all the little things for you that only a husband and lover can do. I want you so very much. The day of our reunion can't possibly come too soon to suit me. Gee, I love you, dearest. My one desire is to make you happy and I know I never will be able to make up to you for all you've missed these last two years, but I will do my best. I love you.

I have answered all my letters, except the one I received from Charlie. I think I'll let that go until next week, because I have to study in order to pass my coming test. I will write an answer to your letter of April twenty-fourth today, and hope that I receive more today.

Your loving husband is well, as usual, and is as happy as he can be, away from you. I hope that you, Jackie and the family are in the best of health, and remain so forever. Poor Forbes had to return to the sickbay. He has it again, I guess. They should send him home, or to a more mild climate. He just can't take it, down here in the tropics. There seems to be no new scuttlebutt going around. In fact, there isn't any. As far as any of us know, we have no orders what-so-ever. That means we may even go somewhere else to do another job, or home. Now, as the war in this area is over, except for a few mopping up jobs, we have a splendid chance of leaving here for home. I have hopes of seeing you soon, my lovely one, but unless we leave here in a week, I don't see how I can keep the date we have for the sixth of June. Gee, wouldn't it be swell if we could? I won't give up hopes until it is too late, so I will keep praying. I kind of wish my letters could be delivered to you daily. Then, when they stopped, you would know I was on the way. But that is too much to expect, as my letters may be delayed anywhere along the line, for a day or two. They may be as much as a week late in reaching you. I will let you know everything that will make any difference to us. That is, of course, if I can possibly do so. Somehow, I will let you know.

Gee, isn't it going to be swell when you and I are together again. Just think, we will be eating with each other, talking over our coffee, walking together, sleeping together. We will be living as a married couple should. It certainly will be nice, even if it is only for thirty days. It may be even less than that. Traveling time may be included in our leave. However long our reunion is, we will make the best of it, and absorb all the happiness we can. My sweetheart, I love you.

Thanks loads for the kiss you sent me by way of the stamp, sweet one. I'll be able to collect for them soon, maybe. I would much rather have your lovely red lips pressing against mine, and have your soft warm body snuggling close to me. Gee sweetheart, I won't be satisfied until I am with you again. My love for you increases as each hour passes. Way down inside this envelope you have a P.S. I've already told you about Vincent. Besides your query concerning his health, you had "I love you, dear, Lou." How I wish I were close enough to you to hear you say that. Its swell to be in love, but so terrible to be separated by so much time and so many thousands of miles from the one you love. If it weren't for your love, I don't know what I would do. Honestly, sweet, I think I'd go nuts if I didn't have you. I depend on you even more than you will ever know.

Sweetheart, I am afraid I will have to close, now. You see, I will have to go feed my face, before the mess-hall closes. I know you will pardon me, while I go get my steak. I'm just guessing as to that steak, but that's what we usually have for Sunday Dinner. Pardon me, my love, I'll be back as soon as I finish. Well, I'm back, but not as soon as I thought I would be. I was detained by a most pleasant circumstance. On the way back from chow (steak etc.) I stopped by the post office and picked up the mail. Believe it or not, there were four lovely letters from you. Boy, was I pleased to receive them. Honey, you're swell. I love you so much.

Your letters were written the nineteenth, twentieth, twenty-first and twenty-fifth and were posted the twenty-first, twenty-fourth and twenty-seventh, respectively. The last three were posted in Millburn, and the first in town. The gals seem to be dropping them more regularly. Here's hoping they keep it up. Could it be that you aren't writing on Sunday? The week of the sixteenth you did well,
very well by me. You wrote for five consecutive days. Boy, oh boy, am I lucky to have such a wife. Sweetest, most adorable girl in all the world, you are divine, and I love you. Now, instead of answering your letter of the twenty-fourth, as I originally stated, I will, the one of the nineteenth, as that is the oldest.

Thanks for the kiss you sent via the stamp, sweetest one. On the inside flap of the envelope you have, "How ya doin', fella! I love you." I'm doin' oke - gal, and yourself? I adore you. I guess that takes care of that, okay. You seem to have been in a very pleasant mood when you wrote that. I am glad to know that you are still able to get in those moods. It is darn seldom that I am able to. I'm at my best when I receive letters from you. Lately, they have been coming almost every time there is mail. We will both be in a happy state of mind when I come home, won't we. It can't come too soon to suit me, either. I've had plenty of these darned Islands, these so-called tropical paradises. I wish I could kiss you.

It is swell of you to take care of Judy while Mil and Gene go out together. You sure are a swell gal. I love you more each time you do something like that for someone else. I know that you have plenty to do, without caring for someone else's children. Gee, you are the best.

Say, sweet, I can't see where you dropped the lid of your Dixie on the paper. What are you trying to do, make me moan? You should know you can't do it with ice-cream. Besides, we have it at least twice a week, so there – now you moan, my lovely one. I had almost a pint for dinner today, but I did give most of it away. I wish I could have given it to you. There are plenty of other things I would like to give you, too, but we won't discuss them now.

Those two kiddies must get along quite well together. I can just about picture that scene in the yard. Judy there on her haunches, industriously shoveling dirt into the pail, and Jackie running around, picking up stones here and there, and dropping them in the pail. Judy would look up, with a disgusted sort of look, each time, and finally become peeved, telling our daughter to stop. Then, Jackie, being more or less of a tease, would merely laugh and continue. She must take after me, because you would be too nice to do anything like that. I didn't think Jackie would be able to see, or rather notice the trains from our place. But I am glad she can. You never told me of her interest in trains before. I wonder how she will like them when she sees one close-up. She may be a trifle scared, don't you think? We'll take her for a train ride, one day, won't we.

I'm glad that Tadone feels much better. He's a grand old man, and I like him a lot. It may take quite awhile for him to completely recover, because of his age. Give him my fond regards and wish him luck and a speedy recovery for me, will you?

Those two little ones sure did have a good day of fresh air and sunshine, didn't they. All morning, and then the entire afternoon. It's no wonder Jackie fell asleep as soon as you put her in bed. The fresh air and exercise made her sleepy. It does her good to have some other youngsters there to play with. It probably did you a lot of good, being out with them, too. What did you do, just sit there in the sun and watch them? I hope that's all you did do, because you need rest and relaxation too. I can't blame Jackie for making a fuss, having to go in at suppertime. I remember how the first days of warmth used to affect me. I never wanted to go in, either.

It must be a relief to you, now that Jackie isn't cranky and irritable. But take advantage of it while you can, my love. It may not last long. She'll be getting another tooth before long, I suppose, then she'll be the same again.

Sweetheart, I found out why you didn't tell me of the accident with the carriage, when it happened. My mom told me that it was her idea for you to keep it from me. I have my doubts as to that. She probably thought I'd be angry with you, and decided to take the blame herself. Am I right, sweet? I sure do love you.

Issue number eight of our local paper is being posted today, my lovely one. I'm glad you like it. It doesn't mean very much to me now, but I have a feeling that it will, in years to come. I don't remember the poem about the fighting Seabees, but there is one in a later issue about all this and twenty per cent that's pretty good. There usually is a pretty good poem in each issue. This week's has one that was taken from one of our previous papers that we had back on Santos. Gee, Lou, my darling, I didn't notice whether the movie schedule was in this one or not. If you care to have a schedule of our movies, I can go copy it from our bulletin board. Maybe I will, one of these days.

Lucia mine, that answers your sweet letter. Now, as I have no further news to impart, I find that I am at a loss for words. Give my regards to all the family and our friends. Here is my daily hug and kiss for our Jackie, sweetheart. All my love is yours. I love you more as each day slowly passes, bringing us more close to the day that I will be able to hold you in my arms and kiss you. Sweetest wife and darling, do you remember all the fun we had when I was there for a brief five days? Well, I want to go through it all again, but for a much longer period of time. Sweetheart, you are mine, and I am yours, forever. Love & kisses.

J.De Roxtro EM2/c   Everlastingly, your adoring *Johnny*

Note on flap: "Sweet, do you mind if I postpone our date. 'fraid I can't make it. I want you to want me."

Monday, May 8, 1944. *No mail. Started to clean out nook in office. Cleaned. Washed. Had Jackie out in pen. Mom went to Newark with girls to see "Aida" at Mosque. Picked up by Clem & Eddie quarter of two.*

[Pavuvu Island, Russell Islands.]
Postmarked May 9, 1944, stamp upside down.   May 8, 1944
                                                                        Somewhere

Hello, Beloved:

I love you miss you and want you. Thoughts of you are forever on my mind. Your lovely vision is eternally before me. I want so much to be there with you, to hold you tenderly in my arms and kiss you. You are the only girl in the world for me. The days slowly drag by bringing us more close, even though we are still separated by many thousands of miles. It can't be long now until we are reunited, my sweet and precious wife. That day can't come any too soon to suit me. Gee, I wish I were home.

I am quite well, and as happy as I possibly can be, away from you. I sincerely hope that you, Jackie, and the family are in the best of health and are happy. I will do my utmost to increase your happiness when I return to you.

I haven't seen Forbes today, so I guess they are keeping him there for treatment and observation. I will let you know how anything turns out, regarding him. Here's hoping he becomes well again soon. He really is one of the swellest guys here, and I hope you get to meet him sometime.

Today I received your letter of the twenty-ninth of April. That one made good time, didn't it. You wrote it the twenty-seventh and it was postmarked the twenty-ninth. That makes it eight days in reaching me.

Tonight I will answer your letter of the twentieth, which is next in order. You very kindly sent me my usual kiss by way of the stamp. I'm going to give them back personally. Would you mind very much? Thanks a million for them, my love. Even though they can't be felt on the lips, just knowing that you want to kiss and be kissed is felt in the heart. Inside the flap you have, "Darling, I love you." Them words is swell, an' dey mean more to me than you think. Knowing that you love me and are waiting patiently for my return, has been all that has kept me from going absolutely nuts. I love you more as the days slowly pass. Did I ever tell you how gorgeous you are? Well, you are, sweetheart. I'm going to do my best to try to be good enough for you, but I doubt if I will ever come close. Gee, you are the best.

So my lovely wife decided suddenly to go to Newark on a shopping spree. Swell, Angel, why didn't you try to do that before. Go as often as you can, even though you never purchase anything. Merely getting away from the household duties will make you feel better. And you always enjoy yourself when you are shopping, so it does you good. It's too bad you weren't able to get what you wanted, but maybe next time you will have better luck. Anyway, that will give you an excuse to go back again. I know darn well that when you have your mind set on a certain thing you won't take any substitutes.

Boy, was I surprised when you said you hadn't gone to the box right after the mailman had been there. You must have been quite busy, or something. Getting dressed to go to the big city, I guess. Here I've been under the impression that you are practically at the door, waiting for the mailman, when he comes. But of course I realize you can't very well do that and your work too. Isn't it funny how my letters arrive there, all mixed up. They should be in closer order than they are. I guess it is because of the way they are handled at the various stopping places.

One of the fellows received a fruitcake from his New Zealand wife, so I just had a piece. It was quite good, only the only fruit in it was raisins. Nothing like ours are. He has a radio, too, and we listen to it all the time, when we are in the tent. No, you don't know him, I've never mentioned him to you before. He just moved into our tent. The only station we can get is the

American Expeditionary Station on Guadalcanal. They have quite a nice variety, and there isn't any advertising. Boy, that's a relief. Ok, the new fellow's name is G.S. Calhoun. He hails from Maryland.

Say, you didn't have very much time for shopping, did you. You left town 11:14 and returned by 5:30. That means only three hours. You couldn't have done much looking around.

That scarcity of Air Mail paper didn't last so very long, my love. There is plenty here now, so, you see, there wasn't any use in asking you to send any. Besides, I am hoping to be gone from here before any package could arrive. Packages never came in less than six weeks, so I'll probably be on my way by that time. I sure hope so. Sweetheart, there isn't any use in doing this, but as long as you want me to ask you for something, here it goes. I want you. Do you think you could manage that? I hope not, because I may not be here when you arrive, so please don't try it. I'll take my chances and wait a little while longer.

No, sweet, I don't remember you ever telling me that you and Jackie had new outfits for Easter, either. That was merely my imagination, sweetie pie. I was so sure that you would get them that I took it for granted. Perhaps it was best to wait until after Easter to get them, but I don't want you to do it again. Look at all the fun you missed when you went to Mass that day. No matter how well you were dressed, I know you felt as if you looked shabby, compared to all the new outfits that were being shown off. There isn't any use telling me that you didn't mind, because I know you did. Here's hoping you finally get what you are looking for. Gee, I love you so very much. Is Mickey better?

That's a swell idea, darling, buying those nursery rhyme records for our little one. It will help her education a lot, don't you think? Don't forget to let me know how she likes them. Of course, she may be a little young for them as yet, but she will be growing up with them. You were bound to get a few little things for Jackie, weren't you. I'll bet you never go out but that you see a little something you would like to get for her. Gee, it must be swell, being able to look around and get little things like that. More power to you, Angel, I hope you are always able to get what you want.

Thank the family for their regards and also Jackie for that hug and kiss. It was really swell of her to send it. I only wish I were there to return it. Gee, I would like so much to be able to romp and play with her.

Naturally our daughter behaved well while she was at Mil's. How could such a well brought up daughter misbehave? I hope she takes after you always. Then she really would be the most wonderful gal in the world. You are now. Didn't I ever tell you?

Give my regards to all the family and our friends. Here's a hug and kiss for Jackie. To you, my dear, I send all my love and wishes for the best of everything. May the day soon come when we will again be reunited. Dearest one, I love you, miss you and want you. I would be lost without you. I adore you.

J.De Roxtro EM2/c   Everlastingly, your *Johnny*

Note on flap: "*Angel mine, you are always with me. I worship you. Hugs and kisses.*"

Tuesday, May 9, 1944. *Letter of May 1st. Card from Mary. Went downtown with Jackie. Bought frame and several picture and storybooks. Call from Vene about having Leslie Ann here. Then Fran called. Would come Friday.*

[Pavuvu Island, Russell Islands.]

Postmarked May 10, stamp upside down.   May 9, 1944

Somewhere

My Adorable darling:

I love you more than mere words can possibly say. I miss you and want you more as each day slowly passes. Gee, Honey, I want so much to take you in my arms once again and kiss you. You are always on my mind, and everlastingly in my heart. Sweetest girl in the world, you mean more to me than anyone ever did, or ever will. I hope and pray that the day will soon come when I will be able to leave this rock and head for you. I have been away long enough. It's time I was there, holding you and telling you of my love. Gee, it'll be swell when we are together again. No mail came today, so naturally I didn't receive any. But I don't care so much. I really did hit the jackpot this week, didn't I. Tonight I will answer yours of the twenty-first of April. The kiss you sent by way of the stamp was very much appreciated. Thanks loads. Oh! Oh! Now, I'm afraid I will have to make up my mind, here and now, whether I will call you when I hit the states or not. You would ask me that question. I could keep you in suspense, and not tell you, but I shall. Honey, do you think that I could keep it from you, at the first opportunity? Hell, the first thing I will do is head for the nearest phone and telegraph station. You knew all the time that I would, didn't you. I love you.

It is swell receiving so many letters, isn't it. Gee, when I think of how tired you must be, sometimes, and you still think enough of me to sit down and write. It's really swell of you, my sweet. I will love you ten days a week when I return home. The only way I could possibly make up for all this lost time would be by making the weeks and days longer, but regardless, I will do my best to make up for all you've missed.

131

Now I am all mixed up. When you told me previously about Jackie walking, I took it for granted that she just stood up when she wanted to, and went wherever she desired. Now I learn that she has just acquired the art of raising herself to a vertical position and not her walking and running all over the place. I guess I overlooked the fact that she had to learn a lot. Oh, well, I can't get things exactly straight in my mind yet. But I sure will straighten myself out, once I see her. And it can't be any too soon to suit me, either. I can understand clearly what you mean when you say that because the little one hardly ever crawls at all now, your wash is much easier and lighter.

Someone, I don't remember who (maybe it was you) told me that Jackie walked differently than most children. She hasn't that waddle that usually comes with the first stage of walking. She would be different, being ours. You are really wonderful.

Why darling, I am afraid that I don't know what you mean when you say that our daughter takes after nobody strange, just because she doesn't go in for sweets. You have always liked them, and I fell in love with the sweetest girl in the world. I wonder who you could mean? I very often eat cake, pie, cookies, and even candy, now. You couldn't possibly mean me, could you? I only eat them to keep from being too hungry, though. I would never think of buying anything like that. Let's see, in a previous letter you mentioned the fact that she likes beer, and in this one, it's saltines. That's a pretty good combination. Maybe she does take after me in that way, but in most of her other ways (good ones only) she follows you.

Boy, would I like to get an egg every morning. The only eggs we have now are dehydrated, and boy, are they ever lousy. Say, sweet, as long as Jackie is tired of her baby food, why not try her on strained fresh vegetables? Or is she too young yet for them? Try anything, sweet, because in order to be healthy, she has to eat. But heck, I suppose she is darn glad to get what she does, when she is hungry. It sure must be tough on my little wife, going through all the trials of being a mother, without any help at all from the old man. I am very pleased to know that our precious bundle now drinks more milk. That's good for her, and will take the place of vegetables she refuses to eat. I adore you.

If you will pardon me, my lovely one, I shall dress and go to chow. After all, one must eat, so here I go. I'll be right back. Here, to hold you until I return, is a hug and kiss. Goodbye for a few minutes, sweetheart. Here I am again, my sweet. I sure didn't eat much of the food tonight. It didn't appeal to me. Maybe because I had a piece of that fruitcake before I went.

Sweetie-pie, did I say that Jackie was fat? Yes, I must have. But I merely meant that she looked healthy and well fed. Heck, I wouldn't care if she was really fat, as long as she wasn't skinny and puny, like some kids. As you say, she may be a little chubby, but to me, she is just right. I love her, and wish I could be there, to play and romp with her. Gee, wouldn't I have a lot of fun with her if I were there? Gee, I can hardly wait to see her. The three of us will have so many pleasant hours together, won't we.

I still can't understand how or why you should have to train Jackie for bladder control, but you know best, sweetheart. I am depending on you, and I know that you are doing everything in your power to bring our little angel up the right way. All this training you put her through must take hours and hours of your time. It's a wonder you have time enough to do all you do. I am at a loss, trying to figure how you can manage caring for Jackie and also the house. That's an awfully large house for you to take care of all alone. When I am home again for good, we will have a nice little place of our own, then things will be a lot easier.

My mental picture of your stroller was entirely different than that. The one I pictured was one of those smaller ones that fold up, so I'm glad you sent the picture of it. It sure does look swell to me, and I'm glad you like it. You were lucky to get one made mostly of steel. Don't worry about the brake, sweet. When I get home, I'll fix that for you. That is, of course, if it hasn't broken off before then. I can do most anything, so I guess that should be simple. Now they'll have to send me home, won't they. How I wish they would.

Well, my love, your letter has been answered, so I have only to tell you that I am well, and I hope and pray that you, Jackie and the family are, and remain in the best of health. Give my regards to all the family and any of our friends you may happen to see. Here is my daily hug and kiss for Jackie, and millions more for you, the most wonderful wife and sweetheart in all the world. How I yearn to be there holding you in my arms and telling you of my love.

J.De Roxtro EM2/c   Everlastingly, your *Johnny*

Note inside flap: "Forbes is feeling much better. Sends his best. I love you. Hugs and kisses."

Wednesday, May 10, 1944. *Letters of April 22,23,27,28.[?], relating to alms, charity, or charitable donations. Went downtown, got pictures, post office, sent money orders to Hellicks, Glendale & Hosp. Wrote to Ralph.*

[Pavuvu Island, Russell Islands.]
Postmarked May 11, 1944, stamp upside down.   May 10, 1944

                                                              Somewhere

Hello, My Darling:

I love you more as each day passes, slowly bringing us more close to each other. I miss you and want you, too, more than you will ever know. I am thinking of you all day, and dreaming of you all night. I long to hold you close to me and kiss you. You are mine, sweetheart, and I want so much to be there with you. The day of our reunion can't possibly come too soon to suit me. I hope and pray that you and I will be in each other's arms real soon. I doubt very much if it will be in time for me to keep that date, but I am still hoping. I refuse to give up hope until the last minute. That will be about a week from today. No matter when it is, I will be satisfied.

In a week from tonight I go take another test for an advance in rating. This time I am trying for electrician first. Maybe that's what I should have done long ago. It is the hardest of all, so I don't know how well I will do. I'll let you know, anyway, whether I get it or not. I should, even though I have not done any electrical work since I've been in the service. Wish me luck, sweetheart. Blosser made his today. Quite a nice anniversary present, no? He was married two years ago today. Just about three months later than us. Are you sorry, sweet? I'm not.

Last night was the first time I have ever left our camp to go to the show. It rained harder than usual, and I sat there through it all, without any raincoat or anything. Boy, did I ever get a drenching. But the picture was excellent, so I really didn't mind it at all. That is one picture I wouldn't mind seeing again. In fact, I intend to, if ever the opportunity arises. If it is possible for you to do so, by all means see it. The name of it? Oh, yes, I had forgotten to tell you. "The Song Of Bernadette." Jennifer James was introduced in this picture, and she is a remarkable character actress. I won't tell you anything about it, because you probably know more than I did. I think it was explained in an issue of Life magazine, so you have probably seen that. I repeat myself, darling, but only to impress you with my thoughts on the matter. The picture was excellent. By all means, make every effort to see it. The picture started at seven, and lasted until almost ten, so you see, it was a long one. To prove how good it is, all I have to do is tell you that not a single person left the theatre when the heavy rains came. Usually, they leave in droves, but last night they were willing to take a wetting. Honestly, honey, that picture is worth seeing, at any price. Let me know if you manage to see it.

I am terribly disappointed today. Carl received six or seven letters, and I didn't even get one. But the other day, when I got those four, he didn't get any. Besides, how could I be anything but pleased when I have you to think about. Sweetest wife in the world, I love you more every day. Gee, it's swell, having you to think of and love. I don't know what would have happened if I hadn't had you, to guide me through this past couple of years.

Tonight I will answer your swell letter of the twenty-fourth of April. I've already commented on the envelope, so I will pass right along and answer your letter. I will, however, thank you again for the kiss you so kingly sent by way of the stamp. Gee, honey, I want so much to feel your lips pressing close against mine. How I love you, darling.

Now, my love, you will have to pardon me while I go to supper. Here's a hug and kiss to tide you over until I return. I will be right back, angel mine. Know what? I love you. Here I am, sweetheart – all we had was spaghetti and meatballs, lima beans (dried) some kind of a sweet salad (I didn't eat any) an iced drink, and a piece of cake. Not bad, but you can bet that I would much rather have some of the swell, well-seasoned food that you would prepare for me if I were home. Boy, every time I think of that parmigiano, or that sauce you make, - oh, me – why the devil did I ever leave home. Gee, sweetie-pie, I'm more hungry for love than anything else.

Angel mine, you may rest assured that I will keep as well as I possibly can. I can't do any more than that, even for you. I take all the precautions I can, so I guess I will remain well forever. I sure hope so, because I want to be in the best of health when I see you again. I wouldn't want you to worry about me, either. Please don't, because I am more safe here than I ever have been. The chances one takes at home, crossing the streets, etc., are more apt to be dangerous than our life out here is. It sure is dead here.

We sure will be happy when we are together again. But gosh, won't the time simply fly by. A mere thirty days, possibly with the travelling time included. But we had better not start thinking about that. Let's concentrate on getting me home first, huh? I want to lie in bed for at least a week. Do you think you could manage to serve my meals in bed? I hope not, because then I wouldn't be with you all the time. Or could that be arranged, too? Maybe someone else could be caring for the little one. Hell no, I don't want to stay in bed. I want to be with my sweet and lovely wife. And when you are busy, I want to play with our daughter. Gee, it sure will be wonderful when you and I are once more separated by only a few layers of clothing (or less) in- stead of by several thousand miles of land and water. Sweetheart, I adore you. I want you.

I sure am glad to know that Tadone feels much better. He must have been in quite a lot of pain, at times. He sure is a grand old man, and I like him a lot. Give both he and Mama G my fond regards, and here's wishing a complete and speedy recovery to Tadone. Everyone who knows Tadone very well would always help him, and I know that all your family will too. It's swell, the way you all care for your grandparents.

135

I didn't inform you of the war bond because I wanted to surprise you with the first one. You should receive one every three months while I am in the service. I thought that it would be a good way to save money for Jackie's college days, or for whatever she wants to do. Right now, I would not care for her to go to school past the high school, but things may change later. I sure am glad that you liked receiving it. That comes out of my spending money. I'm buying a fifty-dollar bond a quarter. That is, I think that's it. I'll let you know.

I can't seem to remember just what I did decide to do. I made arrangements way back when we were on Santos, so, with my memory as it is, well, I just don't remember. In fact, I had even forgotten that I was taking it out.

That, however, wasn't the surprise I mentioned in one of my letters. Boy I sure do hope you enjoy the both of them. Gee, sweet, I wish I could be there to see you. Enough about them. I will wait until I hear from you about them. I like to be always surprising you. Gee, I hope I'm able to keep on surprising you, all the rest of your life.

Forbes just came down from the hill. I asked him how he felt, and he said swell. In fact, there was a nice number on the radio, and he even started dancing, so I have an idea that he does feel better. He also said that he's going to ask the doctor to let him go out to work. He sure has lost a lot of weight. He sends his regards to you, Jackie and Ann.

I don't know the name of the show tonight, but I think I'll go, anyway. I am tired of studying, so maybe it'll do me good. Say hello to all the family for me and give them my fond regards. Here is my daily hug and kiss for Jackie, and many millions of them for you, my precious wife. The show was, "Stand By For Action." It was fair, but a little far-fetched and practically impossible.

Gee, sweet, the day of our reunion can't come any too soon to suit me. I want so much to hold you in my arms and tell you of my love. I want to do those things we used to do. I want to hug you and make love to you. Sweetheart, I will never be satisfied until we are together. I love you, miss you and want to be there.

J.De Roxtro EM2/c   Everlastingly, your loving *Johnny*

Note on flap: "Here's a kiss for Mickey. Hope you aren't jealous. I love only you."

Thursday, May 11, 1944. Received letters of April 28-29. 6th issue of C-Breeze. Brought Jackie out in yard. Catherine and Carol Ann came, stayed for awhile, ice cream. Met Ann in Hoboken 5:45. Shopped at 33rd St. Gimbels. Bought dress, hat, pinafore, 3 dresses for Jackie, missed 9:30 train. Took 10:30.

[Pavuvu Island, Russell Islands.]
Postmarked May 12, 1944, stamp upside down.   *May 11, 1944*

Somewhere

Hello, Beautiful:

I love you, miss you and want you. I am always thinking of you and wishing I were there, holding you real close to me, and telling you how much I love you. Thoughts of you are always in my mind, and your image is everlastingly locked in my heart. More than anything else, I desire to be there with you.

There was no mail today, for anyone, so there naturally wasn't any for me. I still have two to answer, so I will answer one of them tonight, and, if necessary, save the other for Sunday. Yours of the twenty-fifth will be the one I'll take care of now. Thanks for the stamp kiss, sweetheart. I'll collect for them all when I see you again. On the inside flap of the envelope, you have, "Darling, I love you and miss you." That's the way I feel too, sweet, and how I miss you.

This letter contained the clipping from the paper about the town employees receiving a hundred dollar bonus. More power to them. Most of them deserve it, I guess. They are all (or at least, most) underpaid, anyway, so why shouldn't they, huh? I don't know whether to go back there or not, when I return home. It's all according to how things on the outside look. Maybe I'll have to, for awhile. Things may not be so good, after this darn war.

Thanks loads for writing this letter, my sweet, but please don't lose too much sleep by writing me. I would rather you had your proper rest, because it may be that losing sleep would ruin your health. I certainly am glad that you made it a short one, though, but only for that reason. Naturally, I prefer long letters, but at times it is impossible to write them, isn't it. I know that I have difficulty, at times, trying to find something to write about. Gosh, angel, if anything happened to you, I don't know what I'd do. So please take care of yourself, for me, will you?

Was it so much of a surprise, receiving a money order from your husband? I sure am glad that you appreciate it when I send them to you. But I don't think there will be any more, my love, because that allotment is now coming out of my money. Besides that, I have the bond, insurance, and hospitalization coming out. None in itself is very much, but needless to say, the balance left just about meets my demands. That wasn't one of the two surprises on the way, either. Boy, will you be happy (I hope). You have them by now, I'm sure, so I am daily expecting to hear from you about them. Hope you won't get one until Sunday.

137

Lou, dearest, as long as you found a suit that you liked, why the devil didn't you get it? Hell, just because it was priced a little or a lot more than you wanted to pay, that's no excuse. Get it anyway. I want you to look nice, angel, and I won't kick about how much you spend for clothes. But, as usual, I will leave it to you. You're the doctor, and the family exchequer. (Spelling incorrect, probably.) If you want anything, sweet, please don't let the price stop you. Maybe you will have better luck next time. I am wishing you the best of everything, because I love you.

I don't mind the shortness of your letters any more than you do mine. There are times when one just can't write. Now, for instance, I am finished. Your letter has been answered, and I have nothing to say.

As usual, I am in the best of health, and I am as happy as I possibly can be, being separate from you, the one I love, as I am. I sincerely hope and pray that you, Jackie and all the family are in the best of health and are happy. Give my fond regards to all the family and our mutual friends. Say hello to Mary, for me the next time you write to her. She's a swell friend for you. Say, I almost forgot-she is supposed to visit you this month. Here's hoping you enjoy her visit. Here's my daily hug and kiss for our darling Jackie, and millions more to you, my most beloved angel. I love you, miss you and want you.

J.De Roxtro EM2/c   *Everlastingly, your doting* *Johnny*

Note on flap: "Have I ever told you how much I love you? All there is. Here's a kiss for Mickey. I love you."

Friday, May 12, 1944. *No mail. Washed clothes. When Jackie woke from nap, went to Cat's. Gave rubber pants. Walked over to Aunt's on way home. Stopped in Acme. Jackie walked around. Went back to Cat's. Home just before storms. Got few drops on way. Thunder and lightning storm, 1 hour. Jackie weighs 24½ lbs. Fran, Eddie & Leslie came. Les all ready for bed. Stayed 9:15. Baby woke up and cried.*

[Pavuvu Island, Russell Islands.]
Postmarked May 13, 1944, stamp upside down.   May 12, 1944
                                                              Somewhere

Hello, Sweetheart:

I love you, miss you and want you. Thoughts of you are always in my mind. I am constantly seeing you, as visions of you are always before me. I want, more than anything else, to be there with you. I long to hold you tenderly in my arms once again and kiss you. Merely to be able to see you again would be heavenly. I am hungry, so very hungry, for your love. You, and only you can satisfy that hunger. Some day, soon, I hope, we will be reunited.

No mail came for me today, so unless tomorrow brings some, I only will have three letters to write this Sunday. One each to you and my mom, and the one I received from Charlie last week to answer. That won't be so bad - maybe I will have a little more time to study. I have done quite well this week, in receiving letters from you, even though they all did come the first part of the week. I will wait until Sunday to answer the only one I have left. Know what, I didn't get any mail from anyone this week, excepting from you. Gee, angel you really are swell, and I love you. Thanks a million for writing so often. Gee, I want to get home to you. Then we won't have to write, will we? I adore you.

At our local movie area tonight, we were entertained by an army band. It was strictly a military band, but you should have heard those colored boys giving out with the boogy woogy, the blues, and jazz, as well as the marches. They were pretty darn good. They also brought their swing band along, but our piano went haywire, so they didn't perform. I'll bet they would have been good, too. A little entertainment like that helps the fellows out quite a bit. After that show, we had our movie. It was Olsen and Johnson in "Crazy House." It was fairly good, too. A great many laughs. Anyway, it was different than those darn war pictures we've been seeing. I would much rather be there with you, though, than seeing any picture out here.

I'm going to make this the end, my lovely one, because I'm tired, and it's almost lights out time. I hope you don't mind too much. I love you, Lucia mine. Give my regards to the family and our mutual friends. Here's my daily hug and kiss for Jackie. To you, my sweetheart, I send all my love and adoration. I hope and pray that I will be there to keep that date I made, but I have almost given up hope. Dearest one, I am yours forever.

J. De Roxtro EM2/c   Your loving *Johnny*

Note on flap: "Hi sweet. I love you more as each day slowly passes. Here's a hug and kiss."

Saturday, May 13, 1944. *Earrings. Leslie Ann went to circus with Gracie, 1:30-5:30. Went out at 5:45, bought stockings for Mama G, three dresses for Leslie, overalls for Jackie, swimsuit, Home at 9:15. Everybody out. Gave Leslie bath. Thunderstorm.*

[Pavuvu Island, Russell Islands.]

Postmarked May 15, 1944, stamp upside down.   May 13, 1944

                                                            Somewhere

Hello, Beautiful:

No one ever has or ever will love anyone as I love you. You are always in my thoughts, and your image, sweet and lovely, is always before me. I love you so much, my precious one, that no matter what happens, I will always be yours. I miss you and want you. I long to tenderly hold you in my arms once again, to press my lips close to yours, will be heavenly. The feel of your sweet young body against mine, I am anticipating with pleasure. I want to tell you how much I love you. Sweetheart, there are so many things I want to do with you, but I just can't put them on paper. I want you more as each day passes, slowly bringing us more close to the day of our reunion. I am hungry, sweet one, and my hunger won't be satisfied until I am there with you. Gee, darling, won't it be swell when we are able to be with each other once again? Then, and only then, will I be happy again.

There still isn't anything definite about our leaving here, but I still haven't given up hope. We may be able to keep that date yet, but unless we pull out of here suddenly, I have my doubts. In order to make it, we would have to leave by next Wednesday.

There was quite a bit of mail that came in today, but I think most of it was papers and packages. I haven't any of them to expect, so I don't even bother looking, for myself. I do look to see if the other fellows receive any though, so I would see if there were any for me. Besides, I am more interested in receiving letters from you. It is still a little early to get it, so I don't know whether I have or not.

Everything here is about the same, my beloved. I do think it isn't raining quite as much as it used to. It's just about as hot, though. It's so darn hot here, that if we do get a little brown, we sweat it right off. And I ain't kidding. A few of the fellows are quite tan, but most of us aren't. Maybe we work too hard.

I guess this will be a fairly long letter, sweetest, because I did receive a letter from you today. It was written the first of May, and postmarked the fourth in Milburn. That isn't so bad, is it. Enclosed in it were the pictures you took on Easter Sunday. They are swell, honey, thanks a lot. I will comment on them tomorrow, when I answer the letter. Today, I will answer yours of the twenty-seventh of April. That was postmarked the twenty-ninth in town, so you see, it must have been the girls fault that they were being delayed. But who cares, as long as I am now receiving them more rapidly? Gee, I love you.

Gee, sweet, I almost forgot. The paper (C-breeze) was issued this morning, and I didn't get any. I will see what I can do about getting one, though, because I know you like to receive them. If I have to, I'll steal one. Forbes got one, so maybe I can have his. I don't know whether he sends his home or not.

That typed thing you have in with your letter of the twenty-seventh about clearing a title on a piece of Louisiana land was a bit of alright. That guy really went way back there, didn't he.

Thanks a million for the two kisses you so kindly sent me via the stamps. I'll give them back, personally, when we meet again. That sure will be a pleasure. You seem to have forgotten to put a little message of endearment on the inside of the envelope, but I don't mind. In invisible ink, are the words "I love you," written all over the envelope. Thanks my love. You sure are swell.

It seems that you wrote in between the two letters I have. There are two days, and a Sunday, that aren't accounted for. Could it be that you didn't receive any mail from me in three days? Gosh, I hope not. Most of the time, angel, there just isn't anything for you to answer in my letters, because I must depend on your letters for something to say. I wish there was something I could write to you about from over here. Then I could make my letters longer and more interesting. Sorry I can't, Lou. I love you.

It sure is swell, knowing that you are able to find time to go visiting, and for strolls downtown. It sounded funny, to me, the way you mentioned cashing the hundred dollar money order and buying some socks and a pair of overalls for Jackie. I sure am glad that you can use those money orders, sweet. If I had known you needed money, I would have done things a little differently, but it's too late now. You will have to struggle along on the hundred thirty a month you have coming. Sweetheart, I sure did work hard for a couple of hours for that hundred bucks, so spend it wisely. I don't know whatever made me get into that crap game, but I'm not sorry I did. I have never shot crap for large stakes before, and I probably never will again. I want you to enjoy yourself with it, lovely one. I won't be able to send anything for your birthday, so here is my love and adoration, just in case we aren't together.

We are having another show the twenty-fourth of this month (if we're still here). The army is putting this one on. This should be a swell show. I'll let you know more about that when it happens. I hope we aren't here to enjoy it, though. Hell, I expect to be on the high seas before that. One can't figure on a darn thing out here. Our orders may come through tomorrow, or a month from now.

Yeh, I was afraid the club seventy-four, being situated where it is, would draw the loud, boisterous trade. But maybe if they had put a small minimum charge on, things might have been different. It's too bad, because from what you told me, I gathered that it was fixed up fairly nice, and I intended taking you there when I returned home. But we can always find some nice quiet place, can't we. That is, of course, if we want to.

That was a good idea of the *Record's* to print scenes from the town for us. Most of the fellows like to receive them, I guess. As for me, I like to see them, and I take pride in showing them around. We have a nice town, but I didn't realize it until I went through so many others. I sure would like to be back there. Not to see the local scenery, though. All I want to do is to be there with you and our Jackie.

That package from the Holy Name Society sure was a surprise, honey. You did well in keeping the news from me. What I can't understand is, why didn't someone else let the cat out of the bag, or give me an inkling of it. I usually learn of a lot that I shouldn't by reading between the lines of letters.

By the way, tell Gene that a fellow from Caldwell was talking to me the other day. He is quite a bowler, and knows Gene and Nuggi. I forget his name. That fellow Don Crater asked me to say hello to Frank Gannon for him. He is out here, too. The fellow from Caldwell has a name similar to this – Campanatti – That's a rough guess and may be way off, but Gene probably will know who I mean. This fellow was bowling against Harry Girardi in some championship match. Let's see, he bowled on Hoste' team. That's about all.

You mentioned having received the war bond, sweet. I told you about it in my letter the other day. I am purchasing more, lovely one, but I'm afraid it would complicate things if I tried to change them over to Jackie. I had thought about that when I first made application for them, but decided against it. I wanted them made out to you, so that in case an emergency arose, you would be able to use them as collateral, or sell them. We can always hold them for Jackie, so I think it's best the way it is. Of course, if you want them changed, I will see that it is done. Let me know what you decide, angel, and I'll take care of it. It sure is swell, the way we both are thinking the same about our daughter's future. With that money, she can go to college, business school, or of most anything she wants to do. I'm only sorry I am unable to purchase more and larger ones. They are a good investment, aren't they. Dearest one, I adore you.

There was a time, not very long ago, when you said you could never go out and leave Jackie with anyone. Now, you have changed your mind, and you trust your darling daughter with Mil. That's swell, angel. I'm sure glad you do. You are tied down plenty as it is, so make the most of it, and enjoy yourself, honey. But I guess it was only because Jackie was a young baby and all that you didn't care to leave her in the care of anyone else.

That takes care of your letter, my beloved one, so now I'm finished again. It is time that I left this epistle, my sweet, and went to feed my face. Gee, I'm early with your letter tonight, aren't I. I'll let you in on a little secret. I had the after-noon off. Bye for awhile, sweet, see you later. Here I am again, my honey. Pretty good supper.

Well, sweet, there is nothing I would rather do than to be able to make love to you. I long to kiss you, run my fingers through your silken, jet black hair, feel your lovely soft breasts, and touch you anywhere I want to. Lovely one, I want to be there with you. You are mine, and I am yours, forever. I love you with my heart, body and soul. My one desire is to be able to make you happy. I yearn to run my fingers through Mickey's hair, too. She is a lovely little thing. I would like to be there to give her a kiss, too. Regards to all the family & our friends.

J.De Roxtro EM2/c   Everlastingly, your loving *Johnny*

Note on flap: "Here's all my love, hugs and kisses, sweet. Maybe I'll be home soon."

Sunday, May 14, 1944. *Mothers Day. Lovely day. Put Jackie on pot 6:50. Wore new blue suit, hat, to church. Breakfast for Leslie & Jackie. Dressed Leslie Ann for church. Went with Gracie and girls. After dinner gave out gifts. received a card from Jackie and earrings from Johnnie. Joe & Angie came. Took mom, Mama G, Tadone , Gracie to Bernardsville. MdR came. Surprised to see Leslie Ann. Gave her Fran's gift and ours. Miniature of daddy from Vene. Took pictures. Vene and Johnny came to take M.d.R. back. Bonnie walks. Thursday 1st time. Mil called. Judy has Chicken pox.*

[Pavuvu Island, Russell Islands.]
Postmarked May 15, stamp upside down.   May 14, 1944

Somewhere

Hello, My Darling:

I love you, miss you and want you, more than words can ever tell. You are always in my mind, and your lovely image is everlastingly before me. Sweetheart, how I long to hold you tenderly in my arms once again and kiss you. I long to tell you of my love and how much I adore you. You are my guiding light my sweet. I never do anything without first consulting you. Each day that passes brings us more close, even though it is in time only.

How I hope and pray that the day will soon come when I will be able to be there, trying to make you happy. I want to look at you, eat with you, talk and laugh with, and sleep with you. I am more lonely at night than during the day. Each night I kiss you goodnight and pray for your continued health and happiness. Angel mine, soon, I hope we will be together again. I love you more than life itself. You are mine, and I am yours, forever. No one else can ever take your place in my heart.

It is rather early, but as I have nothing else to do, I thought I would start this, and maybe I could make it extra long. I have taken care of my other correspondence, so all I have left is the one letter I received from you yesterday to answer. It is, as you know, the one of the first day of May. It's a nice one, honey. Gee how I want to __ you.

Thanks very much for the double kiss you sent by way of the stamps, dearest one. I'm going to repay you, with interest, when I am once again able to hold you in my arms. On the inside flap you have "Hi, sweet! Here's to an early reunion! Loads of love." That reunion can't possibly come any too soon to suit me. The day we are united once again will be one of the happiest of my life. We have been waiting a long time for it, and we both will make the most of it, when it does come. Just seeing you will more than repay me for the long trip from here to there. We have been separated for close to two years now, and we have a heck of a lot to do to try to make up for all we've missed. We never will, but we can try, can't we. And we sure will try hard. I love you. Gee, it'll be really swell when I am able to hold your sweet young body close to mine again. I am anxiously awaiting the day we leave here.

That picture of Jackie in the crib with the Panda really is something, isn't it. I can't quite make out the expression on her face. She looks as if she just woke up. This is the first time I've seen her with her hair all fluffed up like that. Gee, she certainly does have a bunch of it. Say, was she expecting something when that snapshot was taken? Maybe that's the expression. The Panda is a hell of a looking thing, isn't it. But as long as she likes it so much, it's okay by me. The darn thing is almost as big as she is. I'll bet she can really handle it, though. The picture turned out pretty good, didn't it.

The other picture that was taken on the day after Easter didn't turn out quite as well, did it. Both Grace and Jackie look good, but the background is a trifle light. You can really see Jackie looking at something, out of the corners of her eyes. She looks quite heavy in those winter clothes, and so healthy. My beloved one, you certainly have done a swell job of bringing her up. What a difference between this picture and the other one in which she is in the wagon, July '43. Gee she has grown so much. You have a very intelligent looking daughter, my love. Your baby sister is getting to be quite a good-looking girl, too, isn't she. She seems to have grown up since I last saw her. Maybe it's because she has her hair fixed differently.

The picture of Mike, Mike Jr. and Tadone looks good too. Little Mike is a fine looking youngster, isn't he. Mike looks well, too, but he has aged quite a bit since I last saw him. Maybe married life doesn't agree with him. Tadone looks just about the same, to me.

In these other two pictures, well, I don't know just what to say. It looks as if the two cousins get along well together. Can you imagine, holding hands at their age. It isn't just a hold, but as if they have been doing it for quite awhile. Jackie looks kind of sleepy in the one where they are standing, but that expression she has in the one where they are sitting there on the steps, boy, I never will be able to explain that one. It's a bashful look, but she is happy over it. Maybe I can hit on a better description. Maybe she looks as if she has just been guilty of enjoying forbidden pleasures. No, that isn't correct either. Oh, well, we'll just skip it. All these pictures are swell, angel, and I sure am glad you are able to take them and send them. They mean a lot to me. If it weren't for all these snapshots of Jackie, I wouldn't even know her as well as I do.

Jo and Mike seem to take good care of little Mike, don't they. That looks like a darn nice outfit he is wearing. But then, your brother always liked to dress well, so I guess it's only natural for him to see that his offspring is well dressed too. How come you didn't take a snapshot of Jo?

Today is Mothers Day, sweetheart. It's the second that I haven't been with you. I sincerely hope that you enjoyed the surprise you were supposed to get today. Whether you did or not, my angel, I hereby wish you a very pleasant day. I hope that we will be together for the next one. You've missed a lot by being married to me, sweet, but I will do my best to make up to you for all of it. I want to be there to do things for you, and with you. Oh, sweetheart, how I desire to be there with you. I love you, miss you and want you. You are the most wonderful wife and sweetheart in the world. How proud I am to have you as the mother of our child. You are the best.

Your allotment check seems to have come rather early this month. It doesn't usually come until the fifth, does it? Anyway, I am glad you get it when it's due. I can't understand why you received a letter from Ralph and none from me. Oh, well, mine will come soon, I guess.

There is a gal singing a song I've never heard before. (On the radio). It is "I couldn't sleep a wink last night." It sounds pretty good. It is short, and quite easy to remember. The tune is catchy, too.

That was a good idea of yours to put the little one out in the playpen while you were busy washing windows. She should like being out in that. Most kids do enjoy being out of doors. Anyway, you now know that it will be quite alright to put her out at any time. And leave her there, sweet, whether she cries or not. It might even be a good idea to let her sleep in the pen, instead of the carriage. Then, when she awakens, she can start playing, and she won't bother you.

It must have been a lovely day, that day. Gee, I didn't know she could take her coat off by herself. She seems to be doing better for herself all the time. Gosh, I will probably be surprised so many times, when I am able to be there to see her. Even with all your descriptions, and the snapshots, I know I will have a tough time getting used to her. She sure is a honey, and I love her. I don't blame her for not wanting to wear a hat. I never liked one, either.

Don't take any chances with the weather, yet, sweet. After all, it's still early, and the wee one will be able to stand a little discomfort. Better that than to let her get a cold. She has had enough of them,. As long as that warm spell came all of a sudden, you were right in insisting on a sweater. Honey, all babies sweat during their sleep, in warm weather. Maybe that's why I do. I'm still your baby.

I can't say that I can blame you for not wanting to take on the after effects of the diphtheria shot, along with a cold and a molar coming in. You sure do have your troubles, sweet. Wouldn't it be swell if we could be together to share them. One of these days we will, though.

Don't worry about those ink spots, sweet. I wouldn't care what was on the snap, as long as I received it. Besides, you have the originals, so we can save that for future use. Say, while we're on the subject of pictures, where's the one of you dressed in a sweater? I still have the other one, sweet, and I'll keep it, too. You might have some more made of you with your darling daughter, too. How about it? When I come home, I will have to leave most of these there, so I'll have room for more. That case you sent me is just about full. But don't stop sending them. I will find room somewhere. These little pictures don't take up much space, anyway, and I sure do like to have them. I adore you, the most perfect mother in the world I guess this will be my last page, my honey. Your letter has been answered, and I received none today. It would be swell if this week was as good as last week was. I received five or six letters from you, and none from anyone else. So, all I had to do today was write to my mother, answer Fetzer's letter of the week before last, and write this note to you. Now, I will shave, take a shower, and study until suppertime. I've been most all day on this letter. I was interrupted several times, by getting myself into a conversation. I may even have a bottle of beer before I shave. We have a case here so I may indulge. The only trouble is, that it isn't cold. While on the subject, honey, have you my beer there for me, or will I have to go out for it?

I am as well as I possibly can be, my lovely one, and I sincerely hope that you, Jackie and the family are in the best of health. Give them all my regards, and wish them the best of luck for me. Well, sweetheart, I must now say so long until tomorrow. Hasta la vista. That's close, anyway, but I should have used mañana. Here is my daily hug and kiss for your sweet daughter. For you, on this, your day, I give you my all. I only wish that we were in each other's arms right now.

J.De Roxtro EM2/c   Everlastingly, your loving *Johnny*

Note on flap: *"How would you like to find me there in person, one of these days? Love, hugs and kisses."*

Monday, May 15, 1944. *Letter of May 2,3,5th. Washed Leslie's hair. Dried it in sun out with Jackie. Put Jackie to bed 11:00. Washed clothes. Went downtown. Bought Leslie 2 undershirts, 3 prs. Socks, 1 pr. Summer pyjamas, 1 slip, training pants for Jackie. Took 2 snapshots.*

[Pavuvu Island, Russell Islands.]

Postmarked May 16, 1944, stamp upside down.   May 15, 1944

Somewhere

Adorable One:

I love you, miss you and want you. You are always on my mind, and eternally in my heart. Each and every day brings us more close together, even though we are still many thousands of miles apart. In time we are closer. It can't be too long now, sweetheart, before we are reunited. I want so much to hold you close to me. I long to kiss you and tell you of my love. I yearn to hold your soft young body close to mine, just as I did twenty-seven months ago tonight. Gee, sweetheart, it will seem like another honeymoon when we are in each others arms again, won't it. We have been married over two years now, and I've been away most of that time. I never thought we would be separated this long, did you. But I promise to do my best to make up for all you've missed, angel mine. I love you so very much, sweetest Lucia, that there isn't anything I wouldn't attempt for you. When I return, we will be more happy than we ever were.

I am sort of blue today, my love. I am just about to give up hope of being there for your birthday. I haven't completely given up, but the chances now are very slim. I am still hoping and praying, though. If we leave by this coming Sunday, there is a possibility that I can make it, but it will be real close work, and we will have to go straight through without any stops at all. Gee, I wish something would happen soon. I am getting tired of this waiting. Nothing new has been let out. The skipper has no orders as yet. We may even have to go further up to do another job. I am hoping and praying for an early reunion with you. Happy Birthday my most precious one, in case I'm not there with you. I love you.

No mail came today for me, so I have nothing to write about. We have been out of the states twenty months today. Now we are on the twenty-first. That's longer than any Seabees have stayed out here in the tropics, so our chance may come soon. Maybe we are considered indispensable to the campaign out here, I don't know. Anyway, that is about what's up, so there should be nothing more for us to do unless an emergency arises.

Sweet, I was just thinking of you and wondering how we would greet each other. I could see you, so very plainly, and you were crying. I was on the verge of it myself. You were wearing a nice white summer dress, which had pink flowers on it. I guess you call it a print dress. Gee, you sure did look pretty. The funny part of it was that we didn't rush up to each other and throw our arms around us. We just stood and looked at each other, then you started crying, (probably because of my gray hair) and then, suddenly, I was holding your sob-wracked body so close to me. All this happened out on the street somewhere, too, but I don't know just where. Jackie wasn't around, so I guess it won't happen that way. But no matter how or where it happens, it can't possibly be any too soon to suit me.

I do have a lot more gray hairs than I did when you last saw me. Those two lanes that are growing back from my forehead have almost met, too. Gee, I hope you won't be too disappointed when you see me.

Remember those pictures I told you about, before last Christmas? Well, we are going to get them this week. Our company will get ours on Thursday. I will send you them when I get them.

Give my regards to all the family and our friends. Here is my daily hug and kiss for your darling Jackie. To you, my sweet, I send my all. My heart, body, and soul are yours, but temporarily I am loaned out to Uncle Sam. May the day soon come when we are together again. I love you.

J.De Roxtro EM2/c   Everlastingly, your *Johnny*

Note on flap: "More than anything else I desire to be there with you. Hugs and kisses."

Tuesday, May 16, 1944. *No mail. Vene called, would be down in afternoon, came at 2. Vene used Jackie's carriage (broke handle), we went downtown. Brought film to Sandrian. Tried to get more film. Home at 4:00. Sent out for ice cream. Vene fed children here. Met Johnnie's train. Fran called up. At night went to movies with Mom - "The Fighting Sea bees." Very good!*

[Pavuvu Island, Russell Islands.]
Postmarked May 17, 1944, stamp upside down.

May 16, 1944
Same place

Hello, My Lovely One:

All my waking thoughts are of you, and I dream of you each night. I love you, miss you and want you. My love for you increases as the days slowly pass, bringing us more close together. The day of our reunion can't possibly be far away now. How I long to hold you close to me and kiss you. I want to hold your soft yielding body close to mine while I tell you how much I love you. You are the most wonderful wife and sweetheart in the world. I am more proud of you every day. Gee, I sure was lucky to have gotten you as my sweetheart and wife. Darling, I'm hungry, but not for food. Only being there with you can satisfy my hunger. Sweetheart, more than anything else in the world, I desire to be with you.

Today, I received a nice long letter from my mother, and another wonderful one from my wonderful one. It was six large pages long, and was full of interesting data. That was a swell one darling. Thanks a lot. I am not going to answer it tonight, however, as I must study tonight for my examination tomorrow night. I hope you won't mind too much. Which reminds me. Unless I can find time during the day tomorrow, I may not be able to write. Hell, I can't break my chain of letters to you now, even in order to take a test. Somehow, I'll make time enough to drop a couple of pages anyway.

The letter I received from you today was written the thirtieth of April, and wasn't postmarked until the third of May. Your system must have slipped somewhere. Three days isn't anything, though, so I am not complaining. I'm happy to receive them. I was correct when I said you must have written between the last two I had already gotten. Boy, this was a nice long one, sweet, but still not long enough. But no matter how long you make them, I'll never be satisfied, so don't try too hard. I wish I could write six pages every night. Boy, that would really be swell, wouldn't it. But I can't so there's no use thinking of it.

Some scuttlebutt has broken out, but as far as I know, there is nothing official so far. When there is, I will let you know all about it. I doubt very much if I will be there to keep our date the sixth of next month. But I am still hoping, my love. There is still a bare possibility, but I have my doubts. Whenever it is that we have, I'll be happy and satisfied. Just the thoughts of being with you make me almost happy, so I'm almost always almost happy.

Give my regards to all the family and our friends, precious one.

Here is my daily hug and kiss for Jackie, and millions more for you, the sweetest, most adorable, most wonderful girl in the world. The more I think of you, the more I love you, and the more I love you, the more I think of you, and etc. etc. You are mine, and I am yours, forever. I love you, miss you and want you.

J.De Roxtro EM2/c   Everlastingly, your loving *Johnny*

Note on flap: "Honey I sure do love you. I miss you and want you, too. How's Mickey? "

Wednesday, May 17, 1944. Letter of May 4, 1944. 7th Issue of C.Breeze . Put Jackie out in carriage. Leslie played with paper dolls. Cut the grass, trimmed the hedges. In for lunch. Put Jackie to bed. 2:30 Catherine and Carol Ann came. Sent out for ice cream. Played records for kids.

[Pavuvu Island, Russell Islands.]
Postmarked May 18, 1944, stamp upside down.   May 17, 1944

                                  Somewhere

Lucia, My love,

      I love you, adore you and worship you. I miss you and want you more as each day passes, slowly bringing us more close together. Thoughts of you are always in my mind and your lovely image is eternally before me. I long to hold you tenderly in my arms once again and kiss you. I desire to tell you of my love for you. Oh, sweetheart, I am so tired to being away from you. It will soon be two years since I've seen you. No one knows when we will be reunited, either. At least, as far as I know, no one does. I'm kind of afraid that we (the battalion) will be kept out here for as darn long that the powers that be will simply stick us on another job, figuring we had our rest. That would be a heck of a thing to do, but don't be surprised if it happens. We are working every day, but it is nothing important, and we could drop it all and leave here in a day or two. When we do leave, I am hoping and praying that it will be for the states. Gee, there are so darn many things I want to do with you and for you. But most of all I want to make love to you. Sweetest wife and mother in all the world, you belong to me and I belong to you. We belong with each other, and soon, I hope, we will be happy together. I am hungry. I love you.

      The only mail that came for me today was a letter from Ralph and another from the Reader's Digest. Naturally, the latter wasn't anything important. Your little brother didn't have anything much to say, but he did seem in a more cheerful mood than he usually does.

      I am as well and as happy as I possibly can be, being out here and away from you. I sincerely hope that you, Jackie and the family are in the *best of health and remain so, for the rest of your lives.*

Gee, sweet, I don't know what to say in order to fill it up, but I will think of something. It's almost chow time, and as I have an early after-dinner date with the examiners, I will have to leave for chow soon. Pull me through this one, will you, lovely one? This is the hardest I've ever taken, and I think I'll pass, though not with honors. If I don't make a rate this time, I'm going to give up. I know you'll be pulling for me. I will let you know the result as soon as I know it myself. I know you're interested.

Give my kind regards to all the family and our friends. Here is my daily hug and kiss for the wee one, our adorable Jackie. To you, I only wish I were able to send myself, but as I can't, I send all my love and adoration. You're the best in all the world. I love you.

J.De Roxtro EM2/c   *Everlastingly, your adoring Johnny*

Note on flap: *"Sweetest one, I love you. You are on my mind continually. Hugs & kisses."*

Thursday, May 18, 1944. *Letters of May 6,7.8,9. 8th issue of C-Breeze. Windy. Went to 6:30 mass. "Ascension Thursday." Found Leslie playing with paper dolls on living room floor. Jackie still asleep. Vene called up, said she and M.De R. would be down. Came about three. Gave Les & Jackie a bath. They brought a quart of ice cream and tomatoes. Left at 5:00.*

[Pavuvu Island, Russell Islands.]
Postmarked May 19, 1944, stamp upside down.   May 18, 1944

Somewhere

Hello, My Sweet:

I am more in love with you now than I ever was. My love for you increases daily. My thoughts are continually of you. Your lovely image is forever before me. I love you, miss you and want you more as each day passes, slowly but surely bringing us more close together. I long to hold you tenderly in my arms and kiss you. I long to tell you of my love. More than anything else, I desire to be there with you. Sweetest wife in the world, I was just figuring how many days straight that I have written you. Gee, I didn't realize just how many I had. I've written about one-hundred thirty, and on June sixth, if I am able to keep it up, I will hit the hundred fifty mark on your birthday, the sixth of June. I will have to beg off from that date I made with you. It seems that I will be delayed. The way things look right now, we are about to get another job. I am hoping and praying that we won't but if it comes, there isn't anything we can do about it. So, my lovely one, if mail from me should stop coming, and you have heard nothing from me about returning home, please don't expect too much. It may be only that we have moved. Unless you hear from me, don't rely on anything. I love you.

I took that examination last night and I am quite sure I passed. I know you were with me, because I could feel your presence. Your hand was guiding mine, and therefore I couldn't possibly flunk.

Today, I received the Y bulletin and my Reader's Digest, that's all. I was sort of hoping I'd receive another letter from you, but there was very little or no airmail, so naturally I couldn't expect any. To show you the difference between airmail and ordinary, Blosser received one of the latter today, and it was postmarked March twentieth. Just about two months. What a heck of a long time. Boy, I sure am glad you are sending mine by way of airmail.

Tonight, my most precious one, I am going to answer your one and only letter that I received this week. Maybe I should wait until Sunday, but I may receive more before then. Yes, I think I should wait until Sunday. I would rather make a nice long letter on a Sunday. Somehow, it makes it seem a little more like a day of rest at home. I hope you won't mind too much, Lucia, my love, that I am putting off answering your letter. I wonder why it is that at times my mail comes all in a bunch, and then it strings out like this. I know it isn't your fault, my angel, because I know you are doing your best. It is the way they are held up somewhere along the line. Gee, I love you.

Since I have changed my mind, I will leave this for awhile and go to our local open-air theatre and see the show. At least, I think I will see it. I don't know what's playing, maybe I've already seen it, or perhaps I don't care to see it. I don't want to miss any, in case "The Song of Bernadette" comes here. Gee, honey, I can't seem to get that picture off my mind. It really was a swell one, and I hope you get a chance to see it. I don't think you have, yet, because I doubt if you could have, and not told me anything about it. Gee, I adore you.

Well, I went to the show, and I hadn't seen it before. It was "Here Comes Elmer," with Al Pearce and his gang, Jan Garder and his orchestra, plus the one and only Elmer Blurpp. It was one of the screwiest pictures I've ever seen. It was lousy, but amusing, as well as darned silly. At least it was a darn sight better than those propaganda pictures. They may be alright back in the states, to stimulate sales of war bonds or induce the youngsters to enlist, but we don't need any reminder out here.

There is an Australian program on the radio, and it certainly is entirely different than our programs. Their singers are not as well trained as ours, and they don't seem to have the tone. Not bad, though.

After the show I went up to our ice machine and got a gallon of ice water. *Boy, that stuff sure does go good, when one is so darn hot. Honestly, honey, I take a bath at least once a day, but usually twice, and when I have a shirt on for a couple of hours, I can even smell myself, I perspire so freely. Gee, how I want to get home to you.*

My beloved one, I want as much to be there talking with you and doing things with you and for you. I want to make love to you as I used to. I want to take you in my arms and kiss you. Honey, I long to hear your voice and your laughter. To see the smiles on your pleasant, most beautiful face, and even your eyes, when you are angry. Remember me telling you how they were more beautiful then? They are sweetest one. They seem alive, and full of fire, when you are angry. But I would rather not see them that way. I want you to be happy and smiling always. I intend to do my best to make and keep you happy.

Give my regards to all the family and our friends, my lovely one. Here is my daily hug and kiss for our Jackie, and millions more for you, the most valuable and precious wife a guy ever had. I love you, miss you and want you.

J.De Roxtro EM2/c   *Everlastingly, your adoring* *Johnny*

Note on flap: *"To me, you're the most beautiful and wonderful girl in the world. I love you."*

Friday, May 19, 1944. *Letters of May 10 & 11th. Letter from Ralph. Sent pictures to Mom. Washed Leslie's hair & my own.*

[Pavuvu Island, Russell Islands.]

Postmarked May 20, stamp upside down.   May 19, 1944
                                                                          Somewhere

Hello, Adorable:

You are always in my thoughts and eternally locked in my heart. Your image is before me. I love you, miss you and want you more as each day passes, bringing us more close to the day of our reunion. I long to hold you close to me and kiss you. Sweetheart, may the day soon come when you and I are together. More than anything else in the world, I desire to be there, with you. Honey, you're wonderful, and you are the most adorable wife and mother in all the world. How proud I am of you, sweetheart. I will never regret having wooed and won you. The happiest day of my life will be when we are able to hold each other and talk to each other again. There is so much we have to talk over, isn't there. You probably have plenty to tell me about your lovely little daughter and of yourself, and I have a little to tell you. There is plenty I could tell you now, but I'm afraid it wouldn't pass the censors. How did I ever get off the main subject like that, I wonder? Oh, well, one thing leads to another, and still another. Say, that's something. I was led to you, and we were led to our sweet little rascal, Jackie. Sweetheart, I love and adore you. Angel mine, I long to sit and look at you, to talk to you, and see you smile and hear your merry laughter. I want to let my hands roam all over your beautiful body. I miss you so much. I am terribly hungry, sweetest one, and only you can satisfy my hunger. I want love and kisses from you. I never thought I would ever miss anyone as much as I've missed you these last two years. To be there with you would really make me happy. Gee, I hope I will be able to make and keep you happy forever. This damned war can't possibly last many more years, sweet one, and then we will start all over again. The day of my departure from this island can't possibly come any too soon to suit me. I want so much to feel the warmth of your lips as I press mine against them. To feel the softness of your body as we snuggle closer together in our nice comfortable bed, to be able to do those things for you that a husband should, ah, won't that be swell, sweet, to be a human being again, and not part of a great machine, a machine of destruction. What a contrast to what I want. I desire to build and create life, not tear it down. Heck, honey, if only I could find a way to return to you, without bringing disgrace to you and our heiress, I would leap at the opportunity. I love you, sweetest, and I want you so very much. I'm hungry.

No mail came for me again today, so maybe it's a good thing I didn't answer your letter. I have one more day, and then another Sunday. Gee, it's a relief to get Sundays off, to catch up with ones correspondence, do a few pieces of washing, and then spend the remainder of the day, day-dreaming of the one one loves. I often lay here on a Sunday afternoon and think of lots of things we used to do. I sort of get a kick out of it, but it makes me sad, to think of you, back there alone, with no Johnny. I often wonder if Mickey misses her Johnny as much as I miss you. I know you miss me, too. Could you let me know if Mickey misses her Johnny, sweet? I am very much interested in bringing those two together again, as soon as I get a chance. I think they go well together, and that they both feel swell when they are. It's up to you to let me know all about your views of those two, because I wouldn't want to do anything you would disapprove of. I think you would be satisfied if they were brought together right now, wouldn't you. Mickey might not like me entering my nose into her business, though. Let me know all about her, please, sweet, will you? Only once or twice have you ever mentioned her in your letters. But perhaps you would rather not discuss the matter by way of letters. If that's the reason, sweet, just let me know, and I will refrain from mentioning it anymore.

I got those pictures today, my love, and are they lousy. But from all I've seen, mine turned out pretty good. I must have been a little angry that day, or down in the dumps, because I sure do look stern. That damned grin of mine is still there, though, so it couldn't have been so very bad. I also think I look like a convict, so this is all merely preparation for when you see the picture. But then, you have probably seen that already, so I'll skip it. I have two, both the same, so I'm sending one each to

you and my mother. You two can get a laugh out of them, I guess. Don't forget to tell me how hard the family laughs at it. I sure wish I could hear the laughter and cracks made about it. It certainly would seem more like home, then.

Well, my love, this will be all for tonight, as it is rather late. The boys are already asleep, so maybe I had better turn in and get a little shut-eye also. Pleasant dreams to you, adorable one. I love you. Give my regards to all the family and our friends. Here's my daily hug and kiss for our beloved daughter. I sure would like to see her. To you, sweet precious, most magnificent wife and mother, I send all my love and adoration. May the day soon come when I will be able to hold you close to me and kiss you. I am hungry, my sweet, and not for hugs and kisses only.

J. De Roxtro EM2/c   Everlastingly, your loving *Johnny*

Note on flap: "Sorry I can't keep that date, sweet. All my love."

Saturday, May 20, 1944. *No mail. Went to confession. Went downtown Sat. night. Sandrian closed. Bought supplies in drugstore. Met Albert Pruden. Went up to Pete's jumper.*

[Pavuvu Island, Russell Islands.]
Postmarked May 23, 1944, stamp upside down.   May 20, 1944

Somewhere

Hello, Dearest:

I love you, miss you and want you. You are always in my mind, and eternally in my heart. My one and only desire is to be there with you, holding you in my arms and kissing you. I love you, darling, more than life itself. There isn't anything I would not do, to be able to be there with you again.

No mail came for me again today, my lovely one. Could it be that you aren't using your system of mailing your letters to me? I will know, when I receive the next ones. Maybe tomorrow I'll get a couple. I sure hope so, because so far this week I've only received the one from you. Gee, sweetheart, I'm sure glad I didn't answer that earlier this week. If I had, I wouldn't have had any to answer tomorrow, and I would rather take my time and do a better job on your letters on Sunday. Tomorrow, I will make an earnest effort to answer yours with a nice long one. Gee, sweet, I hope I start this next week *off my receiving at least one sweet letter from you. Gee, I feel kind of bad when I don't receive any mail from you. Oh, well, I really did exceptionally well last week, so I have no room to kick.*

I made a slight error, sweet. Today I received a letter from Grace. I had forgotten all about it until just now. As usual, you know, she had nothing to say.

My beloved angel, in case you are interested, and I know you are, I made a very good grade in my test the other nite. Now, whether or not it means anything, remains to be seen. I made a pretty good mark in the other three, too, but they didn't mean a darn thing. You certainly must have been with me when I took that last one, because I did a lot better than I thought I would. Thanks, honey, for your help.

There isn't anything more I can say tonight, my love. Oh, yes, in case I haven't mentioned it before now, believe it or not, it hasn't rained in a hell of a while. It's been five days, anyway, since we had any. And you can well imagine the difference. It sure has been hot, lately, but we can stand it.

Give my regards to all the family and our friends. Here is my daily hug and kiss for our darling daughter. Don't let that picture I sent scare her too much. Break her in on it gradually. Maybe by the time I get there, she will be used to it.

All my love and adoration is yours, my most adorable darling. I love you more as each day passes, slowly bringing us more close together. I want you.

J. De Roxtro EM2/c   *Everlastingly, your loving* *Johnny*

Note on flap: *"Well, sweetheart maybe I'll do better tomorrow. I love you."*

Sunday, May 21, 1944. *Church. Joe came in morning. Mama G and Tadone up. Dressed Les for church. 1:00 Fran came. Weighs 117. Had dinner at 2:00. Were halfway through when people from Trenton came. Mike home on furlough. Has seven month old baby boy. Finished up beer. Stayed about an hour. Washed dishes. Girls went to play tennis for first time. Took pictures. Poison ivy on [?]. Eddie came. Brought up suitcase. Stayed for supper. Girls came home. Went to movies. Saw "Follow the Boys." Very good.*

[Pavuvu Island, Russell Islands.]
Postmarked May 23, 1944, stamp upside down.   May 21, 1944

                                                            Somewhere

Hello Sweetheart:

I love you, miss you and want you. More than anything else in the world I long to be there with you. I desire to hold you tenderly in my arms and kiss you. I want as much to tell you how much I love you. Each and every minute of the day I am thinking of you and wishing I were home. As the days slowly pass, bringing us closer to the day we will be reunited, my thoughts are of you, more constantly. Dearest one, I am hungry and I don't mean for food. I'm hungry for your love, the feel of your lips as they press against mine in a lovers embrace. You are the only girl in the world for me. I am yours forever, and will love you forever.

No mail came for me again, my lovely one, so all I can do is answer your letter of April thirtieth. It is the only one I have, so here's hoping I get some real soon. You can't even come close to realizing how low I feel when I don't receive mail from you in a week or so. This letter arrived here the sixteenth, as you will know if you check your letters. That's only five days ago, but it seems ages to me. I know you are writing, though, so I will get them in due time. I know how much you have to do, too, so don't try to send any more than you are. I realize how lucky I am to be receiving as many as I do. Gee, sweet, I don't know what I would do without you.

It rained last night for the first time in almost a week. Because of the rain, I guess, today is quite nice. It isn't too hot, and there is a pleasant breeze blowing. I have my trousers on today, so you know it's nice. I don't feel much like writing, sweet. I think that I'll take a shower before I go any farther. Perhaps that'll make me feel better. Pardon me for about a half hour, will you? I'll be back as soon as I finish. Here I am again, my sweetheart, and I feel a little better.

Thanks loads for your two kisses, sent by way of the stamps. I expected pictures, but there was only a lovely letter. It was nice and long, sweet, but I'm still not satisfied. Even if you wrote a book a day, I wouldn't be. Nothing will ever satisfy me, except being there with you. And that can't come any too soon to suit me. I'm ready now, and I have been ready for a long, long time.

So Joe is taking up gardening now, is he? That's swell. Now maybe you can have a few fresh vegetables once in awhile. He will bring things over to you, I know. He's a swell fellow, sweet, and I am glad you picked him as Jackie's Godfather. He will do the best he can for her. It's too bad that Tadone can't do anything with a garden this year. He sure does like to mess around with one, and I'll bet he will be doing something in someone's garden, even if it's only pulling a few weeds. He sure was proud of his garden, wasn't he.

It's swell of your mother to go down there daily to dress his wound. Gee, I sure do hope the poor fellow is feeling much better by this time. But I suppose because he is so old, it will take a long time to heal. Wouldn't it be swell if his arthritis was caused by that abscess and he was able to use his arm freely when it's healed and well again? Give him my fond regards, angel, and tell him I wish him all the best of luck possible. Also give Mama G my best. Honey, you sure do have a swell pair of grandparents. I like them a lot.

A quart of ice cream for the four of you made quite a nice portion each. But as usual, I suppose you had to share yours with Jackie. No, I forgot. It is after eight, and she would be asleep a couple of hours by that time. My mother said that Jackie likes ice cream. Is that right, sweet, or is it only once in awhile that she does? In one of your letters you said that she didn't care very much for sweets. Speaking of sweets, sweet, how would you like to go down to Thodes and sip a sundae with me tonight? You would? O.K. I will be there to pick you up at seven-thirty. How I wish I could say that and really mean it. We would be satisfied with each other's company for awhile, wouldn't we. Gosh, how I would like to be able to take you in my arms again and take you upstairs. I love you.

That sure was a swell idea, sweet, of fixing the office into a sunroom for Jackie. But gosh, it must have been a devil of a lot of work for you to undertake. Boy, I wouldn't have known where to start on that job. All those books and magazines that were on the shelf, and that worktable—how did you ever manage to take that down to the garage? Sweetheart, you didn't do that all alone, did you? Please don't try any tricks like that, will you? Even though you think you can, don't take any chances. After all, your health is much more important that anything like that. But as long as it's done, I guess everything went alright. I still think it's a grand idea. Let's see how good my memory is now. The desk and chair are still in the same place. The shelves also. That leaves about six feet between the windows and the desk. In that space you have nothing but that drawing chair and the box for Jackie's toys. That should be plenty of room for her to play in. I can't seem to remember a typewriter table, though angel. Was that there when I was around. As far as I can recollect, the typewriter was always on the workbench. Come to think of it, what was between the desk and the door? There was something there, but I can't seem to remember it. Maybe that was the table. That bench of Gene's took up a lot of room, didn't it. Glad you moved it.

It would be swell if you could sit the little one on that high stool and leave her there, wouldn't it. But as you say, you can't, because she is liable to fall. The only thing I can say is that you should have started her in the highchair, and then you could have left her. This way, you have to stand there with her all the time she's there, don't you. And that must be a heck of a job for you, too. As long as there are trains and autos or pedestrians moving, she would be easily satisfied, but all too often there aren't any. It's really swell of you to take time out from your work to stay there with her. Gosh, honey, I'm so proud of you. Angel, will you keep anyone from taking Jackie for a train ride until I get there? I want you and I to have that privilege. Everything else seems to be done, by now. But there will be plenty for we three to do for the first time, won't there. Swimming, boating, fishing, and all that sort of thing. Gee, we sure will have a swell time together, won't we, when the three of us are one unit, as we should be.

Sweetheart, you sure had a very busy day, that Sunday. You certainly had plenty of company. I'll bet it was a surprise when you saw Mike and Jr. coming along the avenue. That's tough about Jo having to wear glasses all the time, isn't it. But wasn't she supposed to wear them at all times, when I was home? I sure hope she wears them, now, and doesn't ruin her eyes entirely.

Say, sweet, as long as you are able to eat in peace when you eat later than usual, why don't you always do that. Take care of Jackie and put her to bed, and then sit down and enjoy your meals. Your digestion would be a lot better, and probably your disposition. I know darn well you'll enjoy your meals more, too. Try it, sweet. I'm quite sure the family wouldn't mind.

I can just about picture Joe taking those kids for a ride, and making Mike drive so he could hold Jackie in his lap. I'll bet he really got a kick out of that. He sure does love that wee one of ours. He is good to her, too. It sure would be swell if he and Angie could have a little one. I wonder why they haven't started. Only because of this war, I guess. At times, I am sorry we ever started one, but then when I hear you rave over her and tell me how much you love her, I am not sorry anymore. For myself, I am not sorry, except that I am sorry I can't be there with you two.

I thought Michael Jr. would be a gentlemanly little fellow. I am sure glad that he is careful while playing with children. Gee, I'll bet Jackie really squawked when he stopped pulling her in the wagon. And Joe would jump up and start pulling her. Darn it, he'll spoil her yet, even though he doesn't mean to. And when you tell him about it, I suppose he laughs about it. He would, the lug.

Tell me, angel, when you find that you are forced to spank the little one, doesn't it hurt you quite a bit? Enough so that it sort of draws your hand back as it is on it's way down to the target? Gosh I wonder if I'll be able to do it, when I do have to? That's going to be a tough job, and one that I won't care much for. But I suppose Ill have to do it, sooner or later. It is best that we do, because we wouldn't want Jackie to become a spoiled brat, would we? You are swell, dearest one, and I love you more than anything in the world.

My mother told me that she was down to spend the night with you. She said our bed is very comfortable, and she enjoyed it. The train whistles kept her from getting a decent night's sleep, so she said. Heck, I never even knew there were any trains when I was there. I didn't tell her that I thought our bed was comfortable, too, and that I'd love to be there to do the things we used to do. She might not like that. But boy, how I would love to spend a few nights there with you. The radio is playing, and I am inserting words that I don't mean, so if they make no sense to you, they don't to me, either. So please pardon any mistakes I might make that way. It would be swell if we were able to lie there, side by side, talking and planning the future of our family. How swell it will be, talking with you again. Darling, I love you truly.

That sure was a red letter day, when you were able to get two films. Now I can get that picture of you, showing your profile. How about it, my lovely one? Am I ever going to get that one? I really want a couple more pictures of you, sweet. All the ones I have are rather faded, and I want some new ones. Most of the ones I have of Jackie are alright yet, but some of them are a little faded. I don't mind that so much, because you are sending me pictures of her right along, and how I love to receive them. Honey, you're tops.

That's swell of Mary to send her regards and best wishes to me. Sweet, I thought Mary was going to spend part of the month of May with you. It would do you both a lot of good, too. You could talk over old times, go places and do things.

We very seldom have any pictures that are worth seeing here, so I don't think we would ever see that one you were speaking of. Goodnight, sweetheart, I now send my regards to all the family and our friends. Here is my daily hug and kiss for Jackie, and to you, my beloved wife, the mother of our child I send all my love, hugs and kisses. I love you, miss you and want you more as each day passes. May I see you soon.

J.De roxtro EM2/c   *Everlastingly, your loving*   *Johnny*

Note on flap: "Hi sweet, is this one long enough for you? I would make them all this long if I could. I love you."

Monday, May 22, 1944. *Letters of 13,14,15 of May. 7th issue of C-Breeze. Cat and Carol Ann were over in afternoon. Took two pictures. Started to rain. Short shower. Joe in Hawaii. Wrote to Mary. Wrote to Ralph.*

[Johnny's letter of May 22, 1944 is missing]

Tuesday, May 23, 1944. *Letter of May 12th. Rain & cold. Jackie slept 2½ hours. Fan home at 2:00. We went to doctor's. She must go back in 10 days. Stopped at Dr. Reilly's. Appointment - a* week from Thursday, 4:00p.m. Bought rubber pants for Jackie. Gold earrings. Butcher boy overalls. Wrote to Mrs. Fitzpatrick.

[Pavuvu Island, Russell Islands.]
Postmarked May 24, 1944, stamp upside down.   May 23, 1944

Somewhere

Hello, My Darling:

I love you, miss you and want you more as each day passes, slowly but surely bringing us more close together, in time if not in distance. Thoughts of you are eternally in my mind. You are forever locked in my heart. Your sweet and lovely face is always before me. More than anything else in the world, I want to be with you. I long to hold you tenderly in my arms and kiss you. I want to feel the warmth of your sweet young body as we embrace. Gee, honey, to be there with you again will be divine. Gee, when I think of all the good times we've had together, and will have, I feel well pleased. I am as proud of you and the job you are doing in bringing up our daughter. You are the most beautiful sweetheart, most devoted wife, and most thoughtful mother in all the world. It will be heavenly when we are reunited, won't it. Can you picture the happy home we three will have after this war is over? We will have a heaven of our own, and you will be the boss. Everything in my power will be done by me, to make you and Jackie happy. Your health and happiness will be my goal, always. I love you my darling, and hope to see you real soon.

The weather has been rather nice the last couple of days, sweetheart. It has rained several times, and it hasn't been too hot. I am well, my sweet, and as happy as I can be, being away from you and Jackie. I sincerely hope and pray that you, your daughter and the family are in the best of health, and remain that way, forever.

The scuttlebutt has broken out again, Lou darling, and it all sounds good. If only there was something I could write to you about it. None of it has any foundation however, because someone dreams up a tall tale and tells someone, and it spreads like wildfire. Anything that's good will travel fast, too. Just as soon as I know something definite, I will let you know. I'm truly sorry I led you to believe that I was coming home, my beloved angel, but after all, I told you nothing official had come out. I am still of the notion that we will be home this summer, but it may not be until late. I have been too anxious to return home, I guess, and let my wishful thinking become almost believable. I want so very much to get home to you, my beloved angel. I would give almost anything to be able to see you walking down the street toward me. Those things of mine would be bouncing, and your can would be swinging from side to side. Ah such a pleasant picture that would make. I wonder where

161

it will be that we will first meet. Personally, I don't care where it is, or who is around, I'm going to kiss you, wherever we meet. And I don't mean a measly little peck, either. It will be one of those nice long ones. Would you mind very much, sweet? If we first meet in church, maybe I won't but I don't think we will meet there. It isn't very likely that we could have that luck.

I'm not going to answer either of your letters tonight, sweet, because I don't think I could do justice to it. Your next one is a nice long one, with a blank sheet at the end. I will see what I can do with it on Thursday. Tomorrow night we are having the army show and a picture, so I intend to see that. If it rains tomorrow, I may answer your letter, though. I think I'll go to see the show tonight. "Whistling in Brooklyn" is playing. I haven't the slightest idea what it's all about, but I will go, anyway. I won't finish this until after the show, so I will be able to tell you all about it.

There isn't anything I can tell you, my beloved one, that would be of interest to you, so I don't know what to say. It has turned quite hot since I started this, so maybe it's going to rain. Gee, I love you.

Did I tell you that we are only working six hours a day, six days a week now? My hours are from eight till eleven in the morning and from thirteen hundred to sixteen hundred in the afternoon. That's swell, because it gives me time to have a shower before chow at noontime. And boy, that really makes a fellow feel swell. A nice cold shower, and then a rubdown. It's so refreshing and soothing.

Say, sweet, I heard today that the beer is going to be cut down to three point two. Do you think you could get a couple of cases of it as it is now, and save it for me? If you would and could, I would certainly appreciate it. Let me know, will you, angel, if you are able to manage it? It will make something to look forward to, besides being there with you. That will be swell enough, without the beer, but I would like to be able to have a bottle or two, once in awhile.

Well, my lovely one, it's about time for the show, so I guess I will sign off for a little while. I'll be back later, sweet. Until I return, I will let about a hundred hugs and kisses to tide you over.

Forbes has it again. They should send him home so he could get rid of that darned stuff. He can't seem to shake it off. He sure is trying hard, though. I love you.

I'll start this page before I go, my love, but I'm afraid I won't say anything, except that I love you truly. Here I am back, my lovely one, but I'm afraid I still don't have anything to say. The picture, as usual, was lousy. Red Skelton was the star, and he was as bad as he usually is. It sure was a hell of a picture. Hell, the Palace used to show better pictures than we have here. But the day will come when we (you and I) will be able to go to see a good picture, sit in the comfortable seats, and have a soda and sundae or something after. Gee, that'll be swell, won't it. I am anxious for that day to come, too. It can't come any too soon to suit me, and I can be ready to leave in less than an hour.

Sweetheart darling, I'm afraid I will have to say good night now, as there isn't anything more to say. Give my fond regards to all the family and any of our friends you may happen to meet. Here is my daily special hug and kiss for your beautiful doll baby, Jackie. To you, most precious wife, I send my all. I am yours forever, and I will do nothing to make you sorry you let me talk you into becoming my life-mate. I love you, miss you and want you. I am hungry, sweetheart, and only you can satisfy my hunger.

J.De Roxtro EM2/c   Everlastingly, your doting *Johnny*

Note on flap: "This isn't very long, Lou, but it's the best I can do tonight. I love you more each day."

Wednesday, May 24, 1944. *Rain. No mail. Went to movies. Saw "Lost Angel" Margaret O'Brien. Coal man came. 3 tons of coal.*

[Pavuvu Island, Russell Islands.]
Postmarked May 25, 1944, stamp upside down.   May 24, 1944
                                                                 Somewhere

My Precious Darling:

I love you, miss you and want you. My thoughts are always of you. The most lovely vision in the world is everlastingly before me. As you know, that vision is of the most beautiful wife and sweetheart any fellow ever had. I worship you, angel, and adore you. To be there with you is my one desire. And after I have feasted my eyes on your lovely face and figure, I will then take you in my arms and hold you close to me and kiss you. I intend making love to you as I've never made love before. Your slightest wish will be granted, if it is at all possible to do so. More than anything else, I want to make you happy. My love and admiration for you increases as each day passes, bringing us slowly but surely together. How I wish, hope and pray that the day of our reunion will come soon. I've been waiting a long time for that day, and it can't come any too soon to suit me. My love for you is so great, sweet, that I will never be satisfied until I am able to hold you in my arms. My happiness won't be complete until I can be with you. I love you more than life itself.

I am quite well, my lovely one, and as happy as I can be, away from you. I sincerely hope and pray that you, Jackie and the family are in the best of health and are completely happy. I don't know what I would do if

163

anything ever happened to you. Maybe I'd go nuts, even worse than I am now. But I have an idea I would carry on, and devote myself to our daughter. Let's get off that subject shall we? It isn't very nice, and nothing will.

Today, sweet one, I received another nice long letter from my beloved. It was written the twelfth and postmarked the sixteenth. Just think, our mail now makes a round trip in less than a month. Remember how long it formerly took? Gee, what a difference. I just happened to think of something you put in your letter, in parentheses. You are quite mean, my love, telling me you were having parmigiano for supper. Gee, would I like some of that now. I've just finished my supper, but I could sure make one heck of a dent in one, right now. What are you trying to do, sweet, make me moan? You could have made it a lot worse, though, by telling me how good it was. I'm hungry, but not for parmigiano.

Now, I'll make you moan. Today, as I was coming in to lunch, I happened to see, in a nice isolated spot, a tree full of delicious, almost ripe, oranges. They are as large as small grapefruit, and in just a day or two, I will have plenty. Now, my sweet, it's your turn to moan. I hope no one picks them all before they become ripe, though. I'll let you know how I make out, if I think of it. You know what I would like to be able to tell you? A story similar to the one I told Ann about the pineapple and the bananas. Hell, I haven't seen either here, except the canned pineapple. Fresh fruit seems to be very scarce here, for some reason or other.

We are going to have a stage show tonight, and a movie afterwards, in case you don't remember. It's an army show, called "nuts to you." I don't know the name of the picture, though. I will tell you all about it when I return tonight. A special re-broadcast of the Fred Allen show has just been announced on our radio.

Beloved angel, I will leave you now, for a little while, and return after the show. I have a little job to do before show time. I love you, my Blackie.

Well, my love, the show was merely fair, except for one singer, Michael Strange by name. He was quite good, and he had to sing five songs before the fellows would let him go. He sang several swell songs, but I don't remember the names of them. He was sort of an Irish tenor, I think. The name sounds familiar to me, does it to you? The picture hasn't even started yet. Something went screwy with the machine, I guess. I waited awhile, and became tired, so I left. I just heard the operator call out, "That's all, go on home," so there won't be any picture tonight.

I love you, Lucia my own. I want to be there with you and Jackie. I want to romp with our darling daughter. I want to walk downtown with you on my arm, and Jackie either in the carriage or walking between us. Gee, I sure will be a proud fellow then. I will have the two most beautiful girls, all to myself. While you are doing your shopping, I'll be showing our little one around the shops. I'm afraid I may spoil her though, so you had better keep your eye on me.

Give my fond regards to all the family and our friends, and my daily hug and kiss to Jackie. Here are millions of hugs and kisses for you, the most adorable gal a guy ever had. I love you.

J.De Roxtro EM2/c   Everlastingly, you adoring *Johnny*

Note on flap: "You are the most wonderful girl in the world. I am hungry. Here's all my love."

Thursday, May 25, 1944. *No mail. Letter of 22 returned for more postage. Rain. Drizzle.*

[Pavuvu Island, Russell Islands.]

Postmarked May 26, 1944, two stamps upside down.   May 25, 1944
                                                                                            Somewhere

Hello, Sweetheart:

I love you, miss you and want you. My mind is continually on you, and your lovely vision is eternally before my eyes. More than anything else, I wish to be there with you, holding you in my arms and kissing you. My love for you increases as the days pass, slowly bringing us more close to each other. I want you, sweetheart, and I won't be happy until we are in each other's arms.

No mail came for me today, but I don't mind so very much. I still have these to answer, and as you seem to be writing every three days, I can't expect too many. Tonight I will answer yours of the sixth. You already know when it was mailed, and everything else, so I'll skip all that.

Thanks loads for the two kisses you sent by way of the stamps, honey. As I've said before, and will say again, I intend to collect, with interest, for them, as soon as I see you. Then, after I collect for all you've sent, I will let you collect for all I've sent. Yes, I may even let you have interest, too. Boy, after all those expectant embraces, I will try to make up, as much as I can, for all the time we've been away from each other. I would judge that we are about five thousand kisses behind schedule, so we have one heck of a lot of kissing to do. Gee, I love you.

On the inside flap of the envelope you ask if I expected pictures in this letter. Well, my dearest one, whenever you put double stamps on a letter, I must admit that I do. I'm not sorry, though, because you are doing wonderfully well, by writing such nice long letters to me. I wish I were able to do as well, but all I can do is answer your letters. I am afraid my letters are very much the same, but I am doing my best lovely one. Gee, you're swell.

It sure was swell news, reading that you were able to have the camera fixed. I hope it doesn't cost too much, but even if it is expensive, it will be worth it. I, too, doubt very much if the film will turn out very well. The first couple of pictures might, but I have my doubts. If the light penetrated in any way, the film would be ruined, as you know. You no doubt know by now, whether they did turn out or not, and you should also have the camera. No use my asking you to let me know all about it, because you have probably done so, a couple of days ago. I suppose you should consider yourself lucky to have been able to have the camera repaired at all. Parts must be quite scarce, and very difficult to get. You may even have to wait a week or two longer, but regardless, I hope you manage to make out alright.

You certainly were lucky to have been able to purchase your suit at Saks. I hope that you got what you wanted, sweet. But I should know you did, else you wouldn't have gotten it. As for the coat you got for Jackie to wear in the fall, well, you probably know what you're doing, but I think it's a little early to think of that. She may shoot up like a firecracker, or she may hit a lull in her growing, and remain almost as she is. But what the heck, fall is only a couple of months ahead of us, so I guess you won't have to worry about anything like that. Besides, you may as well get things while you can, because one never knows whether one can get things later on. You probably took into consideration all the facts that I've mentioned, anyway, and a lot more that your loving husband wouldn't think of in a thousand years. The coat sounds swell to me, anyway, and I would like to be there to see it on her. I'll bet she will look swell in it. As for your suit, Lou, my love, I thought you had your heart and mind set on a navy blue one. That light blue must have struck your fancy, in order for you to have even seen it. If I remember correctly, you would never take something even slightly different from your original choice. I love you more each day.

No, sweet, Vincent isn't any better. In case you write to his mother, don't mention his illness, because he doesn't want her to worry about him. Whenever he writes, he tells her that he is well, so please don't do anything to make her feel that he is unwell. Mrs. Forbes didn't write sooner because she wasn't sure of your address. She thought you were from New York. I don't know what could have given her that idea, unless she had you mixed with Fitz's mother. Everyone seemed to like the pictures, so I guess we all looked healthy enough. Don't forget to let me know how you felt when you saw that other monstrosity I sent last week. Boy, I must have been angry with someone or something when that was taken.

It's funny, sweet, reading that it was so very hot there, with the temperature at ninety degrees. Boy, that would feel nice and cool, down here. The average temperature here is one twenty five, and most nights I have to pull a blanket over me about three or four in the morning. You see, we are only about [censored] [it was 9o 11'] off the equator, so you can imagine the heat. If it weren't for an almost continual breeze, it would be unbearable. I love you.

You certainly must have your hands full, trying to keep Jackie from becoming spoiled, when no matter where you take her, people rave over her. She must be even cuter than the pictures of her show. She is the picture of perfect health, too, so naturally everyone is attracted to her. I sure am proud of her and the job you are doing with her. She should be almost perfect, and I have an idea that she is. I certainly would like to see her, but I would rather see you.

Angel mine, as long as I'm so far advanced with this letter, I think I shall go to the show, and finish this later. I know you won't mind, so here's a few dozen kisses to tide you over while I enjoy (?) the movie. I don't know what it is, either. So long for awhile, honey-bun. I'll be back later. Here I am, my sweet. The picture was "A night To Remember." I can't even tell you who played in it. It was a poor picture, one of those crazy murder mysteries. Don't waste any time or money seeing it. I don't know why I ever sat through it, but I did.

Isn't it just like a woman, to be admiring herself in front of a three-way mirror? She certainly is following in your footsteps, my sweet. But I hope she turns out to be as nice and sweet as you are. I'll bet it was funny, to see the surprise written all over her, when she saw three of herself. I can just about picture it, when she looked and saw her image, tripled. I wonder if she (and other girl babies) has a sort of hidden sense that makes them enjoy themselves and be on their best behavior when they are looking over wearing apparel with their parents. It must be, because most bambinos, unless they're ill, take such a peculiar interest in clothes, yet they don't understand what it's all about. Or do they? You probably have noticed, at times, that Jackie does things that make a lot of sense, yet are unreasonable, because of her age. I can't quite put the proper words down here to explain what I'm trying to say, but perhaps you understand. At times like those, as long as she doesn't do any damage to anyone or anything, by all means let her go ahead. She will develop her imagination and learn quite a bit, too. And where would anyone be, without an imagination? As you say, what's the harm in a few fingerprints and smudges on a mirror? They can be removed without any too much trouble. Your adoring husband would certainly be glad to be there to see her in action. How about taking her back there and see if she goes back to that mirror? It would be interesting and we would know how good her memory is. Of course, it may not fascinate her this time, but it's worth a try. Sweetheart, I love you.

I knew, sweetheart, without you telling me, that Jackie wasn't the least bit destructive. How could she possibly be, when she takes after you. She has all your good traits, my sweet. Let's hope she doesn't develop any of my bad ones. As long as she stays like you, she will be loved by all. I didn't know that she was so affectionate, though. I hope her kissing goes no farther than her toys. I wouldn't care to have her being kissed by everyone. I don't mind the family, but outsiders, like my sisters etc., no soap. But again, you probably are way ahead of me, and have taken care of all those details. That she is fond of her dolls and toys is swell, too. It makes it a lot easier on you, and you sure can do with a little peace of mind, knowing that she won't get into mischief at every chance. We are extremely lucky to have such an adorable baby, sweet. My hat's off to you for bringing her up and training her as you have. It would be swell if we could get her a nice small dog as a pet, but maybe it's just as well, for the time being, that we haven't. There is always the possibility of the pup going out into the road and being struck by a car, or worse yet, of Jackie following it out there. Those things happen, sweet. Maybe we should wait until we are in a nice quiet place of our own. Gee, I love you.

We both are of the same opinion about chows, too, my love. I like them, but for some reason or other, I don't trust them, and I wouldn't have let Jackie pet that one, either. You may be right when you say that they almost always have a mean streak in them, but I doubt it. I merely dislike their looks. They seem too damned independent. Maybe because I've never had anything to do with them.

Swell, my beautiful darling. Glad you have finally begun to buy clothes for yourself. Say, honey, the way you said "But that's only the beginning. I intend to get a lot more yet," sounds like a threat. Hell, sweet, I hope it wasn't, because I want you to have all the clothes you want. And I don't care how much you spend for them, either, as long as you don't neglect Jackie. I don't want you to give up something just because you think Jackie should have this or that either. Sweet, I want you both to be happy, and I realize that you can't be happy unless you have new clothes. This is a good time to buy them, too, because you never can tell what will happen later, and we both want you to look your best when we go visiting, don't we. My lovely wife, you are the most wonderful sweetheart in the world, and I love you more as time passes. I thought that would be my last page, but I found I didn't have quite enough room to say all I wanted to. Now, I will have to wrack my brain, what little I have, to fill this one.

Say, what's the idea of inserting the blank sheet of paper in this letter? Are you trying to fool me, or are you too tired, after writing, to tear the sheets off in the proper place? Regardless, I intend to feel that that page is full of the deep love and admiration we have for each other. Nope, there isn't even one word on it. You must have made a mistake, sweet. But as long as you are writing such long letters, I will try real hard, and I will succeed, in forgiving you for not filling that page.

The fellows all send their regards to you, Jackie, and your two sisters. Porky, (the fellow we met at the station), was asking about you three today. You don't remember him. Give my fond regards and best wishes to all the family, sweet, and any of our friends you may run across. Here is my daily special hug and kiss for Jackie. To you, the most beautiful and thoughtful wife and sweetheart in the universe, I send all my love and adoration. I desire to be there with you. I love you.

J.De Roxtro EM2/c   Everlastingly, your loving *Johnny*

Note on flap: "How's this, Lou? I'm getting better all the time. That proves my love is stronger. I'm hungry."

Friday, May 26, 1944. *Letter of May 19, picture enclosed. Washed clothes. Cloudy. Damp.*

[Pavuvu Island, Russell Islands.]
Postmarked May 27, 1944, stamp upside down.   May 26, 1944
                                                        Somewhere

My Darling Lucia:

Each and every hour of the day I am thinking of you and each night I dream of you. The beautiful image of my one and only is before me at all times. I love you, sweetheart, I miss you and want you more as the days slowly pass, surely bringing us more close to the day of our reunion. More than anything else, I desire to be there with you, holding you in my arms and kissing you. I want to do a lot more, but you know that, without me writing of it in this letter.

No mail came again today, lovely one. There was a little three cent stuff, but who wants that junk. It's at least two months old by the time it reaches here. I still have two to answer, so I will see what I can do with yours of the ninth of May. Thanks loads for the kiss, sweetest one. I am sure glad you send them. Whenever I receive one, I imagine the feel of your beautiful red luscious lips pressing against mine, but as good as my imagination is, I would rather have the real thing. I am quite anxious to try that pleasure again. I am also anxious to try something else, since the little girl left there. Are you as anxious and eager as I am, I wonder, to try the duties of married life. Darling, I love you.

Before I forget, my sweet, why don't you and Ann, on your next visit to Newark, go to the Meadowbrook? Surprised? Well, I was talking to a fellow from Newark today, and he told me about it. It, according to him, is fixed up beautifully, and is even nicer than it was before. It is in the basement, under the Mosque Theatre. You may have known this before, but I don't think so, because you never mentioned it. If you do decide to go, tell me all about it, will you? I would rather I were able to go with you, but as I can't, well, I give you my permission, and I want you to enjoy yourself. I can't tell you just where the theatre is, but you can find it alright. It's probably right on Broad St., or just off it.

You didn't have anything written on the inside flap of this one, sweet. You must have been in a hurry, I guess. This letter was a short one, Lou dear, only three pages. I will try to make my answer at least six, but I don't know how well I will do.

My letter of May first really did make good time, didn't it. Yours are coming to me more swiftly now, too. At this rate you could write me, and I could have an answer back to you in about two weeks time. Let's see, that makes more than a thousand miles a day that our letters travel. Come to think of it, that is damn good time.

Honey, I know you are glad of the chance to have Lesley Ann for a weekend, but gee, sweet, you really shouldn't. Heck, you have plenty to do, without burdening yourself with my sister's kid. She probably wouldn't be any trouble, but just the same, I don't think you should. Hell, Fran could have gotten someone to care for her child if she had to leave her somewhere. Let her spend a few dollars on something like that once in awhile. They are making plenty, and can afford it. But it's none of my business, I guess. I do hope you didn't let yourself in for any problems, though. Butch is bound to be a little jealous of Jackie. Tell me all about her stay, please. And don't miss anything.

It kind of looks as if I'm going to have a tough time getting Jackie to like me. Her Uncle Joe sure has spoiled her. But it's a good thing for you that he doesn't live very close. You would really have a spoiled youngster on your hands then. I can just see the bambino clinging to Joe's trouser leg, and crying to beat the band. She was probably looking up into his face at the time, too, with a pleading expression. She will get over all that in time, though, I hope. I sure am glad that Joe loves her so much. In a way, he is a perfect godfather, but I do wish he wouldn't spoil her so. Darling, I adore you.

I doubt very much if we will get a chance to see the picture, "Cover Girl." We don't get those good pictures, because our projector isn't the right size. If the opportunity arises, however, I will see it. I have heard of it, and all reports say it is good. Our show tonight is "Cairo." I think I've seen it, though, back on Santos.

Sweet one, when it is time for our daughter's nap, why don't you put the playpen out in the yard, and let her sleep in that. You wouldn't have to worry about her, and if she did awaken, she would probably start playing, and wouldn't disturb you in the least. That is, of course, if she isn't able to climb over the sides. It won't be long before she does, either.

It was swell of the girls to take your mother to see "Aida," wasn't it. But darn it, why the devil couldn't you have gone? Darn it all, you haven't seen that since we were married. That's one of the disadvantages of being a mother, my sweet. Aren't you sorry, just a little, at times like those, that you married me? Never mind, Lucia my love, we will make up for all that later. At least, I will do my best to do the impossible. We will have plenty of good times together, anyway. I send a kiss to Mickey.

It sure was swell of Eddie and Clemy to drive your mother and sisters home that night. They probably were at Cutters, as you surmised. I haven't heard from Ed in a heck of a long while. I thought perhaps he had left the states before this. Anyway, I am glad he managed a visit to his wife. That's more than I've done, so far. But it isn't my fault. God knows I want to. If you happen to see either of them, tell them I said hello, and thank them for their regards. Eddie sure is lucky, to have remained in the states this long, isn't he. I sort of envy him, but I suppose it wouldn't do me any good if I were stationed there. I wouldn't be able to see you, would I?

I am well and as happy as I possibly can be, away from you, sweet, and I sincerely hope and pray that you, Jackie and the family are in the best of health and are happy. Give them all my fond regards. Here is my daily special hug and kiss for Jackie, and many more to you, the only girl in the world that I could ever love and adore.

J.De Roxtro EM2/c   Everlastingly, your *Johnny*

Note on flap: "Hi Sweet, I hope this isn't too short. Maybe I'll do better next time. I love you, Lou."

May 27, 1944-August 17, 1944 - Allies invade Biak Island, New guinea. The Allied objective was to capture this strategically placed island in order to construct airfields there. This was the first time the Japanese to intentionally allowed uncontested landings for the purpose of creating a kill zone inland. The battle lasted almost three months, but finally resulted in an Allied victory.

Saturday, May 27, 1944. *Letters of May 16, 18. Letter from Mrs. Fitzpatrick. Cleaned house. Out front with Jackie. At night went downtown with girls. Bought stockings and utility bag.*

[Pavuvu Island, Russell Islands.]

Postmarked May 30, 1944, stamp upside down.

May 27, 1944

Somewhere

Hello, adorable:

I love you, miss you and want you. You are forever in my mind, and continually locked in my heart. More than anything else, I want to be there, holding you close to me and kissing you. May the day come soon when you and I will be together, as we should be.

Today I received a nice letter from Ann, dated the sixteenth. I don't know what to call the one I got from you, though. It sure was a swell one, and nine pages long. I think I'll simply call it a novelette, and let it go at that. It was really swell, sweet, and it is the one which you wrote to me on Mother's Day. So we did manage to surprise you, after all. It's a wonder I didn't let the cat out of the bag, isn't it. When I saw the two stamps, I again thought there would be pictures in it, but I was pleasantly surprised to find a long letter. So far, I've read it only three times, but I intend to reread it again after chow.

I will answer yours of the twelfth tonight, lovely Lucia, and the one of the fourteenth tomorrow. I've written quite a few pages so far this week, haven't I. Well, I will start next week off good, by answering yours. I should manage to get at least ten pages out of it. Anyway, I will do my best. Besides writing to you, I only have Ann's letter to answer tomorrow. I always write my mother every Sunday, so that makes three altogether. I love you.

Thanks a million for your kisses, sent to me by way of the stamps. On the inside flap of this envelope you reiterate my thoughts. You say, "Hello, darling, I love you with all my heart." I know you do, sweetheart, but I still like to hear you say it.

Wasn't I a dope, though, to go to all that trouble to surprise you, and then tell you something about it. Darn it, I didn't think about that letter being so close. I am losing my mind, as you see. Of course I didn't mind because you asked Ann for the money in order to buy clothes for yourself. I only sent it to her, because I didn't think you would use it for yourself. Maybe it all turned out for the best, so all is well that ends well. As long as you are happy, I am too. But I sure would be more pleased if I were able to be with you. I'll bet Ann was surprised and a little disappointed, even, to hear that I told you. In her letter today, she said, quote, "And they say a woman can't keep a secret." That means a lot to me, doesn't it you? She was

172

anticipating as much pleasure in the surprise as she expected you to, and was let down. Oh, well, we made up for it in the fourteenth, didn't we. I wish I could surprise you like that every once in awhile, but I can't even do it for your birthday. I am broke, flat busted, and will be until the fifth of June. So all I can send this time are birthday greetings, with love.

Yes, Easter Sunday was a profitable day for me. In fact, I made more in those few hours than I normally make in two months. However, I don't make a habit of shooting crap, so I don't lose much, either. In fact, I am now resting on my laurels. I haven't been in a game since. I'm just as well off, anyway, because my luck isn't consistent, and I would probably lose that and more, in the long run.

No, lovely one, I wasn't at Green Island. A few of our boys went, but they have all returned here, now. They did a wonderful job there, and were back in less than two months. We are a smooth-working outfit and we accomplish things rapidly. I'm kind of proud of this organization, Lou, and glad to be part of it. Naturally, there are some things I dislike about it, but they are unimportant. If it weren't for the Seabees, the war in this part of the world wouldn't be half as far advanced as it is, and the same is probably true of the other theatres of war. I was interested in its location because of the fellows who were there. I will be able to tell you quite a bit about that place, too, when I see you. Some of it is about the marines, so it wouldn't look very good in a letter. You will have plenty to remind me of, when I get home.

I was told today, by one of our men, who is in a position to know, that I finally made my first class rate. I am not depending too much on his word, though. I will have to see it posted on the board before I will believe it. I will let you know all about it, just as soon as I know myself. I sure was glad that you and I were in tune with one another about not wanting it if I couldn't get it on my work. At least my conscience will never bother me, as some should. I haven't asked anyone for anything, and have given more than I have received, so I am very well pleased with myself.

Thanks loads for your information on the word eleemosynary, sweetheart. It was used in a book that we had here, and no one seemed to know the meaning of it. Now we know, thanks to you, my lovely wife. Thanks again.

Sooner or later it had to come, didn't it. I mean Jackie's playing in the dirt. You are swell, honey, in your descriptions of all these things. I could practically see her, from the moment she stepped onto the ground, all through her first contact with the dirt, and sitting there on the log, playing in the dirt for all she was worth. You will surely have your hands full now, with extra washing and all. But then, your daughter will be wearing light summer things soon, and they are much easier to keep clean. I love you.

You sure were lucky to have purchased all those clothes, sweet one. I sure wish you luck in your future tours. Tell me, my love, just what is a pinafore? I can't seem to place them. Are they some kind of a waist? Too bad you had to wait an hour for a train, but you probably didn't mind so much, as long as you were lucky with your purchases.

There seems to me to be only one way to keep Jackie from becoming more spoiled. That is to have her at home, where no one will be able to exclaim over her beauty. That can't be done, though, so you will just have to take your chances and make the best of it. As long as you are now letting her walk around the Acme, you may as well let her push the cart. That way, she won't be into anyone else's. She must be a sketch when she knows someone is watching her. Tell me, sweet, does she show off, or is it natural with her. Gee, I sure do wish I could be there to see her.

I see you were trying to make me moan again, by mentioning parmigiano. That doesn't bother me anymore, sweet. I have had so much of it lately that I am tired of it. But if you don't have some for me when I come home, I may become angry, and only kiss you half a million times, instead of a million. I sure would like some, right now. Or some of your macaroni would go good too. I miss you.

So our wee one has felt the first drops of rain, too. Well, I can guarantee that she will feel plenty more, before the summer is over. I'll bet her expression was one of puzzlement, especially if the rain was cold. She has always been used to warm water, so the drops of cold rain were a bit new to her. Then again, never having been caught in the rain before, she hadn't the slightest idea where it came from. How you ever managed to keep her from being out in it this long is more than I can figure out. You must be exceptionally careful, that's all I can say. As long as you are able to keep her from knowing that you "aren't particularly fond of" electric storms, I think she won't be bothered by them. So, my sweetheart, it's all up to you, now, for awhile until she becomes used to them.

Honey I would be a heck of a one to notice mistakes, when I make so many myself. My spelling isn't what it used to be, and the form of my letters is lousy. I change from one subject to another, and back again. Heck, I don't care, as long as you are able to read and understand them. I only wish I could write longer letters to you. But I can't, simply because my source of information is so small. All I can do is answer your letters and do the best I can to tell you how much I love you.

Surprise, Eddie and Fran came when they were expected, once. But then, you were about to do them a favor, so they would be. Lucia darling, please don't make a habit of doing things for Fran. She will take advantage of you if you let her. She is a swell egg, and all that, but she is all for Fran, and to hell with anyone else. So, my lovely, watch yourself, and do as the de Roxtros do. Look out for

yourself and Jackie first. And I will do all I can to look out for the three of us.

That's all there is to answer of your letters, my Blackie, so I am at a loss for words. The weather has been quite decent here lately, with very little rain. The heat has been bearable, but I am almost used to that now. I am well and as happy as I possibly can be away from the ones I love. I sincerely hope and pray that you, Jackie and all the family are in the best of health and are as happy as possible. Give them all my regards, my one and only. Here is my daily special hug and kiss for our darling adorable Jackie, and to you, the most adorable wife, sweetheart and mother in all the world, I send my all. All my love, adoration and worship is yours, my sweet. Your slightest wish will be my command. I love you, miss you and want you. I am yours forever.

J.De Roxtro EM2/c   Everlastingly, your doting *Johnny*

Note on flap: "Did I ever tell you you have beautiful eyes, especially when you're angry. I love you."

Sunday, May 28, 1944. Took 12:15 bus in front of house, arrived in Springfield 1:00. Eddie came 1:10. Tax. Changed Jackie's dress. Dinner. Very good. Eddie took Mom & girls to see the park. Baby sleeping 3:15 to 5:30.Came back, baby awake. Went with Fran & Eddie Kugler to buy stuff [?] for supper. Had drink in tavern. Supper. Took 8:00 bus home. 9:00 home. Jackie sensed home. Went straight to office. 9:30 Joe & Angie Mama G & Tadone.

[Pavuvu Island, Russell Islands.]

Postmarked May 30, 1944, stamp upside down.   May 28, 1944

Somewhere

Hello, My Angel,

I love you, miss you and want you, more than words can possibly tell. Thoughts of you are continually running though my mind. Your beautiful image is always before me. To be with you again, holding you in my arms and kissing you is my one desire. I will never be happy until I am there. I hope and pray for us to be reunited again soon, and it can't come any too soon to suit me.

I received four letters today, my sweet, but none was from you. I got one each from your mother, my mother, Ralph, and a New Zealander. One of those Maoris I told you about. I am not in much of a writing mood, so I will merely answer your letter of the fourteenth, which I received yesterday. All the others can wait a day, or even a week.

This morning, because I didn't feel like writing, I went for a swim. I was down there about two hours, and when I returned, I took a shower and went to chow. Now, it will take me all afternoon to answer your letter. The water was almost too warm for swimming, but the cold shower felt good. It was quite refreshing.

In Ralph's letter, he said he almost froze his balls off the other night. He was under three blankets and was still cold. The days are very hot there, too. He seems happy tho.

Say, sweet, I thought you said that "Butch" was going to be there for a weekend, not a week or more. My mom, in her letter, said that she (Les) was still there one day during the week when she was down. It's a good thing you did buy those clothes for her, else she would have looked like an orphan.

You fooled me again, sweet, with those two stamps. I expected pictures again, but was pleasantly surprised to receive such a swell long letter. Thanks a million, sweet. This is just about the longest letter you have ever written to me, I think. I would have to go way back, in order to find a longer one. On the inside flap of the envelope you merely told me that you were too tired to mail this letter that night. I don't blame you, darling. It takes a few hours to write a letter like that, and you must have been tired. You also said that you love me, so I am satisfied. I love you.

I wonder why it is that Fran doesn't take better care of her child. Gee, it's a darn shame. Les would be a really beautiful child, if she had decent clothes, and had her hair taken care of. The poor kid can't help it, I suppose, but surely my dope of a sister could. I am willing to bet anyone that our daughter will never be in need of clothes, at least, as long as we can afford them. My lovely wife will see to that. I'm afraid that one of these days Fran and Eddie will separate. I have an idea that they don't get along any too well, any time. All they are doing is staying together, for the sake of Lesley Ann. She will be the goat, no matter what happens. It sure is tough, isn't it.

Boy, I'll bet Grace had her hands full, over at the circus with Lesley. But then, I guess they both had a swell time. Maybe you and I will be taking our little one to the next one. Wouldn't that be something?

It was swell of you to spend your valuable time, running around town, making purchases for our Mothers. My mom said the bag was swell, in her letter today. Honey, I still think you shouldn't have gotten those dresses for Les. But I suppose you would have felt lousy if you hadn't.

That niece of ours sort of pulled the wool over your eyes, a little. She has never been afraid of thunder or lightening. In fact, I don't think she ever was afraid of anything. She is more lonesome than anything else, and with Fran working, she's become worse. You did well in staying with her, though, my sweet, because a little love and understanding goes a long way with a child. Gosh, the way Fran neglects her is a crime. She really is a sweet child, and with the proper care, she would be marvelous. How would you like to have her, if something did happen between Ed & Fran? We may as well forget all about that, though.

Funny, but I had forgotten that you also had a new hat, too. Don't forget to send me a picture of yourself in that outfit. I'll bet our bed was a heck of a mess after those three had been playing on it for an hour. You could probably hear them a block away, too. But what the devil, let them enjoy themselves.

I guess that Fran never insisted that Lesley go to church. Neither Fran nor Eddie go, I guess, so Lesley doesn't either. It could be that she is sensitive about her clothing, too. I think I may remember that straw hat and bag that Grace used to wear. No, come to think of it, it was a white bag she had. The poor kid doesn't even know how to act in church, I guess. I don't know too much about it either, so I shouldn't be talking. I'll learn, though, when we start going together again. Les always did have a good appetite, whenever she was away from home. She used to eat plenty whenever she was at our place, and she would eat anything.

It sure was swell of you to tell the folks that I was sending them that stuff, but sweetheart, you shouldn't. You may say anything is from US, but not me, in person, even though it may make Mama G feel good.

Ann told me how you were just saying that all the mothers were receiving presents but you, when Jackie walked over to you with your gift. She said, "Isn't that just like a de Roxtro?" But I will forgive her this time, simply because she was so thoughtful and used such good judgment in getting you those earrings. I sure am glad you like them, angel. I never would have thought of anything like that. Your sister and I finally did surprise you that time, didn't we. Now who says I can't keep a secret? I love you, my sweet.

I'll bet Vene will catch the devil from my mother for not telling her that Lesley was there. I can well imagine her surprise. She sure does love her grandchildren but next to our little one, "Butch" is tops. You see, my mother and I practically brought both Lesley and Peter up. We did more for Pete than Les, though. Heck, he was with us for quite a few years. He's practically my son, or was, until he went to live with Carl & Nora.

Boy, the disappointment was written all over Joe, I bet, when you remained at home to entertain my mother. You, too, were a little put out, because you would have enjoyed the ride, even if it were crowded. Better luck next time, my lovely one. It's a wonder Fran even thought of Mothers Day and purchased that necklace and bracelet for her. She would have someone else do the work for her, too. I see where you and I will have to remain away from them. They will take advantage of our good nature, and we can't let anyone do that.

Sweetheart, I hope you will forgive me for making this so short, but I just can't seem to write, today. I will see what I can do with your letter again this week. I'm so darn sleepy I can hardly remain awake.

Goodnight, sweetheart, I love you, miss you and want you more as each day passes, slowly bringing us more close together. Give my regards to all. Here is my daily hug and kiss to Jackie, and millions more to you, the only girl in the world for me.

J.De Roxtro EM2/c   *Everlastingly, your adoring Johnny*

Note on flap: "Hi darling, I love you with all my heart, body and soul."

Monday, May 29, 1944. *Letter of May 17. Lovely day. Went downtown. Sandrian, pictures did not come out. Only 2 over-exposed. Shopped on way back. Bought 3 sun suits for Jackie, 2 training panties. Boxers.*

[Pavuvu Island, Russell Islands.]
Postmarked May 30, 1944, stamp upside down.   May 29, 1944

Somewhere

Hello, Dearest,

I love you, miss you, and want you more as each day passes, slowly bringing us more close to the day of our reunion. More than anything else, I want to be there, to remain with you forever. I want to hold you tenderly in my arms and kiss you. I want to tell you how much I love you. Sweetheart, I love you.

This won't be a very long letter, Lucia my love, because I won't have much time. I went to see the marine show, Pacific Panics, tonight, and after that, there was a show "The Son of Dracula." Both were not so hot, but the marine show was the best of the two. Included in it were a trio, singers; hillbilly musicians and a comedian. They put on a pretty good show, for the talent they had on hand, and most of the fellows enjoyed it. They work hard, anyway, and deserve a bit of credit.

No mail came today, my lovely one, so I have none to answer. I will try to do a little better tomorrow, as I think I may have a little more time. I sure didn't feel like writing yesterday.

Sweetheart, the first class rating of mine was posted on our bulletin board today, so I finally made one. It doesn't mean so very much, only eighteen dollars more a month, lots of added responsibilities, and more work.

Now, all I have to do is make another, then I can throw away the monkey suit and wear decent clothes. Then I can wear the fouled anchor, such as you wear on your coat. But to hell with all that, what I want to do is to get home.

Fitz came back today, and he said he would write and ask his brother to make that enlargement for you. He is in good health, and is quite happy out here. Vincent is still in the sick bay. He doesn't seem to be getting any better. About the only thing to do with him is send him back to the states to recuperate. When he does get back, he probably won't be allowed to go home, for quite awhile.

Give my fond regards to all the family and our friends. Here is my daily hug and kiss for Jackie, and many millions more to you, my wife, sweetheart and pal forever.

J.De Roxtro EM1/c   Everlastingly, your loving *Johnny*

Note on flap: "Sorry this is so short, darling. I'll do better tomorrow. Love."

Tuesday, May 30, 1944. Decoration day. Lovely day. Got up at 7:00. Left home at 9:30. Went to Mils, then stopped at Cat's. Saw parade. Came back. Had dinner at Mils. Came home. Put Jackie to sleep 1:45. Cooked. Mom and Mama G here with friends. Jackie awake 3:15. Went to Mils again. Took walk to store. Went back to Mil's 4:30. Stayed until five. Mama G & Tadone up for supper. Girls went to movies. Mom & Mama G went to St. Girard mtg.

[Pavuvu Island, Russell Islands.]
Postmarked May 31, 1944, stamp upside down.   May 30, 1944

Somewhere

Lovely Lucia:

Sweetheart, I love you, miss you and want you. Thoughts of you are forever racing through my mind, and your image is locked forever in my heart. To hold you tenderly in my arms and kiss you would be heavenly to me. I long to tell you how much I've missed you these past long months. Sweetheart, you are the only girl in the world for me. I could never feel for someone else the way I do for you. You are my wife, sweetheart, and companion. To make you happy is my desire. Wouldn't it be swell if we were able to be living together again, as man and wife, in our own little place. Gee, we would be so very happy, most of the time, anyway. There may be times when I will annoy you, or make you angry, my pet, but all you have to do to straighten me up is to mention the South Pacific to me. If anything will make me realize how much I love you, that will. Honey, I don't think I could ever help but realize that you are the sole object of my affections. Dearest one, each day that passes brings us closer to the day of our reunion. It just can't be so very much longer before I leave this damned rock. I love you more as each day passes.

No mail came for me, today, sweet, but Forbes received one from Ann. I have not seen him, but he sent word down to me. He wants me to ask you to tell Ann that he received her most wonderful letter, and will answer it as soon as he feels a little better. The medicine he is taking now makes him very weak, and he has terrible headaches. From what I hear, she really wrote him a love letter this time. You know, Lou, those letters from Ann do Vincent a devil of a lot of good. He receives a letter from Ann, and his morale is higher than ever. Those letters really do him a world of good. He's a swell fellow, and I hope he gets around to see us some time. Or maybe we can get down there, one of our vacations. Forbes also told his fellow to tell me that Ralph was now a private first class. I noticed that, on his letter that I received from him on Sunday. That really is swell, isn't it. Now maybe he will go ahead more rapidly. I sure hope he does, but it isn't very easy, once a fellow leaves the states. That is, unless a guy plays politics, and sucks around the higher-ups. I know, through experience. I got mine the hard way, and I know darn well that Ralph did, too. That brother of yours won't take any crap from anyone, and he won't get rates fast, but when he does, he knows that he has earned it. More power to him. He'll make out alright. I love you.

My lovely one, I don't know what to say. The weather is still rather nice, except for the heat. Did I tell you that Ralph said he had to use three blankets one night, and that he was still cold? I usually have to pull a blanket over me, in the wee hours of the morning, but never more than one. Plenty of nights I don't use any, though. I wont have to use any covers when I get home, though. I'll have my love to keep me warm. Do you think you would be able to sweet? After all, we are out of practice. Boy, I sure don't think if would

180

take very long to become experts again, do you. Gee, I hope I'm not too old to be able to satisfy you. The way I feel most all the time, though, I don't think we will have to worry about that. Right now, just writing about it, I'm in the mood and ready. So, perhaps it would be best to stop.

Sweetest girl in the world, I wish I could truthfully tell you that I would be there by the fourth of July but I can't. The scuttlebutt says that we will be in Hueneme between the twenty-fifth of June and the third of July, but as far as I know, there is no sound basis for it. Someone is supposed to have received a letter from someone already there, saying that we were expected between those times. Something is bound to happen soon, though, so I'm hoping and praying that we'll go home.

Well, I have to fill this page, now, so how will I begin? Oh, yes, something new and exciting has come to me. It's the greatest thing that ever happened to anyone. It's a grand feeling, and everyone should have it. Maybe you have found it, too. It will never grow old or worn out, either, and it gets better as the days roll by. It is love, my darling, and that's really worth writing home about. I'm in love, and have been, for quite awhile now, but it's still new and exciting. I love you, my dearest one, more than life itself. Gee, I wonder how long it will be, before I can hold your sweet loveliness close to me. Soon, it will be two years since I've seen you. Gosh, that's a long time ago, isn't it. This damned war sure raised Cain with our married life, didn't it. But never mind, my lovely Lou, I will try to make up to you for all you've missed. I will do my best to make you happy, forever. Say you never regret having become my wife. I love you.

Give my fond regards to all the family and any of our mutual friends you may happen to meet. Here is my daily hug and kiss for our darling daughter Jackie. To you, most precious angel, I can only send my love, adoration, and millions of hugs and kisses. You are mine, and I am yours, forever. Did I ever tell you how beautiful you are? You are magnificent. I love you.

J.De Roxtro EM1/c   Everlastingly, your darling *Johnny*

Note on flap: "Hi, Sweet, who do I love? My lovely Lucia. I'll always love her. How's Mickey?"

Wednesday, May 31, 1944. Letters of May 22,23. Letter from Ralph. Very warm. Jackie out in yard all morning. Wore sun suit. Washed clothes. Had nap after lunch. Out in yard again. Mill and Judy came over. Girls not coming home. Went to Newark. Wrote to Ralph.

[Pavuvu Island, Russell Islands.]
Postmarked June 1, 1944, stamp upside down.

May 31, 1944

Somewhere

Hello, Beautiful:

I love you with all my heart, body, and soul. I miss you more as each day passes, slowly but surely bringing us more close to the day of our reunion. I want you so very much, dearest one. Mere words could never describe how much I want to take you tenderly in my arms and kiss you. You are mine, darling, and no one will ever take your place in my heart. When you entered, I locked it up and threw away the key. Continually, my thoughts are of you. Your sweet and lovely image is forever before me, and I see your smiling countenance always. You are the most wonderful girl in the world, Lucia, and I am proud to be your husband. In all my life, I was never so happy as I was during those all too short four and one half months when we were together. My happiness won't be complete until we are again living together, as husband and wife should. I want to be able to kiss you good morning and goodnight, and all through the day. I desire to be near you, so that whenever I feel like it, I can hold you in my arms and tell you of my love and adoration. I want to feel the warmth of your young body, as we embrace. I am hungry for all that you can give me, angel mine. Nothing or no one will ever be able to satisfy that hunger but you. We were meant for each other, and together we would be, if it weren't for this darned war.

I wonder how long it will be before we are together again, Lucia? Gee, from all I see and hear, it can't be very much longer now. Hell, we have been separated for close to two years now, and it's time we met again. Who knows, a few more jobs out here, and you may decide that you can get along quite well without me. I can't say that I would blame you, either. But I won't worry about that yet, because I am sure you love me. I probably am more certain of your love than you are of mine, but I can assure you that you are my one and only true love.

The battalion is having a contest to pick a Mrs. 15th C.B., and a Miss. In order to compete, we must submit a picture of our wives or sweethearts, and they will be placed on exhibition in our Recreation Hall. The two winning girls will each receive a bouquet of flowers, and the two of us who submit the pictures will receive a five-dollar bill. I don't know who the judges will be. But I want you to know that you needn't expect any flowers because I won't put a picture of you in the contest. I wouldn't care to have this bunch of wolves gaping at you, and passing all sorts of comments. You are my private property and I refuse to share you with anyone. I do show your pictures to my tent-mates, but not to the whole gang. They are a

182

hungry bunch, naturally, and I don't see how they could help from being. I worship you.

I am not going to finish this letter right now, my sweetheart. I will wait and see if there is any mail this afternoon. If there is, and I should receive one from you, I will answer it. I started this right after lunch, and won't be able to finish anyway before I go to work. So, my adorable one, I now bid you adieu until later. No mail came for me, today, but I did receive that carton of gum from Vene. It is Beechnut, too, and it is nice and fresh. In just a few seconds, there were about six packs gone, so now I have it put away. I don't mind the fellows helping themselves, but if it got around that I had gum, half the boys in the outfit would be down here. It is very seldom that we get any down here.

All the boys came back from Island X Prime today, so maybe something will happen soon. I certainly do hope so. I'm tired of living in the tropics. I want to go home and quickly.

I was talking to Frosty today, and his daughter never mentioned receiving the picture from you. Maybe that's because she didn't know any of the fellows in it. Or perhaps she just didn't think of it when she was writing. He will find out, though and Ill let you know all about it.

Well, my sweetheart, I am as well and happy as I can possibly be, away from you and Jackie. I hope and pray that you, Jackie and the family are in the best of health and are happy. It rained quite hard this afternoon, and I was sort of looking forward to receiving a letter from you, but none came. Naturally, I was a little disappointed, but after all, I can't expect one every day. I am lucky you write as often as you do. I think, because you surely must have plenty to do, without writing to me.

I would like to make another date with you, but I'm afraid I would have to stand you up again. So far, I haven't stood you up, but I sure would have to travel fast, in order to make it, wouldn't I. I could make one for the fourth of July, but I won't, sweetheart, because I may not even be able to make it by then. Let's see, I will ask you for a date for the first nite I am in town. That's definite, and I do hope you will be able to manage it.

Give my regards to all the family and our friends, angel mine. Here is my daily hug and kiss for Jackie, and all my love and adoration to you, the most wonderful wife and sweetheart in the world. I love you, miss you, and want you.

J. De Roxtro EM1/c   Everlastingly, your loving *Johnny*

Note on flap: "Hi, Sweet, all the love in the world is ours. I want you. I'm hungry."

Thursday, June 1, 1944. *Letter of May 25, and allotment check for $80. Very hot. Jackie out in yard with sun suit. Nap. Catherine and Carol Ann over in afternoon. Ice cream. Hot night.*

[Pavuvu Island, Russell Islands.]
Postmarked June 2, 1944, stamp upside down.

June 1, 1944
Same hole

My Gorgeous Darling:

All my love is yours. Without you I doubt if I could go on, out here in this uninhabited part of the world. I think I would go nuts if my thoughts weren't continually of you. Your image, which is constantly before me, keeps me from seeing things I don't care to see. Having such beauty always before me I overlook the un-nice things. Therefore, I see nothing but beauty. Dearest one, I love you more as each day passes, slowly but surely bringing us more close to the day of our re-union, the day that our happiness will get a new start. How I hope and pray that that day will come soon. I miss you and want you. I long to take you tenderly in my arms and kiss you. To look at you will be compensation enough for all I've put up with. I long to be able to talk to you once again. Most precious wife and daughter, you two are all I have, and how I miss you. How pleasant it will be, when we three will be together in our own home, all alone, in a paradise of our own making. Sweetheart, my happiness won't be complete until I am able to hold you in my arms and tell you of my love and adoration. You're swell.

Gee, Sweet, I have just returned from the show. The picture was, "A guy named Joe." I thought it was pretty good, but I hear a lot of the fellows complaining about it. They seem tired of seeing war pictures, and I don't blame them, but personally I think this one was different, somehow. For some reason or other this picture made me think, and I liked it. If I remember correctly, you have already seen it, and you enjoyed it also. Of course, I may be mistaken, but it seems to me that you mentioned it. Spencer Tracy and Irene Dunne played in it, I think. Maybe the fellows that are dissatisfied just don't understand. There isn't any use trying to explain to them, either, so I just let them rave on. Blosser is like that. He complains about most all the pictures we have, and every once in awhile I set him down. For instance, he won't like classical music, or any picture that is a little deep, and that's the kind I like. I never argue about anything, though, because I know you would rather I didn't. I don't let anyone tread on me, either. More than once I've been tempted to sock someone. Gosh, darling, I wonder what I would do out here, if I didn't have you to guide me. I love you more than life itself.

Today I received one letter. It was from Marjorie Frances (x), Vene's girlfriend. You have met her, I think. She assists her father in managing the business. She acknowledged receipt of the order for your flowers, and thanked me for the congratulations I sent with the order. You see, Vene told me in one of her letters that she had married. Marge said that her husband was also in the Navy. I don't know the guy she married, and I doubt very much if I would recognize her if I saw her. Here's hoping you liked the flowers I sent you for your birthday. Those cards were made by a fellow here in my tent. He was not working, so I asked him to make me a couple of cards, in a joking mood, and when I came in for lunch that day, lo and behold, here on my bunk were two cards. One was for Forbes, and the other for me. Honey, I hope you don't mind because we both sent you two sweethearts roses, but Forbes prefers them, and so do I. And, of course, I know that you, the most wonderful girl in the world, would rather have them than anything else, so, as you prefer them, I prefer them, and Forbes prefers them, there they are.

Naturally I would much rather receive letters from you, but it seems that every other week I get them. If I don't receive one soon, I won't have one to answer on Sunday, so here's hoping I do. I sure do love to see letters arrive from you, my lovely sweetheart. The weather has returned to normal lately. For about three weeks it had rained very little and for the past few days it has rained almost continually. Heck, I never mind the weather anymore. I guess I'm used to it now.

As usual, I am in the best of health, and as happy as I possibly can be away from my loved ones. I sincerely hope and pray that you, Jackie and the rest of the family are in the best of health and are happy. I'll have to sign off now, sweet, because it's time for lights out. Give my regards to all the family and our friends. Here's my daily hug and kiss for Jackie, and a million hugs and kisses for you, the most wonderful wife and sweetheart in the world. I love you, miss you and want you.

J.De Roxtro EM1/c   Everlastingly, your adoring *Johnny*

Friday, June 2, 1944. Letters of May 20,21,24. 10th issue of C-Breeze. Check for $50. Brought Jackie to Doctor's. Too hot for injection. Weighs 25 lbs. on way home bought shoes for Jackie - 4E, and some undershirts. Hot.

[Pavuvu Island, Russell Islands.]
Postmarked June 3, 1944, stamp upside down.   June 2, 1944
                                                      Somewhere

Hello, Beautiful One:

I love you, miss you and want you, more than mere words can say. I long to hold you tenderly in my arms once again and kiss you. Sweetheart, if only I could be there with you. I am darn sick and tired of these damned

Islands. More than anything else in the world, I desire to be there with you. One of these days, we will be together again and then, only then, will our happiness be complete. That day cannot possibly come too soon to suit me, either. I am ready and have been ready for many, many months. You are mine, sweetest one, and I am yours. We belong together, and should be together, now and always. Lovely Lucia, you will never know how much I have missed you these past two years. More and more, as time slowly drags by, my desire to be with you increases. May the war end soon, so that you and I together, will be able to raise our family as it (they, sometime) should be raised. I never will be happy until I am there with you. I adore you.

Today I received three letters. One was from Mr. Nuttle of the Y.M.C.A. He invited me to dine with the Rotary Club as his guest, the first Wednesday I am there. Naturally, I will not accept. I will have too much to do at home. A very belated letter came from Ann. It was postmarked the twenty-ninth of March, sent properly, via airmail and I just received it. Now where that one has been is certainly a mystery. Besides those two, I got a nice sweet one from my loving wife. It was written the nineteenth and posted in Harrison on the twenty-third. The train Ann took that day sure was slow in arriving at its destination, wasn't it. No wonder I went almost a week without getting any mail from my sweetheart. It just goes to show you, honey, that if you want something done right, you must do it yourself. I don't mind this one so much, though, because it was only delayed four days, and that isn't so very bad. Gee, they used to take a lot longer than that, didn't they. Gosh, honey, how I wish I could tell you all this, instead of writing it. But then I wouldn't have it to write (or talk) about, would I. Then I would be able to make love to you all over again. Gee, that will be swell.

I most humbly beg your pardon for making your letters so short lately, Lou, but I find it quite difficult to find something to write about. This one will probably end on this page, because of the above, and because it is almost time for lights out. Our tent is the only one still lit up, so it must be close.

I am well, my angel, and I will do all I can to remain in the pink. I hope and pray that you, our daughter, and the family are well and as happy as possible. How I long to be there to see just how well you are.

Goodnight, lovely one. Give my regards to the family and all our friends. Here is my daily hug and kiss for our most adorable Jackie. She sure is a swell kid, and I want to see her so very much. To you, my wife, most precious darling, I would like to send my all. I want to be with you and do my best to make you extremely happy. I desire you.

J.De Roxtro EM1/c   *Everlastingly, your Johnny*

Note on flap: *"Hi Toots! All the love in the world is ours. Here's a kiss for Mickey."*

Saturday, June 3, 1944. *No letters. Fred Camisa died. Got up seven o'clock. Cleaned. Jackie in yard with Mom. After nap took her to Mil's. 2:00 I left for my permanent at Bonne's. 2:30-5:45 Jackie would not eat cereal. Gave her egg. Left at 7:00*

[Pavuvu Island, Russell Islands.]

Postmarked June 5, 1944, stamp upside down.   June 3, 1944

Somewhere

Hello Sweetheart:

    I love you, miss you and want you. More than anything else in the world, I desire to be there with you, holding you in my arms and kissing you. Visions of you are always before me, my dearest wife, and my thoughts are of you constantly are mine. Sorry my beloved one, but it is almost time for lights out, so this will have to be real short. I will do better tomorrow, though. I promise that.

    Today I received a Father's Day card from your daughter, a letter each from my lovely, most adorable wife, and from Fan. Yours was written the sixteenth, sweet and was posted the nineteenth. That will be the one I will answer tomorrow, as it is the oldest I have.

    Enclosed with this letter you will find another issue of our paper. Gosh, I wish there were more minutes for me to write, but I can't finish. I'm working late the last couple of days. I love you, miss you and want you more as each day slowly passes. Goodnight, sweetheart.

J.DeRoxtro EM1/c   *Everlastingly, your adoring* *Johnny*

June 4, 1944 – Allies enter Rome.

Sunday, June 4, 1944. *Took 11:14 train to Newark. Took no. 11 bus to Elizabeth and bus no. 28 & 8 to Roselle Park, Pershing Ave. 1:00 met by Fran and Leslie Ann, Eddie off golfing. Fran packed lunch, sandwiches, hard boiled eggs, pickles, olives. Went to Warinanco Park. Found empty court. Played tennis 1:30. Ate at 2:00. Stopped at 2:45. Had soda & ice cream. Went back to Fran's. Shopped at grocery store to buy supper. Eddie pulls up just as we got to door. Fan & I prepared supper. Didn't realize it was only 4:30. Stayed until 7:00. Eddie drove us to Elizabeth for bus home at 9:00. Joe & Angie here.*

[Pavuvu Island, Russell Islands.]

Postmarked June 5, 1944, two stamps upside down.   June 4, 1944

Somewhere

Most Lovable Lucia:

    I love you, dear one, with my heart, body and soul. How I miss you,

187

especially on these long Sunday afternoons. There is so much that we could do, if we were only together. Most of all, though, I want to be up in our room, alone with you, making love to my gorgeous wife. We belong together, sweetheart, and should be with each other, always. I want so very much to hold you close to me. I want to feel the warmth of your young body as it presses close to mine. I want to feel our lovely luscious lips pressing against mine. Sweetheart, I am hungry and I don't mean for food. Love is what I am hungry for and only your love will ever be able to satisfy me. I only hope that I will be able to do the same for you. Gee, honey, I wonder how much longer I will have to remain on these damnable islands. Wouldn't it be swell if we were reunited this summer? I'm hoping and praying for that day to come soon. I love you more each day.

There was no mail today, but I don't care so very much, as long as I have a couple to answer. Today, I will answer the one I received yesterday, as that is the oldest I have. Many letters should arrive from you this week, because I received only two last week. It's rather peculiar the way your letters come, isn't it. One week I receive plenty and the next, hardly any. Oh well, as long as they come, I will try to be satisfied.

The fellows and I worked around the tent his morning fixing things up a little, so I didn't write any. This is my first for the day. All the others will have to wait. You are first, and most important on my list, always. My mom comes second, then your sisters, and anyone else who writes to me. I have quite a few to write, too, but I don't care, as long as I am able to continue my unbroken chain of letters to you. Boy, I came darn close to breaking it last night, but I did have time to write one page. That's better than nothing. I no sooner finished it, than the lights went out. I even had to address the envelope today. Gosh, angel, I love you so very much.

There seems to be no scuttlebutt going around the past few days, sweet. I guess the fellows are tired of thinking up stuff and nonsense. Some of them really have an imagination, judging from the stuff they put out. I would like to tell you when to expect me, but I just can't. For awhile I was quite certain of being with you this summer, but now, I'm not so sure. Maybe you had better figure around November or December. There has been nothing definite upon which to place my conclusions, but maybe I am a little blue and disappointed today. I had a date with my one and only for the day after tomorrow and I couldn't keep it. I will never make another definite date unless I am absolutely sure of keeping it. It would have been grand celebrating your birthday with you, but it wasn't to be. Maybe we will be in each other's arms soon, lovely one, then we can celebrate all we want to.

Say, darling, thanks loads for the Father's Day card. It's swell. You know, I had forgotten there was such a day. I'll love you eight days a week when I see you.

It has been quite nice here today, not too hot, with a nice gentle breeze. I went for a swim for about a half hour this morning and it really felt good. It wasn't so warm as last week and was more refreshing. Gee, I love you, Lou.

That's about all there is to tell you about myself and this place, so I will now do my best to answer your latest letter. Thanks a million for the kiss, angel mine. As I've said so many times before, I intend to return them all, in person, with interest, when I next see you. That's one debt that I will gladly repay. Do you think fifty per cent interest will be enough? I can almost feel your sweet lips pressing against mine right now. And John Jr. is getting bigger all the time. In fact, right now he is all set to go for Mickey. I wonder how she will react to him this time? They always got along fairly well together before, so I have an idea they will again.

By the way, sweet, you never told me whether my predictions about Mickey were correct. Let's see, I said something would happen about the sixth. Was I right? I'm going in to see her, regardless, when I can. I think she will be glad to see me, even though you never mention her in any of your letters. Doesn't she ever wish I were there, or miss me at all? She should because I miss her, and all the fun we had together. Here's a kiss for her. Tell her I wish, hope and pray that I will be seeing her soon.

On the inside flap of the envelope you have, "Darling husband, I love you with all my heart." The same goes from me to you, too, my lovely one, but you can include the words body and soul. It's swell being in love with a person like you. I have someone to be proud of, besides someone to love and adore. You're tops.

This letter of yours is only four pages, sweet, and there isn't much in it that I can answer, but I will do my best. Even that isn't good enough to suit me. I sure do wish I could do better. Maybe I could if only there was something to write about.

Sweetest wife, you are doing much too much for Lesley Ann. You will never be repaid for your trouble, except maybe in the satisfaction you yourself derive from it and maybe the pleasant way in which "Butch" herself shows her appreciation. She sure is a swell kid, and she does like to look nice. Too bad Fran doesn't take more and better care of her. Darn it, that sister of mine is nuts. With a beautiful daughter such as Les, she doesn't seem to give a darn what happens. She never was any too ambitious with her care of the child, but now that she is working I guess she is even worse. I can, therefore, well imagine the condition of the blond hair. You are too fussy, sweet. But I suppose you want to feel proud of her when you take her out, too. She sure is a beauty. She takes pride and interest in her appearance, too. Maybe that's why she at first didn't want to go to church, that Sunday. Then, after you dressed her up, and she was satisfied with her appearance, she was more than pleased to show off. You know, sweet, I wouldn't mind having her as our own to bring up. I'm quite sure you would want to give her everything you possibly could. But we may have enough of our own, without bothering about someone else's. That is, of course, if I manage to get there before I'm too old. Tell me, sweet, would you be too disappointed if you weren't able to be a mother again? It would not be pleasant to think about, so let's not. As far as I know, I am quit able to take care of all that, for awhile, anyway. Plenty of time to discuss that later. I've got to get home first, anyway. You're beautiful, darling.

I sure am pleased to learn that Les made friends with the Lavada girls. I imagine that she really enjoyed it, too. You know, I don't think she ever had very many friends, little ones, to play with. So, therefore, I imagine she was inclined to be a little bossy. I hope not, though. It would have been swell if you could have sent me a picture of all the kids that I used to know. They probably are quite grown up now, and would be hard for me to recognize.

While on the subject of snapshots, honeybunch, I haven't received any of you lately, and I sure would appreciate one. I love my wife very much, you know, and I never will have enough of her. You know what, sweet, I began writing this right after lunch, and it's now a quarter of four. I may not even finish this short love letter before supper. I must write to my mother today, too. Oh, well, I guess I'll have plenty of time. I've got to shave today, too. In case you're interested. I now scrape my face twice a week. Boy, that really is something isn't it. I intend to gradually get to the point of doing it daily. I know you would prefer me to.

Lucia, my darling, you must be trying to replenish my sister's child's wardrobe, the way you are purchasing clothes. Hell, I don't care, but why should you spend your small amount, when both her parents are working and could afford to better than you? Maybe you will shame them into buying some decent clothes for her. I sure hope you do. I know you like to buy clothes, though, whether they're for yourself or not, so go ahead and enjoy yourself. Don't forget to let me know how Fran reacts to it, though, when she comes for the problem child? She sure is a honey, and everyone must like her. She would think of calling that dress her twin dress, wouldn't she. As most women are, she is vain. My lovely wife isn't, though, for some reason or other. She is vain, but not like other women. But no matter how she is, I love her with all my *heart. She is mine, forever.*

Those two children of yours were not jealous of each other's possessions, my sweet, were they? I'll bet that little one of ours will surely put up a battle for anything she really wants, and Les would be inclined to be stubborn, too. You are the judge, and offered a consolation to Jackie, but she still wasn't any too pleased. She must be a humdinger. That string of babble that Jackie let fly whenever she noticed "Butch" with the package probably was cuss words. Sounds as if maybe she has a temper.

I must have more letters coming from you, sweet, because you haven't mentioned getting the camera back, in any of the ones I have so far received. Maybe you overlooked that, though. I will be anxiously awaiting those snapshots, sweet one, so please don't delay in sending them. Have a couple taken of yourself, too, will you?

What else could you say but yes, when Fran asked you to keep Leslie for the week? Darn it, she's taking advantage of you. Watch her, sweet, she's a tricky one.

Vince felt quite well for a few days, but last night he felt bad again and now he will be detained up there for a week or more again. Damn it, they ought to send that poor guy home. He is no good to us out here, and the longer they keep him, the harder it will be for him to be cured.

So long until tomorrow my sweet. Give my regards to all. Here is my daily hug and kiss for Jackie and my all to you. You are more desirable hourly.

JdeRoxtroEM1/C   *Everlastingly your adoring*   *Johnny*

June 5, 1944 - The first mission by B-29 Superfortress bombers occurs as 77 planes bomb Japanese railway facilities at Bangkok, Thailand. Ninety eight US B-29 Superfortress bombers flew from India to attack the railway yards in Bangkok which had become the Japanese command center on the Southeast Asian front. It was a 2,261 mile round trip. Only 77 bombers made it to Bangkok, the others having to turn back because of engine problems. Bangkok had been subject to air strikes since the Japanese takeover on December 8, 1941. The bombing raids continued until the end of the war.

Monday, June 5, 1944. Letters of May 26,27,30. Mil calls at 8:00. Mom home from work. Took 9:14 train to New York. Stopped at 14th St. and went up to 32nd St. Bought shoes, bag, red checked pinafore for Jackie, blue quilted house coat for Ann. Missed 6:45 train. Took 7:30 train. Home by 8:30. Very tired. Read letters. Stiff joints.

Somewhere in the South Pacific

[Pavuvu Island, Russell Islands.]
Postmarked June 7, 1944, stamp upside down.

June 5, 1944

Somewhere

Hello Sweetheart:

I love you, miss you and want you. You are always in my heart, and thoughts of you are continually running through my mind. I miss you more as each day passes, slowly but surely bringing us more close to the day of our reunion. I want you, too, my darling, so very much. Won't it be swell when we are able to wrap our arms around each other and press our lips together, in a long, loving embrace. Gosh, sweet, when I think of all the swell times we've missed sine I left you, it makes me kind of mad. I should be there with you, doing my best to make you happy. Darn it, sweet, more than anything else in the word, I want to be there with you. I love you so very much, Lucia, my lovely one.

Darling, do you ever tire of reading the same stuff, over and over again? Let me know if you do, and I will skip the beginning of my letters. They are almost all alike, and I know they shouldn't be, but there seems to be nothing I can do about it. Maybe I won't have to write much longer. I sure hope I'll see you soon.

I went to the show last night, and boy, were there a mess of short subjects. None of them were any good, either. However, I sat through them, and then the feature picture. It was "Standing Room Only," and was kind of screwy, but not so bad. At least it wasn't one of those war pictures. I don't remember who played in it, but you probably do. It has been raining quite hard ever since I came from work, but it has just about stopped now, so maybe I'll go to the show tonight. That is, of course, if I am able to finish this letter. I don't know what's playing.

No mail came for me again today, my love. You know, I really expect at least one letter from you every time there is mail, even though I know darn well that I should not do so. There is some mail most every day, but as you can't possibly have time to write daily, I shouldn't expect them. But after I look and see that I have none, I figure well, maybe I'll receive one or two tomorrow. My disappointment is only temporary, my angel, so don't you worry your pretty little head about it. Whenever I do get mail from you, I am practically riding or sailing on air. Gee, it's swell, knowing that you love me and take time to write to me. Darling, you are the best in the world.

I am quite well, as usual, my pet, and am as happy as I possibly can be away from you and our Jackie. My happiness never will be complete until I am there with you to stay. I sincerely hope and pray that you and your daughter are happy and in the best of health. I hope you don't mind when I refer to Jackie as your child, sweet, but I've been away for such a long time and have had nothing whatever to do with her upbringing, that she will never really be mine. All I did was sow the seed, and you did all the rest. I know that you don't want me to write these things, but sometimes, I feel that I must. I don't want to feel this way, either, but after all, the primary training has been done, and you have really done an excellent job. I am real proud of you, sweetheart, and am anxiously awaiting the day when I can actually see the splendid job you've done. I had better stop this right now. I'm beginning to feel worse than usual.

Sweetheart, have you made any tentative plans yet as to what we will do when I arrive home? Let's just stay home and try to make up for all the loving we've missed. Wouldn't it be swell if we had a little place all our own, and could do whatever we pleased, without thinking about anyone or anything, excepting our own immediate happiness? I can dream, can't I? I adore you.

Everything here is about the same, my love. There is plenty of scuttlebutt going the rounds, but none of it is true. As yet, there isn't anything official for me to report to you. Something has to happen quite soon, or else the fellows will crack up. We can't possibly go on much longer, without something happening. I sure do hope for the best, but anything may, and can, happen. Boy, I sure am glad that I have you to think of. If it weren't for that, I think I would have gone nuts long ago. As the days drag by, I find myself wishing more and more that I were there with you. You would be surprised if I told you some of the things I think about. They wouldn't look right on paper, so I won't even attempt to tell you about them. I often think of the times we used to go for those rides when I was supposed to be working, and the potato chips at Madison, the hot dogs and beer at the Red Star, ice cream at Howard Johnsons, the weekly trips to Roselle Park, and oh, so much more. Those most pleasant nights we used to spend on the sun porch and our goodnights standing at the door, gee, they sure do affect me, almost as bad as they used to then. Thoughts of those Sunday afternoon rides are nice to think of, too. Too bad I had to work.

I often wonder how it's going to be, sitting there in the living room with you, after Jackie has been put to bed, both of us listening to the radio, and making love. Or how nice it will be to lie down to sleep in a nice clean, comfortable bed, with you by my side. Gee, it sure will be swell. Do you ever think of things like that?

My source of information has just about run dry, my angel, so I think this will be my last page. I could answer your letter, but I think I had better wait until tomorrow or Wednesday. I may not have as much to write about, so answering a letter will do the job of making one a wee bit longer to you.

Sweetheart, you are the most wonderful wife and mother in the world. How much I miss and want you, you will never know. I long to let my hands roam over your lovely body as they used to. I yearn to feel your lovely warm lips against mine. Sweet, I want to be more than a letter-writing husband. I want to perform all the duties of a husband and be a father to our sweet little one. I love you, Lucia.

Give my regards to all the family and our friends. Here's my daily hug and kiss

for our Jackie. To you, I wish I were able to send myself. I worship you.

J.De Roxtro EM1/c   Everlastingly, your adoring *Johnny*

Note on flap: *"Hi, Sweet! I sure do hope I'm with you soon. Here's a kiss for Mickey."*

[Pavuvu Island, Russell Islands.]
Letter to Mary Petrone, postmarked June 7, 1944   June 5, 1944

Somewhere

Hello, Mom:

I received your letter of May nineteenth one day last week, and haven't had time until today to answer it. Thanks loads for taking time out to write to me. It's swell, knowing that you folks at home think of me.

I am, and have always been, in the best of health. Heck, they can't make me sick or anything. I'm capable of adjusting myself to any condition, so I am one of the lucky ones. I'm as happy as I possibly can be in these conditions, too. It sure is swell, knowing that you folks at home are all well. Give my special regards to your parents, will you? And tell Tadone I wish him the best and a speedy recovery with that arm. Give Mama Gee a tch tch for me, will you? They are a grand couple, and I like them a lot. Every one of my in-laws are really fine people, and I am anxiously awaiting the day when I am able to see them all once again.

Lou sent me a picture of Mike, little Michael and Tadone that was taken on Easter Day. All three of them look well. Little Michael sure does look like a perfect gentleman to me. Lou says he is swell and got along good with Jackie.

It was thoughtful of Jo not to visit you because she had a cold, but that would never keep me away from your home. What the heck, she could have come, and stayed away from Jackie. My Easter Day was the same as any other Sunday, Mom. I did have a bit of luck that night, though, so it was a good day for me. I would rather Lou told you of my luck. She probably has, by this time, anyway.

I'm glad Ralph was able to send some pictures home. It helps you a lot, and you are more certain that he is well. He's a swell guy, and will make out alright, so don't you worry about him. He is in a safe place, too. The place he is in is even more safe than this and I'm more safe than I would be jaywalking around town there. You know where he is, and also where I am, I think.

You know, Mom, it's rather funny and hard to understand, but I never did worry about either Jackie or Lou. Of course, before I heard the news, I was a little anxious, but never really worried. After the baby was born, I was so sure that Lou would do everything in her power to make Jackie healthy and happy that I never worried. Before the child came, I was sure I could depend on you and the girls, in the same way, too. Even when my buddy received that letter from Ann, merely mentioning that Jackie had the accident, I wasn't worried. All I wanted was to get the whys and wherefores from Lou. You see, I have such implicit faith in Lou and her mother that I refuse to worry at all. I realize, too, that I couldn't do any good from over here, so I let nothing bother me. Believe me, it's bad enough having to stay away from my loved ones without worrying about them, too. If I let myself worry, I would have gone nuts long ago, and I can't do that, because I have responsibilities at home.

Your daughter is a swell mother and I am real proud of her. She must take after her mother and her grandmother. They both did swell jobs raising their children, and my wife will, too. I sure do wish I could be there to help her. But maybe I would spoil the little one, even more than her Uncle Joe does. He's a swell guy, Mom. You should be proud of him. He's tops.

You can bet your boots that I will be satisfied with Lou's cooking when I get home. The practice she is getting now will never hurt her, though, so let her go ahead and do it all. Don't give her too much help with the little girl, either. There's no use letting her depend on you too much.

It's great of you to help the red cross, Mom. They sure do need plenty of help. The work they are doing is important, but don't overtax your strength in doing things for them or anyone. If everyone would do just a little, well, it would be so much easier for all.

By this time the weather should be nice and warm, and the flowers all in bloom and everything so nice and green. Gee, it would sure look good to me. How are your nice roses, Mom? I forget just when they are due to bloom, but I mean are the plants healthy?

Thanks loads for all you have done, are doing, and will do for Lou and Jackie. It's really swell of you. Give my regards to all our friends and especially to Mama G and Tadone. I'm hoping and praying that I will see you all soon. So long and good luck.

J.De Roxtro EM1/c   Your son, *Johnny*

June 6, 1944 – D-Day, Normandy.

Tuesday, June 6, 1944. Letters May 28 & 29. 11th issue of C-Breeze. Mom went to Funeral. Went to work in afternoon. Washed clothes. Jackie in yard. Was hanging clothes when Cat came 3:30. Brought me roll of Film. Stayed until 4:00. Started cooking. Roses came 4:15. At 4:45 took bus to town to get mocha cake. Camera. Ralph's pictures. Film. Received only Gracie's gift after supper. Sailor men of soap.

[Pavuvu Island, Russell Islands.]
Postmarked June 8, 1944, stamp upside down.   June 6, 1944

Somewhere

Hello, Darling:

Today, of all days, I wanted to be there with you, but as long as I couldn't, I hope you had a most pleasant and happy day, and enjoyed every minute of it. If I had been there today, my sweet, you would really have had a happy birthday. I am wondering what I would have done for you if I had been there. Would I have had the roses delivered, or would I have done something else? Who knows, perhaps you would have received a nice fur coat, and the roses. I'll tell you what, my love – you let me know how much your choice for a coat is, and I will send you a money order for it. Let's see, though. I had better make a ceiling price on it. Now I'm stuck. I have no idea what a coat is worth. Gee, how can we arrange this? I know, we can consider the coat as a birthday and Xmas present. Just let the roses do for your birthday, and I promise to get you a fur coat for Christmas. Would that be satisfactory, my lovely one? You let me know, and I'll do whatever you say. I can, after the fifth of July, send you two or three hundred, if you think you can do better during the summer. The prices are usually lower during the hot months, aren't they? Ah, I have come to a solution. You pick out what you want, up to three hundred bucks, and I will see that you get what you want. If you want something better, well, it will take a little longer, but I will take care of it. Now, my beloved angel, you know how much I desire to be with you today. I'm not kidding about the coat, either, sweet. All you have to do is inform me, before July the fifth, the price of the one you want. If it is three hundred or less, you will have it by the twentieth. That's the best I can do for your birthday, Lucia my love, but maybe I can do better for Xmas. Besides, you would want your new coat before Christmas, wouldn't you. Gee, I wish I knew the range of prices in those things. Darn it, I'm afraid the three hundred class is kind of low. Do you think you could get a fairly decent looking one for that, sweet? I'll give you another suggestion. You look around in the class I mention, and if they aren't

good enough, let me know how much more I have to save. Come to think of it, you should be able to get a fairly nice coat. Do your best, my love.

My beloved darling, I love you so very much. I miss you more today than I ever have. Sweetest wife in all the world, I long to hold you tenderly in my arms and kiss you. I want to be able

to kiss you good morning, stay with you all day, and retire with you at night. Those nights will be most pleasant, darling. Then, I will be all alone with you. I will make love to you as I never have before. I will hold your lovely body close to mine. The warmth and softness of you will do the things to me I dream they will. You and I will reach the peak of marital bliss, sweetheart, and we will be happy. It's funny, but never before have I felt about you as I do tonight. Honestly, my sweet, I am more happy tonight than I ever have been, since our last parting. Sweetest girl in the world, you are mine, and I am yours, forever. Gee, if we could only have been together tonight, we would have been really happy. Most loveable wife, I love you, I miss you, and I want you. Since being away from you, I have never been quite in the mood I am this evening. It must be because it's your birthday.

I just happened to think of something, sweet. You had better save this letter, sweetest wife and other in the world, because it may be the only one that starts differently than the rest. Now, I will tell you – I love you, miss you and want you, more than anything else in the world. You are mine, and I am yours forever. I long to hold you tenderly in my arms and kiss you, to feel the warmth of your tender young body as it presses close to mine. The feel of your lips against mine will be heavenly. Your pulse beat will entwine with mine, as we make love to each other. Oh, my dearest wife, if only words could really tell you how I feel toward you. To be with you again is my one desire. I don't care if we are the poorest family in the world, we will have our love and it will carry us through, more happy than any other couple ever was. My darling, I am proud to have you as my wife. You are the most desirable girl in the world, even if you are a mother. Sweetheart, more than anything else in the world, I adore you.

Now, I must return to life. No mail came for me today, and I'm not sorry, because there was nothing but that lousy V-mail. Gee, sweet, I'm glad you haven't written that stuff to me. You didn't tell me whether the one I wrote to you was small or large. I mean, the original or the copy. It doesn't matter, though, now, does it. (You will have to pardon me for misspelling the word doesn't, sweet. I notice that in all my letters I spell it the same way, but just to show you that I know better, here it is – dosn't.)(But that dosen't look right, either. Maybe this will look better – doesn't. – That's it – I told you I could.) (But who cares, as long as you know what I mean, what the heck to we care, whether my spelling is correct or not?) My lovely wife, I humbly apologize for my errors in spelling. I know it makes no difference to you, but I would rather not.

For some reason or other, this letter seems more close to you than others I have written. Does it seem that way to you? Gee, I love you.

Gosh, the couple of pages I intended to write turned out to be quite long. Bing Crosby is now singing "Silent Night," in the show. Gee, it sounded swell. I missed this picture, just because I desired to write to you. The name of it is "Going My Way.?" I imagine it is a pretty nice picture, according to the way the boys are taking it. You know, I can tell every time a female enters the scene, the way they raise the whistles, etc. I can almost see the entire show, in my imagination, by listening to the way the fellows take it. Right now, there is some serious conversation going on. I know, because there isn't a sound, other than those coming from the screen. There is an organ softly playing in the background, and it really sounds swell. Gee, sweet Lucia, excuse me for going off the track like that, but I seemed to have absorbed the entire mood of the picture. Sweetheart, have you seen "The Song of Bernadette" yet? Gee, that was a swell picture. I'm still seeing it.

Last night, my sweet, I wrote to your mother, besides my letter to you. This is my one hundred fiftieth letter to you since I arrived on this rock. I am continually hoping and praying that it won't be long before I won't have to write more. Gee, we have been separated so very long, it is time we were reunited. I love you and want you so very much, most wonderful one. You are the sweetest, most adorable wife and mother in all the world. Before I begin to bore you, I think I shall sign off, wishing you and our daughter the best of health and happiness, all the rest of your natural lives, and life everlasting. I love you, Lucia.

Give my fond regards to all the family and our friends. Here is my daily special hug and kiss for our darling daughter and all my love and adoration for you. Most adorable and loving wife, I miss you and want you more than anything in the world. I love you.

J.De Roxtro EM1/c   Everlastingly, yours forever *Johnny*

Note on flap: "Mere words cannot tell how much I love you. Love and kisses."

Wednesday, June 7, 1944. Card from Mary. Brought baby to Mil's. Met girls at corner. Walked to station & took 11:14 train to New York, arrived at 12:45 and looked around 'til 1:00. Met Mrs. Fitzpatrick and her sister. Went for lunch in The Little

White House Res. on 34ᵗʰ St. Talked mostly about Frank. Were together about 2 hrs. Then separated. Girls & I went to Radio City. Saw "White Cliffs of Dover." Irene Dunn. Very good. Also stage show. Took 9:30 train. home 11:00. Very cold.

[Pavuvu Island, Russell Islands.]
Postmarked June 8, 1944, stamp upside down.   June 7, 1944

Somewhere

Hello, Lovely Lucia:

I love you, miss you and want you more as each day passes, slowly but surely bringing us more close to the day of our reunion. That day can't possibly come any too soon to suit me, but I doubt if it will be much before September or October, now. Darn it, I don't know why, but I have changed my mind about being home soon. Everything here is about the same, but maybe I have lost my morale, or something. I am still hoping and praying, though, to be there with you soon. I long to hold you tenderly in my arms and kiss you. Sweetheart, I never will be satisfied until I am there with you.

My morale should be high, Lou, because I received five pieces of mail from you today, and one from my mother. One of yours was a father's day card, and the rest were letters. The dates were the twenty-second, third, fourth, and sixth of May. In one were the pictures. Gee, they really were swell. Honey, I'm going to answer the one of the nineteenth tonight, but I don't know how well I will do with it. Gosh, I love you.

Thanks loads for the two father's day cards you sent me, angel. Both of them are swell, and it was very thoughtful of you to send them. The four kisses that were sent by way of the stamps were really appreciated, too. Gee, wouldn't it be swell if we could deliver our kisses in person? Sweetheart, you will be the most pleasant surprise I could ever expect to receive. To be able to hold you tenderly in my arms and kiss you, ah!! What a surprise I get every time I do that. I love you, my darling, and I'm the one to pull the surprises. Every time I think of it, I am more than surprised as to the reason why I managed to hook you into becoming my lovely wife.

Honey, you shouldn't have gone to all that trouble, cutting the hedge and the grass. Hell, that's not your job, and your brother should have done it. But I suppose he has plenty to do, without bothering with that stuff. Oh, well, I guess it's alright, even though you did become quite tired. That's because you used muscles you aren't usually using. Maybe I'll be home to do it the next time it needs it. I sure hope so.

We have a band over at the theater tonight, and they are pretty good. I decided I would rather stay here and write to my adorable wife. Right now, they're playing the "Moonlight Serenade." I forgot to mention it last night, but during the picture they sang Ave Maria, but it wasn't ours. I'm glad it wasn't because that really does something to me. I really like that song. I never had paid much attention to it until it was sung for you and I.

I suppose Jackie will be real brown when I get there. Gee, I do hope she browns, and doesn't burn, as I do. Don't let her get too much at once, though, because it not only will be sore for her, but you will have extra trouble getting her well again. You always did become brown easily, sweet, so I can imagine that you acquired a nice tan, in the short while you were out.

You know what I think, my love, you are too darned good to have children around. You would spend every red cent on them, and do without things you need for yourself. Darling, you are the most lovely wife and mother in the world, and I'm proud of you.

You seem to be able to get all the ice cream you want, dearest one, two quarts, at different times, in this letter. That's swell, Hon, because I know how much you enjoy it. I suppose our little one likes it now, also. I'll bet Vene's kiddies go for it, too, especially N.G. That was a swell picture of N.G., Bonnie and Jackie, wasn't it. I'll mention them all later on. It was swell of Vene to bring those canned tomatoes down, too. I have an idea she puts too much sugar in them though. Maybe not, though, because she couldn't get much last season, could she.

I'm sure glad Ralph was able to send your mother a few pictures. That's swell, and I know that your mother was surprised, relieved, and pleased to get them. I wish I were able to send you one or two a month, anyhow, but it is an impossibility, my angel. It just can't be done. Printing paper is almost impossible to get out here, so I guess it also is where your brother is. Boy, if he is getting as heavy as most of the fellows, he will really be a man when he gets back. I hope we are there together. I adore you.

Yes, a little care, time and interest in the child, and Leslie would really be a swell one. She has looks, is intelligent, and will go places, in time. If only her mother would take as much interest in her as you do. I have an idea that she would be a totally different child if you took her over for a month. She couldn't do anything but improve, either. It's a darn shame the way Fran neglects Les. Too bad you weren't able to sleep better, though, with Les poking you, and tossing around all night long.

You had a busy night, sweet, and after writing to Ralph and Mary, besides me, well, I guess you were tired. Why didn't Mary come to spend that furlough with you, sweet? I was sure you said she was due there during May some time.

Sweetheart, I don't feel like writing tonight, so this will be my last page. I love you so very much, my dear one. You and I belong together, and we will be, one of these days, and soon, I hope. Give my regards to all the family and our friends. Here is my daily hug and kiss for our Jackie, sweetheart. To you, I send my all. You mean more to me than anyone else in the world. I love you more than life itself.

J.De Roxtro EM1/c   Everlastingly, your loving *Johnny*

Note on flap: "Pardon the brevity of this note, sweet. I'll try to do better tomorrow. Here's all my love. Hugs and kisses."

Thursday, June 8, 1944. Letters of June 2, 1. Letter from Ralph & Vene. Went to dentist. Gracie home with Jackie. Home to cook. After supper gave birthday gift to Ann. A quilted house coat and card. Before supper was out front with Jackie, Mom, and we talked with Mrs. Bianco. Mike comes along, takes Jackie by the hand and brings her to Silversteins for an ice cream cone. Took picture of Jackie.

[Pavuvu Island, Russell Islands.]
Postmarked June 9, 1944, stamp upside down.   June 8, 1944

Somewhere

Lovely Lucia:

Most precious wife and mother in all the world, I love you, adore you and worship you. Mere words never will be able to convey my true love for you. How I miss your smiling countenance before me. I want you so very much, darling. I long to hold you in my arms and kiss you. Gee, honey, to be there at home with you is my one desire. We belong together and we will be, just as soon as I can make it.

No mail came for me today that was important, only a Y bulletin. I have not even opened it yet. By the way, I forgot to mention it last night, but the little thing I enclosed might be of a bit of interest to you. It conveys my feelings, but not as well as I could, if I were there in person. You have my permission to destroy it, if you care to. Just let me know what you think of it.

I am well, as usual, sweet, and I sincerely hope and pray that you, Jackie and the family are in the best of health, and are happy. I'm low again tonight, sweet, so I'll merely answer your letter of the twenty-second. I love you.

This is the one that was returned for additional postage. Therefore, it has three kisses for me from my most lovely wife and sweetheart. You also started putting letters on the outside flap. These were easy to figure out. Here it is. "To the best husband in the world." I sure am glad you think so, dearest one. I wish I could be there with you to prove it. On the inside you echo my sentiments exactly. To be with you soon is my one desire, darling. It can't come any too soon to suit me. Gee, I sure do love you.

Yes, sweet, I actually did steal that copy of the weekly scandal sheet. But I managed to get another, and replaced the one I borrowed. It is quite gratifying to know that you enjoy receiving them. We do have some fairly good stuff in them. Some of the poems are really good.

Some guys get all the breaks, don't they. That guy Pruden is home at least once a month, the lucky stiff. The last I heard of him, he was an M.P. up in New York State. Oh, well, I guess we can't all be at home. I'm glad he was looking better. At least he could stand putting on a little weight. He's not such a bad guy at heart. More power to him. He sure is crazy to prefer action to home leave.

Maybe after I get home, I will be stationed somewhere close, where you and I can be together most of the time. We will have to wait and see, though. Anything is liable to happen, and the unexpected usually does, in this outfit. Who knows, I may prefer foreign duty to stateside, especially if I weren't able to see you every night.

I have to agree with you, my beloved angel. It would be swell if Joe and Angie were able to have a little one of their own. (I don't know why I put that were able in there - they are, aren't they?) Joe sure does love children, and as you say, he would make a swell father and Angie a good mother, too. Your brother Joe has been swell to our little one, and I sort of envy him, even though I am the father. After all, I have as yet to see her, and he has been seeing her and doing things for her, as a godfather should. Honey, every time I think of it, I am more pleased that you picked him. It was swell of Jackie to wake up in time for Joe to be able to play with her for a little while.

Sweetheart, have I ever told you that I think you are the most wonderful girl in the world? I love you more as each day passes. Gee, I want to be with you.

So "Butch" was pleased to go to church the second time, huh? Well, that just proves that you are a wonderful mother. With the proper care from her mother, Les would really be tops, wouldn't she. She's a honey now, and with a little loving care, wow!! She would be sensational. Honey, you are marvelous. You seem to be able to do anything with anyone. You love kiddies, too, don't you. Tell me, Lou, is Jackie worth all the trouble you went through? I just want to hear you say it, sweetheart. Les is quite a chatterbox, and always was. Especially when she has someone to listen, and there is no doubt that her mother was willing to listen, after being away from her for a week. Gee, I sure would like to be able to see all our nephews and nieces again. Honey, I'm afraid I am getting a little old, or something. How do your grandparents like Leslie Ann? They couldn't help but like her. Maybe she annoys them, though?

While on the subject of your beloved grandparents, here is a rare tch tch for Mama G. Tell Tadone I hope his arm is well by now. Gee, I wish I were able to see them both again.

Boy, that sure was a surprise when your relatives from Trenton came, wasn't it. Mama Gee and Tadone were mighty pleased to see them, too, I'll bet. No, sweet, I'm sorry, but I can't remember them very well. I know they are swell, and fine people, but I can't remember them. There were too many, and I was interested in only one. That was you, sweetheart. I remember that there was one of your cousins there, but he left soon after dinner, and I don't remember which one it was. There was another, with a child, but that was your female cousin, I think. We may get to know them better, though, after this damned war is over.

Too bad you weren't able to go play tennis with the girls, but there will be plenty more opportunities, later on. I haven't played since I left. I never got around to it, back on Santos. As long as you were able to take some pictures of everyone, I will be satisfied.

Your mentioning the direction you, Fran and the little ones walked reminds me of our almost nightly walks for awhile. Gee, they were swell. How I would like to do it again. I miss all that, sweet, and you probably do too. Honey, I will do my best to make you happy. I adore my lovely Lucia.

Honey, you sure are learning fast. How the devil did you know that the stuff growing on that tree was poison ivy? It's just as well to take no chances though. I don't remember ever seeing any there when I used to go to that chapel. But that was many years ago, so it could have grown since then. I don't take ivy poisoning, sweet, do you?

It was swell of Fran to invite you all down to dinner. That's the least she could do, though, as long as you were good enough to care for Les for a week. You didn't tell me what she said about the clothes and stuff you bought for "Butch." How could Fran help but notice a change in Les? Heck, you are a wonderful girl, angel, and you work wonders with children. You're my choice to live with forever and a day,

Honey, I'm sorry, but I can't write any more tonight. More and more, I feel it difficult to write, as the days pass, and I can't tell when I am going home to you. Give my regards to all the family and our friends. Here is my daily hug and kiss for our Jackie. Wouldn't it be swell if I could send myself to you, instead of these letters. I love you, miss you and want you, my sweetheart.

J.De Roxtro EM1/c   Everlastingly, your *Johnny*

Note on flap: "Honey, you are mine and I am yours forever. Here's a kiss for Mickey."

Friday, June 9, 1944. Letter of May 31st. Went to movies. Saw Uncertain Glory. Fair.

[Pavuvu Island, Russell Islands.]
Postmarked June 10, 1944, stamp upside down.   June 9, 1944
                                                              Somewhere

Hello, Sweetheart:

Today I received three lovely letters, one from Vene, which contained two snapshots of her daughters. Gee, Bonnie doesn't look half as good as Jackie, does she? N.G. looks well though, and they both have nice blond hair. They are a nice-looking pair though, and I would like to see them. The other two were, of course, from the most wonderful wife and sweetheart in the world. They were written the twenty-fifth and thirtieth of May, and even postmarked the twenty-sixth of May and the first of June, respectively. That's really swell, darling. It's so much better receiving your swell letters so soon after you write them. Just think, sweet, only ten days ago, you were writing the letter that I read today, and if I answered it tonight, you would receive the answer less than twenty days after you wrote it. Thanks loads for making them come to me more promptly, angel. Gee, I have a swell wife. That little trick of mailing them yourself makes all the difference in the world. Honey, I love you.

204

All the love in the world is ours, Lucia, and I am anxiously awaiting the day when I will be able to hold you real close to me and kiss you. I long to feel the warmth of your lovely young body pressing close to mine as we embrace in the privacy of our room. I long to tell you of my love and adoration, too, and to look at you. Honey, I love you, miss you and want you. Thoughts of you are forever in my mind and your sweet image is eternally before me. May the day soon come when we will again be able to act as a loving married couple should.

I am in the best of health, and am as happy as I possibly can be, being so far away from you and our little one. You are always with me, sweet one, but in spirit only. That helps a lot, but it isn't satisfactory. I want to be able to see you, talk to you, and tell you of my love. Won't it be swell when we can actually touch each other? I can hardly wait for that day to come. Here's hopes and prayers that you, Jackie and the rest of the family are well and happy. Maybe I'll be home soon. I adore Lucia.

Thanks loads for your kiss, which came by way of the stamp. All you have on the inside of your letter is "Darling, I love you," but that means so much to me. I don't know what would happen if you ever stopped loving me. I would be lost, forever, because there can never be another to take your place.

Your letter of the twenty-third is a short one, my lovely, so this, in answer to it, will have to be short also. Right now it is longer than yours was, so perhaps I can manage a couple more pages. By the way, in case you are interested, I am feeling not quite so low tonight.

Over at the theatre, Joe Louis and Billy Conn are being shown on the screen. All I can hear is the crowd yelling, but from the sound of that, it must be a good fight. After this fight, they are showing a western of some sort. So, I am sitting here in my sack, penning this little note to you. You mean more to me than anything else in all the world, Lou, so be sure you take good care of yourself, and our daughter, too. You two are my sweethearts, and my only ones. I hope you don't mind sharing me with Jackie. I love you both.

You may think my letter of the twelfth of May was short, but what did you think of the shortest one? Boy, I hope I never have to make another one that short. I am actually ashamed of it. But I had to write you, didn't I. I couldn't break this chain of daily letters now. Heck, I've written over one hundred fifty since the battalion landed on this rock.

It's too bad you had to light the furnace, sweet, but there are days like that, when everything is damp and the air is sort of raw, especially as the month of May isn't the best or warmest in the year. At any time, up to about the middle of June, you can sort of expect those kinds of days. You're lucky you are able to do it, I guess.

Here's hoping there is nothing very seriously wrong with your teeth, sweet. You never have had much trouble with them, have you. Maybe you will now, though. Sometimes that happens, after a girl becomes a mother. Anyway, my love, let me know all about it, please. Doc Reilly must really be a busy guy, if you had to wait over a week for an appointment. I'm glad he is, and I hope he is collecting his bills. He's a swell guy.

Lucia, if you do meet Fitz's mother in New York, let me know everything about her, will you. She is a little bit of a thing, too, I think. Well, I sure hope you had a swell time, and got everything you went for.

Your letter has been answered, sweetheart, and now, I don't know what to say. Gee, wouldn't it be swell if we didn't ever have to write letters to each other? Right now, you and I would be together, maybe at a show, maybe just sitting in the living room listening to the radio or reading, or perhaps we would be up in our room, lying there beside each other, talking and planning the future of our family. No matter what we are doing, we will be in love with each other, and we will be the most happy couple on the earth. Honey, more than anything else in the world I want to be there with you, doing all I can to make you happy. Wouldn't it be swell if this war would end soon, so that we could be together, doing all the things that we should be doing? I want very much to be able to make love to you again.

There is still nothing definite that I can pass on to you, my love. I only wish there was. I want to put right here, just when I will leave this damned island, and about when you can expect me, but darn it, I don't know. No one knows, and we are all just waiting. It isn't the most pleasant thing to do, but we have no choice. All we can do is wait. Let's hope we don't crack before we hear whether we are going home or not. I won't be one of the ones to go nuts, though, simply because I have you to think of. I never will regret the day we met and married. It sure was my lucky day. I adore you. Sweetheart, you are the most wonderful girl in the world. I still can't see what you saw in me. Love must be blind, or else you would have taken a second look. It's too late now, though, you're mine and I intend to keep you.

Give my fond regards to all the family and our friends. Here is my daily special hug and kiss for our daughter, and millions more for my loving, patiently waiting, adorable wife.

J.De Roxtro EM1/c   Everlastingly, your *Johnny*

Note on flap: "You are beautiful, sweetheart, I love you more as each day passes. Here's lots of hugs & kisses."

Saturday, June 10, 1944. *No letters. Tonite Fran called. Told about baby. Expects it in Jan.*

206

[Pavuvu Island, Russell Islands.]
Postmarked June 13, 1944, stamp upside down.   *June 10, 1944*
                                                            Somewhere

Lovely Lucia:

Today, I received two more sweet letters from you. They were written the twenty-seventh and eighth of May, and were postmarked the thirty-first. Boy, I sure hit the jackpot again this week, didn't I. Thanks loads, honey. Gee, it's swell receiving so many letters from you.

I'm sorry, my love, but I won't have time to answer any of yours tonight. I am not allowed to have our light lit during the show. It must bother the fellows, so, I will now have to either go to the show every night or lie here in the dark and think of you. I will have to make some other arrangement, so that I can keep up my correspondence to you.

Sweetheart darling, I love you, miss you and want you. Each and every day your lovely image is before me, guiding my every move. I am eternally thinking of you, too, and how I long to be there, holding you in my arms and kissing you. It will be so nice, being able to look at you, talk to you and touch you. More than anything else, I want to be there with my lovable Lucia.

Honey, I've just been looking over my mail, and you wrote seven days straight. If you wrote the twenty-ninth and I have an idea you did, that makes nine. I don't know how many more you have written since then, because I haven't received them yet. Gee, if you have started writing daily, I sure will have a job catching up. In fact, the only way I could do it would be to answer two at a time. However, I will have to wait and see. Tomorrow, I will try and write a nice long letter to you.

Out where we are working, some fellow took a candid shot of a couple of us and I saw the picture today. Boy, was I surprised. You should see what I was doing. He is going to have a couple made so he said, and will give me one. However, I won't send it through the mail, because you might show it to others. I don't mean it that way. I know you wouldn't. What I mean is, you may leave it somewhere where someone may see it, and neither of us would want that. You would never put it in your album, either. Just forget that I even mentioned it, sweet. I think I'll destroy it, if I do get one. Sweetheart, I'm ashamed of myself. But one does things out here, that he wouldn't even think of doing back home. Hell, who ever would have thought that someone was taking a picture? Oh, well, it's done now, so I'll grin and bear it.

I had a couple of cold beers this evening after supper, and boy, did they taste good. Somehow or other, the beer we get out here isn't as good as it is at home, but it's better than nothing. Have you any beer waiting there for

207

me, sweet? I'm not going to have much time for drinking, though, so I don't care so much. I'm going to spend most all of my time making love to you, all over again.

If I remember correctly, there was something in one of those weekly sheets of ours concerning Ernie Moore's cream puffs. We had more tonight, and they were really good. He put some kind of chocolate inside, and it improved them. We sure are lucky to have such good bakers. If it weren't for them, I would go hungry plenty of times. There are times when I am unable to eat the food and if it weren't for the bread, well, I would be lost. They make rolls daily, too.

While I'm on the subject of food, I may as well tell you that we had fried eggs and sausage for breakfast the other day. That is a rarity, over here, and boy, did I receive a surprise when I went in to dinner. Of all things, we had fried chicken, and I got a drumstick and second joint. I wouldn't have but I told the guy it was your birthday and he piled it on. And, believe it or not, it was your birthday.

The lights just blinked, so I guess I will have to finish this tomorrow, or stop where I am. I will keep on writing, though, until they put them out. I haven't even addressed the envelope yet. I'll do that now. There, that's done. Now all I have to do is try to finish this, if I can. Give my regards to all the family and our friends. Here is my daily hug and kiss for our daughter. For you, my lovely wife and sweetheart, I never will be able to give you enough. All my love and adoration is yours. The day of our reunion will never come too soon to suit me. You are the most wonderful girl in the world.

J.De Roxtro EM1/c   I adore you, Lou. As ever *Johnny*

Note on flap: "My Darling, here's hoping we will be together again real soon. I love you. Here's all my love."

Sunday June 11, 1944. *Joe & Angie here in afternoon. Took Jackie for ride. Fitz's birthday, 24 yrs. Jackie says OK, Hey you! Boo!*

[Pavuvu Island, Russell Islands.]

Postmarked June 13, 1944, stamp upside down.   June 11, 1944

Somewhere

Hello Sweetheart:

I love you, miss you and want you. How I long to hold you tenderly in my arms and kiss you once again. Each and every day my love for you grows stronger. Your sweet image is before me always and precious thoughts of you are continually running through my mind. Dearest one, you mean more to me than anything or anyone else in the world. My one desire is to be there doing my best to make you happy.

Today I hit the jackpot again, sweet. I received a letter from Ralph in which he reminded me that he has now been out here a year and has but one more to go. It doesn't seem that long ago since he came out, does it. Time does go by fast, even though we think it lingers and draws slowly on. It's almost two years since I've seen you, too, and at times it doesn't seem so long. At other times it seems much longer than that, though. No matter how long it has been since I was last holding you in

my arms, it has been entirely too long to suit me. Besides the letter from our brother, I received two from you, the most loyal loving wife a fellow ever had. I am one of the luckiest guys in the world if not the luckiest. I think I am at the head of that list.

Your letters were written the first and second of June and were postmarked the third and fourth. Gee, it won't be long before I receive the one telling me about your birthday, and about your trip into New York the day after. Both those days were less than a week ago and already I am expecting to hear about them. Boy, I sure am glad the mail is coming so fast. Let's see, in the one of the second you mentioned receiving mine of the twenty-fifth. That's only seventeen days ago. Swell time for me to receive an answer, isn't it. But how much more convenient it would be if we were able to converse with each other. Gee, I want to hear your voice so much. I want to look at you and feel you and do things with you. I adore you. I had better hurry and answer all these letters I have from you, as long as you are writing daily. I'll never catch up this way, will I? But I'll do my best so here goes with an answer to yours of the twenty-fourth of May.

Thanks loads for the kisses, sweet. I wasn't disappointed by not finding snapshots in this one, because there were some. You sealed the envelope with love, hugs and kisses, in letters. I, too, love you very much and want you more each day, as you said on the inside flap. You are mine and I am yours forever. I want you.

Before I start, honey, I thought that perhaps you would be interested in knowing that I've answered Ralph's letter and written to my mother. I still have two from Ann and one from Fan to answer, but they will have to wait until I get time. Tell them my intentions are good and I will answer them as soon as I possibly can. They will understand, I guess. Maybe I will have a few minutes after I finish this, but I doubt it.

This picture of the three cousins is kind of cute, isn't it. Boy, that little one of ours sure is a honey and plenty healthy looking, too. She even shows her teeth in this picture, but they aren't very plain. Judy looks better, too, doesn't she. Michael looks nice and tidy but a trifle uncomfortable with that coat buttoned like that. The next one is of the other three cousins – meaning, of course Vene's two blonds. You know, Jackie looks more at home with Bonnie and N.G. She seems to be more satisfied, or something. She and Bonnie are about the same size, aren't they. All three of them look happy and healthy, too. You are a marvelous mother. I am really proud of you, my sweet. So this is the picture that caused you to break the camera, huh?

Come to think of it, sweet, I can now fix most any size film to fit your camera, merely by cutting the spool a little. When I get home, I'll show you how so you won't have any trouble later on getting films to fit. It's simple and you will be able to do it easily.

These two of the wee one standing beside the stroller are swell, too. She seems to be in a thoughtful mood. In the one taken of her in the carriage, it looks to me as if she sees something attractive across the street and is expecting something interesting to happen. All the pictures are nice and I love to receive them. I still want one of you, though, my angel. I'm waiting for that one of you in a sweater, sweet, but I don't insist on it. I would like to receive more pictures of you, though.

It is almost supper time, I guess, because I smell the guys preparing fish in bacon grease. Our Sunday night suppers are never very good, so the fellows usually go fishing and have a fish fry. Boy, I have been invited to a few and it really does taste good. Nice and brown and well done. Can you imagine all the fellows around, eating fish with their fingers and drinking coffee? It's swell and everyone enjoys it. I never help, so don't attend regularly. I could, of course, but I wouldn't feel right, horning in on someone else's good time without assisting in some way. I don't have time to spare from my writing. So, I always wait for an invitation, and don't always accept that.

Before I start answering your letter, I wish to take this opportunity to inform you that the picture at our local cinema this evening is, believe it or not, "Cover Girl." It is supposed to be pretty good and a picture worth seeing. I'm going to chow now, and will be returning right after chow. Here I am, my sweet one and I ate everything they gave me. I must have been hungry. But my hunger isn't satisfied and it never will be until I can be with you for a night or two.

Yes, it is best to purchase from the same dealer all the time. Consumers is a good company and their coal is of the best grade most of the time. They were always the ones to supply us, too, when we needed coal. They will do their best to keep their customers satisfied, too. If you make a complaint about the coal, they will do their best to help you by suggesting different methods of firing the boiler, and I have even known them to take the coal out of the bin and replace it. As you say, they're good.

Maybe the picture, "The Lost Angel" will come out to us. If it does I intend to see it. That little girl, Margaret O'Brien was really good in "Journey for Margaret," so she should be good in this one. By the way, our show tonight is not the afore-mentioned one, but "Girl Trouble." It sounds familiar, and I have an idea that I've seen it. I may go because we are having three boxing bouts before the show. Now, I have just one more thing to say about motion pictures and then I will quit. Jennifer Jones won the Oscar this past year for her performance in "The Song of Bernadette." I don't know yet whether you've seen it, so I thought this might be an incentive.

Honey, you know darn well that I would like these pictures. I like them all. That little gal of ours sure is a sweetheart isn't she. The coat your mom made sure looks good to me, too. Gee, I want so much to get home.

Your letter has been answered, my darling, so now, I will close. Give my fond regards to all the family and our friends. Here is my daily special hug and kiss for Jackie. To you, my sweetheart, I send all my love and adoration, plus millions of hugs and kisses.

J.De Roxtro EM1/c   *Ever, your adoring* *Johnny*

Monday, June 12, 1944. *Washed clothes. No letters. Mary called. Would be up in afternoon with Lena 3-5:30. Ice cream & cake. Got period. Cramps. Gene put in shower. Wrote to Ralph.*

[Pavuvu Island, Russell Islands.]
Postmarked June 14, 1944, stamp upside down.   June 12, 1944

Somewhere

Sweetheart:

You are the most wonderful girl in the world. I love you, miss you and want you. Thoughts of you are forever racing through my mind and I am lucky enough to have your sweet and lovely vision before me at all times. Gee, I want so much to be there with you. I long to hold your vibrant, youthful body close to mine and kiss you. To be there, trying to make you happy is my one desire. Sweetheart, I adore you. May the day soon come when I leave this damnable hellhole and head for home. It can't come too soon to suit me.

I didn't even to go chow tonight, my angel. A few of us, ah, acquired some bacon, bread, potatoes, salt, ketchup and so forth, and fried some bacon, French fried some potatoes and had coffee. Honey, it really tasted swell. After the French fries were done, I made myself some potato chips and ate them. They were pretty good too, only not as good as the ones we used to get in Madison. I burned the last batch and tossed them out.

Out on the job today, that fellow I told you about gave me the picture I was telling you about. Yes, that's it, the one I said I wouldn't send to you. Now, I have changed my mind. If you want me to, I'll send it on to you. After all, we have no secrets from each other and I love you. So, let me know if you want it and I'll send it. I feel that I must warn you, though, once again, just how good it is. I showed it to Fitz, and he said if it was his, he would tear it up and throw it in the bay. Maybe I should, I don't know, but anyway, I will wait till I hear from you. I depend so much on your good judgment. Honey, you're beautiful.

There was hardly any mail today, my lovely one, but I received one. Boy, I really was surprised. It was from you, naturally, and was written the twenty-ninth of May. Now all I have to do is get the one of the thirty-first and I'll have them all. I have an idea you are writing daily. Thanks loads, sweetheart. How can I ever thank you enough. You are the sweetest wife in the world, and mine.

I fixed my pancho across the end of the tent so the light wouldn't shine on the customers of our local theatre, so now I can write to you during the show. At least no one has come around so far. I will know tomorrow whether it's okay or not. Now, angel mine, I will answer your letter of the twenty-fifth of May.

Thanks loads for the kiss you sent my way of the stamp. Just thinking of all those lovely kisses makes my mouth water. How I could stand a few now. Here's all the love in the world for you, my darling. I love you. That's what you had on the inside flap of the envelope, sweet, and I feel the same about you, only more so.,

Honey, it must have been raining a little harder than usual, if, by carrying the wood from the garage to the house, it was too wet to burn easy. In fact, it must have been raining almost as hard there as it usually does here. And boy, that's hard, is what I mean. My guess is that it wasn't only the damp wood that kept you from getting a good fire going. There was probably no draft, and oh, there could be ever so many things. I sure don't think it was your thought, though.

Of course, I'm terribly frightened by your statement concerning how adept you have become with the axe. Maybe you also think I've been letting myself become soft and flabby on this cruise around these beautiful South Pacific Islands. I've learned a few little tricks myself and letting a little blood would never bother me now. So you swing your axe, my darling, if you want to, but you had better make the first swing count. (heh heh –haw haw w w w - That's supposed to be Raymond's double). Sure I remember that inner sanctum sweetheart. How could I ever forget, when I had you in my arms most of the time. Gee, I wish I could do the same things now.

Darling!! I'm surprised!! How did you ever manage to say damn in a letter? My, how you have changed. That's about the first time you've used that word, I think. It sounds good to me, though, and keep it up, will you? No one ever reads your letters but me, so you can let yourself go and say anything you want. It may do you a lot of good and you may feel better. Honey, I want you to tell me anything and everything you feel like, and tell me in your very own words. After all, I'm your life-mate and you love me. I adore you.

I noticed, as you know by now, that your letter of the twenty-second was delayed because it was sent back for insufficient postage. But it doesn't matter, because your mail is coming to me very rapidly now. Thanks loads for getting them posted so soon. My sweetheart, I love you more than life itself.

Angel mine, have you doubts of my love and adoration for you? It sort of sounds as if you do, when you say, quote, "The most important is the fact that I love you and knowing that you love me. And don't forget it!!" unquote. Now, if that isn't a threat or something, I want to know what it is. Way down deep, you know that I love you and also that I always will. That's enough for that, because I don't think you really meant it as a threat to me. Oh, my sweet, what a mistake I've made. As soon as I wrote those last two words I realized what you meant. Stupid me, I should have known that all you wanted to do was impress upon me the fact that our loving each other as we do is more important than anything else in the world. You see, sweet, how my mind is weakening. I love you.

Yes, our little one is growing fast and I haven't seen her at all, yet, except in the many snapshots you have so thoughtfully sent to me. I want so very much to be there to see both of my loved ones.

Now, sweetheart, I've run out of words again. Hell, I wish I were able to put down my innermost thoughts, but I can't even start, because I know I would only bawl everything up. When I am there with you again I will tell you, and then we will be happy. Just think, sweet, one of these days you and I will be united and the three of us, maybe more, will have a home of our own, and you and I will bring our children up the best we can. Give my fond regards to the family, Mama G, Tadone, and any of our mutual friends you may happen to meet. Here is my daily special hug and kiss for our Jackie, and millions more for you, my darling wife and sweetheart. Give Mickey a pat or two for me and tell her I'll be there soon to make her happy again. I love you, miss you and want you, dearest one.

J. De Roxtro EM1/c   Everlastingly, your loving *Johnny*

Note on flap: *"This will have to do for tonight, my love. Hope you don't mind. I love you and am hungry for you."*

Tuesday, June 13, 1944. *No mail. Went downtown. Mailed package to Johnnie.*
[Pavuvu Island, Russell Islands.]
Postmarked June 14, 1944, stamp upside down.

                                                          June 13, 1944
                                                          Somewhere

Hello, Sweetheart:

I love you, miss you and want you more as each day passes, slowly but surely bringing us more close together. Dearest one, I long to take you in my arms and hold you close to me as I try to smother you with kisses. I want to be able to talk to you. I'm tired of these Islands, and I am tired of being away from you. Sweet, I adore you.

I received only one piece of mail today and that was from my mother. I don't care, though, because I still have seven of yours to answer. If I answer one a day, I will finish the last one next Monday. By that time, I'm almost sure to have more to answer. Gee, wouldn't it be swell if I never was here long enough to receive any more from you? But there isn't any chance of that. It's possible, of course, but highly improbable.

Yours of the twenty-sixth is to be answered tonight, sweetheart. Thanks loads for the kiss. On the inside flap of the envelope you hope it won't be long before you see my face before you. You aren't the only one, sweet. That day can't possibly come too soon to suit me. It may become a truth in the next month or so. Maybe they're holding us out so we can be home for Xmas.

Lovely one, I'm not in much of a writing mood tonight and I don't know why. I feel as though I could lie right down and be asleep within a very few minutes. I am well, darling, and I sincerely hope and pray that you, Jackie and the family are in the best of health and are happy.

I have just re-read your letter, (the one I am going to answer now) and there is nothing in it I can say much about. All you did was tell me how much you liked the picture I sent and how the others liked it. I am glad you liked it, sweet, even though I wasn't smiling, and, according to your letter, Jackie also liked it. You must have her well trained, Sweet, the way she reacted to the picture shows that. Too bad you had to take it away from her, but a few tears will never hurt her. I was quite sure the girls would get a laugh out of it, simply because they have a laugh over most everything.

Sweetheart, you won't be too disappointed if I don't make this any longer, will you? I simply can't write any more. I'm truly sorry.

Give my regards to all the family and our friends, will you, sweet? Here is my daily hug and kiss for our daughter and to you, my angel, I can't send enough love and adoration. I want more than anything else to be there with you.

J.De Roxtro EM1/c   Everlastingly, your loving *Johnny*

Note on flap: *"Lou, darling, I'm sorry this is so short. I'll try to do better tomorrow. I love you. Love, hugs and kisses."*

Wednesday, June 14, 1944. Letters of June 3,4,5, C-Breeze. Call from Jo 10:30. Came at 10:45. Rain. After lunch, about 2:00 Vene & M.d.R. came. Jo went to McKenzie Rd until 9:30. Waited for bus with her. Belated birthday gift from Fan. L'amour perfume.

[Pavuvu Island, Russell Islands.]
Postmarked June 15, 1944, stamp upside down.   June 14, 1944

Somewhere

Hello, Sweetheart:

I love you, miss you and want you. Thoughts of you are continually in my mind. Your beautiful image is constantly before me. Each and every day my love for you increases. Darling, I hope and pray that the day will soon come when we are able to be together. More than anything else in the world I want to be there with you to do my best to make you happy. I want to hold you tenderly in my arms and kiss you. You never will know how much I've missed you, honey. Twenty-one months ago today was the last I had my feet on our good old American soil. Tomorrow morning at ten in the morning, twenty-one months ago we sailed from San Francisco out through the Golden Gate and headed out in this direction. I'm afraid I would not be allowed to give you any of the details of our trip, but I can tell you that it was not uneventful. We had some fun, but nothing to amount to much. I will tell you all about that when I see you next. I have plenty that I can tell you that I can't put in black and white. I may be unable to get everything in the proper order, but it won't make much difference. Maybe I won't even feel like telling anyone (not even you) about my life in the service. I love you, sweet.

No mail came for me again today, my angel. There was very little, anyway, and most of it was rather old. I am sure I have all you have written, but of course, there may be one or two somewhere that I know nothing of. For instance, you never have told me what you thought of the picture "The Fighting Seabees." So maybe that will be the next one I receive. I'm not worrying about them though, because I still have a few to answer. Boy, it sure is swell to have such a loving wife as you are. You are the best in the world.

Our movie tonight is "The Falcon's Brother." That should be quite interesting, don't you think? Hell, I never would go to see that, but the news is read to us every night before the show, and tonight we are to see some Navy pictures about and of the Seabees. I will go to see them anyway, and probably I will stay to see the other thing. It's tough, sweet, having nothing to return home to, after a day's work. By home I mean this damned tent and it's a hell of a place to call that. The darn thing leaks and, oh, hell, it's no use telling you about it.

Sweetheart, I love you so very much. I want so much to be there with you. I want to make love to you again.

Well, I guess I will have to answer our letter of the twenty-seventh tonight. It's only two pages long, so my answer can't be long, either. Thanks loads for the kiss you always sent by way of the stamp. It helps a lot and they do make me feel a lot better, even though the contact, the personal touch, isn't there. That's what I long for.

Say, sweet, just how were you to know Mrs. Fitzpatrick when you saw her? Or how was she to know you? Gosh I hope you didn't have any difficulty in knowing her, or should I say, recognizing her? It's swell that you were finally able to make arrangements to meet her. I have an idea that she is a swell person, and you will like her.

It would have been much better if we were able to celebrate your birthday together, but we can't, so I sure hope you had a lovely time. Angel, my mother's birthday is sometime between the second and seventh of July, so will you find out the correct day and give her a little something for us? I think it's the third, but I'm not sure. It's either that, the fifth or the seventh. I never could figure them out because George, Fran, my mother and father all have birthdays then. I know that George's is the second, but I'm not sure about the rest. Don't bother with anything for the other two. They're not worth it. Honestly, honey, I worship you.

Well, my adorable one, that's all there is to answer in your letter. I wish I could have done better, but, well, I just couldn't. I don't seem to be able to write so very much anymore. Wouldn't it be swell if I were in the mood to write nice long interesting letters every night? Those moods are becoming more rare as time goes by, though, and there seems to be nothing I am able to do about it. Whether I write sweet nothings or long dull comments on everything you mention in your letters, Lovely Lucia, I want you to know that my love for you has increased daily and I long to be there with you. Gee, honey, I want so very much to be there, doing everything in my power to make you happy. I love you so much.

This will have to be the last page of this letter, sweet, and I am truly sorry that I can't make it longer. I'm just not in the mood for writing, anymore. I guess I've been out here too darn long.

216

I hereby send my fond regards, through you, to all the family and our friends. Here is my daily hug and kiss for our darling daughter and millions more for you, my most wonderful wife and sweetheart. Darling, I am hungry, and you are the only one in the world who will ever be able to satisfy me. I adore you.

J.De Roxtro EM1/c   *Everlastingly, your loving* *Johnny*

Note on flap: *"Hello, Angel – you are the most magnificent girl in the world. All my love is yours. I adore you."*

June 15-July 9, 1944 – U.S. Marines invade Saipan in the Mariana Islands. By this time, the Allies had re-captured the Solomons, the Gilberts, the Marshall Islands and the Papuan Peninsula of New Guinea. This left the Japanese holding the Philippines, Carolines, Palaus, and the Marianas. The Japanese expected an attack on the Carolines and built up forces there, but the Allied forces hit Saipan in the Marianas as that location was well within range of an air offensive using the B-29 long range Superfortress bombers. After a bloody series of battles that left the Japanese in a hopeless position, Lt. Gen. Yoshitsugu Saitō ordered a final suicidal banzai charge, the largest banzai charge in the Pacific War and ended in failure for the Japanese. Saitō along with commanders Hirakushi, Igeta, and Vice-admiral Chuichi Nagumo, the naval commander who led the Japanese carriers at Pearl Harbor, all committed ritual suicide in a cave. For the Americans, the victory was the most costly to date. Among the American wounded was future actor Lee Marvin who was hit by shrapnel from Japanese mortar fire, awarded the Purple Heart, and received a medical discharge.

June 15, 1944 – The first Superfortress B-29 bombing raid on Japan. 47 B-29 bombers based in Bengal, India target the steelworks at Yawata. This was the first air raid on Japan by strategic bombers since the Doolittle raid in April 1942.

Thursday, June 15, 1944. *Letters of June 6,7,8. Rain. Man came to put in light. Fixed vacuum. Belated birthday card from M.d.R. with $1.00. Grace graduated yesterday. Gave birthstone ring. $1.25 from Mom, $1.00 from Ann, ($.90 + $1.25) $2.15 from Fan.*

[Pavuvu Island, Russell Islands.]

Postmarked June 15, 1944, two stamps upside down.   *June 15, 1944*

Somewhere

Hello, Darling:

All the love in the world is ours. How I long to hold your sweet soft lovely body close to me and kiss you. You are all I desire, sweet one. I am hungry, and nothing but being with you can satisfy me. You are the most wonderful wife and sweetheart I, or anyone else, ever had. You are mine and I am proud to have you as my wife. I love you, miss you and want you, my darling. More than anything else in the world, I want to be there with you. May the day of our reunion come soon, my Angel. That day can't come any too soon to suit me, and I am anxiously awaiting word for me to prepare to sail. That will be a swell day for me, but gosh, the trip across the beautiful blue Pacific will be all too slow to suit me. The hours and days will simply drag by, and I will probably become cross and irritable. On all our other trips I managed to find myself a nice steady job, so the time didn't drag so slowly. Here's hoping I can do as well the next time. Gee, honey, I hope I haven't led you to think I am practically on my way, because I'm not, and as far as I know, we have no official orders for anything. I still think and hope that we will be back this summer, but as the days go by, my hopes gradually diminish.

Forbes came back down from the sick bay yesterday and he has gone back to work. He feels quite well now and I hope that this time he will stay that way. He asked me to say hello to you for him. Right now he is lying in his bunk, resting. After such a long siege he tires easily and I make him take it easy, nights. He really is a swell guy and I know you will like him. I am quite sure he will come up to visit us after this crap is over. He may even come up during his furlough. I told him he would be welcome at any time. He thinks the world of you and Jackie and he is continually talking of Ann. Whenever he mentions her, his face lights up and he is smiles all over.

Our movie tonight is "The Meanest Man In The World," with Jack Benny. I was going to see it, providing I had gotten far enough along with this letter, but now that it's raining so hard, I know I won't. There is no use sitting through a heavy rainstorm, just to see a lousy show, is there? I did it often, though, and I probably will again, sometime. If "The Song of Bernadette" plays again and it is even snowing down here, I will see it. It sure rained the night I saw that picture, but it was worth getting wet for. I love you.

When I came in after work this afternoon, upon my sack lay a letter. Naturally it was from you, my adorable one. It was written the fourth of June and postmarked the seventh. It was a swell letter, angel, and I'm sure glad you enjoyed yourself so much at the park playing tennis. But I will comment on that when I come to it. Did you write the third, sweet? I have not received any for that day, so far, but there is still plenty of time. I still think you are writing daily and it pleases me greatly. Gee, you are swell, dear one, you're the tops. I love you more than life itself. There is nothing I wouldn't do for you, I love you so. Just think, Lou, all these hours we've spent writing to each other could have been most pleasantly used by us making love. Boy, that's a good many hours of love-making, isn't it. But we probably would have spent a lot more than those we spent writing, in that most delightful of your past-times, wouldn't we. I sure would like to be able to do all those things we used to do, now, wouldn't you?

I guess that's about all I have to write about now, so I guess I will proceed to answer your letter of the twenty-eighth of May. This is a short one, sweet, so my answer will have to be the same. You wrote only eight pages this time. The way I started off, mine may equal, or even pass that. I love you.

Thanks loads for the two kisses, Lou. You know this practice of inverting the stamps is really a childish gesture, but I kind of enjoy it, don't you? And another thing I have forgotten to tell you, I no longer expect pictures in the ones with two stamps. Now, instead of expecting pictures merely by looking at the stamps, I feel the envelopes instead. I love to receive those pictures, but somehow, I would rather have all these nice long letters. Don't stop sending either, though, my lovely wife, because I would be lost without them. Gee, you're swell, and the more I think of you the more I love you, and I am forever thinking of you. I'm so glad we were married before I entered the service, instead of waiting until I came home. I love you, Lucia my own.

On the inside flap of the envelope you send our daughter's special hug and kiss and also wish that you could give me something special. If that means what I think it does, I wish you could, too. I sure could use a little, even though I do dream once in awhile. Those dreams aren't worth anything to me, though. I never dream, as you know. I often daydream of you, though, and before I know it I'm ready for action. I sure hope I will be able to satisfy you. Honey, if I could only hold you close to me, as I used to and kiss you as I used to. If I could only have you, and feel the warmth of your lovely young body under mine, gee, I would think it were a second heaven. I miss all that passionate lovemaking and hope to be able to take off where I left off before. Do you think we will be able to do as good as we did when I had my five days, angel? You know, we went riding about eighteen times then and would have gone more only you wouldn't let me. Do you remember that, sweetheart? That's just about two years ago, now, and I know darn well that I will be willing to try better this time. Why don't you come out in some of these letters and tell me exactly what you feel and think about these things, darling? After all, we are married and we have done nothing to be ashamed of, because it's only natural to do those things. Again I say, no one but me ever reads your letters and I want to hear them. I love you so very much sweetheart. Each day, my pride in you as my wife and the mother of our child increases by leaps and bounds.

It has stopped raining and the show hasn't started yet but I still don't think I'll go. So far, I haven't even started to answer your lovely letter. Maybe I had better start, else I won't finish before bedtime.

Yes, we used to pay Fran and Eddie a visit most every week and we both enjoyed them very much. I used to like the ride down more than anything else, though, didn't you? Remember how we used to stop at Madison for potato chips, then eat them all before we reached there? And how I used to love to have you lay your head on my shoulder as we were driving down there. Or have you lay your head on my lap and go to sleep. I wasn't obeying the law very much when my right hand wasn't on the wheel, either, was I? Gee, those were the good old days, weren't they. Do you remember where my hand was, most of the time? I do, and I sure would like to put it there once more. Sweetheart, you certainly are a swell wife, and I've enjoyed to the utmost every second that I have been there with you. Let's see, what was the excuse we used to use for going down there? Oh yes! We were going down to listen to the Saturday night operas. Or was it Sunday nights? I've forgotten but we didn't really care, as long as we were together, did we. You know, before we were married, the evenings couldn't possibly come soon enough to suit me, even though I did see you during the day, usually. Our romance was rather short, but well full, wasn't it. I wasted plenty of time, though, before I asked you for a date, didn't I? I adore you.

Your letter is mostly about your trip down to Roselle Park, sweet, so there may not be very much for me to answer in it. I will do the best I can, though, because I love you.

Jackie sure is a lucky one to be able to get a breakfast like that. We usually have a cereal every morning, but I never take any. One morning there were a few worms in the oatmeal and I have never taken any since. But, to tell you the truth, I never took any cereal before, either, and I didn't have any the morning the worms were served. I do quite well on a cup of coffee, and that's usually all I have. Once in awhile I have bacon, or an egg, and whenever they serve doughnuts I eat one. Say , what's all this got to do with answering your letter, huh? To come back to earth, I sure am glad to hear that our sweet daughter has a good appetite. That'll do her the world of good and keep you from worrying about whether she's getting enough to eat or not. From the looks of her you have no cause to worry about that, though. She looks plenty healthy to me. Gee, she's a little angel. My mother used to give us prunes every once in awhile, too, and we seldom had to take anything to keep our bowels loose or regular. Personally, I haven't taken a physic in such a long time that I forget what they taste like. By the way, sweet, how is your regularity?

Every time you mention something about the gang there getting ready for a visit somewhere or anything sort of special I can practically see and hear those two sisters of ours running up and down stairs yelling to each other, singing, laughing at each other and everything else. I can picture Grace begging and pleading with your mother to comb or brush her hair (I suppose she does that herself by now) and all the other familiar noises of a happy home. How I will enjoy hearing, seeing, and being a part of that noisy madhouse.

Our wee one can't be anything but a healthy baby, as long as she enjoys each novel experience as she does. You are extremely lucky my sweet one and you alone deserve all the credit for the well being of our child. I would like to have been able to see her on that first bus ride, but as long as you are able to describe things so well to me I am satisfied. By the way, Lou, forget what I said about saving Jackinelle's first train ride for me. If the opportunity arises, by all means, let her get the most out of it. I wouldn't want her to grow up and tell people that she never had a train ride, because her old man never got around to doing it. There will be plenty for me to do, anyway, with her and for her, so let anything that comes up happen. Honey, I think you are the most beautiful girl in the world.

How you ever managed to get off the bus at the correct place is more than I can understand. But then, you are one of the most intelligent girls in the world, so it isn't so surprising, is it. But, because you had only done the same thing only once before, I have an idea that you weren't any too sure and I can imagine that the girls and your mother were becoming nervous, were they not? But maybe they were too interested in Jackie and the way she behaved on the bus. She must be the best baby in the world.

It's raining again, so I'm glad I didn't go to the show. The boys haven't returned yet, though, so it must be a pretty good show. Ok, Oh !! I spoke too soon. Mr. Forbes has just returned and as it's raining harder now I have a feeling Blosser won't be far behind.

The meal sounds pretty fair to me, but I wouldn't care so very much for the cherries and pineapple on the ham or the candied sweet potatoes. That sort of thing never did appeal to me very much anyway. Fran is a good cook when she feels like cooking and her meals are usually good and well planned. I have an idea she has to be good, in order to keep Eddie satisfied. You should consider yourself lucky, sweet, because even though I really enjoy nice food, I am not too particular and prefer plain food.

The wind is quite strong, now, and I am having my hands full, trying to keep these papers from blowing away. So, if a blot suddenly appears, blame it on the wind. I'm sure not going to stop now until I finish this letter.

I'll bet that "Butch" was glad to see you folks again. Hell, whenever you are around she is a little queen and she is smart enough to know it. And who wouldn't be glad to see her. She is a honey, alright.

Well, as long as that guy Tex stayed to listen to the ballgame and you remained in order to be there when Jackie awoke I sure am glad that Fran stayed. Not that I don't trust you, sweet, but one never knows what may happen and I am a little jealous. But I have something to be jealous of. Your love means more to me than anything else and I wouldn't want anything to break it up. I'm sorry, sweet, I shouldn't have written that, but I can't help it. Please don't be angry.

Jackie sure did have a nice long sleep, didn't she. The bus ride and the excitement probably made her more tired than she usually gets. She must be a well-behaved youngster, too. You are never saying anything but praises for her. It's no wonder you love her so very much. I love you both and want to be there to share your happiness. I want you.

I'm glad your mother had a nice warm place outside in which to read the papers. That trip probably did her loads of good. Too bad she couldn't do it, or something like it, more often.

I am not going to say anything much about your next paragraph, sweet. It's only about your ride out for food and beer. How is the draught beer now, lovely one? Is it as good as it used to be? I heard the alcoholic content was supposed to drop to three point four. That's even better than we get, though. Ours is three two. Your mentioning buying beer by pitchers makes me think of another question to ask. Can't you purchase beer by the quart anymore? Or was that one of Eddie's quaint ideas, in order to save paying the deposit on the bottles? Sweetie-pie, did you have a dance while you were at the tavern or was it just one of those small places with no room for dancing? Never mind, my love, we, you and I will have our fun later on. Gee, I'm glad you are able to get around a little, and have a little fun. I love you, Lou.

Come to think of it, angel, that was the first time Jackie was ever out after dark, wasn't it. No wonder the lights fascinated her. Gee, I wonder how she'll act when she sees all the Christmas lights, like some people used to display? That is, of course, if they ever light up their places again. I hope so, don't you?

My beautiful one, as long as you write lovely long letters like this one, I don't care who you visit with, as long as it isn't someone who is competition to me. Mama G and Tadone are the salt of the earth and to me they are tops. Always give them my special regards, even though I don't mention it.

I was quite surprised to learn that Jackie recognized the place as home. I didn't think she was smart enough for that, yet. But I guess she takes after you, after all.

That takes care of your letter, Lou darling. Now, I have something to ask you that I almost forgot. Did Father Sheerin become Monsignor or is that just scuttlebutt? I have an idea it's not true, because certainly you would have told me. But perhaps you did, and I haven't received the letter as yet. I heard that he did, so please inform me of the truth. In case you have told me, there is no need to repeat, because I'll get the letter soon, I hope.

This will be my last page, sweetest, because I have nothing more to say. I would like to write all night, but alas, my source of information has run dry as an old well. So, my beloved one, give my regards to all the family and our friends. Here is my daily special hug and kiss for our Jackie, and many more for you, the most wonderful wife and sweetheart in the world.

J. De Roxtro EM1/c   Everlastingly, yours forever, *Johnny*

Note on flap: "Hey, Sweetness, how do you like the length of this one? Here's all my love and a kiss for Mickey. Always yours."

Friday, June 16, 1944. *No mail. Very hot. Washed clothes. Jackie out in yard. Jackie drinks from glass at 15 mos.*

[Pavuvu Island, Russell Islands.]
Postmarked June 19, 1944, stamp upside down.   June 16, 1944

Somewhere

Hello, Beautiful:

I love you, miss you and want you, more and more as the days slowly pass, bringing us slowly but surely together. To be there with you is my one desire. I long to hold you tenderly in my arms and kiss you. If I could only have you before me, to do as I desire and attempt to make you as happy as possible. You are mine, sweetheart and I am yours, forever. I am hungry for you and I won't be satisfied until I am able to be with you. Dearest one, I love you.

Tonight, instead of going to supper, I found a large can of bacon on the beach, located a blowtorch, coffee, something to prepare my bacon on, some nice strong onions, some bread, and proceeded to the place to prepare my feed. There were four of us and we had quite a nice feast. There were a couple bottles of beer for each of us, too. Gee honey, those couple of bacon and onion sandwiches tasted so much better than the usual chow we have for supper. Who knows, maybe you and I will be able to go on a trip sometime where I can do the cooking. Some nice trout, for instance, or a rabbit. Anything that will taste good and appease our appetites. Think Jackie would like, huh?

223

No mail came today, angel, for me. Some of the other fellows received some, but I guess maybe you've been too busy to continue your daily letters. Thanks loads for all you've done, sweetie pie. I never did expect them all. I sure hope I am mistaken in assuming that you have stopped your daily writing. You know, it was tough, at first, when I started this chain of daily letters, but now it's sort of become a habit. No matter what I'm doing, or where I am, I find myself longing to get here and start writing. Even those days when I don't feel like it, I am ever anxious to drop a line or two, just to keep the chain unbroken. I love you, my beloved, and will write daily as long as I possibly can.

Tonight I will answer your letter of the twenty-ninth of May. Enclosed herein was a poem about your wishes. They are mine, too, sweet. Gee, I wish I were there to hold you tight. I kind of mixed up a couple there, but you know which one I mean. I wish I may, I wish I might, etc. Thanks loads for the kiss sent via the stamp, angel. Gee, I don't know what I would do without them. On the inside flap you say you love me and miss me more each day. Boy, I, too, wish I could be there to make love to you. I miss you and want you so.

This letter is only two pages long, sweet, so mine won't be much longer. I am quite sure that when I leave here, I will be headed for the states, home, and you. That's what I really want to do and honey, you had better look at the floor as much as you can because when I return, all you'll see is the ceiling. I want you so very much, my darling. I'm in love with the most wonderful wife and sweetheart in the world.

Say, sweet, as long as Ann's camera is out of working order, let's you and I give her a new one. I can spare a few bucks and you can give it to her as a belated birthday present. You find out if you can get one and how much it's worth, and I will send you a money order for the same. I didn't know her camera was on the bum, else I would have suggested this before. Let me know what you think about this, honey, will you? If you do get her one, get one that takes the same size film as yours, so that if anything goes wrong, you can use hers. That would be looking ahead, I guess, wouldn't it? Personally, I don't think there is much use in trying to repair her camera because it is awkward and inconvenient to carry. Just trade it in for a new one and you can use it sometimes, too. I love you, Lou.

Forbes sends a hello back to you, honey, and says to tell you that he is feeling much better. He looks better, too. Maybe the poor guy is finally cured. I hope so, because it must be hell lying around all day with nothing to do. He is looking for a letter from Ann every day and is disappointed when none comes. He thinks a lot of that sister of ours, sweet. It would be nice if they could meet each other, wouldn't it. Who knows, maybe they would click and stick.

How long is it since Woolworths haven't been wrapping purchases, sweet? This is the first you have mentioned it, so I guess it's just a recent innovation. You can just stick things in the carriage, though so it doesn't bother you.

What is the proper spelling of the contraction of does not, sweet? I've been spelling it wrong all this time, I'm afraid.

Here comes the end of the paper, so I now ask you to give my regards to all the family and our friends. Here is my daily hug and kiss for our Jackie, and·many millions more for you, the most wonderful wife and sweetheart in the world. I'll always love you. You are mine.

J.De Roxtro EM1/c   Everlastingly, your loving *Johnny*

Note on flap: "Hello Lovely Lucia. All my love and adoration is yours. Here's loads of hugs and kisses."

Saturday, June 17, 1944. No mail. (took 2 snaps) Very hot. Dressed Jackie in panties. Cleaned house. Went to play tennis 6:00. Came home at 8:00. Had ice cream. Fell asleep in chair 1:15.

[Pavuvu Island, Russell Islands.]
Postmarked June 19, 1944, stamp upside down.

June 17, 1944
Same Place

Hello, Honey:

All the love in the world is ours and I sure do love you. I miss you and want you, too, angel mine, and the day of our reunion can't possibly come too soon to suit me. If hopes and prayers have anything to do with my returning to you soon, then I will be there soon. As the minutes roll up the hours and the hours, days, so my love and adoration increases. More than anything else in the world, I desire to be there holding you in my arms and kissing you.

Tonight I am a little disappointed because no mail came from you, but I will soon get over it, so neither of us should worry. I have a couple to answer yet, so I won't have to wait so very long for another, I hope. By Tuesday or Wednesday, I feel sure, I will have more of your sweet letters to answer.

Let's see, tonight I will answer your letter of the thirtieth of May. The one for the thirty-first hasn't arrived yet. Thanks loads for the kiss sent by the stamp. When I get home I'm going to count them and pay them all back, with interest. Boy, won't that be a long job. That should last me the duration. On the inside flap you asked about my examination. By this time you know all about it, or at least you should, so I won't repeat here. I love you.

That G.I. poem written by Dooling from Morristown sure is correct for the army, but not quite so for us, although it would describe us too. The last part is best. Gee, I wish that I were home with you.

That must have been a parade in itself, with the three of you mothers with children and Grace. But I'm glad you were able to take Jackie to see it. Now I know something else. Our Jackie dances, too. I had never thought of it, but it's only natural that she would. It's in the family on our side and yours too. She is bound to be a dancer. And we all love animals, too, so it's no wonder she liked and was fascinated by the horses.

You seem to have made a day of it at Mil's. More power to you, sweet. Get around all you can and enjoy yourself because it may possibly be quite awhile before I am there to entertain you. When you are happy, I will be happy too. Dearest one, I adore you.

Sweetheart, this letter will be short, because I have to go on duty. After I'm finished it will be too late to write, so you will have to be satisfied, my sweet. I am sorry and would rather make this much longer, but I just can't. Always remember, though, that I love you and think of you always, even though some of my letters seem to be short.

It's too bad you weren't able to go to the show with the girls, but your time will come one of these days and then you'll be happy. Give my regards to all the family and our friends, beloved angel. Here is my daily hug and kiss for our sweetheart, Jackie, and millions more for you, my beloved wife and sweetheart. Here's hoping and praying that we are together soon. All my love is yours. I want to be there, trying to make you happy.

J.De Roxtro EM1/c   Everlastingly, your loving, *Johnny*

Note on flap: "Dearest One, I love you more with each breath I take. Millions of hugs & kisses."

Sunday June 18, 1944. "Father's Day". Very hot. At dinner gave Tadone $3. Joe and Angie came up. Pinafore on Jackie. Jackie waiting at door. Brought her chocolate bars and lollipops. All went out for a ride. Girls and I went to movies. Saw "Tender Comrade." Sad. Home at 8:00. Jackie still up. Ate. Then put her to bed.

[Pavuvu Island, Russell Islands.]
Postmarked June 19, 1944, stamp upside down.   June 18, 1944
                                                           Somewhere

Hello, Beautiful:

I love you, miss you and want you more as each day passes, slowly but surely bringing us more close together. Each and every day my love for you increases. My thoughts are continually of you. Your sweet and lovely image is always before me. I long to take you tenderly in my arms and taste the kisses that I love so much. To feel the warm softness of your tender young body as it presses close to mine, ah, won't that be swell. I miss all the things we used to do together, sweet. I want so much to be there with you. The day of our reunion can't possibly come too soon to suit me. And once again, I feel that it can't possibly be too much longer before I leave this blasted place and return to make love to you.

It's a beautiful day, today, sweet. I can hear several out-boards out in the lagoon and whenever I look in that direction I can see the sail boats sliding gracefully over the deep blue waters. There are four fellows down here pitching horseshoes and a couple having a catch. Over to the left is the rec hall and some fellows are in there reading while at the right, more boats are being built. All the boats are home-made so one can see all shapes and sizes. This place is becoming the playground of the Pacific. But the boys of the fifteenth seem to be the only ones who have the time to build boats and such. There are quite a few of our fellows who haven't anything to do at present, so in order to kill time they build boats and go out riding in them. I just looked down at the dock and there are about a dozen fellows in swimming. The water is always warm and even I go in once in awhile. The other afternoon I was in for about an hour straight, swimming all around the lagoon. Away out in the middle, I went down under, and gee, the water is such a beautiful blue. It's almost impossible to describe the multi-colored fish that are in these tropical waters. The only trouble with swimming now is that we must wear our trunks. That has been in effect the last couple of months. Our officers, a couple of them, have boats, and they often bring some nurses down to go boating, so, sure we must of a necessity become modest. When I get home, I will be able to tell you more about these nurses. I wouldn't be allowed to put in writing what I think about them. There must be some nice ones, though, but in the eyes of the enlisted men, they are all alike. We can go nude in our quarters, though. And, as you have probably guessed, your loving husband is in that condition most of the time. It's a lot cooler and after all, comfort is the hardest thing to get here. Gee, it's going to be swell, when you and I will be able to do as we please, in the privacy of our own little room. Darling, I love you and desire so much to be with you.

Well, there seems to be nothing I can say to describe things further. Blosser is here at the foot of my cot shaving, Forbes is getting dressed, a fellow named John Harder, another ten-mate is fast asleep and I am writing to my adorable angel. Forbes must be feeling much better, because he went out and played a couple of innings of baseball this morning. Here's hoping he never has to return to the sickbay again. He had to go up last evening for a check-up, but I think the results will be negative.

Now, my sweet and lovely one, I guess it's time to start answering your letter of the first of June. As usual, honey, I send my thanks for the kiss you sent by way of the stamp. Boy, they are mounting up, and it will take me a long, long time to return them to your lovely ruby lips. On the inside flap you apologize for not making your letter longer. That is unnecessary, lovely, because I realize that at times it's almost impossible to write very much. I will be satisfied with only short ones, if you write daily. Heck, I'll be satisfied with any.

Lou, darling, it may seem hot to you back there, and it may seem that way to me here, but boy, wait till we get together. That's when we will really think it's hot. And how I am looking forward to it. Are you?

How could Ralph do anything but like the snapshot of Jackie and Michael Jr. together? They are really swell. No one could help but like those pictures.

Heck no, I don't want our daughter to be a sissy, but after all, simply because she is a female, I want her to be a little lady. But her playing in the dirt won't hurt her. In fact, I think it will do her a lot of good. The only trouble is you have extra work trying to keep her clean. But even that could be worse. Supposing she didn't like to be bathed? Then your troubles would be doubled. You had better not give her bottles to play with, though, sweet? Isn't it possible that one may break and she become cut on it? You have probably thought of all that, though, but I just can't help reminding you of it. If I seem a bit bossy at times, or out of line, just overlook it, will you? It's only because I have the interests of both of you at heart. I mean well, and can't help but make suggestions about some of the things you mention. I would like to be able to be there with her, playing in the dirt. Gee, what a kick

I would get out of playing with our wee one. I'm missing a lot. I love you both.

I'm glad to learn that Judy doesn't look as bad as the pictures of her. Maybe she is just one of those kiddies who don't photograph well. Our Jackinelle takes a swell picture, though, doesn't she. Say, Hon, I thought you said that our bambino doesn't care for ice cream? But I guess children change in likes and dislikes, too, as they do in most other things. You were lucky that day, if only because Judy didn't like her black raspberry ice cream. You and I will have lots of cream when I get home, but what's most important, will have lots of love.

Honey, my letters of the twenty-second and twenty-fifth were nice and long, as you say, but there probably won't be anything in them to answer. No mail came again for me, so I have reasoned that you weren't able to keep up with your daily writing. I may be mistaken and I hope I am, but that's the way it looks.

It would be swell if we were able to tell each other of our love and adoration without writing, but actions speak louder than words, so maybe we won't even have to talk. Most of the time I'll have your lips sealed by a kiss, anyway, so you won't be able to. I love you.

Well, sweetheart, this will be my last page for today. Your letter is answered and all I can say now is that I am as well as usual, and as happy as I could possibly be, away from you.

I am hoping and praying that I will be there with you this year, and the sooner the better. I am terribly hungry, my little lotus blossom, and only being there with you can satisfy me. I want to feel the thrill of kissing you. I want to feel the steady rhythm of your pulse as I hold your sweet, lovely, warm body close to mine. I want to be able to feel your lovely breasts, kiss you on the neck, cheeks, shoulders, nipples, belly and navel. Dearest one, I want to be able to do the things to and for you that a husband should. I love you so much, Lou. There isn't anything I wouldn't do for you. Darling wife, sweetheart, and mother, I am more proud every day to be your husband. Never a minute goes by that I am not thinking of you and wishing I were there.

Give my fond regards to the family and any of our mutual friends you may happen to meet. Here is my daily hug and kiss for Jackie and a kiss for my Mickey. To you, my sweet, I would like to send my all, but you will have to be satisfied with my undying love and adoration. Always your dutiful slave,

J.De Roxtro EM1/c   Your loving *Johnny*

Note on flap: *"Hi, Sweet, this isn't very long but it's the best. I love you eight days a week now. Hugs & kisses.*

June 19-20, 1944 – The "Marianas Turkey Shoot" occurs as U.S. Carrier-based bombers shoot down 220 Japanese planes, while only 20 American planes are lost. US carrier forces located and practically wiped out the Japanese carrier fleet and Japanese air attacks which were launched at various times and from different land-based operations. "This was the largest carrier-to-carrier battle in history" (Wikipedia.org, Battle of the Philippine Sea), where approximately 1,350 carrier-based aircraft picked off the Japanese planes "just like an old-time turkey shoot down home," according to a remark by a pilot from the USS Lexington.

Monday, June 19, 1944. *Card from Mary. Rain. Very dark at 10:00. Wrote to Ralph.*

[Pavuvu Island, Russell Islands.]
Postmarked June 20, 1944, stamp upside down.

June 19, 1944
Same old place

Most Precious Darling:

You will never know how much I love and adore you because mere words couldn't even come close to explaining my feelings for you, and, honey, by my actions you could never know, either, because I'm so darn clumsy when it comes to delicate, delightful things such as love-making. So you will have to be satisfied with me saying that I love you more than life itself. Sweetheart, you are the only girl in the world for me and no one will ever be able to take your place. I miss you so very much, too, my lovely one. I miss all those little things we used to do together and all the things about you, yourself, that I like. For instance, your eyes that sparkle with joy when you smile and are comparable to the hottest fires of hell when you are angry. They are beautiful eyes, either way, my love, and although I prefer them laughing, I also like to see the fire in them when you are angry, but that is so seldom, it wouldn't hurt me any. My angel, I want you. I desire to hold you tenderly in my arms once again and kiss you. The pleasant feeling of your luscious lips as they cling to mine still remains with me, after all these long months. I long to see you and talk to you. I desire to touch you and let my hands wander all over your beautiful body. I yearn to sate the hunger I have, partly by letting my eyes feast upon your lasting beauty. May the day of our reunion soon arrive so that I can be happy in your company and do my best to make you happy too. The sooner the quicker and I am, and always have been, ready to head for home. Hell, if I remain much longer, maybe Ralph will have his two years in and be there the same time I am. That would be swell, but I hope I don't have to wait that long.

Today I hit the jackpot again. I received four lovely letters. One was from my mother and the others were all beautiful epistles of love and adoration from my most precious wife and sweetheart. They were written the sixth, ninth and tenth of June and were postmarked the tenth, eleventh and twelfth. All these had two airmail stamps on them and only one had pictures enclosed. Thanks loads for the kisses, honey, but thanks over and over again for that snapshot of you. It's really swell and, darling, you are more beautiful than ever. Gee, I sure am lucky. I will mention more about those pictures when I answer the letter they came with, but I feel that I must comment on the snapshots of Jackie, too. In every one of them she is smiling and she also gets more beautiful every day. Darling, I love you both and want so much to be there with you. I am real proud of you, my beloved wife, and I sho' does loves yah, honey.

There is a musical playing at our local theatre this evening so I think I'll go. So, my sweet, pardon me for a short while. I will be back soon. I love Lucia. The picture was College Rhythm and it was a fairly decent piece of light entertainment. I rather enjoyed it but I wouldn't care so much for it back in the states. I don't know who the players were, even though I've just seen it. You know how I am about those things.

I received another picture today, too, Lou. It isn't of me, or anyone else whom you would know. It is of a machine that another fellow and myself made up out of junk parts of different pieces of machinery while we were back on Santos. It is a machine that cuts threads on pipe, thus saving much time and labor. You probably would understand it, but I intend finding out if I can send it home. If I can, I want you to preserve it for me. It's one of my brainchildren and I am proud of it. You may show it to Gene or anyone else if you care to. The picture itself isn't very clear, but maybe I will be able to describe it to you when I see you. There were three pictures taken of it and I'll try to get the other two. It's really quite a piece of machinery and as heavy and large as it is, we brought it along with us. So you can readily see how valuable it is to the battalion. But I am boring you, so I will dispense with my self-praise and rest on my laurels. Or isn't that what I rest on.

Your letter of the second of June is next on my list, so I will answer that tonight. It's a good thing it isn't too long, else I wouldn't be able to. 'Tis rather late, you know, and I may have to stop rather abruptly. Here's hoping I won't, but I will take time out now to address the envelope, put the stamp on, and seal it with a kiss. Time out for that, my adorable angel. Always remember I love you. That's done, so here I go, my sweet.

Thanks millions for the kiss. You tell me inside the flap, that you love me and miss me and send love and kisses. Gee, angel, those little notes are really swell, aren't they. Just like passing love letters to your beau in school. Or didn't you ever do that? I love you.

That changing of mind really was a wonderful thought for you to have, lover. If you had had Jackie injected that day, as it was so warm you would have had your hands full. You are about the most thoughtful wife, mother and sweetheart in the world. Every day I become more proud of you and my love and adoration increases. You're swell. You know, our bambino must take after you. She knew there was something at the doctor's office she should remember. That's really remarkable, sweet, and she's as yet so young, too. One would never have thought she would remember, after an absence of almost two months. She's smart, like her mother. You're darn tootin' she's solid. I was comparing her legs with "Butch's" today and they look about the same size to me. She is a healthy, husky babe and right in the groove. I'll bet she's hip to a plenty, too. (tch! Tch!)

You may as well forget all that stuff you tell me about ration books, coupons, and such, dearest one, because I'm an old man and haven't the faintest idea what it's all about. Anyway, I seem to know that the less coupons you get rid of the more you have and that's supposed to be good. That means, I suppose, by not forking out a coupon for Jackie's shoes that you will now be able to get another pair for yourself. Am I right? Don't bother going into too much detail about it, though, because I will soon learn the whys and wherefores of rationing when I get home.

Most of this letter was about your trip to the doctor for Jackie's routine inspection and general checkup, so now that I have answered it all, I will be able to say something I've intended to for quite awhile, but have forgotten until now.

You know, sweet, I am kind of pleased that we don't have an automobile anymore. Now, when I come home we can remain at home and if anyone desires to see me or us, they can come there and we can be out if we want to. It may be more inconvenient, though, I don't know. Let me know what you think about the situation, honey, will you? Maybe we can make some kind of arrangements to acquire a car, if you want to ride, once in awhile.

Good night, sweetheart, I love you. Give my regards to all the family and our friends. Here is my daily special hug and kiss for Jackie, and millions more for you, the only
girl in the world for me. More than anything else in the world, I want to be there making love to you. Sweetheart I love you, miss you and want you.

J.De Roxtro EM1/c   *Everlastingly, your loving* *Johnny*

Note on flap: *"Did I ever tell you how beautiful you are? The most in the world. Loads of hugs and kisses."*

Tuesday, June 20, 1944. *Letters of June 9, 10, 11, C-Breeze. Vene called up this morning. Washed clothes. Cooked sauce. Jackie awoke 1:30. Ate. Vene came at 2:00. Went to bank and then to see Nana 3:00-4:30. Had ice cream. Beautiful place. Came home at 5:00. Read letters. Made fruit salad. Pulled in clothes. Sent package to Ralph. Bill from Dr. Wade - $35.00.*

[Pavuvu Island, Russell Islands.]

Postmarked June 21, 1944, stamp upside down.

June 20, 1944
Same hole

Lovely Lucia:

I love you, miss you and want you more as each day passes, slowly bringing us closer together. Gee, honey, I hope and pray that it won't be long until I can hold you in my arms once again and kiss you.

Tonight we are having a stage show. It is supposed to be quite good. There are a few nationally famous personages in it, as you no doubt have noticed in our local paper. I'm going, whether I finish answering your letter of the fourth of June before show time or not. If I don't, I will take a chance on returning in time to do so. I may stay for only the stage show and return before the picture is over. I'll see how things work out, though. I may even have time to tell you about the show. I'll do my best, anyway, because I love you.

No mail came for me again today, most precious one, but I can hardly expect them every day, can I? I sure did well yesterday and I have taken your picture down dozens of times today and looked longingly at it. Thanks again, sweetheart. I have the most thoughtful wife in the world, and I adore her. I sure wish I could have been there all these months instead of out here in the tropics. The two best years of my life have been spent on these damned tropical islands. I want so very much to be there making love to you. I am hungry.

Clere's daughter is sixteen years old tomorrow and he wants each of us to write a page to her, like we did last year. I will, of course and I'm quite sure all the others will. I hardly know what to say but somehow I will find a way. It would be a lot easier if I knew her, though. He always refers to her as his baby girl and I have an idea that she wouldn't like it if she knew. Frosty has shown us pictures of her and I must say she is a beauty and quite well-developed, almost over-developed, for a girl so young. Why he refers to her as he does I can't imagine.

Now don't get excited or get your hopes raised too high, because there is nothing official about the following bit of scuttlebutt. Dame rumor

233

has it that we are leaving here about the eighth of next month. Boy, how I hope and pray that it's the truth. Wouldn't it be swell, honey. That would mean we would be in each other's arms about the first of August. It seems almost too good to be true, and it probably isn't but here's hoping. One of these days someone will hit it right, though, and whenever it is that we leave this rock it will be okay with me. As I said before, it can't come any too soon to suit me. Oh, darling, how I long to hold you close to me. I want to feel your soft warm yielding body close to mine, to feel those soft luscious lips against mine and to do all those little things with you and for you that we used to do. I am in love with you.

Thanks so very much for the double kiss you sent by way of the stamps, angel. Do you ever have to put extra postage on any of my letters anymore? I try to keep them all stamped correctly but sometimes I may slip up a little. You never mentioned it any more and I was wondering. On the inside of the envelope you tell me of your love. I feel the same about you, angela mio. You also asked me to say hello to the boys for you. They all said to answer with a hello and send thanks for your interest in them. Also, they send their regards and best wishes to both you and Jackie. Every time I receive some snapshots they are almost as eager as I am to see them. Naturally I show them around as soon as I look at them. When they saw the last one of you they all wondered how an ugly old man like me ever managed to get a beautiful wife like you. They said you must have fell for my line. Did you fall for my line, or me, darling? All the fellows think the world of both you and Jackie, sweet, and I honestly believe some of them are jealous. I do have the most beautiful wife and daughter in the world. And I also have the most loving and most thoughtful wife. Angel, I am proud of you. More than ever before, I want to be there with my wife and daughter. I love you both and should be with you. I'm hungry. Gee, Lou, this letter of yours is eight pages long and I never could answer it before show time. So, I will have to skip the show and take care of my love life. You are the most beautiful girl in the world, sweet. The stage show has just pulled in so I guess it's about time for it to start. There isn't so very much I can answer to your letter, I see, so I will go, anyway.

So you held out on me, huh? Well, I'll overlook it this time. And I'm glad you were not able to wear your shorts. You should know I don't want anyone to look at your legs, (above the knees, I mean.) but me. All kidding aside, honey, I'm sure glad you were able to go down to Roselle, and more glad that you had a good time. In a way, I envy you. That's a heck of a long bus ride just to play a couple of sets of tennis, though. I don't think I would care so very much for it. With you by my side I would be bound to enjoy it.

Say, sweet one, if you care to, you and I can beat Ann and Fan in a game of doubles, so why not challenge them? You will have to do most of the playing, though, I'm afraid. After all, I'm an old man now, and not as spry as I used to be. I haven't even had a racquet in my hand since the last time I played with you and that sure is a long time ago. You see, I'm alibiing already.

Well, sweet, I have just started my last sheet of writing paper, so I'll have to get more tomorrow. I'm not taking chances of running short anymore. It's five of seven, right now, lovely one, so I think I will close temporarily and go see how the show is. It's supposed to start at seven.

No I don't know anything about Elizabeth, sweet. I've been through there once or twice but I don't remember anything about it. Which reminds me, Elizabeth is supposed to be a good place to shop. How would you like me to take you one of these days? The prices are a little higher than most places, though, so I hear. But who cares about that as long as you get what you want?

Come to think of it, sweet, maybe it's a good thing it wasn't very warm that day. Can't you just picture how uncomfortable you would have been had it been hot? And how you would have imagined you smelled to others in the bus? Yes, for your sake, I guess it was all the better because it was cool.

I've just returned from the show, my pet, and I say truthfully that it was the best all-service entertainment we've had so far. In my estimation, it rates second only to Ray Bolger and Little Jack Little. It was really magnificent and the fellows all appreciated it. I can't remember names very well, or else I would tell you more than I am. There was an eight-piece band, made up mostly of members of famous name bands, a pair of comedians, four members of the star dusters (You've heard of them) and as master of ceremonies, a fellow named Jack Hart, formerly on the N.B.C. Oh, I almost forgot, there were also two Irish tenors who were also very good. The instruments in the band were a piano, trap drums, bass fiddle, accordion, trombone, cornet, and a saxophone. They were all swell, too. A show like that back at home would go over big and would draw quite a crowd. I'm glad I went, sweet. There were naturally quite a few jokes but I couldn't repeat them here. They aren't allowed by the postal authorities or our censors.

Thanks, sweetheart, for pardoning me while I went to the show. It was swell of the swellest sweetheart and wife in the world. Now, I will take up where I left off and see what I can do with the remainder of your letter. Sort of looks as if this one will have two stamps on it, too. Honey, do you like long letters, or would you rather I wrote shorter ones and wrote more often?

There's no need to answer that one. I know you prefer more letters. More long ones, that is, of course. But I'm afraid I won't be able to write more often. Sorry honey, no can do.

Gosh, honey, I don't know what I would do without you. It has been practically impossible all my life to remember birthdays, anniversaries and such. Heck, I didn't have the faintest idea that Fran's anniversary was in June. I'm depending more on you each day and you are continually surprising me by reminding, no, surprising me with these little things. How do you ever manage to remember them all, Lou? I can't even figure how I ever remembered your birthday and our anniversary and Jackie's birthday and even Ann's birthday, but I did, and it even surprises me. I guess being in love with the most gorgeous girl on earth does those things. Or could it have been the threat you issued one time when I told you I might forget. Do you remember that? You said I had better remember those things about you or else. I don't know what the ultimatum might have been, but I wasn't taking any chances. Oh, my sweet one, I wanted so much to be there with you on those special days, but it wasn't to be because of this damned war. Never mind, angel, we'll make up for it later one if it is possible, won't we. Sweet, I want to do so much for you but at times I am afraid I won't be able to do all I want to. Sweetheart, I love you more as each day passes and I am hungry for your love.

Gee, it's so refreshing to hear you say you had such a swell time down at Fran's. Honey, you don't know how much I enjoy reading about those little excursions you are able to make. I only wish you were able to make more of them. Maybe the three of us can do things later on. I sure hope so.

Fran would pack a nice lunch and she always uses quite a few of those delicacies like pickles etc. When she wants to be, Fran is swell and an excellent mother as well as a good housekeeper and wife. But most of the time she just doesn't give a darn and lets things slide.

That park sounds like a swell place to me and I agree that it would be a swell place to take our children. It would be lovely if we had a park similar to that in your back yard. There are plans for connecting Lake Pocahontas into a beautiful park, you know because of the war. One of these days though who knows, maybe our local board of aldermen will awaken from their deep slumbers and do something. I think maybe I should run for alderman, some day and awaken them rudely. I love you.

You are bragging, my sweet, and it isn't becoming to you. You do play a good game of tennis, though, and you do everything else well, too. I can beat you at tennis, though, without half trying. That is, of course, providing and so forth. I would like to play a game with you though. I keep my balls low, too, and my service is terrific. I haven't tried my backhand in quite awhile though, so it probably is worse than yours. And don't get me wrong, censor, I'm writing of tennis.

Playing for such a long time must have been quite tiresome, wasn't it, sweet, especially as it was your first time this season. Boy, I'll bet you were stiff the next day and a bit wobbly in the legs, too. I wonder what I'll feel like when I start going about on sidewalks, etc. My sweet wife will probably walk me to death, not realizing that I am unused to city streets, etc. All I've walked on is coral, coral, and more coral. And I wear out a pair of shoes in a little less than two months. That includes the resoling job I have done, too. I sure am glad I don't wear my shoes out as quickly back at home. It would keep me broke, buying new shoes. As you know, I am very easy on shoes too. You should see some of these guys. Shoes last hardly any time at all, and they aren't easy to get, either. Sweet, I love you.

Isn't it funny that Fran never mentioned that park to us before, sweet? Hell, I never even knew there was such a place until I received this letter. And boating, reminds me, would you care to go rowing at Branch Brook Park and take colored snapshots? You see, every once in awhile I am able to remember something nice. But, as usual, you have to start me off with a suggestion or a hint.

Let's see, Fred Camisa was the one who was a gardener at some private estate, wasn't he? I remember him and I liked the poor guy loads. Too bad about his demise, but we must all go sooner or later to meet our maker. I sincerely hope and pray that he will rest in peace.

Gee, seven o'clock at night is kind of late to dine, isn't it? It doesn't give you or the girls much time to prepare for an evening out, does it. But it's swell of the rest of you to wait for her, though. You folks really do get along swell together. I wish I were there.

So, you are prettying up. A permanent, now. I suppose you have to look pretty for your boyfriend, is that it? Well, you have better or I'll break your lovely neck. No sweetheart of mine deserves anything but the best, and I have an idea you needed one. How's about a picture, huh? I still want more and I never will get enough. I do want you to keep yourself in clothes and well groomed, Lucia. You deserve everything you get and more, so, for me, pretty up often, will you?

Darn it, I had intended ending this all too short note on the preceding page, but there wasn't quite enough room. Now I will have to bore you with another page. Oh, well, you promised to take me for better or worse, and you got the worst of it.

Say, angel, have you taken the little one to a swimming hole yet?

237

I'm kind of anxious to learn how she behaves. Who knows, maybe she'll learn to swim this year? That really would be a novelty, wouldn't it? But our child is capable of anything and it wouldn't surprise me in the least if she was a child wonder at something. Say, those last pictures of her are swell. I love them. They are the first I have of her in summer clothes, aren't they. Gosh, if only I could get home this summer. Wouldn't it be swell.

I am so tired I can hardly keep my eyes open. Every once in awhile I have to stop writing for a half second or so and close my eyes because everything becomes blurry. And the picture isn't over yet, either. I must be aging more than I thought.

Give my fond regards to all the family and our friends. Here is my daily hug and kiss for our Jackie and many million more for the most adorable wife and sweetheart in all the world. I love you, miss you, and want you forever.

J.De Roxtro EM1/c   *Everlastingly, your faithful* *Johnny*

Note on flap: "*Hi Darling, Did I ever tell you how much I desire to be with you? I love you.*"

Tuesday, June 21, 1944. *Letter of June 14. Rain. Cleared in late afternoon. Judy came over with Gene. Girls went to Newark. Ann gave me my birthday present - a pair of pyjamas.*

[Pavuvu Island, Russell Islands.]
Postmarked June 22, 1944 – two stamps upside down.   June 21, 1944
                                                              Somewhere

Hello Sweet:

I love you, miss you and want you. Each and every day that passes brings us more close together, even though it is in time only. How I long to hold you tenderly in my arms once again and kiss you. My most precious one, the day we are reunited can't come any too soon to suit me. I am continually hoping and praying that we will be together soon. My sweet, my thoughts are continually of you, and your image is always before me, guiding me in everything I do. Most lovable wife, I adore you.

No mail came today, Lou, and I don't have anything more to tell you, so I will go right ahead and answer your letter of the sixth of June. That will leave me only two more to answer, so unless I get more, I will save one for Sunday. I am not expecting any, though, for awhile now. Those last ones came across so fast the next ones won't come for another few days yet. Maybe I will get one Saturday or Sunday.

After supper tonight I went down and pitched a couple of games of horseshoes. I didn't do as badly as I thought I would but I sure was lousy. I did manage to win a couple of games, though. I may go down more often and practice a little.

Thanks loads for your kisses sent by way of the stamps, sweet. This letter is a nice long one; ten pages. I hope I will be able to do as well. I sure do hope the hunch you have that we will be together soon comes true. This is what you had on the inside of the flap. To be truthful, my sweet, if things go as they are now, we are liable to go farther north to do another job. We are raising the devil with those little yellow men right now, so maybe it won't be long before we are home for good. I know I've been away long enough. I want to get home to see my adorable wife.

Yes, sweetheart, you and I have been away from each other for two of your birthdays and probably will be for two more, but even that is better than having the Japs there, fighting in our country. I want so very much to be there with you, but if it was fighting at home or out here, I would rather it was here. Gee, wouldn't it be terrible if we were being invaded by some foreign power? I think I will get off that subject. It isn't pleasant, is it?

Sweetheart, you may be getting older, but never will you be anything but my little sweet one. To me, you will always retain your youth, while I grow older and older. I love you, my darling. Do you really wish you were eighteen again, Lou? You are more beautiful now than you were then. You have a loving husband and an adorable baby, too. You don't have to wonder what your boyfriend will be like, or anything. So, if you really do wish you were eighteen again, you would probably do things differently. I wonder what you would do, if it did happen. Would I have met you, wooed you, and won you? I doubt it. Someone else would be there with you and where would I be? Let's see, if I were single and seven years less old I would be in the air corps, if I could be. If not, I would be aboard a can (destroyer) or some other small boat that sees plenty of action. Oh, hell, we can't possibly become younger, so why am I carrying on like this. The main thing is we never grow old until we begin to feel old. And you don't feel any older. That's swell! Most of the time out here I feel old, but I know it's nothing that being with you won't change. Seeing you again will be as good as finding the fountain of youth. One glance of your lovely face and wonderful figure and I will be completely rejuvenated. Say, dearest, did I ever tell you what a wonderful shape you have? It's the best I've ever seen and I've looked them all over. I love you.

No, sweet, I haven't said anything to Fran about you purchasing those clothes for Lesley Ann. I know you didn't have to buy them. You are just too darn good for your own sake. Anyone as good-natured as you are would have done the same. I'm not blaming you, lovely one. In fact, it's little deeds like that that make me love you more. So, honey, we will just forget about that little incident, shall we? I was a bit put out at first, but soon I got over it.

Yes, my precious one, I've just taken one more step toward the top, but you are over-rating my powers. This next step is a lot harder to make and there are plenty of other guys here that will keep themselves in the eyes of the powers that be more than I will. However, I intend doing my best and who knows, one of these days I may be able to wear clothes and not the monkey suit. That really would be swell and a lot more comfortable. And even though there would be no gold on my hat, I would then try hard for that. But let's not be in the service that long, shall we. What I want more than anything else is to be there with you. Sweetheart, I would be willing to leave here as an apprentice seaman if they would let me go home. I've had enough of the navy. I adore you.

Yes, Fitz and I have been separated for two or three months, but now he is living in the tent next to me. He is doing alright as is Forbes. I told you he is well again now, didn't I? He went out to play ball for our company today and does a good days work each day, so I guess he is finally rid of the malaria. Here's hoping he stays well the duration of our stay out here in the tropics.

By this time you have received the news of the pin-up girl contest by the scandal sheet. If I had entered your picture you would have been Mrs. Fifteenth Battalion now. There were only about thirty entries altogether including wives and sweethearts. Most of the fellows wouldn't put their wives and sweethearts on exhibition and I know darn well that I wouldn't. I have been thinking of that baby contest, myself. It would be kind of risky, though, because plenty of us have little ones we've never seen, and naturally we're all proud of our families. There would be a great deal of jealousy and hard feelings would spring up. Naturally I wouldn't want a bunch of fellows sore at me. Our Jackie would win easily, I know, because I've seen most of the others and I'm not saying that merely because she belongs to us. She really is a beauty. If they did hold a baby contest I would enter a picture of Jackie. I don't know which one, though. It would either be one of these last ones or the one you took of her on her toidy. It wouldn't make much difference, though, because she would be certain to win.

You poor darling! You do have to go through plenty, don't you. I wish I could have been there to see Jackie upset the basket of clothespins, get whacked, and then start on the clothes. Ha Ha! I sure would have liked to have seen it. It sounds as though she were thinking - hm - spank me, will she?

Gosh, that spanking hurt! I'll get even though – I'll make her rinse the clothes again – I'll get another spanking, but it will be worth it. Besides, it hurts my mommy more than it does me! How's that, sweet? I'll be it does hurt you to have to spank her, doesn't it. I know darn well that it would really hurt me. I have my doubts if I would be able to do it. It was nice of her to help you at first, though, wasn't it. And cute, too.

All you have to do is leave a child out in the yard and she'll get into the dirt, alright. I'm sure glad she does, though. Wouldn't it be terrible if she didn't like to play in the dirt: Heck, that wouldn't be natural, would it. It keeps you busy trying to keep her clean though, doesn't it.

No angel, you don't know the fellow who made those cards. His name is John Hardie, and he is in the tent with me now. Not right at this minute, though. He was on light duty or something and I asked him if he would make them for me. He was kind enough to do it and he did do a swell job. All he had were two colored pencils and a fountain pen. He is always doing something like that. He is a pretty fair guy but a little too much of an old maid to suit me. However I figure that it's only for a short while so I can stand him or anyone else. Out here one has to do things once in awhile that aren't particularly nice.

I like to surprise you, angel, and I know you like being surprised. That's the only reason I sent the roses without telling you. I did tell a little white lie, though, about being broke, but I know that you will overlook that. Anyway, my love, I am pleased to know that they arrived in time, this time, and that you like receiving them. I specifically ordered small red rosebuds, because they always last longer and are nicer to look at. I made out the order for both Ann's and yours, and had both sent the sixth, in order to save the florist gasoline. I hope Ann didn't mind too much. I know you didn't, love. I'll have to remember that you like those Mocha cakes for your birthday. That will be my next birthday present to you. You are bound to have it and would even make a special trip to get it. So, in order to keep trade the old mill inn temporarily moved in to Day's huh? Oh, well, I can't say that I blame them very much.

And Sandrian's finally had your camera fixed. Swell, now maybe I can get more pictures taken with that good camera. Say, who took these last ones, angel? Especially that one of you? Whoever did held the camera crooked. I didn't notice whether the ones of Jackie were or not! I'm glad those negatives of Ralph turned out good too. He probably won't show any weight he may happen to put on because it is probably going into muscle. It's possible he may grow a little taller, too. Personally, I've lost about ten pounds, but don't miss it at all. I am still able to jump up onto a table from a stand, turn

241

handsprings and everything I used to be able to do, so I have an idea I will live through all they can dish out. I am lucky enough to be able to adjust myself to any conditions that exist. I would like a decent meal once in awhile, though. By that I mean a good home-cooked meal like we used to have. Our meals are good, but there's no place like home. I love you.

That pair of sailors that Gracie gave you must have been cute. The verse is pretty good, too. She is quite a thoughtful gal and does her best, doesn't she. You know, that little sister of yours must have changed quite a lot since I've seen her. Heck, she has become almost a young woman by now and she was still a little girl when I last cast eyes upon her. You can be sure that your mother and sisters will come across with a little something or other for your birthday. They, like you, would rather give than receive. You folks get quite a kick out of giving each other presents. It's a swell way to be and I love you for it.

Another trip to New York. Boy, you sure are doing a swell job of it, honey. Make the best of it while you can, sweet, and enjoy yourself all you can because someday you won't be able to do all those things. Not because I won't let you or don't want you to, but just in case you may not be able to. Did you go down for anything special this time or just for the sake of going? I remember when you two gals got those housecoats. That was a mighty long time ago and I guess you did need them. Both of you made good use of them and you, maybe, a little more than Ann. Why didn't you also get one for yourself, sweet? I adore my wife. Ann is bound to like that coat, sweet. You both like the same things (maybe even me) and if you like it, she will, I know. Her other one was blue, too, wasn't it, and yours red? I'm not any too certain of that, but I think I'm right. You said you bought a pair of white shoes, a white bag, and a pinafore for Jackie. Honey, what the devil is she going to do with a white bag. She's a little too young yet to be carrying a bag, isn't she? And as for the shoes, you were taking quite a chance, buying them without trying them on. I hope they fit alright. Let me know. I still don't know what a pinafore is, so I can't very well comment on that. But as you know what you're doing, it's okay by me. What a jackass I am. You bought the shoes and bag for yourself. How could I have thought the other, even though that's the way your letter read. Pardon my dumbness, sweet. That's one of my many faults.

That ends your letter, so this page will end mine. Two nights in a row and I've written at least ten pages. Must be love. I hope I don't bore you too much.

Give my fond regards to all the family and our friends. Here's my daily special hug and kiss for our darling daughter and millions more for you, the only girl in the world for me.

J.De Roxtro EM1/c   Everlastingly, your loving *Johnny*

Note on flap: "I'm in love with you, Lou. Here's lots of love, hugs and kisses. As ever."

Thursday, June 22, 1944. Letters of June 12,13. Lovely day. Sent Gracie to store for meat. Came back with Mary. Cooked sauce. Put baby to sleep & went to dentist. Had a molar pulled. Went to Mil's in afternoon with Jackie.

[Pavuvu Island, Russell Islands.]

Postmarked June 23, 1944, stamp upside down.   June 22, 1944

Somewhere

Hello, Sweetheart:

I love you, miss you and want you. Your lovely image is always before me, guiding my each and every move. Without you, I would be lost. My thoughts are of you continually. Gee, I often wonder what I would be like, out here, if I hadn't have had you as my mate. I know darn well that I wouldn't be as quiet and easy-going as I am. Several times I've felt like blowing off a little steam but I figured you would rather I didn't, so I worked it off. And boy, can I work when I'm angry. The trouble is, I make the others work harder and faster in trying to keep up with me. But that doesn't happen very often, so it's not so bad. I guess we all have to release the pressure once in awhile. There, you see, I am able to change from one subject to the other with the greatest of ease.

How I long to take your lovely young body, hold it close to me and kiss your luscious lips. Ah, the memory of our last embrace is still with me, and I am anxiously awaiting our next. May the day of our reunion come soon so that we can make each other happy again.

I'm not in a writing mood tonite, Lucia, my own, so I don't think I will answer either of your letters tonight. I have written a short note to Charlene Clere wishing her a happy birthday and that really was a tough job. I couldn't possibly think of anything to say. I really made a mess of it, but what the heck do I care. I only did it because Frosty asked me to. Say, I hope you don't mind because I wrote to another girl. She's a nice-looking gal, too, and has a nice shape. You should see her in a bathing suit.

I think I shall go to the show tonight and finish this after I return. Maybe I'll be in a better mood after. I don't know what is playing and don't care a heck of a lot. I know that it's something about the blues but I don't know what kind of blues.

Honey, did I ever tell you that you are the most adorable wife and sweetheart in the world? You are, and I am more proud of you all the time.

243

How I would like to be able to be there with you soon, wooing you all over again. Most precious one, I love you and I am hungry for your love. To me, you are the best. I adore you.

Sweetheart, I couldn't remain at the show. I honestly tried, but it was lousy, with a capital L. First there was a short, with some gal singing nursery rhymes to us, then the feature picture, "Swing Out With The Blues." Boy, I've seen bad pictures but never one as bad as that. Such a stinker I've never seen. Just about half the guys have left but there are some who always remain. Some fellows would sit through anything. Enough for that, my love. No use boring you.

No mail came for me today, honey, but I don't expect any until Saturday or Sunday, although the stuff that has arrived since I got my last ones from you was postmarked up till the seventeenth of June. I love to receive letters from you, but after all, I can't expect too much, can I? I consider myself very lucky to receive as many as I do. I hope you don't mind if I don't answer yours tonight but I just don't feel like writing.

The news of the war sounds quite good, now, doesn't it. And that fellow who predicted the Germans would be licked by November, Armistice Day, sure stuck his neck out, but I hope he's right. As for the news down here, well, we will be able to take care of the Jap fleet, unless they run again.

A week from Sunday we are to have a regatta here, with sailboat racing, motor boat races and swimming meet all combined. All the boats are homemade out of scrap lumber and discarded machine parts and they really are quite good. Our executive officer designed and built the funniest looking boat you've ever seen and it runs just about as funny as it looks. Any minute everyone expects it to suddenly plunge to the bottom with all hands aboard. He isn't very well liked so it boosted the morale quite a bit. That's the best I can say for it. I will tell you more about it when I see you. Maybe there will be a poem or something about it in our scandal sheet this week. If there is, and it is veiled, somehow, I will underscore it for you.

The scuttlebutt still says that we are leaving here between the third and eighth of next month, but I doubt it. If hoping and praying will help any, I know we will, because I've been doing both. The sooner we leave here, the sooner I will be there holding you close to me and I am ready to leave now. The scuttlebutt remains consistent, anyway. Gee, lovely one, to hold you in my arms and kiss you would be heavenly. More than anything else in the world, I desire to tell you of my love and adoration.

Honey, I've finally found out the name of the shell those salt and pepper shakers are made of. It is Paua, pronounced powa. Look that one up in your dictionary or encyclopedia. Maybe it's in there, but I am not sure it would be.

I think I may be able to surprise you again one of these days with a matching set of. But if I tell you about it, it won't be a surprise, will it. Besides, I am not sure I am able to get it. And I won't know for at least a month, so you just forget it. I probably will, too.

Darling, I'm honestly and truly sorry that this letter has been so uninteresting and short but it's the best I can do tonight. I'll try and do better tomorrow. Maybe I can even make up for the brevity of this. I'll try. Even now, I'm stuck for words, sweet. I can't seem to be able to think of anything to say in order to say goodnight. I only wish I were there to take your shoes and stockings off, as I used to, and watch you while we prepared for bed. Remember how I used to sit on the floor and rest my head in your lap? Or how we used to cuddle up on the sofa in the sun-porch, or in the big chair Sunday nights, listening to the radio? Gee, all those little things I desire to do again. I want to kiss the back of your neck, your lips and hug you. Goodnight, sweetheart. I love you, miss you, and want you.

J.De Roxtro EM1/c   Everlastingly, your loving *Johnny*

Note on flap: Here's my daily hug and kiss for Jackie, and more for you. I sure do love you.

Friday, June 23, 1944. *No mail. 11:00 went to Acme. Baby food and vegetables. Took two snaps of Jackie after lunch & put her to bed. Made potato salad. When Jackie awoke, went down to Sandrian's. Home just before it rained.*

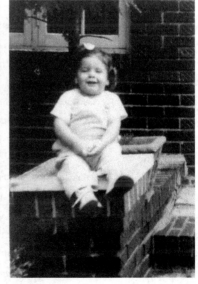

[Pavuvu Island, Russell Islands.]
Postmarked June 24, 1944, two stamps upside down. *June 23, 1944*

Somewhere

Hello, Lou:

I love you, miss you and want you. My thoughts are continually of you. Your sweet and lovely image is always before me. I long to hold you close to me and kiss you. More than anything else in the world, I yearn to be there talking to you and making love with you. I hope and pray that we will be together soon, sweetheart. Each day brings us more close together, sweet, even though it is in time, and not distance.

I did fairly well on the mail situation, today. I received a letter each from Ann, Grace, Ralph and Joe Gannon. Besides those four, I got two from my honey. They are worth more to me than all the others, too. They are dated the twelfth and fourteenth and both are postmarked the fifteenth. Thanks, angel, for being so thoughtful. Those letters mean a lot more to me than you can imagine.

Ralph didn't have anything much to say. In fact, all he did was comment on my first class rating. You know, it takes my mail anywhere up to two weeks to reach him and I receive his in three, four or five days at the most. I can't understand it, myself. I love you.

As usual, Joe didn't say anything. All he ever does is tell me where some of my friends are now such as Eddie Leary. By the way, he is now in California so perhaps he will be shipped out this way soon. Things are hot out here now, so I hope he doesn't hit one of these hot spots right off the bat. Most of the fighting has been done by the Navy lately, but the army and Marines have been doing quite a bit, too. I wish I could foretell the outcome of the present Naval engagement. That will turn the tide of the war a lot and then it won't be long. I think we will take care of most of the Japs fleet, this time, and a lot of their air force. Boy, I'm sure glad I'm not in that one. I've seen enough, anyway, and I'm ready to return and take up my duties as a civilian where I left off. But that will be impossible because this past two years will never be made up for, no matter how much we try.

In one of your letters today you asked me if there was anything you could send Forbes. Well, I asked him and he said the only thing that would do him any good now would be Ann. He wants you to wrap her up in a package and send her out. He's been bothering me ever since I began this, asking me if I had told you yet. Now I'll tell him it's in and have some peace. I adore you.

Well, my lovely one, before starting to answer your lovely letter of the ninth of June, I wish to inform you that I am I the best of health and am as happy as I possibly can be away from the ones I love. I sincerely hope that you, Jackie and the family are, too, in the best of health and are completely happy. I want you to be happy. Thanks loads for the two kisses you sent by way of the stamps, sweetie. Although only one of these was inverted, I know that you intended doing it, but for some reason you didn't. All you have on the inside of the envelope is "Sweet, I love you." But that is all I want to hear. My dearest one, to hear you say that instead of merely reading it, would be like the breath of angels whispering in my ears. Now I will proceed to answer your sweet letter.

Most of your letter is about your trip to New York and meeting Mrs. Fitzpatrick. I'm so glad you were able to meet her, my sweet, and I'm also pleased to know that you had such a swell time in the big city. Even though you had only two hours with her, you probably had quite a chin-fest with both of you showing off your bambinos. You, Jackie, and Mrs. Fitz., her grandchild, and both bragging about each other's and telling each other how cute they are and all the time thinking, oh, mine is much nicer.

That picture she showed you was one of the storekeepers and the supply officers. Forbes formerly was a storekeeper and so was Frank. As you know, I never was one and I couldn't possibly be in that picture. Frank is now a mechanic and Vince is a carpenter. They both quit the previous job and took ones more to their liking.

Sweetheart, did it make you feel good when you were talking to Fitz' mother and as she spoke of him her face would shine ad she would swell up with pride. I know I would feel good at something like that, although, I would probably become a little embarrassed. Still, it might have made you feel good to talk of me to someone else, too.

Now, sweetheart, I feel that I must put you straight about something. I don't and never have, advised or tried to advise, any of my boys. I may drop a gentle hint once in awhile or talk their problems over with them but I can safely say that I have never advised them as to anything. I haven't the faintest idea where you got the idea that I was Fitz's adviser but you are mistaken. I'm not half the swell guy that you and a few others seem to think. Sorry to sink your dreamboat, my love, but it would be possible to sail that into perhaps dangerous waters. I wouldn't want you to. I love you.

I know that Fitz didn't write very often and I have tried to get him to drop a line or two to his mother but I know not whether it did any good or not. Also, I decided the best way to tell him about this plea from his mother was to let him read this letter of yours, which I did. Now, the results are up to him. I conveyed your birthday greetings and he sends his thanks. He's a swell kid and I can tell you the reason he doesn't write. He is too active to sit down for even a few minutes to write a letter.

247

You inquire as to the location of my body when the picture aforementioned was taken. Well, as that was taken on a Sunday morning, my body may have either been in or out of the sack, at work, or in a chair, writing to my lovely wife. But my mind was back there in Jersey with you, my most desirable wife and sweetheart. You may well ask why I am so sure of that, simply because my mind hasn't been off you since I've been away from you. My darling, you are mine and I am yours, forever. I adore you.

I've heard the picture "White Cliffs of Dover" was good and I am glad you enjoyed it, too, and the stage show was good, too. The day was most enjoyable in the City. You are lucky you are able to get away as often as you can and enjoy yourself. My lovely one, I am happy, too. I love you more each day.

Vene wrote and told me that she saw a Seabee pin on the nurse you mention and I asked her to get you one. Now, the rascal gives it to you as a birthday present. Oh, well, as long as you got it, that's the main thing. I'm glad you did. How about describing it to me, honey? I've never seen one, you know. All I've done is heard about them and I would like to know what they look like. This time of year is a busy one for the farmers and the Naughtons are farmers in a sense of the word. Anyway, it was nice of her to write you a letter. I don't blame her for returning as soon as she possibly can to those little ones of hers. Heck, she probably leaves them with some young gal and pays her by the hour for minding the kiddies. She'll be down one of these days and then you can thank her in person for it. 'Twas nice of you to answer her letter and send her thanks. I knew you wanted one of those pins and would be glad to get one. I'm glad.

Gee, I'm sure glad you aren't going to have any bad trouble with your teeth. Two small cavities and one extraction isn't bad at all, is it. I wonder why you women have trouble with your teeth after adding to the population of mankind.

I knew that Ann would like the housecoat, sweet. How could anyone but help liking what you pick out? You have such wonderful taste, sweet. Why, I would even trust you to pick out my clothes, and that's something I never would let anyone do. I am not particular as to color schemes and such, either. I either like a tie or I don't, and if I like it I will wear it with anything and if I don't well, I will just put it away and forget it. But why am I telling you all this? I have not worn decent clothes in so long I've probably forgotten how to tie a tie, even. But it won't take me long to learn. Do you realize that a week from tomorrow will be two years since I shed my civilian clothes and donned G.I.? Sometimes it doesn't seem that long, does it.

248

I wonder if Mrs. Bianco was really out there waiting for Mike, or just trying to pick up a little gossip? Now who's being catty? Gee, I sure have changed. So our little Jackie readily agreed to go bye-bye with Mike, huh? Well, she certainly is friendly and isn't too particular is all I can say. It probably makes the old folks feel good when she is so friendly, though, so as long as she doesn't go too often for ice-cream you may as well let her cater to her public. Two in one afternoon is quite a lot for her, isn't it, sweet? And in one of your letters you said that she didn't care much for sweets. Heck, now I'm a little disappointed. She doesn't take after me, after all. Not even in that small way.

I am anxiously awaiting those new snapshots, sweet. Not only because they are the first ones taken since the camera was repaired, either. They are also taken of our wee one, and I'm mighty interested in her growth and development. Gee, I sure wish I were there to see her grow up. But as it was impossible, the pictures are the next best thing. I love to receive them. How about a couple more of you, precious one? After all, I want to see you, too, you know.

I think I will save your next letter and answer it Sunday, sweet. It is much longer and contains the latest pictures, which I have yet to talk about. Hence, my letter tomorrow may be fairly short. I hope you don't mind, honey. I probably won't receive any more from you in a couple of days, now, so I'll make these last.

Give my regards to all the family and our friends. Here is my daily special hug and kiss for Jackie and many million more to you, my wonderful wife.

J.De Roxtro EM1/c   *Everlastingly your loving* *Johnny*

Note on flap: "*Hello, Beautiful. I love you with my whole heart, body & soul.*"

Saturday, June 24, 1944. *Letter of June 15, washed clothes. Rain in afternoon. At night went to movies. (Community - Gaslight - Boyer & Bergman.)*

[Pavuvu Island, Russell Islands.]
Postmarked June 26, 1944, stamp upside down.   *June 24, 1944*
                                                                Somewhere

My Beloved Darling:

All the love in the world is ours and we aren't there together to make use of it. I want so much to be there, to hold you tenderly in my arms once again and tell you of my love and adoration. I miss those smiling eyes of yours and your tender caresses. Sweetheart, I miss all of you. More than anything else I desire to be there with you. I want to make you happy sweet, and keep you happy the rest of your days. Beloved one, I won't be happy until

I am there with you in my arms. I am hungry, sweetheart, and only being with you will sate my appetite.

Tonight we are having another U.S.O. show. It starts at nine o'clock after the movie. As yet, I don't know what the show is. I may have seen it and if I have, I will return here and complete this letter to you. I will then return to the theatre to see the stage show. Our movie starts at 19:15 tonight, instead of the usual time 19:30.

Beloved angel, I am sending this week's issue of our scandal sheet free, because I now have some plain envelopes. It will take a bit longer to reach you, but I'm quite sure you don't mind. If you do, let me know and I shall return to the use of airmail. I sure am glad you aren't expecting this to be a long letter, Lou, because I am not in the mood for writing. I'll do a lot better tomorrow, though.

I've just returned from the show and the picture really was pretty good for a change. It was "Silver Queen." I don't know who was in it, naturally, so I can't tell you. As for the stage show, well, the U.S.O. should be proud of that one. The show started alright and was going along fine until the master of ceremonies became disgusted and gave up, simply because the boys called for another encore from one of the girl singers. They only called her back three or four times and, although they were a little unreasonable, it wasn't asking too much. Hell, we darn seldom have any female entertainers, so what can anyone expect from us? The show is on again now, but most of the fellows have left and won't return. I know darn well that I wouldn't go back. It could be the best show on earth but boy, they couldn't drag me back. Personally, I think it was a lousy thing to do and these folks should be sent back to the states. No, it was only the master of ceremonies that caused the trouble. The rest of the show is alright. I wish I knew the name of it and the number so you could report the dirty so and so for me, but we may as well forget it. The show is over now and it didn't last more than ten minutes after they came back. Boy, such a flop that was. Enough of that, though, maybe the guys will forget it before many days are done. Perhaps they were all drunk. Certainly the accordionist was and the M.C. The girls could have been, too. Some of our fellows may have been a little tipsy, too. But they weren't obscene or in any way boisterous. They were gentlemen, every one. Funny, my raving on and on like this about a mere show, but I couldn't help it. Honey I want to be there with you.

Let's see, shall I give you the latest scuttlebutt? Yes, I may as well, so here it is. In two months we will be back in the states and put on inactive service. That's a lot of hooey, though, so pay no attention to it. Here's some more, just to show you what we have to put up with. In two months we will be headed for the Philippines to build and fight. That, too, is a lot of bunk, so don't believe a word of that either. What really is going to happen, no one knows, as far as I know. One of these days our orders will come through, however, and then I will let you know all. That is, of course, if it's at all possible. Gee, honey, I don't know what to tell you. Anything can happen and when it does, it comes fast.

Tomorrow, sweetheart, I will write you a fairly long letter to compensate for the shortness of these too short ones. At times I find it rather difficult to write, so those times you will have to bear with me. I think I do fairly well, most times, and find so very much in your letters that I can write about. They (my letters) are probably quite boring to you most of the time, but I do try hard.

There's a fellow in the tent next to us and he really is a card. He rattles on and on day and night and he is witty. He entertains everyone in the area and even I have to laugh (out loud) at some of the things he says and does. He's just a natural born comedian, I guess, always smiling and laughing and raising hell in general.

Well, sweetheart, I don't know what else to tell you. I am well and as happy as I can be, away from my most adorable wife and darling daughter. I sincerely hope and pray that you two and all the family are in the best of health and are happy. Sweet Lucia, please give my regards to all the family and our friends and wish them the best of everything for me. Here's my daily special hug and kiss for our sweetheart and daughter and many more to you, my adorable, darling wife.

J.De Roxtro EM1/c   Everlastingly, your loving   *Johnny*

Note on flap: *"Hi darling, I love you, want you and miss you."*

Sunday, June 25, 1944. Rain. Tadone and Mama G up. Gene got consent of living here. Joe & Angie called up. Would not be here. Went to movies. Saw "Ladies Courageous." Took picture of myself.

[Pavuvu Island, Russell Islands.]
Postmarked June 26, 1944, two stamps upside down.   June 25, 1944

Somewhere

Hello, my Sweetheart:

I love you, miss you and want you so very much. You are always in my heart and your lovely image is eternally before me. I miss your happy laughter and your smiling face. I miss hearing your sweet voice and looking into your beautiful eyes. Dearest one, I want, more than anything else, to be there with you. I long to hold you close to me and kiss you. I want to hold my hands and arms around you and tell you of my love and adoration.

251

Sweetheart, if I were only able to do the things with you that I used to do. One of these days I will leave this rock and head for the states. Then and only then will our happiness be complete. To be there with you is my one desire. Gosh, lovely one, I adore you.

There seems to be nothing new that I can tell you today. No mail came again, for me, but I expect some tomorrow. I have answered all my correspondence and now, my darling, I can devote my entire afternoon to you. I have shaved and taken a bath and feel very much refreshed. There is a pleasant breeze today so it isn't so unbearably hot. In fact, Lucia, it would be a swell day for you and I to be together, laying out in a park somewhere watching Jackie enjoy herself, playing in the grass. Or it would be swell riding around the lake, somewhere. Even sitting at home, listening to the radio would be alright. Anything, as long as I were there with you.

I am well and as happy as I possibly can be being so far from my loved ones. I sincerely hope and pray that you, Jackie and the family are in the best of health and are completely happy   .

As there isn't anything more for me to say, I shall now attempt to answer your letter of the tenth and comment on your pictures. Thanks loads for the two kisses sent by way of the stamps, honey. I'm going to collect, with interest, for all of them. Are you going to do the same for me? On the inside flap you told me that I was right about the stamps this time. But I wasn't. I looked for a nice long letter and was pleasantly surprised when I read your envelope p.s. Immediately, I removed the pictures and I honestly believe my heart skipped a beat when I saw that one of you. Gee, darling, thanks loads for that.

A fellow next door just yelled over and said, "Hey, Pop. Tell your wife that you are the only guy I've ever seen who could write letters while in a horizontal position." When I said okay, here goes, he asked me not to. I do get in a comfortable position when writing to my sweetheart and I don't care who knows it. I get as comfortable as I can so naturally I am absolutely nude, too. Every once in awhile I have to cross my legs, though, because something happens, over which I have no control. I think you will know what I mean. Right now, I can feel it starting and I sure do wish I had a place to put it. Have you a receptacle handy, which I could use? It sure would be nice, wouldn't it?

Those pictures of Lesley Ann and Jackie turned out swell, didn't they. Gee, there is so much difference now that she doesn't have all those heavy clothes on, isn't there. I am now looking at the one where they are both sitting on the steps. Les has her arm around Jackie and the little one is sitting there with her fingers entwined as if she was praying. She has such an angelic look on her face, too. Jackie has a lot of hair and gosh, isn't she chubby and nice. A more healthy-looking child I've never seen. She is ours and I certainly am proud to be the father of such a fine child. The eyes of "Butch" are so blue that she seems to have none at all. Her hair looks nice, too. I think I told you before that all four legs look to be about the same size, didn't I? From the looks of Les, Fran should have her adenoids removed. She seems to be breathing through her mouth. Or did she have a slight head cold? No, that couldn't have been because you wouldn't have let her be so close to our lovely specimen of childhood. In the other two snapshots of the two of them there isn't much I can say, except that Jackie seems to be very happy. She really is smiling in them, isn't she. She really is turning on the charm and personality, alright. You know, Hon, Annette looks so nice and stands so straight, it's almost unbelievable. Most bambinos are inclined to be a little bowlegged. She's a sturdy little rascal and looks well cared-for. Lesley stands nice and straight, too. Fran and Eddie should be as proud of her as we are of our Jackie and take better care of her.

Now I come to the one in which our family is standing alone. Gee, she's so big and I haven't even seen her yet. But I sure am glad you are able to send these snapshots. Golly, without them I wouldn't have the faintest idea what she was like. Now wouldn't that be something. I just can't say anything more about this picture, sweet. It's really swell. We have a honey of a daughter and more than ever I want to get home. I am more proud of you than ever, too, my sweet. You certainly have done a swell job of raising our family, that's why I often call her your baby. After all, I had nothing whatever to do with her life, except to sew the seed and maybe send some financial support to you. You did all the rest. I love you.

Finally, I have come to the picture of my one and only. Gosh, sweet, how did an ugly old geezer like me ever manage to hook you? Say, are you losing a little weight? Somehow or other you don't look quite as heavy as you used to. You are the most beautiful girl in the world. Your skin looks so smooth and nice, Lou, how I would love to kiss those luscious red lips. Your eyes are swell, too, but you could use a little more sleep. Looks like dark rings under your eyes. Honey, you are adorable. I wish I were able to caress you. The feel of your firm round breasts under my hand would really be swell. Darling, I want you. I am so very hungry and only you can satisfy me. Sweetheart, I can't say any more about this snapshot except that I love it and want you to include one of yourself every time you send a batch out to me. Will you, please, sweet? After all, I love you and want to see you. As I can't, these pictures are the next best thing, so please send me more. That outfit you have on is very becoming, too. I prefer seeing you in a skirt and blouse (or sweater). That bow in your hair looks nice and is also attractive. Sweetie-pie, you are mine and I love you very much.

Dearest one, I will now go ahead and answer your letter. It is only five pages long, but I may be able to make this a nice long one. I know you prefer them long, as I do. I can't quite see the three of you remaining home on a Saturday night, even though it was raining. That's rather unusual, isn't it, sweet?

Lou, I don't think Fran is going to have another child. She probably missed one period and jumped to conclusions. Besides that, neither she nor Eddie wanted another, I know. She always took precautions against it as you probably know. I don't know what she used or anything but I do know that she did. Personally, I don't think she should because she doesn't care for Lesley, so how could she care for another? But looking at it another way, this new addition, if it is, may change both of them and cause them to get along better together. No matter how it turns out I am looking for a break, someday, between the Kuglers. I hope they stick it out, though, for Lesley's sake.

Your letter previous to this one was a nice long one and I sure appreciate it. I like to receive long, loving letters from you. I read them over and over again and I always will. Those letters, like you, will never grow old. My sweetheart, I love you with all my heart.

Sweetest one, I knew that Pyro was something to do with fire, but I hadn't figured that thing was the gremlin of fire. Yes, I know all about the Gremlins. They are Yahoodie's children and are there where they aren't wanted always doing something wrong, or good. They are unpredictable and pop up in the strangest places. Who knows, maybe we had a couple in Esmeralda, during her last days. We sure did have something, and even Ralph didn't know what or how to get them out. But what I can't figure out is the why and wherefore he was on the envelope. I can't see the connection. And why wasn't it on more than one of your envelopes? Oh, let's forget it, sweet. I don't care, but it seems as if I did care enough to write a few lines about it. Oh, well, lets just skip it again, shall we? When you answer this letter, please refrain from saying anything about this letter. (The gremlins must be here, too, in my pen.) Those evasive little men. Look what it got me doing, now. Writing words I can't even think of and causing me to make so very many mistakes. Darn the gremlins, anyway. How did they get in here. I love you.

Say, lovely one, I don't think you ever told me anything about Tadone having three abscesses all on the same shoulder. Gee, the poor guy must be down quite a bit, and here I was thinking he would be good as new again by this time. I guess he is quite weak. It's a good thing he is able to get around, though. He is a good sport and is taking it well, I can imagine. It sure would be a good thing if the two of your grand parents could and would come up there to live with you. But Mama G is stubborn and she hates to move from her home. I can't say that I blame her, either. After all, there is no place like home, and don't I know it. I've had plenty of away from home experience and I don't care very much for it. By all means let me know how things turn out. I'm quite interested, you know.

Do you mean that you and the others would drink my beer, that if you bought some for me now, you wouldn't even save it for me? But I realize how things are, angel. As long as you are able to get some in for me, I will be satisfied. You see, I am not interested in leaving you for a beer or two. I want to have it there, where I can get it, and won't have to leave you for a minute. After all, we have so much to make up for we won't have time to be separated, even for a minute. I love you, most precious angel, and want to be there with you in my arms, forever. May we soon be there together. I adore you.

Darling, I will have to close now, in order to eat supper. I will return and finish this afterwards, so if you will pardon me, I will prepare for supper. There is a fly walking around on [me] and I can't chase him away. It must be a female. It is quite uncomfortable. Here's about a half million kisses to tide you over until I return. Remember, I love you, miss you and want you. Now, as I have returned from the usual Sunday evening meal, I will proceed with my answer to your lovely letter. I am now fully clothed but not because it is my choice to be so. Rules and regulations must be lived up to, you know, and by adhering to these rules and regulations I am less likely to become inflicted with malaria as are the unlawful ones. And honey, your loving hubby is taking no chances. It seems that the malaria-carrying mosquito is only out between the hours of five in the afternoon and six in the morning. They aren't very numerous here, though, so very few men have that disease. Now I wonder what brought that on. Sounds a little like a lecture, doesn't it, but it isn't, my sweet. It must be them gremlins again, behaving as they shouldn't.

Well, it looks as if the boys caught a load of fish today. After the sorry supper we had, I think I'll stroll up that way, after I finish this letter, and have a few bites. They will really taste good to me.

As long as your mother is able to get all the beer she wants, there isn't much use in you getting any, and saving it for me. Besides, a dozen or so bottles a week is enough for you. You may over-indulge if you have more there, easy to reach. It's a good idea to have beer on hand, I think. Let Jackie have a little once in awhile if she still wants it, will you, angel? It won't do her any harm and may do her some good. It'll give her an appetite and also make her sleep. So you prefer *Pabst Blue Ribbon* to any other kind, eh? That's a pretty good beer. I like it, myself, but I prefer ale to beer. The kind you prefer will be suitable to me, though, so have that on hand when I return to my lovely wife and sweetheart.

Here I thought I was telling you something you didn't know and you knew it all the time. Why didn't you tell me about it. But of course I should know better than ask you that question. Why should you, when it means absolutely nothing to you. I was quite sure you would have gone there in preference to the Flagship, so therefore I thought you hadn't known about the Meadowbrook being in Newark. I might have known that you would know all about it, though. Have you ever been there, sugar-puss? If it's as nice as I heard it was, you would like it. Maybe we can go, when I get home. I sure do love my wife.

That answers your letter, sweetheart, and now I will have a heck of a job trying to find something with which to fill this page. I'll see what I can do.

Oh, yes, we now have another radio in the tent. Now, unless the guy who owns it decides to sell it, we will have music and the news. The war news sounds pretty good to me.

The pleasant breeze, which I mentioned this afternoon has died down. In fact, it has become quite calm. Perhaps we will get some rain. It doesn't rain quite as much as it used to out here. Maybe the rainy season is over.

Know what, Lou? I have only six sheets of this paper left, so after my letter of tomorrow night you will be receiving my letters on paper similar to that upon which I wrote to Ann and Grace today. This paper is lighter, I think, so I reserved it for use in writing to you. I thought I had plenty more, but I am fresh out as I now see. Oh, well, I have two packages of the other, so that will last me another week or so. And I will get more tomorrow or the next day. You see, we aren't allowed to purchase more than one at a time. It has to do for all and the supply is limited, but we have plenty.

Give my fond regards to all the family and our mutual friends. Here's my daily special hug and kiss for Jackie and millions more for you. I love you.

J.De Roxtro EM1/c   Everlastingly, your adoring *Johnny*

Note on flap: "I'm looking forward to seeing you soon. I love you. Here's a kiss."

Monday, June 26, 1944. *2 letters from Ralph. No mail. Lovely day. Went to Cat's and then went down to park. Took pictures of children. Went back to Cat's until 4:30. Bought ice cream for kids. Came home and cooked. Call for Ann from Rose Condon. Asked us to go down. Went and had soda and mocha cake. Very nice room at Community Club.*

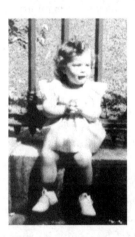

[Pavuvu Island, Russell Islands.]
Postmarked June 27, 1944, stamp upside down.   *June 26, 1944*
                                                                    Somewhere

Hello, Dearest One:

I love you, miss you and want you more as each day passes. As those days pass they bring us more close together even if it is in time only. I long for the day to come soon when we will be able to stop writing and let our actions proclaim our love and adoration for each other. How I wish I were able to hold you close to me and kiss you. You are mine, sweetheart, and I love you. Your lovely image is always before me and I am continually thinking of you. We belong together and will be, one of these days.

Today, your letter of the fifteenth arrived at its destination. It was postmarked the seventeenth and was not long, but it sure was sweet. It was five pages long though, so that isn't so bad, is it. Thanks, my adorable one, for writing as often as you do. Gee, it sure would be swell if we were able to stop writing and be together.

Your letter of the twelfth is next in line for me to answer, sweet, so here goes. Thanks loads for your kiss. On the inside flap of the envelope you hope that we'll be together soon. Boy, how I hope and pray that we are, too. Wouldn't it be swell, dearest? I could make love to you the way I should then, and receive some cooperation. I love you.

Enclosed herein was a picture of Mary. She looks happy and contented, doesn't she. She looks real well in her uniform, too. I see by her stripes that she is a sergeant. She got ahead pretty fast. But, knowing her as you do, you probably aren't surprised. Well, sweet, when you write, give her my regards. She's a swell egg and will be a good lifelong friend to you. Sweetheart, would you like me to return this picture to you? It won't be worth keeping if I retain it here. For some reason or other, pictures fade to beat the band out here. Most all of the ones I have faded, but I still have every one you or anyone else has sent me. I get quite a thrill looking them all over. It was raining last night and I went over every one of them again.

Gee, it was tough for both of you when Mary wasn't able to stay over for a few days as planned, wasn't it. But as she was able to drop in for the short while she did, well, that was better than nothing. She may be going overseas but I doubt it. Someone was probably taken ill or something, and she was needed back there. Plans for embarkation aren't made in such a short time, Hon, so I doubt if she will be going over. Just what kind of work does she do, sweet? Is she a secretary, or something? I know one thing, though. She nor any other wave, waaf, other than nurses will come out here.

No, sweetheart, I hadn't realized that it had been fourteen months between visits of Mary. I had even forgotten that she had seen Jackie, when she was only a month old. Those things never remain in my mind, but if reminded of them I remember. How could Mary or anyone else think our daughter anything but adorable. She is a honey and everyone will think so.

You had expected Mary to visit you during the month of May, hadn't you? I wonder why she didn't get her furlough in that month, instead of June. If she had, you two could have had a swell visit together and would have chinned most all day and night, I'll bet. As it was, either your or Mary's jaws were moving a mile a minute, I'll bet. I'm sure glad I wasn't there to have to listen to it. Maybe I would have taken a sneak and gone for a few brews. You would never have missed me, either, I'll bet.

I don't know why Mary should send me her love, but thank her for it anyway. She's a bit of alright, too. It's a good thing she doesn't know me, else she wouldn't think me as swell. But you do too, so perhaps there is something okay about me. I have yet to find out what it is, though. Must be my personality or my handsome puss, or my manly build, or any number of things I don't have. Your imagination must be really good, in order to fall in love with a dope like me. I love you, darling.

I guess I'll go to the show tonight, sweet. I don't know what's playing, but there are a few boxing bouts preceding the show. I'll be back later, so until then, here's a little lovin' and kissin' to tide you over for a short while. The show was George Raft and Pat O'Brien in Broadway. It was pretty fair, but I had seen it before back on Santos. Preceding the show, there were three boxing bouts and all three of them were pretty good. The fellows don't go in to knock the other out, though. It is all clean fun and everyone enjoys them. Of course there are a couple bloody noses every once in awhile but nothing very serious. I enjoyed myself quite a bit tonight.

I didn't think there was anything wrong with Jackie's eyes, but I wanted to make sure. So her eyes are smoky-blue now. Why haven't you told me this before? I could see by her pictures that she has nice long lashes. I wonder why I never mentioned that before. Some things just pass us by, don't they. And she weighs twenty-six pounds. The last I heard a week or so ago, it was only twenty-five pounds. She is growing up fast isn't she. I do hope she doesn't spring up and be a tall girl, don't you? Most people prefer small gals and I know that I do. I hope she grows up to be just like her mother. Then everyone will love her.

Boy, that was a surprise, knowing that you three remember Porky. He will be surprised when I give him your regards, too. But he won't remember, I'm sure. I don't see him very often anymore, but when I do, I will do the honors. He's just as fat and chubby now as he ever was.

As you know by now, Vincent is in the best of health again and has gained back some of the weight he had lost while he was ill. Maybe he is finally rid of that malaria. I sure hope he is. In fact, he went out this afternoon and starred for C company in a ball-game, by knocking out a three-bagger. He's a bit of alright, don't y'know?

Our hospital is nothing but a fairly large room with cots and things in one end and a sort of a clinic at the other. There is nothing private about it but it is clean and our doctor is darn good. He really takes an interest in the patients and is very conscientious. I'll tell you more about it later, maybe. It may not pass the censors, sweet.

This is all for tonight, honey. I don't have time for another page and no news. Give my regards to all and my daily special hug and kiss for our sweet Jackie. Sweetheart, I love you with all my heart.

J.De Roxtro EM1/c   Everlastingly your loving *Johnny*

Note on flap: "Hi Wifey!! Here's all my love and adoration. You're marvelous. I adore you."

Tuesday, June 27, 1944. Letter of June 18th. Cooked sauce while Jackie slept. Awake at 3:00. Went downtown. Post office and Sandrian.

[Pavuvu Island, Russell Islands.]
Postmarked June 28, 1944, stamp upside down.   June 27, 1944
                                                                Same old place

Hello Lucia My Love:

How I hope and pray that the day will come when you and I are together real soon. I long to hold you tenderly in my arms once again and kiss you. I want to hold you close and never let you go. I love you, want you and to kiss you. (It seems as if I am making quite a few mistakes in this one.) Sweetheart, if only we could be together once again, to do all the things we used to do and gee, would I have fun with our little one. You're swell, Lou, and I never will regret having married you. I grow more proud of you every day. Your lovely image is before my eyes constantly and my thoughts are eternally of you. Each day that passes brings us more close together, and when the call for me to start my homeward journey comes, I will be ready. In fact, I am ready now, and have been ever since I left the states. Gee, angel, how I hope we are reunited real soon so I can try my best to make you happy. I love you so very much.

Gosh, darling, there seems to be nothing more to say. Do you remember in one of the scandal sheets, our doctor predicted that we would leave here in four months? Well, he is reputed to have said, just the other day, that we would be out here another six months. That's all scuttlebutt though, so don't you worry about it. I still say don't expect me until you see me, then you won't be disappointed. I feel quite sure that we will be home this year, though. Of course, it is quite possible that we will be needed up farther. If we are, we will have to go, and we will do a good job. The success or failure of this present push is what we are waiting for, I believe. If the condition of the places taken is good, we wont have to go, but if they need roads and airfields in a hurry, well, anything can happen. We are just being held here for an emergency outfit, so perhaps, when things up above are in better shape we will head for home. Boy, won't that be a swell day? It's close to two years since I've seen you and believe it or not I am hungry for your love and kisses.

I am not going to answer your letter this evening, darling, I will save it and answer it tomorrow. Then, your other one will be saved until Sunday unless I receive more mail from my most precious darling.

We have a movie tonight that I haven't seen yet, so I'm going to the show. The picture is "Moon Over Vermont," or something like that. I've never heard of it, so I haven't the slightest idea whether it's good or not, but I will let you know when I return. Here's a few thousand hugs and kisses and lots of love to tide you over until I return to my sweet sweetheart. My most humble apologies, my sweet. The name of the picture was, "Moonlight In Vermont," with Gloria Jean. It was pretty good, but nothing to write home about. So who am I? Well, I thought you might be interested. Preceding the show we saw about dozen short articles. Heck, honey, my can became so darn tired from sitting on that coconut log, that a couple of times I had to stand up and stretch. Those nice comfortable seats in our theatres back home will sure feel swell to me. Perhaps I'll fall asleep in them. If I do you will have to awaken me.

There is to be another U.S.O. show here tomorrow night, and we were asked to behave like gentlemen even though we did have cause for booing as we did the other night. I never expected our officers to agree with us and I presume it was as much of a surprise to the majority of the fellows. I am quite sure there will be no repetition of the previous performance, either by us or the M.C. I'll let you know how it all goes.

Lovely one, this will be the last page of my letter because I am without information of any kind to forward to you. Your loving husband is in the best of health and is as happy as he possibly can be away from you. Here's hoping that you, Jackie and the family are in the best of health and are completely happy. Your happiness means more to me than anything else. How about another picture or two of yourself, honey? I love to look at your face and figure and try to figure how I managed to hook such a shapely beauty into marrying me. Gosh, I love my wife. Give my fond regards to all the family and our mutual friends. Here's my daily special hug and kiss for our Jackie and many million more to you, my marvelous wife.

J.De Roxtro EM1/c   *Everlastingly, your loving* *Johnny*

Note on flap: "*This is a little short, sweet, but I'll try to do better tomorrow. I love you. Hugs and kisses.*"

Wednesday, June 28, 1944. *Letters of June 16,17,18. Hot. Issue of C-Breeze. Sent Gracie to store in morning. Cooked pot roast. Jackie slept until 9:00. Would take nap after lunch. Put to bed at 1:15, slept 2:30. Woke at 3:30. Dressed and went to Mil's. Made brown gravy when I came home. Cleaned off shelves in office. For supper we had pot roast & brown gravy, mashed potatoes, buttered cauliflower, veg. salad, applesauce and lemonade.*

[Pavuvu Island, Russell Islands.]
Postmarked June 29, 1944, two stamps upside down.   June 28, 1944
                                                                Same hole

Hello, Adorable:

I love you more than you will ever know. You become more desirable every day. How I long to be there, able to hold you tenderly in my arms and kiss you whenever I want to. I miss you, sweetheart and want you. Your sweet and lovely image is always before me and my thoughts are eternally of you. More than anything else in the world I want to get home to make love to you.

As you were told previously, we are having another U.S.O. show tonight. I'll let you know whether it's any good or not. It starts at nineteen hundred, so I won't have much time to write before then. I will see what I can do after the show. It might be too late to write then because we probably will have a picture also.

Today my adorable angel, I received five letters, one each from Herb, my mother, and your younger sister Joan. Besides these, I also get two from the most wonderful wife and mother in all the world. Yours were written the seventeenth and nineteenth of June and were postmarked, respectively, the twentieth and the twenty-first. That last one left our post office one week ago today. That's good, no? Thanks loads.

The picture of Ralph was really swell, wasn't it. He looks very well, too. I'll bet your mom was pleased when she saw it. I've been trying all afternoon to figure the reason why you sent me that page out of the comic section. Is there a hidden meaning, or did you sent it merely because you thought it was good. I imagine it was Nancy you wanted me to look at, but I can't see any reason, unless you wished to remind me of our boat ride at

Branch Brook Park. An explanation from you to me is in order. I'll admit I'm stuck on this one.

Say, darling, you probably know one of Mr. Tuttle's sons. He is about nineteen, I think. Anyway, I heard today that he is stationed here at the hospital. Hell, I've been working there for the past six months and didn't even know it. I probably don't know the kid, but maybe he will be pleased to see someone from his old hometown, so I'll drop in and see him one of these days. I will let you know the results of my endeavours. Even if you don't know him, perhaps Fan or Ralph would.

Vincent received another letter from Ann today and he is now answering it. He sure is happy when he hears from her. Maybe it's love??

There isn't anything new to relate to you from here, so I will try to answer your letter of the fourteenth of this month. Thanks loads for the upside down kiss you sent, angela mio. You are the sweetest girl in the world, and I love you. I said hello to Fitz and Forbes for you as you requested on the flap of the envelope and their response was "hello, mom." You see, as I am pop, you have to be mom. Some fun, did you know you had two grown boys before? And only a year or two younger than you are. My, you certainly started young. I hope you don't mind them calling you that. They mean nothing by it, so don't let yourself feel aged all of a sudden. Both these youngsters of mine think the world of you. In fact, I heard Fitz tell someone he was going to name the boat he is building, "Lucia." Both Frank and Vincent are swell fellows and I hope they will meet you someday soon. It will be easy enough for Fitz to visit us, but for Vince, it will be a little more difficult. Somehow I think he will make it his business to get there to see Ann and then you will meet him.

Forbes told me Ann was vacationing the last week in July, so wish her a pleasant time for me, will you? She's a swell sister-in-law.

Honey, you should know that I will write daily, even if it is only one page, unless it is absolutely impossible. Do you think it would be an easy matter for me to break this chain of daily letters now? Well, it would be, but I won't do it. It seems to have become a habit but I really want to write you, even though it is very difficult at times. I love you too much to stop now.

Well, the show is about to start, lovely one, so I will bid you farewell for a while and return later. I may not stay to see the picture. Here's a few dozen kisses and loads of love to tide you over for an hour or so. I wish I could deliver those kisses in person, though. If I could, it wouldn't be merely a few dozen, though. Boy, how grand it will be when I can kiss you again. So now, darling, if you will pardon me, I will take my leave. I adore my wife, very much.

Well, here I am again, my love. The U.S.O. show was quite good. There was a nice orchestra, an accordionist, a singer, a juggler, and a fellow who gave a sort of a spiel. The whole thing was well planned and all the fellows seemed to enjoy it. The orchestra wasn't sent out with the show, though, of course. It was an army unit, traveling around here with the entertainers. A pianist, bull fiddle, clarinet, banjo and drums comprised it. They were good, though.

As you probably have guessed, I didn't stay for the movie. I still don't know what is playing, but it doesn't sound familiar to me. Your elder sister should feel honored. Forbes came back in order to complete his letter to her. It must be love.

Now, back to your letter. Yes, honey, it would be swell if we were able to write nice long letters to each other all the time, but as you say, at times it's impossible. I try hard, real hard, some days and I still can't find anything to write about. Do you find it the same way? It would be so easy to find something to talk about if we were together, though, wouldn't it. But we wouldn't be talking, we'd be acting, if we were together. And boy, that would suit me to a tee. How I long to make love to you again and be amorous. You know, angel, at times I'm sort of afraid; afraid that when you see me again you will be a little disappointed with me. I've probably changed a lot and don't know it. You would soon know it though, in fact, you would notice it immediately. Gee, I wonder if you have changed much. You have changed in looks darling. You used to look sort of girlish and now you are a beautiful young lady. Sweetheart, you are more beautiful now than you were before. You look as if you are not afraid of anything and nothing could get you down.

No, Lou, I don't shave twice a week anymore. That was only a flash in the pan. I now go through that arduous task three times weekly. You see, I am getting in a habit of shaving daily. At least, that's my intention now. I may, of course, drift back into my old routine any time. It isn't necessary to shave so often out here, but the work I am doing sort of demands it. So, for safety's sake, I do shave at least once a week. I wouldn't want my beard to catch fire and burn my handsome (?) puss a little, would you? Besides, I don't shave very close, so it isn't so very bad. I don't know why I ever started doing that sort of job. It's plenty hot here, just standing around, without working over a hot fire all day. And the fire is really hot. In fact, it's hot enough to melt iron and steel. I'm pretty good at it, too, even if I do say so myself. I'm glad you think it's so wonderful for me to shave as often. Wait until I get home to you. Then, my darling, you will see me close-shaven every night. You might ask why at night. Well, you see, I may have a date every night with a good looking girl, and I probably will have. You are the most wonderful sweetheart a man ever had and I grow more proud of you every day. I love you with my whole heart, my body, and my soul. You are mine, to have and to hold, forever. I adore you.

Now, I think I have an idea what a pinafore is. It's a smock, with low-cut neck, ruffles, and buttons down the back, instead of the front. It has no sleeves and sounds quite comfortable to me, for hot weather. You never had one, did you, my most lovely angel? I can't seem to remember anything like that. Besides, I prefer my buttons down the front. Maybe that's why I never did notice anything such as you described as a pinafore to me. No matter what they are, or what they look like, as long as they're comfortable I am sure glad you got them, both for Jackie and yourself. May I be home in time to see them on you. Want me to undo the buttons for you? They must be quite difficult to reach.

Your surprise at hearing Jo's voice was no greater than mine was when I read that she was paying you a visit. That's something that was never expected by me. She never did like living in Morristown and was so glad to get away from it that I never expected to hear that she had voluntarily returned, even for a visit. Oh, well, anything can happen, can't it. Too bad it rained, though, and spoiled your visit. And my mother would come down the same day, so that you wouldn't be able to see your aunt, too, wouldn't she. It was swell of you to give up paying a visit to remain at home and entertain my mother and Vene. Jo probably felt as if she was getting a raw deal, too. Oh, well, I'm glad you decided to see my mom. Also glad that she looks so well. But after not seeing your mother-in-law in a month, she is bound to look good.

You gals must have gone on a permanent spree, sweet. To be truthful, I don't know whether it's good or bad to have a short one. You will have to inform me when next I see you with one. Regardless, I'll bet anyone, anything, that you look better in yours than Vene does. Say, sweet, we won't let Jackie have a permanent for many years yet, will we? If she takes care of her hair, she won't need any, I hope. So our sweetheart has nice long soft hair, huh? Gee, that's swell. And you all had ice-cream again, too. More power to you, sweet. It's a lot cooler with plenty of that, isn't it. Gee, my lovely one, I want so much to be there, so I can buy you those buttered pecan cones like I used to and do all those other little things for you. I love you more each day that passes. Goodnight, sweet one. Give my regards to all the family and our friends. Here's my daily hug and kiss for our daughter and more for you.

J.De Roxtro EM1/c   Everlastingly, your adoring *Johnny*

Note on flap: "This isn't so very short, sweet, but I can't do any better tonight. I love you, sweet, and am very hungry. Love & kisses."

Thursday, June 29, 1944. *Letters of June 20, 21. Very hot. Stayed home. Saw "Snow White," with mom.*

[Pavuvu Island, Russell Islands.]

Postmarked June 30, 1944, two stamps upside down.
        June 29, 1944

        Somewhere

Hello, Sweetheart:

I love you so very much. I miss you and want you, too. Darling, you and I should be together, always, and one of these days we will be. How I long to take you tenderly in my arms once again and kiss you. I want so very much to tell you how much I love you. Sweet, the day of our reunion can't possibly come too soon to suit me. I want so much to get home.

The scuttlebutt has died down again, so there is nothing I can tell you about that. I am in the best of health and I hope and pray that you, Jackie and the family are well and completely happy.

Lovely one, there has been something on my mind, lately, that I've meant to tell you, but it always slips my mind when I am writing. It is about me calling Jackie your baby. I feel that I have hurt you and I wish to apologize. Naturally, I am not sure that I have, it's only one of my hunches. I'm terribly sorry if I have, angel. You know I wouldn't do anything like that intentionally. As you have already received my explanation of that, I won't repeat it here. I can promise never to refer to our child as solely yours. I love her and want to share her. Now, it's off my chest, Lou, and I feel a lot better. Honey, you're the most wonderful wife and mother in the world and I desire to be there with you, more than anything else. You are mine and I am yours forever. Please forgive me for any mistakes I've made because none of them were intentionally done.

I'm finding it rather difficult to write tonight, sweet one. The light is very bad tonite, and I'm in one of those can't write moods. So, I am going to answer your letter of June fifteenth. It is nice and long, even after you have written so regularly. Thanks for the kiss, sweet. Say, what's the idea of calling me a sailor? I'm a Seabee, sweet, and proud of it. I am no more a sailor than the marines are. I wear the same uniform, but I could wear a marine uniform just as easily. Now don't get me wrong, please. There isn't anything wrong with being a tar. They're swell fellows most of them. As for the marines, well, they sure do have a good publicity man. I can tell you a lot about them when I return. I'm sure glad I didn't join that outfit. But you may call me a sailor if you so desire. I really don't care because I am a part of the Navy. Better off than the army, too.

Shirley Temple is playing tonight, but I haven't the faintest idea the name of the picture. I think I will go to see it. If I do, I will tell you all about it when I return. You know how much I like the movies, so I may stay here and write to you. I don't especially care for the shows, but as long as I have to dim the light, I may as well go.

Well, sweet, I will draw enough tomorrow so that both you and Jackie can have a new winter coat. You may, of course, use your own discretion as to whether you buy them now or later. And you may consider it as a Christmas present from me. If you do, though, I guarantee that I will too, and give you nothing else. I will send you a money order for one hundred tomorrow and save the other. Anytime you want some, though, just let me know and I'll send it. Or would you rather have it there? Your idea for our new home is a swell one, sweet, but I have my doubts as to whether we can have it as soon as I leave the service or not. I, too, would love to be able to have a home for the three of us to move into. Gee, won't it be swell, sweet? Say, do you mean our own home, or a rented one? I prefer to own one, don't you? But that will take a little longer than the war lasts, won't it. So, my lovely one, you can expect a money order the day after you receive this, or the same day. You can do with it as you desire, my sweet one. Buy your coats or save it, I don't care. What's mine is yours, lover, and what's yours is mine. I'll tell you what let's do. I won't send you any money, anyway, unless you ask me for it. I will let it accumulate on the books (with the exception of what I want or need) to use for our home. Let me know what you think of these plans. Here's the other one. I can send everything to you, and you can put it away or use it, as you see fit. It might be best that way. Then, in case of an emergency, you would have it handy. I, too, have been thinking quite a bit about a home of our own, darling, so we are together once again. It's funny how we think about the same things so often, isn't it. It must be love. Have you been thinking about a new car? I have, and I've been sort of debating whether it would be a car or a home. The home has a little edge now. I've just about decided to walk to work for a little while, until we see our way clear to get another one. It would be nice having a car, but the home is the better investment, don't you think, sweet? We can get a car anytime and a house, well, the sooner the quicker. I love you.

Honey, of course we'll have a shower in our own place. Maybe one in the basement, too, for me to use when I come in from work all sweated and dirty. That's not a bad idea, is it? I'm sure glad Gene finally installed one for you. You really appreciate it, I know. Swell of you to think of getting it while in New York, too. Whatever made you think of it? But then, you think of a lot of things that I never would. You're reliable, sweet. Maybe that's one more reason [why I love you].

Boy, your description of the installation of the light by the front door is very complete. I can almost see it from here. You must have been right there, watching him while he put it in. That was a complete detailed description, my lovely one, and very accurate. I couldn't have done better myself. You folks certainly are making a few improvements in the old homestead, aren't you. Swell, honey, keep up the good work. It will mean less for me to do when I get there. Better have someone fix the front porch up a little now, and get the woodwork painted. Leave it to me to fix things up for a job for someone. Just like me, isn't it, to find a way to spend some money. I adore you.

Boy, is it raining right now, or is it raining. The wind is very strong, too. The rain is blowing all the say across the tent, inside. It hasn't even rained this hard before out here and it certainly has rained hard. Oh, well, I guess it won't last very long. Most of the fellows who were at the show have returned. A few of them will stay, though, even if it is raining so hard that they won't be able to hear the thing. The name of the picture was "Gung Ho", and I doubt very much if the aforementioned star shines in that. I must have been misinformed, I guess. It has slowed quite a bit now and the wind isn't blowing so hard. Why, I can even hear the sound from the theatre. Mixed with the sound of rain on the tent and ground, it is nothing but a jumble of sounds, though.

Ten bucks was reasonable for installation of that light and repairing the vacuum, wasn't it. Why, I would have charged more than that for the material used, as scarce as it must be. Or did your mom already have the fixture? I know darn well that you are glad to have the vacuum repaired. After all, you do all (or most of) the work, I think. Why the devil did you wait so long to have it fixed? You could and should have gotten someone in to repair it long ago, even if you had to pay for it out of your own money. It would have made it a lot easier on you, too. If you were waiting for me to come home, well, you really had a long wait, didn't you, and I'm still out here enjoying myself among the beautiful palm trees, basking in the sun, and being entertained by the wonderful, exquisite South Sea Islanders, with no idea when I'll come home. Gee, I sure do hope it's soon though, don't you? I just thought of something, angel. How would you like a picture of one or more of these native women? You would? Okay, I'll see what I can do. It's very seldom I have an opportunity to see any, because I don't visit their villages. Some of the fellows do, however, and have taken a few snapshots. I'll get one, somehow, and then you can compare for yourself these and the kind you see on the silver screen. Boy, will you be surprised. I may be able to get a few pictures of different things around here. You may be interested in some of them. Boy, I sure changed the subject in this paragraph, didn't I. It's so easy to skip from one subject to another that one hardly realizes he has done so. You're beautiful, darling, and I worship you.

So our little one was frightened when you started the vacuum cleaner. Well, I'm not very surprised at that, because it is noisy and on her sensitive ears, well, I imagine it almost hurts them. She'll get over it in time, though. Don't give up using it though, will you Hon? Heck, I know darn well you won't. Does Jackie understand when you explain things like that to her? Maybe she does, but it seems hardly possible. You may have a way of looking at her or perhaps she can tell by the tone of your voice that it is a necessity and won't hurt her any. There must be some sort of an understanding between mothers and their young, though, because of the unexplainable things done. But, we have an exceptionally smart baby, so it would be quite easy for her to understand. Gee, I sure am proud of both of you and long to be there with you. My wife and my daughter are my two sweethearts. I love and adore them both. I'm only sorry that I have had to be away such a long time.

Regards to all the family and friends. Here's my daily hug and kiss for Jackie and many more for you. I idolize my Lucia.

J.De Roxtro EM1/c   Everlastingly, your loving *Johnny*

Note on flap: "Hi, sweet, you are the most wonderful girl in the world. Here's loads of hugs and kisses. I love you."

Friday, June 30, 1944. No mail. Went to Martha's with Jackie. Richie in England. Very hot out. Sent Gracie to store. Made salad & parmi. In morning. Ann home from work early. Helped me to cut grass and hedges. Gene over at night two valises. Going to Boston (St. Louis) for 3 weeks.

[Pavuvu Island, Russell Islands.]

Postmarked July 1, 1944, two stamps upside down.   June 30, 1944

Somewhere

Hello, Beautiful:

I love you, miss you and want you. My thoughts are of you eternally and your lovely vision is continually before my eyes. You are the most wonderful girl in the world and my one desire is to be there with you and make you the happiest girl in the world. Gee, it'll be swell, being there with you again, holding you close to me and kissing you. One of these days we will be together and then we both will be happy. Each and every day that passes brings us closer to the day of our reunion, so maybe it won't be too long now. At midnight tonight I will have been in the service exactly two years. You know, sweet, the time has passed quickly, yet it seems to drag all the time. In the past two years I've only seen you five days, and that short five days hasn't been enough. I want you so very much, sweetheart. We belong together and when we finally are able to be with each other, we will be for life.

Enclosed in this letter you will find a money order for one hundred dollars. You may use it for those winter coats or any other way you desire. I still have the other two on the books and won't be able to get it until the fifth of next month, so if you need any, don't hesitate to let me know and I will see that you do. I hope this is sufficient, sweet. I adore my lovely Lucia.

I have nothing further to relate to you, my adorable angel, so I will see what I can do with your letter of the seventeenth of June. Thanks loads for the kiss, sweet. On the flap of the envelope you say that you wanted me very much that night. I always want you, lovely one, very much, but at times my want is more great than others. That must be how you felt that nite. Your letter is very short, only two pages, so maybe this will not be long. I will do my best to think of something to tell you, though. I could wait, see the show, and tell you about that, couldn't I. Maybe I will.

Two lovely letters came for me today. Both were from you, naturally, and were really swell. They were written the twentieth and twenty-first and were postmarked the twenty second and third, respectively. Two pictures of our sweet little sweetheart were in one of them, but all I will say about them now is, they are swell. I'll comment further on them when I answer the letter. It was the one of the twenty-first they came with. Gee, she sure is a honey, and I love her. You'll have to pardon me for about an hour, sweet. The boys are starting to clean up for inspection tomorrow, so maybe I should help them. We have to swab the deck and generally clean the tent. It never gets real dirty, though, because we always remove our shoes before entering and sweep quite frequently. I'll know how to keep house for you when I return to you. I sure do love you.

Well, that's that. No one cares to co-operate, so I'll be damned if I will do it alone, all the time. To hell with them. All my things are in order and so are Vincent's, so the other three can suit themselves. I'm sorry, sweet. I shouldn't unburden my domestic troubles on you. You have enough of your own. Forbes just came down with a bucket of water, so I guess he'll do his corner. Here I go again. I'll help him. Here I am again, and I hope I'm not interrupted again, until chow.

I wonder why it is that you don't receive letters from me every day? Of course, it's too much to expect, but I still wonder. I write daily, and you should receive them that way. They are probably held up over here somewhere, maybe until they can find room on a plane, or maybe they only have three trips a week out of here, or something like that. Anyway, I'm sure glad you are receiving them. Say, honey, have you gotten all of them, or are there some days missing. It would be easier for you to check up than me, because some of mine are put away. Besides, they are all inside your epistles somewhere and it would take too long for me to find them. What the devil brought that up? You must be getting them, else you would have asked why etc. You know, sweet, I'm getting to really enjoy writing to you, most of the time, anyway. At times it is rather difficult, though.

Angel, don't forget to send me a snapshot of our wee one in nothing but panties. It's swell that she doesn't get a heat rash or anything like that, isn't it. Or does she? Anyway, I hope she doesn't. You should see some of the fellows out here. Boy, they have it bad and does it look sore. I don't get it and I'm thankful for that. I have a few places on my shoulders where the pigment seems to have left the skin, but it's nothing to worry about and doesn't bother me any. Some other fellows have it and it sure does look funny. Just as if we had white freckles under a light coat of tan. You can imagine a coat of tan like that, can't you? I just happened to think of something. Sweet, if you were out here, people could really call you Blackie. We have a couple of dark-skinned chaps and boy do they take a tan. If you were here a couple of years you'd become black. I would still love and adore you, though, so you had better get out in the sun with our Jackie. I want my wife and my baby to be healthy and the rays of the sun really help a lot. Have you taken my Jackie swimming yet?

Sweet, I will have to sign off now and go feed my face. This, my sweet, will be my last interruption, I think. If I'm still writing, I will stop and go to the show, though. This has been a heck of an afternoon, hasn't it. Oh, well, it doesn't happen very often so I'll ask your pardon for another half hour, while I eat. Here's a few kisses, though. I love you.

Now, lovely you, I have returned from a meal of corned beef and cabbage, potatoes, apple pie and coffee. Naturally the corned beef was canned but the rest of it was fresh. The cabbage tasted good for a change, and there is no use in me telling you that I enjoyed having coffee for supper. You see we don't have it very often, maybe because most of the fellows don't care for it. They claim it's too hot to drink it in the evening. I will have to admit, it makes the perspiration run, but heck, I don't mind that. I would much rather have hot coffee than any iced fruit drink.

Gee, honey, it was swell of you to let Jackie stay the tub for awhile after she had her bath. She probably had a lot of fun and you had to stay there all the time, too. You're a swell mother. You must be as good a mother as you are a wife. You couldn't possibly be any better simply because you are the best wife in all the world and I love you. Gee, I am proud of the swell job you are doing for Jackie. Our baby, under your personal care, will be the smartest,

271

most lovable child in the world. I sure do wish I were able to be there to help you raise her. Hell, it seems as if you are doing very well without me, but we could talk little things over. I would be your moral support and adviser. Who knows, I might even make some suggestions that you hadn't thought of. But I doubt it very much, because you are doing such a bang-up job of raising her. I'll bet you would have a spoiled child on our hands if I were there. Sweetheart, do you think I could keep from spoiling her when I do see her? If you tell me how, I may try not to, but gee, it's going to be tough. Her Uncle Joe does all the spoiling that's necessary, though, so I won't have to. I don't see how you keep her from becoming too spoiled, Lou, with all those uncles and aunts around. You must be the perfect mother as well as the perfect wife. I sure am the most lucky guy in the world. I adore you.

Gosh, sweetie-pie, how the devil were you able to stand two hours of tennis after it was so hot all day? You must have energy and vitality to spare. But it must have been very refreshing, taking a nice cold shower after your last sets. Or don't you enjoy cold showers? Personally, I really enjoy them, especially when it's so hot out here. At home I used to take a real hot shower to cleanse myself, then a cold one to stimulate myself. It's wonderful, sweet, and so refreshing.

Lucia, my love, it looks as if this short note will have to be interrupted again, because I think I will go to the show. I haven't seen one in quite awhile now and besides, I would like to hear the news. The daily events of the war are read to us each night, now. I don't know what the name of the picture is or who is playing in it, but I'll let you know afterwards. When I started this, I thought I would have to see the show in order to find something to write about but it sure doesn't look like it now, does it. Perhaps the stuff about the show will help me fill the eighth page. That may be the last, though because I've already answered all but one paragraph of your letter and I doubt if I will be able to make it any longer. I'm sorry I have two paragraphs to answer. Did I ever tell you how wonderful you are? No? Well you are the most wonderful girl in the world and I long to be there holding your beautiful young body close to me while I intermittently kiss you and tell you of my love and adoration. I want so very much to caress your lovely curves. You belong to me and I to you. I idolize you, Lou.

Dearest one, our Jackie couldn't help but get more smart every day with you there to teach her, talk to her, and try to make her understand everything. I would like to have been there to help in any way I could, but it was impossible. One thing I am sure of, and that is, that you are doing a much better job than I ever could if the situation was reversed. I become more proud of you every day, sweetheart, and I want to be there with you. Dearest one, if I were only there we could discuss those little problems as they come up. I know you would feel better knowing that I agreed with you on some small but important things. I have never doubted your judgment in the slightest thing, but still I would like to be there to assist in my small way. One of these days we will be together, darling, and then we can decide a lot of little things. Won't it be swell, after the day has ended, to lie there in our nice bed, side by side, and talk over the events of the day and make plans for the following day, while holding hands. Every once in awhile I will kiss those pretty lips of yours and tell you how much I love you.

All that was in answer to only one line of your letter. So you see, if I was in this mood all the time I would be writing continually. I hadn't heard before that Jackie, our delightful and lovely sweetheart, could say "hello" and "atta girl." She is coming right along and will be chattering like a magpie before very many more weeks go by. One of these days she will let out a string of words and surprise you. So you and the rest will have to watch your language or you might be teaching the wee one some cuss words. She will learn and use them soon enough. Do you actually think it will take a couple more months before Annette speaks quite well? I don't! I'll make a little wager with you. Let's see, I'll bet she knows and uses at least a hundred words before the end of July. The bet will be a quarter bag of potato chips from "Wulff's" delicatessen in Madison. Let me know if you accept the terms, will you? Or, if you prefer, I'll bet you an extra kiss, or anything you say, sweet. You name the bet and I will agree. Naturally you will have to be the judge and sole counter of the words. Just take a guess, it will satisfy me. You will know whether she uses a hundred words or not, easily. Win or lose, I expect to collect or pay off as soon as is possible after our reunion. I adore you.

I know darn well that this will be my last sheet. It's getting quite late and the lights are about to go out any time now. I think I have about a half hour, though. Sweet one, you don't have to apologize for writing short letters. Heck, I do the same thing. It just can't be helped sometimes, and others, well, the words seem to form themselves without even half trying. Take today, for instance, I sat down expecting to be through with this at five or six o'clock, and here it is going on for eleven. Tomorrow I may have to sweat and struggle in order to write three or four pages. I will be satisfied or try to be, as long as I hear from you. So, my love, if you aren't in the mood sometimes, just think about me and the next time you are in the mood, you can throw in an extra page. I'm hoping and praying that you and I won't have to write letters very much longer and will be entwined in each other's arms making up for lost time. Boy, won't that be swell? I'm ready my sweet one, and have been for almost two years now.

Looks like I'll have to write another page anyhow, sweet. Forbes just asked me to send you, Jackie and Ann his regards and love. He had to stop writing to Ann the other night because of a bad itching somewhere I shouldn't tell you about.

The show tonight was "Captains Courageous," with Lionel Barrymore and Spencer Tracy. It was very good but I had seen it before, many years ago. I rather enjoyed seeing it again, though. I should have humbly begged your pardon and asked you to bear with me awhile while I went to the show, but I was in a hurry to see the beginning of the show, so I left everything and high-tailed it over there. I hope you will forgive me, my angel.

I am well, as usual, and in the best of spirits and I sincerely hope and pray that you, Jackie and the family are in the best of health and are completely happy. Our daughter certainly looks happy enough in all the pictures I have of her and you, my sweet, look exquisite. Give my fond regards to all the family and any of our mutual friends you may happen to meet. Here is my daily hug and kiss for our sweet little bambino and many million more to you, my beloved wife, the only mother my kiddies will ever have. Darling, I love you more than life itself and would do anything in order to be there with you, to love, honor and obey, until we are parted. I love you, miss you and want you.

J.De Roxtro EM1/c   Everlastingly, your adoring *Johnny*

Note on flap: "Hi, Darling, it's only fifteen hundred. I should be finished before chow. I love you. Here's a kiss."

Saturday, July 1, 1944. *Letter of June 23. Cleaned sun porch. Jackie out front with Joey. Took picture. 5:30 girls went to play tennis. I couldn't go. Nobody home. Came back for supper. Then went downtown. Bought gift for M.de.R., a slip. Stopped in Thodes for ice cream.*

[Pavuvu Island, Russell Islands.]
Postmarked July 3, 1944, stamp upside down.

July 1, 1944
Somewhere

Hello, my love:

I love you, miss you and want you. Your lovely image is always before me and my thoughts are continually of you. How I long to be there holding you close to me, kissing you and telling you of my love and adoration. Gee, Lou, it will be swell when you and I are able to see each other and talk to each other instead of having to write letters. Darn, I wish I was home all these past months instead of way out here away from my lovely wife and darling daughter. One of these days I will be there though, and then our happiness will be complete.

No mail came in today, my sweet, so it is only natural that I didn't receive any. Maybe I'll get one tomorrow or Monday. I will answer yours of the nineteenth today and that will leave me two yet to answer. That isn't so very bad, and I'm quite sure of getting some before next Sunday. So, I will answer one tomorrow and one Monday and trust to luck for the rest of the week.

Thanks loads for the two kisses sent by way of the stamps, sweet. I only wish they could have been delivered in person. Boy, I'm ready and waiting for those kisses of yours.

This letter is only five pages long but it contains Ralph's picture and the single half sheet containing the comics Nancy and Mandrake the Magician. I still can't figure any other reason for you sending that to me unless you expect me to keep building even after I'm home on my leave. That could be it, but I doubt it. That sailor rowing probably reminded you of our boat ride, the same as it did me. That was a swell afternoon we had, wasn't it. Do you have those colored pictures we took? How would you like to do it again some time?

Ralph sure does took good and he didn't get fat like most of the army fellows do. His hair is nice and curly, too. Maybe this climate agrees with him. Sweet, would you like me to send this picture of him back so it won't become faded too much? Or perhaps you have a duplicate of it. Anyway, if you want it, I'll send it in my very next letter to you.

I have about a half hour before chow so I will start answering your letter. On the flap of the envelope you have told me how much you wished I were there that night. Honey chile, you all aren't the only one. My thoughts are always of you, my sweet. I love you so very much and want to be there all the time.

I forgot to tell you something. In celebration of our second anniversary as the fifteenth Construction Battalion, we are getting three bottles of beer per man tomorrow, for nothing. That is very generous of them isn't it. I wish they were quart bottles, though, instead of those small ones. I could go for a few cold ones now. I'll tell you what - you have one when you read this and I'll burp now. Okay?

You know sweetheart, one of these days this damn war will be over and then I'll have only six months or less to serve. That last six months will really pass slowly but at least we will know what to expect, won't we. By that time perhaps I will be a chief and won't have to wear my monkey suit.

It's chow time, my honey, so I will leave you now and return a little later. Here's my all to keep you company for the short while I'm gone, plus a couple million hugs and kisses and _____.

Here's that man again. The chow, as usual, was lousy, but I guess I can wait until I get home to have some of my wonderful wife's good cooking. I'll have to, I guess, cause it's a hell of a long swim from here. You are a good cook, sweet, and I am anxiously awaiting the day when I can sit beside you and eat. I'm hungry for love, too.

It's really a swell idea of you folks to give your grandparents cash instead of presents on occasions like birthdays and such. Mama G can get what she wants, then, and can probably get it more reasonably. Tadone probably turns all the cash over to her anyway. They are a swell couple and I like them a lot. I like your whole family, sweetheart. Every one of them are aces, but you're the best of all. You are my ace of hearts.

Joe and Jackie sure must be fond of one another. He is always bringing her something and she is smart enough to know it. He spoils her and knows he does, but he can't help it. She is darn cute and such an angel, how could anyone help but spoil her. I'm glad that Joe is so good to her and brings her things and takes her for rides, but just between you and I, darling, I'm a little bit jealous. That should be my job, but as long as I'm not there, I'm glad she doesn't have to do without all those things. Joe is swell and you really did a good job when you picked him for our little one's godfather. You couldn't have done better. I do wish I were at home so I could enjoy our daughter's tricks. I can almost see her as she opened the bag and found the chocolate bars and lollypops. Grinning all over her face and body.

The name of that show you gals went to see sounds familiar to me. I must have read about the picture somewhere or other because I don't think I've ever seen it. If it comes out here I will see it on your recommendation. You shouldn't let your emotions run away with you, though, and cry through almost the entire picture.

Some of those nights back there are really too hot for sleeping and when it is so terribly hot, it won't be necessary to put Jackie to bed so early, will it? It will be easier on both of you if you let her stay up a little while longer. Soon she will be staying up late anyway, so why not start now. Besides, she is sure to get enough sleep either later in the morning or longer during her nap. You can suit yourself, though, my lovely one. Anything you do or say will be okay by me.

The nights here are quite cool, sweet, so I am able to make out alright. The days are really hot, though, and I perspire something awful. I have sweated away about ten pounds, though, so I am not too fat to stand the heat. I'll put it back on just as soon as I hit the states and you. Your cooking will help a lot too. I am anxiously awaiting the day of my departure from this damned island. I can't possibly arrive home any too soon to suit me. I'm waiting patiently, my sweet, and won't be satisfied until I am there with you in my arms.

Honey, I'm afraid I won't be of much help in your problem. I can't understand why you should be afraid either and see no reason for it. If we knew what you were afraid of perhaps we could straighten things out. Let's see what we can do about it, shall we? You and Jackie are both healthy and in no danger, so that's not the reason. You may be afraid something is going to happen to me, but you should know better, so we'll eliminate that. Now, as far as I know there is only one thing more that may trouble you. You are afraid you aren't able to keep giving proper care to Jackie. In other words you are afraid of what tomorrow may bring, or the future. Or perhaps your responsibilities are weighing too heavily on you. I can't see that I can be of much help in either case, except to tell you that you will be well cared for as long as I am able to do so. That's for many years yet, too. All I can say about your responsibilities is for you not to worry and share your little problems with me, or perhaps someone closer to you. Please, sweet, don't worry yourself sick. That'll only make things worse. Do your best to hold out awhile, sweet, cause I'll be home soon and then we'll talk this over and find and remedy the trouble. Give my regards to the family and our friends. Here's my daily special hug and kiss for our Jackie. I love you, sweetheart, and want you.

J.De Roxtro EM1/c   Everlastingly, your loving *Johnny*

Note on flap: "To you, my lovely one, I send my all. I want so much to be there with you and Jackie. I love you."

Sunday, July 2, 1944. Lovely day. Mama G & Tadone up. Mike came. I cooked dinner. Joe & Angie came afterwards. Took

Jackie for ride. We went to movies. Saw "See Here, Pvt. Hargrove." Very good.

[Pavuvu Island, Russell Islands.]
Postmarked July 4, 1944, two stamps upside down.   *July 2, 1944*
                                                          Somewhere

Hello, Sweetheart:

I love you, miss you and want you more as each day passes, slowly but surely bringing us more close together even though it is in time only. Your lovely image is always before me and my thoughts are of you constantly. I long to hold your soft yielding body close to me as I kiss you and tell you of my love and adoration. Soon, my sweet, we will be together, doing the things every married couple should do and telling each other of our love instead of having to write it in letters. Writing is alright, I suppose, but it is so unsatisfactory. I desire to be there with you, and remain forever.

As you know, today is the day of our regatta. I've already written four pages to you, describing the races this morning, as well as writing to Fan and my mother. Not bad for a half days work, huh? I don't know whether I will answer one of your precious letters today or not, because this may be plenty long without it. The sailboat races start at thirteen thirty and I will try to describe them to you as I did at the motorboat races this morning. I hope they don't bore you too much. I thought you might like to hear or rather read about them. With the stiff breeze that's blowing today I may miss a lot of the happenings but 'll do my best. Besides, by writing it all out in longhand I have to remember quite a bit and put it down during a lull in the proceedings. Furthermore, while I am writing, I can't be watching the races, so I have to tell a lot from sound. I see that Fitz now has Lucia in the water, trying her out, but she looks kind of sloppy to me. He may become used to her, however, by the time the race starts.

No mail came for me today, lovely one. I really can't expect some every day, can I? I'm doing very well, I think, to receive what I do. It's really swell of you to write as often as you do. There isn't anything new that I can relay to you, so, as I have about a half hour before race time I will see what I can do about answering your letter of the twentieth. This one brought me three kisses from you, my adorable angel. Thanks loads. I will return them with interest when I see you. As you know, Forbes is doing well and has had no relapse in three or four weeks now. Perhaps he has finally gotten rid of the malaria. He had his share of it, anyway, and needs no more. All the fellows say hello right back. They all think you must be the swellest girl in the world and I quite often assure them of that fact. I know that you are the most wonderful girl in the world and I am really proud to have you as my wife and the mother of our daughter. Sweetheart, I love you more than life itself and I would do anything for you. I adore you and worship you.

This letter of yours is real short, too, so maybe I will be able to answer it. It's only nine pages long. Boy, I think perhaps I should answer this one in installments. Some today and more tomorrow. With all the racing news there won't be much room for an answer to this letter. I find it hard to make up my mind whether to leave the racing news out, or what to do. I'll see how things go. The sailboat racing course is too far away for me to see, so I will go ahead and answer your letter and just give you the results. Both races have started and they looked very well, getting under way. Just between you and I, I don't think Fitz has a chance. He didn't have enough time to try his boat out. I'll give him hell for naming it after you. Those two fellows are still skiing out there. I think I'll watch it for awhile. The breeze has died down considerably and these races will last quite awhile. I will interrupt my ramblings to bring you the results as they are brought in. One of those skiers just went all over head and boy, did he plop. He is quite alright, though, and is returning to his fun.

Your mother and the girls may disagree with you about your feelings, but I agree with you perfectly. As long as Dr. Wade sent a bill, why didn't he make it correct in the full amount. Damn it, we don't want any charity and never will. I, too, appreciate his trying to help but hell, why couldn't he send the bill every month as he should? Besides he needs the money. He must have plenty of outstanding bills and can use it.

A fellow by the name of Swab, sailing a boat named Queenie, came in first in the class 'a' race, having just completed the course. Don Smith, in Dottie, is second, and I don't know the rest of them. My interest is on my boy, in the other race. I haven't heard anything about those boys as yet.

To return to your letter, why not find out what brand of cigars the doc smokes and give him a box sometime. No, better not. Just let it ride the way it is and maybe some day we will be able to do something for him. Our day will come and we can repay all the folks that have done us favors.

I'm glad you had an opportunity to get up to the place where my mother is. I never corrected my error about the location of that place to you. You know now where it is, so you will see that I was mistaken. I do know where it is, though. It is really a beautiful place and must be wonderful at this time of the year. As you say, it's the kind of a place you often dream of but never acquire. It takes a pile of dough to get a place in that condition and a lot more to keep it up. It takes a lot of hard work, too. Our place will be almost as nice, even though it will be on a much smaller scale. We, together, will have an exceptionally nice place and will be the envy of all our neighbors.

We'll have a nice lawn, a nice flower garden, a vegetable garden, a playground for all the kids in the neighborhood, and plenty more besides. We will have a home, darling, not merely a house in which to live. I love you.

Fitz was dropped from the race for some reason or other. He just came back and I see he has his rudder in his hand. It must have broken loose. Too bad, because he sure would have felt good even if he hadn't won. Fitz worked hard on that boat and it's too bad he didn't do better. Oh, well, it's over now and he will have plenty of fun sailing around in his off time. He's a good kid.

Sweetheart, that wasn't the scandal sheet which had postage due on it, was it? If it was, I will try to do better in the future. But I now have some plain envelopes, so I can send them free. Gee, I didn't think that any of my letters were overweight. I've been using plenty of stamps and always thought I was within the weight limit. Sorry honey, I'll try to do better from now on. But as you know, even I make mistakes once in awhile. I'll bet you were anxious to get home so you could read my letters. I'm also kind of anxious to get home from work in the afternoons, too, and that makes the afternoons drag slowly by. But I get here and if there is a letter from you, my day has been a good one, and if not, well, I'm disappointed. Not too much anymore, though, because tomorrow is another day, and if none comes then, well maybe the next day some will.

Well, as long as you are so interested in our local news, I may as well keep sending them. Most of the thing is worth reading and naturally I am more able to understand it than you are. I will, some day, explain different things in it to you. No, Honey, our chaplain isn't Catholic. I think he's a Presbyterian or an Episcopalian. He's quite a sweet guy and all the fellows like him. He will play cards with the men, throw darts, or anything. He is the best one we've had so far.

Sweetheart, I'm going to quit now and leave. I have been invited out to a little beer party, so I think I'll go. I've been wanting a few for a quite a little while and now that the chance has come I will take it. I hope you don't mind, lovely one. I will answer the remaining part of your letter tomorrow. Besides, this will be plenty heavy as it is, so unless I stop now, I will have to use three stamps instead of two. I don't intend drinking too much, though. Maybe I'll play a few hands of poker, too. There usually is a game up there.

Good night, my love, I will see you tomorrow at the same time. Give my fond regards to all the family and our friends. Here's my daily special hug and kiss for our bambino and many million more for you, the sweetest girl in all the world. Wishing I were there, I remain,

J.De Roxtro EM1/c   Your ever faithful, *Johnny*

15TH C.B. SAILBOAT RACES

The sixteen horsepower outboard race just started, with the Yellow Bastard and Gypsy B entered. Yellow Bastard is leading at the quarter and will be a certain winner, unless something happens to his motor. This is a two-mile race and anything can happen. Two boats were scratched because of motor trouble. Coming into the half, the Yellow leads by about fifty feet, with Gypsy keeping the race a close one. Around the turn, the Yellow does best, but the Bakers has more speed on the straight away and closes in. It is still anyone's race, but personally I think the Yellow will win. At the mile, Yellow is leading big a little more. Round the turn the Bakers closed in to close the lead but the Yellow stepped out again and is still leading. At the far turn, which I can't see, anything may happen. I will give you the mile and a half standings now. Only one more lap to go and the Yellow leads by about a hundred feet. Around the near turn, the Gypsy lost more ground and Yellow seems to be a sure winner. The finish is about in sight and it is the Yellow Bastard piloted by Sellers, the winner by about seventy-five feet. Too bad the other two boats were scratched, it might have been a closer race.

Fitz put his Lucia in the water this morning, and she looks like a sea-worthy craft. The power boat race is about to start, and as this is a handicap race, I won't be able to give you the winner until it's announced. I will, however, do the best I can to describe it to you. Paul Andrews has a windjammer entered in this race, so I hope he wins. I have my doubts, though, as the competition is too keen.

Fitz seems to be having a little trouble getting his mast and other rigging set right. Perhaps he won't be ready to sail this afternoon.

Powerboats are now lining up for a start. They are off and this should really be a race. A little yellow boat with an unprintable name, is leading at the quarter, but has a ten second penalty for rounding the buoy the wrong way. He's broken down. Sea Breeze is now leading by seven lengths. Green picking up. The Sea Breeze, with all it's horse power, is doing fair. A little more zip and the second boat has a good chance. Paul Andrews is out, you might say, having just finished the quarter with the Sea Breeze finishing the half. At the half, it's all the Sea Breeze, with no, or very little competition. Skinner, in the second boat, is still nineteen seconds ahead because of the handicap. Lets hope he wins. Sea Breeze is walking away, though. The yellow boat developed motor trouble and is definitely out of the race. At the mile and a half mark, with one lap to go it is the Sea Breeze out ahead, but the green boat is giving him a good race. The Sea Breeze, piloted by Lt. Commander Bowers is a sure winner, but here's hoping he breaks down, the rat. At the finish, it's the Sea Breeze first, with Skinner's boat second, but just announced was Skinner the winner by four seconds. The handicap did the trick. In third place will be the Typhoon, piloted by Andrews or Williams.

Next race consists of a variety of boats; an outboard, an inboard, and the Typhoon, Jr. The Lucia is back in the water again, but I doubt if she will be ready to sail. He has plenty of well wishers, Fitz does, so I hope he gets in it and wins.

In the next race, the entries are by Gansdorf, Williams, and the Typhoon Jr. I don't know who's piloting it. The crowd is tense and is enjoying every minute of this day. There are several hundred spectators down on the beach in front of me, and all are very hot. It isn't so bad, here in the tent, with a nice breeze blowing.

The race is about to start. Here they come toward the starting line. They're off. Williams is off to a good start, maybe because I worked on this boat a little. Around the buoy, it's Williams, Gansdorf, and the Ty. Both Gansdorf and the Ty have a two minute handicap, so it's really the finish that counts. Williams is way out in front, with G and T racing bow to bow for second place. This is the last race of the morning, so I will give you the results and go back and finish answering Fan's letter. I interrupted it to give you the races. There is a stiff breeze today and the sail boat races should be good, if the breeze holds out.

Williams is way ahead at the half, but the other two are racing neck and neck for second. Neither has much of a chance to win, but they are evenly matched and are making a race of it. Gansdorf is a little ahead of the Typhoon, but it's still a race. Williams is finished, but as he is handicapped by two minutes, he hasn't won yet. Here the finish, Williams first, Typhoon second and Gansdorf, whose motor conked out, last.

The last race of the morning will be a free for all or chowder race with various entries. I'll have to wait and see the entries before I can tell you anything about them. They are now lining up for the start. There are only three entries. They are, the Yellow which won the first race, another green boat which had motor trouble and was scratched from the first, and one other and I don't know which one, though. Oh, yes, it's Skinner's boat, which also was a winner this morning. This should be a good race.

A couple of the fellows made water skis and they are having a swell time out there, being towed behind a fast power boat. It looks like a lot of fun. Maybe I'll try it sometime. The sailboat races will start at thirteen thirty this afternoon, so I shall return and give you the blow-by-blow description of that. It really should be good.

Skinner's boat is scratched, so it is a race between Sellers and Warner. It may be a little too fast for me to record, but I'll try. This is only one mile and will be fast. They're off. Sellers took the lead by starting by a length. Sellers is way ahead and should win easily. It must be getting close to chow time, too. I'm getting hungry. Chicken and French fries today, so the announcer said. I have my doubts though. At the half it's Sellers way out in front and Warner is about an eight mile behind. It looks as if it's over, with Sellers winning by about a quarter mile. Not much of a race. So long. I'm in love with my wife. I'm hungry for love and kisses and _____.

Monday, July 3, 1944. *Letter of June 22 & checks for $80 & $50. Went downtown. Cashed checks $130. Went to post office. Mailed package to Johnnie & M.d.R.*

Carol Lavata, Jackie

[Pavuvu Island, Russell Islands.]
Postmarked July 4, 1944, stamp upside down.

July 3, 1944
Somewhere

Hello, Lucia:

I love you, miss you, and want you. You are locked forever in my heart. Your lovely vision is constantly before me and my thoughts are continually of you. I long for the day to come soon when you and I will be in each other's arms. It'll be swell when I am able to hold you close to me and kiss you. You are mine and I am yours, forever. We belong together and will be together one of these days. I am so very hungry for your kisses and loving. I am hungry for something else, too, and you are the only one who can satisfy my hunger. I adore you, Lou.

I received three letters today, honey, one from Grace and two lovely ones from you. Both were short, but as long as I get them I don't care so very much. They were written the twenty-second and twenty-third and postmarked the twenty-third and fourth, respectively. Your system is still working well, sweet. Thanx loads for being so considerate and thoughtful. Did I ever tell you how wonderful you are? You are the most wonderful wife and sweetheart in the world and I idolize you. I am more proud of you as the days roll by and I yearn to be there with you. I love Lucia.

I returned to my sack about ten-thirty last night and I had won two dollars. All I had was a half dozen bottles of beer, too, so I was quite sober. There was some liquor at the tent, too, but I only took a sip of that. This climate doesn't agree with heavy drinkers. They all acquire stomach ulcers or other troubles so, in order to return to my wife and family in the best of health, I don't indulge in the stronger more potent drinks.

Now, I'll see where I left off with your letter and finish this. By the way, some new scuttlebutt came out today. Some of it is good, and the other is bad. I won't bother going into detail because neither has any foundation and is almost impossible.

Your birthday certainly did mean something to somebody, and I don't think they enjoyed it as much as I did, even. If you remember, my sweet, the sixth of June was the day of the invasion, too. That day will be remembered by many, and quite a few will not be able to remember anything. Taken all in all, I have been quite lucky and I have no complaint. I've seen very little action and hope I never see anymore. I don't want to be a hero; all I want to do is get home, healthy in body and mind, to my waiting wife and daughter.

I'm sure glad to learn that Mike Jr. is a little gentleman and all boy. That's swell, isn't it. I, too, think Jo shouldn't strike Mike so very hard.

A whack on the behind will do just as much, or more, good, and it won't cause any permanent injuries. It is a relief knowing that you don't believe in that, too. When I was small, I used to feel more hurt from a scolding than a spanking, anyway. Maybe you were the same, too. We have plenty in common and may find plenty more, later on. All boys like to play with hammers and nails and it doesn't mean a thing. He may never be a carpenter and he still may possibly be.

I'll take your word for it that Judy is quite pretty, but you can't prove it by any pictures I have of her. As you say, she may be un-photogenic. (Boy I wonder where that word came from.) As for her being smart, well, I guess I'll have to take your word for that, too. I will find out both when I see her, though, won't I. I'll bet you anything that she isn't as pretty as our Jackie, though. It may be that Jackie is as pretty as her pictures, though. I'll still bet, though. Our little one is really a honey and smart, too, I'll bet. How can she be anything else with you for her mother.

You know, Jackie must have a good disposition, too. Else the other children wouldn't like her as much as they seem to. I'm glad that she gets along so well with other kiddies. It saves you a lot of worry and grief. Because they do get along so well, you can let them play without keeping such a strict eye on them. Isn't it funny that our wee one should consider Bonnie a baby, when there is so little difference in their ages, and she prefers to play and associate with N.G. [Nancy Gardiner] Perhaps she is using N.G. for an example and is sort of trying to imitate her. It's swell, knowing that those cousins are able to see each other and be with each other before they grow up. That way, they will grow up together and be fast friends.

Now, sweet, I will try to tell you how to make almost any size film fit your camera. The next time you have both yours and Ann's empty, take the empty rolls out and compare them. You will find that they are the same length and have the same holes for winding. The only difference is that one roll is a little larger in diameter than the other. The metal end pieces, I mean. Now, all you have to do is cut that end piece down to the same size as the smaller one. Why don't you try it? Don't unwind the film, though, or expose it to the light in any way. If you do, it will become "n.g." as you know. The spool on which the film is bought is the one that should be cut down. Even though you can't make it fit your camera, it will still be usable in Ann's, so you won't be wasting it. Come to think of it, films for your camera should work in Ann's. Try interchanging the spools and you will find out. Maybe Ann's will fit yours, too. You may even ask the fellow or girl in Sandrian's about cutting the spools down, or get them to do it for you. It seems to me that they could and would do it for you unless there is some great difference in the profits on a roll of film. If you find out anything further along this line, please let me know, will you, darling? In order to cut the ends of those spools down you will need a pair of tin snips and a strong right hand.

Whoa, sweet, back up! I'm not going to stop my writing to you, even if I have to go hungry most of the time. These daily letters have become sort of an institution with me, and I intend keeping them going just as long as I possibly can. Fish-fries and everything else can wait. Letters to you come first. I love you, my sweet, and I can live on that. Did you honestly think I would let these letters go, just so I could attend a lousy fish fry? No piece of fish can ever take your place and you know it. I can go up any time they have one and eat all I want and no one will ever say a word. In fact, I now have a standing invitation to any and every feast they have. But I don't go, simply because I don't assist in any way. There have been plenty of times when I could have, but didn't. Heck, it's seldom that I go up anyway. I am in a position to do little odd jobs for some of the fellows and just to pass the time away I do them favors. My pay is the invitation and I still don't feel right going to them. Enough of this. If I keep on I'll have you all bowled up. I just want to say that it isn't you who is keeping me away, but myself. I'm an independent cuss. So you don't have to feel badly about it anymore.

By all means, sweet, see "The Song of Bernadette," if you possibly can. No, see it, even if it's impossible to do so. Seeing that picture would be worth any price and I know that you will enjoy it. You should know darn well that it's a good show, just because I remember it. That gal, Jennifer Jones, played a wonderful part and had a swell cast with her. I would like to see it again, myself. I love you with all my heart.

In this letter you say you have some more snapshots being developed. Does that mean that I can expect more of my beautiful wife, as well as more of our elegant bambino, or just more of Jackie? I hope there are more of you. That last one was swell, darling, and even though I couldn't see my things out in front, I love it. You were standing alright, but somehow they didn't show up so good. I really don't care, as long as I get a picture of my sweetheart every once in awhile. So, keep 'em coming, will ya huh? As for your "if they turn out alright," well, I'm not worried about that because they most always do. It's darn seldom you have any worthless ones. I don't think I can remember even one, can you?

I, too, wish I were there so Jackie could get to know me before she gets much older, but that depends entirely on persons other than us. I also wish I were there so that I could return Jackie's good night kiss and say "nite nite" to her too. One of these days I will be, though, and then we will all be completely happy. I love you both so very much and desire to see you. Give my fond regards to the family and our friends. Here's my daily special hug and kiss for our little one and to you, my all. I yearn to make love to you again.

J.De Roxtro EM1/c   *As ever, your ever loving* *Johnny*

Note on flap: "Hello, wifie, dear. Here's lots of love, hugs and kisses from your loving hubby. How's Mickey? I adore you."

Tuesday, July 4, 1944. Everybody home. Mil & Judy here for dinner. Also Mama G and Tadone. Took pictures of Jackie & Judy. Thunder shower. Gene came over to supper. Rained again. All left at nine o'clock.

[Pavuvu Island, Russell Islands.]
Postmarked July 5, 1944, stamp upside down.   July 4, 1944

                                                                    Somewhere

Hello, Sweetheart:

All the love in the world is ours. How I long to be there soon so that I can prove it to you. Thoughts of you are continually on my mind. Your lovely image is always before me, guiding me in everything I do. How I want to be able to hold you tenderly in my arms once again and kiss you. My love for you increases daily. I am hungry, my darling, but not for food, and only you can satisfy me. Each day brings us more close to the day of our reunion, but, gee, how much longer I'll have to remain out here I would like to know. I still feel that we will be in each other's arms soon, but I wish I could tell you when. I love you so very much, miss you and want you too. We belong together and should be together. My happiness won't be complete until we are, either.

No mail came for me again today, so I now have only three to answer. Tonight I will answer yours of the twenty-first. Thanks loads for writing so often sweetheart. I really appreciate it, because I know darn well that you don't have much time to spare from your duties there at home. You are writing almost daily, too. Gee, I have a loving wife. Thanks also for the kiss you always sent via the stamps. I adore you, sweet, here's a hug and kiss.

On the inside of the envelope you inquired about Forbes. He has been out of the sickbay for three weeks, I think. I told you all this before, though, so you should know it by now. Up until yesterday he felt quite well, but suddenly he felt ill and right now he has gone to see the doctor. If he returns before I finish this letter, I'll let you know the results. The poor guy feels bad, but he doesn't show it.

Enclosed in this letter were the two latest snapshots of Jackie. She sure is a honey and her old man wants so very much to see her. In the one picture she really is busily engaged with that flowerpot, isn't she. Each picture I receive our little one seems to have grown so. She must be growing like a weed. She still is the finest looking babe in the world, though. Gee, she has a lot of curly hair and such nice attractive eyes. And besides being good-looking, she also looks very intelligent. Cute little nose, too. Gee, I wish I were there to see her and her me. I love them both. You know, if I don't get there soon, our little one will be too grown up for me to romp with. Heck, she'll be a big girl by the time I arrive. Here's hoping she isn't more than a month or two older, though. Everyone I show her pictures to think she is swell, too, so she must be the best in the world. You know, I adore you two.

I acquired myself a spring bed today, so I expect to have a decent night's sleep tonight. Boy, I sure am glad to get rid of that cot. You know, you feel more tired, bodily, than you do when you go to bed at night. They're most uncomfortable and someone could make a fortune inventing something as handy, but more comfortable.

Forbes just came down and he seems to think he has it again. The doctor took another smear, too, so when Forbes returns tomorrow morning, he will know for sure. I hope he doesn't have malaria again. I'll let you know tomorrow night the results.

I thought my mother's birthday was the third, but I wasn't sure. As for Gracie's birthday, well, I had forgotten all about it. I don't know what I would do without you to remember those things for me, my lovely one. I never could remember days. Vene or my mother used to remind me. It's a wonder I even remembered your birthday, Jackie's birthday, or even our wedding date. Love, and love alone must be what's reminding me of these things. Gee, I sure am lucky to have such a swell wife.

Forbes just asked me to ask you to relay his love and adoration to Ann, as long as he isn't able to be there himself. He's talking to a guy next door about her, now. He said "hello" to you.

I, too, often recall those last five days we spent together, sweet, and I sure would give a lot to be able to return and go through it all again. Five days wouldn't be very long, after two years away from you, but it sure would help. Sweetheart, more than anything else I long to be there with you to remain forever. I love you.

Now, dearest one, if you will pardon me I will now go to the show. I don't know what's playing, or who is in it, but I think I will go anyway. I haven't been in quite awhile. Who knows, maybe it'll be a good one. We sure have had a lot of stinkers, lately. Mostly horse operas, too. I like higher-class stuff than those darn things. Here's a few hundred hugs and kisses to tide you over until I return. I love you. ***** Here I am again, sweet. I sat through as much of this one as I could and had to leave. The name of it is "The Uninvited," with Ray Milland. Boy, it sure is a stinker. I just couldn't stand any more of it. The rest of the boys are still there, though. They would sit through most anything.

Heck, honey, as long as the ground is warm it won't hurt our wee one to sit on it. Besides, she enjoys it more that way. All kiddies seem to and she's no exception. Gee, you sure do have your hands full trying to keep our Jackie clean, don't you. Maybe it's healthy to play in the dirt while one is a child. The wee ones that weren't allowed to are usually puny, sickly grown ups and are never healthy. You can see it whichever way you turn. So, my dear one, even though it means more work for you, let her enjoy herself as much as she wants to. I know darn well that you will, anyway. One thing we will have to have is a washing machine, wont we. All our other little ones will get dirty, too, and we will have to have plenty of clean clothes for them. Say, lovely one, that reminds me of something. You never have told me how many children we are going to have. So when you answer this letter, tell me all about it. I will try to satisfy you, but I am getting older, you know. We will definitely wait till the war is over and we are together, though, because that's what you and I both want. I don't want you to go through all that again without being there beside you through it all.

I guess this will be all for tonight, sweet. I've answered your letter and have nothing more to say to you, from this base. I love you more than life itself, my darling, and desire to be there with you. Our happiness will be complete when we are together again, and that'll be soon, I hope. Regards to all the family.

J.De Roxtro EM1/c   As ever, your adoring *Johnny*

Note on flap: *"Here's Jackie's special hug and kiss, and many more for you. I love you, my darling."*

Wednesday, July 5, 1944. *Letters of June 27-28. V-Mail poem from Ralph. Up at 6:30 to catch Alderney milkman. Mistake in bill. In afternoon went to post office for Fan. Girls in Newark. Mil came after supper. Aunts came with people from Ohio. Stayed until 9:30. Martha & I walked Mil home. Wrote to Ralph. Jackie trained for bladder control. 16 m.*

[Pavuvu Island, Russell Islands.]
Postmarked July 6, 1944, stamp upside down.

July 5, 1944
Somewhere

My Darling Lou:

I love you so very much. You will never know how much I've wanted to be there with you all these many long months. I miss you and want you, too, and each night I pray that we will be together soon. As the days slowly drag by, though, we are brought closer together, even though it is in time only, and one of these days, my orders to come home to you will surprise me. I am ready, though, and when they do come I will be prepared. I long to take you tenderly in my arms once again and kiss you. Your lovely vision is always before me and my thoughts are eternally of you. These last few weeks would have been almost unbearable, sweetheart, if I hadn't had you to think of. I'm so glad we were married before I left the states. I'm selfish, I know, but knowing that you are there, waiting for me, has helped me over quite a few rough places along the way. You have had it tough, though, and I will do my best to make up for all we've missed together. I love you, Lou, and want to make a home for you and our family. You're the most wonderful wife and sweetheart in all the world and I am proud of you. I am also proud to have you as the mother of our little one. No one else could have done such a swell job. Gosh, darling, I still can't see how I ever managed to win you, but you can bet your boots that I'll never be sorry. I love you more than life itself and will do everything possible to make you more happy and satisfied with life. I adore you.

No mail came for me again today, so I guess I can sort f expect some tomorrow or the next time some comes in. I still have two letters of yours to answer, so tonight I will answer the one of the twenty-second of June and save the other until more comes. Your letters have been coming very good lately and I am so very proud of you. How I hope that soon we won't have to write these letters. Won't it be swell when we can tell each other of our love and adoration? Boy, will I be a happy husband then. Pucker up, honey, here's a kiss.

Forbes said he was feeling a little better today. He won't know the results of the malaria smear until tomorrow or the next day. Right now he is up at sickbay, but only for a visit to the doc. That poor kid has had tough luck ever since we've been on this rock, so I hope he is well real soon and doesn't have that illness again. He asked me to say "hello" to you and sends his love to both you and Ann. Frosty, Fitz and Carl all send their best to you and expect to meet you soon. Frosty still hasn't heard from his daughter about that picture, so maybe she never received it. He has written and asked her about it, though, so he should receive a reply very soon. As soon as he lets me know about it, I will tell you all.

We, the whole gang of us, may have a chance to have a picture taken all together. I would like to have one as a keepsake and so would the rest of the fellows. Know what, sweet? I love you.

There seems to be nothing further that I can say about things over here, so I may as well try to answer your letter. Oh, yes, I slept very well last night and today I got up feeling swell. I brought another bed in this morning and gave it to Forbes. He has had so much sack duty he will appreciate a little more comfort. Besides, he has been complaining of not sleeping well nights, so maybe this will help. Honestly, I felt more rested this morning than I have in a long, long time.

Well, Vincent just returned and he said that the doctor wanted him to turn in to sickbay tonight. But he asked the doctor to let him return down here for a couple of days so that he could use his new spring bed. And the funny part of it is, the doctor allowed him to. That guy has a wonderful disposition and everyone likes him a lot. He seems to be able to do most everything he wants to do with those doctors. He even asked the doc if he could have a couple of days off from work and the doc told him he knew damn well he could, without even asking for it. Vincent is afraid he has the malaria again, though.

Thanks for the kiss you sent by way of the stamp, sweet. As I've said before, I intend to repay you, in person, with multiple interest for all these kisses you've sent me. That is, of course, unless you would rather I didn't. If you want, I will kiss you over and over again. I love you loads.

On the inside of the envelope you told me how much you miss me. You don't miss me any more than I miss you, I'll bet. Honey, I miss you and want you so very much. I love you very much and desire to be there with you, more than anything else.

Honey, you must have had quite a time with your tooth. Gee, after all that drilling, it still had to come out. That's tough, and I can imagine it really did hurt you terribly. The drilling hurt, naturally, but the extraction itself wasn't so very bad, was it? At least, not for quite awhile afterwards. I know the reason you turned so pale, sweet, you were in such pain while the doc was drilling that you sort of expected pain when he pulled it and sort of became faint. Now, the main reason you became faint is because you didn't eat anything that morning. I should give you the devil for that, but I won't because it was there for you, and if you didn't eat, that's your business. But you should have known better, my love. I'm sorry it happened, though, sweet. Gee, I love you, miss you and want you. Here's hoping you don't have to have any more pulled or extracted. I don't want to see you hurt. Maybe you shouldn't have any more children, sweet. Cause if you do, you will probably have more trouble with your teeth. Speaking of teeth, angel, what is causing Fan to have more trouble with her teeth than you are? Gee, she used to have nice strong teeth, didn't she? I love you, sweet.

My darling, there are some questions you shouldn't ask. You will have to use your imagination as to where and how we acquired our food for that little supper. There are ways we can do things, sometimes, and we don't take any unnecessary chances. Maybe we found the articles on the beach, or maybe we dug them out of the ground. Regardless of where we got them, we have enough for a little snack once in awhile. And it really tastes good. There are times when we simply don't care for our chow and then we make our own. We can always get bread and we can find the other stuff easily, the second time. Right now, I can go for a five-minute walk and have quite a feed. Yes, sweet, I helped quite a bit on this one. I was official cook and bacon slicer-upper. You see, I had all my letters taken care of, so I had plenty of time.

Well, my dearest, don't expect me to send that picture to you, because I don't know whether you'd like it or not. I will save it and bring it home with me. Then I will find out.

The name of the show tonight was, "You Are Always In My Heart." I didn't see it tonight because it was raining. I did see it back on Santos, I think. Anyway, it sounded familiar to me. I've been writing and shooting the bull with the fellows in the tent, intermittently. Now I will continue this uninterrupted, until I am finished. It is getting late and I have another page to write to the only girl in the world for me. I love you.

Sweetheart, I am in the best of health as usual, and am as happy as I can possibly be separated by so many thousands of miles away from you. I sincerely hope and pray that you, Jackie and the family are in the best of health and are completely happy. My happiness won't be complete until I am there, holding you in my arms and kissing you or telling you how much I love you and adore you. That day may come soon, or it may not be for a couple of months, but when it does come, we both will be more happy than we've been for a couple of years.

Your letter has been answered sweet, and all I can do now is thank you for the clipping about the two old gals looking at rugs. Those cartoons are usually darn good, and I enjoy them. So, thanks again. Give my fond regards to all the family and any of our friends you may happen to meet. Here's my daily special hug and kiss for our daughter and many more for you my adorable angel. I love you so very much, my sweetheart, and desire more to be with you than I ever did.

J.De Roxtro EM1/c   As ever, your loving *Johnny*

Note on flap: "Hi, sweet!! I wonder when you and I will be together. I love you."

Thursday, July 6, 1944. *Received letters of June 24,25,26,29. Card from Mary. When Jackie awoke from nap we went to Cat's and downtown. Cat looked for gift. Stopped in Whelan's for fudge sundae. Home again to Cat's. Drove down to Lidgewood. Watched kids in pool. Stayed 15 min. came home. Had cooked sauce in morning. Girls went to movies. I sewed dress for myself.*

[Pavuvu Island, Russell Islands.]
Postmarked July 7, 1944, stamp upside down.   July 6, 1944
                                                             Somewhere

Hello, Sweetheart:

I love you miss you and want you. Thoughts of you are continually on my mind and your lovely image is eternally before me. I long to hold you tenderly in my arms and kiss you. Each day that passes brings us more close together and you can believe me when I tell you that they can't possibly pass quick enough to suit me. My darling, mere words could never describe my true feelings for you. I want so much to be there with you, to do my utmost to make you comfortable and completely happy. That is my job and I should be there doing that, instead of being way out here away from you and our lovely daughter. Sweet, I love you.

Today I received five letters. One was from my mother and the rest were from my sweet and lovely wife. Gee, it sure is swell receiving so many letters from you. The ones I received from you today were written the twenty-fourth, fifth, sixth, and seventh and each was postmarked two days after you wrote them. That's swell, dearest one. Your system was a success right from the start. One of these today was postmarked in Orange, too, so Fan must have remembered to mail it, after all. You know, sweet, it makes you seem so much closer to me when your mail comes through so quickly. What a difference between now and the first few months I was over here. Do you remember how long it used to take your lovely letters to reach me? You're the sweetest girl in the world.

Now, my love, I have some news that you won't like to hear. I am almost out of paper and try as I would, I wasn't able to acquire anymore. I do have enough to last me a couple of days, so maybe I will be able to get more tomorrow, or the next day. Anyway, I will see what I can do, and I'll keep writing even though I have to use toilet tissue, I have plenty of envelopes so I feel sure I can get some paper somewhere somehow. A single package of writing paper doesn't last me very long, anyway. I should get all I can whenever I have the chance. Oh, well, I'll learn one of these days. I love you, sweet.

Nothing new has happened lately so I will go on and answer your letter of the twenty-third. This is only three pages, but it tells me that you love me and are patiently waiting, and oh, so very much more, that you never could put in writing. No one ever could, sweet, cause there just aren't any words to explain it. It's so deep and means so very much to couples in love, that they can only feel it. Thanks loads for the kiss you sent by way of the stamp, sweet. I really like to see them and even though there is no external feeling, it means a lot, deep down inside, where my love for you resides. Some day we will be together and then we can have the pleasure of indulging in the young American's favourite pastime, pitching woo. Lucia, my love, I really wish I could answer that question you asked on the inside of the envelope. Boy, wouldn't I like to say the end of this month, next month, or any time this year and mean to keep it. I can't make any definite date with you, angel, but you know darn well I would like to. I love you.

Sweetest girl in the world, I have just made a recount of my stock of paper and I have only enough to write five pages tonight, and six tomorrow. That's all, so I had better get busy and try to locate some tomorrow. I'll let you know how I make out.

Thanks for the clippings you so thoughtfully enclose with your letters once in awhile, my sweet bundle of love. The Gremlins are really quite good, aren't they. Say, I just happened to think that it's about time we got a decent picture here, so I think I'll go tonight and see. As usual, I haven't the slightest idea what's playing, though I will let you know when I return.

Sweetheart, you are writing more often now than I expect you to, so don't you worry your pretty little head about it. You are writing almost every day, so what more can you do. I honestly don't expect you to keep it up, my love, but I sure do like to receive your epistles of love and adoration. It's only natural that I am disappointed when I don't receive any mail from you, but I think your disappointment is a little greater than mine is. After all, angel mine, you know I am writing daily so you are sort of expecting them. As for me, I have no way of telling whether you are writing daily or what, until I receive the letters from you. Then again, I have a lot more time to write than you do. I do love you and even if you did write daily, I wouldn't be satisfied any more than you are now. Neither of us will be, until we are in each other's arms again.

Sweetheart, don't you ever become tired of people stopping you, just to talk to and rave over the beauty of our Jackie. Heck, maybe it's a good thing. I'm not there cause sure as I was born I would be quite insulting to some people and make some of them quite angry. I can't take all that kind of blarney even though it is well meant. Perhaps I would be changed, though, by realizing that it was our bambino they were raving over. I could take most anything now, though, just as long as I were there with you.

Our little one will soon be old enough to go to the store alone and I still won't be there to see her, you know, Lou darling, sometimes I can't quite get it through my thick head that she is so big and able to walk around and all that. Gosh, even though I have all those pictures I feel that I will be so surprised when I see our sweetheart. Your descriptions are almost perfect, too, yet I don't understand her and the things you tell me about her. She must be a remarkable child, alright. Damn it, why the hell can't I get home so that I can see our bambino before she gets too far out of the childhood stage. Unless I get there soon, she will be a little girl instead of a baby. Oh, sweetheart, I want so very much to be home to see you and our family. I love you both and should be there with you two beautiful little girls. Honey, it's about time for the show to start, so I will close temporarily, offering you many millions of hugs and kisses to tide you over. Bye now.

I sure would have liked to have seen our little one, when she was walking around the Acme, pushing that cart around. I'll bet she certainly does draw a lot of attention, though. I love our daughter and I want to be there to see her as well as her mother. Darn it, my sweetheart, I want to get home. Gee, she really did walk a long ways, didn't she. There is plenty I don't know about our little one. Every letter I receive from you teaches me plenty and I still don't know very much about her. I sure wish I did, though. Honey, you shouldn't have moved that heavy flowerpot, just to take a picture of our little one. Those things are entirely too heavy for you to move. I'll bet those pictures will really look good, though, and different. Tell me, darling, weren't you a little scared that she might fall off? Especially when she was standing up on the post. Or has she learned when to stand or sit still. She probably does, though, by now.

Honey, I sure do hope your teeth are and always remain in good condition. My teeth are pretty fair yet, but I sure am sorry that I didn't take better care of them when I was younger. By this time they (your gums) are really healed, though, and I hope that's the last you'll lose. Give my fond regards to the family and all our friends. Here's my daily special hug and kiss for our darling Jackie and millions more for the most wonderful wife and sweetheart in the world. I love you more than ever.

J.De Roxtro EM1/c   *Everlastingly, yours forever* *Johnny*

Friday, July 7, 1944. *No mail. Very hot. Stayed with Jackie out in yard. Worked on my dress. Mil came over after supper.*

[Pavuvu Island, Russell Islands.]
Postmarked July 8, 1944, stamp upside down.   *July 7, 1944*
                                                                  Same place

Hello Beautiful:

I love you, miss you and want you more as each day passes. Thoughts of you are constantly in my mind and your eyes are before me always. Such beautiful dark eyes in such a pretty face. How I long to be there, looking into those eyes. I want to hold you tenderly in my arms and kiss you, too. Oh, my sweetheart, I love you so, and want to be there more than ever. As each day passes, we are brought more close together, even though it is in time only. We are bound to be together one of these days and then we will be happy together.

As you know, this will be only six pages long. I managed to acquire four packages of writing paper this afternoon, so I will be able to continue my daily epistles for another month. By that time I hope and pray that I will be on my way to you, my loving wife. According to the scuttlebutt, the latest, we are to leave about the first week of August. Wouldn't you feel swell if I were able to tell you that, truthfully. I know darn well that I would feel good. One of these days I will be able to tell you when to expect me and then I will really be in form. I love my sweetheart and wife and our little daughter. I want more than anything else to be there trying hard to make you two happy.

No mail came for me again today but I don't care. I have four to answer now and I am quite happy and pleased that you are able to make time to write so often. It's really swell of you, honey, and I appreciate your efforts. Tonight I will answer your letter of the twenty-fourth of June, which I received yesterday. Thanks loads for the kiss you sent by way of the stamp, angel. I wish I could be there, so that we wouldn't have to write letters and send kisses that way. How's about a nice warm embrace with a nice long kiss and all the rest, sweet? Would you like that? Boy, I would. Thank our little daughter for the hug and kiss you sent me for our daughter and yourself. I'll pay them all back when I reach home and I may even pay a little interest.

Sweetheart, I know how you felt when you wanted to get out of the house so you went to the movies. I feel that way quite often, but there isn't anything I can do about it. You have me beat that way, but I can get away from things merely by concentrating on my love life. I am always thinking of you, though, so it isn't so bad on me. I'm glad you enjoyed the picture, though. Tonight we are having the show "Up In Arms." It is supposed to be a pretty good picture and a late one so I think I will go. I hope you don't mind too much. I'm not going yet, so don't expect a few million hugs and kisses to tide you over. They're only a present.

Yes, my sweet, it is nice receiving long letters but darn it, most of the time it's almost impossible to make them very long, and still make them interesting. I wish I could make them all at least twelve pages, but I can't. Besides, if I did that, the censors may ask me to write less often, and that would really be bad. I think you'll agree on that. I sure love hearing from you and I know darn well that you will be more pleased with me if I write more often and longer. I love you.

Sweetest one, I am taking the best possible care of myself and I think I'm fairly lucky. Hmm—I don't exactly know what to say about your next sentence but I feel that I should. You ask me to be good and not to do anything you wouldn't do. Let's see, you know that I'm always good and as for the other, you can use your own judgment. There are some nurses here and they are allowed to date enlisted men, now. So, it's quite possible that I may have a date one of these days with a nice nurse. But my love, you know darn well that I will remain true to you, no matter how long I've been away. I am yours and will be yours forever. I want no one but you and I will take nothing from anyone but you. I know you were kidding when you wrote this and I started off that way when I wrote about the nurses. The above is all true, and some of the fellows may have dates with them, but your old man will wait a little longer. After I've waited this long, I'm sure I can wait longer.

Angel, I'm sorry, but that's all there was of your letter to answer, so this may be a little shorter than I expected it to be. I'll try as hard as I can to make this six pages, but I don't have anything to write about, so I may be unable to.

There's quite a bull session going on here in front of the tent and it's really bull. A couple of the fellows are feeling pretty good and some of the stories are really good. In fact, they're so good that I couldn't write them. The paper would burn up if I wrote them.

Forbes just came in and the result of the first smear was negative. That's swell but it doesn't mean anything yet. Maybe the next will be positive. Hope not though because he sure has had enough hard luck with sickness, etc. He is feeling a little better today but he isn't quite right yet. He sends his regards to both you and Jackie and he wants you to give his love to Ann. He also wants you to ask her to write to him because that's the only medicine that does him any good. He's due for a letter from her any day now, I think, and then he'll be happy again. He really is a swell guy and he almost always has a smile and a good word for everyone. No matter how bad he feels he always has regards for the other persons feelings. He is a swell guy and I, too, hope you are able to meet him in the very near future. I know that you and the rest will like him loads.

Well, it's just about time for the show to start, so I will now offer you a few million hugs and kisses to hold you until I return from our open-air theatre. Right now, the news is on and soon afterwards the chaplain will read the articles of the Navy, and then the show will start. I've read the news and heard the articles read as darn many times that I don't care about either. I will be there in time for the show, though. So long for awhile, sweet. I love you and want you. ******* Here I am again, my sweet. Here's a couple million hugs and kisses to hold you through the rest of this letter. The show was pretty good but it was really crazy. I enjoyed it though for a change. I still don't know who the players were, so I can't tell you. I'm sorry about my lack of knowledge concerning the actors and actresses in the cinema but as you know, I never was very good at that. I like to see some of the pictures, but I can't seem to remember anything about them shortly after I've seen them. I do remember "The Song of Bernadette," though and a few more. The last picture mentioned has left the island and may not return while we are here, so perhaps you and I will be able to see it together when I come home. It's really a swell picture, sweet, and I'm going to see it again, if I am able. I love you.

Blosser just asked me if you ever said anything about me returning home. Can you imagine that? I told him that you merely ask me when I'm going to make a date with you and keep it. That satisfied him and now he's in bed. Forbes is also in his and John Harder, the fellow who made those birthday cards, is over in his corner snoring. I will soon lie down to rest my weary bones and think of how nice it would be if you and I were side by side in our own most comfortable bed. Gee, how I wish I were there now instead of way down here on an island with no towns or villages and no loving wife to return to after a hard days work. You know, honey, I miss you more at night than I ever did. Perhaps it's because I spent more time with you at night.

298

I just heard the whistle blow and a few cheers so I guess someone made a basket. Oh, I never told you that we now have a basketball court, did I? It's quite nice and a lot of the fellows are playing. I never was any good at basketball so I don't play. Besides that I'm a little old to waste energy on something like that. Especially down here. Give my fond regards to the family and our friends. Here's my daily special hug and kiss for Jackie and to you, I send my all.

J.De Roxtro EM1/c   *Everlastingly, your loving* *Johnny*

July 8, 1944 - Japanese withdraw from Imphal, India, the turning point of the Burma campaign.

Saturday, July 8, 1944. No mail. Hot. Ann home from work. Cleaning. Mom worked half a day. 5:00 went downtown with Jackie & girls. Bought dress. Left girls to go to Crane's. Came home & went to play tennis. 8:30. Period.

[Pavuvu Island, Russell Islands.]
Postmarked July 10, 1944, stamp upside down.   July 8, 1944

                                                                Somewhere

Hello, Beautiful:

Gee, darling, I love you so very much it hurts, way down inside. The feeling I have for you is unexplainable. Mere words can never portray my feelings for you. I long to put my arms around you, hold my lovely wife close to me and kiss you. In between kisses, I want to tell you of my love and adoration. Your lovely image is always here in front of me and I am always thinking of you, my dearest one, more than anything else in the world, I want to be there. I love you, miss you, and want you.

After supper tonight, Lou, I was in an un-writing mood. So, I sat here on the deck gazing out over the lagoon. All the while I was there, I was sort of daydreaming of you. It was really beautiful, angel. There was a nice breeze and about a dozen sailboats were skimming noiselessly across the dreamy blue water, graceful as swans. The trees across the way caught the last rays of the setting sun and the fronds were glistening while waving gently. I could picture you and I together out in one of those boats enjoying life as we should be. Gee, sweetheart, I want so very much to be there with you and Jackie. Honestly, lover, I was sitting there until I was rudely awakened by one of the boys inviting me to go to the show. I had no idea that I sat there so long. It was dark when I was disturbed, but I was still looking toward home and you. Anyway, I went to the show and saw "Salute to the Marines." It was pretty good, but damn it, those guys are very much over-rated. Hell, the Seabees are just as good if not better. At least we have no press agents taking pictures of our every landing and deed. This sounds like professional jealousy, I guess, so I will knock t off. I'm sorry if I have bored you. You know it was entirely unintentional if I did. I love you too much to bore you. You are the most marvelous wife and sweetheart in all the world and I long to be there with you.

Frosty is here shooting off his mouth trying to pester me. He just said he was a sad sack and wants to go home. His daughter is five feet, one and one half inches tall and weights one hundred five pounds. She's a honey, according to her pictures, and he thinks the world of her. He is just about always talking of her and at every word you can hear the affection coming out. I love ours, too.

I'm not going to answer any of your letters tonight, mainly because your next one is six pages long and I want to write you a long letter tomorrow. I didn't intend writing any answer tonight, anyway, so I haven't lost anything, have I. Besides, it is too late now to start answering one. So, my sweetheart, you will now know why this letter is so short.

I received another sweet letter from my honey today. It was written the twenty-eighth and postmarked the following day. Gee, honey, that's swell. I will love you at least ten days the first week I am home. Your system is working swell, too. Gee, darling, thanks loads for writing so often. That makes about ten days straight that you have written to your distant hubby. You're the most remarkable girl in the world and I love you.

Next to me in the tent on my right, the fellows are playing knock rummy or poker, or some other game and two tents away on my left there is a hillbilly playing his homemade guitar. It sounds pretty fair but he is no musician and plays the same chords with every song he sings. It's a constant pling, plang, plung, whenever he is around, but most of the fellows enjoy it, so who am I to complain. I can stand it as long as anyone else can. Besides, I have my lovely wife to think of, so I don't care what goes on around me. Darling, I love you very much.

Well, my adorable angel, this will be my last page but I'll be darned if I know just how I will ever fill it up. There isn't any news from here that I can relay to you. All the scuttlebutt is good, though, so maybe something will happen soon. I'm still hoping and praying for the best, though, and I always will. Gee, it'll be swell when I am there able to hold you tenderly in my arms and kiss you again. I adore you.

Forbes asks to be remembered to you as do Carl and Frosty. Forbes wants you to give Ann his regards and love. He said he is thinking of her tonight, especially because it's Saturday night and he would like to be out juking with her. Clere is telling the boys a few stories about a friend of his and boy, such stories you've never heard and probably never will. There are lots of these things I will forget, my love, but I'll remember quite a bit of it and tell you when I return.

My most magnificent sweetheart, I love you more as each day slowly passes gradually bringing us more close together. Give my regards to all the family and our friends, sweet, especially Mama G and Tadone. Here is my daily hug and kiss for our sweet daughter and many more for you my adorable angel. I want you, sweetheart. I love you more than ever.

J.De Roxtro EM1/c   Everlastingly, your loving *Johnny*

Note on flap: "Hello, darling: I love you more than life itself. You are mine and I am yours forever. How's Mickey?"

Sunday, July 9, 1944. Mama G & Tadone up. Tadone trimmed moustache. Joe & Angie not up. Jackie sick. Temp. Teething. Girls went to movies. People from Trenton.

[Pavuvu Island, Russell Islands.]
Postmarked July 10, 1944, stamp upside down.   July 9, 1944
                                                                Same old place

Hello, Beautiful:

I love you with all my heart, body and soul. Your sweet face is always before me and you alone are locked forevermore in my heart. I've locked my heart and thrown away the key. But instead of staying there, quietly, as I had an idea you would, you are growing and growing until I want you almost too much. My love for you increases daily and more than anything else in the world I desire to be there, trying to make you happy. You and our darling daughter are my one and only worthwhile reasons for living.

It's a beautiful day today and it is nice and cool, with a strong breeze. The sailboats are cavorting like sheep in a pasture. The boys are having a sporting time and it looks like a lot of fun. Maybe I'll try it sometime. Quite a few of the boats have turned over, but that's nothing. No one ever gets hurt, though, so it's perfectly safe.

Two lovely letters came for me from you today. They were written the twenty-ninth and thirtieth of June and were postmarked the day following the writing of each. Neither were very long, so there won't be much of a letter in answer, but I am satisfied, my sweet, as long as you write. I am receiving more mail from you than I thought I would, anyway. Sweetheart, I am the luckiest guy in the world to have such a lovely wife as you. I adore you. Together, you and I will bring up a lovely family and we will be happy and contented in our new life. How I long for the day to come when we are able to be together. I love you and want you, my dear.

Thanks loads for the two kisses you sent to me by way of the stamps, dearest one. Your letter of the twenty-fifth was six pages long, but it wasn't necessary to put two stamps on, was it? Or were you just paying safe, by making sure it would go. You know, I have five or six letters of yours to answer now and I don't know how I'm ever going to answer them all providing I don't receive any more for a week or so. I will continue my daily letters, though, and do the best I can. I love you, my dear. On the inside, you merely say that you love me, but oh, how much those words mean to me. I love you, too, and one of these days you and I will be together again and then you and I will be happy together. Sweetheart, more than anything else in the world I want to make you and our little bambino happy. I want to be able to take you tenderly in my arms and kiss you. I want to make Jackie happy by romping with her. In doing these things I will then become happy. The happiness of you two sweethearts of mine is of more concern than you realize.

There seems to be nothing more that I can say about anything out here, because there just isn't anything. No news is good news, they say, so maybe I will be on my way soon. So, because I have nothing to say, I will merely answer your letter. It's too bad that your grandfather is unable to eat during the hot weather, but he is rather old now and most persons when they become aged, lose their appetites. I'm glad that his arm is getting along alright. He's had quite a siege of it now and it's about time he was pulling through. Here's hoping he doesn't have any more trouble with it this winter.

Gee, I don't know what to say, now. You and Jackie are my responsibility and I should have a home for you. Of course I'm pleased that Mama G and Tadone are going there to live, but it's going to mean quite a bit more work for you. I know that you feel strange now, and sort of out of place. Honey, it will be perfectly alright with me if you look around and get a little place of your own. But I doubt if you would care for that, as long as I'm not there to be with you. Gee, I'm sorry, sweet, but being away from you as I am, there is absolutely nothing that I can do. Darn it, why the devil did I have to enter the armed forces.

Gene's idea of converting the office and pantry into a room for the girls sounds alright to me, but how about the two ice-boxes? Will you put them out on the little porch and make that the pantry, or what are his intentions? Fixing that room for the girls will be much better than letting them go up in the top of the house. That way, there will be a room for Ralph when he returns. It would have made quite a problem the other way. If I only knew exactly when I was coming home, we could then plan on moving. But maybe we had better wait until I am home for good before we even think of that. I don't think it's at all silly of you to think the way you do. After all, you aren't in that family anymore, but head of a family of your own. It does make a difference to your feelings and I know it. Sweetheart, I've caused you nothing but pain, worry and uneasiness so far, but I promise to do my best to make you happy and contented when I come back to you. I, too, am looking forward to a place of our own, where we can do as we please and bring our children up the way we want to. Our home may be a small apartment, or even perhaps a half house, at first, but in time we will have our own home and all the things we have always dreamed of. You know, darling, at times I am so afraid that I won't be able to do enough for you. I'll try hard and do my best to keep you and our family as best you deserve, but I'm still afraid I won't be able to make you as comfortable as I desire you to be. With your help and advice I can do it, though. Things will change again when we are united.

I suppose your mother and grandparents were quite disappointed because Joe was unable to visit you that Sunday afternoon. They all look forward to that visit and naturally would be. Tell me, does our bambino miss him and expect him, or is she a little too young for that yet? Your afternoon sounded quite dull and quiet to me, but gee, it sounds so restful and peaceful, I couldn't help but wish I were there beside you, reading the papers or making love to you.

It's swell, knowing that you enjoyed the double feature again. Sweetheart, it does you plenty of good to go to the show and enjoy yourself. Our picture tonight is "Destination Tokyo." It is supposed to be quite good but I suppose it is more of that damn propaganda stuff. The picture last night was fair, but then, I told you about that. I'll see the show tonight and if it's worthwhile, I'll tell you all about it tomorrow.

This is my second letter today. I wrote to my mother and now this, to you. Besides not being in the mood to write, I was reading my June Reader's Digest which I received a couple of weeks ago and never took time out to read. So, this morning, I decided to take time out to do that. I have a letter from Grace to answer yet, too. Darn it, I wish I could get in a writing mood more often. Honey, here's hoping you and I will be able to stop this writing soon. I love you so much.

You're telling me that there's nothing like making yourself comfortable. But I am able to go further toward my natural self than you are. All you can do is remove your shoes and loosen your clothing, while I can remove everything and usually do. It is much more comfortable that way.

Oh, oh!! I seem to have made a slight error. My remark about you knowing where to remove the carcass from the bus in Springfield was not meant to be sarcastic, but to be truthful. I was surprised that you were able to do it. You never were too bad that way, but sometimes you were a mile off your course. But that happens to anyone once in awhile, even me. Honestly, I can get lost so darn easy. I have no memory for towns passed through or anything like that. Heck, honey, you are sure swell. Maybe it's a good thing that your mother and the others didn't know you weren't too sure about where to get off. Gosh, if they had known, they would have pestered you to beat the band.

No, angel, you never told me about Father Sheerin becoming Monsignor, but then, you may have, and the letter hasn't arrived or has become lost. Anyway, I didn't know about it until my mama done told me. Will he remain at St. Margaret's? Give my regards to all the family and our friends. Here's Jackie's daily special hug and kiss from her daddy.

J.De Roxtro EM1/c   Everlastingly, your loving *Johnny*

Note on flap: "Hi, sweet, here's loads of hugs and kisses for the most wonderful wife in all the world. I love you. How's Mickey?"

Monday, July 10, 1944. *Hot. Sun. Nite hardly any sleep at all. Had baby in my bed. Letters of June 30th, July 1st. Money order for $100. Letter from M.de.R.$1.00 enclosed for Jackie. Went to dentist. Fannie home from dentist. Baby crying continually. Called doctor. Came just as I finished bathing baby. Teeth coming, top & bottom. Tonsils inflamed.*

[Letter from Johnny of July 10 is missing.]

Tuesday, July 11, 1944. *No mail. Hot. Washed clothes. Jackie much better. Will eat only fluids. Fan working overtime. Ann & I went to movies. Saw "Cobra Woman." good.*

[Pavuvu Island, Russell Islands.]

Postmarked July 12, 1944, two stamps upside down.   July 11, 1944

Somewhere

Hello, Sweet:

I love you, miss you and want you. You are the most wonderful wife, sweetheart and mother in all the world. You mean more to me than anyone else in the world. Of course when I say that, I mean that you are even more important than our little one, but she runs a close second. So close, in fact, that I refer to you two as one. More than anything else in the world, I desire to be there with you. Your lovely face is always before me and your soul has united with mine, way out here in the Pacific, to bring you more close to me. Sweetest girl in the world, I'm hungry for your love and kisses and you. I want you so very much. You are mine, I am yours, and we belong together. Someday we'll be reunited though, and then we'll be completely happy.

I received two letters today, my sweet. One from a beautiful well-shaped sixteen-year-old lassie named Charlene Clere, and a wonderful long letter from my one and only wife. Gee, sweet, it was really swell, hearing from you again. I really hadn't expected another quite so soon. Yours was written the first of July and postmarked the third. I know why this wasn't posted the second. It was dropped in a box where they don't have Sunday collections, or if they do, they merely put the letters accumulated away until the following day and then work on them. How's that for getting to the bottom of the cause of delay, huh? But who cares why your lovely epistles of love are delayed, as long as it isn't any longer than that? I love my darling and hope and pray I will be with her soon.

Charlene's letter was in answer to the one I wrote wishing her a happy birthday. I think I told you about that, didn't I? Anyway, when I wrote, I asked about the picture, whether she received it or not, and she did. She said she intended writing you, thanking you for it but never got around to it, finally forgetting all about it. When I wrote her, I told her that both she and her daddy were invited up to our place after the war. She said her dad intended taking her to New York City and she would be pleased to meet me, you, and our darling daughter, as she said she just loves children. She has never been to New York or seen an ocean. Complainingly, she said the farthest she has been from West Virginia is Chicago. Frosty has a brother there. He is married and has a daughter about the same age as Charlene, so Skip (Clere's daughter) visits them a couple of weeks each summer. She sounds like a swell kid to me and I think you two would get along alright. Frosty thinks the world of her and continually refers to her as his little girl. Maybe he doesn't realize that she is a young lady now. Well, enough about that. I love you very much, Lou.

Let's see, what else can I tell you before I answer your next letter, the one of the twenty-seventh of June. Heck, I can't think of anything, sweet, so I'll start. If I do think of anything, I will interrupt this and tell you. It seems there has been something that has slipped my mind. Oh, well, here goes. Thanks loads for the stamp kiss, angel. I'll repay you someday. On the inside of the envelope you wish I will be home soon. Honey, you aren't wishing any harder than I am. I am ready and have been for many, many months. You also told me that you love me. Gee, I'm sure glad you do, cause I don't know what I would do if you didn't. Knowing you do helps me more than you realize over the rough spots. I love you too, my most precious one. Your letter is four pages long and I am already on my third, so this looks like another six-pager, at least. Who knows, I may even manage to make it twelve. But before you get too excited, I must tell you that I'm not in the mood to write very much tonight. Right now, it is getting close to chow time so I will have to stop soon and go get my chow. Most of our stuff has been lousy lately, so I

305

hope they have something decent tonight. Boy, I sure did twist this paragraph around, didn't I. But what's the difference. We aren't supposed to be literary inclined, we are merely two people in love. I adore you, my sweet.

No explanation is necessary for my letters being misspent, because it is one of those impossible happenings. Someone made a mistake, and away it went, to the wrong destination. As long as you finally received it, we don't care where it went, do we. It wasn't delayed very much, either, so all is well. When I get to be postmaster general those things won't happen. That isn't a bad average, though, is it. Two letters misspent out of five or six hundred. Our main desire is to have our letters reach their destination and we don't care what route they take as long as they aren't delayed too long. Do you agree, my lovie-dovie? I could explain why it went to Jersey City, but this is enough about the subject, so I will refrain from commenting further.

The picture you mention is on the way with the latest issue of our scandal sheet, so you will have it soon. There won't be any use in your showing it to anyone because they won't know what it is or anything about it. You can't see much of the thing in this picture. Just put it away in the back of your album and I don't care if you don't mount it. You may do as you please about that. I intend trying to get a couple more taken from different angles. As for me being smart, well, I'm glad you think so. Here's a few dozen hugs and kisses till after chow, love.

Believe it or not, sweet, after chow I went down and played a couple games of horseshoes and I did fairly well. I hope you don't mind. But then, I know you don't. You're swell, sweet, and each day that passes I find myself more madly in love with you.

Ah Hah!! So you have a past, which you have kept from me all these years. A few more little innocent questions and I will have your complete history. You had a steady from the fourth through the seventh grades and even one in high school. You don't surprise me any though, sweetheart. How you ever were free and un-entangled when I met you is beyond understanding. I won't bother you with anymore of your previous loves, though. Anything and everything that you do, have done, or intend to do is of utmost importance to me. I want to learn all I can about you so I can do better for you. So, how could you bore me? You've never done it yet and I doubt if you ever could. I'm interested in you, my adorable one. I want to know what things you like best (other than red rose buds), how you like them and when. I'm learning a little all the time but it takes so long while we are separated this way. If we were together, I could find out a lot more about you and then I could do more to make you happy. But I'm repeating myself. I will not bother you with any more of this. I adore you, my darling.

Well, sweet, you win. We will get one of those two cars you mentioned and take a few nice rides out in the country somewhere. That is, of course, if the weather is okay. It was rather selfish of me when I mentioned something about staying home, wasn't it. What I do want is to be there with you so whether we are at home together or out riding together, what difference does it make, huh? Just being with you will be satisfactory to me. But please don't ask me to take you to New York, will you? Right now, I don't think I would care much for crowds. I want to be alone with you and Jackie. It's swell of those two brothers-in-law of mine to offer to loan me their cars. But let's forget all this until we are together again, shall we? Besides what you say about the gasoline rationing doesn't sound so good.

Sweetheart, don't you keep all the originals of these pictures I have? Wait a sec! I'll get all straightened out and begin over. Don't you have a duplicate of all these pictures? If not. Let me know which ones and I will send them back to you so you can have another print made of each. Hmph! What the devil is the matter with me tonight. All of a sudden I'm going around in circles. Maybe it's my yearly shot in the arm. It doesn't bother me though, as you know. Just forget all the previous drivel about prints and reprints. I'm just a little crazy, I guess. I know I'm crazy about you. I love you.

Angel, as long as I receive those pictures I don't care how long they are in coming. I'm glad you have been sending so many, sweet, and they sure have turned out swell, every one of them. I'm glad you think the last ones are swell, too. Just send them along whenever you get some and you can depend on me appreciating them. I don't know why you send the originals, though. Tell you what, sweet, why not get both sets and compare them, then send me the poorest ones. That way you have the best to put in your album. That's what I was trying to say on the last page but couldn't get it out. While on the subject of snapshots, sweet, do you have more than those you've sent me? I sure hope you do, because I want to see all I possibly can of the growth of our daughter. Don't send me too many, though, because I'm afraid they will spoil out in this damp heat; just enough so that I am able to see how Annette is progressing and once in awhile one of yourself, too.

The light became so bad that I'm afraid I will have to stop until after the show. It's almost show time anyway, so I won't lose much time. I have nothing further to report from this side of the world, anyway, except that I am in the best of health, as usual, and am as happy as I possibly can be away from you and our darling daughter, Jackie. I love you both so very much and desire more each day to be there with you. I love you more than life itself, and I would do anything to be with you.

Darling, I don't know what the name of the picture is, or who plays in it, but I will go and give you a report on it a little later. It's show time now, so here's a few thousand hugs and kisses to hold you while I go. I'll be back as soon as it's over. Gee, I sure could go for a few beers tonight and then a lot of you. I'll be seeing you sweet after the show. I'll have to get some water to quench my thirst, but there is nothing I want, other than you, to satisfy my hunger. Did I ever tell you how wonderful you are? You're pretty, too. I'm in love with you and intend to meet you just as soon as I possibly can. Here's hopin' and prayin' for an early reunion, my sweetheart.

The picture was "Nine Girls." I still don't know who played in it. There were nine of the second raters, I guess. Anita Louise was one, I think. Anyway, it was one of those lousy mystery pictures, where half the time you never could see anything on the screen. They are making a lot of those things lately. Maybe that's to conserve power and light for defense. I wish they could send some good pictures out here. The fellows would all appreciate it. Whoever picks those pictures for us sure doesn't know the kind of shows we like. Maybe they just send the ones that have no box-office appeal. Tomorrow we're having "Crime Doctor." We saw that one over a year ago back on Santos and most of us won't even go to see it. Oh, well, they give us something to do.

Looks like I'll have to do a little more thinking than usual in order to fill this page. Of course, I could end here, but then you would be a little disappointed. Forbes is in bed and probably asleep. Carl is reading a magazine, which he received in the mail today and the other two fellows are abed. That's where I'm going just as soon as I finish this short note.

I haven't told you much about the weather lately. That's because it's been quite nice, I guess. Anyway, it has rained very little in the past month. Not more than once a week. So that's pretty good for us, out here. It has been quite warm, but that's to be expected. I can manage no matter how things turn out and will be in good health when I return home, which is very soon, I hope. If we don't get something to do pretty soon I'm afraid we will be put to work somewhere else. Now that Saipan has been secured, most anything can happen. We may be in the next bunch that moves forward but I sure hope not. When we leave here, I want to head for home, you, and our sweetheart.

Well, angel child, give my fond regards to the family, your grandparents and any of our friends you may happen to meet. Here's my daily special hug and kiss for our sweet adorable Jackie. I love you both and desire more than ever to be there, doing my best to make you happy and satisfied with life.

J.De Roxtro EM1/c   As ever, your loving *Johnny*

Note on flap: *"Here's a few million hugs and kisses, sweet. Tell Mickey I'll be home to play with her soon. I love you."*

[The letters from Johnny from July 12, to October 1, 1944 are missing. We know they were written and received because Lucia mentions them in her journal entries.]

Wednesday, July 12, 1944. *Letters of July 2 & 3rd. letter from Mary. Hot. Baby better. Eats solids. Varnished desk. Sam Mirabello free.*

[**Sam Mirabello** was born in Morristown in 1918 and attended Morristown High at the same time as Lucia. The families knew each other from the 'old country.' Sam and a few of his buddies enlisted in the US Army in 1940, was captured and detained in POW camp 59 just south of Florence, Italy until 1943 when he escaped. Sam and about four other men hid in the Italian hillsides and sought refuge with Italian farmers. Finally, on March 14, 1944, they made contact with an American Patrol on the Anzio beachhead.] (camp59survivors.com)

Thursday, July 13, 1944. *Letter of July 4. 10 days to come. Varnished desk, 2nd coatings. Went downtown for pictures, baby food, fruit, socks. Moved desk to front. At night went to movies with girls. Saw Deanna Durbin in "Christmas Holiday". Did not like it. Storm Wed. nite. Did not last long.*

Friday, July 14, 1944. *Letters of July 5,6,7. Writing out in front.*

Saturday, July 15, 1944. *No mail. Varnished coat rack, chair, umbrella rack. Cleaned house. Vene came at 4:30. Brought string beans. Said M.deR. might come down Sunday. At night went downtown with girls. Bought swim suits and riding breeches for their vacation. Had coke at Thodes.*

Sunday, July 16, 1944. *Church. Baby slept 'til 8:00. Mom went to N.Y. early this morning. Girls busy packing. Grandparents not up. Dinner at 12:00. M.deR. came at 2:30. Very pleased with Jackie. Joe & Angie came. Brought Jackie for ride. Stormy, windy. 4:45 Vene, Johnnie & kids came for M.deR. 5:00 Joe brought girls to station. Came back. I took Jackie's supper and went down Mama G's. Supper there. Stayed until 8:00. Jackie very sleepy. Baby girl born Sat.*

Monday, July 17, 1944. *Letters of July 8,9,10. Letter from Ralph. Went to dentist 3:00. Filled tooth. Then went o Sandrian's. Jackie can imitate dog, cat, lamb, train whistle.*

Tuesday, July 18, 1944. *Letter of July 11, 1944. Cards from girls. Home all day. (Br. Hurting)*

July 19-August 10, 1944 - U.S. Marines invade Guam in the Marianas in the second battle of Guam. Guam, the largest island of the Marianas, had been a US possession since its capture from

Spain in 1898 until it was captured by the Japanese in 1941 who had formed a large garrison there. After Saipan was secured by the Allies, Guam was the next step in "Operation Forager" and fighting continued until August 10 when the Japanese resistance collapsed. Guam was declared secure, but 7500 Japanese soldiers were estimated to be at large in the mountain caves. On January 24, 1972, almost 30 years later, a Japanese army sergeant was discovered by hunters on the island. He had lived alone in a cave for 28 years. (Wikipedia)

Wednesday, July 19, 1944. Letter of July 12. Washed. Home.

Thursday, July 20, 1944. C-Breeze issue. Picture. 2nd $50 war bond. Rained during night. Damp in morning. Clear in afternoon. Home all day.

Friday, July 21, 1944. Letter of July 14. Joey here to play with Jackie (asked about daddy). Read book "A Tree Grows in Brooklyn." Up until 12:00.

Saturday, July 22, 1944. Letter of July 13. Lovely day. Joey came to play with Jackie 9:00. Out in yard. Went over to Julia's. Saw room. Jackie got Pluto from Joey. While asleep did cleaning. When awake both took bath, washed hair. Gracie & Mom to Newark. Stayed until 12:00.

Sunday, July 23, 1944. One stamp was a mistake. Church. Jackie up. Jo Ann & Carol over to play with Jackie. 11:00 sleep. Woke in time to eat with us 1:00. Dressed Jackie then went for walk 4:00. Joe & Angie came and took Jackie for ride to Burnham - ducks - cows on James St and South St. corner. Had ice cream. 6:15 Call from girls. Joe, Grace & Jackie went to station. Girls have nice tan. Pail. Nursery rhyme book. Dog for Jackie. Change purse for me. Picture folder for Johnnie.

Letter from Ralph postmarked July 24, 1944.
July 23, 1944
Hello Lou,

I received your letter of the 5th a few days ago. It was good hearing from you again.

I received the package today about 15:00 (3 p.m.) It was all out of shape but there wasn't very much damage done. Somehow the top came off of the long end and they were all broke into small pieces. I don't use a pencil very much anyway so I guess there's no harm done.

I was glad to get the paper. I really needed that. If you will notice the stationary I used in my last letters home was pretty heavy. It was all I had at the time because the P.X. ran out of light paper. I got this paper in a package that I received recently from Joe Cerilla. He sent me a capacolle with some candy and gum and peanuts. I had to throw the candy and peanuts away because they were spoiled. By the way you sure sent me enough paper. I guess that should last me for the duration and then some.

It's been a lousy day today. It was supposed to be our day off but we had to work because they needed the trucks in a hurry. I didn't mind working though because it was raining pretty hard all day.

I didn't go to the show because I don't feel like sitting in the rain and mud so I stayed home and wrote some letters. If it's nice next Sunday I'll take some pictures.

If you can get some more film I would like to have them very much. That's something you can't buy over here for love or money.

I was certainly surprised to learn that grandma & opa consented to come and live up there. Boy, I'll bet someone must of did some tall talking to convince them and that it would be for the best and I sure am glad that they are coming up.

I was sorry to hear about the Biancos not receiving any letters from Arkie but you know how that guy is. I have a letter from him now that I received recently that I haven't answered as yet and one from Martha also. Yes, he was busted but don't think anything of that, Lou, because I've seen men busted for practically nothing. For instance, if an officer doesn't happen to like a certain man, he can usually have him busted for something or other with no trouble at all. That's the way the Army is. By the way, Lou, being busted is not something to be ashamed of unless its because of a serious offence. I was glad to hear that you wrote to him and encouraged him to write home & I'm sure he will do so.

I received the pictures and thought they were swell. Jackie sure looks big not to mention Lesley. She sure has grown since I saw her last.

Well, Lou, this will be all for this time. Give my love to all. So long for now.   Ralph

July 24, 1944 - U.S. Marines invade Tinian, part of the Mariana Islands. A little over a year later, the planes that dropped the atomic bombs on Japan took off from Tinian.

Monday, July 24, 1944. Letters of July 15,16,17. Issue of June 24 C. Breeze. Went to Sandrian's. Stopped in drug store for supplies & film. Went downtown to post office. Bought stamps. Sent money order to Grolier Society. Bought green apples at Sandelli's. Judy here for afternoon. 9:00. Mil's birthday.

July 25, 1944 - Allied forces finally "breakout" from the costly hedgerows campaign in Normandy.

Tuesday, July 25, 1944. Letter of July 18. Issue of C.Breeze, July 1. Bad storm during night. In morning went to Acme. Gracie & Jackie. Baby food, cereal, crackers. Right after lunch took bus and went to Aunt's. brought tax bill up. Jackie played piano. Swing. Took 2:00 bus back. Found Cat at door 2:30. Put Jackie to sleep 3:00. Cat stayed until 4:30. Drove over to station. Took 4:52 to Hoboken. Met Ann at terminal. Waited for Fan. Took tubes to Hudson terminal. Met 4 girls, 2 Bettys and Dot and

Ruth. Went to little German place to eat. Way down on 57th street. Took cab. Complete dinner with Manhattan. Walked to Radio City. Tried to sneak in line. Dot got through. 10 minutes. Sat in 3rd mezzanine, first row. Stage show lovely. Show, "Dragonseed" good. Lasted 2 ½ hours. Missed 12:30 train. Next 2:30. Had drink in Quesinada's [sp.] with 2 Bettys. Left. Took tubes back to Hoboken. 2:15 train left 2:30. Reached Morristown 3:20. Slept most of way. Home at 5:45. On vacation.

Wednesday, July 26, 1944. No letters. Awake at 7:45. Washed clothes.

Thursday July 27, 1944. Letters of July 18,20,21. Made sauce in morning. Hot. Cat went to movies. When Jackie awoke, ate & went to Aunt's. Played with Carol in sandbox. Aunts gave pail to Jackie. Had supper there. Wrote to Ralph. Razzi drove us home. Aunt filled pail with sand.

Friday, July 28, 1944. Issue of C Breeze. Hot. Out in yard with Jackie.
Saturday, July 29, 1944. No mail. Joey over to play with Jackie. House cleaned while Jackie slept. Ate. Bath. Mil called to go over & finished at 3:30. Went downtown. Bought swing and went to Mil's. Had piece of Blueberry pie. 5:15 kids had supper. Brought Judy here 6:00. Put up swing. 8:30 M.de.R. called. Worried about not receiving letter. We'll see tomorrow.

Sunday, July 30, 1944. Church as usual, late. Met M.de R. after mass. Jackie still sleeping when I got home. 8:30. Gracie & Mom stayed overnite at Jo's. After Jackie was fed, started dinner. Mama G and Tadone up. Gene & Judy. Gene went to get them. Had dinner at 12:30. Put Jackie to sleep at 1:30. Washed hair then sat in front with M.G. & T to wait for Joe. Jackie slept until 4:00. Joe & Angie came at 4:30. Girls & I got dressed and went to Newark. Glad to see us. Had lemon ice. Supper. Beer. Stayed until 9:00. Jackie not sleepy.

Monday, July 31, 1944. Letters of 22,23 of July. Went downtown to post office and Sandrian's. Bought Jackie toy dog Shulttes. Met Vita. Ann called Penhurst Hotel Atlantic City. 3 in room $54, $18 per person. Says "more" "eat" "moon."

Tuesday, August 1, 1944. Letters of July 24, checks $80 and $50. Notice of moving change of address of Mary. While kids played with Jackie, washed clothes, then ironed. Made sauce. Mil & Judy came over. Judy stayed. Mil-Gene - Mon. went to movies.

Wednesday, August 2, 1944. No mail. Rained all day. Period.

August 3, 1944 - U.S. and Chinese troops recapture the strategic city of Myitkyina in Burma, after a two month siege.

Thursday, August 3, 1944. Letters of July 25-26. Cloudy and damp in morning. Clear in afternoon. Mama G came up. Brought cookies for Jackie. Went out in yard. Jackie on swing. At night went to movies. Park. Fair.

Friday, August 4, 1944. *Letters of July 27,28. Letter from Ralph. Cooked eggplant while Jackie slept & took shower. Dressed, fed Jackie. Went downtown to bank. Bought veg. at Sandelli's. Went to Mil's gave money. Glass of beer. Jackie stamped foot and said "No" first time at 17 mo. Very hot out. Brought Judy home here. Cooked. Sent Judy with Grace to meet Mom in coming. Mil over while we were eating supper. Then Gene. Mom & Gene went to wake (Gervasio Woman). Mil & Gene stayed until 8:30. Took picture of Jackie & myself.*

Saturday, August 5, 1944. *No mail. Call from Vene last nite. Jackie woke 6:45. Got up at 7:00. Stayed outside for awhile, then started cleaning. Finished by 2:00 Fan came home and then Ann. Put Jackie to bed after lunch. Slept only an hour, 3:30. Jackie and I went downtown. Girls tennis. Bought gift for Sundi's baby and one for Leslie Ann. Very, very hot. Temp. over 100. Came home. Supper. Went to confession. Brought baby. Ice cream.*

Sunday, August 6, 1944. *Hard time sleeping. Late for church. Met M.d.R afterwards. Baby awake when home. Cooked. Mama G & Tadone up. Joe & Angie not up. Jackie asleep after lunch. Awoke 3:00. 4:30 went to movies. Saw "Going My Way." Bing Crosby. Home 7:30. Big rain storm. Fan took my picture.*

Monday, August 7, 1944. *C. Breeze. Letter of July 29. Ann home from work. Took 10:14 train to N.Y. Brought Jackie to Mil's. Took tubes to 33rdSt. Found coat in Macy's, $89.95. Bought toy for Jackie & Judy. Training pants. Garment bag. Took tubes to 14thSt. Bought pay shoes, bathing suit. In terminal early, had sandwich. Took 7:30 train home, 8:45 home. Found letter waiting.*

August 8, 1944 - American troops complete the capture of the Mariana Islands.

Tuesday, August 8, 1944. *Letters of July 30-31. Vene came at 8:30. We went to Lake Hopatcong to visit Fran & Eddie 10:05. Nice bungalow. (Tumble Inn) Had a sandwich before going to lake. (Pails alike). 1:30 went down. Small spot with us and shallow water. Grand for children. Jackie likes water. Fell in. Sat on dock. Went back 2:30. Put Jackie to sleep. Slept until 4:00. Sat on porch for awhile. Left at 5:30. Home at 6:30. Supper for Jackie, soup. (found letters).*

Wednesday, August 9, 1944. *No letters. Received Book of Knowledge Annual. Washed clothes. Put Jackie to bed. Thru by 2:45. Went to Mil's. Cooked corn. Stayed until 5:00. Mom & Gracie went to Newark. Girls went to Newark. Ate supper alone. Stayed out with Jackie until 7:30. Bed at 8:00. Gracie took my picture & Jackie's.*

Thursday, August 10, 1944. *No mail. Garment bags came. Mom worked half a day. Went to say Goodbye to Mama G. Left at 5:30 with my Aunt going to Ravena, Ohio for three days. Mil brought Judy over in afternoon, then went downtown. M.d.R & Vene came down. Vene brought Nan to doctor's. Quart of ice cream. Says "doll" "comb."*

Friday, August 11, 1944. *Letter of Aug. 3. Hot. 10:00 went to Mil's and then downtown. Gene to be Godfather for Sundi's baby. Sunday. Stopped in at the Pizzeria for lunch. Came home & put Jackie to bed. Cat called. Wanted to take some pictures of Carol Ann. 4:00 went there and stayed until 5:00. Went to Acme. 8:45 Herb called. Eleanor gave birth to a girl. Took*

314

pictures of Carol Ann & Jackie & myself.

Saturday, August 12, 1944. *Letter of August 4. Very hot. Storm 2 hrs. Lights out. Cleaned house. Jackie with Gracie out front. Mil & Judy over in afternoon. Judy here for supper. Mil & Gene here until 8:30. Brought ice cream cone for Jackie & Judy.*

Sunday, August 13, 1944. *Hot sleeping Sat night. After church met maids. Cooked dinner. Mama G not up. Put Jackie to bed after dinner. Gave bath when she awoke. Only in panties. After supper Joe and Angie came. Girls went to movies. All went to Mama G's. Stayed until nine.*

Monday, August 14, 1944. *Letters of Aug. 1,2,5,6. Hot. Out in yard with Jackie. Put Jackie to sleep after lunch. 3:00 went downtown. Brought roll to Sandrian. Bought slippers. Tadone must go to hospital for Penicillin treatments. Mon nite, could not get ice cream. Very hot. Jackie says "dirt" "chair" "church."*

Jackie and Richard

August 15, 1944 – Allies invade southern France.

Tuesday, August 15, 1944. *No mail. Mom came home 1:30. J was awake. Had just put Jackie on the pot. Told her about Tadone. In morning Mom went down. Ironed clothes. Hot. Mom & Gene went down again at nite. When they came home, Mom told us about her trip to Ohio, Revena, Warren, Akron. (Sam Mirabello).*

Wednesday, August 16, 1944. *Letters of Aug.7th,8,9. Hospitalization notice. Birth announcement of Susan Jane de Roxtro. 9:00 Gene and Mom took Tadone to the hospital. Came home 11:00. Put Jackie to bed after lunch. Woke at 3:00. Mama G up for supper. Girls went to Newark. 7:00 thundershower. Mom, Gene, M.G. went to hospital. Gave Jackie bath. Put to bed 8:15. Raining lightly. Little cooler. Jackie says "no more".*

Thursday, August 17, 1944. *Letter of Aug. 10. Washed clothes. Jackie out in yard with Joey. Gave bath after lunch. Bed 1:00 - 3:00. Finished clothes. Cooked. Gracie took Jackie to store. Caught in rain. Mama G up for supper. Mom, Gene, & Mama G went to hospital. Aunt Santa & Carol Ann came. Had just put*

Jackie to bed. Home until 8:40. Went to movies with girls. "Two girls & a Sailor." New top tooth on Aug. 10, other side Aug. 19.

Friday, August 18, 1944. *No mail. Cool. Put Jackie to bed after lunch. Cat called while I was dressing. Went over and took pictures of Carol Ann. Went downtown. Bought material for peasant skirt. Cat paid elect. bill. Had ice cream. Bought eggplant. Home at 4:30. Cooked eggplant. Ann home at 5:30. Sent Gracie & Jackie to store. Mom with them when they came back. Mama G up for supper. Mom, Gene, Mama G, Ann, Fan, went to hospital.*

Saturday, August 19, 1944. *Letter of Aug. 11, and issue of C-Breeze. Did cleaning, ironed and prepared Jackie's clothes for the week. Packed bag.*

Sunday, August 20, 1944. *Took Penn. train to Atlantic City. Arrived 1:05.pm.*

August 21, 1944 - Battle of Falaise Pocket was the decisive engagement of the Battle of Normandy. A pocket was formed around Falaise, Calvados, in which the German Army Group B, with the 7th Army and the Fifth Panzer Army were encircled by the Western Allies.

August 22, 1944 – Japanese retreat from India.
August 25, 1944 – Liberation of Paris.

Monday, August 21 - 25, 1944. *On vacation.*

Saturday, August 26, 1944. Last day of vacation.

Sunday, August 27, 1944. Took 5:00 train to Newark. Home at 9:00 found letters of Aug 12,13,14,15,16,17. [Letters missing.]

Monday, August 28, 1944. Received letter of Aug 20. Letter from Mrs. Fitzpatrick with pictures enclosed of Fitz and Forbes. Went downtown. Brought watch to Lee's. Will cost 9:00 to fix. Paid 5:00 ready in a month.

Tuesday, August 29, 1944. Letter of Aug 21, 1944. **Johnnie coming home.**

Wednesday August 30, 1944. M.DeR. up for three quarters of an hour.

Thursday, August 31, 1944. No mail. M de R up for an hour.

Friday, September 1-5, 1944. [diary pages missing.]

Wednesday, September 6-8, 1944. No entries.

Saturday, September 9, 1944. Letter of Sept. 1st.

September 9, 1944 - Pavuvu - Johnny, along with the 15th CB Battalion, boards the U.S.S. Cape Bon and heads for the Florida Islands.

Sunday, September 10-15, 1944. No entries.

September 11, 1944 - The U.S.S. Cape Bon arrived at Tulagi Island, in the Florida Island group.

September 12, 1944- The U.S.S. Cape Bon arrived Guadalcanal, Lunga Point.

September 15 - October 13, 1944 - U.S. troops invade Morotai and Peleliu, in the Palaus.

Saturday, September 16, 1944. Ann, Fan and I gave Mom and Tadone a surprise birthday party. Whole family was here except Mil.

317

September 17-26, 1944 - Operation Market Garden in the Netherlands, the largest airborne assault operation of the war.

Sunday, September 17, 1944. No entry.

September 18, 1944 - U.S.S. Cape Bon crossed the International Date Line.

Monday, September 18, 1944. Mom home. Jewish holiday. Letter from Ralph.

Tuesday, September 19, 1944. Went to N.Y. with Mom and Ann. Rain. Took 9:14 train. Paid balance of my coat, $79.94. Bought dress, identification bracelet for Ralph, overalls for Jackie, an umbrella and stockings. Home by 5:45. Letter from Mary and Mrs. Fitzpatrick.

Wednesday, September 20, 1944. Clear weather.

September 25, 1944 - U.S.S. Cape Bon arrived Pearl Harbor, Hawaii.

Thursday, September 21-October 1,1944. No entries.

October 1, 1944 - U.S.S. Cape Bon arrived San Francisco, California.

THE DREAM COMES TRUE . . . OCT. 1ST. 1944 . . . AFTER 24 MONTHS . . . 11 DAYS

Monday, October 2, 1944. Western Union from Johnnie. Will be home in two weeks!

Tuesday, October 3 - Thursday, November 9, 1944. No entries.
[Johnny home on furlough before returning to California.]

October 5, 1944
"New Caledonia"
Hello Lou,

    I received your letter of the 20th and I was glad to hear from you. I'm sorry if I seemed to neglect you with my writing but I guess I had a spell when I just couldn't get to write.

    I received the snapshots which you enclosed in your letter and thought they were swell. I sure was happy to hear about Johnny. It's been quite some time since I've heard from him last. I hope it's true. Gee, I wonder what it feels like to know that you're going home again. Boy, I won't mind that boat ride at all if I know it's going to the states.

    By the way, Lou, guess what? I got a good conduct medal or it's a ribbon now. It's not as hard to get now as it was before because you only have to put 1 year good behavior but before it was 3 yrs. I think I'm getting a driver & mechanics medal pretty soon.

    Boy, Lou, I'll have 2yrs in pretty soon. The time sure does fly, thank God.

Well, Lou, I'll have to close now. Give my love to all & kiss Jackie for me.

So long for now,
Ralph

P.S. Thought you might be interested in this clipping. Maybe Johnny did some. R.

Ralph, Age 21

October 11, 1944 – U.S. air raids against Okinawa.

320

Photos taken October 17, 1944, Johnny home on furlough.

October 18, 1944 - 14 B-29s based on the Marianas attack the Japanese base at Truk.

October 20, 1944 - U.S. Sixth Army invades Leyte, Philippines.

Photos taken on October 22, 1944, Johnny home on furlough.

October 23-26, 1944 – Japanese battle fleet destroyed at Leyte Gulf resulting in a decisive U.S. naval victory.

Photos taken **October 23/24, 1944.**

October 25, 1944 – the first suicide air Kamikaze attacks occur against U.S. warships in Layte Gulf, Phillipines. By the end of the war, Japan will have sent an estimated 2,257 aircraft on suicide missions.

Photos taken November 10, 1944

The Gang: Joan, JoAnne, Carol Grace, Jackie, Marilyn

Vincent Forbes

[There are no letters from Johnny for the remainder of 1944. He was deployed to the West Coast where he remained until spring of 1945.]

Friday, November 10, 1944. Back to Jo's by 2:00 A.M. Raining lightly. Went right to bed. Awoke at 7. Mike came home. Left at 10. Took 10:18 train home. Jo came with me to Station. Home at 11:20. Took bus. Slept for ½ hour while Jackie napped. Ann home from work early. (place being painted.) Packed bag for Mom to take to Fan. Ann and Mom went to hospital.

November 11, 1944 - Iwo Jima bombarded by the U.S. Navy.

Saturday, November 11, 1944. Jackie awoke at 7:40. Stayed in bed until 8:30 (called for daddy). Ate all of breakfast for first time since you left. Carol Ann here to play with Jackie while I cleaned. After her nap, I brought Jackie out to the swing. Cold.

Sunday, November 12, 1944. went to 7:00 mass. Jackie slept until 9:15. Met MdeR. as I was going in. Read papers until Jackie woke. Would not eat much dinner. Gave bath and washed her hair. At 3:00 Joe & Angie stopped in to bring Mama G to hospital. 4:30 both Aunts and Carol Ann came. 5:00 Joe & Angie came back. Aunts left at 5:30. 6:00 Gene and Mil brought Fannie home. Looks good except that she was tired. Put Jackie to bed at 7.

Monday, November 13, 1944. Letter of Nov. 10. Jackie woke at 8:45. Mil called at 9:30. Went downtown with Mil. Brought film to Sandrians & got one roll. Brought pants & suit to cleaners. On way home stopped in Acme. Mil & Judy came here. After lunch we baked an apple pie. 3:30 Vene & M.d.R came. Anxious to hear about you. Martha & others were here too. Fan came downstairs after lunch.

Tuesday November 14, 1944. *Lovely day. Jackie woke at 6:00 & 8:30. Washed clothes. Tried to keep Jackie upstairs with Fan. She came down & I stood her on stool near washing machine. Stopped to feed Jackie at twelve. Put Jackie out to sleep. 1½ hours. Finished washing at 2:00. Cloth on roller not so good. Started yellow sweater for Jackie while resting. Cooked sauce for supper. Forgot to mention ident. tag.*

Wednesday, November 15, 1944. *Went to church. Jackie woke at 7:35. Letter of Nov. 14. Vene called. Going to hospital tomorrow for appendicitis. Put Jackie to bed 11:30. Ironed clothes 1:30. Prepared lunch. Ironed again. Prepared supper. Jackie on chair. Called daddy. Cyst on ear. Johnnie called 8:00 P.M.*

Thursday, November 16, 1944. Johnnie called 8:40 A.M. Leaving for coast today. *Waited until 1 A.M. for call. Knitted on Jackie's sweater this A.M. Went to church. Rain. Remind Johnnie to write to father Sheerin. Knitted on sweater after supper. Vene operated on for appendicitis.*

Friday, November 17, 1944. *Went to mass. 10:30 took Jackie downtown to Post office, stockings, cleaned house in afternoon. Put red snowsuit on Jackie. Fits perfectly. Took her to Acme. Mil and Judy over for supper. Johnny N. came for bed jacket for Vene. Jackie and Judy out with Gracie. Walked Mil & Judy home. Ann & I went to movies. Saw "Gypsy Wildcat" Maria Montez.*

Saturday, November 18, 1944. *Went to confession & communion. Took 11:44 train & met Ann in Hoboken to do Christmas shopping. Went first to 33rd St. and then to 14th St. Bought gifts for most of the children. Home by 8:00.*

Sunday, November 19, 1944. *Went to 8:00 mass with Ann & Fan. Mama G & Tadone not up because Tadone sick in bed. 4:00 Joe & Angie came. Just finished giving Jackie a bath and washing her hair. 2 Aunts were with Joe. Drove Aunt M. [Micheline] home and stayed there for 15 min. Wants always to write. Jackie remembered piano. Joe looked at the lock. 5:00 we all went down to Mama G's. Stayed until 7:00. Gene came while we were down there. Jackie had a lot of fun with the cat.*

Monday, November 20, 1944. *Went to church. 9:30 it started to snow. Changed to rain an hour later. Washed Jackie's clothes. Hung them to dry in cellar. Cleaned house. Knitted on sweater.*

Tuesday, November 21, 1944. *Went to 7:30 mass. Snow, rain, slush. Finished Jackie's sweater. Fran came to visit Vene. called me from bus station. Came here for lunch. Cooked sauce. Then both left for the hospital. Fran brought bed jacket and I brought a box of Fanny Farmer choc. candy. Took bus from Lofts to hospital. Stayed with Vene 1½ hours. Saw Fran off on bus. Came home. Took pictures of Jackie in house. Started period.*

Wednesday, November 22, 1944. *Clear. Went to 7:30 mass. Received post card and folders from Johnnie, also souvenir for* myself and Jackie from Kansas in morning. Wrapped Christmas presents. **Received call from Johnnie 12:50.** After lunch, Fan, Jackie & I went downtown. Brought proofs back to Thomas. Got suit and pants out of cleaners. Fan took 3 pictures of Jackie & me.

Thursday, November 23, 1944. *Thanksgiving Day. Went to church with Fan. Came home and started cooking. Pot roast, mashed potatoes, brown gravy, corn, veg. salad, Lasagne, ate dinner at 1:30. Got up at 3:00. Sat around until 5:00 took some pictures. Went to movies. Picture terrible. Came home to find Forbes here. Had something to eat, then talked for awhile until 11:00. Forbes slept on couch.*

November 24, 1944 – Twenty four B-29s bomb the Nakajima aircraft factory near Tokyo.
November 24, 1944 – B-29 raids begin on Japan from Tinian.

Friday, November 24, 1944. *Went to church. Were very quiet so as not to disturb Forbes. Jackie woke about 9:00 and Forbes about the same time. Dressed Jackie & brought her down. Saw Forbes from stairs and stared at him. He took a bath and dressed before breakfast 10:00. After, he brought Jackie out in the swing (wore suede jacket) and for a ride in the carriage while I cleaned. Came in for lunch. Very cold. Ann home at 1:30. We all went downtown & brought his suit to be pressed. Went down for film. Only 3 came out. Forbes got a roll in Mack's. Walked down to Municipal building then came home. Cooked supper, then he and Ann went to movies. Forbes to sleep in the girls bed. Fan sleeps with me.*

Saturday, November 25, 1944. *Baby woke at 7:15. Before I went to church. Jackie woke Fan & Grace up but Forbes slept until five of nine. Took Jackie on his knee while he ate breakfast, egg eaten by Jackie. Afterwards she called him daddy. Forbes wrote two letters while I cleaned upstairs. Then I sent him to Johnnie's barber. Was home at 1:15. Brought white teddy bear for Jackie, candy for Ann. Went downtown after lunch. 4:30 stopped in Pizzeria. Came home. Took Ann to Newark.*

Sunday, November 26, 1944. *Went to 8:00 mass with Ann, Fan, and Vincent. Met Mrs. De R. & introduced Forbes. Had breakfast then took 11:14 train to Hoboken and a bus to 42nd St. Walked to Radio City 1:20. Bought tickets. Too early for show so we had dinner at the Brass Rail. Very good. Went back to R.C. 3:00 and saw "Together Again" Chas Boyer & Irene Dunne. (ice skating) After show, stopped in 42nd St. Café (popcorn) for beer (2 glasses). Found bus at terminal. Took 8:00 train home.*

Monday, November 27, 1944. *Rain. Went to church. Ann had day off. Letter from Jack. Breakfast. Decided not to visit the Fitzpatricks. Letter from Johnnie. Called F.P. about 1:00 to let them know. Insisted that we visit them. Took 3:15 train out of Morristown. Raining very hard. Vincent called a cab to take us to station. Made many changes. Arrived in Flatbush at 6:00.*

Mr. F.P. waiting in front of house. Were glad to see Vincent. At supper & afterward Fitz' Aunt, Uncle & cousin Joan came. Left there 5 of 9. Uncle drove us to subway station. (Vince switched milk pitchers.) Came home different way. Went from Flatbush Ave to 33rdSt. Stopped in at Penn Station to inquire about Vincent's train. Took subway to Hoboken and train to Morristown. Stopped in for 2 glasses of beer at Cutters 11:30 - 12:30. Stopped in at Carbello's for Pizza and beer (2 or 3). Ann feeling good. Left at 2:30. Home. Had coffee. Bed 3:00. Stopped raining.

November 28, 1944 - Antwerp port opened.

Tuesday, November 28, 1944. Went to church 7:30. Vincent up at 9:00. Cooked spaghetti for lunch. Ann home 1:00. Dressed & then took pictures. Left 4:45, walked to station. (no cab). Had to change at Summit. Went into the Penn, N.Y. terminal. Made it with 5 minutes to spare. (had shot of Harnwoods before leaving house) Saw Vincent off. Ate supper. Home.

Wednesday, November 29, 1944 Went to church. 11:00 Fan, Jackie & I went to post office to mail Xmas gifts and Forbes' sweater. Wrote to Mary in afternoon. Finished after supper. Had glass of beer for Forbes - His beer.

Thursday, November 30, 1944. Rained all night & morning. Went to church. Cleared in late afternoon. Wrote to Ralph.

Friday, December 1, 1944. Went to church. Home. Fed Jackie breakfast. Went to Newark with Fan. Took 10:15 train. Used Christmas club money. Bought the rest of the children's gifts. Home by 5:00. Left Jackie with Mil. Found letter from Johnny. Letter from Forbes. Allotment check for $80.

Saturday, December 2, 1944. Went to church. 8:45 was about to feed Jackie when doorbell rings. Vincent home on 57 hour pass. Brought me a (C.B.) pillow case. Gave me a (C.B.) book of matches, went downtown to cash check with Fan. Vincent went out later with Ann. Came home with a doz. bottles beer. 12 films. After lunch he went to sleep. Slept until 5:30. Went with Gene & Mil to dinner and to a show. Had coffee & lemon pie at night.

Sunday, December 3, 1944. 8:00 mass. Cold. Vincent slept until 9:00. Made breakfast for Vince. Started cooking sp. sauce. Dinner at 1:30. Mama G & Tadone up. Took picture of Vince & myself. Joe & Angie not here. 5:00 5 of us went to Naster's for ice cream. Came home, had coffee and sandwich. Gene came over, drove Vincent and us to Station. 5am Vincent off at Grand Central Station. 9:00, train at 9:45. Went into Child's for coffee and sandwich. Went back to station to take subway. 11:00 train home.

Monday, December 4, 1944. Went to church. Letter from Johnny & check for $50. Washed clothes. Jackie would not take a nap. Went downtown with Mil & Judy. Cashed check. Stopped in

Acme. Came home & cooked. Met Cat. Carol Ann had a convulsion. Went to Mil's after supper. Were going over to see Cat but Gene came home too late. Stayed until 10:00.

Tuesday, December 5, 1944. Went to church. Lovely day. Received letter of Dec. 1, put Jackie to sleep after lunch then wrapped Xmas gifts. When Jackie woke up we went out in the swing and stayed out front. Came in to cook when Grace came home with the meat. Grace stayed out with Jackie.

Wednesday, December 6, 1944. Went to church. Lovely day. Went downtown in afternoon. Sent money order. Stopped for my pictures in Thomas. Shopped on way back. Stopped for Judy. Mil here for supper. Finished writing out Xmas cards. Jackie's cutting in 3 back molars. Keeps saying what are you doing? How are you, and Look, Mommy, Look! See!

Thursday, December 7, 1944. Went to church. Lovely day. Jackie knows all about Santa Claus.

Friday, December 8, 1944. Went to church. Rain. Ann had day off. We went to New York to shop. Left Jackie with Mil. Took 10:14 train. Rain. Took 4:14 train home. Bought things for Jackie's stocking.

Saturday, December 9, 1944. Went to church. About to feed Jackie when Vincent comes. Had coffee. 57 hr. leave. Got in 12:00 last night. Went to Hotel. Talked while I fed Jackie. Helped me clean up & had lunch. Letter from Forbes. Went downtown (Fui called) to get pictures. Came right home. 5:00 girls came home. Had gone shopping in Newark. Sat. nite went downtown. Stopped for ice cream in Jane Logan parlour, then went to Community 2nd show. Lana Turner, "Marriage is a Private Affair." 11:30 out. Picture good. Stopped in pizzeria for sandwich and beer. Home 1:00.

Sunday, December 10, 1944. Went to 8:00 am mass. Jackie awake early 6:30. Put her back to bed. Awake when I got back. Fed her then started cooking dinner. Vincent down by 10:00. Breakfast. Dinner at 1:30. Mike & Mike Jr. came. Left house

331

2:45. Took 2 pictures of Vincent. Went to station. Vincent's train at 3:14. Came home and learned that photographer had come with proofs. Joe & Angie came. 8:45 everyone left.

Monday, December 11, 1944. Went to church. Letters of Dec 5-7. Xmas card from Mary. Went downtown with Mil after lunch. Went to bank, Sandrians, Whelans, ice cream. Morris St., Industrial Enterprises. Mr. Benson not in. Cold and raw out. Came on home. Met Cat with Carol Ann. Stopped in at Acme. In sight of home when it started to rain. Cooked. (Teddy bear - drink!)

Tuesday, December 12, 1944. Went to church. Dark rainy dismal in morning. Shower in afternoon. Christmas card from Marge. Ironed until 1:45. Vene called. Mil & Judy over. Mil went shopping after lunch. Went out in yard with kids. Took 3 pictures. Mil & Judy here for supper. 4th back molar out.

Wednesday, December 13, 1944. St. Lucy. Went to church. Cold. Jackie still asleep 8:30. Cleaned house. Put up curtains. After lunch went downtown with Jackie & Judy. Got pictures at Sandrians then went to post office. Mailed pkg. & bought stamps. Went to five and 10, bought peanuts and fed squirrels in Park. Jackie unafraid. Judy timid. Came home & cooked. Jackie locked herself in bathroom. Unlocked door herself.

Thursday, December 14, 1944. Went to church. Jackie still asleep. Ann & Fan went to New York shopping. 11:00 went downtown to Post Office, mailed rest of packages. Home by 12:30 fed Jackie, then gave bath and washed her hair & mine. Put her to sleep. 2:00. Pkg. from Nora. 2 pairs of silk stockings & powder. Cooked. Girls came home. Showed pkgs. Put Jackie to bed. Started on pair of white mittens for Jackie.

December 15, 1944 - U.S. troops invade Mindoro in the Philippines.

Friday, December 15, 1944. Went to church. Card from Nana with $1 enclosed. Gas man came to fix pilot. Washed clothes. Put Jackie to bed after lunch. Worked on glove. After supper went downtown. Bought gift for Mom..

December 16, 1944 - January 25, 1945 - Battle of the Bulge in Belgium.

Saturday, December 16, 1944. Went to church. Confession. Finished Jackie's mittens. Cleaned house. Through early. Ann & Fan home 2:00. Went downtown with fan. Bought Ann's gift. Joe & Angie's. At night 3 of us went downtown again, bought things for Jackie's stocking.

December 17, 1944 - U.S. Army Air Force begins preparations for dropping the Atomic Bomb by establishing the 509th Composite Group to operate the B-29s that will deliver the bomb.

Sunday, December 17, 1944. Went to 8:00 mass. Communion. Cleaned room. Cat came at 4:00, left 5:00. Joe & Angie came. M.de R. stopped in for two minutes. Gave me envelope. I gave her gifts. Dressing to go to the movies. Lucille comes. All went together. Ride home.

Monday, December 18,1944. Went to church with Ann. Jackie slept until 10:00. Letter of December 15 and card from Vene & Johnnie and Mrs. Forbes. 11:00. Lucille came up to see Jackie. Stayed for lunch. Ann called. Took 2:14 train to Hoboken. Ann got on in Harrison. Bought Fan's gift and Gracie's. Pair of gloves and stockings. Through by 6:00 had sandwich in Hoboken Terminal. Took 6:45 train home. When we left N.Y. it was just beginning to snow. Pulled into Morristown. Found an inch of snow. Snowed all night. Got card back from E. Blosser.

Tuesday, December 19, 1944. 3 or 4 inches of snow on ground. Went to church. Cards from Betty & Joe Vigilante. M.de R and Carl & Evelyn. Went out to clean side walk, brought Jackie out. Carol was pushing her on sled. Judy & Mil came over. Mil went downtown. I pulled kids until 11:30. Took two pictures. Jackie cold. Jackie took nap in afternoon. Went downtown with Fan at nite. Bought wallet. Was looking for tissues & Lux every store in town.

Wednesday, December 20, 1944. Went to church. Card from Martha & Jackie got a card from Nan & Bonnie and Fan. Went downtown in afternoon. Mailed wallet. Brought prints to

333

Sandrians. Gracie took Jackie out on sled. Wouldn't come in. Left her out with Carol Ann and the kids. Came in 5:00. Went to movies with Fan. Got period. Took two pictures, Jackie on sled.

Letter from Mary Lukawitz, postmarked December 24, 1944
Somewhere in New Guinea

20 December, 1944

Dear Lucia,

It's the first time I've used a straight pen since way back in the days when I was in the States. Dot just put a new point on and it writes very smoothly. Now to get back and really say something. Lou, I can't thank you enough for the snapshots you sent me especially the one of you. I didn't take the ones I had of you for I didn't want to cut them to fit my wallet. However, this little one you sent me will fit in the small picture frame. I can keep it on my little dressing table, made out of a wooden ration box about 2' by 12" by 12". Of course I put in a shelf, but my satin slip which I had no use for and made a nice drape, with lace on the bottom. Now I made shorts from my P.J's the rest of the material I made another set of drapes.

I'm so happy to hear that Johnnie finally got home and that both of you enjoyed every minute. I really hope and pray that there may be a slight possibility that he remains closer to home. Ah, I bet you were in your glory. Sorry to hear Ann was sick at the time. Don't forget to give my regards to Johnnie, Ann, Fannie, your other, and a kiss and hug for Jackie. She is so sweet.

Ah, Lou, you know what? One of my brothers is now also in New Guinea. So near and yet so far away. They're hoping we can get to see each other. No luck unless he can get a leave. I haven't seen him in five years.

Remember Joe? I haven't heard from him in a long time. The last time he really was peeved to learn I came overseas. Said he could spank me good and hard. Now, I've heard from my girlfriend, Nora that he came home. Isn't that grand? He was badly wounded at one of the beachheads. Ah, I'm really happy to hear of boys getting the chance to go home. Most of them really deserve it, too.

The weather as usual is hot during the day and "gobs" of rain at night. Still go in for a dip of the ocean and am beginning to be as dark as a native more and more. We went to a native village some time ago, and it was quite interesting. Must try to go during full moon, then is when they hold ceremonial festivals, lot of dances and such.

Must go to Mass now Lou and will remember you, Johnnie and Jackie in all my prayers, especially tonight. I try to go every night since it's so convenient. The chapel is very small, open, with grass-covered roof, but yet it's so sweet. As soon as I can get some pictures taken developed etc. I'll send you a set of them. Really, I wouldn't give anything for the things I've seen and places I've been. Yes, even here. I'll grant you every precaution has to be taken, but then this is not the States.

Tonight we went to the movies – saw Gary Cooper & Ingrid Bergman in Saratoga Trunk. Very good. The other night we saw an old picture "Anthony Adverse". I hadn't seen it before but it was a wonderful picture. Now

I hope that I can see "San Francisco" which is coming this week. But I'm C.G. at the office.

Now and then we have band concerts and the music is heavenly. It brings me back to the nights I attended the concerts at the huge auditorium in San Antonio. They really have a grand band. I enjoy standing retreat and marching to work. Always did.

Last night the sky was clear so I searched the heavens for the Southern Cross. I found it and showed it to Blanche who had never seen it before. When you first see it, it's disappointing. Has only four stars in it. Haven't found the teapot since the time we were on the ship. The SS Lurline was a huge and wonderful liner. Always will remember the pleasant voyage over here.

Lou, you'll have to forgive me for using two shades of paper in one letter. I kind of started it at the office but didn't bring enough paper to complete it.

Ah, I'm enclosing a pound note as a Xmas gift to you and Jackie. It's a little late. It's worth about $3.22 in American money. Someday I'll see if I can send you a few small coins that we use also.

Here I've been rattling on and haven't even thanked you for your most welcomed letter of November 29. Full of news too. Mail has been few and far between. So every letter means so much to us.

Gee, it's unbelievable that my little girlfriend will soon be two years old. Ah, I wish I could get her something from here. They don't have a thing. Maybe if we ever go forward, I may be able to. So just tell her to wait patiently. I'd appreciate it very much if you could send me a bra size 34, B-cup. Just slip it in an envelope. It'll get here much more quickly.

Just finished eating a Babe Ruth bar – was very delicious, but now I'm thirsty. Still the same old Mary. I went with a M/Sgt twice since I've been here, but there's nothing to do but sit on the beach and talk. And I'm not a talker. Say, how's about letting me in on a secret or maybe a suggestion as to where I could find a boy like Johnnie. Lou, you are really a fortunate girl. And may God grant that Johnnie will come home for good and the two (I mean three) – mustn't forget my sweetheart – of you be as happy as the time I last saw you together.

Now I must end my letter and hope that I made it interesting. May God's choicest Blessings descend upon you. Though a little late but, Merry Christmas and a Very Happy New Year. Here's a hug and kiss for Jackie, too.

P.S. Bathing, swimming – no snow for Xmas.   *Love,   Mary*

Thursday, December 21, 1944. Went to church. Put Jackie out to play in snow 10:00. Joey came over (with pail & shovel) watched them while I ironed clothes. Jackie came in when she got too cold. Played inside. Put her in crib but didn't sleep. Cards from Mil & Gene, Fitzpatrick, Kuglers, Jackie, Ann, Potts, Ronald & Richard, Leary, Gannons, Vita, cards for Jackie from Ann, Fan, Judy, Grandma, Gracie. At nite 6:00 went to buy Christmas tree with Gene, $1.75. Put Jackie to bed. Went downtown with mil. Stockings, ice cream.

Friday, December 22, 1944. *Went to church. Cold. Card from El & Herb. Cleaned house & attic. Ironed clothes. At nite went downtown with Ann. Very cold. Mr. Sandelli killed by car.*

Saturday, December 23, 1944. *Went to church. Cold. Snow. Jackie awake early. Ironed all morning. Mom home from work. 5:45 went to movies with Ann and Fan (Community). Saw "The Song of Bernadette" very good. Stayed until 11:30.*

Sunday, December 24, 1944. *Went to 8:00 mass. Mama G & Tadone up. Jo & Mike and Michael came (to stay over) at 3:15. Joe & Angie came 5:30. Mil & Gene & Judy 4:30. Had supper 5:30. Ann, Fan & I started to trim Tree at 8:00. Jackie went to bed 7:30. Michael, too. Finished the tree 11:30. Mil & Judy went home 9:00. Everybody else here. Joe passed his jokes around, and his gifts. Woke children and brought them down for Joe's satisfaction. Had only the tree lights on. Jackie stood enthralled, just remarked on tree lights, then the balls. Then she noticed her toys and didn't know which to go to. Loved everything. Played with toys until 1:00. Everybody opened their gifts. All were happy. Gene took Mama G & Tadone home 1:30. Jackie didn't want to go back to bed. Thought it was time to eat breakfast. All up until 2:30. Had coffee & cake.*

Monday, December 25, 1944. *Christmas. Raining heavily. Went to 8:00 mass. Rollers came while others were at church. (Roses came at 10:00). Jackie played with toys while I got her breakfast. She and Michael played together very nicely. 12:30 went to Sandelli's then went to visit Aunt on Columba St. all the gang. We had a 22lb. turkey. Ann got it at work. Had dinner at 2:00. 3:30 Vene & Johnnie & kids dropped in. Vene gave Jackie her gift. Stayed for about 5 or ten minutes. Everybody full and sleepy after dinner. 5:00 both Aunts and Uncles came over. Aunt M. gave Jackie a dollar. Stayed until 6:00. Everyone still full from dinner so we all had a cup of coffee. Then afterwards we played put and take. Lost $.55. Sat in chair listening to carols. Fell asleep. Awoke at 12:30 went to bed. Too nasty out. Jo & Mike stayed over night. Mike to take day off.*

Tuesday, December 26, 1944. *Day clear and cold. Slept until 9:00-9:30 for Jackie. Jo & Mike left at 11:00. House is mess. Cleaned up. Took 3 pictures. Had lunch. Gracie took Jackie to store. Mil & Gene came over to open their gifts. Fixed tree lights.*

Wednesday, December 27, 1944. *No mail. Dark, dreary, cold. M.d.R came at 2:30. Stayed until 4:45. Taxi. Showed gifts & talked. Snow. Wrote to Vincent.*

Thursday, December 28, 1944. *Ice and snow. Gracie took Jackie out on the sled for an hour. Came in for lunch. Put Jackie to bed. Gracie went to movies. Started to cook. Went to movies with girls. Saw "Kismet" good.*

Friday, December 29, 1944. *Very icy. No mail. Washed clothes. Rinsed by hand. Went to Mil's in afternoon to see Christmas* tree. Came home to cook. After supper Gene & Mil came over. Gene put rollers in [washing] machine.

Saturday, December 30, 1944. Up at 9:30. Mom home. Fire out. Could not get into garage. Found pieces of wood. Got fire going. Cleaned up a bit. Lunch. Put Jackie to sleep. Went downtown with Ann & Fan 3:30. Home 6:15. Letter from Johnnie & Mary. Headache. Jackie tries singing "Santa Claus is coming to town."

Postmarked January 2, 1945, letter from **Vincent E. Forbes C.M.3/c**, Co.C. 15th N.C.B. Camp Parks, Shoemaker, Calif.

December 31, 1944

Dear Lou,

I received your letter yesterday & was glad to hear from you. Well, Lou, I've been on a lot of parties lately "fun parties." I tried to catch malaria again, but it won't come back. I stay out all night drinking & work the next day, trying to get malaria, you see Lou I have a very good reason for wanting it so bad. I told you that I was going to get 6 months duty in the states, well, they are trying to pull a fast one, by that I mean the Doctor says I need to get a "pastin-malaria smear." If I don't I may go back overseas with the 15th. The last five times that I had malaria, it wasn't put in my health record. I see now by drinking that it won't come back on me, a lot of the fellows get drunk and it shows up the next day. I'd just as soon go back with the 15th as stay. I know that I couldn't get in another Batt. as good as ours. If I do get duty in the states, I hope it's in Rhode Island, too. Yes, Lou, your hunch about "Pop" coming home for Xmas was a good one, but he was hoping to be there for Xmas, maybe next year. I gave him your picture, identification tag & the nail clipper. Well, Lou, I remembered some of the questions, but there's one that I haven't & that's what you mean by "cats." Every time I see him I forget to ask him. We are not in the same companies now and I don't see him very much. Clere and I are still in C. Co, the rest of the boys are transferred to different companies. You said something about not hearing from him for over a week. Try not to worry about him too much, he's in the best of health, he's working most of the time and I know that's the reason that you haven't been hearing from him. Gee, Lou, I know that you and everyone at your house had a swell Xmas. I remember where you had the desk, I bet the tree was beautiful with all the trimmings. I bet "Jackie" was really thrilled with everything. Glad to hear that Jackie likes the little teddy bear. I'd really of loved to of been there and seen her on Xmas morning. I know that she was very happy. I have a good idea how she was acting when you started opening the presents. I wish I could have been there when it started snowing. I'd of loved to of taken Jackie for a sleigh ride, that would have been something new for me. I bet she does love it. If I don't get back this winter, maybe I will after the war. I'd like to go on a sleigh ride myself. Glad to hear that the pictures turned out good. Yes, Lou, I had a swell Xmas, although I wish I hadn't drank so much on Xmas eve. I went to "mass" on Xmas day with Fitz. No Lou, I don't mind a bit about the envelope being upside down. Well I guess I had better close, it's chow time again. Tell Ann & everyone hello for me. Give that cute little Jackie a kiss & hug for me.

Bye for now Vincent.

P.S. Thanks for the nice card, Lou.

Sunday, December 31, 1944. Went to 8:00 mass. Rain. Feeding Jackie. M.D.R. calls to ask about J.De R. Gene brought Mama G & Tadone up after dinner 3:00. Joe & Angie at 4:00. Called up Mike to let him know we'd be down tomorrow. Mil, Gene & Judy came over. 9:00 Joe & Angie left. Took Mama G & Tadone home. 9:30 Gene & Mil left. 10:00 played Put n take. Always won at first - then luck changed. Won 8 cents. Played until a quarter of twelve. Went in and listened to radio. 12:00 all had a shot to the New Year. I had four shots. Listened to radio for awhile then went to bed 1:00 A.M.

Chapter 4
1945
Johnny Pleads With Lucia to Visit Him

Monday, January 1, 1945. *New Year's Day. Went to 8:00 mass. Rain, drizzling, foggy. Fan had to go to work. Family invited to Jo & Mike's. Ann and I took 12:13 train, rest went in Joe's car. Reached there 1:15. Had dinner 2:45. Raining heavily. Wonderful meal. Ate too much. Stayed until 8:45. Fan had come in 3:30. Ann, Fan, Gracie & I took 8:13 train home. Stopped raining. Fog lifted. Began to snow. Home 9:00. Caught bus just as we reached station. Reached front door, Joe pulls up. Jackie asleep all the way. Woke up and wanted to start playing with her toys. Jo gave me a half bottle of eggnog to take home for Jackie. All went to bed 10.00.*

Postmarked January 2, 1945, stamp upside down.   *Monday, January 1, 1945*
[Camp Parks is 23 miles east of Oakland, CA]   *Camp Parks*
Hello, Sweet!

May my love and adoration for you increase this year as it has in the past. A very happy and prosperous year to you, my lovely one, and may we be united permanently before this year has progressed very far. I love you more than ever, my darling, and want so very much to be there, holding you in my arms and kissing you, while telling you how much I adore you.

I spent quite a nice New Year's Eve, my adorable angel. I went to town, sat in a joint drinking until midnight, and then came back and hit the sack. This morning I arose at five thirty, went over to the galley and prepared the vegetables for today's meals. We had a delightful repast today, everything from soup to nuts. Shrimp cocktail, candied sweets, cauliflower, peas, cranberries, turkey, dressing, a salad, celery, pickles, olives, fruit and practically anything else you could name. All of it was pretty good, too. After we finished eating and were on our way out, a small paper bag was handed to us, containing mixed nuts, a package of cigarettes, and a cigar. That's all, except that there were more fellows in to eat than were planned for, and the latecomers got no turkey or sweets. Instead, they had a pork chop and French fries. I have just returned from supper, and shall retire as soon as I finish this letter and shower. I am quite tired, believe it or not.

Your letter describing your Christmas at home came yesterday, and boy, it certainly was a swell one. How I wish I could have been there, watching Jackie, and making love to you. To be truthful, sweet, tears came to my eyes as I was reading it, but they didn't last long. I'm so glad you were able to have a nice day and also that you enjoyed the flowers. It was the best I could do, Lucia mine, but I will try to do a little better in the future.

My cold is practically gone, but the way the weather is continually changing out here, I wouldn't be surprised if it didn't come back. Every time I go out I either have to wear or carry my pea coat. Gosh, I never thought I'd have to do that, especially in California, the land of liquid sunshine. Gosh, what a place. I love you.

I thought I told you about my cyst, sweet, but I guess I didn't. All I did was squeeze it, and now it's alright. That happened a week or so after I got out here and it hasn't bothered me since. It hasn't filled up again yet, either. Who knows, perhaps I won't have any more trouble with it.

Gee, I wish I could think of something to say, but life is so humdrum and monotonous here that there is nothing to write about. Forbes told me he received a letter from you the other day. He is still hoping to be transferred to Rhode Island, but seems to be making very little headway. I sure hope he does make it.

Oh, the latest scuttlebutt has us leaving here about the first of March. If we do remain until then, I am quite sure of getting a pre-embarkation leave. Here's hoping I'll be able to get home to my lovely wife and sweet daughter. I love you both so very much. The seventh battalion, which has been in the states for such a long time, has moved from this base. I am not sure whether they have left the states or gone to another base, though. They left for here before we went to New Zealand, lucky fellows.

Speaking of New Zealand, the women and girls around here are just about as bad and loose as they were, and maybe a bit more infected. It sure is a hell of a way to be, but heck, I suppose they are tired of doing without their men and want to have some fun. The married ones are worse than the singles, too, and several fellows have been living with them as husband and wife. All this makes me appreciate you more, my sweetheart, because I know that you are to be trusted and won't let anyone take my place. You can be sure of my love for you, too, as I've told you before. My one desire is to be able to soon return to you, to live as a married couple should. I don't know what I would do without you now. You certainly have changed me, for the better.

Well, my lovely wife and adorable sweetheart, as I have nothing more to write about I will close, hoping and praying that we will be together before many more days have passed.. Give my fond regards to all, and my special hug and kiss to our Jackie. To you, my own precious darling, I send my all.

J.De Roxtro EM1/c   Eternally, your loving *Johnny*

Are you coming out?

Note on flap: "Sweetheart, you are the swellest in all the world. I love you."

Tuesday, January 2, 1945. Jackie and I up at 8:45. Gave Jackie eggnog. Thought it was milk. Cleaned house in the morning. Very cold out. Received checks for $80 & $50. Also New Year's card from Johnnie. Eugene brought gift from Trenton. Was a Zebra. Put Jackie to sleep after lunch. 3:30 Grace took Jackie to the store to buy veg. for supper. Mom & Gracie went out. Girls went to movies. Home alone. Sat in chair and read a magazine.

January 3, 1945 – General MacArthur is placed in command of all US ground forces and Admiral Nimitz in command of all naval forces in preparation for planned assaults against Iwo Jima, Okinawa and Japan itself.

Wednesday, January 3, 1945. Stayed in bed until 9:00. Jackie slept until 9:45. No mail. Mildred called. Went downtown 11:30 to cash checks. Meant to buy Jackie's shoes, forgot ration book. Had lunch at Mil's. Home at 2:30. 3:15 Vene came. Brought Jackie & me downtown. Looked all over for Jackie's shoes. Settled for brown pair in Van's, size 5½. Vene didn't come in. Went to Mills St. 5:30 Jo drops in. Had been to see Masterfano lady. Had supper. Took 8:05 bus. Took picture of Christmas tree.

January 3, 1945 – British occupy Akyab in Burma. The Allies continued their unsuccessful attempts to completely free Burma from Japanese occupation until the end of the war. Japanese forces had Burma well-fortified and the only reasonable staging point for the Allies was from the island of Akyab. Repeated attacks by the Allies all resulted in failure, but Japanese forces on Akyab had weakened under continued assault and they finally evacuated Akyab on December 31, 1944, enabling Allied forces to land and occupy the island without resistance.

Thursday, January 4, 1945. Received letter of Jan. 1st from Johnnie and a letter from Forbes. In all day. Washed hair. Not very cold out. Gracie went to the store with Jackie. Wrote to Ralph. Took picture of Jackie on horse.

Friday, January 5, 1945. Woke by ringing of telephone. Breakfast, then took tree down and cleaned room. Lovely day out. Jackie helped untrim the tree. Sent her to store with Gracie. Cooked. At nite went to movies with girls. Saw "An

American Romance" with Brian Donlevy and Ann Richards. Very good.

Saturday, January 6, 1945. Cold. No mail. Cleaned up a bit. Washed clothes. Put Jackie's swing in cellar. Went to Paper Mill Playhouse, "The Student Prince." Took 7:14 train to Milburn. 12:20 train. Home 1. Play very good

Sunday, January 7, 1945. Snowing. When awake went to 8:00 mass. Jackie awake when I got home. Cooked after I finished with Jackie. Still snowing heavily. After dinner I started on white sweater for Jackie. Gene, Mom, Gracie & Judy went down Mama G. Lucille came at 5:00. Stayed until 9:00. Knitted on sweater & listened to radio until 12:00. Went to bed.

Postmarked January 8, 1945, stamp upside down.
Co.A. 15th N.C.B.-Camp Parks, Shoemaker, Calif.   January 7, 1945
Hello, Sweetheart:

All the love and adoration I can possibly give goes to you, my sweet. Never a moment goes by that your lovely image isn't before my eyes. Thoughts of you are continually running thru my mind. You are my one and only, darling, and I want so very much to be able to hold you again in my arms, to press my lips against yours and to tell you of my devotion. Dearest one, if it's at all possible, will you try to get out here to see me and stay with me? Even if it's only for a couple of weeks, honey, I want to be with you. If it isn't possible, well, remember that my thoughts are always of and with you. Some day, this darned mess will be over and the three of us can be together again. Let's hope and pray that it will end soon.

There isn't anything new for me to tell you, my angel, so this will probably be a very short letter. The only mail I've received this past week was a letter from Ann. She wrote it the twenty-seventh, the same day you wrote that nice long one. Gee, I want you.

Don't worry about me drinking too much, darling, because I've stopped. All I've had since New Year's Eve was two bottles of ale. I kind of decided I wasn't bring quite fair to you, or to myself either, by doing so much of it, so I decided to refrain. I haven't definitely gone on the wagon, but I surely won't drink as much as I have been. See what you've done to me, my lovely one? You've made a better guy of me and I love you more for it.

I am unable to get down to the shipyard very often and when I do I am usually an hour or two late, so I'm not doing as good as I thought I would. What I make down there, along with my Navy pay, just about permits me to make ends meet. I'm able to purchase enough cigarettes and a decent meal once in awhile, so I'll get along.

Honey, you never mentioned receiving that Christmas card from me. Didn't you get it? You couldn't have, else you would have mentioned it, cause it probably was a complete surprise. If you did, I hope you liked it. I shopped around for two weeks trying to find a better one, but I couldn't. I love you.

The weather here has been bad lately; rain, fog, and raw as the devil. Even with my pea coat on I am chilly. So you know darn well that it is cold. Must be the dampness that makes it so hard to take. It doesn't do my cold any good, either, but thanks to proper medication, it isn't getting any worse. We should be getting an embarkation leave next month, because we've been back almost four months now. Gee, I hope we don't ship off before we are eligible for that. A few more of the fellows are being transferred so I may be one of them yet. Darn it, I wish I knew something definite. This uncertainty will eventually drive a guy nuts, especially if he hasn't much to keep him occupied. Every chance I get I go down to the yard to work, so I keep pretty busy. I may lose my mess cook's job, too, because the men who have their wives here are getting the preference. But I wouldn't mind that. Hell, give the guys a break. I'd want someone to do the same for me. That would mean I couldn't make work at all, though, so it wouldn't be so good that way.

Give my fond regards to all the family and our friends. Here is my daily special hug and kiss for our darling daughter Jackie, and very many more for my dearest wife. Gee, I want you so very much and I am hungry for your love, hugs, kisses, and everything.

Eternally, your loving *Johnny*

Note on flap: "Here's a few more special lovings. You are adorable. Love."

Monday, January 8, 1945. *Stopped snowing. Woke by fire whistle. Fire at Silversteins. 8:15. Fan home from work - headache. After lunch we three went downtown, post office, wool, met Catherine and Carol Ann. Home at 3:00. Sent Gracie to store. Took Jackie along. Cooked. At nite went to movies with Ann & Fan. Saw "I love a Soldier." Very good.*

January 9, 1945 - U.S. Sixth Army invades Lingayen Gulf on Luzon in the Philippines.

Tuesday, January 9, 1945. *Jackie awoke at 8:00. Mil called 9:30. Went downtown. Home at 12:30. Lunch. Put Jackie in crib but did not sleep. Sent Gracie to store with Jackie. After supper knitted on sweater until 10:00. Went to bed. Wrote to Mary.*

Wednesday, January 10, 1945. *Very cold out. Received letter of Jan. 7. Mom went to N.Y. with Ann and Fan. Met them in Hoboken. Gracie went ice-skating after school. Mil, Gene & Judy came over after supper 5:45. Stayed until 9:30. Grate from furnace came out. Kept fire going until 1:30 then went to bed. Left note for Mom. Very cold.*

January 11, 1945 - Air raid against Japanese bases in Indochina by U.S. Carrier-based planes

Thursday, January 11, 1945. *Very cold. Ann home from work. Lit oven to warm up kitchen. After I fed Jackie I went out and tried to open the garage doors. Worked one loose. Finally gave way enough for me to squeeze thru. Filled wood in wheelbarrow. Kindling great help. Lit fire place at 12:00. Went down and started fire in furnace. House all warmed up by 3:00. Shelly came for boiler. Mil & Gene came over after supper.*

Friday, January 12, 1945. *Ann home from work. Took 9:44 train and we both went to New York. We each bought a dress. Home by 5:30. Mom home from work because they had no heat in the factory. She said Jackie was very good all day. Gene brought the welded grate over tonight.*

[Camp Parks, Shoemaker, California.]
Postmarked January 13, 1945, stamp upside down.   *Friday, January 12, 1945*

Same Old Place

Hello, Sweetheart:

I love you, miss you and want you more as each day slowly passes, bringing us closer to the day of our next reunion. Sounds like my same old way of starting, doesn't it, but as the old saying goes, my love for you will never grow old. I do love you more now than I ever have, my sweet, and I am even more hungry. I long to take you in my arms once again and kiss you. Your voice would be like music in my ears and your smile would really brighten my life. Gosh, won't it be swell when we are finally settled in our own little home? I am anxiously awaiting that day and I know that you are too.

Since New Years, I've only had two bottles of beer, so you don't have to worry about my drinking anymore. I was going at it too often, but I couldn't help it. Maybe it was because you were so near me and yet so very far away. Anyway, I spent a heck of a lot more than I was earning and my conscience will bother me now until I pay all that I owe. It will take quite a few weeks but I'll get it done. I managed to get in another full day at the yard this week and I plan on going in tomorrow if possible, so that will help. Maybe next week I can make three days. Boy, what I wouldn't give to be able to work down there for about six months, every day. That would pay me about eighteen hundred bucks. We could surely use that as a little nest egg, couldn't we, but I can't, so there's no use in even thinking of it. We'll make out somehow, and whatever happens we will be happy together. Gee, I wish the darned mess would end soon. I love you so very much, my adorable one. I want you. I'm hungry. You must forgive me for always asking you to come out here, darling. I know that it's almost impossible, but I do want you to. As long as you can't, sweet, well, I won't bother you like that anymore. I'll just

346

hope and pray that I get a long enough leave to come home to you and Jackie before shoving off.

Everything is about the same here, so I haven't any news to tell you. I did manage to get one of my blue uniforms washed today and right now it's hanging here in the hut to dry. Maybe tomorrow morning I'll have a chance to press it. No, I can't do that because tomorrow is inspection and we aren't allowed in the area. That means I'll be late for work down at the yard, too, 'cause I won't be able to get in to shave or change clothes. Oh, well, what the devil do we care, huh?

I received a couple of letters from you this week and enclosed in one were the pictures. They were swell, sweet, and the little snowsuit looks good, doesn't it. You look happy, too, and that helps a lot. My second collection of pictures has a fairly good start now. Here's hoping it never has a chance to become as large as the first one was. Gee, I love you. There isn't anything in your letters to answer, cause I've answered all your questions in previous letters, so I am now at a loss for words. This will be another short letter, my lovely one, but I promise to do better Sunday, if I possibly can. I will try to write to my mother, too, at that time. You are the only one I've written to in a heck of a while. I am kind of neglecting my social duties and will have to take time off to make amends, one of these days.

Give my fond regards to all the family and our friends. Here's my special hug and kiss for our Jackie, and millions more for you, the most wonderful wife and sweetheart in all the world. I love you, miss you and want you.

As ever, your loving, *Johnny*

Red snowsuit   With Gracie   On sled

Saturday, January 13, 1945. No mail. Changed Jackie's crib. Cleaned rooms. Went to confession and then downtown. Got dress out of cleaners. Beginning to snow. MdR called on telephone.

Sunday, January 14, 1945. *Snowing heavily. Received communion. Knitted on sweater. After dinner Mom and I went to the movies. Saw "Mrs. Parkington" with Grace Gasson. A good picture. Nite time put Jackie to bed. Knitted and listened to radio. Finished sleeve. Stopped snowing later in evening. Jackie's 4ᵗʰ molar broke through.*

Monday, January 15, 1945. *About six inches of snow on ground. After lunch brought Jackie out in yard with pail & shovel. Took a walk to mail box. Gave her a large box to put snow in, then I came inside. Became tired of shoveling snow in box so she threw it on her head. Stayed out an hour. Called to come in. Put her to bed but did not sleep. 3:00 Catherine & Carol Ann comes. Dressed Jackie. Went outside. Wrote to Vincent. Took 3 pictures of Jackie in snow. Took others with Carol Ann. Took kids for sleigh ride around the block. First time for Carol Ann. Started to snow again at night.*

Letter from Mary Lukawitz, postmarked Jan. 23.

New Guinea,
15 January 1945

Dearest Lou,

You know that I can't thank you enough for the bra that you sent me. It's lovely and will wear a long time I know. Yes, it's the right size too. Thanks loads. Maybe someday I can repay you for all that you have done for me. The letter came in less than two weeks which really broke the record of any of my regular letters. If all of the letters would come that fast, then I would be one of those girls whose morale is sky high. Right now it's on the level.

Couldn't wait to find out if I had any today since I'm on duty at the office. I eat early chow, then stay in the office while the rest of the office force has theirs. Today we had a very tasty lunch -Swiss steak with butter (un-meltable), slices of canned pineapple, and iced tea.

Will be waiting for the long letter that you are going to write me, in the meantime I'll scribble a few lines (type, I mean) to let you know everything is fine. The weather as usual is as hot as ever. The only cool spot is the ocean, or one of the offices that have a fan. Luckily our office has, so at the present time I feel very comfortable. I have sent you a bracelet which I hope you will like, though I was a little disappointed since they wouldn't engrave your name on it. I do hope that you like it. If I think of it I'll mail you some of the coins that we use here. One of the boys made me a lovely bracelet out of them. I wish I could get a shell bracelet – they are pretty. Most of the things are made by our own boys. Of course the natives make the grass skirts and rugs which I don't like at all. Other than that there isn't much to send home as souvenirs.

Yesterday we had lots of fun. Went to the beach for several hours and stayed in the sun, also went swimming. The water was very warm, but felt wonderful for it was so hot. I did some ironing when I got back to the barracks; got a shower from perspiration while doing it too. Took a shower afterwards but even that didn't cool me off. One of the girls made a stove so we had coffee and soup along with our meal last night. One of the girls opened a large can of fruit cocktail that she had which was our desert. Almost like a campfire picnic except that the cooking was done outside and the eating inside.

Now I must close. Will really write a long one as soon as I hear from you. Give a big hug and kiss for my sweetheart. Tell her I have her picture on top of my little homemade dresser. She's a doll. You know I think I'll just have to get a bracelet for Jackie like the one I sent her Mother.

Best of luck and happiness to all.

Love, Mary

January 16, 1945 – Battle of the Bulge, Belgium. Allies link up. German commander ordered to surrender.

Tuesday, January 16, 1945. Snowing heavily. No school for kids. Baked two lemon pies. Knitted on sweater until 11:00 went to bed. Jackie came downstairs standing with help of bannister - 23 months.

[Camp Parks, Shoemaker, California.]

Postmarked January 17, 1945, stamp upside down.

January 16, 1945

Concentration Camp

Hello, Sweetheart:

I love you more as each day passes, my darling, and how much I miss you and want you you'll never know. I long to take your soft sweet lovely body in my arms once again and press my lips against yours. Oh, sweetheart, if only we could be together again, living as a married couple should. Just the three of us, for awhile, and then maybe more. Gosh, we're sure losing a lot of time, aren't we. But the way the news sounds now, perhaps it won't be too long before we are able to be in each other's arms again.

There is no news from here that I can think of, my sweet, so all I can do is comment and remark on our letters, the last of which I received today. I have about an hour before I go back to my duties at the galley, so maybe I will be able to get this finished. Enclosed in your lovely letter today were three pictures; one of Vincent, one of our family, and one of you and Jackie. Gee, darling, you sure do look good to me. You seem to be taking a better picture lately, else I'm not able to see correctly. Anyway, they don't flatter you; they are real honest pictures. By the way, I met Evelyn Sunday afternoon at chow and showed her your pictures. She thinks both you and Jackie are swell, too, as everyone else does. She seems to be a likable gal, herself. I was only talking to her for a few minutes, so I can't tell you anything about her, other than she is okay by me. She has a pleasant face and nice figure and seems to have a nice personality. That's all I know, except that she may become a mother about September. I don't think I had told you that before had I. Carl told me quite awhile ago, but I had forgotten all about it until just this minute. It's costing them about five dollars a day to keep her here, so maybe it's just as well that you weren't able to come out. If you had, we would have used all that you have saved for our future. It sure would be swell if we could have been together all this time, though, wouldn't it. But we'll be together again before I shove off, I feel sure. It will be a terrible disappointment if we're not. You will have to send me dough enough to get there and when I have my chance, though, so I hope you have it where you can get to it easily. About fifty bucks should get me across to you safely. I won't worry about returning here until I have to.

350

The P.S. on your letter sure came as a surprise to me, honey. I still don't know anything about Fitz being engaged. I do know that he appears to be going quite steady with a wave he met out here, but I hadn't heard or even thought that it was going that far. I will see him about it and let you know what I learn. He was going with a nurse or something while he was home on leave and seemed quite interested in her. Gee I want you.

By the clippings you sent in a couple of your nice long letters, it looks as if the fire department had a busy day. The poor guys seem to be earning their money this payday, for a change. Poor old Si had a little trouble too, didn't he. And I'll bet it seemed funny having the fire department there in the neighborhood and not at the flats, didn't it? Many people were really surprised at that, I'll bet. You know, I always thought that Silversteins owned that building. Thanks loads for the news from the home front, sweetheart. I was glad to see that the Salvation Army finally received some praise for something, too. They are on the ball, alright. To me, they're a hell of a lot better than the Red Cross.

Say, honey bunch, how come all those pictures of Forbes came out cloudy. That must have been a poor film or something, I guess. I have not seen him since I received them, but as soon as I do, I will show them to him. Several times he has asked me about them.

I'm terribly sorry, my pet, but duty calls and I must return and make my little individual salads for the boys. That's a hell of a job and takes quite awhile to make over nine hundred. I'll leave this open and maybe after supper Ill have time to write more. I'm going to do my washing first, though and get it over with. So long for now, sweetheart. Regards to all, my hug and kiss to Jackie and to you, all my love. I love, miss you and want you.

Everlastingly, your adoring *Johnny*

Note on flap: "I'm hungry, sweet. Can you help me out? Love."

Wednesday, January 17, 1945. Received letter of January 12. No school for kids because of snow, 15 inches. Grace took Jackie out on the sled in the morning. She would not take a nap. Slept all night long with bandage on thumbs. After supper went to movies with Ann & Fan. Ann treated. Saw "Climax " in Technicolor with Susanna Foster. Very good.

Thursday, January 18, 1945. Cold. Jackie awoke at 7:45. Sun came out at noon and about 3:00 took Jackie out sleigh riding. Carol Ann was with us. Stayed out until 4:30. Had sauce all done. At nite I knitted on Jackie's sweater. Took 2 pictures of Jackie in snow.

Somewhere in the South Pacific

[Camp Parks, Shoemaker, California.]
Postmarked January 19, 1945, stamp upside down.

January 18, 1945
Same Old Hole

Hello, Sweetheart:

All the love in the world is ours, as the days slowly pass, we are brought more close together. I will be satisfied with life only when I am able to hold you once again in my arms and kiss you. My thoughts are always of you, my darling, and I long for your sweet company. I want you so very much, dearest one, even more than I did when I was out on the islands. We belong together, my sweet, and when we are finally living together, I will be completely happy. I long for your kisses and warm embraces, and all else that goes with marital bliss. I'm hungry, Lou darling, and only being with you will satisfy my hunger. I adore you, precious angel.

Tomorrow, Clere starts home on a fifteen-day emergency leave, but it won't be pleasant for him. His mother is quite ill and he was granted that special leave. When he went to ask the chaplain about it he said why not wait about six weeks and then we would all be going home. That means we would be having our embarkation leave in about six weeks. One can't believe anything he hears, though, so don't let yourself hope too much. I am hoping and praying that we won't be kept apart much longer. One of these days official word will come out and just as soon as it does, I will let you know. Gee, sweet, I love you.

I haven't seen Fitz as yet, but another fellow told me that he is supposed to be engaged to the nurse I told you about. I doubt if she means very much to him, though, because he sure is rushing this wave. She even comes to see him when he can't leave the camp. That's how come I met her, last Sunday afternoon.

My cold is back again, sweet, but it isn't very bad. I have some nose drops and some pills to take, besides using the Vicks, so maybe it will be chased before very long. I've never had one to hang on as long as this one has. But I'll at least keep it from becoming worse.

I've about decided to give up working at the shipyard, my sweet, because I can't get there as often as I would like to and besides, it's costing me more for transportation than I make.

Tell my mother I haven't had time to write, but will at the first opportunity. Regards to all and my hug and kiss for our Jackie. To you, all I can send is my all, and that only by words. How I wish I could also send my body. I love you, miss you and want you.

Eternally, your *Johnny*

Note on flap: "*My dear wife and sweetheart, I am yours forever. I love you.*"

Friday, January 19, 1945. No mail. Turned out to be a lovely day. Washed clothes in morning. Put Jackie out after lunch. Carol LaVato came over to play with her then gave her a ride on the sled. When Gracie came home from the store she took Jackie along with her until 5:00. After supper, Mom, Ann and Fan went out. I finished Jackie's white sweater. Turned out swell. Sings and knows almost all of "Little Bo-Peep" "Little Jack Horner" "Pussy cat, Pussy cat" "Ring Around a Rosie".

Saturday, January 20, 1945. Received a pkg. from Mary. Bracelet and shells from New Guinea. Took 12:15 train to Newark. Met Fan on train and then met Ann & Del in front of Proctor's Theater. Saw "Winged Victory," very good. Sad. Tickets were compliments of McKiernan Terry Corp. After show Ann & Del went to banquet at Terrace Room. Fan and I looked around for awhile, had a sandwich in Childs and then came home. Gracie took a picture of me in the snow.

Sunday, January 21, 1945. Lovely day. Gene brought Mama G and Tadone up in time for dinner. M.d.R. called while I was bathing Jackie and washing her hair. 4:00 went to Community with girls to see "Thirty Seconds Over Tokyo." Very good.

Postmarked January 24, 1945, stamp upside down.   *January 21, 1945*

<u>*Camp Parks*</u>

Hello, Sweetheart:

I love you, miss you and want you. My thoughts are continually of you. More than anything else in the world, I desire to be there with you. Gee, how I would like to be able to hold you in my arms once again and kiss you. Lovely one, if you can possibly make it, please come out to me. Even if it's only for a week or two, I surely would appreciate it. I want you so very much. Most adorable angel, I see all these fellows around with their wives and it makes me long for you even more than before. Perhaps next month you will be able to make it. Anyway, keep trying, will you sweet? But be sure you let me know when to expect you, if you do come. Maybe you could bring Jackie along, if you can't get someone to take care of her. Besides, I sure would like to see her, as well as you. If only I could get stationed somewhere in the states for about a year, we could be happy together again. Gosh, wouldn't that be swell? But it's almost too much to even pray for. But enough of that. I know you would be here if it were at all possible. Gee, I love you so. Because you aren't here, I lost my easy mess cook job, so now I can't even work down at the ship-yard anymore. Now I won't even be able to repay the fellows what I owe them, until we hit the islands again. But most of them don't mind because they'll have enough to tide them over. Besides, I only owe about fifty. You see, sweet, when I was drinking so much, whenever I got paid, I would spend it on the cursed liquor, at fifty cents a drink, and wasn't able to pay my debts. Then when I decided to go to work, I would have to borrow to provide transportation to and fro, and buy my two meals. Then, if I had anything left, I would buy my cigarettes, if it was possible. That's the explanation for my indebtedness and I'm really ashamed of myself for it. But I've now practically stopped drinking and you have no need to worry any further. The only time I drink now is for sociable reasons only. And then I only use beer. That runs into dough too, at twenty cents a bottle. Especially when there are eight or ten in a party, and I'm sap enough to come up for a round. So, sweetheart of mine, if you ever have a little extra cash lying around, I won't be too angry if I receive some from you. But whatever you do, don't run yourself short.

In practically all your letters you ask why I don't write more often. Well, I simply don't have anything to write about. Everything is so damned dull and monotonous around here. And besides, I have been quite busy. But I do love you.

Forbes is being transferred tomorrow, but only out of the outfit. He will remain here in camp for at least three days and then he may go back to the east coast. From all reports I hear, those men who had malaria will be shipped to Maine, so don't be surprised if he walks in on you in a month or two.

Blosser and Andrews are both on mess-cook duty now, so they can see their wives for about twenty hours, every other day. Hell, I don't mind giving up my racket so the fellows with their wives out here can get a few extra hours with them. I was put on regimental guard this morning and that will last for a week. After that I don't know what will happen, but I hope I don't have to go through commands training. To be truthful, I don't think I could stand it. When I finish this letter I have to sew my rating badge and CB patch on my undress blues, in order to go on duty. Then I shall take my shower and retire, thinking, as always, of my most precious wife and sweetheart.

Angel mine, at supper tonight we had macaroni and I was thinking that maybe you could send me some sauce. The stuff they make here is lousy and I can't even force myself to eat it. I doubt whether it would keep, though. What do you think about it? I could always go in the galley and warm it up, but I wouldn't be able to take time enough to make it. I can acquire the macaroni easily too, so don't send that. Let me know what you think about it, will you my love? While on the subject of sending, if anyone wants to know what I need, besides money, of course, tell them I can always use more of those black socks and maybe a half dozen pair of shorts. Mine are just about gone. In fact, I had two pair lifted off the clothes line since I came back and now have only two. I don't know what happened to all the rest, either. That's all I really need, except to be with you. Boy, if I could only get that last, I wouldn't care what else I had or didn't have. Gee, I love you.

Your letters don't seem to be coming very often, either, my lovely one. Can it be that you are writing only when you receive one from me? Well in that case, I can expect more, because I will now be able to write more often, if I can find something to write about. I'm really sorry that I haven't been writing more often, sweet one, but you can rest assured that you have been on my mind continually. If only I could hold you in my arms and caress you, I would be happy. To seal our love with a kiss would seem swell to me too. You are my one and only, Lou, so never worry your pretty little head about that. No one else can ever take your place and so far I haven't seen one that would even appeal to me. I love you too much to let anything like that come between us. Even if you never knew about it, I'm afraid it would be on my conscience all the time. Please come out here to me, my darling, if you possibly can. I love you and want you so very much. We could manage to get along somehow. I need you.

Forgive me, darling, for pleading with you to come to me. I know you would if it were at all possible. I will manage to get along as long as you and Jackie are well cared for. Your health and happiness means more to me than anything else. Regards to all the folks. Here's my special hug and kiss for our little one and many more for the most desirable girl in the world, my wife. I love you, miss you and want you.

As ever, eternally your loving *Johnny*

Note on flap: "Here's a kiss for Mickey. Have I one from you for Johnny? All my love."

Postmarked Jan 24, 1945 from Ralph.

Jan 21, 1945
"New Caledonia"

Hello, Lou,

I received your letter of the 4th a few days ago. Boy, it sure is about time you remembered to write me. Don't tell that during the time you didn't have a chance to drop a few lines.

Well, I was glad to hear from you anyway. It was raining all day today and I don't feel like going to the show in all the mud. So I just stayed home tonite and decided to get rid of some letters. This is my third one. Say, what do you mean, "why didn't I answer your last letter?" I answered that one right away and told you the pictures were swell.

Before I forget I want to thank you for the swell bracelet and the package you sent from Jackie and you & Johnny. Everything got here O.K. I got your package & bracelet Dec. 30th.

Say, I just heard that about 6,000 guys went over the hill because they were coming overseas. It just came over the radio in the news from the states. Well, I can't say I blame them too much.

I was glad to hear that Jackie really enjoyed the Christmas tree. I'll bet it was good to see her face when she saw it.

About that letter from Johnny, I couldn't understand it at all until you explained it. Here it is Jan and he was home in Oct. and I just got his letter. I couldn't figure it out. I'll write to him as soon as I can. Boy he sure had a swell time from what he says. Of course his daughter was the smartest one in the world (so he sez) It sure made me feel good to read it. He told me of all the changes and how things are in general.

No, I don't want any of the pictures I sent you. The one you sent of you & Jackie sure came out swell and you're both looking good. I'll have some more pictures to send home in a couple of days.

Well, Lou, I guess I'll quit for this time. Give my love to all and a kiss to Jackie. So long for now.

Love, Ralph

Monday, January 22, 1945. *Received letter of Jan. 16th, also war bond. Started to snow after lunch. Didn't amount to very much. Ann & Fan went to movies. Mom went out. Gracie & I home alone.*

Tuesday, January 23, 1945. *Jackie woke at 7:30. Kept saying to me "Mommy get up. Put shoes on." Cooked sauce and soup in morning. After lunch went over to Mil's. Went to Acme. Bundles in carriage. Jackie walked back to Mil's. Threw snowballs at each other until 5:15. Kids were having a lot of fun. Came home.*

[Camp Parks, Shoemaker, California.]
Postmarked January 24, 1945, stamp upside down.

January 23, 1945
Sunny(?) California

Hello Sweetheart:

My love and adoration for you increases greatly as each day slowly passes, as does my longing and desire to have you in my arms again. Wouldn't it be swell if we were able to settle down in our own little home right now. Gee, the three of us would certainly be happy, wouldn't we. To lie down beside my sweet and lovely wife again would be divine. I love you so very much, sweetheart.

There isn't anything I have to tell you, lovely one, so this letter probably won't be very long. I will do my best though to make it interesting as well as lengthy.

Thanks loads for the latest pictures, my love, but there were none of you or our Jackie. That one of Ralph really turned out swell, didn't it. And I was kind of surprised when I noticed that he was a corporal. When you write to him, offer my congratulations and wishes for an early promotion to Sergeant. Pardon incorrect spelling. He sure does look well and happy, doesn't he. Those two of Forbes came out better than the others too, didn't they. I haven't seen him in the last couple of days, so I can't tell you any more concerning his transfer. If and when he does move out, you probably will learn about it from him via a letter. However, I will also inform you of anything I learn. I may have time to go over and see him tomorrow.

I was on guard duty just outside the guesthouse this afternoon and I think you may be interested in hearing about one of the little incidents I saw and overheard. The fifty-fifth battalion started their leave today and there were ever so many wives, sweethearts and mothers there to meet their men. Boy, all the kissing and tears of happiness I've seen there today. Service men aren't allowed in the front door, so all this was going on outside, within five to ten feet of me. One fellow came running up the road and tried to get in, but I had to stop him. I asked who he wished to see and he kept telling me his wife. I had to ask him about four times for the name and he was becoming quite angry. Anyway, before he told me who she was, she came out the door, very slowly and shy like. In her arms was a pretty little blond baby girl, about eighteen months old. When the poor guy saw her and the bambino, he just stood there and I could actually see him shaking. He looked at his wife, said hello to her, and then tried to talk to the bambino. Right away as soon as she looked at him, she started to bawl. Gee, he looked so sad and disappointed. I really felt sorry for him. Then he put his arms out to her and just touched her and she really turned on her temper. All this time I could see the tears welling up in the wife's eyes. After about a couple of minutes of the guy trying to become acquainted with the baby, the wife finally broke down and asked the guy if he wasn't going to kiss her. He got a sheepish look on his face, looked at me, and when I winked and half turned my head away, he gave her a short, rather cool kiss. Then she started crying also and tears came into his eyes too. And, darn it, they started in mine and I had to turn away from them. In a couple of minutes they left and got in their car. Gee, what a welcome he gave his poor wife. I hope I didn't treat you as badly, sweetheart. I don't think so. What a difference between their welcome and ours. Gosh, wouldn't it be swell if we could do it again real soon? Then there was a chief came strolling up the street. His wife came out of the guesthouse and they happened to meet right in front of me. He didn't even touch her. All he said was "who ever though you'd wait that long for a husband." They walked up to the car, got in, pecked once and drove away. What a difference there is in people one sees.

Then there was a nice-looking young fellow there and he just stood there while seven girls took turns kissing him. One was his sweetie pie and the others were his sisters and her sisters. They simply got in line and as soon as they were finished, they would fall in at the end of the line again and came back for more. Cars would pull up in front of the place and the girls would be so excited and in such a hurry to get out that they would show every darn thing they had, their dresses would ride up so high. There were darned few with panties on, either. More than one little patch of hair I saw today. But it only made me want you more, honey, so don't worry about it. And don't say that I shouldn't have looked, because I couldn't help it, sweet. It was my duty to stand there and how the devil could I help it. I didn't stare or anything like that, though. And just between you and me, my love, I didn't see even one who could hold a candle to you. For some reason or other, the girls out here all seem to look hard and sort of "don't-give-a-damnish," if you get what I mean. That turned out to be quite a long incident, didn't it. I saw the usual welcoming embraces also, both passionate and cool. That's about all there is to tell about my latest detail. When I go on again at midnight I will probably get a different post, so I'll tell you in my next letter about anything interesting that occurs. That is, of course, if I think it would interest you. You perhaps were rather bored with the foregoing narrative, but I thought maybe you would like to hear it.

I haven't been to a movie or anything like that since I left you, honey, and doubt very much if I ever will. Somehow I can't get interested in anything. I've only been bowling those times I told you about while at Endicott, and the alleys here are supposed to be real good. I haven't even gone roller-skating and there is a rink here also. I love you.

Don't pay too much attention to me please, for you to come out in my letter of the other day, sweet. I had the blues, I guess. But gosh, I sure do wish we could be together again. I love you so very much and want you more than you will ever know. The latest scuttlebutt has us leaving here in about three weeks to a month, so if you decide to come, you had better do it soon. There may be nothing to the scuttlebutt but there always is the possibility that it may be true. However, if I do have to leave the states without seeing you or Jackie again, you can be sure that I will remain true to you forever.

My love and adoration for you will overcome all temptations. But gosh, there is no use going on along this line. It's bad enough for me to think about it without telling you. A guy just came in and said he had some good straight stuff. Here's what he said, "Well, boys, my wife will have to go to work now, cause we're not leaving till May." Boy if that's the case, we'll be getting an embarkation leave. So you see, there isn't anything we can actually depend on. Tomorrow there may be an entirely different story.

Now I seem to be at a loss for something to write about, my pet. Maybe you won't mind so much if I just tell you once again how I want to act when we are together again. No, I don't think you like to read that too often. Anyway, you know how I feel about it, so there is no use in repeating it too often.

Give my fond regards to all the family and our friends. Here is my special hug and kiss for our darling daughter and many million more for you, the most lovable wife and sweetheart in all the world. I still can't figure how I ever managed to get such an adorable wife. Dearest one, I love you, want you and miss you. I'm hungry for your love, hugs, kisses and _____. Oh, my angel, if only this darned war would end so that we could be reunited again, for good.

Everlastingly, your loving hubby, *Johnny*

Note on flap: "Here's all my love, sweet. Also, a kiss for Mickey. I am really Hungry."

Wednesday, January 24, 1945. Letter of Jan 18th. Ann home from work. After lunch started to go downtown with Jackie. Acme. Too windy. Changed my mind. Went to Cat's and then to Mil's. Came home to cook.

[Camp Parks, Shoemaker, California.] January 24, 1945
Same Place

My Adorable Darling:

I love you, miss you and want you more as each day slowly passes. To hold you in my arms once again and kiss you is my one desire. I want you near me always, as we used to be before the service called to me. I want to be able to put my arms around you and tell you of my love and adoration. We belong together, sweetheart, and one of these days we will be. Gee, I actually miss you more now than I did when we were so many miles farther apart. Maybe it's because I had another sample of your charms. And even you must admit that our marital relations were a lot nicer and more satisfying this last time than they were previously. Gosh, when I think of all the times we could have sown the seeds, how I wish we could have been together from then on. By this time we would have had another on the way. I don't want Jackie to be too old before she has a brother or sister, do you? But a month from today she'll be two years old and it looks as if she'll be five, at least before we can have another child. Oh, well, you're the boss and if you don't want another until I can be with you to go through the trials if childbirth, then I can stand it too. And to be quite truthful, my sweet, I want to be around, too. I want to be with you during your pregnancy and I also want to help you bring up the little one. Hell, I want to change diapers, have the baby wet on me and all the other little things that go with child raising. But we've gone through all this before, so why should I be repeating it now. Forgive me, sweet, but as I sit here and think, I write of anything that comes into my mind. So if I repeat myself too often, bear with me. One of these days I will think of something new, and dwell on that for awhile. I adore you.

I didn't see Forbes today, so I can't tell you anything new about his future. The last time I saw him he promised to come around to see me before he left. As for Fitz, I haven't seen him in about two weeks. The only ones I see anymore are Blosser and Andrews. I probably would not see them if we weren't all in the same hut. Gee, I wish I could think of something to write about.

My guard duty last night was really tough. From midnight till four this morning all I had to do was walk and run up and down the road, trying to keep warm. I had my undress blues on, a sweater underneath, and my pea coat. The collar of my coat was turned up and I even had the chinstrap buttoned. Boy, it sure was cold. A very heavy frost was all over the place and where my warm breath created moisture on the collar of my coat a slight frost formed. And my feet, encased only in a pair of dress shoes, were cold also. So when I complain of the cold, you know what to expect if you come out. It isn't the cold as much as the dampness, though, I think. It seems to penetrate clear through clothing of any kind. Some of the fellows had long underwear on and a pair of dungarees under their dress blues and they were still cold. But if you were here, we wouldn't be out at that time in the morning, would we. You and I would be tucked away in a nice warm bed somewhere together. Right now, we would have every other night together and every other weekend. Even that would be better than nothing, wouldn't it. It sure would be lonesome for you on the days I didn't get out, though, but you could always go shopping. By the way, they have some lovely children shops out here. So if there is anything special that you'd like for Jackie that I might get, let me know and I'll do my best to fulfill the order. Sweetie pie, I'm very hungry.

To prove to you that your loving husband is being a good boy, I was entitled to liberty at 10:00 this morning and didn't even bother taking it.

Several fellows even offered to finance my trip to town, but I refused. Darn it, it's hell staying here in camp but it's worse knowing that you wouldn't be any better off, owing money all over the place. Sweetheart, I sure am a darn fool and can't figure why you ever married me. Love must be blind. But I'm not quite as bad when you are around as my inspiration. At least I don't think I am. You know, angel mine, if I was ever confined to camp for a period of time I think I would go nuts. I slept most all day today, so it wasn't so very bad. I will have to do my washing tomorrow before I go on duty, so that won't be so bad either. Then on Friday I'll have to go down to the shipyard and quit and pick up my clothes. I'll have to borrow some dough in order to do that, but a couple of bucks will do for that. As it takes most all day to quit and say my farewells, I won't be bored too much. I have a check for five hours coming, but that won't mean a thing, because I will have to pay for a couple tools that someone borrowed from me while I was not around. Some thief broke into my locker and lifted them. An investigation was made, but naturally they were never found. Oh well, maybe I'll be better off away from that place, anyway. But it did keep my mind occupied somewhat. Now that I am unable to work, I will probably be able to write you more often. That won't make you mad I know. Darn it, if only I had a little something of interest to write about. Those guys down at the yard are a swell bunch and I enjoyed working with them, but all good things must come to an end, except one thing and that is my love and adoration for you.

I'm afraid this will be the final page, my love, cause I've been sitting here thinking of something to write about for the last half hour and can't do it.

Just now I realized that I never said anything about something in one of the pictures you sent. It's the one where you are standing on the porch with Jackie. It was taken the third of December. Now here it is. You look wonderful in that coat, sweetheart, and if you think you don't have nice legs, just look at that picture and see for yourself. Why, darling, all the fellows think so. That coat does look very nice and I'm sorry I never mentioned it before. Gosh, but I have a beautiful wife. How I wish I were there with her, or she here with me. You are getting more beautiful every day, my beloved, and I mean it. Gee, I'm sure a lucky guy to have gotten beauty, intelligence, nice personality and even a good cook for a wife. Not only that but comradeship and understanding as well as everything else any fellow could desire. If only we could be together again for the remainder of our days on the earth. No matter what happens, my sweet, I have a feeling that we'll always be happy together. We both give in a little to each other and get along swell. You aren't a nagging wife and oh, hell, darling, you are the most perfect wife, sweetheart, and mate any man could ever wish for. I only wish I could become good enough for you. You've made a new man of me already but I doubt if I'll ever become as good to you as you are to me, sweetest, most adorable girl in the world. I will always love you, with all my heart, body and soul.

Give my fond regards to all the family and our friends. Here's my special hug and kiss for our Jackie and all my love and adoration for you. My love for you is the only thing worth living for, sweetheart, always. I will be living to make you happy.

Everlastingly, your loving *Johnny*

P.S. Can you satisfy my hunger tonite? Here's more hugs and kisses. J.

Note on flap: "Sorry sweet, but I have no stamps until tomorrow. I love you."

Thursday, January 25, 1945. *Very cold. Temperature 0. Had trouble getting the house warmed up. Kitchen pipe froze in afternoon. Mom melted it by a candle. At nite went with Fan to movies. Saw double feature. Good. Very cold. Jane Nesbit called.*

[Camp Parks, Shoemaker, California.]
Postmarked January 26, 1945, "Free."

January 25, 1945
Same old place

Hello Sweetheart:

I love you, miss you and want you. Never a moment passes that I don't think of you. Gee, how I long to take you in my arms once again and kiss you. I want to make love to you and do all the things a husband should do. Darn it, why the devil did this war have to come along? If it weren't for that, we would really have a swell time. But we are separated and there's nothing we can do about it. Just remember that I love you and always will. No one will ever be able to take your place, my most adorable angel. You are the most wonderful girl any fellow could possibly have and you can bet your bottom dollar that I am proud of you.

Your letter of the twenty-first arrived this afternoon while I was out on guard duty and enclosed were the three pictures of Jackie and Judy. Gee, honey, they turned out swell, didn't they. And both of them look so happy and healthy. You kind of surprised me when you told me about her being able to say the nursery rhymes. Gosh, she sure has progressed since I was there. But then, she will progress more rapidly now as she grows older. Thanks loads for those pictures, sweet. I sure do love to receive them. I would like to have a few more of my lovely wife, though, if you could arrange it.

You didn't tell me about Mary asking you for a bra. I can't see why she would want one out there, though. Hell, what's the difference if she has one on or not? I doubt very much if the other girls wear them and I'm darn sure

362

I wouldn't if I were there. The less one wears in those places, the more comfortable it is. But I suppose she feels undressed without one. I love my wife. Besides, if I remember correctly, Mary has plenty to hold up. Now don't get me wrong, my lovely one, all I did was look at the bulges under her clothes. Anyway, sweetie pie, it was swell of you to send her one. She is a swell gal and you can depend on her as a lifelong friend, I think. Maybe she doesn't want the boys down there getting too familiar. You know, angel, it must be tough on a girl being in a place like that, with so darn many love-hungry guys. I wouldn't want you to be in a place like that. But Mary will manage to make the best of it there, you can bet on that. And, just between you and me, she will probably do more than her share of the work to be done. She's welcome at our home anytime.

In one of my previous letters, I mentioned that I hadn't written to anyone but you and asked you to tell my mother any news my letters may contain. There is absolutely nothing wrong with me as you should know. I have given you the reasons for my not writing before too, so I won't bother going into that again. In the future, I will try to do better. I may even find time to write to other persons, too. I owe Ann and Vene each a letter and also my mother. Gee, I have so darn much to do besides write, that I don't have much time for writing. I will try to do better in the future, however. Please offer my apologies to all, will you, honey, until I have time to do so for myself? I will love you thirty hours a day, eight days a week, if you do.

I heard about the blizzard you folks back in the east had. It sure must have been a bad one. Gee, I can just about picture the wind howling and the snow blowing against the windowpanes and the intense dry cold. Boy, it must have been swell. Did our little one like it, sweet? Gee, I love you so very much, my Lucia.

That sweater you knitted for Jackie was bound to come out swell, honey. How could it help but that, when you were the maker. Hell, honey, everything you ever made yet was the best, except for me. I hope it wasn't a mistake. Do you think so, my lovely one?

No, my sweet, I haven't heard from Ralph since I returned out here. I can't say that I blame him for wanting to come home. It's hell, being away, but he can and will stand it. He has no choice, so he may as well make the best of it. He'll make out okay, angel, so don't worry about him. I've felt the same many times. Ever since I've been home, I've felt that way, but what's the use in talking about it. I've even felt that being back out on the islands would be better than this, but I soon changed my mind. Here, at least, I am closer to you.

Say, sweet, how come you always send hugs and kisses from Jackie, but never from yourself. Can it be that you wouldn't want to hug and kiss me? I doubt that. That little note you put on the inside of the envelope tells me better than that. I know you're waiting, sweet, and I am more than willing to come, but the distance between us is a bit too much, even for me. Maybe in March or April, or when you come out here. I'm still hoping and praying for something to bring us together, my beloved.

Give my regards to all the folks and my special hug and kiss for our sweet little Jackie. To you, most lovely one, I send my all, millions of hugs and kisses and all my love and adoration. I am very hungry, my sweetheart, and I need you.

Everlastingly, your loving Johnny

Note on flap: "Angel, mine, I want you so very much. I'm hungry. Will you come out? I love you."

Friday, January 26, 1945. *Cold. Zero weather. Kitchen drain plugged up. Letter of Jan 21-23. Mil & Judy came over in afternoon. Stayed for supper. Drain frozen. Mike came over to help. Held torch under pipe. 2 hrs. Could not fix.*

Saturday, January 27, 1945. *Still very cold. Drainage still frozen. Vene called. Fran & Eddie, baby girl born in morning. Cleaned house. When girls came home went downtown.*

January 28, 1945 – The Burma road is reopened.

Sunday, January 28, 1945. *Lovely day. Jackie awoke early with slight temperature. Became worse towards afternoon. Would not eat dinner or supper. Cried a lot and was very fussy. Took temperature, 102. Called doctor. Came around six o'clock. Cold and sore throat. Gave me two tablets for her to take. Prescribed Citralka. Mama G & Tadone up. Joe & Angie came too, for 1ˢᵗ time in four weeks. Joe brought 8 packs Camels for Johnny. Went to drug store for cit. started to snow.*

[Camp Parks, Shoemaker, California.]
Postmarked Feb 3, 1945, "Free."

January 28, 1945
Still here

Hello, my lovely one:

All day, every day, I am thinking of you and wishing we could be in each other's arms again. My love and adoration for you continually increases. How I long to be able to live there with you and our family. Gosh, wouldn't that be swell, honeybunch? All the little things we would be able to do together and what fun we would have doing them. I love you, darling, miss you and want you. To be able to be with you again is my one desire. That desire will carry me through this war and anything else that may come up. Darn it, I want to get out of here and home to you.

Your letter of the twenty-fourth came yesterday and enclosed therein were more pictures of our Jackie playing out in the snow. Gee, she looks well and happy and so does Judy. It looks as though they both like to eat the white fluffy stuff, too. You certainly are a swell mother and I am really proud of you. I'm the luckiest guy in all the world to have you as my wife. You're one in a million.

I was talking to Forbes today and he is really a disappointed boy. It seems as if he is getting a raw deal over where he is now and there is nothing he or anyone else can do about it. He is to go up to request mast tomorrow, so maybe he will be able to tell me something more definite the next time I see him. Here's the best of all good luck to him. I'll let you know all about it later.

I can't make this very long tonight, sweet, cause my cold is just about killing me. That regimental guard sure fixed me up. Darn it, and it was almost gone, too. I'm going over to the sickbay now and see what they can do for me. Whenever I cough it hurts clear down in my stomach. I have chills and headache, my back hurts, and I don't know what else. Otherwise I'm alright, so don't worry about me. Gee, sweet, I love you.

Here it is another night, my lovely one, and I am feeling much better. After I came back from sickbay last night I went right to bed. I coughed very little all night and had a fairly decent night's sleep. All day today I've been feeling much better, too. I've been coughing very little and my body feels better. I'm still sore a little and my throat isn't quite well, but I don't have chills anymore, anyway. You see, my sweet, for you I will take care of myself. The corpsman gave me a half ounce of something or other to drink, swabbed my throat, and gave me a few pills to take, one every four hours. I don't know what the drink was but the swab had three different kinds of stuff in it, one of which was argyrol. The pills were nothing but morphine. After I finish this letter, I am going over again and get another treatment. So, sweetie-pie, by this time tomorrow I should be quite myself again. Boy, I never did have a cold affect me as this one did. Here's hoping I never have another one. Maybe it's just as well that I didn't finish this last night, cause I know darn well that you would have been worried. In fact, I started this Sunday night. That was interrupted by an argument about religion, which was followed by a debate. Naturally I was in on it. Then last night, I was just too darn sick to write. Have I your forgiveness, my angel?

I received your letter of the twenty-fifth today and although it was short, it was swell receiving it. And boy, it sure must be cold there now. But I would still rather be there than here. This dampness is sure hell. No matter how much clothing I wear, I am still chilly, even when I'm well. As much as I

365

want you to come out here, I still tell you things like that about the weather. Will you come, sweet? We aren't to be ready to leave the states until the fifteenth of May, according to the last reports, so maybe later, huh? Gee, it sure would be swell to be with you again. I love you.

I was talking to Blosser today and he said that Evelyn wanted to know when you were coming out. I simply told him the truth and let it go at that. After all, what more could I do? He said she has asked several times and he just thought to ask me today when I asked him if he told her about your Christmas card to her. He had told her, so that's taken care of. Gee, I sure do wish you were coming out, though.

Back again after a bar of candy and a coca cola. One of the fellows in the hut has a birthday today so another guy [treated] us all to the aforementioned articles. Such a way to celebrate a birthday, no? Blosser and Andy just came off mess-cook duty, and they are now preparing for liberty. In an hour or so they will be with their wives. Gosh, I envy them. I don't know how they do it, but somehow they manage to get out most every night. We aren't supposed to get but every other night and every other weekend. More power to them, though. You can bet your boots that I would do everything possible to get out if you were here. Everything but through, over or under the fence, that is. In other words, everything possible to get out legally. Just think, my adorable one, every other night sleeping together, every other afternoon out walking together, or just merely being together every other afternoon and night. Boy, it sure would make California a heck of a lot better place to be in. Oh, well, even if you don't get out, if we stay until May, I should get an embarkation leave, but even that may be turned down by then. All we can do is wait patiently, hoping and praying for the best. Gee, I adore and worship my lovely wife.

Before I forget, Nelson wanted to know my address so as to mail me a form to fill in so as to be eligible for the new municipal employees retirement system. All I have to do is decide whether to return there to work or not first. Gee, sweet, I can't make up my mind whether to or not. We can't live very well on that small salary, but at least it's a steady income. I think I will fill the form in, as if I decided to return there, and let the future take care of itself. That's all I can think of right now, cause jobs, good ones, may be rather difficult to get after the war is over. That's one problem even you can't help me out on, my sweet. The system will be retroactive to the day I started, too, so that isn't so bad. Not only that, but the town will pay all my back dues and keep paying them until I return to work. While on the subject of the town, I don't know whether that two hundred dollar raise affects me or not but I imagine it does. I was wondering how he found out my newest address, but I might have guessed.

That's all there is to answer in your letter so I guess I'll have to bore you with what I've been doing lately. (Meaning yesterday and today.) Yesterday morning at muster, our warrant officer read off several lists of men going out to build places for navy personnel and their families to live. I was the last one on the plumbers list so I am doing plumbing work again. I'm with the same old gang with a few of the old guys gone, so we get along very well together. Because of my cold, the chief put me inside our tool-room to straighten things up. So I haven't been doing very much of anything except sitting by the fire keeping warm and dry. I may have to go out tomorrow, though, because I have everything in pretty good shape now. Boy, it sure was a mess when we took over. Some other outfit was working there and messed everything up. Most of their work had to be torn out and redone. Somehow or other our outfit seems to get all those jobs but no credit. Even in the book, Can Do, the fifteenth isn't mentioned but a lot of the jobs we finished up on were. Some other outfit always seems to get the credit when we do the work. But we don't care for anything except to get home.

Gosh, honey, I don't know how I'm going to finish this side of the paper let alone the other, but I'll do the best I can. I can't seem to be able to get in a writing mood anymore. I still haven't written to anyone but you, not even my mom, and I know darn well that I should. Maybe I'll be able to write Sunday, cause I'm not going out. I will try to answer Vene's two letters, too.

Most of the guys are out tonight again. Three of them are up in the corner playing knock-rummy, one is in the sack already, and one other fellow is writing. There are twenty of us in a hut, so that isn't a bad average of fellows going out, is it. Some are at the show here in camp, some at the basketball game, and some on liberty. As far as the rest, well, they're just out. I haven't been out in over a week now but I don't feel any better for staying in. If you were here I know darn well that I wouldn't stay in.

I don't know whether you know what a Quonset Hut is but these homes we're building are made of them. Those half-round things you see in the pictures are them. I am living in one now. They are about twenty feet wide by about fifty feet long. These we are fixing up for homes are partitioned across the center. Each has a bathroom, kitchen, and at least one other room. I haven't been inside a finished one as yet so I'm not quite sure about them. I do know that the Navy furnishes them completely, even to bed clothes and linen. Not only that, but they run a bus to the commissary for the ladies to do their shopping. At the commissary, they pay the same prices for food stuff as the Navy pays. They do have to use ration points as you do, however. I heard today that T-bone steaks were thirty six cents a pound. I love you.

Now don't get your hopes and expectations up too high, sweet, cause there may be nothing to the following. A fellow just came in from the ballgame and said he got it from a pretty reliable source. Here it is, but as I said before, don't depend too much on it. Half the battalion will get their embarkation leave the first of May and the other half, the fifteenth. That sounds pretty good to me, as it does to you, but darn it, I wish I had it officially. That's a long time to wait, sweet, but I'm willing, as long as I get to see you again before we shove off.

You know, sweet, it's nine o'clock now and I've been writing this since before six. Boy, it sure is taking me a heck of a long time, isn't it. Maybe that's because I'm not able to think very much anymore. But now maybe it looks as if I'll be able to finish this note of endearment before the lights have to be extinguished at nine-thirty. I think I'll interrupt this in order to address the envelope. Say, sweet and lovely one, I hope you don't mind my sending these letters via free mail but I have no stamps and no money to buy any. My most humble apologies for appearing so cheap, but at least it's better than none at all.

More confirmation on the good scuttlebutt previously mentioned in this letter. I don't have room or time now to tell you but it confirms previous statement. Boy, oh, boy, oh, boy. How I hope it's true. Better have about a hundred bucks ready for my traveling home to you about the middle of April, my sweet, cause I may need it. Regards to all, hugs and kisses to our Jackie, and all of me to all of you. May I see you again soon. I love you, miss you and want you. I'm hungry.

Eternally, your loving *Johnny*

Note on flap: "Here's much love & many kisses. I am yours forever."

Monday, January 29, 1945. More snow on ground. Letter from Mary. Jackie much better. Woke every half hour during nite. Kept her in bed all day. Wouldn't eat very much. Went to movies with girls. Saw "Hollywood Canteen." Good.

Tuesday, January 30, 1945. Received letters from Ralph (23) and one from Johnnie, Jan.24. Warmed house up. Dressed Jackie and brought her down for lunch. Did not eat much. Ironed after lunch. Cooked sauce. Martha mailed the cigarettes out to Johnnie. Prepared spaghetti and sauce for Johnny in jar.

Wednesday, January 31, 1945. Received letter of Jan. 25. Ironed clothes in afternoon. Mil & Judy came over. Stayed for supper. Gene went bowling. Walked them home. Ironed Jackie's little dresses until 10:30. Went to bed.

[Camp Parks, Shoemaker, California.]
Postmarked February 1, 1945, stamp right side up.   *January 31, 1945*
                                                          <u>*Same old place*</u>

Hello, Sweetheart:

Just to keep up with you, or rather get a little ahead, I will write again tonight. I promise that I will finish this one tonight, though, so you can bet it won't take me three nights to finish one measly letter.

You see, my sweet, I can start a letter differently. But now, before I go too far, I will revert to form. I love you more than life itself. You mean more to me than anything or anyone else in this world. I miss you, sweetie pie, and want you more as each day passes. How I wish you and Jackie were here with me. I'm hungry for your love and adoration, angel mine, and won't be satisfied until you, Jackie and I are together again. Darn this war. It's caused us a lot of trying times, hasn't it. But some day we'll be reunited and happy and then even California will look rosy to me because I'll be there with you. Boy, wouldn't it be swell if the war ended now and I got my discharge first? Boy, am I a dreamer. But it costs nothing to dream and I'm always daydreaming of our pleasant past and future. And I guarantee it will be as pleasant as I possibly can make it. You and Jackie and any others we may have in the future are mine to keep the best possible way. I love you true and I know I will love any and all of our kisses almost as much as I love my beautiful, adorable wife and sweetheart. No one can ever take your place in my heart cause the largest part of it where you are, is well insulated and locked against invasion. You are my one and only, my sweet. I adore you.

Nothing new has happened here. I am still in the tool shed out on the job because of my cold, which is much better, by the way. I haven't coughed hardly as much today. Very soon, though, I think I shall be welding again because we have to put in a pipeline and the chief asked me today if I would like to do it. Naturally I said yes, if only for the experience.

I have nothing further to report from over here so I will answer your most interesting letter, which I received today. You folks sure must be having cold weather there for the drain from the sink to stop up. Next time it does, just get some rags or something, soak them in real hot water, and wrap them around the trap. That's where all the water lies, so the foot or so of pipe is all that needs thawing. Or pour boiling water in the sink, let it stand a couple of minutes, sponge it out, and redo it until the stoppage releases itself. After the water starts running, though, you must continue to use two or three pots of hot water, else the remaining ice may cause the drain to freeze completely again. The hot rags are best, though.

You know, I kind of forgot all about the Kugler's blessed event. I

369

thought it merely another figment of the imagination. But come to think of it, Fran was quite large when I was there. I don't have to ask you to send my congratulations, cause you've probably done that already. I sure do wish the little one all the best of everything and although I hate to say it, she will probably need all she can get. But perhaps this will change things for the better down there.

Forget about sending the sauce out, sweet, cause it would never keep, I'm afraid. I would like to have some good sauce, though, so if you desire, you can try. At least we would learn whether it would keep or not. Maybe it would even keep long enough to send overseas. But that is asking a little too much. Out there, you could send the makings, though. Gosh, why didn't I think of that before? Can you imagine what those fish fries would have been like with a good mess of spaghetti? And I can make the sauce even though it won't be as good as my sweet and lovely wife makes. That good scuttlebutt I told you about last night is still going strong with no important changes. One of our chiefs wanted a special leave so as to get married and the skipper told him to wait until April because someone had to remain here while the rest of the outfit were on leave and that would make things very pleasant all around. That's the confirmation I told you of.

You know, sweet, I was wondering why the special delivery stamp was on this letter and I didn't find out until I reached the third page. And that little note you put on the inside of the envelope had me fooled for awhile too. I was beginning to think you meant I'd be surprised that you loved me. But eventually I found out the meaning of both. You shouldn't keep me in suspense like that, my love. It's bad for the heart, you know, but all kidding aside, sweet, that's even better news than what I told you about last night. Boy, make reservations as soon as you can and get here as quickly as possible, if not more quickly. That will give us about two whole months together before I get my embarkation leave. Won't that be swell, honey? Gosh, I can hardly wait. According to your letter, you can't possibly arrive here until about the tenth of March. The weather should be just swell here by then, too. Don't worry about me getting someplace for you to stay, either, because places are even advertised in the paper now. You see, there were quite a few battalions here that have recently left the states and rooms are plentiful right now. I can't guarantee an apartment for you, though, but I will look around and inquire. Maybe I can arrange to get one of these places on the base? Then we could be together every night. But from what I hear, only those families with two children are allowed those homes. However, I will find out just as soon as I can and let you know.

As for transportation, or rather, the best route to take, from what I can gather, is the northern route. You take the Pennsylvania to Chicago and the Southern Pacific from there to Oakland, California. It sounds easy, my love, but it's a tough trip to do alone, so it must be worse with a baby. You will have to figure on your meals coming across, too, don't forget, and some reading matter or something to pass the monotonous hours away, while Jackie is sleeping. Here's hoping you manage to get a decent riding companion. Naturally, you know you should get a lower, in case Jackie has to go or something during the nite. And don't worry about privacy, either, cause those curtains are nice and snug. Gee, I sure wish I was coming with you.

As for being reimbursed for your traveling expenses, well, you should have that back in about a month or six weeks, I think. There is a notice on the bulletin board about that right now, so I will also enquire about that.

I'm sure glad you decided to come out and bring the baby, even though it will be more tough on you, coming out here. If you had come and left Jackie, you would always be worrying about her, so I agree with you that it's better this way. Gosh, honey, it'll be wonderful having you with me again. I love you so very much, my sweetheart. That part of your letter about we three being together as long as we are able sounds swell to me. Here's hoping we are together until the end.

I can manage to get some fairly decent place where the rent is reasonable, too, so don't worry about that. I won't start looking quite yet, though, cause there are about four more outfits leaving very soon. That will give me just that much more of a variety to choose from. I will want to find a place quite close to camp, too, so as to save carfare and time. Oakland is about as far from here as New York is from home, so that is entirely too far away. Would you mind living in a small village around here, or would you prefer a small town? Let me know just about what you desire, my sweet, and I will do my best to secure it for us. You will want to do your own cooking if possible, too, won't you.

Now, if there are any further questions, angel, don't hesitate to ask them of me. Oh, yes, I almost forgot. Merely purchase your ticket to Oakland, California. Whatever time you arrive, day or night, I will be there to meet you. But you will have to let me know about when to expect you so I can make arrangements beforehand for a special liberty, if I'm meeting you. You can wire from Chicago, and maybe Reno, Nevada, as to exact time.

Love to all and all my love to you. A hug and kiss for our darling daughter, and millions more for the swellest wife a fellow ever had. I love you, darling, miss you and want you. I will always remain your loving hubby,

Johnny

371

Note on flap: "*Here's all my love. You made me very happy today. I love you, my sweet. Yours forever.*"]

Thursday, February 1, 1945. *Check for $80. Ironed more clothes. Holding up a pair of Gracie's old shoes Jackie said, "Whose shoes are these?"*

Friday, February 2, 1945. *Check for $50. Bill from Dr. Riley. Washed clothes. When Gracie came home I went downtown. Bought gift for Fran's baby, a pink bathrobe, blouse for Jackie. Went down to Sandrian's. Came home 5:00. Started to cook. Wrote to M.de R.*

[Camp Parks, Shoemaker, California.]
Postmarked February 3, 1945, stamp right side us.

February 2, 1945
Same Mud Hole

Hello Adorable One:

I love you, miss you and want you. Your lovely image is always in my heart. Each day, every day, all day, my thoughts are of you. You are my one and only and no one will ever be able to take your place. You are mine, darling, to have and to hold and so I will be able to do both. This next month will pass very slowly for me and this time next month I will be looking forward to seeing my lovely wife and family very, very soon. Gee, Angel, it's going to be swell, being with you and Jackie again. I hope you will be happy and satisfied out here, and that we are able to be with each other for the duration of our stay on earth. Gee, darling, I sure do love you.

It's been raining quite hard for the last couple of days and the mud out where we are working is only about ankle deep. I'm still in the tool shop, though, so I only have to get in the mud going in and coming out. But that's enough for me. The other poor guys are out in it a heck of a lot more than that, even though they are working inside the huts. Nothing much has happened here, so I haven't much to tell you.

Forbes was over today and the poor guy is really disgusted with the outfit he now is in. He is thinking of trying to get back into this battalion or else getting in the station force as a storekeeper. He thinks he can pull strings to do either. Boy, someone sure gave him a run-around, talking about sending all malaria patients back to the east coast for recuperation. He came over today to see our doctor, to give him hell or something. He really got a tough break.

Now, I have a surprise for you. Mr. Fitzpatrick is going to marry his wave girlfriend. She's the one he met out here and has been going with ever since. They are to get married just as soon as they possibly can. That means as soon as they can get their birth certificates from the east coast. The girls name is Ruth, and she comes from Newark. I can't give you any more information about her, because, although I met her, I didn't pay any particular attention to her. She seemed to be okay, though, and they've been seeing each other as often as they could. Both have told their parents and have their blessings. Fitz was over here after work this evening and told me all this himself and even showed me a letter he received from his father. It seems that both he and Mrs. Fitzpatrick were quite surprised and he asked Fitz a lot of questions about the intended daughter-in-law. Frank must have been very brief, as usual, in his letters. The future Mrs. F.X.F. is going to leave the service as soon as possible because she doesn't want to be shipped overseas. Right now, the waves are in the naval reserve and can't be, but they are to be transferred to the regular navy and then will be sent wherever they are needed. Fitz said he told her how the nurses were out there and that she has decided not to go. They are to be united in holy matrimony here at camp by a priest. All arrangements have been made and they are only waiting for the papers, blood test, and license. There is no three-day law out here so they will only have to await the results of the blood test. Naturally, I told him that they both would be welcome at our home any time after we got settled. I meant out here as well as after this darned war is over. I also told him I would do all I could to help him out and if he wanted anything, I would do my best.

That's all the news I have to tell you from here, my lovely one, so I will now tell you what I've done, so far, in regards to having a residence for you and Jackie to stay in after you arrive out here. All I've been able to do is file application for one of these compact apartments here on the base. The fellow told me that there probably wouldn't be a vacancy for sixty days but that just as soon as new places were completed they would be readied for occupancy. I know darn well that these huts we are working on now will be ready in less than a month and that there are about twenty apartments to be opened this week. So, maybe we will be lucky enough to get one. We can only remain there for thirty-one days, though, so in the meanwhile I will look around for something more suitable. These places cost only a dollar per day with three dollars for laundry service for the month and that would really help us out a lot, wouldn't it. I only draw twenty-five a month out here, sweet, so if you lived in town, it would cost me about all of that to travel so you'll have to be satisfied to live closer, in a small village. I love you.

I won't be able to get out until this coming Monday on account of financial reasons, so it will be Tuesday or Wednesday before I will be able to let you know anything further in regards to what I've been doing about a place to park the body. But don't worry about it, sweet, because I know darn well that I will be able to find a fairly decent place for my loved ones, even if you have to remain in a hotel for a couple of days. But I doubt very much if that will be necessary because rooms are really quite easy to get right now. All you have to do is get here, but don't forget to let me know when to expect you. I will send you a surprise for one of these ex-happy days of ours. But don't expect too much because it'll only be a birthday card for our Jackie. Maybe I'll call you sometime around the middle of the month. Or shall I not and save you that dough? Yes, I will merely remember our day of days. Give my fond regards to all our friends and the family. Here is my special hug and kiss for Jackie. I wonder if she will recognize me. To you, the most remarkable wife and sweetheart in all the world, I send my all. I love you, miss you and want you.

Yours forever, Johnny

Note on flap: "Will you be welcome out here? And how!! Here's a kiss for Mickey until I see you. I love you.

February 3, 1945 - U.S. Sixth Army attacks Japanese in Manila, Philippines. American troops landed on Luzon and rapidly made their way to Manila where they promptly freed the mostly American POWs. Japanese forces put up a fierce fight in which the opposing forces fought block by block, building by building, and floor by floor, frequently hand to hand. Finally by March 3, 1945, the Allies were victorious and General MacArthur turned the city over to the Filipino government.

Saturday, February 3, 1945. Letter of Jan 30. M.deR. called 9:00. Vene came at 12:00 noon. Rode down to station. Took bus to Springfield 1:11. Changed to Elizabeth bus 1:20. Reached hospital 2:10. Fran looked very well. Saw baby. Eddie came. Vene went down and they came up again. Stayed until four o'clock. Went home with Eddie. Vene cleaned while I cooked some bacon & eggs and fried potatoes. Hadn't eaten since morning. Eddie drove us to Springfield 6:00. Two buses passed us up. Took next one 6:45. Johnnie [Naughton] met us at terminal. Very cold.

February 4-11 - Yalta Conference, USSR to enter the Pacific War. The Yalta conference was held in the Russian resort town of Yalta, Ukraine in the Crimea (an island in the Black Sea) attended by US President Franklin D. Roosevelt, British Prime Minister Winston Churchill, and Soviet Premier Joseph Stalin. Knowing that an Allied victory in Europe was inevitable, the US and GB convinced Stalin to enter the war against Japan, and in exchange, the Soviets would be granted a sphere of influence in Manchuria.

Sunday, February 4, 1945. Went to 8:00 mass. Jackie slept until 9:30. Gene brought Mama G and Tadone up for dinner. Judy here for afternoon. Gene took Mil out to dinner. Started to pack bags.

[Camp Parks, Shoemaker, California.]
Postmarked February 5, 1945, 'Free.'

February 4, 1945
<u>*Same place*</u>

Hello Sweetheart:

I love you, miss you and want you more as each day slowly passes. My thoughts are of you continually. How I long to take you in my arms and kiss you. My one desire is to be with you. My adorable angel, you are the only girl in the world for me and I will patiently await the day of our reunion.

Gosh, sweet, I don't know how to tell you what I feel I have to. When I do get it down, you will realize why I'm not in a letter-writing mood and why this letter will be a very short one. Prepare yourself for a slight disappointment, my lovely one. But it may turn out alright later. Everything was swell up until two o'clock yesterday afternoon, and then the bottom dropped out of everything. Official word came for the battalion to be ready to leave here for Port Hueneme between now and the twentieth of this month. That's all the orders said. I haven't seen them, so it may be alright. As far as I know, and can find out, it is not scuttlebutt, but the truth. No one seems to know the reason for the sudden change in plans or what we are to do after we get there. Our skipper is supposed to be doing all he possibly can to find out. We may be going down to do a job or perhaps we are to become station force there. As soon as I find out something definite, I will naturally let you know all.

Now, as far as you coming here is concerned, I suggest that you make your reservations as far as Los Angeles, but don't purchase your tickets until you hear more from me. I don't know much about the trains or anything down that way, but L.A. is only about fifty miles from the base, so that won't be so bad. Darn it, why the devil couldn't we have stayed here for another few months instead of being transferred down there. As for rooms and places to stay, it should be more easy to locate something definitely nice around that section. There are quite a few small towns close to the base and living is quite a bit cheaper. I am only telling you what I know or have learned from different fellows so I may, of course, be mistaken about the price of living. At its worst, though, I can't see things costing quite as much as they do out here in the bay area. I do know that the people down there are more friendly and hospitable. At least they were a little over two years ago when we were there. And things weren't quite as expensive there then, either. That's all I can tell you right now, my precious one, but you can expect something more definite in my next letter, which will be of tomorrow night, if I can make it. I was going to write last night but I wanted to make certain of the preceding things. After all, I do want you to come out here very, very much.

The weather down around Hueneme is much nicer than it is here, too, so you will enjoy yourself more. And the scenery is just as good, if not better. Let me know just what you decide to do, my pet, as soon as you possibly can. I will be awaiting your answer, as I await the arrival of all your mail. Gee, this would have to happen to us, wouldn't it. And just when things were beginning to look so rosy. Oh, well, it just goes to prove that you can never be quite sure of anything the Navy says or does. They are worse than women when it comes to changing plans. I love you.

This morning all I had time to do was my laundry and after dinner I showered, shaved, washed my hair, and started this letter. While I was shaving a fellow came in and started telling me that his wife was coming out to camp this afternoon and that he had to work. Softie that I am I volunteered to work for him so that he could be with his wife. It will only be for about an hour and a half, though, so I don't mind. He probably would do the same for me and I know darn well that I would want someone to do it if you were going to visit me at camp. After I told him I would work, he even offered to pay me for taking over for him. As if I could accept anything for that, as bad as I need the dough.

I may drop a few lines to my mother and Vene after supper, cause I owe them both a letter. Perhaps I will feel more like writing then. Gee, I haven't written my mother in so darn long, she probably feels that I've forgotten her.

Give my fond regards to all the family and our friends. Here is my special hug and kiss for our Jackie and any million more to the sweetest most lovely wife in all the world. I love you angel, more than you will ever know.

As ever, your *Johnny*

Note on flap: "Hi, sweet, hope this isn't too disappointing to you. I love you."

Monday, February 5, 1945. Ann home because of her teeth. Started to clean out office while Ann went to dentist in morning. After lunch Ann stayed with Jackie while I went downtown. Took all my money out of bank, $324.00. Deposited $40 for Mil. Called for Judy's medicine at drug store and brought them back to Mil. When Gracie came home, Ann & I took the 3:45 train to Newark to Penn Station. Arrived too late to put in request for Pullman reservation. Bought two dresses on way back.

Tuesday, February 6, 1945. Letter of Jan. 28th. This morning called to put in Pullman reservation. Lower berth, to Oakland California.

Wednesday, February 7, 1945. *No mail. Packed a few more things. Put them up in dresser. Wrote to Mary.*

[Camp Parks, Shoemaker, California.]
Postmarked February 8, 1945, 'Free'   *February 7, 1945*
                                                                                      <u>*Same Place*</u>

Hello, Sweetheart:

I love you, miss you and want you more as each ay slowly passes. I long to hold you tenderly in my arms, kiss you, caress you and tell you of my love and adoration. Gee, dearest one, if only we could be together for good. More than anything else in the world I desire to make a happy, comfortable, loving home for you and our family. You are my one and only, my precious one, and no one can ever take your place in my heart. It sure is hell, being away from you.

My humble apologies for not writing since Sunday, darling, but I've been quite busy trying to find out something about conditions down around Port Hueneme. Here is the result of my quest. Homes, apartments, rooms, trailers and everything else a person could live in are as scarce as hens' teeth. There are several hundred families there with no place to live. They are sleeping in hotel lobbies and anywhere else there is a little protection from the weather. So, until I get down there to see for myself just how things are, you had better forget about coming out here to the west coast. Looks like you waited just a little too long, angel and I am really a sorry, disgusted Seabee. I was looking forward to spending a few weeks with you and now it looks as if we won't be able to.

When I arrive there, I will look around and see what I can do, but I don't have much hope. Darn it, why the devil couldn't we have stayed here for a couple more months. Then we would have been together again, even if only for a short while. However, there is one ray of sunshine in our lives, and although it isn't definite, I feel quite certain that I will get an embarkation leave after we are at Hueneme for awhile. We aren't entitled to one until we are back from our leave four months, so you can hope and pray that I get it. The nineteenth battalion, which is going down there with us, has been promised fifteen days shortly after they arrive there. They came back to the states about a month previous to us. That means that we are due our leave about a month later than they. We will probably get ours after they return from theirs. Gee, it sure will be swell being with you again, even if it is for only five days. That isn't much to look forward to but it is better than nothing. Enough for that, my lovely one. It makes me feel badly enough just trying not to think of our bad luck. Perhaps it's just as well, though, because this weather out here wouldn't be any too good for our Jackie. She seems to have quite a few colds and the change of climate may cause her to be more susceptible. I love you.

I saw Fitz today and he said that his papers came in this morning's mail. He hasn't set the date yet though, so I have nothing more to report on that subject. Forbes hasn't been around lately so I can't tell you how he is progressing, either. He is still trying hard to return to the battalion though. Blosser and Andrews are quite undecided what to do with their wives although both have relatives down around Los Angeles. Personally, they would be damned fools if they didn't take their wives down there. I know darned well that there would be no doubt in my mind as to what to do. And Andy is also wondering whether to take his car down, or to sell it. He hasn't found out whether he can get gasoline or not, or if he can drive down. Boy, I would surely have most of that all settled by now, that is, if it was at all possible to do so. But that isn't my headache, I have my own to care for. Gee, I sure wish you were coming out.

That's all I have to tell you from here, my adorable one, so I will answer your last two letters. They are the ones of January thirtieth and February second. Before I go any farther, you might be interested to know that my cold is just about gone again. Very seldom do I cough and I have no sore throat or anything else. My nose doesn't run as much as it formerly did, either. Maybe it's because I've been eating a lot of raw onions. Gosh, but I love you.

Gee, Jackie sure seems to have a lot of colds and stuff lately, doesn't she. I don't blame you for calling the doctor, angel. I'll bet my sweet little wife worries plenty when something like that happens, too. Darn it, why the devil can't I get there so as to be a help to you. I probably wouldn't be anything but moral support, but that would help you, perhaps. Swollen glands, a sore throat, and a cold. Gosh, no wonder she didn't feel like eating anything. I doubt very much if I would care to eat, either. But I'm glad she is feeling much better now and is more able to eat a little. (That's a hell of a composing job, isn't it. The sentence, I mean.) Gee, sweet, it must be tough on you when our little sweetheart isn't feeling well. But, dear, believe it or not, I am never in the least bit worried about Jackie because I know darn well that she has a mother who will do her best. I'm proud of you, my pet, and love you more than you will ever realize.

That package you sent to Mary sure reached her in good time, didn't it. And as they are probably scarce out there, she probably was glad to get it. But I still can't see why she would want one. She's a swell gal, though, and I'm glad you two are corresponding. She'll have a lot to talk to you about when she gets back, I'll bet. But maybe she'll be like some others and not care to talk of her experiences. I adore my lovely wife.

That sure was a delayed letter that Ralph received from me, wasn't it. Gosh, it's no wonder I haven't heard from him. I don't have the slightest idea how that letter ever got out into the office, but anyway, I'm glad that you found it and sent it on with a note of explanation. I'll be looking forward to receiving his letter and will be sure to answer it as soon as I possibly can find time to.

As I told you, precious one, you didn't have to put the spaghetti in with the sauce, but as long as you did, it's okay by me. I also hope the jar doesn't break and that the sauce keeps until after I consume it. Then I don't care what happens to it. I will be anticipating it with relish. Thanks loads, sweet. Thanks also for acquiring so many cigarettes, my love. I hadn't any idea that you were sort of passing the hat for me. But as they are still quite hard to get, I will enjoy them immensely. About all I can ever manage to get are the off brands, such as mentholated Spuds, Pall Malls, wings, etc. Camels are very hard to get so here's hoping that's what they are, but any of the three most popular brands will be graciously accepted, and smoked. I won't give any away, either. Thank all the donors for me, will you, and tell them how much I appreciate their thoughtfulness? We may be able to get them down at Hueneme. I'll let you know all about everything down there as soon as I find things out.

As you start your letter of the second by mentioning that special delivery letter you sent me, I want to inform you that one of those stamps doesn't help any at all when the mail is coming to me. The only time it would save from me to you would be from the local post office to you. In other words, instead of waiting for the regular delivery, the letter is delivered personally, as soon as it reaches the post office to which the letter is addressed. So don't bother to send special delivery mail to your loving hubby anymore. It's a needless expense. We don't even have to sign for them out here.

You may as well go to Fran's with Vene because there isn't much sense of going down there via buses. That would be asking a little too much, especially in the weather you have been describing to me lately. Let me know how everything is down there, and if there are any visible changes. Did you now that Fran told Vene that she intended asking me to be Godfather to the new little Kugler? She hasn't asked me yet, however, as I think maybe she has changed her mind. I would probably have to become so by proxy, however, so maybe it would be better if she had someone else.

I did finally manage to write to my mother and Vene on Sunday, so both of them will be more pleased with me now. I also offered my apologies for not writing sooner. They are the only ones who write so the rest can wait for mail from me. Vene also is trying to get a carton of Camel's from the fellow across the street for me. Boy, I sure do have a few friends back there, even if they are most all on your side of the family. To be truthful, I think a heck of a lot more of my in-laws than I do most of my family. But then, as you are as much sweller than I am, your family also should be better than mine.

Gosh, what a memory I have. I had forgotten about Mil being with child. Maybe I should jot these things down once in awhile. Don't you wish, even a little, that you were in the same condition? Gee, it would be swell for Jackie to have a little playmate just about now. But you're the boss, sweet. Anything you say goes. And I DO want to be there when our second little bundle of loveliness comes along.

Glendale's has been sending that bill to my mother for the past couple of years, off and on and as she swears that it has been paid, well, I guess it will continue to be sent. I don't even now what it's all about but it sounds like a corsage, or something, for only three dollars. Forget it, my sweet.

Our daughter certainly is progressing rapidly, my love. That sentence was very well constructed, even though her diction wasn't quite perfect. It sure was a surprise to me to read of it so I can imagine how you felt when you heard it. But this business about her picking my socks up and calling them mine sounds a little far-fetched to me. Are you quite sure that you didn't mention them in any way? She may have associated the color with her pappy, never-the-less, and remembered. She probably has forgotten me before this, so I won't look forward to having her remember me. It certainly would make me feel good if she did, though. She's a remarkable child, sweetheart, and you are doing a wonderful job of bringing her up. I am more proud of you with each advance Jackie makes because you are teaching her, even if it's only by mimicking you. I can truthfully say that I have the most wonderful wife and sweetheart in all the world.

That answers your letters, sweet, but I must remark on what you put inside the envelope. Oakland is the last stop on the line and you could have depended on me being there to meet you. I would have met you no matter where you landed. I thought I made that clear in my previous letter. But that's right, you hadn't received my answer to your special delivery letter at the time of writing, had you. Not only that, but you may now stop being nervous because you don't have to travel. (Damn it!) It would be too tough on you bringing Jackie across country anyway, so perhaps it's just as well that things turned out the way they did. But that doesn't help my personal feelings any, nor does it yours. You won't have to worry about me overindulging in alcoholic beverages anymore, either, because I've realized what a fool I was. In the past two or three weeks I haven't had more than a dozen small beers. Last night I went over across the compound with a couple of guys and had four beers. That's all I could stand, believe it or not, because I was so darn full, I couldn't take another, even if they paid me to take it. One of them drank five and the other seven and they were both satisfied. It was Pabst beer, too, so you know darn well that I could have gone for more. I ate just before we went over, though, so that's what caused my fullness. The beer hall is about a mile from here and we have to wear undress blues in order to get in. The place is open nightly from five-thirty until eight o'clock. There are quite a few fellows who go over every night they don't have liberty, too. They can't do without the stuff, I guess.

Gosh, sweetie pie, I almost forgot to tell you some news that may be interesting to you. It suits me fine, or rather, it will, if it happens. Harold Gibbons, a fellow from New York who runs around with Fitz once in awhile works with the plumbers. He came up to me today and asked me if I was going to stand up for, or with, Fitz. Boy, you could have knocked me over with a steam-roller, or something. I told him that the prospective bridegroom hadn't asked me yet but that I would be glad to, if he did. It seems that Fitz said he was going to ask me. I sure am becoming popular, aren't I. He may ask someone else, though, so don't depend on it. He is a changeable fellow, alright. I think I'll try to get to see the ceremony, if I can arrange it, even though I am not the best man. Then I could tell Mr. and Mrs. Fitzpatrick all about it. I will also inform my closest pal, my adorable wife, all about it, too. Too bad they can't have a nice wedding and reception like we had, but the war has made many changes, hasn't it. Ours sure turned out swell, didn't it.

My fond regards to all the family and our friends, my sweetheart. My special hug and kiss for Jackie and millions more to you. Thanx for sending your hugs and kisses too. You are the most magnificent and lovable girl in the world. I love you,

Sincerely, your adoring *Johnny*

Note on flap: Sweetheart, I adore you. Here's a kiss for Mickey. Is she itching for me? Love.

Thursday, February 8, 1945. Received letter of Feb. 2 and Hospitalization bill. Woke to find it snowing very heavily. Ironed all day. Could not get reservation for the 26th. Train's all sold out.

Friday, February 9, 1945. No mail. Called to make reservation for March 9th. Lovely day. 4 inches of snow on ground. Brought Jackie out in morning while I shoveled walk. Took one picture. Mil & Judy over for supper.

Saturday, February 10, 1945. *Letter of Feb 4ᵗʰ. Jackie slept until 10:00. Cleaned house. Put Jackie out side with Grandma in afternoon. 5:00 went downtown with Ann and Fan. No reservation for March 9.*

Sunday, February 11, 1945. *Went to 8:00 mass. Very slippery out. Gene brought Mama G & Tadone up in morning. Joe and Angie here at 2:00. Jackie very sociable with everyone. Started to knit sacque. We think Jackie has the measles.*

[Camp Parks, Shoemaker, California.]
Postmarked February 15, 1945, 'Free'

February 11, 1945
Same Place

Hello, Adorable:

I love you so very much, my sweetheart. I long to hold you tenderly in my arms and kiss you. You are the most wonderful girl in all the world and I am proud to call you my own. I long to be with you. I miss you and want you more each day, dearest one. Just to be able to hold you in my arms again would seem heavenly. We belong together, adorable one, and the sooner we are in our own home the more happy I will be. But this war will soon be over, lovely one, and then our life of happiness will begin. I will do my best to make you the most well-satisfied wife in all the world. I adore and worship you, my dearest one.

Thanks loads for sending all the cigarettes, darling. They really are coming in handy. I have to keep them hidden, tho, cause if I left them out, someone might help themselves and I desire keeping them myself. I received both packages and the spaghetti the same day. But, as I feared, the starch in the spaghetti caused it to sour. I think the sauce itself would have kept alright, though. Thanks for trying it though, my sweet. I must say that you packed it well, too. Don't bother trying it again, darling, because it's too much trouble for you. I can wait until I am with you, anyway, and I know darn well that all my food tastes better when you are sitting across from or beside me. That's a swell cigarette case you sent to me, angel. Thanks loads for it. I promise to keep it and take good care of it. It's darned seldom they are large enough to hold a pack of cigarettes, either. This one is ample, holding even a couple more than a full pack. All the fellows like it, too. And as you were so thoughtful in having it initialed, even if it is lost, it may be returned and there is less chance that it will be "borrowed." Thanks again, my love. I am even using it during working hours because it keeps my cigarettes from becoming mashed. Oh yes, unlike other cases, the springs in this one aren't so strong that they cause the butts to become mashed in the case. All in all, this is the best case I've ever seen and I even prefer it to the ones with the lighter attached. Thanks again, angel, for everything. Gosh, but I love you.

Lou, darling, I'm sorry I haven't written more often this week, but I just couldn't make myself. I'm quite down-hearted about not being able to have you here with me but perhaps it's all for the best. And after you went to all the trouble of withdrawing your hard-saved money, made reservations and all that, too. You probably have done a lot of packing or preparing of wearing apparel, too. Darn it, sweet, why the devil can't they let us know exactly how long we are going to remain in one place, so that we are able to make plans. There is a notice on the bulletin board saying that there is a <u>possibility</u> that we <u>may</u> go to Port Hueneme and that the battalion has found that dwellings of any kind are very hard to find close to the base. Both words that I have underlined are the same in the notice as are several more. Again, there is a possibility of future changes, so perhaps you had better forget all about coming out here with Jackie. Anything is liable to happen so there is no use in you taking a chance on my being here or wherever I'm supposed to be. I wish I could get transferred to the east coast. Anywhere along the east coast would be much better than being stationed here. The notice I mentioned before also said that we <u>may,</u> also underlined, be down at Hueneme for several months. That is rather encouraging but also very indefinite. Damn it, sweet, I want to be there with you. Maybe I'll call you the fifteenth, but even if I don't you will know I was thinking of you. Here's hoping the cards arrived on time. I even sent one to the Kuglers congratulating them on the new arrival. I hope you don't mind. I know that you sent one but I merely happened to see one and sent it. Birthday cards were received from Ann, Fan, and your mother, by me, besides the ones sent by my wife and lovely daughter. That's all I received, too. None of my family remembered, so far, but it is expected. Perhaps Vene and my mother will send one but I really don't expect one from mom as it's probably hard for her to get around to do any but important shopping.

I haven't seen Forbes since I last wrote you, but I think he is still around, trying to get back here. Fitz hasn't become united with his wave yet because she hasn't received her necessary papers from home yet. Perhaps her mother doesn't approve and decided not to send them. I can't blame her for being anxious about her daughter's future, though, can you? But they are both old enough to know what they're doing so why not let them go ahead, with blessings. Gosh, I'm rattling on as if you were the one holding things up. I'm sorry, sweet.

I can't think of anything to write about, unless it's what you had on the envelope of your last letter. Boy, oh boy, do you think something like a little cold would keep me from doing my best to satisfy you? Hell, honey, even a pair of broken arms couldn't do that. I'm not ashamed of anything I've done with you and intend doing it all again sometime. And the sooner it can be, the more satisfied I will be. Besides, my cold has practically disappeared and I am taking better care of myself, for you and only you. I love you.

I was working on the chow line again today because Paul Andrews wanted to be with his wife. Maybe I'm a little too generous with my time but I couldn't say no when he asked me. I think I would even do that for my enemies, if I had any. I know darn well that I would want someone to help me out if I was working so I understand his feelings. I often wonder if I would ask someone to work for me, if you were out here. Do you think I would, sweet? At times I doubt it and at others I am quite sure I would. But I don't have to worry about that now, do I. I wouldn't worry about it anyway cause I know darn well that I would be doing all I possibly could to be with you every possible moment, for as long as possible.

We have a radio in the hut again now and the darn thing is continually going, even when there is no one here. There have even been times when I've come into an empty place and it's been blaring away wearing itself out with no one listening. Some of the guys even want to hook it up so we can play it after the lights have to be turned out at nine-thirty. Not only that, but few of the folks are satisfied with the program on and someone is always changing it. Seldom does a program start and finish, unless no one is paying attention to it.

Thursday is going to be another extra blue day for me, angel. Gosh, we've been married all this time and have only been together on our wedding day and none of our anniversaries. We haven't been together any Xmas' or Jackie's birthdays, either. Darn we haven't been together hardly at all, have we. But someday we will start making up for all we've missed and we'll keep trying until we are old and ready for the next world. Never will we be able to catch it, though, cause our lives will be too full of happiness and love to let any extra in. Complete happiness will come for me only when you and I are together again. I love you, miss you and want you, my adorable angel. Give my fond regards to all the folks at home. Here is my special hug and kiss for Jackie, and millions more for the swellest girl in the world, my wife.

As ever, your devoted *Johnny*

Note on flap: "Darling, I love you more than life itself. May we be together sooner than you or I expect. I love you."

Monday, February 12, 1945. Johnnie's birthday. Received Anniversary & Valentine cards from Johnny and a birthday card for Jackie. A valentine for Jackie from Carol Ann. Letter from Mary. Washed Jackie's clothes, knitted on saque. Ann made reservations for Los Angeles, Mar. 9, and from Chicago Mar. 11. Brushed teeth for first time with toothbrush.

[Camp Parks, Shoemaker, California.]
Postmarked February 13, 1945 'Free.'

February 12, 1945
Sunny California

Hello Sweetest:

All the love in the world is ours. My happiness won't be complete until I can once again hold you in my arms and tell you of my love and adoration. I miss you and want you, my sweetheart. I am now another year older, so here's hoping I am not too old to satisfy you when I return home. The way I feel right now, I never will become that way. My day today was very much like every other day, except that I drank about eight or nine cups of coffee and I received another letter from you, my precious wife. It was dated only three days ago and postmarked the day before yesterday. Gosh, wouldn't it be swell if I could cross the country that fast? Boy, that would give me eleven days with you instead of five, as we'll have. Darn, that five days will pass rapidly, won't it. But it's a lot better than not being with you at all, won't it. Maybe after I get to Port Hueneme I will find out that we can be together for a month or two, but we'll have to wait and find out about that. If you only had someone to leave Jackie with, I would ask you to come out to Los Angeles, anyway, even if you had to come out all the way by day coach. Would you do that, just to be with your ever-loving husband? I'm hungry, sweet.

We are leaving here a week from Wednesday for our next camp. Liberty will be secured on Monday morning of next week, so these fellows with their wives here are trying to get out every night this week. I let one of them have my liberty card tonight and unless something important comes up in the meantime, I will let him have it Wednesday and over the weekend. It's hard telling what Fitz may do this week, so I can't be sure. Another fellow told me today that he intended asking me to be his best man, so maybe he will. If he does, I sure will. When I see him next time I will offer your congratulations and best wishes. I intend asking them to have a picture taken, too. Not only for you, but also for their parents. They will both be welcome at our home anytime, too, so I will tell them that, too. (Gee, I sure am using bad grammar or something, aren't I?)

My new address is:

John de Roxtro, EM1/c, U.S.N.R.
15ᵗʰ .C.B., A.B.D.
Port Hueneme,
California.

That may be the same as it was the last time I was down there. I can't seem to remember just what it was way back then. Anyway, it doesn't matter very much. As long as that U.U.W. doesn't come around very soon, I will be quite satisfied, especially if you and I are able to be with each other. I've been over there long enough, so I'll be satisfied to remain in the states for another year or so.

As I don't have anything more to write of from over on this side of the continent, I will merely answer your letter and close. Gee, sweetheart, I sure wish we could be in each other's arms again, to remain forever. I want so very much to perform my duties as a hubby. Sweetest, most adorable wife in the world, I am hungry for you, and only you can satisfy my hunger. Gosh, darling, you are the most wonderful girl in the world and I adore you.

As you may have noticed, I am not using my pen tonight. This is a very small one I borrowed cause I dropped mine and the point bent. So, I will have to get another nib put in. It still writes and holds ink but I'm afraid if might catch and splatter ink all over the paper. So I merely borrowed this one. While on the subject, you will have to pardon the indelible pencil used on the cards. You see, I was downtown to purchase the cards, and that's all I could get ahold of while down there. I had intended taking my pen down with me, but as usual, I forgot it. Hell, I'm always forgetting something. I can't forget you, ever, though.

I hadn't intended writing you about how badly I felt when my cold was so bad but I thought you might be interested in knowing why I hadn't written.

Sweetheart, I don't know what to say about you coming out now because I don't know just what to expect when we get down there. Some people say rooms will be impossible to get and others that it will be easy to get one. So, you see how things stand. Maybe you had better forget the whole thing and just wait for me to come home to you. I sure would like to have you with me, though. Damn the Navy for not letting us know what we can expect. Be sure to give my thanks to both Ann and her girlfriend Cleo for helping you and that I am also sorry I put them t so much unnecessary trouble. Darn the Navy and the war again.

Adorable angel, my utmost desire is to be with you. I want so much to be able to kiss you and make love to you as I should. I long to feel your lovely body close to mine. Sweetheart, I am more than ready and I know that you are also. For five days and nights we will be in bed for as long as we possibly can, won't we. But what if your girlfriend is there? What will we do then, but make love?

Regards to all. Hugs & kisses to you and Jackie. Eternally, your loving,

Johnny

Note on flap: *"That kiss below is meant only for all of you, not everyone. I'll kiss your entire body when next we meet. Dearest one, I miss you and want you. Here's a kiss for all of you. Love, JdR"*

February 13, 1945 – Americans and British fire bomb raids on Dresden, Germany and kill 25,000.

Tuesday, February 13, 1945. *Michael Petrone Jr.'s birthday. Received letter of Feb 7. Valentine & birthday card for Jackie & anniversary card for me from Ann. Anniversary card from Martha. Started to snow in morning. Cold. Turned to sleet in afternoon.*

Wednesday, February 14, 1945. *Michael Petrone Sr. birthday. Received Valentine for Jackie from Michael Jr. and a bracelet from Mary. Ash Wed. Ann, Fan, & I went to 7:00 mass. Received Valentine cards from Michael, Bonnie & Nancy, Grace, Grandma. When Gracie came home went downtown, post office, Sandrian's, drugstore. Mil & Judy here for supper. Walked them home.*

[Camp Parks, Shoemaker, California.]
Postmarked February 15, 1945, stamp upside down.   *February 14, 1945*
                                                                    <u>*Same place*</u>

My Adorable Darling:

I love you, miss you and want you. You are my Valentine, sweetheart, and always will be. Our hearts have been intertwined for only a short while but they are welded together forever. Sweetest girl in all the world, little Dan Cupid sure scored a bulls eye when he aimed your arrow at me and you can bet that the love and adoration that was on that arrow tip was deeply imbedded to remain forever. I long to hold you tenderly in my arms once again and kiss your luscious lips, to feel your lovely body pressing against mine as we, entirely unclothed are performing our duties as a married couple should. Oh, my angel, how I long to be able to awaken in the morning and look beside me and find you. That would really be heavenly. Adorable one, after we are reunited permanently, we will be so completely happy. The three of us and maybe more, will be so happy together then. Angel, I worship you.

No mail came from you today, my lovely one, but I did receive a birthday card from my mother, and, believe it or not, a letter from Ralph. He told me how pleased he was to hear all about home from me, in my own way, just as I saw it when I returned, and how he was glad everyone was so well and happy. He didn't even seem very sad or down-hearted in this letter so I guess he was temporarily down-cast when he wrote that letter to you. He was also talking about his two years being up in another four months. Gee,

387

wouldn't it be swell if he could get to come home this summer? Then I'm quite sure he wouldn't have to return out again. Maybe, if we remain in the states for another six months or so I won't have to go out again either. Here's hoping I never have to leave these shores again. Of course, if we decide to take a little ocean voyage together, that would be a horse of another color. I would like to take you for a little trip sometime. My sweetheart, I adore you. I'm hungry.

Forbes finally got back into the battalion again and he sure is happy about it. He looks much better than he has for a long while, too. He was put in company B, so he won't be with me very much. We probably will be out on different jobs and everything, but I'm quite sure we won't be separated completely. That is unless he has to leave the outfit again because of his malaria. He told me again that he still owed you a letter, and that he would get it off just as soon as he can get in the mood. He must be similar to me in that he has to get in the mood before he can write. Anyway, he's a swell fellow and I wish him the best of luck.

Fitz is getting married on Friday, the sixteenth. Too bad it couldn't have been on Thursday instead, then it would have been another reason for celebrating so much on our day. But maybe it's just as well, because after all, that day is ours, and nothing should come on that day. We should be together tomorrow, my sweet, but our Uncle Sam seems to want to keep us apart awhile. So far Fitz hasn't asked me to be best man, but he did ask me not to go out Friday night. There were always quite a few fellows around whenever he saw me, so maybe that's why he didn't say anything about it. He seems not to want too many fellows to know about it, but most of them do by now, anyway. Gosh, sweet, I hope they are as happy as we have been, are now, and always will be. Most precious, you are my dream girl.

When the sixth battalion was down at Port Hueneme they got twenty days leave so maybe we will too. Boy, that would give us ten days together. Honey, I sure do wish we were going to be together longer than that. I want you with me wherever I go. I love you so very much, angel mine, that it hurts terribly to be separated from you. And you have no idea how I miss our Jackie, either.

Give my regards to all the folks at home and tell mom about Ralph feeling more satisfied with his lot. Here's my special hug and kiss for our Jackie and millions more for you, the swellest girl in all the world. I adore you.

Everlastingly, your loving *Johnny*

Note on flap: "Angel, I miss you more as each day passes. Here's a kiss for Mickey. Pet her a little for me tonite. I adore you."

388

Thursday, February 15, 1945. Received Anniv. cards from Mil & G. and Eleanor and Herb. Went to church 7:00. Lit candle. Home all day. Mama G up today. Brought anniv. gift of two pillow cases for me and a box of Torrones for Johnny. Also two dollars for Jackie's birthday. Rain.

February 16, 1945 - U.S. Troops recapture Bataan in the Philippines.

Friday, February 16, 1945. Anniversary of Fitz & ____Fitzpatrick. Went to church. When Gracie came home from school I took 4:14 train to Newark. Met Ann at Kresge Department Store. Went to Penn Station to purchase reservation ticket. Couldn't get it until they contacted Chicago. Will go again either Sunday or Monday. Met Fan in station. 6:00 took bus to Jo's house. Mike just going to work. Jo took us out to Star, had antipasto, pizza, beer. Took 7:45 train home.

Saturday, February 17, 1945. Received letter of February 14 and a birthday card from Uncle Joe and Aunt Angie for Jackie, $2.00 enclosed. Mom and Gracie went to Newark after lunch. Girls went to Movies. Judy here and Mil & Gene went out to dinner.

Sunday, February 18, 1945. Went to 8:00 mass. Mama G and Tadone up. Tadone not so well, another boil coming out. Joe and Angie did not come. 4:30 the girls and I went to the Community to see "Frenchman's Creek." Good.

[Camp Parks, Shoemaker, California.]
Postmarked February 19, 1945, stamp upside down.   *February 18, 1945*

Same Place

Hi, Sweets:

I love you more than life itself. I long to hold you tenderly in my arms and kiss you once again. You are the most adorable girl in the all the world and to be with you again is my one desire. Sweetheart, you are adorable. Gosh, my sweet, you mean more to me than anything else in the world. You're wonderful.

I'm not in much of a mood for writing tonight, my sweet, so this may be quite short. I'm glad you received the cards in time and that you liked them. They were about the best I could find in Oakland and I sure looked all over. It took me about two hours to select them, too. I do think once in awhile of those little things that make you more pleased with married life, don't I. Gosh, but you're swell.

Fitz got married Friday night at nine o'clock and I was the best man. Your best wishes were conveyed to the newlyweds, too. I was in the sack, reading, when a messenger came down from our OD's office saying I was wanted at the base chaplain's office immediately. So naturally I arose, dressed in my dress blues, and went up. That was the shortest and most uninteresting ceremony I ever witnessed. The girls were in their uniforms and wore corsages of gardenias. The bride wept afterwards, too. That's all there was to it. Merely a few words spoken by the chaplain and they became man & wife. Gee, I sure am glad we had a nice wedding. You were so beautiful in all your finery. Even now, after all you've had to go through, you are the most beautiful girl in the world. More and more, as time slowly passes, I love you.

My cold was gone, most completely, but this morning I awoke with the sniffles again. I'll take care of it though, so I should be rid of it before the end of the month.

Adorable one, I'm sure glad you are coming out here to me. Gosh, but it'll be swell holding you in my arms again. As you know, it may be quite difficult to find a desirable place to reside, but I promise to do my best. Naturally, I will meet you in Los Angeles. The powers that be will give me a special liberty to do that, I am positive. All you will have to do is let me know when you are due in. By that I mean the day and approximate hour. I'll be there, so don't worry about that anymore. As for there being rooms or anything around the terminal at Chicago, I wouldn't know sweet but I am sure you won't have any trouble finding a place to stay overnight. You can find out by asking at the information desk. The terminal is similar to ours but much larger, I think. I haven't seen much of it, myself.

I still don't know exactly where we will be stationed down south so I can't tell you anything more about that. As I told you before, we are leaving Wednesday evening and should arrive there sometime Thursday morning. L.A. is about four hundred miles south of here.

You should receive this before the twenty-sixth, so you will know what I am going to do, at least, as much as I know. No, I wouldn't advise trying to secure reservations any earlier than the ninth, because even then, I will only have a couple of weeks to locate a place for my two sweethearts to live.

Please don't be nervous my lovely one, because you won't have any trouble at all. Oh, yes, you can easily find the track from which the train leaves by consulting either the boards in the lobby, or asking some conductor or other employee. All trains are announced over a public address system anyway, so there's no need to worry about that.

I'm glad you were able to get a lower birth from Chicago out anyway, and it won't be too bad as far as Chicago. You will only have one night in the upper anyway. Gosh, sweet, I'm anxiously awaiting your presence.

I am anxiously awaiting your arrival out here, my beloved angel.

Won't I be a happy Seabee when the three of us are together, though. I can hardly wait for you two lovely girls here. Gosh, I love you, Lou. And I'm going to have such pleasant times with you. I may not have much time to play with our Jackie but at least I will have some weekends to play with her and maybe, if I can get you located close enough to me, she won't be in bed before I arrive. Say, if I can't get an apartment or two rooms, how about a room with two beds? I'll just take a room, if possible, until you arrive to pick out a place for yourself, but if I can find a nice place, I'll grab it quick. My most adorable angel, I adore you, and can hardly wait until you are with me again.

Give my fond regards to all the folks back at home, especially Mama G and Tadone. They're swell people, my sweet. The lovely daughter of ours will be kissed by her daddy in person soon, but give her my special hug and kiss anyway. To you, sweetheart, I give all my love and adoration. May we be together real soon and be happy much longer than we anticipate. I love you.

Eternally, your loving hubby, *Johnny*

Note on flap: "Adorable, I love you. Here's many hugs and kisses. Yours forever."

February 19-March 16, 1945 – U.S. Marines invade Iwo Jima.

Monday, February 19, 1945. *Cpl. Ralph Petrone's birthday. Received letter of February 11 and Feb 12th. Grace home for the week. (fuel conservation). Ann couldn't get reservation. Must call for it again, tomorrow. Wrote to Ralph. Got period.*

Tuesday, February 20, 1945. *Call from Penn. Said they had a lower berth for me from Newark to Chicago. Call from M.deR. Coming to see us on Friday. Ann picked up ticket for me. Packed sauce to send to Johnnie.*

[Camp Parks, Shoemaker, California.]
Postmarked February 20, 1945, stamp upside down.

February 20, 1945
Pneumonia Valley

My most adorable Darling:

Honey, a long time I didn't see from the peoples. I am longing to holding your so lovely body close to mine. Skip all this, my sweet. I'm not in the mood to keep it up. Love you, miss you and want you so very, very much, sweetheart. You are the most adorable girl in all the world and you're mine, to have and to hold, very soon, I hope. I won't be completely happy until we are together again. Gee, won't it be swell, honey, when we are able to eat and sleep and be with each other once in awhile again. I can hardly wait until we are once more entwined in each other's arms. Just think, in a few more weeks we will be holding hands and making love. You're the swellest wife any fellow ever

391

had, my sweet, and I'm the lucky guy to have won you. I still don't know how I ever managed it, but you can bet your boots that I'll never regret it. Also that I'll do my best to make you as happy as you possibly can be. You and I together will be envied by all our friends and neighbors, because we have such a delightful family. Won't it be swell when we are able to live in our own home and never be bothered by another mess like this. I adore and worship you, my lovely angel.

Your letter of the fifteenth came today, sweet. Thanks for the anniversary wishes, angel mine. I'm only sorry that we couldn't have been together. Maybe next year we will be, lovely one. Here's hoping that we are reunited before then, long before.

Jackie may have a slight touch of measles, but I doubt it. All that rash probably is from something she has eaten. Measles etc., usually start breaking out on the body where there is more warmth, don't they? I'm not too certain of that, but I think so. Anyway, don't worry about it because she will have all those things during her life as a child, anyway, so the sooner she gets over them, the better. A few of the fellows out here have them too, but nothing is being done about it, as far as confinement is concerned.

Blosser was in town with his wife the other night and was taken so ill they had to call the ambulance out from here. The doctors haven't told him what's wrong as yet, but I think he is worrying too much about Evelyn's pregnancy. He always did have bad digestion, anyway, so it's probably nothing but nervous indigestion. Someone told me that the doctors seem to think he's only goldbricking.

I'm glad you got the tickets and everything, sweet. You may be taking a chance in coming out but we can find someplace to live even if it's only a temporary place until we can get something better. I'll do my best to locate a decent residence for you two sweethearts of mine and I intend putting my problem before the Red Cross and the A.W.U.S., if I have to. Our chaplain may be able to help a little too. He seems like a pretty decent fellow. Hell, he even eats with the men, instead of the officers. But that may be only to create an impression on us. For some reason or other, I don't trust those gold-braid very much. Must be my suspicious character or something, I guess. But all this is beside the point. I'll have some sort of a place for you, so come on out.

I heard today that some of us are to start our pre-embarkation leave the first of March, with the rest following later. I won't take mine until after you are out here, my sweet. Don't think too much about the title of this leave, because even if we stay here a year, we get one every four months. We may be here a long while.

If you think of it, my darling, will you throw my black shoes and my sweater in one of your bags or trunk? Also my shoe-polishing outfit, will you? I have just about worn my shoes out and unless I get another pair, I can't leave them to be repaired. Just bring them out with you, or send them, if it's easier. That's all I can think of for you to bring. Oh yes, don't forget the marriage certificate and your hospitalization card. Here's hoping you won't need the latter but one can never tell and it's best to be prepared. You can have your mail forwarded to me until we find out your future address too. You can either change it at the post office or have Ann or someone else send it on to you.

I sure do remember that candy you speak of in your letter. It certainly is good and you can give my hearty thanks to Mama G right now, because I know darn well how good it will be. I didn't tell you before but there is an Italian fellow here and he received some from home a couple of months ago. I had some then, too. I intended telling you about it but I never remembered. I love you.

I was talking to Pete Dionisis today and I invited him out to our place sometime when you are having macaroni or spaghetti. Is that okay with you? He's the Italian I previously told you about. He is from New York and quite a swell guy, although a bit dark. But who cares as long as he is a gentleman, huh? We will have to have my gang up sometime too, especially Forbes and Fitz, Andy and Clere. Blosser too if he is around. Andy's a swell guy, sweet. I'm sure you will like him. He's full of the devil most of the time but until you get to know him, he may be quiet and almost bashful.

There is only one more item in your letter that I can comment on and that is the receipt of the bracelet from Mary. It was very thoughtful of her to send it and I am quite sure that our little one will appreciate it when she is a little older. Mary's a swell friend to you, sweetie pie. You're lucky to have such a faithful and thoughtful one. I doubt if I could name one as good and I think I have one or two good ones. We'll have to write her after you come out so I can put my personal thanks on it. I adore my wife.

Sweetheart, please try to keep from getting too nervous and excited about coming way out here with Jackie. Everything will be alright, my sweet, so don't you worry about it at all. Oh, sweet, I almost forgot. Perhaps you should in some manner make reservations at a hotel or something for your overnight stay in Chicago. There may be a scarcity of living quarters there, too. I don't know just how you would go about it but you can find out somehow. There is a U.S.O. in the terminal at Chicago, too, so you could always inquire there. Everything will turn out swell, honey, so don't worry yourself sick about it. Another thing, you may get a break, going from New York to Chicago. Some kind-hearted soul may exchange berths with you. It has been done before, you know. And if you don't accept, I'll beat your ears off. Just a little anyway.

Give my fond regards to all the folks at home and don't forget to thank Mama G for that candy. Here's my special hug and kiss for Jackie, and to you, my adorable one, I send my all. You're the swellest girl in all the world.

Eternally, your loving *Johnny*

Note on flap: "This is my last from here, my sweet. I'll write as soon as I can. Love."

Wednesday, February 21, 1945. *Card for Jackie from Carol Ann. Went to mass. Rain all day. Rain at nite.*

Thursday, February 22, 1945. *No mail delivery. Raining all day. Fan had day off. Went to confession and communion.*

Postmarked February 23, 1945, stamp upside down.

February 22, 1945
Port Hueneme

Hello Sweet:

As you see, I arrived safe and sound, but a little sleepy. We left Parks at five yesterday afternoon and got in here about ten this morning. Believe it or not, it took us five hours to come the last thirty miles, the freight traffic was so heavy. We were riding on old day coaches without room enough to stretch our legs out so you can easily enough see why I am a little sleepy. What with getting squared away and cleaned up, I haven't had any sleep today either. So, as soon as I finish this letter, I am going to hit the sack and I have an idea that I will sleep like a log. This place has really changed since we were here last but I will tell you all about that in the future.

Now, my lovely one, I will tell you all about what you are most interested in, next to my love and adoration for you. I haven't had much time so far to do much inquiring, but rooms etc. aren't too hard to find. At least, you and Jackie will have a nice room. The first chance I get I am going out and look around for something. First of all, I'm going to see what our chaplain has to offer. He's supposed to find out about those things for us, and as we probably won't be able to get liberty for a couple of days, he should find out something.

Who knows, perhaps he can tell me exactly where to go to find a room, I mean. There are a lot of new places going up, I know, because I saw them under construction while on the way down this morning. We may be here only a couple of months, too, because all the work on the base here is being done by civilians. There are even civilian girls going around checking material on hand. Boy, the unions even have the Navy tied up. They sure are powerful

394

here on the West Coast. The Navy can't even build on their own property. So evidently all we are here for is more training.

I'm telling you all this in case you want to change your mind about coming out. I hope you don't, though, as I really want you. As I've told you before, to be with you is my one and only desire. I love you truly.

I love you, darling, with all my heart, body and soul. I miss you, my angel, more than you will ever know and I want you, I long to hold your lovely body close to me and tell you of my love. To feel your soft luscious lips as they press against mine will again be thrilling, and adorable one, when we are lying in bed together, doing those things which a married couple should do, my happiness will be almost complete. Complete happiness won't come until this war is over and we are finally together in our own home. Sweetest sweetheart in all the world, please don't change your mind about coming out here. I love you so very much, and I'm looking forward to being with you. A fellow just came in and said the latest scuttlebutt is that we are to do a four month job down here. That seems almost too good to be true, though, so don't think about it too much.

If today is a sample of what the weather is like down here, I'll be satisfied. The sun was shining bright and it was quite warm. The dampness isn't in the air, either, so my cold may disappear entirely. It feels much better tonight, anyway.

Give my fond regards to all the folks at home. Here's my special hug and kiss for Jackie and millions more for the most wonderful girl in all the world, my wife and sweetheart. Adorable angel I love you, miss you and want you.

Everlastingly, your *Johnny*

Note on flap: "Sweet, all the love in the world is ours. May your happiness continue forever. Love."

Friday, February 23, 1945. Heard for first time that Carol Ann was in hospital for a week with infected tonsils. Letter of Feb 18th from Johnnie. M.deR came at 4:30. Vene called. Nancy broken out in chicken pox. Cards from M.de R - $1.00 for Jackie, $5.00 for me. Had supper with us and stayed until 10:00p.m. Jackie went upstairs and turned on faucet in bathroom for first time. Said she was washing her hands.

Saturday, February 24, 1945. Today is the birthday of Jackie de Roxtro. Went to church. Dressed and fed Jackie and then went to see Carol Ann. Came home. Did housework. Mil and Judy came in afternoon. When girls came home, prepared for Jackie's party. Decorations in red & green. Birthday cake, baskets and surprise packages. Gene and Mil went out to supper. Jackie slept until 4:45. 7:00 had party. Jackie thrilled with *everything. Received gifts from Ann - a green jumper, Fan, a green and brown butcher boy ensemble, Judy - two pink slips, money: $2 from Uncle Joe & Aunt Angie, $2 from Mama G and Tadone, $1 from Gracie, $1 from Nana, $5 from Grandma. Jackie up until 8:30. Gave her Milk of Mag. Tablet*

February 24, 1945, 2 years old

Sunday, February 25, 1945. *Fran's baby christened. Went to 7:00 mass. Met M.d.R. Gave me shoe coupon. Mama G & Tadone up. After dinner M.de R. and Vene dropped in. Stayed until 4:30. 5:15 went to movies with Ann & Fan. Saw "Music for Millions." Very good.*

Postmarked February 26, 1945, stamp upside down.　　*February 25, 1945*

Port Hueneme

Hello, Sweetheart:

　　I love you, miss you and want you very much. You are the most desirable girl in all the world and I really consider myself exceedingly lucky to have wooed and won you. I long to hold you tenderly in my arms once again and kiss you. Also I desire to feel your soft lovely body close to mine. When I awake in the morning, I want to be able to roll over and kiss you. Adorable one, to have you out here with me will really be swell. Even if we are only able to be together for a few short weeks, I want you to come out. I am quite certain of getting about ten or fifteen days with you without having to return to camp, when I get my embarkation leave. Boy, won't that be swell, honey? Even after my leave is up, there is no definite assurance that I will be shoving off right away, so I don't want to return east with you. I want you to stay out here until I get my orders to leave the states. Are you willing to do that? We can talk that over after you get here, though.

　　Don't forget to bring the alarm clock, angel, cause I'll have to get up early in order to get back to camp on time in the morning. Gosh, that's going to be terrible, cause I won't be able to see you until the following night. But even that's a lot better than it is now. Gee, it's going to be swell having you with me again. Why the devil didn't you come out sooner? But you had quite a decision to make and I'm satisfied that you have finally decided to increase my happiness with your lovely presence. I am anxiously awaiting your arrival, sweet. How would you like to go to Hollywood with me after you get settled and a little rested from your trip? We could make it some weekend, easily.

I haven't been out yet because I don't have any dough but this week I intend to borrow some so that I can look around for a place for you and Jackie. Several outfits left here yesterday so I should be able to find a nice place. I'm going to try tomorrow. Saturday will be the first chance I'll have to get out during the day though, so don't expect me to do too much until then. Most of the fellows have found a place already, so it can't be too difficult. I asked Andy to look around over this weekend so maybe he will have some places for me to look at. I suggested that he, his wife, you, Jackie and I live together in an apartment. His wife wants a place where she will be able to cook, too. The trouble with that is I haven't seen her yet, but he's a swell fellow, so she must be okay. Hell, we'll put up with a little discomfort for awhile, won't we. That arrangement may not be satisfactory to either of you gals, though. But don't worry about anything, my lovely one. I will have a place for you even if it's only a trailer. They are quite nice, too, even though they are rather small. I know darn well that you would be able to make it comfortable, but enough of this. I really shouldn't bother you with anything on this end. I'll take care of everything and maybe even have a few groceries in the place for you. I love my wife.

Guess what, angel. Yesterday I received a letter from, believe it or not, Joe Gannon. I sure was surprised. He does write once in awhile. That's more than most of my so-called friends will do. He didn't have much to say except that he was sort of anxious to return to Philly. Seems as if the town etc. are too dead for him. The darn fool doesn't know when he's well off. Why, he even was thinking of joining one of these outfits. Oh well, that's his business. If I was in his place, I know what I'd do. I also received another birthday card from our Alma Mater. That's two this year. Someone must have made an error.

Tomorrow morning we are to start more military training so your old man will probably be very tired tomorrow eve. I haven't had any so far because when the rest of them had it at Parks, I was busy with my mess cooking. I guess it won't hurt me any, so I'll go out and learn to march. At least, they'll try to teach me to do it. Maybe I'll be too dense to learn. I'm not used to walking though, so it won't be easy on poor me.

I just interrupted this little note to go out to the head and drain my kidneys, and I met Forbes. He went to sick-bay this morning to get something for his cold and came back to get a few things to take to the hospital with him. He has the measles. He showed me his stomach and it's covered with the rash. His neck also has same on it. He said there were about a dozen fellows over there with them. So, our buddy will be confined for another ten days. He sure does get the breaks, doesn't he. Gosh, I hope they don't quarantine the entire outfit. But they wouldn't do that. Measles aren't caught very easily by adults. Besides, most of us have had them during childhood, so aren't liable to get them again. By the way, how did the rash on Jackie turn out? It must have disappeared, else you would have mentioned it in this last letter.

The nights are quite cold here, but the days are nice and warm. So bring your warm clothing with you, my angel. I don't think playsuits, or rather, light snow suits would be too warm for Jackie during the early morning and evening, either. I'm going to have my pea coat cleaned this week and one of my uniforms. Then later, the other uniform. I'm afraid I'll have to purchase another pair of shoes, too, sweetheart, even though I intend having these repaired this week also. All of this is going to take some money, but it's a case of necessity so I'll have to have it done. Before we can leave camp, we must subject ourselves to a personal examination so we will look decent. It's a good idea, too, because some of the fellows don't care how they look. I'm not too meticulous, but I don't let myself become too sloppy, or do I?

As that's about all I have to tell you now about things here, I will see if there isn't something to answer in your letter of the nineteenth. I know you will tell me all about Jackie's birthday so I won't say anything about that, except that I wish her a very happy and healthy one. One of these days we are going to be together, the three of us, to celebrate some day. Maybe we'll be together for Easter. That isn't a personal day for us but it's a day to celebrate, anyway. And if we pray hard enough, we may be together to celebrate the fourth of July together.

Mail just came in. Here's hoping I will receive one from my darling adorable wife. I love her. No such luck, angel. Maybe tomorrow, or this afternoon, or Tuesday. I'll just have to wait, I guess, cause there's nothing I can do to speed up delivery of my contact with you. Besides, I don't really care very much, because I'll be seeing you in person very soon and then we'll make up for all our disappointments brought via the mailman.

I still don't know whether you got your reservations through to Los Angeles or not, so I presume you haven't. Or at least hadn't when you wrote this letter. You said you were to return Monday but I guess maybe you hadn't been able to.

That was darned swell of Jo to treat you three gals at the Star but you shouldn't have let her. Heck, honey, I don't want you to become obligated to her or anyone else, or give them a chance to say they did this or that for you. But we'll be able to repay them all some day so I guess it's alright. Besides, I'm glad you were able to get down there again. That place is alright and the food is pretty good for a restaurant, even though you do have to wait quite awhile for it. While on the subject of food, a lot of the fellows are seeking an invitation out to our place so that they can sample some of your food. Perhaps I've been talking too much, as usual. But I'm only asking about half a dozen and not all at once, either. To hell with the rest, I want to be alone with you and Jackie. They are even talking of taking up a collection so you won't have to spend anything. Forbes has been telling them what a good cook you are, too, so you have quite a rep as a good cook and a marvelous, ideal wife. I even think some of these guys envy me. I guess I'll have to keep a good watch over you, or someone will try to steal you. And I couldn't stand that, at all.

It's too bad that Tadone has another carbuncle coming out. He must have something in his blood or system somewhere that causes them. Here's hoping this will be his last one and that his health will improve. Wish him the best of heath for me and also Mama G, of course.

I'll bet Joe and Angie miss coming out to your place every Sunday. They both seemed to enjoy their visits so very much and Joe liked our daughter a lot too. Does Jackie miss him those Sundays when he didn't show up and not realize it?

This is turning out to be quite a letter, and I'm afraid I'll have to interrupt it to go to chow very soon. And I haven't said anything yet, either. Here's hoping this one will be long enough to suit you, but if you are like me, you could go on reading forever. They can't be too long to suit me.

Gee, I can't quite believe that a whole month passed without you going to the theatre, but anything can happen, I guess. You may go longer than that, even, after you get out here. But if you so desire it, my love, we three will go every night we are together.

Don't bother sending me any sauce, sweetheart, because I will be willing to wait until we are united again and you are sitting across the table from me. Besides as I am not working around the mess hall, I may be unable to heat it, or to acquire the macaroni. If you have already sent it, however, I will make sure that it doesn't go to waste. Even if I have to eat it cold, without anything but bread. Besides, it's quite a bit of trouble to you. Darling, I love you.

Dearest one, I really do like this cigarette case very much and wouldn't part with it for anything. I also prefer it to the leather cases because they allow the cigarettes to become mashed, almost as bad as the ordinary package does. This case just fits in my pocket and there is practically no chance of losing it, it fits so snugly. Thanks again for being so thoughtful, angel. I've used the case ever since I received it, whether working or not. And as you will see when you come out, it has seen some hard use. Quite a bit of the black on the back has already chipped off but as the case underneath has been chromed, it's alright. It won't rust or anything. In fact, it's an ideal case, and you used expert judgment when you picked it out. Thanks again and here's a few kisses in part payment for your thoughtfulness. You are the most wonderful wife and sweetheart any fellow ever had and I love and adore you. May your happiness be complete very soon. My angel, I want you. I worship you.

Well, beloved, I have returned from my noon chow, so I will continue with this letter. I won't tell you what we had, but the chow here isn't quite as good as it was when we were in Parks. It is just fair, although the coffee is better and I drink plenty.

As for you coming out here, sweet, let's look at it this way. You and Jackie are coming out to California to take a little vacation. And while here, you will be visited by your loving hubby. You will be together every other night and every other weekend, and we will all be very happy. After I receive orders to ship out, you and Jackie will then proceed home, if you so desire, or remain here on the coast. All those details will have to be taken care of later, however, so the main thing is for you to get out here. You will receive this and previous letters on or before the first of the month so I won't bother using the phone and causing you more expense. Besides, you never told me what the last call cost, and I asked you to. Regardless of anything else, you come out, quickly. You know how much I want you, my angel, and I feel that I don't want to wait much longer, now that you have made up your mind to come out. I am looking forward to the middle of March with anticipation, so please don't disappoint me. Even if we can only be together fort a few weeks, I think your troubles and efforts will be well worthwhile. You may never get another chance to visit the West Coast, either, so you may as well take advantage of this one. Many girls, both wives and sweethearts, would be glad of the opportunity you now have to make this trip, so please, Lou, come out to me, as soon as you possibly can. I'll take care of everything on this end and we'll have time to be together, but not quite as much as I want to.

Well, adorable, that takes care of everything, so I'll not start another page. Give my regards to the families. Here's my special hug and kiss for our Jackie and many more to you. Dearest, I love you, miss you and want you. *As ever, your Johnny*

Note on flap: *"Please don't change your mind. I love you & want you. Hugs & kisses"*

Monday, February 26, 1945. *Letters of Feb 20 & Feb 22. B.card from Michael. Rain. Waited for Gracie to come home from school. Went to New York.*

Tuesday, February 27, 1945. *Went to church. Started to rain. Planned on going to N.Y. with Ann and Fan. Left Jackie with Gracie. Took 9:20 train. Met Fan at Orange. Met Ann in Hoboken. Took a cab to Stouffers (opposite Grand Central), meal very good. Took cab to Radio City. Saw, "A Song to Remember." Good. Stopped raining when we came out. Caught 11:35 train to Morristown, very tired. Trip was anniversary gift from Ann and Fan.*

Postmarked February 28, 1945, stamp upside down. *February 27, 1945*

Port Hueneme

Hello, Sweetheart:

I love you, miss you and want you more than ever. As the day of our reunion slowly but surely approaches, I am becoming more anxious than ever to hold you tenderly in my arms and kiss you. Gee, darling, it's going to be swell, having you with me again. Just to be with you will be swell, angel. I can hardly wait, so please don't change your mind at the last minute. I want you so much.

I haven't been out yet, to look for a room, but I will get out tomorrow at one in the afternoon and I hope to have one before nightfall. I will let you know as soon as I have all arrangements made. And please don't worry about anything on this end, cause I'll take are of everything.

Now, I have some news that may be good to you. I think it is, so let me know what you think about it. Today, I went back on mess cook duty. Every other day I get off from one in the afternoon until ten the following morning. The other days, I can get off after supper is cleared away, which will be about six-thirty until five forty-five the following morning. I won't get any weekends but that doesn't matter very much, does it. Boy, we will be able to be together almost every night. That sounds good to me, how about you? Not only that, but I have an idea that shortly after you arrive we will have about ten or more days together. Sweetheart, I'm so glad I won't have to spend them days traveling, just to be with you for five days. But I'd do it, if only for one day with you.

Your train is due in Los Angeles at seven on the morning of the

401

fourteenth, according to the timetable. That, I believe, is a Wednesday morning. I will be there to meet you, angel. I'm quite sure I will be able to get off. But I have plenty of time to make those arrangements. My main concern is getting a decent place for you to reside.

The little town I have in mind to start looking is named Ventura. It has plenty of lemon trees around and there is a swell beach where you can take Jackie in the afternoons or mornings. There also is a place to hold picnics, if one is desirous. It's a nice clean town and I think you will like it. That's where I'm going tomorrow, first of all. It's only twelve miles from here and transportation is no problem. Hitchhiking is easy, too, so I won't have any trouble getting out and back. Besides, Andy has a room out there and he is working the same shift that I am.

Don't worry about bringing Kleenex with you, because most every day we can purchase them, and Ponds tissues, here at camp. I went down to the store with Andy today and we each bought a five-hundred single tissue box of Ponds, for his wife. Twenty cents a box, is that much? I can get cigarettes here, too, so far.

This will be all for tonight, lovely one. I'll drop a few lines again Thursday to let you know all. Give my regards to all. Here's my special hug and kiss for Jackie and many more for you, my most adorable angel. I love you, sweet, more and more.

Everlastingly, your adoring, *Johnny*

Wednesday, February 28, 1945. Rained in morning. Cleared in afternoon. Jackie received gift (a blouse) from Eleanor and Herb, card enclosed. Washed clothes in morning. Went downtown in afternoon. Cashed check for Mil. Bought white shoes for Jackie & Saddles for myself. Reached home just before it started to snow. Large flakes.

March 1, 1945 - A U.S. submarine sinks a Japanese merchant ship loaded with supplies for Allied POW's, resulting in a court martial for the captain of the submarine, since the ship had been granted safe passage by the U.S. Government.

Thursday, March 1, 1945. Letter of Feb. 25. Washed clothes in morning. 2:30 p.m. went to Acme with Mil & Judy. Nite, went to movies with Fan.

March 2, 1945 - U.S. airborne troops recapture Corregidor in the Philippines.

Friday, March 2, 1945. Letter of Feb. 27. Letter from Eileen. 11:15 went to Aunt's on McKenzie Rd. Stayed until 1:00. Home for few minutes then went to bank to cash allotment checks.

March 3, 1945 – U.S. and Filipino troops take Manila.

Saturday, March 3, 1945. Took 11:45 train to Newark. Went to Penn. to make Hotel reservation. Pulled in Penn. St. 1:15. Saw Mrs. Cunnion. Agreed to have T.A. representative to meet me in Chicago and also to get hotel reservation. Paid deposit of $10.00. Met Ann & Fan in Lobby. Took bus to Jo's. Stayed until 5:45. Went downtown. Bought brown non-rationed shoes.

Sunday, March 4, 1945. Lovely day. Girls and I went to 8:00 mass. Saw M.deR. Gave back ration book. Mama G and Tadone up for the day. Joe & Angie came in afternoon. Joe took Jackie and me up to say goodbye to Nana. Then brought Jackie to see the ducks. Went to movies with Ann and Fan. Saw Loretta Young in "And Now, Tomorrow."

Monday, March 5, 1945. Went to mass in morn. In afternoon brought Jackie to doctor's for check up. Weighs 26 lbs., height 33 ½. Asked doctor about contraception. Waited in office until 3:00. Through at 6:00.

Tuesday, March 6, 1945. Cat brought dress for Jackie. Aunt M. made it.

March 7, 1945 – Battle for the bridge at Remagen, Germany. Until its collapse on March 18, the Ludendorf Bridge at Remagen provided the Allies an unexpected opportunity to move forces across the Rhine River.

Wednesday, March 7, 1945. In morning went to bank to get $250 worth of travelers checks. Cost $2.00. Vene dropped in.

Thursday, March 8, 1945. Vene Naughton's birthday. Received letter and check from Travelers Aid.

March 9, 1945 – Fifteen square miles of Tokyo in flames after massive incendiary bombing raids by 279 B-29s.

Chapter 5
1945
California

On March 9, 1945 – Lucia and Jackie left for California. No journal entries until March 15th.

March 10, 1945 - U.S. Eighth Army invades Zamboanga Peninsula on Mindanao in the Philippines.

Sunday, March 11, 1945
Sunday (on train)

Hello Mom, Ann, Fan, Grace!
    It's 1:00 P.M. - Jackie is asleep and it's raining out. We just passed the Mississippi River. Gave me quite a thrill - after hearing and reading so much about it. You're all probably anxious to hear how the first half of our trip went along - so here goes!
    The name of the train I took in Newark was The "Golden Arrow." This train is the "Pacific Limited." I felt very badly when I left all of you people there - nervous and a little frightened. If it weren't for Jackie, I would have been bawling all over the place. She was grand! Our berth was all made up. The porter brought the ladder (the train is rocking terribly!) and we climbed up and prepared for bed. Jackie was very good. When the porter held her (the train has stopped) while I climbed up, she told him she was going to California to see daddy. When she was all ready for bed she fell asleep in two minutes flat. I'm certainly glad we have a lower from here out. I didn't like the upper at all. It was so enclosed. I hardly slept at all, all night long. Oh, by the way, I tipped the porter $.50 when he carried my bags in. Sat. Jackie slept until 7:00. When she opened her eyes and looked around she became frightened and started to cry. She said she wanted to get down. I quieted her down, finally dressed her and then rang for the porter. I brought her to the ladies room and kept her there for a while. I met a woman there who told me her berth was opposite mine. (The train has stopped again for the servicemen to eat lunch. Jackie is sleeping through the lunchtime on the car here, so I'll have to feed

405

her what I have left in the box.) You'd be surprised how handy the sandwiches were. I wish I had packed more. I only have one left besides the orange and apple! Well, to continue - when we came back from the ladies room, the woman told me to stay with her (she had a lower) instead of climbing up into ours again. (Jackie just woke up. She slept for two hours and 15 minutes.) Guess what! When the soldier across the way came back, he brought me some coffee and a sandwich! So far, the upper berth is unoccupied so Jackie and I have the whole space to ourselves. There's no one else with the soldier either. When we first came in, we talked for a while and he offered me his lower berth if I had an upper. Oh, Golly!, I'm always changing the subject! Anyway, we stayed with the woman and it was so much better. Jackie was busy looking out the window. The woman was a lovely person, somewhat on Eileen's style. We went into breakfast with her and she showed me what to do. When we came back, the lady in the lower berth of our space was still sleeping so we sat with the woman in her space. Her upper berth was unoccupied so we sat in the opposite chair. When she got off at Canton, we had the whole space to ourselves for the rest of the trip. We didn't even bother going back to our seat. When Jackie fell asleep I just lay her across the whole seat.

The breakfast cost me $1.20 and $.25 tip. I didn't have my change purse with me so I borrowed a quarter from the woman. When we came back I wanted to give it to her but she refused. She said to put it in Jackie's bank.

I didn't bring Jackie in the dining car that Sat. afternoon. Instead I rang for the porter and asked him to bring me a table and a glass of milk for Jackie. The milk cost $.15 with $.50 tip for the porter. I won't go into much detail from here on. The soldier said if I had this finished by the time we hit the next station he would mail it for me.

So, let's see, - at Fort Wayne, I set my watch back 1 hour. We pulled into Chicago at 6:30 P.M., two hours late. The T.A. rep. met me as soon as we got off the train. Everyone on the train was very nice and Jackie was friendly with all of them. When I got off the train a man even carried her for me. I gave the porter $.75. The T.A. representative took me to the T.A. Station in the terminal. The head woman told me what to do Sunday morning. (She wasn't half as nice as Mrs. Cunnion). The rep. was nice tho and she got me a cab outside the terminal. You may not believe this but when I got off the train my nervousness had disappeared, nothing frightened me anymore.

Our Hotel room was very, very, nice. We even had a radio! Hotel rooms are very scarce!!! On the desk was a sign -"Rooms by reservations only! Boy! I sure was thankful for our room!

I put Jackie to bed at 7:30. She was quiet but she wouldn't go to sleep. I took time out to write a couple of cards home and then I got ready for bed. Jackie kept pulling the same old line for an hour so to hush her up I brought her in my bed so we had to sleep together after all. You know, when I was on the train I had such cramps that I thought I was going to get sick to my stomach. I had headaches, too, but I kept taking the aspirin and I pulled through all right. But in the Hotel, every time I bent my head a little, I became so dizzy. I couldn't understand that. I'm all right now, and the riding doesn't bother me at all. I'll continue on in my next letter. The train has just stopped. Jackie is playing with Cathy on the opposite side of me. She's always going over to talk with the soldiers. She isn't bashful at all. She even sings for them.

Well, so long for now. Love,

Lou and Jackie

Thursday, March 15, 1945. Awoke at 8:00 A.M. For breakfast, Jackie had 2 eggs, milk toast, (eggs $.50 doz, milk $.14 a quart). 11:45 went into town of Oxnard. We missed the bus - took us 30 minutes to walk. Pretty nice town. Small though. We shopped around in different markets for food and came home very tired. It was a very windy day. For supper we used the sauce I sent to Johnnie. (Spaghetti out here not so good.) Jackie drinks a lot of milk here at the farm.

Friday, March16, 1945. It was very cold during the night. Jackie wet the bed. We warmed the room up with the hot plate. For breakfast, Jackie had a bowl of cereal, 2 eggs, toast. She plays with the ducks and chickens. Is lonesome for Judy. 2:00 had vegetable soup for lunch. It started to rain. Out here on the farm there are orange trees, calla lilies, large cauliflower patch, avocado trees, loquat trees. Many beautiful birds, ducks, chickens, dogs. It rained all night.

Saturday, March 17, 1945. We were up at 8:30. Clear Day. 11:30 we went into town. Got a ride in. Bought food and brought baggage home by taxi. Paid $1.34 for express from L.A. to Oxnard. $1.75 for taxi.

Sunday, March 18, 1945. Bonnie Reed Naughton's birthday. Passion Sunday. Missed mass. 11:30 went into town. Stopped at U.S.O. to look for rooms. Walked around town and came upon a carnival. Jackie had rides on the Merry-go-round, airplanes, and cars. Liked them all very much. Didn't want to leave. Visited Santa Clara church on 3rd St. All went in to say prayers. I lit a candle. Came home by bus. Johnnie went back again to U.S.O. No luck. Took two pictures.

Monday, March 19, 1945. lovely warm day. Up at 7:45. Left house at 11:00. Took bus into town. Looked around for rooms. Did some shopping for supper. Johnnie went back to U.S.O. Had supper and then went back again. No luck.

Oxnard, California, Jackie in front of Mission View Inn. She is standing in front of geranium plants

March 20, 1945 – British troops liberate Mandalay, Burma.

Tuesday, March 20, 1945. Johnnie went room hunting all day long. Warm day. Jackie getting sunburned. Got period! Johnnie came home with a room for us. 185 S. Figueroa Street, Ventura, California.

Wednesday, March 21, 1945. People who owned room came back at 7:30 A.M. It was raining heavily. Came into room and talked with us for awhile. Liked Jackie and they did not stay. Went on to L.A. (swab). Johnnie paid bill $10 for room. Johnnie and I packed our bags and cleaned the room up. While walking in rain, got ride into Ventura. House owned by Mrs. Eva Cecil, Mission View Inn. Our room was large but I wasn't satisfied with it. No cooking privileges. Cot for Jackie to sleep on.

Thursday, March 22, 1945. Arose at 9:00. Went to U.S.O. after we had our breakfast. We stayed there for half hour, then walked out to Main street. Met some friends of Johnnie's, Buddy and anther fellow. We bought Jackie a pail and shovel & 2 new panties. Came back to house (2 blocks from ocean). Johnnie went back to U.S.O. to ask about a room - no luck!

March 22, 1945 – Arab League declares war on Axis.
March 22,23, 1945 – Patton and Montgomery cross Rhine.

Friday, March 23, 1945. We were out by 10:00. A very windy day. We went first to U.S.O. and then visited Church - San Buenaventura. Afterwards we walked around the town and stayed in the park awhile. We cashed travelers check of $20.00 at the bank and bought souvenir pillow case to send to Mom and Mrs. De Roxtro. Cost us $4.10. We came back to our room 6:00 p.m. and Johnnie went back to the U.S.O.

Saturday, March 24, 1945. Johnnie borrowed a car to bring our bags to Ventura from Oxnard. Jackie & I went back to Oxnard with him to return the car. After looking around Oxnard we took the bus back to Ventura. After supper we met

Paul and Marion Andrews. We went for a ride as far as Ojai and rode to the top of a high mountain. The view was beautiful! Later we went for some ice cream and were home by 8:30. Johnnie stayed until 10:00 p.m. It was the last night of his leave. Paul called for him. How I hated to have him go.

Sunday, March 25, 1945. PALM SUNDAY! Jackie and I left the house at 9:30 A.M. We had breakfast at the coffee shop and then attended 11:00 mass at San Buenaventura church. Jackie's first mass. She behaved very well. Service lasted one hour. We walked up to buy the Sunday papers and then went back to our room. We have dinner at McKauley's and stayed in the park for an hour and a half - then went back to room. Johnnie came in at 4:00 P.M. He was with us until 3:00 A.M. the next morning.

March 26, 1945 - U.S. Marines and Seabees land on the Kerama Islands that surround Okinawa, Japan.

March 26, 1945

Hello Mom, Ann, Fan and Gracie:

Certainly have plenty to tell you! I hope I can remember everything, because I know you're interested. I'll continue from where I left off in my last letter.

We left the Harrison Hotel at 8:15 A.M. (By the way, I got a refund of $.50, the room was only $3.00.) We took a cab to the North Western Station and when we got there I went straight to the Traveler's Aid to check in because the woman was told to expect me. I left my bag there and Jackie and I went down to the main floor to have some breakfast. While we were eating an ensign came to hang his coat on the rack in back of us. When Jackie saw him she looked at me and said, "Mommy, that's a sailor!" The guy smiled at her but when he passed, I had to laugh; imagine an ensign being called a sailor! For some reason or other Jackie is more interested in sailors than in soldiers. And it was the soldiers who were so nice to her on the train.

Well, anyway, we went back to the T.A. and at 9:25 the lady brought us right through the gate where quite a few people were waiting, had the ticket master check my ticket, and brought me right up to the car I was to get on. We were the first ones on the train.

You girls would certainly be surprised about the berth business. I know I was. I won't go into too much detail, but I'll tell you something about it anyway. The Pullman car is divided into sections. On the train from Newark to Chicago there were only six sections, three on each side. On the train to L.A. there were ten, five on each side. In these sections, right where the seats are, the berths are made up, the upper and the lower. Our car wasn't crowded at all. There were about ten or eleven people. Our berth was next to the last. There was a soldier across from us and two more in back of us. There were only four women in the whole car, including myself. On the other end of the car was a man very sick with T.B. His berth was always made up because he was in it most of the time. I had quite a job keeping Jackie away from that end of the car but the two older women in front of me and the soldiers helped me a lot. Jackie behaved wonderfully. She became cranky and irritable the last couple of days but that was only to be expected.

A girl named Gladys got on at Council Bluffs, during the night and when the train stopped at Cheyenne, Wyoming, she walked with Jackie and me. You'd be surprised how warm it was out there. As far as I could see, the place was as large as Morristown. There was so much you could buy if you had money. The girl I was with was only married for three months and her husband is in the Air Corps.

Here's what struck me funny. She comes from Nevada and she thought I had an accent! When we were in one of the five and ten's she said, "Ah just love-e-e yore accent. Ah could just listen to it all day!" Can you imagine!! I thought I was going to have hysterics. She got off at Salt Lake City, which we pulled into during the night. Our soldier friends got off there, too. I set my watch back for the second time in Wyoming. This is how far we got when Jackie started to get cranky. That night she wet the bed for the first time. She didn't wet much tho, because I caught her while she was doing it. The next day approaching the end of Utah, Jackie took a nap for 2¾ hrs. When she woke up she had one of those crying tantrums. She couldn't be touched. One of the conductors happened to be passing by and he stopped and started teasing her about crying. Ooooooo!! Did she get mad!! I just had to let her cry it out.

At the end of Nevada we passed through the Grand Canyon. [not **THE** Grand Canyon in Arizona.] It lasted one hour and we went through forty tunnels. Sometimes the rocky walls, or rather, mountains, were so close to the car you could reach out and touch them. The scenery was really beautiful. There were snowcaps on all the mountains.

At Caliente we stopped for fifteen minutes. This place was sure a disappointment to me. I expected it to be a large town and instead, it was a very small valley with one large modern building in which was the Hotel, restaurant, Railway Express, post office and everything else a
town is supposed to have. The few surrounding houses were only small shacks. Jackie and I walked up and down for a while with one of the ladies in our car, which, by the way, was called, "The Villa Clara."

Tues. night, 7:30 P.M. we pulled into Las Vegas, Nevada. (I can't finish this today, I'll have to continue on, tomorrow.) Johnnie just came in and he has some mail for me. I'm so glad!)

******

Well, here I am, back again. I'm down in the U.S.O. lounge. Jackie is here with me, of course, and is busy looking at a coloring book some little kid must have left here. She's very friendly with these boys here. Mostly all of them are Seabees and regular navy. She's talking to a sailor right now. You know it's a funny thing, nine times out of then, when anyone asks her what her name is she always says "Annette." She saw a sailor's hat on the chair and asked me if it was daddy's hat. The sailor just asked her where her daddy was and she surprised him by answering, "He's at the camp." Everyone out here thinks she's so smart and so many people stop to admire her and say how pretty she is.

I almost felt like ending this letter on that last page but I think I'd better finish telling you about the trip. Let's see, where was I, Oh, yes, Las Vegas! Quite a few people got on here that night. Gee, the city looked swell, lights and action everywhere. I wanted to get off so badly. We stopped here for about forty five minutes. I had just put Jackie to bed so I had to be contented by just looking out of the window. Jackie was looking with me.

The berth across from us was taken by a woman and a little girl. Boy, was I glad it was our last night! The kid was crying and wouldn't sleep and Jackie couldn't sleep because she heard the kid. It must have been about 10:30 before she did fall asleep. Jackie, I mean, the little girl kept crying throughout the night. The little sleep that I was getting I didn't get at all that night.

Wed. morning of Mar. 14th I awoke at six o'clock. I dressed myself first and then I woke Jackie up at 6:30. We were all ready by seven and the train pulled into the L.A. Station at 7:30 A.M.

Johnnie was there to meet me as he said he would and I sent the telegram off first thing. Jackie wasn't strange with Johnnie at all. She seemed to take him for granted. We arranged to have our baggage sent out by express and then we went to have breakfast. After breakfast we rode in a Greyhound bus for two hours. We passed thru Hollywood and mostly every building you saw was a studio of some kind or other.

In Oxnard we had to change to a Port Hueneme bus and rode for about 10 or 15 minutes. This place we first went to belongs to another couple that was going away for the fellow's leave. The guy is a Seabee and a friend of Johnny's. It wasn't a bad place at all. The building was a converted chicken coup, which the owners had fixed up for the Seabees and some air force fellows. All the rooms were taken before Johnnie knew about it. There was one kitchen, which the five couples had to share. When we were there, there were only two of us who had to share the kitchen. The other couple was Mary and Bob Lang. All the others were spending their leaves somewhere. Everything was newly built and the bathroom had a shower. On one side of the building there was a huge cauliflower patch and up away from the rooms was a chicken coop and the house of the owners out in front. They have orange trees, cherry trees, avocado and a pecan tree. The woman had two dogs and two ducks. Jackie was out from early in the morning until it was time to go to bed. She loved to chase the ducks around, but if they ever turned toward her she'd cry like the devil. When we first arrived, the weather wasn't nice at all. We had a lot of rain and the days were pretty cold. We had to go to Oxnard for my bags and what a shock I got. Jo and Mike's bag is ruined! The paper is off in several spots and the corners are all banged up and the handle was off. When I saw it I was almost sick. You can tell them about it when you see them and tell them I'll pay them whatever the bag cost them. The other bags are O.K., a little banged up but nothing much. I wish it had happened to one of ours, instead of theirs. I feel terrible about it. The one time I borrow something I have to regret it. Oh well, so much for that.

All the time we were there we had fresh eggs and milk. Jackie had two boiled eggs every morning. The eggs were $.50 a dozen and the milk $.14 a quart.

As soon as we'd have our breakfast and finished cleaning the room, the three of us would go into the town of Oxnard. When we missed the bus we started walking and someone would always stop to pick us up. We did walk it one day, tho, and it took us thirty minutes. Oxnard is a little smaller than Morristown. The park is situated just like ours and the stores are all around.

The second day after we arrived, we opened up the jar of sauce that Johnnie had been saving all this time. We bought some spaghetti (some American brand) and that night we had spaghetti. It was very good, Mom, and we sure enjoyed it.

Meat is very scarce out here and when they do have it, people form lines blocks long. However, just before we left the place, I cooked one good dinner for Johnnie. We were lucky enough to get two T-bone steaks. And the only way we got it was because Johnnie asked the butcher if he had any meat salted away, and to our surprise, we got some.

The most common flowers out here are geraniums and calla lilies. The geraniums grow about four and five feet high and the lilies are the most beautiful I've ever seen. I think I'll end this here and continue on in my next letter. I haven't felt much like writing and I still haven't sent out cards to everyone. Please offer my apologies and tell them I will, one of these days. Goodbye for now and love from us all.

Lou

Monday, March 26, 1945. We went out for breakfast at 9:30. Were back at 11:00 to wash clothes. (used washing machine) We went out to lunch at 1:00. Shopped in stores for an hour - came back to room. Jackie took a nap. Slept 1½ hours. 5:30 Johnnie came home. He brought letters from Ann & Fan. We went out to supper. Met Fitz for first time at U.S.O. 7:00 P.M. He came back to our room with us. Stayed 10 minutes. He's very nice.

March 27, 1945 - B-29s dropped mines in Japan's Shimonoseki Strait to interdict shipping.

Tuesday, March 27, 1945. Johnnie left for the camp at 7:45. Jackie and I had our breakfast then went to the U.S.O. No luck in finding a place to live. Stayed at U.S.O. until 1:00 P.M. Man gave Jackie two oranges. We went out for lunch. Home for rest. Cleaned room, then went to Park. Johnnie joined us there at 5:30 P.M. We all went to dinner 6:00 P.M. On way back to room I met several of Johnnie's friends. They all liked Jackie. Johnnie went back to U.S.O. No luck - stayed until 3:00 A.M. Took bus back to camp. I paid room rent - $10.00. $2.00 a day.

Wednesday, March 28, 1945. *Jackie awoke at 10:00. We went out for breakfast. Back to U.S.O. We watched the waves for awhile. Brought Jackie to playground. She rode on the swings. Then we went into the U.S.O. lounge room. We met a girl named Ruth Greaves and her 3½ yr.-old son, Buddy. Johnnie found us there at 12:45. While we were going to supper we met Paul and Marion. They took us for a ride and we had supper in Santa Paula. Afterwards we rode around until 9:15 P.M. Jackie was very good.*

Thursday, March 29, 1945. *Beautiful day. We went out to breakfast then to U.S.O. No luck with room. Johnnie got off at 12:00. He brought letters from Ann and Fan.*

Friday, March 30, 1945. *I awoke with a sore throat. We went to breakfast, then to U.S.O. Met Ruth and Buddy in afternoon. All went to the beach. Jackie played with her pail and shovel. Then we went to the park. Stayed there with Ruth until Johnnie came at 5:00. Went to bed early. I felt very sick. Johnnie left for camp at 3:00 A.M.*

Saturday, March 31, 1945. *Jackie and I had breakfast in room. (Rice Krispies and milk). Stayed in until 1:00. Went to dinner then sat in park until 5:45. Had our supper and just in front of house I met Johnnie. He had a package for Jackie from Ann. Bunny Rabbit for Easter. We went back out for a little walk and in front of mission we met Ruth and her husband, Burton. Came back to room again and at 7:30 Paul came up and asked us to go riding. Visited Santa Barbara and Carpinteria. Johnnie left for camp at 5:45 A.M.*

April 1-June 21, 1945 - The Final amphibious landing of the war occurs as the U.S. Tenth Army invades Okinawa. [According to Wikipedia, the invasion of Okinawa on April 1, 1945 was the largest amphibious assault in the Pacific Theater of World War II. The invasion was led by U.S. Army, U.S. Marines and 18,000 U.S. Navy personnel, mostly Seabees and medical personnel. The 98-day battle lasted from March 26th until July 2nd, 1945.]

Sunday, April 1, 1945. *EASTER DAY! It was lovely out, nice and warm. Johnnie came at 10:00 A.M. We all went to the 11:00 mass. Jackie was very good. We bought a paper and then came back to room. After reading the paper, we went out to dinner. Afterwards we walked out to the park and took six pictures of us all. Then we went to the movies and saw "Sunday Dinner For a Soldier." Johnnie and I both enjoyed it. Jackie fell asleep. We felt our first earthquake during the movies (First time Jackie went to the movies.) Had supper. Went for a walk to the U.S.O. (wore aqua dress, black accessories). U.S.O. crowded with servicemen. We stayed for a half hour and then came on home.*

Monday, April 2, 1945. 11:00 I washed the clothes. 1:00 Jackie and I went out for lunch. 2:30 we went to the park and met Ruth and Buddy. Johnnie met us there at 4:00, but left us to go room hunting. Ruth and I exchanged our home addresses and she left at 5:00. Johnnie came back at 5:30. No luck. We met Jim Higley & wife in the park. They invited us up to their place. 6:30 we went to have our supper. Jackie climbs the stairs alone & without holding on. - 2 yrs. 6 wks.

Tuesday, April 3, 1945. Johnnie left for camp at 5:00 A.M. I gave Jackie a bath and then we went out for lunch at 1:00 and afterwards we went out to the park where we met Ruth and Buddy. They had brought their own lunch so Ruth gave Jackie a hard boiled egg, milk, and a banana. Johnnie met us there at a quarter of five. Ruth left shortly afterwards so we went for our supper and then headed for home.

Wednesday, April 4, 1945. We left room at 11:30 and went to the park. Ruth came at 12:30 with lunch for us all. Johnnie came at 1:45 and we stayed in the park until 4:45 P.M. We had our supper. Got our snapshots at the store and then came home to put Jackie to bed at 7:30.

Thursday, April 5, 1945. Johnnie left at 6:30 A.M. I arose at 8:15. Jackie was still sleeping. I packed a lunch for us to picnic in the park. It was a lovely day. Ruth came at 12:00 noon. We ate our lunch and then went shopping in town. We separated at the corner and we came on home. Jackie took a nap at 4:00 until 5:30. When she awoke we went out to supper. Johnnie came in at 7:00.

Friday, April 6, 1945. Johnnie left at 5:00 A.M. I packed a lunch this morning and Jackie and I had lunch in the park. Johnnie met us there at 12:30. He had a letter for me from Ann and a gift for Jackie from Fannie (a white pinafore & panties). He brought his pea coat back to the room and while he was gone Paul and Marion came. When Johnnie came back we all decided to go to Hollywood to see a circus. We left 1:33 and arrived 3:15 too late for the afternoon performance. Next show was at 8:30 P.M. To kill time we went to the movies. Saw "Belle of the Yukon" and "Keys of the Kingdom." Jackie was very restless and would not sleep. We left show to have something to eat. Then went to circus, good seats. $2.00 a piece. Circus was very good. Jackie enjoyed it but was very sleepy. She fell asleep at 11:30 P.M. Circus over at 11:30. On way home she slept for a half hour then woke up and cried. We stopped for something to eat. Jackie fell asleep again. We brought her in from car and put her right to bed 1:30 A.M. As souvenirs we bought a bird on the stick - Frank Puck Pistol Holder. Program.

April 7, 1945 - B-29s fly their first fighter-escorted mission against Japan with P-51 Mustangs based on Iwo Jima; two U.S. Carrier-based fighters sink the super battleship Yamato and several escort vessels which planned to attack U.S. forces at Okinawa.

Saturday, April 7, 1945. Johnnie went back to camp 6:30 A.M. Jackie slept until 10:15. We went out for lunch at 1:00. 2:30 we went to the movies. Saw "I'll be seeing you" Ginger Rogers, Joseph Cotton. It was good and Jackie behaved very well. 4:00 we went to the park and stayed there until 5:30. We had supper at 6:00, and when we were coming home we met Johnnie at the corner (7:00). Ruth, Burton and Buddy came to visit us. They stayed until 10:15. Jackie said "Darn it" while she and Buddy were playing and kept repeating it until Johnnie told her to stop.

April 7, 1945
Ventura, Calif.

Hello Mom, Ann, Fan and Gracie!!

And so I begin another letter. Not to waste words, I'll start right off with the morning of Mar. 18ᵗʰ, Passion Sunday. Since I didn't know where to find a Catholic church, I had to miss mass. We went into the town of Oxnard at 11:30. We walked all round the place and what do you think! We came upon a carnival!! Of course, we went in, don't be silly!!

The first thing we put Jackie on was the Merry-Go-Round. We didn't know just how she would take it so Johnnie went on with her. She seemed to enjoy the ride but she wasn't relaxed. Next came the airplanes (for children) and we sent her in to the man, alone, and he strapped her into one of the planes. This she really enjoyed and every time she passed us she laughed and waved. And then there were those little cars. You know the kind - racers, fire engines, etc. We put her in a fire engine. This she really loved. She stayed on for another ride. Then she wanted another ride on the Merry-Go-Round. We let her go on alone this time. She liked to ride on the horses but I think she's just a little bit afraid. There wasn't a cry of fear out of her, though, and being alone on the rides didn't seem to bother her at all. Only when she realized that we were leaving the carnival did she put up a fuss. We walked around the different Streets and we finally found a Catholic Church. We went in and lit a candle and said some prayers. That's the third time Jackie was in church. The first two were at home. She was very good and knew she had to be quiet. We caught the bus just as we got out to the corner and came on back to the farm.

We've been looking for rooms ever since I got out here and we finally found this place that we have now. Johnnie learned of it through one of his friends. Let's see, Johnnie got the room on Mar. 19ᵗʰ and the next day we moved in. It so happened that on that day it had to rain. We left the farm anyway and walked down the road to the bus station. But before we reached it a car picked us up and gave us a lift all the way to Ventura. That was a break because we would have had to change buses in Oxnard and it was still raining. It cleared up by the time we reached Ventura so it wasn't so bad after all. We left all our baggage at the farm except one bag which we brought along with us. This room that we have now is large and bright but we're still not satisfied. It's costing us $14.00 a week with only washing privileges. She furnishes the bed linen and towels but anything outside washing is an extra privilege and for extra privileges there are extra charges. Cooking is out of the question. Ironing is an extra privilege and so far I haven't done any ironing. I can't do it in the room because there isn't any base plug. However, the room light we have could overcome that handicap if I had a plug. We have two light bulbs and after looking around a week I found a double socket for one of the lights but for the life of me, there isn't a screw in plug in town. I've gone in every 5 & 10, hardware and electric store in Ventura and not a one was to be found. I was told that they were a scarcity. See if you can get one

416

for me and please send it to me. You know the kind I mean, Mom, the plug that goes into the double socket where I can plug the iron into. There's a cot or daybed that Jackie sleeps on and she's only fallen out of it once in all the time we've been here. We've been having our three meals a day in restaurants and believe me it gets pretty tiresome.

After we had our breakfast, Jackie and I would go down to the U.S.O. to see about getting a room but they never had anything for us. What made it worse was that nobody wanted children. Afterwards we'd go into the U.S.O. Lounge and spend the rest of the morning there.

This house in which we are now living is situated at the end of the street. The beach is two blocks down and at the other end of the street. On the other side, is the Catholic Church, "San Buenaventura." It's an old mission over 160 years old. This house we're in is called "Mission View Inn." Johnnie was able to borrow a car from one of his friends to bring our bags here from Oxnard.

Sat. Mar. 24th, I met Paul Andrews and his wife, Marion. We met them as we were returning from having our supper. Paul has a car and he took us for a ride and then we rode to the top of one of the high mountains above the Mission. There is a huge cross right on the top and at night it's always lit up. We stayed up for quite a while looking over the lighted city. The view was beautiful! Afterwards we went and had some ice cream and then came home at 8:30. Johnny stayed until 10:00 P.M. It was the last day of his leave.

Paul "Andy" and Marion Andrews

Palm Sunday, Mar. 25th, we, Jackie and I, left the house at 9:30, had breakfast, and then walked back to attend the 11:00 mass at the Mission. This was Jackie's first mass and she behaved fairly well. She became restless towards the end of the hour but she didn't talk.

About eight blocks from here there is a beautiful large park. That's where Jackie and I went and passed a couple of hours the first day we were away from Johnnie. We've gone there every day since. It gives Jackie a chance to run and yell all she pleases and there are always children there to play with. Palm Sunday, Johnnie came home at 4:00 in the afternoon and stayed until 3:00 in the morning. The buses to Oxnard run at 3:35 A.M. and at 5:30 A.M. Johnnie has to be in at five so he had to take the early bus.

Monday, Mar. 26ᵗʰ, when Johnnie came at 5:30 P.M., he brought me letters from Ann, Fan, and the one from Mary. There were also the Easter cards from Ann and Fan. Thanks a lot, kids, it felt swell to hear from you.

After supper, that Monday nite, we went to the U.S.O. and finally met our friend "Fitz." Johnnie said he had arranged to meet us there, but Johnnie didn't say anything to me about it and yet, when I saw him with Johnnie, I recognize him instantly. He looks just like his pictures. You see, the three of us didn't go into the lounge together. Johnnie went upstairs to the housing desk to see about a room with kitchen privileges, and Jackie and I went into the lounge. Fitz told us later that he recognized Jackie and me as soon as we came in the door and that he was coming over to ask if I was Mrs. de Roxtro. Johnnie came in just then so we were introduced. He likes Jackie and thinks she's swell. He came back to our room with us and he carried Jackie the whole seven blocks. She calls him Uncle Fitz and liked him right off. He only stayed with us about fifteen minutes because he had to go back to the base. His wife is in San Francisco and he goes up to see her on weekends.

I've met several of Johnnie's friends and they all think he has a peach of a daughter.

There's a playground down in back of the U.S.O., with swings, a slide and a merry-go-round like the one that used to be at the Speedwell Park. You remember, Ann. Jackie's only been on the swings, though. Once she gets on she never wants to get off.

Now I'll tell you a little about the U.S.O. This is an old Spanish building (at least that's what it looks like to me) made of yellow stucco. It's quite a big place. Upstairs is the housing desk (where they're supposed to help you find a place to live. I was given a wives' registration card there, which made me a member of the U.S.O.) Upstairs is also the place where they give dances for servicemen. Downstairs is the lounge, very large, with fountain service and the Ladies and Men's room. There are even a couple of offices in the back and then there's the beach. This is where every one comes to stay. There are benches where people can sit down, and away from the benches is the sandy part. Jackie and I have sat on those benches several times to watch the waves. Jackie loves the beach.

Wed. Mar. 28ᵗʰ after we had watched the waves for a while and Jackie had a ride in the swings, we went into the U.S.O. I met a girl there whose name is Ruth Greaves. She has a three-year-old boy named Buddy. Ruth's husband is an F2/c and is stationed at the airport in Oxnard. (that airport was right next to the farm where we stayed for the first week and a half.)

Ruth and I have been palling around since that day we met. Buddy and Jackie get along very well together, too. He's a well-mannered boy. He treats Jackie just like Michael does. That day we met, we all went to the park and Johnnie met me there at 12:45 P.M. That night after supper, we met Paul and Marion who were looking for us and they took us for a ride out to Santa Paula and all around. We rode until 9:15, and then we came back to our room. The only time we go any place is when Paul and Marion take us in their car. Thurs. Mar. 29ᵗʰ I didn't feel well at all. I had a touch of the flu. My throat hurt me terribly and my body ached all over. I even had a temperature. Fortunately, Johnnie got off at 2:00 that day and he took care of Jackie. Friday, I just hated to get up and go out, but that's what I had to do. We had breakfast, went to the U.S.O. Met Ruth there and then we went to the park. Gee, I was feeling miserable. But Jackie had to be out of the room and the park was the best place for us both. Maybe the sunshine helped me to get well so quick. That Friday night after we ate our supper, Johnnie and I stopped in a market and bought some milk and Rice Krispies to feed Jackie in the room the next morning. It worked out swell and I've been doing it ever since. You don't know what it is to rush right out in the morning so that it won't be too late for Jackie to have breakfast.

Sat. Mar. 31ˢᵗ Johnnie didn't come until seven o'clock. We met him just as we reached our place. He was carrying a package, and, it was the bunny rabbit you sent, Ann. I opened it without Jackie seeing because I wanted to give it to her on Easter Sunday. It's darling, thanks a lot for sending it.

We had to go out again that Sat. nite and on the corner we met Ruth and her husband. He seems like a nice guy. Ruth and I, Buddy and Jackie walked on ahead while Johnnie and Burton walked behind talking. We had just gotten in when Paul came up and asked if we wanted to go riding. It was only seven thirty, so we went. We rode out to Santa Barbara and through several other towns.

Easter was a lovely warm day. Johnnie managed to get off early and was here by 10:30 A.M. We all went to the 11:00 mass together. Outside of being restless, Jackie behaved very well. We

419

took pictures in the afternoon, the ones I've enclosed, and then we went to a movie, "Sunday Dinner For a Soldier," and "The Fighting Lady" was playing. We just went into see the one picture because this was the first time for Jackie. (And don't think Johnnie didn't remember about being the first to take her.) The picture was good. Even Johnnie enjoyed it. Jackie fell asleep and woke up just before the end.

When we first went in she was so interested in the screen that after a while we even forgot that she was there, she was so quiet. When she saw the kids and the chicken she'd laugh out loud and wouldn't take her eyes off the picture. She fell asleep when it was about the soldier and the girl.

After the show we went for a walk and then we went to the U.S.O. We didn't stay there long because the place was crowded.

Johnnie and Jackie get along swell together. She'll kiss him and say, "I love you." And when she sees him coming to meet us in the park, she always runs into his arms. The other day she said, "That's my daddy, see."

Easter morning I gave her the Bunny you sent, Ann, and she loves it. That night when I put her to bed and she was all settled with Cathy and Raggedy Ann, she got up suddenly and said, "give me my bunny rabbit, please, mommy." She has to sleep with it every night now. I wanted to send it home again so that it wouldn't get dirty around here. Johnnie and I gave her a large tin pail and shovel with Easter things fixed on top. We were lucky to find it because we haven't seen any in all the stores. There were only a couple when we bought it, too, and we bought it about a week and a half before Easter. The pail is blue and red and has pictures around the outside.

This will have to be all for now. Give our regards to every one and especially to Mama G and Tadone. Here's a kiss from Jackie.

Love, Lou

Sunday, April 8, 1945. Jackie and I went to the 11:00 mass and had dinner at 1:30. Afterwards we went to the park to pass some time but it was cold and windy so we came on back to the room. Johnnie came home at 7:00. I was so glad to see him.

Monday, April 9, 1945. Johnnie went back to camp 5:45 A.M. Jackie slept until 10:15. 12:30 we went to the bank to cash a ten-dollar travelers check. We had dinner in the coffee shop. Came straight home when we were through. Johnnie came at 3:00. He brought me two letters from Ann and the allotment checks. 6:30 we went to U.S.O. to meet Forbes. On our way we met Fitz at the corner. Forbes was waiting for us in front of U.S.O. He made his 2/c rating. We walked out to Main Avenue. Met Fitz again and both boys came up to the room with us, but first they went out and bought 8 bottles of beer and a bag of popcorn. They stayed for an hour, until 9:00. They didn't want to keep Jackie up late. She went right to town on the popcorn.

Tuesday, April 10, 1945. Jackie and I had lunch in the park and met Ruth and Buddy there. We walked out to Main St.

Cashed my allotment checks and shopped around for a while. I mailed a package to Ann & Fan. The pin cushion dolls. Then we all took a bus up to Ruth's house. I left a note for Johnnie telling him where I was. Jackie and I stayed for supper hoping Johnnie would come for us, but he didn't. We took the bus home 8:30 and found Johnnie asleep on the bed. He said he didn't have any carfare to come out.

Wednesday, April 11, 1945. Lovely day. Washed clothes and washed hair. Johnnie came at 1:00. We had lunch in the room and then Johnnie went out to inquire about a room. While he was gone Jackie took a nap. At 4:30 we went out for supper. We met Fitz in the Coffee Shop. After supper we went to the movies saw "Can't Help Singing" with Deanna Durbin. Pretty good. Jackie was very interested in the color and music. She really enjoyed the cartoon. On way home we met several of Johnnie's friends. All liked Jackie. (paid rent today).

April 12, 1945 - President Franklin Delano Roosevelt dies, Vice President Harry S. Truman sworn in as President of the United States.

Thursday, April 12, 1945. Jackie slept until 12:15. We dressed and went out for lunch. Afterwards we went to the park for awhile then came back to room and ate supper. Johnnie came in at 6:15 P.M.

April 12, 1945
Ventura, Calif.

Hello Ann:

Received your letters and was most glad to hear from you. Thanks for sending out the checks. I could hardly wait 'til they came.

Your Easter outfit sounded swell. You sure made me moan! I would have liked to have had one of those coats. I don't feel dressed up at all out here. I don't have a decent hat to wear to church and I had to wear either the blue or the brown jacket on my dresses. I'd like to have that cherry jacket of mine. That's a lot more dressed up than either these two that I have.

I'm disgusted about the stockings. There's a scarcity of hose out here and I had to go all over town before I found a pair of seamless, 42 gauge. They were that shiny streaked rayon. Awful!! And yet I had to wear them because I needed stockings. I sure was glad to know you were sending me some. Listen, Ann, keep track of what you buy me, and the cost, and when I come home I'll settle with you. I can't send you the money from here because I need every cent I can get. I can't even put my fare back home away and I should because Johnnie told me the latest scuttlebutt was that they were leaving sometime in May. I don't know whether to believe it or not.

What about your leg, Ann? You didn't mention it anymore. Does it still bother you? Gee, I hope you're not going to have any more trouble. Did Mom like the pillowcase we sent her? We sent one to Johnnie's mother too. Both of them cost us five dollars. I don't know what to send for Mother's Day. There isn't anything nice out here and what they do have is so very expensive. How about a (orsage-cay?) I was thinking of sending one to Mom and Johnnie's mother. One of you has thought of it, have you? Let me know as soon as you can. By the way, did you give that ten dollars to mama G and Tadone for Easter? I had it in my night table drawer. Incidentally, you never did tell me how you spent Easter back home. Did Mom ask anybody up?

We haven't found a place where we can cook yet, but we're still trying. We did have a lead on a place but the woman didn't want any children.

Glad to know you've included the dishes for Jackie in the package. I tried to get her some out here but couldn't. When I did locate a set, it was so large that it cost $4.50.

How stupid of me!! Here I just asked how you spent Easter and I've just remembered about the Aunt passing away on Good Friday. Yes, it was quite a shock to me. I could hardly believe it. It was pretty awful about the way she died, wasn't it. I kept thinking about it all day. I imagine Aunt Santa is taking it pretty hard. I feel sorry for them because they lost a whole lot in losing her. Maybe now they'll appreciate all that she did for them.

When does Mil expect her baby? Be sure to let me know as soon as it happens. So glad to hear about Tadone! Have the treatments made him any stronger?

Oh, say, I found out the correct spelling of hysterics after I had sealed the envelope. For the life of me, I couldn't remember which was right, either the 'I' or the 'y'. Johnnie wasn't around but then, he never is when I write my letters. I haven't written to anyone but you people back home. I don't have much time to write. Sounds funny doesn't it. Here's what I mean. I try to keep Jackie out in the air as much as I can. If she sleeps when I take her home for a nap, then I can write, but if she doesn't, I can't. She wants me to read to her or to help her color, etc. I can't write out in the park because I have to keep my eye on her all the time and then I have Ruth to talk to. So there you have it in a nutshell. I was relieved to know how Jo and Mike took it about their bag. I winced every time I looked at it. I don't feel so bad about it now. Crazy, aren't I?

I didn't want to start off on another page but I guess I'll have to because I don't have much room left on this one. I've sent out cards to quite a few people but haven't written to anyone else yet.

Oh, I don't think I've mentioned it before but Jackie climbs the stairs by herself now. She let go one day as we were coming up to our room - we live on the second floor. She talks a lot more now, too.

How did you like the pictures I sent home? Be sure to put them away in the desk or in my box in the office. I don't want them to get lost. I want to send the negatives and the Easter cards home, but I couldn't find one of those manila envelopes. And oh, Ann, the next time you to go Newark, will you buy me another of those bags to carry the potty in. This one I have is practically worn out. I take it with me everyplace we go. I don't want her to go near any of these dirty toilets out here. Maybe Shulte's still has them. You can try there first.

The weather out here isn't any too warm yet. I guess you can compare it to our spring. Jackie still wears her overalls and sweaters except on Sundays, then I dress her up. I suppose if I could iron anytime I wanted, I'd put more dresses on her. By the way, if you make up another package, include that box of perfumed starch of mine that's down in the cabinet.

I don't have any thing else to tell you so I will close sending our regards to all of you back home.

Love, Lou

Friday, April 13, 1945. We had lunch in the park and at 1 Ruth and Buddy came. We stayed in the park together until 3:30. Ruth and Buddy went home and Jackie and I went back to our room. We went out for supper at 5:15. Then came back and waited for Johnnie to come. He came in at 7:00.

Saturday, April 14, 1945. Johnnie has weekend off. He came in at 12:00 with a letter from Fan and a pkg. (Easter gift from Grace to Jackie, 1 pr. Stockings, my blue slacks and sweater, a little blue dress for Jackie from Ann and Fan, dishes for Jackie and my white hat.) Jackie liked the little lamb and her dishes. The first jelly beans since we've been out here. We went out to lunch and then to the park where we stayed until 4:30. After shopping in market, we came back to our room. All the stores and restaurants are closed in tribute to Pres. Franklin D. Roosevelt.

Sunday, April 15, 1945. We arose at 9:00, dressed and went to church, 11:00 mass. Came back to room and then went out to lunch. After lunch we went to the park. (a very warm day. No coat on Jackie.) I took four snapshots in the park. We stayed there until a quarter of five. We had supper at 6:00. Ate at the "State." While we were eating we met Frosty Clere and Forbes. They sat down with us. Both were slightly stewed. Clere paid our bill (I had two Tom Collins). After we left the restaurant we all went to have a drink together. Left at 8:00. Came home and put Jackie to bed.

Imitating Machine Gun

Monday, April 16, 1945. *Johnnie left for camp at 5:30 A.M. After I fed Jackie breakfast, we went to the Chinese market. Stopped on our way back to watch the school children. Then I fixed lunch and we ate in the park. Ruth and Buddy came at 1:30. We left at 3:45. Went shopping around town together, then Ruth went home and we came back to the room. Johnnie came in at 5:00. We ate supper in the room.*

Tuesday, April 17, 1945. *Jackie got sick to her stomach during the night. Johnnie left for camp at 3:00 A.M. After he left I brought Jackie into bed with me. We got up at 9:00. Jackie wouldn't eat breakfast. Drank some orange juice. Johnnie came in at 11:00. He was worried about Jackie. She seemed to be all right, tho. I bathed and washed her hair at 10:00. At 12:00 we all went out for lunch. Went to the park afterwards. Met Ruth and Buddy. We shopped at the market. Then came home. Jackie took a nap 4:00 - 5:30. We went out for supper. Met Fitz in coffee shop. We ate together. Fitz paid our bill. Came on home. Fitz stayed for a half hour.*

Wednesday, April 18, 1945. *Jackie woke at 7:30. 9:00 I washed the clothes. Was through at 10:30. We ate lunch in room. Jackie not feeling well. After lunch Jackie took a nap. She slept all afternoon. Johnnie came in at 5:00, went out for supper.*

Thursday, April 19, 1945. *Johnnie left at 5:30 A.M. Jackie woke at 7:30. 12:00 we went to Ruth's for a spaghetti dinner. I bought meat at the butcher shop on the corner, tomatoes, tomato paste and cheese. We got there at 1:00. I fed Jackie chicken soup. Johnnie came at 5:00 feeling high. He had a rose for Ruth and me. We had supper at 6:30, spaghetti turned out fair. Jackie ate very well. Both Johnnie and Burton ate a lot. We came home at 8:00. (Johnnie had a plug and a roll of film)*

Friday, April 20, 1945. *Johnnie had the day off. We went out to lunch and after lunch we bought a hot plate and a steel cooking kit. We met Ruth on way home. Told us about being able to get plugs in the New York Store. We went there and bought three. Came back to our street and Johnnie bought me a banana split. Came on back to room 3:00. Using the plug, I ironed my clothes until 5:30. Used the hot plate and fed Jackie chicken soup. Went out for supper. Stopped in at the market. Bought pastine, carrots, butter, milk. Home and then to bed.*

Saturday, April 21, 1945. *Johnnie left at 5:30 A.M. Jackie woke at 10:00. I used hot plate for first time. For breakfast Jackie ate: Hot oatmeal cereal, ½ slice toast, 1½ bananas, glass of milk. Lunch: pastine & egg, whole bowlful, milk, ½ slice toast. Paid rent, landlady told me about having a room empty around 30th. I took a walk with Jackie to look at house. Came back through town, bought a few things, came back to room. Johnnie came in at 5:00. I fed Jackie then we went out to eat. Johnnie home for weekend.*

Sunday, April 22, 1945. *We went to 11:00 mass. Had lunch in restaurant. Came back to room. Jackie took a nap 2:30-5:00. Fed her supper, then went out to restaurant for our supper. Through at 6:30. Went to movies. There was too much of a line at "Bring On The Girls" so we went on to another theater and on the way we met Ruth, Burton and Buddy. At the Mayfair we saw, "Crime Doctor" and "Eadie was a Lady." Very good. We had to leave before the picture was finished. Jackie was restless and began to cry.*

Monday, April 23, 1945. *Johnnie left at 5:30 A.M. We got up at 9:00 & fed Jackie her breakfast. For lunch Jackie had macaroni with butter. 1:00 Johnnie came in. We went to post office. Mailed package to Grace (pig) received a letter from Ann. We went to the park and stayed until 4:15. Took four pictures there. Then came back to room. Fed Jackie her supper then went out to restaurant. Came right back and put Jackie to bed.*

With stray puppy

Monday, April 23, 1945
Ventura, Cal.

Hello Mom, Ann, Fan and Gracie:

Here I go again! Hope you are all well at home and have managed, somehow to get along without me and my daughter. Say, did I ever tell you about the movies out here? No, I don't think I have. Well, there are four movie houses here and none have matinees during the week, only on Saturday and Sunday and, open of course, every night during the week. But isn't that strange? Johnnie says it's because not enough people attend during the day. One Saturday afternoon after Jackie and I had our lunch, we went to a movie and saw "I'll Be Seeing You" with Ginger Rogers and Joseph Cotton. It was a double feature program but Jackie can only last one picture. Whenever we go to the movies we always have to pick which one we want to see and go in at the beginning. The picture was pretty good. We went in at 2:30 and were out by 4:00. I wasn't expecting Johnnie home until 7:00. Some nights he can't get away until after chow, but gee, I don't care how late it is, as long as he can come. Most every one out here only sees their husbands every other day. I've been seeing Johnnie every day so far. Sometimes he gets away real early on his days off. He's here by 12:00 and on the other nights he manages to get here by 5:00 so we have a lot of time together.

Well, to get back, after we came out of the show we went to the park for awhile, stayed until it was time to go for supper and then came on home. We met Johnnie right on the corner of our street.

That night, about 9:00, who should come to visit us but Ruth, Burton and Buddy. Jackie had been asleep for an hour and had just awakened for a drink of water. When she saw Buddy it was no more sleep for her so I put on her slippers and housecoat and let them play. Ruth loved Jackie's little housecoat. Johnnie likes it a lot, too.

Guess what! While Jackie and Buddy were playing, I heard Jackie say, "Oh, darn it!" and kept saying it every time something went wrong. Johnnie put a stop to it. That's the first time she ever said anything out of the way like that. Ruth and Burton stayed until 10:15 and Jackie went right to sleep after they left.

When Johnnie came home Monday afternoon of April 9th, he told me he had made a date for us to meet Vincent Forbes at the U.S.O. 6:30 P.M. So----- right after we had our supper that night we started out for the U.S.O. Before we got very far, however, we met Fitz at the corner. He said he was waiting for a friend of his. We talked with him for a while (Jackie wasn't very friendly or talkative) and went on our way. Forbes was waiting for us outside the U.S.O. building. He's as healthy as can be and is so very tanned. He asked about all of you and sends his regards. He wanted to know how Gracie made out with her boy friend. (??) While Forbes and I were talking, Johnnie went up to the housing desk to see if they had anything for us - no luck. I don't think Jackie remembered Vincent because she didn't show any signs of recognition. Forbes told me that he had tried to see me before and I

426

know it was true because I had heard about it. He was up to our room twice, once with Fitz and once alone. Both times I was out. Another time, they both tried to meet me in the park. Jackie and I were having lunch in the restaurant at the time. When Johnnie came home that night he asked if I had seen them. You know what! Forbes made a 2/c rating while they were at Camp Parks! Isn't that swell! Fitz couldn't make his, tho. I felt sorry for him when he told us about it. (But, to get back to our meeting). Forbes walked out to the main avenue with us and Fitz was still at the corner, waiting. When he saw us, he came over and started walking with us, too. They wanted to take us for a drink but Johnnie suggested buying beer and taking it to our room. Johnnie came home with me and the boys went to buy the beer. I wanted to give them the money for it but they wouldn't hear of it. Oh, yes, we met several other boys of the 15th Batt. that night, too, and they all thought Jackie was so pretty. The boys brought back 8 small bottles of beer and a large bag of popcorn.

By the way, they ought to call this place, "Popcorn Town," they sell so much of it out here. And does Jackie love it!! She always wants Johnnie to buy her some. Oh me! Why do I always have to stray away from a subject! I was undressing Jackie for bed when the boys came back. When Jackie saw that bag full of popcorn which Fitz was carrying, she certainly became friendly enough. It was so nice seeing the three of them together. They were afraid of keeping Jackie awake so they left at 9:00. There were four bottles of beer left and a half bag of popcorn.

The following afternoon, Jackie and I had our lunch in the park with Ruth and Buddy. After shopping around downtown for awhile, Ruth asked me to go up to her place. Since I didn't expect Johnnie until seven, I said I would. I went home first and left a note for Johnnie telling him where I'd be and instructions on how to get out to Ruth's room. We took the bus in front of the old mission where we go to church.

I had taken a blouse and slip along which I ironed when we got there. Ruth asked us to stay for supper and I accepted. She has quite a nice place out there, not bad at all. Burton came in at six and I was so sure Johnnie would come out that I stayed on even after supper. But he never showed up. We left at 8:00. Burton, Ruth, and Buddy walked out to the corner with us and waited until the bus came along. When I came within sight of the house, our room was dark. I couldn't imagine what had happened to Johnnie. When I opened the door of the room, there he was sprawled out on the bed fast asleep!!

Wednesday, April 11th was a lovely day. I washed the clothes ten o'clock in the morning and when I was through I washed my hair (in the bathroom sink). It was Johnnie's day off and he was here by 1:00.

Some fellows in the outfit told him about a room with cooking privileges. Johnnie went to inquire about it but the woman didn't want children, so that let us out again very nicely.

We usually eat our supper in the Ventura Coffee Shop and

427

that night we met Fitz there. He sat down in our booth and ate with us. He had a date to meet some fellow at 6:30 so he left before we were through. After supper we decided to take in a movie because Jackie had slept two hours during the afternoon. We went to see Deanna Durbin in "Can't Help Singing." It wasn't half as good as the rest of her pictures but it wasn't too bad. Jackie was very interested in the picture and was as good as can be. We think it was the singing and the Technicolor. Then they had one of those Terrytoon cartoons. It was about some little white lambs and some wolves. You should have heard Jackie!!! Laugh!! Right out loud, just as though no one else were around. Then she'd say, "Oh, look a dat! Oh, look a dat," and laugh to beat the band. The people around us all got a kick out of it. At the end of the Terrytoon they all turned around to look at her. Johnnie and I were laughing so hard that our sides ached. It was the first time she ever saw one of those cartoons.

On the way home we met several of the boys from the outfit. Johnnie introduced us and, as usual, they all commented on Jackie.

Thurs. April 12th, Jackie slept until 12:15!! When she awoke I dressed her up and we went out to eat. Johnnie came at 6:15 that night.

Friday, April 13th, we had lunch in the park. Ruth and Buddy came at 1:00. It was a lovely day and we stayed in the park until 3:30. After we had our supper we came back to the room and waited for Johnnie. He came at 7:00. He had to work late Thurs. and Friday because he was having the weekend off. The first since we've been here. Sat. he was here by 12:00. He brought me a letter from Fan and a package from Ann and Fan. Thanks for everything, kids. I sure needed those stockings! The blue dress is adorable. I love it. Johnnie liked it too.

Gray, thanks for Jackie's Easter gift. You should have seen how happy she was when we handed it to her. She loves the little lamb and calls it her "Lambie." I was so glad to see those jellybeans! They're the first she's had since we left home. I couldn't find any at all out here for her. And the dishes!! We didn't tell her what was in the bag. We just handed it to her. She peeked in, cocked her head on one side, gave us one of her looks and said, "Oh, my dishes!" Then she brought them over to the side of the bed, looked in the bag again and squealed with delight. Johnnie and I stood there watching her and laughing. It was funny! Right away she had to give us a cup of coffee. Johnnie's been the victim so many times, since. I was also glad to get my "Good Housekeeping Magazine," my slacks and sweater and my hat. Thanks again!

All the stores and most of the restaurants were closed, Sat. in tribute to Pres. Roosevelt. Were they at home, too? Sunday it was very warm out. We got up at 9:00 - fed Jackie her breakfast and went to the 11:00 mass. After lunch we went to the park and stayed there until a quarter of five. We took four pictures while we were out.

As we were eating our supper, who should come in but Clere and Forbes. They sat down with us while we ate and I had a

Tom Collins with my meal. I certainly was surprised in Clere. You remember my speaking bout him, Ann and Fan. He's a couple of years older than Johnnie and he's _fat!_ Johnnie says he got fat just while he was home in the states. Forbes asked about you, Ann and asked if it would be alright if he wrote to you again. He said he was pretty busy while he was at Parks and didn't write to anyone and now that he's here, he's ashamed to write. He thanked me for the pictures I sent him and told me his mother raved about the one of him and Jackie, together. When we finished eating, Clere took our bill and paid it. They walked down the street with us but didn't come up to our room.

Oh, dear, this letter is so long that I'll just have to sign off here. Give our regards to everyone especially Mama G and Tadone and here's a kiss for all of you from Jackie. She remembers and thinks of you all.   So long for now, Lucia

Tuesday, April 24, 1945. Johnnie left at 6:15. Jackie slept 'til 10:45. We ate breakfast and lunch in room. 2:00 we took a walk out to the park. Stayed for an hour because it was raw and windy. We came back to room and I ironed. Johnnie came at 7:00.

Wednesday, April 25, 1945. Jackie slept until 7:15. We had breakfast in our room. Johnnie came at 1:00. Jackie took a nap 2:-4:30. 5:30 we went out for supper. Intended going to movies afterwards but we met Paul and Marion so we went for a ride. Paul took us to a place called, "Hollywood-by-the-sea." It used to be a nice summer resort. Now it's practically deserted and sand dunes everywhere. Stopped in for ice cream and were home by 9:00.

Thursday, April 26, 1945. Lovely day. Washed clothes 9:30. Through at 10:30. Went to market and bought something for lunch to eat in room. Then we went to the park. Came home for supper. Johnnie came in at 5:30.

Friday, April 27, 1945. A lovely day. Had breakfast and went downtown to P & H market. Came home and had lunch. 2:00 went down to the beach with Jackie. We took her pail and shovel. Stayed there until 4:15. Came home. Started cooking supper for Jackie. 5:15 knock on door. I thought it was Johnnie. In walks landlady - husband & sailor downstairs. Catches me with hot plate. Cooking potatoes. They carried in a new mattress for our bed. Johnnie came at 7. We went to market for milk and then came home.

Saturday, April 28, 1945. Jackie awoke at 6:00. Stayed in bed with me until 9:00. I fed her breakfast. Then cleaned room up. Prepared Jackie's lunch and Johnnie came in at 12:30. He brought me a letter from Ann, letter dated April 23. We went to park 1:30. Stayed until 3:00. Came home to have Jackie take a nap. We had supper in room.

Sunday, April 29, 1945. I went to the 11:00 mass. Jackie was naughty all day long. We ate lunch in restaurant and at 2:30 we went to the movies. Saw "Meet Me In St. Louis." Jackie fell asleep for 2 hours. We came back to room and I boiled Jackie two eggs. Went to restaurant for sandwich. Came home & put Jackie to bed. Jackie doesn't feel well and my throat hurts.

April 30, 1945 - Hitler commits suicide as Allied forces close in on Berlin.

Monday, April 30, 1945. Jackie woke at 9:00 feeling much better. She stayed in bed all morning and we had lunch in our room. Johnnie came in at 12:30. He had swapped days with one of the other cooks. We took a walk out to the park. Came out on Main St. and shopped in markets. Brought things back to room and then took a bus to Ruth's place. She asked us to stay for supper. We had a grand meal and stayed until 8:30 P.M. Ruth, Burton, and Buddy walked out to the bus stop with us. Jackie was good all day and when we came home she fell right off to sleep.

Tuesday, May 1, 1945. Jackie awake at 9:30 A.M. We had breakfast. 11:30 went to market. Came back and had lunch. Jackie took a nap. We had supper in the room. Johnnie came in at 6:30 P.M. The guy next door asked Johnnie to wake him up in the morning.

Wednesday, May 2, 1945. Jackie woke at 10:15. Had breakfast. 12:00 Johnnie came home. Brought $123.27 for our fare from the gov't. We sure needed the money. $10 left & rent due. 12:00 Ruth and Buddy came. 1:30 we all went out. We were going to eat at a restaurant but Ruth invited us to her place. We stayed for supper too. I gave Ruth red points and $1.00. We had a lot of fun. Jackie was very good and ate swell. We were home at 8:45.

May 3, 1945 - Rangoon, Burma, liberated.

WORLD WAR II Soon after the Japanese attack on Pearl Harbor and America's subsequent entrance into World War II, it became apparent that voluntary conservation on the home front was not going to suffice this time around. Restrictions on imported foods, limitations on the transportation of goods due to a shortage of rubber tires, and a diversion of agricultural harvests to soldiers overseas all contributed to the U.S. government's decision to ration certain essential items. On January 30, 1942, the Emergency Price Control Act granted the Office of Price Administration (OPA) the authority to set price limits and ration food and other commodities in order to discourage hoarding and ensure the equitable distribution of scarce resources. By the spring, Americans were unable to purchase sugar without government-issued food coupons. Vouchers for coffee were introduced in November, and by March of 1943, meat, cheese, fats, canned fish, canned milk and other processed foods were added to the list of rationed provisions.

430

Every American was entitled to a series of war ration books filled with stamps that could be used to buy restricted items (along with payment), and within weeks of the first issuance, more than 91 percent of the U.S. population had registered to receive them. The OPA allotted a certain amount of points to each food item based on its availability, and customers were allowed to use 48 'blue points' to buy canned, bottled or dried foods, and 64 'red points' to buy meat, fish and dairy each month—that is, if the items were in stock at the market. Due to changes in the supply and demand of various goods, the OPA periodically adjusted point values, which often further complicated an already complex system that required home cooks to plan well in advance to prepare meals.   Despite the fact that ration books were explicitly intended for the sole use by the named recipient, a barter system developed whereby people traded one type of stamp for another, and black markets began cropping up all over the country in which forged ration stamps or stolen items were illegally resold. By the end of the war, restrictions on processed foods and other goods like gasoline and fuel oil were lifted, but the rationing of sugar remained in effect until 1947. (from INSIDE HISTORY website, www.history.com/news/food-fatonng-in-wartime-america)

Thursday, May 3, 1945. Jackie woke at 11:00 had breakfast and then lunch at 2:00. 3:30 we went to the park and then to market. Home by 5:15. Had supper at six. 7:30 put Jackie to bed. Johnnie came at 9:15 P.M. He had to take an I.Q. test which lasted two hours. Had another shot. Paid rent.

Thursday, May 3, 1945
Ventura, Calif.

Hello Mom, Ann, Fan, and Gracie!!

How's everything going back there? Jackie's lying on the bed. I doubt very much whether she'll sleep because she just woke up at eleven o'clock. Pardon me! She's not lying anymore. Now she's sitting up with one shoe and stocking off and she's cleaning her toes. That'll keep her busy for a while. Maybe I'll even be able to finish this letter - maybe!

I'm sending home some pictures that we took a couple of weeks ago. After you've finished looking at them, put them in my album or any other safe place where I'll be sure to find them. Do you like the way they turned out?

Thanks for the two letters you wrote me, Ann, those of Apr. 18ᵗʰ and 23ʳᵈ. Sure was glad to hear from you! You needn't bother about sending the plug anymore. I already have one, but I'll tell you about that later. Send the stockings by all means!! I'm on the last pair that you sent me.

No, I haven't met Carl and Evelyn Blosser. Carl is still in the hospital - gall bladder and appendicitis. He's very sick. Evelyn is expecting in a couple of months and was about to go home when I came out here. Whether she did or not, I don't know.

So glad to hear about Tadone! I hope he'll be completely well by the time I come home. Jackie remembers and speaks of Mama G and Tadone quite often, but then, she speaks a lot of all of you. For example: she tells me she's watching Gracie wash the dishes or that she wants Gracie to put her shoes on. She's in the stage of "Make believe" now. She was sitting on the pot and I heard her say, "I have to do wee wee, Aunt Fannie. I told you I had to do duty, Ann!" She says "I told you" a lot. Johnnie says she got that from me. Then she'll say, "Good-bye Mommy, I'll be right back." I'll ask her where she is going and she'll say, "I'm going home to Grandma's house, or it'll be to school, or to the store. She keeps going on like that all day long. Uncle Joe and Aunt Angie are a big part of her life, too.

When we first came out here, everything belonged to Uncle Joe. He owned just about every car on the road. She even mentions Uncle Gene and Aunt Mildred a lot - and, of course, Michael and Judy. Aunt Josephine and Uncle Mike are right in there, too. Why, one day, I even heard her talking to "Mrs. Bianco"!! She has quite a vocabulary and speaks very well. Johnnie is very pleased with her manners. She says please, thank you, and I'm sorry. Gray, she still says, "Don't cry. You be a good girl, now."

Those pieces of material you enclosed in your letter <u>are</u> lovely, Ann. I particularly like the two aqua's. The dresses out here are so expensive and they're not even worth all the money!!

I hope you didn't send my purple coat out. I wanted my cherry jacket because it's a little dressy and it goes with most of the clothes I have. That blue coat you kids bought when I got my purple one would go fine, too.

I don't know just how much longer I'll be out here. It may be for only a matter of weeks. Anyway, I'm staying as long as I can.

I might know you'd forget about that ten dollars for Mama G and Tadone!! It's a good thing I thought to remind you!!

I wrote Mrs. De Roxtro a 13-page letter the other day. I didn't think she expected to hear from me, too, as long as Johnnie wrote her. She sent Jackie two dollars for Easter enclosed in a cute card. She even enclosed $2.00 in a card for Johnnie and me. We've only had one letter from her, though. Maybe she'll write when she gets my letter. If I'm still here. I'll have to stop now. It's three o'clock and I want to take Jackie out to the park for some fresh air and exercise. It's not even a nice day. Looks like it's going to rain. The weather's been terrible, lately. It's funny how the dampness out here affects me. I have another sore throat. Jackie's alright, tho, and I'm thankful for that. Bye now.

<u>6:45p.m.</u>

Well, here I am back again. We had our supper and pretty soon it'll be time to put Jackie to bed. She's reading a book now. That's how I'm able to write. Johnnie's going to be late tonight. His name was posted, along with several others, saying he had to go to school tonight at 6:00. He didn't know much about it so I don't either.

One night Jackie woke up calling me and said, "my throat, my throat." I didn't know what could be wrong so I picked her up and just in time for she up-chucked all over her nighties and my pyjamas. She had a temperature and Johnnie and I were worried.

And that was one of the few mornings when Johnnie had to leave at 3:00 A.M. When he left, I brought Jackie in bed with me and she slept until 9:00 A.M. She wouldn't eat any cereal so I didn't insist. Instead, I squeezed some oranges and we both drank orange juice. Johnnie came home at 11:30 that day. He said he told his chief that his little girl was sick and he got off early. I was both surprised and glad to see him.

We went out for lunch at 12:00 and then afterwards we went to the park. We met Ruth and Buddy there. Jackie was all right when she saw Buddy and started right in to play with him. We came home early, though so that Jackie could take a nap, which she did. 5:30 we went out to supper and while we were eating, Fitz walked in. He ordered and ate his supper with us and when we were through he paid the bill. He came back to our room with us and stayed for a half hour. Two weeks ago, on a Thursday, we went to Ruth's house for supper. We had planned on having a spaghetti dinner, with me doing the cooking. We chose a day when both men would be off. Jackie and I went to Ruth's at 12:00 noon. On the way, I had stopped to buy some round steak, tomatoes & tomato paste and some cheese. When we got there we had our lunch with them. I made a meat roll because I couldn't get chop meat.

Johnnie came at 5:00 that day. He had gotten his first shot. Burton came at 6:00 and we ate soon afterward. I don't think it turned out so well, but everybody else seemed to enjoy it. I cooked a lb. and a half of spaghetti just for the four of us and the two kids, and every bit of it was gone. Johnnie and Burton ate so much that afterwards they looked like two bloated pigs. And Jackie!! You should have seen Jackie. She ate her dish full and then asked for more. She just dove right in to it and didn't say a word until she had finished. I didn't like the way it turned out, tho. In the first place you can't get any of our spaghetti around here. Only the American kind which cooks in seven minutes and you know what that's like. By the way, when you do send me a package, stick in a lb. of La Rosa spaghetti. I may still have a chance to use it.

Oh, yes, Johnnie finally was able to find a plug at the base. And - he also won a roll of film!! They had about 11 rolls of 616 for the whole Battalion and who ever was interested put their names in a hat and the eleven names drawn had the chance to buy the film. It cost them a quarter. Wasn't Johnnie lucky!!

The next day, Friday, Johnnie had off. He wasn't supposed to either, but his boss told him he could have liberty because he had enough men there to do the work. Incidentally, that was our lucky week. He even had the weekend off, too, which he wasn't supposed to. But to get back to Friday, we didn't have much of the money from the allotment left but we decided to buy a hot plate just to cook food for Jackie. So that afternoon we bought one. We also bought a Boy Scout all steel cooking kit for $2.30. It consists of a small pan with a cover, a flat pan, (shaped like a pie tin, only smaller and deeper), a cup and a frying pan. It all fits together and comes in a cloth kit which I use for my clothespins. We were quite lucky to come across it because pans are quite hard to get out here. On the way home we met Ruth and Buddy and Ruth told us about

433

seeing a plug in a little store down the street. We all went down to the store and Johnnie bought three of them. They're not just the female plugs. It's everything in one with a chain. Know what I mean, Mom? These plugs had just come in that morning. We came back to our room and I ironed all my clothes. Took me two hours and a half. That night I fed Jackie chicken soup with noodles. I used the hot plate for the first time. After she ate we went out to supper. She eats much better, now, although her appetite isn't what it used to be. Just the same she's put on two lbs. since we've been out here. And she seems to be getting chubby. The first morning I gave Jackie her breakfast using the hotplate, she ate: hot oatmeal cereal, ½ slice of toast, 1½ banana, glass of milk, and for lunch, a whole bowlful of pastina and egg, ½ slice of toast and a glass of milk. Is it any wonder?

Last Saturday, the Landlady told me she may have a vacancy in one of the houses with cooking privileges. Haven't heard anything more about it. I've asked her about it several times. She doesn't know just when the people intend moving out. They were supposed to have moved by the end of April. If they're going, I wish they'd hurry up, before it's too late to do any good.

Last weekend, Johnnie had off so we decided to take in a show. Jackie slept quite a while Sunday afternoon so we planned on seeing "Bring On The Girls," with Sonny Tufts. When we got there, we saw two long lines waiting to get in and right at the end was Ruth, Burton & Buddy. They didn't feel like waiting in line either, so we all went to the "Mayfair" and saw "Crime Doctor" and "Eadie Was A Lady" with Ann Miller. We saw all of "Crime Doctor" and half of the other when Jackie became very restless. She wouldn't stay anymore, so we had to get up and leave. Gee, I sure hated to, because it was pretty good. When I saw Ruth again, she told me how the picture ended.

Wed. after supper we met Marian and Paul Andrews and they took us for a ride. We went to a place called "Hollywood-by-the-sea." Ever hear of it? It must have been all right at one time but now it's a deserted summer resort piled high with sand dunes. There are still people there but I told Johnnie it looks like a ghost town.

Last Friday the Landlady caught me with the hot plate on. I was boiling potatoes for Jackie. It was a quarter after five and I heard a knock on the door. I thought it was Johnnie for he usually knocks and then walks in. So when I heard the knock I went right on with what I was doing and who should walk in but the landlady, her husband, and another guy, carrying a new mattress. For a couple of seconds, neither of us spoke. Then she said, "I hope you don't mind if I strip your bed. I have a new mattress for it. It really didn't matter whether I minded or not because she was taking off the bedclothes as she spoke. They laid the new mattress on top of the old one and went out. Not a word was said about the hotplate. By the way, the mattress was hard before, but now it's even harder. It's the most uncomfortable bed I ever slept in.

Last Sunday we went to the movies and saw "Meet Me In St. Louis." It was swell!! Jackie slept through it all. Lasted a good two hours, too.

Monday was Johnnie's day off and he was here by 12:30. About 4:00 in the afternoon we took the bus out to Ruth's house. She was glad to see us and asked us to stay for supper. Burton came in at 6:00 and he was glad to see us too. They make us feel so much at home. Ruth cooked us a grand meal and after we had the dishes done they walked out to the bus stop with us.

Johnnie just came in!!! One moment, please. Johnnie just told me about that school business. He had to take an I.Q. test, which lasted two hours. He also received another shot.

Time to say goodnight to you all and regards to everybody, especially to Mama G and Tadone. Guess what!! Johnnie even brought me home a banana split!! Here goes another couple of lbs!!! Here's a kiss for all of you from Jackie.   Love, Lou

Friday, May 4, 1945. *Jackie awoke at 8:00. 10:30 I washed the clothes. 12:00 Jackie and I had lunch. 1:00 Johnnie came home. Brought me a letter from Gracie. 1:30 Jackie took a nap. Slept until 3:00 P.M. We dressed and left the house at 4:00. Caught the bus in front of the old mission. Went to visit the Phlegars, Wanda & Hunter. We were invited for supper. Johnnie did not tell me. Very nice meal. Jackie very bashful at first. They shared apartment with Julia and Raymond Lash. Both very nice couples. Made such a fuss over Jackie. Jackie took to Wanda but couldn't make up her mind about Hunter. We stayed there until 9:30. We made a date for next Wednesday. A spaghetti supper. Hunter took some pictures of Jackie.*

Saturday, May 5 1945. *Jackie awoke at 9:00. It was a lovely day. After we had our lunch in the room, we went to the park and stayed there until 4:30. We came back to room and had supper. Started ironing clothes and Johnnie came at 7:00.*

Sunday, May 6, 1945. *Chipper Petrone's birthday. Missed Mass. Had breakfast. Jackie slept until 11:30 A.M. 11:45 gave Jackie a bath and washed her hair. 2:30 went out to eat in restaurant. 3:45 went to movies. Saw "Naughty Marietta," very good. Jackie just about lasted it out - 5:30. On way home we met Johnnie. We came back to room for awhile, read papers and then went out to supper (paid $5.35 for steak dinner). Coming home we heard Burton calling us. They came up to our room and stayed until 9:30 p.m.*

May 7, 1945 – Germany surrenders. Victory in Europe Day.

Monday, May 7, 1945. *Got up at 9:00 A.M. Was very surprised to see Johnnie come home at 10:15 A.M. He brought checks and a letter from Ann, & stamps enclosed. Jackie was still sleeping. She woke at 10:45.   Johnnie shaved and then went to ration board to see about shoe stamps for Jackie. When he came back we went to the bank to cash allotment checks and then had lunch in the coffee shop. When we were thru we went to Ventura R.R. station to inquire about a reservation. Were told to come back in a couple of days. We walked out to Main St. and took bus to Ruth's. We were invited for supper. Grand meal - stuffed ourselves like pigs. Lots of fun when we go there. They walked out to bus stop with us. Had to wait 45 minutes. We were home by 10:00 P.M.*

Tuesday, May 8, 1945. *V.E. Day - Victory in Europe. Jackie awoke at 10:00. (rained during night). Had breakfast, then dressed her up. 12:30 Ruth and Buddy came to visit us. We stayed in room for awhile and then the four of us went downtown. We asked S.P.'s if men would be restricted at the base. Said no. 3:30 we went back to room. Jackie took a nap at 4:00 and slept until 6:00. Johnnie came in at 5:30. I didn't expect him until 7:00. We had supper in room and then went to* market, bought tomatoes and other groceries. Jackie not sleepy at all. Johnnie & I played with her on bed. 9:15 Paul and Marion came to our room. Paul was supposed to have been restricted at the base (dirty linen). They stayed until 10:30 P.M.

Wednesday, May 9, 1945. Jackie woke at 11:00 A.M. Johnnie came in at 12:30P.M. Brought letters from Ann and Fan. Left house at 2:00. Went to market for beautiful piece of top round to make brasciole and to cook spaghetti at the Phlegars. (especially for J.& J.) (such appetites those two have).We bought all the ingredients. Cooked a lb. and a half of spaghetti and it was almost all eaten up by the four of us. While dinner was cooking, I etched names on my bag pull and on Jackie's spoon and fork. Johnnie engraved his cigarette case and lighter. Gosh, but it was fun. Think I'll get one later. Had nice time. Then we went out and took pictures. The spaghetti turned out pretty good. We had a very nice time. Were home by 9:00 P.M. Received negatives & took pictures of all of 5/4/45.

Thursday, May 10, 1945. Johnnie left at 6:30 A.M. Jackie woke at 10:00. Fed her breakfast. Wrote a letter to Mil. 12:30. Right after lunch, Ruth and Buddy came up to the room. We all went out to the park. 3:00 we left and came home through town. Jackie and I had supper in room at 6:00. Johnnie came in at 7:30. Had double shots in arms. Not feeling well.

Friday, May 11, 1945. Johnnie left for camp at 3:00 A.M. Jackie awoke at 10:00. Fed her breakfast. 10:30 I washed the clothes, had lunch. In the mail we received our ration coupons; 80 blue stamps and 48 red. Shoe coupon for Jackie. In afternoon went to bus depot to buy round trip tickets for Johnnie and myself. They cost $3.95. Planned on going to L.A. with Ruth and Burton. Came back to room. Pulled in clothes and ironed them all. Johnnie came at 7:10. He went out to buy milk, brought Jackie along and brought me home a banana split. Ruth, Burton and Buddy came to visit.

Saturday, May 12, 1945. I got up at 7:00. Got dressed then woke Jackie up at 8:00. Fed her breakfast and then dressed her. We were ready by 9:00 A.M. Johnnie came at 9:15. Brought package; P coat, hangers, choc. bars, stockings, doll, marbles, ball bag, starch, pro-curler, etc. Left here, after opening package which enthralled Jackie. Arrived at bus station 9:30. Met R.B & B. Boarded 9:57 bus for L.A. Slow, uneventful trip, very crowded. J & B stood all the trip, very crowded. Stopped at Thousand Oaks for refreshments enroute. Lay over twenty minutes. Quite a nice rest. Drank soda (Johnny too) watered Jackie, etc. Arrived Hollywood at about twelve thirty. First stop U.S.O., where we had refreshments(coffee & doughnuts), signed Navy wives' register and inquired about room. Went to Sunset Motel where we got a duplex room, large enough for six of us. Two full size beds, two nice armchairs, dressers, but rug full of lint. Beds quite comfortable, too. Nice fairly clean place. (Price $1.50 per person, excluding children.) Left room after cleaning up a little. Passed C.B.S. - N.B.C. - Radio City - Hollywood Canteen, Brown Derby - Grauman's Chinese Theater, Earl Carroll theater and several others, including Hollywood Hotel again. Lunched at a cafeteria, enjoyed a pleasant moderately priced meal. Johnny, Jackie and I all ate for about $1.50. Shopped in novelty shops and five and tens all afternoon. Gee, it was swell. Bought paper after learning that there was no stage show at Grauman's, in order to locate one. Decided to go to Orpheum Theater, which turned out to be in L.A. Looked over Chinese theater. Nice fountains with pools of goldfish, which Jackie didn't want to leave. Many stars have their foot and handprints right in the cement sidewalk in front of theatre. John Barrymore even has his profile there. Jackie fell asleep in Johnny's arms and slept all the way to L.A. on a street car. After riding about ¾ of an hour, arrived at end of line (subway terminal) at 6:30. Jackie wide awake now, and full of pep. Buddy also slept on way. Did more shopping, mostly window and sight-seeing. Nothing of interest seen. Saw monkey, which intrigued children. Got quite a kick out of his scratching. Jackie said he had an itch. Decided to eat before seeing show. Went to another cafeteria. Don't have much variety here, like New York. Picture was good. "Forever Yours" with Gale Storm and Johnny Mack Brown. Couldn't find seats together for picture, but afterwards we did. Sat in last row of balcony. Stage show was very good; Ross sisters, Allan Jones, Connie Haines, Jack Marshall, with Al Lyons band. Ballerina sure was comical. Don't miss the Ross sisters. They're good. After show, returned to Hollywood by street car. In L.A., Jackie & Buddy walked hand in hand down street singing at tops of voices, and did they attract attention. Did I ever laugh. At destination in Hwood, we again had coffee & hamburgers, then returned, very sleepy & tired. Jackie slept in bed made by pushing two chairs together. And so, goodnight.

Sunday, May 13, 1945. Received card from Johnny, arose at ten o'clock, dressed and left room about noon. Caught bus. Rode to destination (C.B.S.) learned time of departure (3:10PM) of

Greyhound bus. Went to take pictures for awhile. Johnny & Burton entered Hollywood canteen and tired but happy, we all rode bus back to Ventura. We parted at bus depot. Came home, cleaned up a little and went out to eat (again). Returned to room, put tired daughter to bed and now, I am ready to do likewise. Adios.

Greaves family

Monday, May 14, 1945. Arose at 10:30, had breakfast. After lunch 1:30 we went out. Lovely day. Met Ruth & Buddy at park. Stayed there until 4:00. Came home 5:30, had supper. Johnnie came at 7:30. We all went to market and then came back to room.

Tuesday, May 15, 1945. Jackie & I awoke at 9:00. Had breakfast. 10:15 Johnnie came home. (not much to do. Had gone to see about reservations - not come in yet.) Brought Mother's day card from M.de R. $1.00 enclosed. All went out at 1:00, mailed polo coat, then took pictures in the park. 2:00 went to the restaurant for lunch. Came home, put Jackie to bed for nap. Had supper in room then went to movies. Saw Bing Crosby in "Here Comes the Waves." NOT enjoyable. Very warm night. Stopped in for ice cream.

439

May 15, 1945
Ventura, Calif.

Hello Mom, Ann, Fan and Gracie!!

How's everything going back there? I haven't spent very much time in this room lately, that's the reason for the lateness of this letter, or should I say, 'book'?

I have quite a bit to tell you so I may as well start right off. Jackie woke up at 9:00. I fed her breakfast, dressed her up and now she's playing. This is Johnnie's day off and I expect him to come about noon so that leaves me an hour to write.

Two weeks ago, May 2, to be exact, Johnnie came home on his day off, 12:00 noon and he handed me an envelope. In it was the money which the government reimbursed me for my fare out, $123.37. It wasn't as much as I paid but it was more than I expected. And did it come in handy. We didn't have any money at all left from the allotment and I was all set to cash one of the few travelers checks which I have left. I put $1.00 of that amount away and we used up the rest.

Ruth and Buddy came up at 12:30 that same day. It was a Wednesday. Ruth was surprised about my getting some money back. She didn't know anything about it. She said she was going to have Burton apply for hers.

440

1:30 the whole bunch of us went out. What do ya know!! Johnnie just came in!! He said they didn't have much work to do so he came on out. He stopped at the post office and brought me a Mother's Day card from Mrs. De Roxtro. It's a lovely card and on it are the words, "Because you are a mother." She even enclosed a dollar in it. Wasn't that nice of her!! Johnnie doesn't want me to write any more. He said it's so beautiful out that he wants us to get out of the room. It does look nice out. The sun's been shining since early morning and it looks quite warm out. I've been told that the real hot weather starts about June. It'll be just like me to be gone when it does start. Guess I'll have to call it quits, now. I'll continue on as soon as I can

May 16, 1945

Well, here I am again. Jackie is still asleep so I may be able to write quite a bit this morning.

I started telling you about that Wednesday with Ruth and Buddy, so I'll continue on with that now. When we finally did go out, none of us had had our lunch yet so we invited Ruth and Buddy to come to the restaurant with us. Ruth didn't want to eat in a restaurant so she invited Johnnie, Jackie and me out to her place and asked us to stay for supper, too. I didn't want to go because I didn't feel right about eating at her place so much, but she kept insisting, so we went. We stopped in at the market first and I bought the ham and paid for it. She wanted to pay me for it but I wouldn't take the money. Burton always comes home at six, so when he came, we were ready to eat. We had a swell meal. Ruth had bought three large veal steaks. Jackie ate very well and so did the rest of us. We had a swell time out there. Johnnie and Burton are two of a kind. Each tries to outdo the other in wit and foolishness. They keep Ruth and me in stitches. They walked to the bus station with us and we were home at a quarter of nine. Before I left, I gave Ruth a dollar and ten red points.

Friday, May 4, Jackie woke up at 8:00 A.M. I fed her breakfast and dressed her up and then I went down to wash the clothes. I was through by 12:00 so we came up to the room and had our lunch. Johnnie came at 1:00 and he brought me a letter from Gracie. I was very glad to hear from you, Gray. Yours was the only letter I had received that week. I'm glad you liked the pig I sent. It's really hand painted and comes from Mexico. I thought you might like to keep it as a souvenir.

No, the jelly beans weren't hard when we got them. They were just right and they didn't last long, either. I certainly do remember those pictures I took of you and Mary. I'd love to have one of them if you'd send it out. Don't worry about writing me any more. As long as one of the family writes, it's O.K. by me. I'm glad you thought enough of the little pig to write your thanks.

By the way, Ann and Fan, didn't you ever receive those dresser dolls I sent you some time ago. Even before I sent Gracie the pig? Neither of you mentioned anything of them in your letters so I gathered you didn't get them. Let me know!

Now to get back to Friday, May 4th. Jackie took a nap at 1:30 and slept until 3:00. We had been invited out to supper by another friend of Johnnie's who works with him in the spud locker. His name is Hunter Phlegar. He said his wife was anxious to meet Jackie and me. Her name is Wanda Mae. They live out in the same direction as Ruth and Burton and when we were on the bus, Jackie thought she was going to see Buddy and when we got off she began to cry when she found out we weren't. I had told her right from the beginning that we were going to see Hunter and Wanda, but because we took the bus in front of the old mission and turned off the same road, she was sure we were going to see Buddy.

Wanda and Hunter were outside the house when we got there and as we approached them he snapped our picture. I'm enclosing all the snapshots he took of us in this letter. Be sure to take good care of them and put them away for me. By the way, doesn't Hunter look like George Sanders? He talks like him, too!! Wanda is very nice. She comes from West Va.! And has a southern accent.

The house in which they live has three rooms, two bedrooms and a kitchen. The kitchen is between the two bedrooms and they share the place with another Seabee of the 15th. His name is Raymond Lash and his wife's name is Julia. Julia comes from Georgia and such a southern accent I never did hear!!! It's terrific!! They're both very nice couples. Jackie was very bashful at first but after awhile she was herself again. They just raved over Jackie and think she's so sweet and lovely. I dressed her in the red flannel skirt and white blouse and that pink sweater with the short sleeves that Mom gave her. Remember it, Mom? It fits her swell and looks darling over her dresses. Speaking of dresses, all those dresses of hers that I packed are too short. I have to take the hems down on all of them.

Wanda prepared a lovely meal for us. She had steak for the fellows and fish for me because Johnnie had told Hunter I don't eat meat on Friday.

Jackie liked Wanda and was very friendly with her but she couldn't make up her mind about Hunter. He was falling all over himself trying to win her over. He tried so hard that I think Jackie became suspicious. Julia and Raymond made a fuss over her too. Julia is pregnant, but Wanda can't have any children unless she undergoes an operation. They're waiting until after the war is over.

We were there until 9:30 and just before we left, Hunter made up with Jackie. They say "Hug ma neck, sugar," and "honey chile" and etc. They told us we were welcomed to come at any time. Johnnie asked them if they liked spaghetti and they said they did. So when we left we made a date for Wed. when I'd cook a spaghetti dinner for them.

Sun. May 6th, Johnnie didn't have the week end off so after Jackie and I had our dinner in the restaurant we went to the moves and saw "Naughty Marietta." It was quite a long picture and Jackie just about made it. I enjoyed it very much, though. We were out by 5:30 and on the way home we met Johnnie. He had gotten out at 4:30 and was looking all over for us. We came on back to our room and then went out for supper. All they had was steak and fish so Johnnie ordered steak and when the bill came it was $5.35. On our way back to the room we heard someone whistling and calling Johnnie's name. It was Burton, Ruth and Buddy. They had seen us from the corner and had tried to catch up with us. They came up to our room and stayed until 9:30.

Monday, May 7th I got up at 9:00 and I was surprised by Johnnie coming in at 10:15. He brought me the allotment checks and a letter from you, Ann. Thanks for the stamps you enclosed. I was fresh out and about to buy more.

Jackie was still asleep and didn't wake until 10:45. Johnnie shaved and then he went to the ration board to see about getting a shoe stamp for Jackie. When he came back, Jackie and I were all dressed and we went to the bank to cash the allotment check. After we had our lunch in the coffee shop, we went to the Ventura Railroad station to see about getting my reservation back home. Johnnie told me they were leaving around the end of this month. So we're trying to get a reservation for June 1st. If Johnnie does leave by the end of the month I may have to wait here until my reservation comes through. I won't leave before he's restricted anyway. Maybe something will happen to keep them from going over again. At least, that's what I'm hoping and praying for. The man told us he hadn't had a lower in weeks and told us to come back in a couple of days - that he would try to get one for me. When we were through there, we walked out to Main St. and took the bus to Ruth's house. She had invited us to supper. We reached there at 4:00 P.M. We had a grand meal and Johnnie, Jackie and I ate so much. And as usual, we had a swell time. Tues. May 8th - V.E. Day - Ruth and Buddy came up to our room at 12:30. We had just finished our lunch. We stayed in the room and talked awhile and then we all went downtown. Ruth asked the S.P.'s if the men would be restricted at the base. They told us, "no." Johnnie said if they were restricted, he wouldn't be able to come home for 72 hours. We were glad to know they weren't being held up. I came back to the room at 3:30 and at 4:00 Jackie took a nap. She was so tired she could hardly keep her eyes open. Johnnie came in at 5:30. I was surprised because I didn't expect him until 7:00. Jackie woke at 6:00.

We had our supper and then we took a walk to the market. I don't think I've ever told you, but the market we always go to is run by Chinese. At first, I was afraid to go there by myself, but it doesn't bother me a bit, now.

To get back to the subject—When we came home again, Jackie was very wide awake so Johnnie and I played with her on the bed. My gosh!! Johnnie is so rough with her! And she loves it! He holds her way up in the air sitting on his feet and when she's as high as she can go, she topples over. That's the object of the game, "falling from the mountain." As I told you before, they get along swell together. Johnnie spoils her in some ways, but he also disciplines her, too. In fact, she obeys him more than she does me. When she's naughty all he has to do is look at her and tell her to do what ever she won't, and she does it! If necessary, he even spanks her. So you see, she isn't a "spoiled brat." Even now, she and

443

Johnnie were playing on the bed for quite a while. I gave up. She tires me out. Johnnie loves to roughhouse her up. He lets her walk on all the ledges, he races with her, he swings her in the air and encourages her to climb up things. Honestly, sometimes they drive me crazy! At 9:15 there was a knock on the door and who do you think it was! Marian and Paul! (The first time Marian's been up to our room. She always waited for Paul down in the car.) Well, anyway, they came in and visited with us until 10:30. Paul was supposed to have been restricted at the base for a week. At inspection, his bed linen was dirty. Johnnie's is dirty, too, but once a month, just before inspection, he shakes the dust out of the sheets and turns them over. I told him he better not take any chances like that. It would be just like him to get caught. But to get back again, Paul was friends with the M.A. on duty and he let him out every night.

Wednesday, May 9ᵗʰ, Jackie awoke at 11:00 A.M. This was the day we were supposed to go to Wanda's and Hunters to cook the spaghetti dinner. Johnnie came home at 12:30 and he brought me letters from Ann and Fan. Thanks for sending me the cards, Ann, but I had already bought and sent mine out when I received yours. They're very nice and I certainly would have used them. I was lucky enough to find the other two, like you sent me, and bought them a month ahead of time. I can't send you the money for the hospitalization, Ann, I thought we'd have a place by this time, but it didn't come through, so we're still stuck here. It's costing us $1.50 a month to live the way we are now. I was so glad to know that Mil had a baby boy, but then, I knew it would be. I wrote Mil a short letter of congratulations and sent Gene a card.   Thanks for your letter, Fan. You made it nice and long, too. See what you kids are going to send me in return for this! Certainly was surprised to hear about Paul being home. No wonder I didn't hear from you. If Ann hadn't written I wouldn't have known what was going on! Sorry Jackie and I had to miss him. I would have liked to see what he was like. (That doesn't sound so good but right now I'm at the stage where I'm just writing.) Now to continue on with my narration.

After I read both your letters, Jackie and I got dressed and the three of us left the house at 2:00. (I had told Wanda I would be there early). We went to the market to buy whatever we needed and the chinks had some nice round steak. I bought two and made two meat rolls out of them. Cost me $1.05 -18 pts. We paid for everything. They wanted to reimburse us but we didn't take the money they offered. We got to the Phlegar's house about 3:00. Hunter took more snapshots of us. The spaghetti dinner turned out pretty good. Better than it did at Ruth's. Johnnie certainly did eat a lot. I cooked a lb. and a half just for the four of us, and Jackie, of course, who didn't do so bad herself.

Hunter has an engraving machine and Johnnie engraved his cigarette case and lighter. He wrote on them, "To Johnnie, with all my love - Lou" After he got through putting Jackie's name on her fork and spoon, I engraved our names on my brown bag pull and also on my key chain. It was a lot of fun doing it. We had a very nice time at the Phlegars and were invited to cook again.

Thurs. May 10. Ruth and Buddy came up to our room at 12:30 and we all went out to the park. We stayed there until 5:00 and then came back to our room. Ruth & Buddy had left earlier. Jackie and I had our supper in the room and Johnnie came in at 7:30 P.M. He had gotten two shots in his arms and wasn't feeling very well.

Fri., May 11. I received a shoe coupon for Jackie, through the mail. I've already told you about Johnnie applying for it. Earlier in the week, Johnnie and I had planned to go to L.A. with Ruth and Burton, to spend the weekend. So, Friday afternoon, Jackie and I went to the Greyhound bus depot and bought two round-trip tickets. They cost us $3.95. When we came back, I pulled in the clothes I had washed in the morning and when Johnnie came home at 7:15 I had them all ironed. We had a visit by Ruth and Burton and Buddy that night, too.

I'll tell you about my trip to L.A. in my next letter. In this, I want to have room enough to tell you to send my mail to the post office in Ventura. Then I can call for it myself in case Johnnie leaves, and I'm still here. Give my regards to everybody and here's a kiss to all of you from Jackie.

Love, Lou

Wednesday, May 16, 1945. Jackie awoke at 10:20. Lovely day. After lunch, 2:00, we went out to the park and stayed until 5:00. Met Janice & Gary there. Went to market to do shopping and met Johnnie on S. Figueroa St. Had been out since 4:20. Came to room and gave Jackie her supper. Then Johnnie & I had our supper in restaurant. Came back to room. Very warm night.

Thursday, May 17, 1945. Jackie awoke at 9:00. Had breakfast in room. Waited for Johnnie to come 12:00. 1:30 Ruth and Buddy came. Jackie about to take a nap. She wouldn't stay in bed any more after she saw Buddy. Ruth stayed until 2:30. Dressed Jackie up, yellow dress, and walked out to corner with Ruth and Buddy. On way back, saw Johnnie. Walked up to meet us. 2:45 went to park for awhile. Had supper in Maddox 5:30. Came home 7:00. Paul came up. Johnnie asked him if he were going to L.A. Put Jackie to bed 8:00. Paid rent. Ruth took 6 negatives.

Friday, May 18, 1945. Lovely day. Jackie awoke at 9:30, had breakfast. Landlady brought us clean linens. 11:30 washed clothes. Almost through when Ruth and Buddy came. Helped me hang out clothes. Ruth had brought lunch. Intended eating in the park. Ate in room instead. Johnnie came at 1:30 not feeling well. Went out with Ruth and Buddy. Went to Sears to look for film. Came home at 3:30. Fed Jackie supper in room. Johnnie & I went out to restaurant for our supper. Came back and pulled clothes in, then went to market for milk. (got period.)

445

Saturday, May 19, 1945. *Jackie awoke at 10:45 A.M. Had breakfast then cleaned the room. Had lunch at 1:00. Dressed. Johnnie came at 2:00. Went to park. Paul and Marian stopped by, got in car and went to "Goebel's Lion Farm" an hours' ride from Ventura. Beautiful place. All kinds of animals, mostly lions. Jackie very much interested. Liked monkeys best. I was sprayed by lion. Left there at 5:45. Came into Ventura and had supper in Maddox. After supper Paul took us to Wheeler Springs, past Ojai, high up in the mountains. Saw "Believe it or not Ripley's Smallest Post Office in the U.S.A." Stayed there at lodge until 10:00. Jackie very good. On way home, Jackie fell asleep. In by 10:30.*

Sunday, May 20, 1945. *Jackie awoke at 9:30. Missed mass. Johnnie came at 1:00. Fed Jackie her lunch and then we went out to the restaurant for dinner. After dinner stopped to buy Sunday papers and came back to the room. Jackie took a nap from 4:00 to 6:00. All went out for supper then went to movies. Saw "A Guy, A Gal, A Pal" and "The Three Caballeros." Jackie too tired to see all of it. Not much good anyway.*

May 20, 1945 - Japanese begin withdrawal from China.

Monday, May 21, 1945. *Jackie awoke at 7:15. I told her it was too early to get up so she went back to sleep again and slept until 12:00 noon. Had lunch. 2:00 went to railroad station to find out about reservation. Man told me I was still on the waiting list. On way back, stopped at the park and stayed until 4:00. Shopped in market on way home. (Found shopping bag in restroom) came back to room and ironed. Had supper at 6:00. Johnnie came in at 7:30 with milk and bottle of beer. Johnnie has a bad cold.*

Tuesday, May 22, 1945. *Jackie awoke at 9:00. A lovely day. Had breakfast then dressed and went out. Took Jackie in schoolyard for a ride on the swings. Came home at 12:00. Ruth and Buddy came as Jackie was about to take a nap. They stayed until 5:00. Jackie and I walked out to the corner with them and then came back to the room and had our supper. Johnnie came in at 8:30. Waited since 6:00 for a ride.*

Wednesday, May 23, 1945. *Jackie and I got up at 9:00 and went to buy the milk. Came back and had breakfast. Johnnie came in at 10:30. (not much work) (received 4 rolls of film from Seabees.) We went out for lunch and went to park. Took pictures of us all. 1:30 Paul and Marion came along. Stayed with us for a while in park until Jackie said she wanted to go for a ride. We rode up to Wheeler Springs. Stopped at the store for a while and then rode on up the mountain. 28 miles. Stopped on bridge and boys walked down below to take some pictures of the mountains. While we were looking, some rock fell just missing the car and us. Marion moved the car further up and Jackie and I walked back to the bridge. No sign of the boys. We walked back to the car and Jackie started to throw rocks down the mountain into the water below. Boys came back* *after a while. Each with cuts on their fingers. Johnnie had climbed to the top of one of the cliffs. As we were riding up my head was getting dizzy and my stomach weak. Coming back it was just like an elevator. Had same sensation. Stopped at store on way back for hamburger and then came on home 5:30 P.M. All of were very tired.*

Thursday, May 24, 1945. *Jackie got up at 10:30. 11:30 we left to go to Ruth's. Got there at 11:45. While we were having lunch at 2:00, Johnnie comes. 4:00 Ruth, Buddy & I went to the market. I bought the meat. Came to $1.12 & 21 pts. Burton came at 7:00 and we ate a few minutes afterward. The meal was very nice and we all ate a lot. We stayed there until 9:30. Were home by 10:00. (washed Johnnie's jumper at Ruth's.)*

May 25, 1945 - U.S. Joint Chiefs of Staff approve Operation Olympic, the invasion of Japan scheduled for November 1, 1945.

Friday, May 25, 1945. *Got up at 9:00. Woke Jackie up at 9:30. Washed clothes at 10:00 (washed bedspread, too.) Through at 12:00. 12:10 Hunter Phlegar comes. Told me he and Johnnie had arranged for us to spend the afternoon with Hunter and Wanda. Said he would wait while Jackie and I dressed. (He went downtown.) He came back just as Jackie and I were walking down the stairs. Took bus to their home and cooked Jackie some lunch when we got there. Wanda cooked a meal for Hunter and me. It was very good. Johnnie came there at 3:45. We spent a very nice afternoon with them and left at 6:30. Reached home 7:00 and at 7:30 Paul and Marion dropped in. They stayed until 8:30. (Johnnie expected to be secured Monday.)*

Sharon, Jackie, Lynne

Saturday, May 26, 1945. *Got up at 9:00. Jackie woke at 10:00. (Jackie has a cold and so have I, Johnnie, too.) 11:30 we went to post office to see if we had any mail (none). Home again by 12:00. Waited for Johnnie to come. We had our lunch and I ironed the clothes. Johnnie came at 2:45P.M. 4:00 Jackie took nap. Wanda and Hunter came at 6:15 just as Jackie woke up. We left the house at 7:00 and went to the bus station to take the bus to Oxnard. We were going to the Carnival. Pulled into Oxnard 8:00. Bus left at 7:30. The Carnival was quite large. There were rides for the children and grown-ups. Jackie had two rides on the Merry-go-round and one ride on the little cars. She loved riding and didn't want to get off. We bought popcorn and I had an apple on the stick. Johnnie and I rode on the Ferris Wheel and we took Jackie with us. She wasn't a bit afraid. Left Carnival 10:30. Got on 11:00 bus. Driver stepped on starter and blew a fuse. Had to wait for 11:30 bus. Reached home 12:00. We had a very nice time.*

Sunday, May 27, 1945. *I went to 10:00 mass. Jackie stayed home with Johnnie. Wedding before mass. 11:30 we went out for breakfast. 1:00 went to park. Met Ruth and Buddy. Took* pictures. Marion and Paul came by 2:00. Ruth and Buddy went to movies. Marion & Paul went home and Johnnie, Jackie & I went to the restaurant for our lunch. 2:45 P.M. we came back to room and tried to get Jackie to take a nap, but she wouldn't. After we had our supper in the room (we're low on money), we took the bus out to the dairy to buy a milk. While we were there we had some ice cream. We walked home and were in by 8:00.

Monday, May 28, 1945. *Jackie awoke at 11:30. Had breakfast and finished by 12:00. Johnnie came in at 2:30. We went to post office to see about mail. Letter from Ann (May 19). Went into park. Met Ruth and Buddy. 3:30 they went home and we went to the R.R. station to see about reservation. All booked up for a month. No cancellations. Will try now from the 15th to the 30th. Came back and had supper in restaurant. Only 6:00 so we brought Jackie in schoolyard for a ride on the swings and stayed until 7:30.*

Tuesday, May 29, 1945. *Johnnie came in at 10:30. Jackie and I were having our breakfast. 11:30 Johnnie brought Jackie out to the store and I took a bath. We fed Jackie her lunch in the room and then we went out to the restaurant for our lunch. (Johnnie said there was a notice on bulletin board saying they would be restricted Friday 7:30 A.M.) Met Ruth and Buddy as we were going out. They were going to have their lunch in the park. We said we'd meet them there. Finished our lunch 2:30 and went to park. Sat on bench with Ruth. Paul Andrews joined us shortly after. Marion had gone to Beauty Salon. Ruth left at 4:00 and we left at 4:30. Johnnie and Paul went out for some beer. Fed Jackie supper in room. Cleaned up and then went to the schoolyard with Jackie. Johnnie found us there 6:15. Stayed until seven. Went to market and then came back to room. Put Jackie to bed 7:30.*

Wednesday, May 30, 1945. *Memorial Day. Jackie and I got up at 10:00, had breakfast in room and then cleaned up. (Jackie likes to wear my high-heeled shoes.) Had lunch in room and then went to park. Stayed until 2:30. Came back to room because it was too cold in the park. Johnnie came in at 4:00. I was surprised to see him. We fed Jackie her supper in room and then we went out to the restaurant. Paul came in just before we*

451

were being served. Said they'd be waiting for us outside. We finished eating at 7:00 and joined Marion and Paul. We went for a ride to Port Hueneme. Boys wanted to get a look at Transports. Stopped in at the Dairy on way back. Had ice cream and bought bottle of milk. (Johnnie has change of address.)

Thursday, May 31, 1945. Jackie woke at 6:30 A.M. Did not go back to sleep again. Had breakfast and lunch in room and at 2:00 we went to the post office and to the park. Johnnie came in at 5:15 just as Jackie and I were eating. I had bought hard sausage at the chinks so I cooked that in egg for Johnnie and he enjoyed it very much.

Friday, June 1, 1945. Johnnie left at 6:30. Jackie awoke at 8:00. Washed clothes 8:45. Finished at 10:00. Had lunch at 12:00 and at 1:00 left the house for the bus terminal. Went to Camp Rousseau to visit Johnnie (1ˢᵗ day of restriction). Reached there at 2:00 and was with Johnnie until 9:15. Visiting hour was over at 7:30 so we went to the camp show but Jackie was too tired and wouldn't stay so we had to leave. We took the 9:30 bus home. Jackie fell asleep on bus and I had to carry her all the way home. Put her in bed without even changing her. In room at 10:15.

Friday, June 1, 1945

Hello, Folks:

I'm sorry about not writing but I haven't been in the mood. Johnnie's being restricted today and he expects to be gone by Sunday. Jackie and I are going out to the camp this afternoon to see him.

I'm writing this to tell you to forward my checks to Ventura cause I sure need them. Nothing at all has come through on my reservation and I have no idea when it will. When I went down the other day, he said he would try for the 15ᵗʰ to the 30ᵗʰ of June. I hope I won't have to wait any longer than that.

I haven't heard from any of you for a long time. Please don't stop writing until I tell you to. I may have to wire home for some money although I hope not.

I finished my wash a little while ago and now I've got to get Jackie something to eat. So long for awhile,

Love, Lou

P.S. Make sure you write the "De" in my name plainly. It's been filed under "R" the last time I got a letter. L. De. R.

Saturday, June 2, 1945. Jackie woke at 9:00. Gave her breakfast and then I started to pack my clothes. 11:00 we went to bank, cashed the checks, and then went to post office to mail pkg. (yearbook), $1.05 insured it. Then went to R.R. station. Have reservation to Chicago on June 17, upper birth. Came back to room and then left at 1:00 for bus station. Reached Camp Rousseau at 2:00. Johnnie waiting in guest house with Hunter and Wanda. Stayed in guest house all afternoon. Johnnie got me a reservation through chaplain, ($111.) all the way through to Newark for June 8th. (Fitz came to visit with us for a while.) For supper, Johnnie went to the spud locker and brought us back three meat loaf sandwiches and an apple. We were together until 7:30. Took bus home and were in room at 8:30. Ruth & Burton came at 9:00.

Sunday, June 3, 1945. I woke Jackie at 8:30 A.M. (sprinkling rain). Left house at a quarter of nine. Had breakfast in bus terminal. No 9:30 bus. Had to wait for 10:45. (planned on going to church with Johnnie at the camp 10:00). Johnnie was waiting when we got there 11:15. Went and sat with Wanda and Hunter. 12:00 Wanda, Jackie & I went to Oxnard for dinner. Came back at 2:00. Boys had to get special permission to stay out after 6:00 muster. (Forbes came and visited with us). Jackie very cranky. Took 1 hour nap at 5:45-6:45. 7:30 left quest house to go to movies. Met Porky in theatre. Movies over at 10:00. Seabees not allowed to leave theatre with guests. Said good-bye to Johnnie, and Hunter and Wanda and I and some other girls went to get the bus home (raining lightly). Bus crowded. Girl gave me her seat. Jackie fell asleep on bus. Pulled in 11:15. Carried Jackie asleep all the way home. Rain had stopped.

Somewhere in the South Pacific

Chapter 6

Johnnie Sent to Okinawa, Hiroshima & Nagasaki Bombed

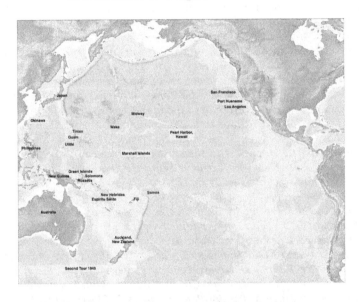

June 4, 1945 - The 15th Construction Battalion boarded the U.S.S. Comet and departed from Port Hueneme, California for the Pacific. The voyage lasted 40 days.

Monday, June 4, 1945. Jackie awoke at 9:30. Raining. Hazel loaned me an umbrella to go across the street to get a bottle of milk. Came back and had breakfast. 11:00 took bus to Wanda's. She wasn't there. Took bus back and stopped at chinks market. Could not get any eggs. On way home met Ruth and Buddy. They stayed in room with us until 2:00. Ruth helped me pack. I washed some dirty clothes of Jackie's and then I ironed. 4:30 Jackie took a nap. We had supper in room and I put Jackie to bed at 7:30.

Tuesday, June 5, 1945. Jackie awoke at 9:30. Had breakfast in room. Then cleaned up and finished packing. (received birthday card from Johnnie). Had lunch and then went out. Met Ruth and Buddy coming down to our place. Walked to Market with them and then we parted. I sent a telegram home, went to express agency, and then went to Station. Came back.

stopped at post office. Letter from Ann and Fan. Shopped in stores for last minute things. Had supper in room and put Jackie to bed at 7:00. She was very tired.

Wednesday, June 5, 1945
Ventura, Calif.

Hello Folks,

This is it!! I sent a telegram this morning telling you I was coming home. Johnnie left for overseas, yesterday. The three days he was restricted at the base, Jackie and I went to see him while I was applying for a reservation home. Johnnie was also trying to get me one through his chaplain. That's how I got it. I leave here or rather from L.A. June 8th 6:30 P.M. I have to leave here by Greyhound and then take another bus to L.A. Station. I went down to the station (Ventura) today to cancel the reservations they were making for me and I showed him my ticket. It's a good thing I did because he told me it was all mixed up. You can imagine how I felt. He said the way it was made out I wouldn't have time to make the connection in Chicago. So he did some inquiring and told me to change at Englewood instead of Chicago. It would give me about 45 minutes to make the connection. I'm coming by upper berth all the way. It's the best the chaplain could do. From L.A. to Englewood I'll be in a tourist Pullman. And then from there on I have a standard berth. I'm a little nervous about making the trip home but I'll soon get over that as soon as we're on the train.

I'm sending home a big box full of things that wouldn't fit in my bags. It's coming by express. Gee, I sure hope I get my checks before I leave. I need money badly. I went to the post office today and received a letter from Ann and Fan. It's been quite a while since I last heard from home so I was pretty glad to get the mail. Tell Mrs. De Roxtro about my coming home, will you? I'm not in the mood to write to anyone. Oh, and by the way, I'm coming by Southern Pacific and then by Pennsylvania. If I have time, I'll send a wire when I change. Try and get someone to meet me.
Love, Lou

Wednesday, June 6, 1945. Jackie woke at 8:00. Had breakfast, then went out to Greyhound bus depot to find out hours of departure of buses on Friday morning. Man very abrupt and not helpful at all. Told me he wouldn't guarantee me passage because the busses were full and I couldn't get standing room with the baby. Came back and talked to Hazel and Mrs. Cecil. Mr. and Mrs. Cecil took my bags down to the station for me and I had them checked on my ticket, decided to go by train after all. Train leaves 6:05 A.M. Friday morning. Went to post office. Received allotment check of $80. Cashed it. Came back to room to wait for express man to come. He came at 2:30. Sent package collect. Took bus and went to Ruth's house for supper. She baked a cake for my birthday and gave me a card and a gift. During afternoon Jackie became sick. Came home right after supper and put Jackie to bed. She kept waking up all night long. Temperature.

456

Postmarked June 10, 1945, addressed to 219 Speedwell Ave. [Aboard the U.S.S. Comet]

June 6, 1945

Hello, Sweetheart:

You have no idea how much I miss you and want you. I miss you more now than I ever have, my most precious angel. Today is your birthday and I hope you are more happy than I am. In fact, my sweet, I wish you complete happiness and health on this day of days. Today, as every day, my thoughts have been of you. I love you, Lou darling, so very much. Never again will I have to leave you, I hope. That last parting was almost too much for me to take. The tears welled up in my eyes, as you probably noticed. That was very sad, that night, but you took it very well, my darling, and I'm proud of you.

After we left you that night, Hunter and I walked, sat, and talked for about an hour. I lit one cigarette after another and neither of us dared speak for the longest time. Gosh, I never want to feel like that again. Both Phlegar and I got so we could talk after awhile and he told me quite a bit. I can't very well tell you what he said, tho.

Everything went off as per schedule and I'm on my way. The scuttlebutt is good, and I'll be home with you soon, I hope. Regards to all. Here's a kiss for Jackie and many more for you.

J.De Roxtro EM1/c   *Eternally, your loving, Johnny*

Thursday, June 7, 1945. Jackie woke at 9:30. Girl in back room went out to buy me a quart of milk. Gave Jackie milk and rice Krispies. Kept her in bed until 11:30. Does not feel much better. 12:00 took bus to Ruth's, had lunch there. Jackie ate hardly anything. Ruth fixed egg salad for me. Was home by 2:45 and Jackie took a half hour nap at 3:30-4:00. I mailed another package by railway express. Came back and borrowed alarm clock from girl next door. Jackie wouldn't eat any supper. Put her to bed at 6:00 but she didn't fall asleep until 7:30.

June 8, 1945 - U.S.S. Comet boiler "blew up" and became completely useless. The ship drifted at four knots and finally managed to crawl into Pearl Harbor four days later for repairs. Johnny was aboard.

Friday, June 8, 1945. Got up at 4:30A.M. went down to call up taxi. Woke Jackie up at 4:50A.M. Dressed and then went down and waited in hall. Jackie was in a good mood and feeling much better. Her temperature had gone down. 5:15 the taxi had not arrived so we went out and waited out front. A cab just back from Hueneme stopped and brought us to the station. ($.50) Jackie was a little afraid at first but once we were on she was all right. We pulled into the L.A. (Union Terminal) at 8:35

457

A.M. Made friends with a woman on the train and stayed with her for awhile. First thing, I checked my bag and lunch box. Very heavy. We spent all day in the station. Jackie became very tired and I was also. 4:30 she could keep her eyes open no longer and she fell asleep in my arms for ½ hr. 6:00 P.M. we got in line in front of the gate where we were to leave. Jackie very cranky & tired. Gate opened at 6:15. Could not get porter. Had to carry bags all the way to train, Jackie crying after me. Train left at 6:45-15 minutes late. We had upper berth. Soldier got on at Yuma (lower). Jackie woke twice during night. Went to bathroom.

June 9 1945 - Japanese Premier Suzuki announces Japan will fight to the very end rather than accept unconditional surrender.

Saturday, June 9, 1945. Jackie woke at 7:00, still very tired and cranky. Had breakfast in diner. Waited in line 1 hour. Stopped for 15 minutes at Tucson, Arizona. Put in a terrible day. Jackie crying and cranky. Very hot. Appetite poor. Naughty. Pulled into El Paso, Texas 9:30 P.M. Went out with girl in opposite berth. Only to terminal.

June 10, 1945 - Australians invade Borneo.

Sunday, June 10, 1945. Jackie woke at 9:00. Slept all through the night feeling much better. Went into diner for breakfast. Waited in line an hour. Through at 11:30. Jackie fell asleep at 2:00 and slept until 5:00. I got my period during afternoon. Woman gave me a napkin and Tampax. Stopped in Liberal, Kansas for 20 min. Jackie very good all day. Went to bed at 10:30. 11:00 stopped at Kansas City.

Monday, June 11, 1945. Got up at 8:30. Jackie slept until 9:45. Girl across aisle brought back some milk from diner. Train pulled into Englewood 11:40. Had five minutes to make connection. Penn train (The Manhattan) 17 minutes late. Gave Jackie lunch in car. Fell asleep at 2:00. Slept until 5:45. Very nice porter. Treated us very nice.

June 12, 1945 - U.S.S. Comet arrived Pearl Harbor, Hawaiian Islands for repairs to the boiler.

Tuesday, June 12, 1945. Woke Jackie at six o'clock, dressed her and waited for train to pull in to Penn Station. Arrived at 7:10. Red cap brought bags down to street. Took cab to Newark Lackawanna. Had to wait 1 hour for train to Morristown. Left bags in Penn Station. Called Mom up at a quarter of eight. Just leaving for work. Waited for us. Got in about 9:30. Took cab home. Gracie opened door. Jackie not frightened but a little shy. Did not take long to overcome it. Got along very well with Grandma & Gracie. Had breakfast. Jackie had two eggs. Ran around house jumping and laughing. She was so happy. Had pastine for lunch and drank lots of milk. Mom had called girls up and they came at 1:30. I had put Jackie to bed because she was very sleepy. Called Mil and Vene up in afternoon. Jackie awoke at 4:00, and Vene, MdeR and children came to see us. MdeR very disappointed about Johnnie not writing her sooner. Left at 5:30. Gracie cooked supper. Spaghetti. Very good. Jackie enjoyed it very much. Gene and Judy came at 7:00. Jackie went outside to play with kids. All glad to see her. Girls brought cake home. After supper Grace gave me a card and a pair of stockings for my birthday, Ann, a pair of pyjamas, aqua. Put Jackie to bed in crib. Went right to sleep.

Wednesday, June 13, 1945. Jackie & I slept until 10:15. Felt very rested. Gracie home all day. Mil called in morning. Mom came home to lunch. Washed hair and in afternoon Mama G came up. Gave me two dollars for my birthday. Express man came with pkg. ($4.79) (Jackie's toys, hot plate, pans.) Jackie wasn't too friendly with Mama G. Mama G stayed until Mom came home at 5:30. It rained heavily during afternoon. They told me it rained everyday out here. Today was quite warm. At supper Jackie ate wonderfully. After supper she went out in yard with Mom, planted tomatoes. Put her to bed 8:00. 9:00 Martha and her mother came over. Brought two records Archie had sent home. In Germany. Played them on Victrola. Very nice. (Girls had gone to Newark.)

Thursday, June 14, 1945. Woke up at 8:30. Stayed in bed until nine. Woke by hearing the teddy bear play. Put sun suit on Jackie. Very hot out. Gracie went to school for exam. Last day of school. Came home at 11:00 with girl friend, Mary. (Robin's nest in tree). 11:15 Jackie and I went to Mil's. Chipper is adorable. Jackie was a little strange but she played with Judy. We had lunch there and came home 2:00. Put Jackie in tub and washed her hair. I cooked the sauce and made ice cream for desert. After supper, Fan & I went to movies. Saw "Bring On The Girls" with Sonny Tufts. Pretty good. Mom said Jackie woke up once and cried her head off.

Friday, June 15, 1945. I awoke at 10:00. Did not sleep well. We had breakfast and then at 11:00 Joe Petrone came with a bagful of lollypops for Jackie. He stayed for a while and talked to me and Jackie. Jackie was a little bashful, but she answered him when he talked to her. Joe brought Jackie and Gracie for a ride to Burnham Park. He left about 12:30. Jackie ate a very good lunch. Since she's been home she eats much more.

Saturday, June 16, 1945. Got up at 9:00. Left Jackie still sleeping in my bed. Very hot day. We had breakfast and then she went out in the yard with Grandma. Gracie went to work on farm. I started my first letter to Johnnie. Jackie had no appetite for lunch. Drinks lots of milk, though. Mom went down Mama G. Jackie & I home all afternoon. Cleaned kitchen then gave Jackie a bath and took one myself. Gracie came home at 6:00. Made $1.91. Mom came home at 7:30. Paid Mom money I owed her $32.91. Ann & Fan went to Jo & Mike's. Fan bought me a bra $.79. I owe Fan $1.39, bra & movies.

[Aboard the U.S.S. Comet.]
Postmarked June 16, 1945, stamp upside down.

June 16, 1945
Somewhere

My Darling Wife:

Please forgive me for not writing sooner, but I just couldn't get around to it. My thoughts are continually of you, my sweet, and I carry your image in my heart. All the love and adoration in the world is ours. How I wish we were still together. I miss you more this time than I did before, too, though I don't see how that is possible.

I am in the best of health, sweet, and my cold is all gone. I am eating the best of food and not working too hard or long. Boy, what a racket I have "working" in the Officer's Galley. (Pots & Pans)

We were detained en route, hence the letter so soon. Don't expect any after this for awhile, my dearest one, because I have an idea we will be moving along soon. Most of the fellows received mail, but I haven't, with the exception of the father's Day card. Thanks for that, anyway, and please write often. I'm homesick a little. I'm kind of anxious to find out how everything came off about you leaving California, too, so I'm anxiously awaiting news from you.

This will have to end now, because we're allowed only 2 pages. Regards to all and the best of everything to you and Jackie. Here's a bunch of hugs & Kisses for you two.

J.De Roxtro, EM1/c   *Eternally, your loving Johnny*

Note on flap: *"Here's a little more love and stuff for you. I love my wife."*

Postmarked June 17, 1945 three stamps upside down.

June 15, 1945
Ventura, Cal.

Johnnie Darling:

Hello, this will be the first of my letters. It may be months before you receive it but I couldn't keep from writing any longer. Honey, I love you and miss you so much.

You're probably anxious to know about our trip across, so I'll tell you all I can. When Jackie and I left you that Sunday night, it was raining lightly. (Just to make matters worse.) We walked with Wanda and some other girls to the bus and on the way home Jackie fell asleep. The bus was terribly crowded but a kind and thoughtful girl got up and offered me her seat. I was feeling perfectly miserable and cried most of the way home. No one could see with the lights out and I just couldn't hold t back. We pulled into the bus station 11:15 P.M. Jackie was still asleep so I had to carry her all the way home. What a time I had! Fortunately it had stopped raining so that helped a little. When we got into the room, I flopped her on the bed, took off her shoes and stockings and her coat and let her sleep as she was. I cried myself to sleep that night, darling. I felt so lost and lonely.

I awoke early Monday morning and Jackie slept until 9:30 A.M. It was raining again. As Jackie and I were on our way out to buy a bottle of milk, Hazel, the two little girls' mother, loaned me her umbrella. We came back to the room again and Jackie had breakfast. I couldn't eat a thing. The food wouldn't go down my throat. About 11:00 we took the bus out to see Wanda but she had already left. So we came on home and stopped in at the chinks' market. Coming back we met Ruth and Buddy in front of the firehouse. They stayed in the room with us until 2:00. Ruth helped me to pack some of my clothes. When she left, I washed all the dirty clothes I had and then I ironed them. Jackie took a nap in the meantime. While Jackie was eating her supper I'd find myself looking out the window like I used to when you were due home, and every time a sailor passed, a terrible aching lump would swell up in my throat. Oh, honey, how I missed you!!

Tuesday, June 5, I got up very early, cleaned the room and finished packing. Later in the morning, Lynne came up with the birthday card you sent me. I was very happy to receive it, hon. I had even forgotten about my birthday coming. We had our lunch in the room and then Jackie and I went out. There was so much to do yet. On the way we met Ruth and Buddy coming down to our place. Ruth told me she couldn't stay out very long. She had just come down to do her shopping. We walked up to the P & H market together and then we parted. I went to the Western Union and sent a telegram home, then Jackie and I stopped in at the Express Agency and I learned that they don't express baggage or packages short distances, like from the house to the Station. I was making up a couple packages to send home so I told them to stop by anyway. There were quite a few things I couldn't get into my bags. We went to the post office from there and I received a letter from Ann and one from Fan. Next, we went to the station. And guess what, Johnnie! The ticket agent told me that my reservation was all mixed up. June 8th was stamped on all the tickets and it should have been stamped June 8th from L.A. and the 11th from Chicago. He said the way the ticket was made out I wouldn't have time to make the connection at Chicago. We were due in Chicago 11:18 and the train from the Penn Station left at 11:30. You can imagine how I felt when I heard that. He said he would straighten it out for me so he called up their agent at the base. They talked for quite a while and then he told me to get off at Englewood and that would give me 15 more minutes. The Penn train was due in Englewood at 11:45 and he said I wouldn't have to change stations. I asked him about going on the Greyhound to L.A. and he attached another part to the ticket. I won't be able to finish this letter tonight, dear. It's late and I'm tired. I'll write more tomorrow. I love you with all my heart.

Saturday, June 16, 1945

Hello, My Darling:

Here I am again. I hope this time I'll be able to finish. Last night, Jackie woke up and cried and cried. Why, I don't know. She said she wanted to sleep with me so I put her in our bed intending to put her back, but I fell asleep and when I awoke it was so close to morning that I left her there. It's almost impossible to sleep with her, though. She, somehow, manages to cover the whole bed and when I got up, she was sleeping crossways, right smack in the center of the bed. Johnnie, it's terribly hot out here, awful!! And yet when I came home they told me all they had for April and May was rain and cold weather. The day I came home was the first nice day they had. But before I tell you anything more about this place, I want to finish telling you about my trip.

Wed. June 6ᵗʰ (the birthday I don't think I'll ever forget!) Jackie awoke at 8:00. We had breakfast in the room and then went out to the Greyhound bus depot to find out the hours of departure of the buses on Friday morning. The agent was very abrupt and not helpful at all. The buses left at 7:52 and 9:52. He said he wouldn't guarantee me passage because the buses were too full and I wouldn't be allowed standing room with the baby. I told him I had reservations to catch a train in L.A. but he said it didn't make any difference. He was really quite nasty, Hon, and at any other time I would have stood my ground and told him where to get off, but having him talk to me as he did made me so angry that instead of talking I just turned away and cried all the way home. If you had been with me he would have probably been as nice as pie. And I needed help all the more just because you <u>weren't</u> with me. That meant I had to go by train after all. When I went back to the house I met Hazel and I told her about the change in my ticket and while we were talking (in the kitchen), Mrs. Cecil came in, so of course she had to know what it was all about. I was going to call a cab to take my bags to the station but Mrs. Cecil said her husband would take them down for me. I was certainly glad to hear that and about noon we went down and had the bags checked on my ticket. The train we were to take left at 6:05 in the morning. On the way back, they left Jackie and me off at Blair's restaurant and afterwards we went to the post office. I received my allotment check of $80. Was I ever glad and relieved to get it!! It was too late to wire home and I don't know what I would have done if it hadn't come on time. Ann only sent the one check and when I came home I learned that she had sent the other out, too.

When Ruth had come down Monday, she had invited me to supper at her house for my birthday. So Jackie and I went back to the room to wait for the express man to come, which he did at 2:00, and then we took the bus to Ruth's. It was swell being there again and for the first time since I last saw you I was beginning to relax. Ruth gave me a birthday card and a gift of a pair of bookends. Jackie, too, was glad to see Buddy and they were playing down in the yard, as usual. Later in the afternoon, about five o'clock, they came up to play in the room - and—Jackie suddenly became sick. She had chills and temperature and was always crying. I couldn't imagine what was wrong!! I was so worried! I couldn't enjoy myself after that and could hardly wait until we went home. Ruth had prepared a lovely meal, even a birthday cake for me. As soon as we finished eating we left. Didn't even help Ruth with the dishes. I put her to bed as soon as we reached home and all that night she hardly slept at all. She'd sleep for a half hour and then wake up and cry. She kept that up until about 5:00 in the morning and then she slept until 9:30. In the morning I didn't know what to do about breakfast. We had to have milk but I wanted to keep Jackie in bed as long as I could. I thought perhaps if she had a good rest, she'd feel better. I saw the girl in the back room going out and asked her if she was coming right back and told her why I wanted to know. She said she wasn't, but that she wouldn't mind going across the street to buy me a quart of milk. She's the one with the little blonde girl. So for breakfast, I gave Jackie milk and Rice Krispies. When the girl came back, she stayed in the room with me and we talked awhile. You know, she told me that Mrs. Cecil got in trouble with the O.G.A. about the rent she was charging the people in the back house. So now they don't even pay the $10 they had to. I had to keep paying the $2.00 a day because of the extra bed in the room.

Jackie wasn't feeling much better at all but we had to go out to eat because I had packed the hot plate and I hadn't brought any more food. She stayed in bed until 11:30 and then I dressed her up. Ruth had promised to make me some egg salad to take along on the trip so instead of going to a restaurant, we took the bus and went out to Ruth's. I had brought out the dozen of eggs when I was there Wednesday. Ruth opened up some soup for the kids but Jackie wouldn't eat any of it. I boiled the eggs and Ruth made me the salad and we put it in a small empty jar. You should have seen the lunch I packed!! All in little jars I had; butter, jelly, egg salad, old fashioned cheese spread and several cans of baby fruit. Then I took along a half loaf of bread and some crackers, five hard boiled eggs and four oranges. That box was as heavy as the suitcase. We left Ruth's at 2:00 and when we came home, Jackie lay on the bed and slept for a half hour. I still had one more package to get off and I intended taking it to the post office and making out a change of address form. When she awoke at 4:00 we started out. She didn't feel any better after her nap and she wanted me to carry her. I tried making her walk because the package was terribly heavy, but Jackie was whimpering and crying and her face was so flushed that I picked her up and carried her **and** the package. My arms ached so much that instead of going on up to the post office, I stopped in at the express agency. So I never did get to the post office. When we came back, I borrowed an alarm clock from the girl next door. I tried to give Jackie some Rice Krispies and milk and canned fruit for supper but she wouldn't eat anything but a glass of milk.

Friday, June 8th, I awoke at 4:30 A.M. I went downstairs and called up a taxi and told them to be there at 5:00. Then I went up again, finished dressing and woke Jackie up at a quarter of five. How worried I was about Jackie, honey. She kept waking every half hour again and finally fell asleep at 2:30 A.M. I prayed so hard that her temperature would be gone by morning. When I did wake her up she was swell. Not cranky at all. Her head was warm but not as burning as it was. I was so thankful! Jackie's being sick helped me to get myself back under control and made me stop crying over you. As soon as we were dressed, we went down and waited in the hall for the taxi. 5:15 and it hadn't come yet, so we went out and waited on the walk. I had left the lock on the door open in case I had to go in again. We weren't there long when a taxi passed, but not the one I had called for. This guy was on his way home from Port Hueneme and when he saw us standing there, he asked me if I wanted a cab. Of course we took it and were down at the station 5:25 A.M. The train came promptly at 6:05. Jackie was a little afraid at first but once we were on she was just fine. We pulled into the L.A. station 8:35. First thing I did when we got there was to check my bag and the lunch box. Then we had our breakfast. Oh, Johnnie, what a day we put in!! Jackie became so very tired and so did I. I found out what gate our train was leaving from and then we hung around in the station all day. 4:30 Jackie could keep her eyes open no longer and so she fell asleep in my arms - for a half hour. She woke because I tried to lay her on the bench because she was so heavy to hold. Of course, she woke cranky and crying and wanted to sleep some more in my arms. 6:00 we got in line in front of the gate. We were one of the first ones there. Jackie was very tired and wanted me to hold her up. So I sat on my suitcase and held her in my lap. The gate didn't open until 6:15. People were crowding in from all directions and pushing Jackie and me out of line. Can you picture me holding Jackie and the suitcase and box? I thought my arms would drop off. The people were pushing so hard that Jackie began to cry because she was being hurt. That did it! I got really angry and said to Jackie, "O.K. Jack, we'll fix them!" (You were supposed to have your ticket out so that the attendant at the gate could look at it before you were admitted.) I heaved Jackie up a little higher in my arms, got a good grip on the suitcase and box, lunged forward and didn't give a damn who I pushed. I got through that gate so fast the attendant didn't even see me go by. I couldn't get a porter so I had to carry my bags all the way out to the train. I had to put Jackie down, though. I just couldn't hold her any longer. She ran after me with the tears streaming down her face. I felt so sorry for her because I knew she wasn't well. She had been very good during the day, considering how she felt. We found our car and the porter carried my bags in for me. The train left at 6:45- 15 minutes late. When the conductor came around, I asked him if I could have a lower berth. He told me forty people wanted lower berths and none were available. At Yuma, Arizona, a soldier got on to occupy the other half of our section. I thought you said a Mrs. Colby was to have it?? The soldier didn't even offer the lower to me. Jackie woke twice during the night and once to go to the bathroom.

June 9th, Saturday, Jackie woke at 7:00 A.M. She was still very tired and cranky but she had no temperature. We had breakfast in the diner after waiting in line an hour. That turned out to be a terrible day. Jackie seemed to be crying all the time and her appetite was very poor. Saturday night she slept without waking and Sunday morning she awoke at 9:00. We dressed and went into the diner for breakfast and by the time we got through it was 11:30! Jackie took a nap at 2:00 and slept until 5:00!! She was feeling much better. More like her own self. And Johnnie, what do you think! I got my period Sunday afternoon! I wasn't due until the 20ᵗʰ. One of the women in our car was that way, already, so she gave me enough napkins to last until I got home. Monday, I felt terrible but Jackie didn't give me any trouble. She slept until a quarter of ten. It was too late for us to go into the diner, but earlier in the morning I had asked the woman across from us to bring back some milk for me so I had that for Jackie and also some Rice Krispies. You don't know how glad I was about packing that big lunch!

Our train was due to pull into Englewood 10:45 and we didn't pull in until 11:40. The train from Chicago was due 11:45. That gave us only five minutes to make the connection! Luckily, the train was seventeen minutes late so we had plenty of time. There were no porters around so I had to carry my own bags, but how I rushed poor Jackie. Englewood was so different from what I had expected. The tracks were all out in the open air. There was an attendant out front to tell you where to go.

Oh, Johnnie! What a difference there is between the tourist car and Pullman first class! The tourist Pullman, coming out, was terrible. Hot, stuffy and dirty. Even the porter was lazy. He wasn't around half the time. But that first class Pullman - ahhhhh. That was Heaven! Everything was so nice and clean and there was a nice thick rug on the floor. It felt swell to relax after those first three nights and two days. The car wasn't crowded but all the lowers were taken so we still had to have an upper, and the porter was swell!! Jackie liked him even. After I fed Jackie her lunch in the car, she fell asleep and slept for three hours and three quarters. During the night she woke once to go to the bathroom. We pulled into the Penn Station, Newark, 7:10 A.M. There was no one to meet me because I hadn't sent a wire saying when I'd arrive. The reason I didn't was because I didn't know whether I'd be able to make the connection. The porter came out on the platform and whistled and called for a red cap to come down for my bags and he carried them right down to the street. We took a cab to the Lackawanna and as luck would have it, we just missed the 7:22, so we had to wait for the next train, 8:27. Jackie was tired and hungry and that hour seemed like five. I called the house up and Mom was just leaving for work. She was so surprised to know it was I calling. She wanted to come to Newark to accompany me home but I told her it wasn't necessary, so she said she would wait for me. I had such a job keeping Jackie awake on the ride home. When we reached Morristown, a man on the train carried my bag down the stairs for me. We took a cab home and got in about 9:30. The sight of the house looked so good, Johnnie! Gracie opened the door for us and was so glad to see us, especially Jackie. Jackie was a little shy but it didn't last long. We had our breakfast and then Jackie ran around exploring. She was running through the rooms and laughing and then she came into the kitchen jumping and said to me, "Mommy, I'm jumping!" I guess she thought it was really something that I didn't tell her to stop. She was so happy, honey! She ate a large dishful of pastine and drank lots of milk. She didn't even want to sleep anymore; said she wanted to play. But I put her to bed just the same and she slept until 4:00. Mom had called the girls up and they came home at 1:30. For a while there, we had a regular pow-wow. I had called Mil and Vene up after lunch. You know, your mother quit her job last week and is staying with Vene. They said they would be down as soon as the children woke up from their naps. They came just as Jackie woke up at 4:00. Nancy and Bonnie have grown so! Jackie was strange with Vene and your mother and wouldn't make up to them. I was sorry but there was nothing I could do. Both Vene and your mother look very well. Vene said Johnnie was going to be detailed in Pennsylvania for a couple of weeks. He'll be able to come home on weekends, won't he? Gee, honey, your mother was very disappointed because you hadn't written to her during our last weeks together. She said if she had known when you were leaving, she would have come out to see you. She said she wrote me a letter telling me that, but I never received it. Your mother thinks I've changed, Johnnie. In what way, I wonder. They stayed until 5:30 and Vene wants me to go up to see them by bus. She said the bus passes right by their house. We had spaghetti for supper and Gracie cooked it. She said she was the one who cooked on Tuesdays and Thursdays. The sauce was very good, too. I had a big dishful and Jackie ate a lot too. Gene and Judy came over while we were eating. Jackie was bashful with them, too, although she was friendly. After supper Jackie went out front with Gracie and played with the kids. They were all glad to see her. For my birthday from Ann I received a pair of pyjamas, from Fan a cherry blouse, and from Gracie a pair of stockings. They gave them to me after supper. I still have to get a gift for Ann. I'll go downtown next week and see what I can buy. When I put Jackie in the crib she went right to sleep.

This is all I'll write for now, darling. I didn't think it would turn out to be so long. I hope it hasn't bored you too much. You know, Hon, they didn't receive one of my letters in which I had enclosed a set of pictures. I wonder what happened to it?

I miss you, darling, so very much and I'm thinking of you always. Our room looked so good when I first entered it and our bed felt like heaven. Johnnie, darling, how I hope it won't be long before we are together again. I love you and want you. Good-bye for now. Say "hello" to Hunter when you see him. Here's a great big hug and kiss from both Jackie and me. I love you, my darling.

Always and Forever,
Lou

Note on flap: "Hi, Sweet! It'll probably take an hour to read this book. I hope you don't mind. I love you."

Sunday, June 17, 1945. Fathers' Day. I went to 7:00 mass. Jackie slept until 10:00. Gene brought Mama G and Tadone up. Tadone feels very well. Gave Gene checks for my bags. Jackie friendly with Tadone. Very hot out. In afternoon, 3:00, people from Trenton came. He took them all out for a ride to Burnham & then to Budd Lake. Jackie very friendly with Joe.

While they were gone, girls and I went to Community. "Affairs of Susan." Pretty good. Home by 9:00. Jackie still up. Gene had brought my bags home. Paid $2.40 for storage. Joe & Angie, Mama G & Tadone went home 9:30. Gene & Judy 10:00. I stayed out in front until 11:30. Then went to bed.

Monday, June 18, 1945. *Received back Christmas card I sent to Archie. Jackie & I arose at 8:30. Very hot. Cleaned house up and cleaned room. Changed it around a little. After lunch gave Jackie a bath and washed her hair. She wore only panties. Unpacked bags.*

Letter from Mary Lukowitz, postmarked June 20, 1945.

Oro Bay, New Guinea
16, June, 1945

Dearest Lou,

I have wanted to write you before this but hesitated for I was uncertain as to the length of your stay in California. I did get your card that you sent about April 6. And yesterday your grand letter of May 22 that you wrote while in California. That's swell. Thanks for both.

Have been quite busy of late at the office so have to do a lot of my letter writing in the evening. The other day I started a letter to Mother and since we're allowed to tell of the places we've seen – hell, I wound up with about twenty pages. Took me 'til after midnight to complete it. In as much as the mail comes in bunches, there's busy spells trying to answer all of them. I've tried to scatter them by answering a few at a time, but it doesn't do any good. So, I just let them come and answer them whenever I can.

Several weeks ago the new ball field was opened. What a turn out these nights. Both the boys and girls play at night under lights. It's really something else to look forward to in the way of entertainment. Before, all we had were movies and were getting tired of seeing them, especially where a group of poor ones would be shown. I think I told you that we sit on benches or on chairs carried from our office and out in the open, in the fresh air under the stars (no covering whatever) to see the movies. The first few months very seldom did we see a movie without getting wet - - it just poured. Sometimes it came down so hard they had to stop the movie cause you couldn't hear a thing. Lately, however, it's been swell. A cool ocean breeze stirs up and it's heavenly sitting out in the open watching a movie. Last week we saw a good one, Betty Davis in "The Corn is Green." The one last night "The Picture of Dorian Grey" had superb acting throughout the whole movie though I personally didn't care for the story itself.
9:30 P.M.

Just got back from the ballgame. We lost again. The boys game was a very good one. The score was tie 2-2 after the 7th inning so another had to be played. I sure enjoyed it.

Several of our bulbs blew out and can't seem to get any, so have to use candles most of the time. It's not too good for reading or writing, yet I like to for it makes it seem so homey.

Am sending you two prints of me. They're not very good, however. I sent another set home to have prints made and will send you some of them when they come. The one I'm enclosing of me is taken next to one of our barracks. Margie and I wore the dress one of the girls borrowed from Special Services. Just for the heck of it, had our pictures taken.

I'm glad that you liked California and that you were able to be with Johnnie if for a short period. Say! I don't think you ever did tell me what he thought of my sweetheart, Jackie, when he first came to the house. I'd like a picture of her now and then, so I can see her growing up into a "lady." I bet you're proud of her.

The only spot of interest that the average individual has heard or read about in this location is Buna which is not too far from here. I had the opportunity of seeing it– a mass of dense, dark jungle, thousands of shot off tree tops, holes of all sizes from artillery shelling, foxholes, and pillboxes. Unbelievable that so *much had happened on that little spot, and really nothing to show for all the fighting that was done– no towns, villages, no civilization, nothing except jungles. That's the kind of fighting our boys have done on this side – just land. Wonder what a store, a building, or even a child would look like to most of us, especially the boys who have posted their third year overseas? Bet it would be a glorious feeling. Sometimes I feel we'll forget how to act when we get back. Most of the time we'll just stare at things we just ignored at one time.*

The **Battle of Buna–Gona** was part of the New Guinea campaign in the Pacific Theatre during World War II. It followed the conclusion of the Kokoda Track campaign and lasted from 16 November 1942 until 22 January 1943. The battle was fought by Australian and United States forces against the Japanese beachheads at Buna, Sanananda and Gona. From these, the Japanese had launched an overland attack on Port Moresby. In light of developments in the Solomon Islands campaign, Japanese forces approaching Port Moresby were ordered to withdraw to and secure these bases on the northern coast. Australian forces maintained contact as the Japanese conducted a well-ordered rearguard action. The Allied objective was to eject the Japanese forces from these positions and deny them their further use. The Japanese forces were skillful, well prepared and resolute in their defense. They had developed a strong network of well-concealed defenses.   Operations in Papua and New Guinea were severely hampered by terrain, vegetation, climate, disease and the lack of infrastructure; *** the Allies faced a severe shortage of food and ammunition. This problem was never entirely resolved. The battle also exposed critical problems with the suitability and performance of Allied equipment. The combat effectiveness of US forces, particularly the US 32nd Division, has been severely criticized. These factors were compounded by repeated demands from General Douglas MacArthur, Supreme Commander of Allied Forces in the Southwest Pacific Area, for a rapid conclusion to the battle. The demands were more to politically secure MacArthur's command than for any strategic need. In consequence, troops were hastily committed to battle on repeated occasions, increasing Allied losses and ultimately lengthening the battle.   The remaining [Japanese] garrison fought to the death, almost to the man.

The resolve and tenacity of the Japanese in defense was unprecedented and had not previously been encountered. It was to mark the desperate nature of fighting that characterized battles for the remainder of the Pacific war. For the Allies, there were a number of valuable but costly lessons in the conduct of jungle warfare. Allied losses in the battle were at a rate higher than that experienced at Guadalcanal. For the first time, the American public was confronted with the images of dead American troops. (From Wikipedia, the free encyclopedia)

As for food, I must say it's been very good. Within the last few weeks we've had steak, fresh pork, chicken, eggs, apples (fresh), and fresh potatoes. Boy, did they ever taste good. I have been able to have bananas often – which I love. Must say adieu. Want to write to a friend who's in Manila. May this find you in good health
and God's Blessing to you and your family.
Love, Mary

June 18, 1945 – Japanese resistance ends on Mindanao in the Philippines.

Postmarked June 19, 1945 stamp upside down.   *June 18, 1945*
My Darling Husband:
You are all that I think of morning, noon and night. I love you with all my heart and miss you more than ever before.
The weather back here is so very hot, honey. All Jackie wore today was a pair of panties. I gave her a bath this afternoon and washed her hair. She gets two baths a day and sometimes three. The first thing we did when we came home was to take a bath and wash our hair. I sure do appreciate our bathroom, now, sweet. It sure feels good to take a shower in your own bathroom every day.
Guess what! This morning I received back the Christmas card I sent to Archie Bianco! Was I surprised! When Willard saw me waiting for the mail he laughed and said I was a little ahead of myself. I know I shouldn't expect any mail just yet but I can't help it. I'm so anxious to hear from you.
I cleaned the house up today and even changed our room around a little. The house wasn't kept any cleaner since Jackie and I were gone. They had a nerve to blame it on us. Boy! I was sure tired when I got through. Not used to such hard work anymore.
You know, the day after we came home, Jackie and I slept until a quarter after ten. And Gee! Did I feel rested. Jackie slept during the night without waking and she looked so well the next morning. You'll never know that she hadn't been feeling well for a week.

Gracie wasn't taking any exams until Thursday, so she was home all day Wednesday. That was June 13ᵗʰ. Mil called me up in the morning and Mom came home for lunch. Later in the afternoon, Mama G came up and she gave me two dollars for my birthday. She brought me some popcorn and some tootsie rolls for Jackie. Jackie was very shy but she melted a little after Mama G was here awhile. I told her not to expect Jackie to be a friendly as she was before she went away and Mama G understood. She was glad that Jackie didn't forget about her entirely. She wanted to know all about you and felt so bad because you had to go out again. Mom told me she had brought some cigarettes up for you and they had forgotten to enclose them in our last package. They were Raleighs, all she could find. The thought was nice, though, wasn't it?

The express man came that afternoon with one of the packages I sent home; the one with Jackie's toys, the hot plate and pans and a lot of other stuff. Guess how much I had to pay for it! $4.79!! I haven't received the other package yet, and I even paid for it already. Mama G stayed until Mom came home at 5:30. It rained heavily that afternoon and Mama G said it was like that every day for the past two months.

Jackie ate a wonderful supper that nite and after supper she went out in the yard to help Mom plant tomatoes. Honey, she follows Gracie and Mom around like a shadow. She's crazy about Gracie and wants to go everywhere with her. I put Jackie to bed 8:00 and at 9:00, Martha and her mother came over. Archie had sent two records home from Germany and they brought them over for us to hear. Darling, they're swell!! He speaks to them just as though they were before him and then he plays his mandolin. He's improved so much since he's been in the army.

Thursday, June 14ᵗʰ I woke in the morning by hearing the musical brown teddy bear. Jackie loves it and added it to her sleeping collection. It was terribly hot that day too. Gracie had to go to school for the last exam. It was the last day of school, too. Gracie goes into the 10ᵗʰ grade next year and she's only fourteen years old. She came home about 11:00 and her girlfriend, Mary, was with her. Jackie loved being with them. It helps me a lot too in not having her around all the time. Maybe it will make her lose her shyness. 11:30 that morning we went to see Mil and Chipper, the new baby. Johnnie, he's adorable! I held him while Mil prepared some lunch for us. I almost wished I had one too. We stayed until 2:00 and, Hon, on the way home, Jackie said to me, "maybe Daddy'll be home, Mommy." I didn't answer her the first time so she repeated it. I tried to explain to her that she wouldn't see you for a long time but she doesn't understand. She thinks you're still at the camp. That last week we were in California, she often asked about you. She misses you, honey. She kisses your picture goodnight and says, "I love you, Daddy." I didn't tell her to say that, either. After she kissed you, she looked at the picture a long time and _then_ said, "I love you, daddy."

I cooked supper that night and for desert I made ice cream. Didn't turn out bad at all. Ice cream is very hard to get out

471

here and Jackie eats up a whole Dixie cup or a cone every chance she gets. Isn't that just like her!! Just because it's scarce out here, she likes it!!

I went to the movies Thurs. night, with the girls and saw "Bring On The Girls." That's the picture I wanted to see that night when we went out with Marion and Paul. Remember? I'm glad we did go out with them, now, because the picture wasn't as good as I had expected it to be. Mom said Jackie woke up while I was gone and cried her head off because I wasn't there.

Joe came to see us Friday morning and he brought a bag full of lollypops for Jackie. She was bashful before him, too, but she answered him when he spoke to her. He brought her and Gracie for a ride to Burnham Park and Gracie said she was very friendly. Joe was so glad to see her. He thinks she grew a lot.

Mom overslept, Saturday, so she didn't go in to work. After breakfast she went out to work in the yard and Jackie went right with her. Mom was planting some gladiolas and Jackie was helping her. Mom said she really helped, too. Gracie wasn't home. She went to work on a farm and made $1.90. Mom said she's been going since I went away. Mom went down Mama G's in the afternoon and Jackie and I were home all alone. I put Jackie to bed and then I gave the kitchen a good cleaning. I paid Mom all the money I owed her, $32.91. (that last telephone call you made was $19.91.) I settled with Ann, too, $12.00. I owe Fan $1.39.

Gene brought my bags home for me last night, and after I finished cleaning today I unpacked them. Honey, Mike's bag is completely ruined, now!! The seams of the brown bag came apart, also.

Goodnight, Darling, I love you so very much. How I wish we could have been together longer. I was so happy there, with you, dear. Regards from the family and here's Jackie's (X) hug and kiss to her daddy. I send mine to the best husband in the world.

Yours Forever, Lou

Tuesday, June 19, 1945. No mail. I awoke at 7:00 but didn't get up until 9:30. Jackie woke at 10:15 A.M. Had breakfast and dressed. 11:30 we went downtown, bought rubber pants for Chipper, 2 barrettes for myself, glue, oversize box, white socks for Jackie. Were home by 1:30. It had started to rain while we were in the park. Bought peanuts for squirrels. Gracie made sauce, then went swimming. We had lunch at 2:00. It rained for the rest of the afternoon and night. Fed Jackie supper before we had ours. Roof leaks in Pantry hall. Gene came over to look at it. Thinks Ralph is in Leyte, Phil. Started reading Valley of Decision.

June 20, 1945 - The USS Comet departed from Pearl Harbor, Hawaii.

Wednesday, June 20, 1945. Stayed in bed until 10:00. Jackie woke at 10:15. Dressed and had breakfast. At lunch, heard Jackie saying to Gracie, "Don't spill it, hon. Don't spill it honey." 1:00 Gracie went swimming with girls and Jackie and I went to Mils. Brought her baby pants, some clothes for Chipper

472

and five dollars for Chipper. Jackie played nicely with Judy. We stayed there for supper. Came home at 7:00. Mom and Gracie out. Couldn't get into house. Tried side porch door. Could not get down. Called Martha. Tried several keys. Mike B & Fed came over with ladder. Tried windows on Bianco's side. Fed climbed in window and opened door. Martha came in and stayed until 9:30. Girls came home at 9:15 with pizza and beer.

Thursday, June 21, 1945. *Both Jackie & I got up at 8:00. Had breakfast and Jackie went out in the yard to play. Mil called in morning. Received belated birthday card. Jackie went out to the store with Gracie. I stayed in all day. Read more of Valley of Decision. Washed blouse for Ann and ironed it. Girls went shopping in N.Y. Started to rain 7:00 and rained all night. Put Jackie to bed. Sat near window to watch storm. Jackie frightened by thunder. (Jackie said, "Where's Mommy's house?")*

June 22, 1945 - Japanese resistance ends on Okinawa as the U.S. Tenth Army completes its capture. General Ushijima and his Chief of Staff, General Cho, committed hara kiri (ritual suicide) and Okinawa was secured by the Allies. The 15th Construction Battalion is on its way.

Friday, June 22, 1945. *Jackie and I got up at 8:00. Had breakfast, then started to wash clothes. Big wash. Jackie outside playing with dirt. Finished washing at 2:00. Gave Jackie a bath. Jackie took a nap 2:30. Washed my hair and while it was drying read more of "Valley of Decision." Started to cook at 4:30 - Jackie woke at a quarter of five. When Gracie came home, Jackie went to the store with her. At suppertime, received a call from Vene. MdeR taken to hospital (stomach hemorrhage). Wrote to Ruth.*

Saturday, June 23, 1945. *Woke at 7:15. Got up 7:45. Received allotment check. Birthday card from Fan. Letter from Johnnie, June 16. Vene came 2:30. Went to Hospital to see Mother de. Looked pretty well but pale. Internal hemorrhage. Found George there. MdeR to have x-rays taken tomorrow morning. Transfusion Monday afternoon. All drove back together. George treated Vene & me to ice cream. George dropped in to see Jackie. 6:00 Herb called me up from Cutter's. Said he would be up to see me. 7:00 after I put Jackie to bed I went downtown with Ann & Fan. Bought writing paper for Ruth. Home by 9:15 P.M. 10:50 Herb came up to see me. Staying over at Vene's until Monday. Took two pictures of myself.*

June 24, 1945 – The U.S.S. Comet crosses the International Dateline.

Sunday, June 24, 1945. Went to 7:00 mass. Lovely day. Gene brought Mama G and Tadone up in the morning. Jackie out in yard playing. Ann went to wedding. Jackie did duty and emptied potty. Mil & Gene came over with Chipper. Christened today. After dinner, dressed and waited for Vene to come. 3:20. Johnnie was with her and Herb, also Nan & Bonnie. Johnnie & Vene went in first and then Herb & I. We only stayed ten minutes. MdeR wasn't feeling very well. Herb came home with me and stayed 'til 7:30. Joe & Angie came at 6:30. Joe brought broom for Jackie. He drove Herb to Hospital with Jackie along. Jackie very friendly with Joe. Came back and brought them all out for a ride. The girls and I went to the movies. Jackie touched Joe's face and said," Uncle Joe, you got a beard!" Took two pictures of myself.

June 24, 1945
Sunday

Hello My Darling:

I went to the 7:00 mass this morning and since Jackie is still asleep I decided to take this opportunity to write you. It's beautiful out now, but by this afternoon it's going to be really hot.

It's been quite a while since my last letter so I'll pick up where I left off.

June 17 was Fathers' Day. Gene brought Mama G and Tadone up to spend the day with us and Tadone looks great! His appetite is so much better and he's even more active. They're always asking me about you and never fail to send you regards and best wishes.

When Gene left for Newark that morning, I gave him the checks to get my bags at the Penn Station.

In the afternoon, our relatives from Trenton came. They were surprised to know that I had been in California. How in the world did I ever forget to send them a card!! Joe and Angie came at 5:00. They stayed for a while and then Joe took everybody out for a ride to Burnham Park and then out to Budd Lake. Mom said Jackie enjoyed herself very much and was pretty friendly with Joe but she still doesn't treat him the same as before we went away.

While they were gone, the girls and I went to the Community to see "The Affairs of Susan." It was a pretty good picture—light entertainment. When we returned home at 9:00, Jackie was still up. Judy was here and Gene had brought my bags. He said I had to pay $2.40 for storage (the five days they were there.) That wasn't bad, was it. It would have cost more to have had them sent out by express. Jackie was tired and sleepy so I put her to bed almost as soon as I got in. Mama G and Tadone went home with Joe and Angie at 9:30. Gene and Judy left at 10:00. It was so terribly hot that night, honey. The others all went to bed but I sat in the sun porch until twelve and then, I, too, went to bed. I love you, darling.

****

Tuesday morning, 11:30, Jackie and I went downtown. After I finished what shopping I had to do, I bought some peanuts and Jackie and I went in the park. (Now Jackie always calls it the Morristown Park.) She was so happy over the squirrels and loved to feed them the peanuts. We couldn't stay there very long, though, because it started to rain so we had to hurry home. It was just as well because Jackie still had to have her lunch. The rain stopped just as soon as it had begun and didn't start again until we were home for about a half hour. But when it did, it rained for the rest of the afternoon and all night. The roof over the pantry hall was leaking very badly so Mom called Gene up. He came over, found the leak in the roof and covered it. We received a letter from Ralph, Tues. saying he was somewhere in the Philippines. Gene thinks he's in Leyte. Ralph said it took them 33 days to reach their destination. His new A.P.O. number is 718. Wednesday morning I stayed in bed until 10:00! I would have stayed later if Jackie had slept longer. Jackie's appetite has picked up wonderfully, dearest. For breakfast every morning she has a glass of orange juice, either cereal or two eggs, toast and milk. While she was having her lunch I heard her saying to Gracie, who was eating the same thing she was, "Don't spill it hon. Don't spill it honey." Right after lunch we went to Mil's. I brought Mil some of Jackie's baby clothes for chipper and I also gave her our gift, (five dollars in an envelope) for the baby. Jackie and Judy got along very nicely together so when we were invited for supper, I accepted. (The girls were

475

staying to shop in Newark, so no cooking had to be done). I called Grace up so that she and Mom wouldn't wait for us. We were home by 7:00, _but_ - I had forgotten my keys and nobody was home. Mom and Gracie had gone out and all the doors were locked! I felt pretty sure that the door of the little porch was open so I climbed up on the little ladder I found in the yard. It was about as high as a step ladder and just about cleared the space under the porch where the window was. I hoisted myself up to the window and the door was locked, also the kitchen window. _Now_ I _was_ in a fix. Jackie was waiting for me down in the yard and I couldn't get down. The only thing to do was to call Martha and ask her to call Gene. When she saw me stuck up in the porch she called her father and he brought a long ladder so that I could get down. Instead of calling Gene, they tried to help me get in. They brought over several keys but none of them worked. Then we tried the windows in our driveway. _They_ were locked. So we went over to the other side and Martha saw that the living room window was unlocked. Ted, Martha's boyfriend, climbed up the ladder and opened the front door for us. Martha came in and stayed until 9:30. I had put Jackie to bed and she fell asleep just about as soon as she closed her eyes. The girls came home at 9:15.

Thursday, both Jackie and I arose at 8:00. After breakfast Jackie went out in the yard to play. (I wish we had a sand box for her, honey) I found a wooden box, filled it with dirt, and she played there all morning. In the afternoons she goes to the store with Gracie. Just before I put Jackie to bed Thurs. night, we had a thunder and lightning storm. (a small one) She was frightened by the thunder so we sat by the window and watched the rain. She was all right after a while so I put her to bed and she went right to sleep. Yesterday I had a very busy day. I washed two and a half long lines full of clothes. I started at 10:00 and didn't get through until 2:00. After lunch I bathed Jackie and she took a nap. While she slept I washed my hair and while it was drying I read a little. I'm reading a very good book, hon. It's called "The Valley of Decision." The movie is playing at Radio City now. I started supper at 4:30 and Jackie awoke at a quarter of five. She had a very good nap. I wrote a letter to Ruth last night and also sent her a birthday card.

Saturday morning while I was out in the yard with Jackie, Willard called me and gave me quite a bit of mail. I received the allotment check that had been sent to Ventura and also a birthday card from Fan. Besides that, two nursery Rhyme books Ann had sent Jackie, **_AND_** I received your letter of June 11th! Darling, I was so happy to hear from you! Were you writing from Pearl Harbor? I'm enclosing the pictures we took in Ventura with this letter. The originals turned out swell. You remember, the ones we sent to Hollywood to be developed. They all turned out but I'm only sending you a few.

Darling, I love you and miss you with all my heart and want you to be home so much. Love and kisses from Jackie and me.

Always Yours, Lou

Pictures Ralph sent home:

Philippine boy he wanted to adopt

Hanging around.

The Camp Puppy   Basketball Court

Monday, June 25, 1945. *No mail. Very hot day. Jackie woke at 8:00. After breakfast went out to play with Gracie. After lunch we went downtown. Cashed allotment check. Went to post office. Mailed gift to Ruth. Bought airmail and defense stamps. Went through park to see squirrels. Stopped at Greenbergers to buy pants for chipper and pyjamas for Jackie. Very warm. When we got home (stopped in Acme) I sent Gracie out for ice cream. Cooked supper at 4:30. Took picture of Jackie. Finished "Valley of Decision. Very good book.*

Letter from the Greaves, postmarked June 26, 1945 from Oxnard, California.
June 25, 1945
Monday 3:30 P.M.
Dear Lou,

I was so glad to get your letter today. We had been wondering how you made out on your trip home. I'm sorry to hear how terrible it was, but at least you are home. One of these days, you'll be laughing about all the trouble you had.

I hope that soon you will get a letter from Johnny. That will relieve your mind considerably.

Buddy mentions Jackie quite often but he has taken it for granted she won't be back. Friday night we rode past the Old Mission on the bus. Buddy said to Burton, "That's where Jackie lived, but she's in New Jersey now at her 'grandmudder's."

We haven't been down to the park since you left. I'm usually too busy through the daytime. I am still watching Mrs. Taylor's little grandson. I don't mind at all, because he is such a good baby. The extra money comes in handy too. Last week I made $3.75, which made our rent for the week only $4.75. It's a big help.

The 2 gals downstairs have become quite talkative lately. One even went so far as to come up to visit me last Thursday. She brought me some magazines to read. Both have invited me downstairs to visit them but I have never troubled myself to go. I don't care to get too chummy with them.

Burton doesn't want to get too friendly with them either. They drink & carry on too much. Besides, Hazel's husband made a rather dirty crack to me the other night. Burton was plenty peeved about it. He never did like men who made suggestive remarks to me. He's very jealous of me, but he needn't be. I never saw any other man I'd care to have. What it was that Hazel's husband said to me was, "Is Burt home tonight?" I said, "Yes, he's upstairs." Enno said, "I thought if he wasn't I'd come up & keep you warm tonight." I was just coming up the stairs when he said it. I never said any more to him. I came in the room & Burton was sure red in the face. He had heard what Enno said. We never mentioned it after that night but I don't get near the man. I don't trust any man. I've learned not to.

I think Hazel & Ellen are moving back East next month or in Aug. Their husbands are supposed to go overseas. I hope they do move, then I can have the nice room downstairs. Besides, maybe we will have some nice couples in here to chum with.

We never make definite plans, though, because we don't know whether Burton will be transferred or not. They are moving all the Navy men and "Seabees" from Port Hueneme. The Army is going to take the place over in July.

Of course, Mira Loma isn't Port Hueneme so Burton may get to stay here. I hope so. His mother is coming down next week. I'll surely be glad to see her. She sent me a nice pair of pajamas for my birthday. She also sent Buddy a couple more new suits, some anklets, & some money. She sent Burton 4 pr. black socks for Father's Day. I bought him socks also. Now he has 20 good pairs again.

He got me a beautiful chenille robe & slippers for my birthday tomorrow. He said we would go out for dinner tomorrow night & then to a movie, so I guess my birthday won't be too boring.

We finally got my radio but it isn't working yet. We can't find the right kind of tube yet. That's all it needs. I'll be glad to hear a radio again.

I have finally quit gaining weight. I still weigh 125 lbs. How about you? Did your folks think you looked better & that Jackie had grown? How is the weather there? It's still the same here, except more fog. We didn't see the sun for a week.

We spent all day Saturday up at Ojai. We did have a good time. Burton & I went to the club up there. He taught me how to play pool. I just love it. I made a couple darn good shots too. We also played some tennis and table tennis.

Yesterday we spent the day at the beach. The sand was so nice & warm. We couldn't go swimming because there was too much kelp & seaweed in the surf. It made the water look black. Oh, yes, one night last week we went to an old-fashioned square dance. Gosh, it was fun.

It's time for me to get supper started so had better quit for now. We are having beef & noodles, fresh green beans, escalloped potatoes, coleslaw, & watermelon. Wish you were here to eat a bite with us. We did enjoy having you eat with us.

Don't wait too long to write now. I think of you often & wonder what you are doing, so write & tell me.

Who knows, maybe we will all be home for Xmas. If we are, we'll run over to New Jersey & throw a snowball at you.

Your friends, Ruth, Burton, & Buddy

P.S. Can't get eggs at all now. Guess we'll have to find a couple old hens to be nice to. No shortening or lard either. Very little oil. Still lots of meat, but never enough points.

Tuesday, June 26, 1945. Ruth Greaves birthday today. Letter from Mary. Jackie up at 9:30. Raining. Ann home from work. I ironed all morning and afternoon. Day cleared in afternoon. Gracie went to store with Jackie. Wheel on carriage broken. After supper, Gene brought Mom to see Willard Jones' father who died Saturday. Judy was with Gene and Gracie and Jackie went along for the ride.

Wednesday, June 27, 1945. Lovely day. We received a letter from Archie. 11:00 called Vene up. She said Mother de was much better. Stayed in all day. Wrote a letter to Ralph. Jackie can climb in her high chair alone. She also goes up to the bathroom to do wee wee or duty by herself. Climbing up on the Toidy seat!

June 27, 1945

Hello Darling:

I love you with all my heart. I miss you more than life itself. I am thinking of you always and wanting you.

I just finished writing an eleven-page letter to Ralph tonight. It's the first I've written him since I went away.

Chipper was christened Sunday. Mil's sister Nancy was Godmother and Doc's son Buster was Godfather. After the christening they stopped over here for a while to show us how Chipper looked before they went to Newark. Then the four of them went to the Chanticler for dinner. We were having our supper when Joe and Angie came. (6:30). Joe brought Jackie a little broom. He wanted to bring Jackie to see the ducks so all but the girls and me went along. Ann, Fan, and I went to the movies. It sure is swell to be able to watch a picture without Jackie wiggling around. When we came back, Mom told me Joe had won his place back with Jackie. She said Jackie was very friendly and laughed and talked all the time. And also that while they were riding, Jackie touched Joe's face and said, "Uncle Joe, you got a beard!" Mom said Joe got such a kick out of her. She talks even more now than she did out in California, honey, and she really uses good sentence structure. You know, during the first week we were home, we were in the living room and Jackie says to me, "Mommy, this is Grandma's house." And after I answered in the affirmative, she said, "Well, where's Mommy's house?" I was too astonished to answer her at first and she kept repeating her question until I did. She still asks a lot about you and can't understand why you don't come home any more.

Monday was very warm. After lunch Jackie and I went downtown to cash the allotment check I had received back, and then we went to the post office for some airmail stamps. On the way back we came through the park and stopped to watch the squirrels for a while.

Jackie needs summer pyjamas and I couldn't find any for her. She takes a size 3 and Greenbergers had one pair in a size 4 so

I took them anyway. They're awfully cute, but they're too big for Jackie. Maybe they'll shrink a little when I wash them. We stopped in at the Acme on the way home and as soon as we were in the house I sent Gracie out for some ice cream. Jackie never refuses ice cream any more. She loves it. It's quite hard to get out here, too. The girls rave about the suppers I cook for them and you should see them eat! I'm back in the same old routine again and I sure miss the freedom I had out in California.

I finished the "Valley of Decision" Monday night. It's a wonderful book, darling. I enjoyed every bit of it, 640 pages!

Tuesday was Ruth Greaves birthday. I had already sent her a birthday card and Monday I mailed a gift to her. I bought her some lovely writing paper.

I received a letter from Mary yesterday. She enclosed two snapshots of herself and she looks simply grand! She lost a lot of weight, too. She's in Oro Bay, New Guinea and has been to Buna.

It rained all yesterday morning and cleared up in the afternoon. Gracie took Jackie to the store in the stroller and when she came back, the back wheel of the stroller had broken off completely.

Willard Jones' father died Saturday, after a long illness and last night Gene brought Mom to the wake.

This morning Mom received a letter from Archie thanking her for the Christmas package he had just received. Can you imagine!!

To give you an idea how much Jackie has progressed since we've been home, listen to this. She climbs into her highchair by herself and she goes up to the bathroom, climbs up on her toidy seat and does her business. Isn't that swell!!

Time to say "goodnight," dearest. I love you, miss you, and want you. Regards and best wishes from the family and loads of love, hugs and kisses from Jackie and me.

Longingly yours, Lou
Note on flap: "Dearest: I love you so very much. I miss you terribly."

June 28, 1945 – MacArthur's headquarters announces the end of all Japanese resistance in the Philippines.

[On board the U.S.S. Comet heading for the Marshall Islands.]
Postmarked June 28, 1945, stamp upside down.   *Still en route*
My Darling Wife:

Each and every moment of the days and nights I am thinking or dreaming of you. You are constantly with me, even though we are so many thousands of miles apart. I love you more than ever and my desire to be with you is beyond all possibilities of description by mere words. I want you and miss you, my adorable one. No one will ever be able to take your place as wife, sweetheart, or mother of my children. We belong together and only the necessity of foreign entanglements could possibly keep me from your side. In a short while, I hope, (but doubt very much), we will be together again for good.

481

According to scuttlebutt, the navy is planning to inaugurate an overseas period of three years maximum. If that becomes true, you can expect me home about a year from now. But let us hope we won't be separated for that long.

This trip is quite similar to my previous crossings, with the exception that I am now in a position to eat very well, without waiting in line. In fact, I am doing mess cook duty (washing pots and pans) for the officers' galley. I am well, and as the ocean has been fairly calm, very few of the boys were ill.

It is twenty days since my last letter to you and I have no excuse for not writing, except that there isn't anything I am able to say. Perhaps after we arrive at our destination I will have news enough to enable me to write daily letters, as I used to.

Please write as often as you possibly can, Lou darling, and tell me everything. I want to learn more about our Jackie and everything else. Once again, I have to tell you what a marvelous job you did in bringing her up. She's a sweetheart, alright, and I'm proud of you both.

Necessity forces me to close now, so with all my love and adoration,

I remain, as always, your devoted and ever loving,   *Johnny*

J.De Roxtro EM1/c

Note on flap: *"Here's a few more hugs and kisses. I love you."*

June 28, 1945 – The U.S.S. Comet arrived at Eniwetok Island in the Marshall Islands group.

Thursday, June 28, 1945. Both Jackie & I up at 8:00. Lovely day. Jackie drank orange juice and went out in the yard to play. Called her in to eat her cereal and then went out again. Fixed Jackie's swing under the tree. After supper was cooked I went upstairs to dress and waited for Vene to come. She came at 7:30 and the girls & I went to the hospital to visit Mrs. De Roxtro. While we were there, George and Estelle came. Started to rain while we were there. Home by 9:15.

Friday, June 29, 1945. Jackie and I up at 7:30. After breakfast Jackie went out in the yard to play. Brought Album up to date but ran out of mounting corners. Vene came at 1:30 with children and went to hospital and left kids here. Children very good. The three played together nicely. I washed my hair. 4:00 cooked eggplant. Very hot day. After supper went to movies with Ann and Fan. Very good.

June 29, 1945

Dearest Johnnie:

I just got in from the movies. I went after supper with the girls. It's pretty late to start writing but it's even too hot to go to

482

bed. This will be a short letter anyway. First of all, I hope this finds you safe from any danger and in the best of heath. Has your chest bothered you anymore, darling?

The days have been so hot, lately. The kind of heat that takes all the life out of you.

I fixed Jackie's swing under the tree yesterday morning and she was as happy as a lark. She plays outside all day long. It rained quite hard last night but it was nice and clear this morning. We were both up at 7:30. After Jackie had her breakfast and went outside to play I tried bringing our album up to date. I would have finished except for the fact that I ran out of mounting corners. I love you and I miss you, darling.

Vene came down here at 1:30 this afternoon. She wanted Jackie and me to go along while she did her shopping so that I could watch the kids. I told her I couldn't go because I wanted to wash my hair and then I had to start cooking. I suggested she leave Nan and Bonnie with me, which she did. The children got along very nicely together, hon. Jackie behaved wonderfully about sharing her toys. They all took turns on the rocking horse and also on the swing, while I was out drying my hair. When Vene came back, she brought a quart of ice cream and boy, did it hit the spot! You should have seen the kids tackle their dishful. I was frying eggplant for supper tonite and if I let them, Nan, Bonnie and Jackie would have eaten it up as fast as I fried them.

I have nothing else to tell you, dear. I'm sorry for the shortness of this letter but perhaps I can make up for it in my next one. Loads of love and kisses from _your_ family.

Always, Lou

Note on flap: "Darling I think of you always and love you with all my heart."

June 30, 1945 – Luzon declared secure. [fighting continued]

June 28, 1945 – The USS Comet departed Eniwetok Island in the Marshall Islands, headed for Okinawa.

Saturday, June 30, 1945. Up at 9:00. Very hot. Jackie had breakfast and went out to play. Received letter of June 6th. Read part to Jackie. Told Jackie I was going to New York. She thought and then said "Are you going far away?" Took a shower & dressed. Waited for bus 11:45. Martha drove me to station. Met Fan at Hoboken. Ann at 14th St. Did quite a bit of shopping. Gift for Gracie and Mrs. De Roxtro. Took 6:15 train, home by 7:30. We were very tired. Bought pop gun like Buddy's for Jackie. Liked it very much. Sent Gracie out for ice cream. Took a shower 11:30 & then went to bed.

Sunday, July 1, 1945. Went to 7:00 mass. Very hot day. Jackie woke at 8:30. After breakfast I gave our room a thorough cleaning. Gene brought Mama G & Tadone up 11:00. Ate dinner 12:30. 2:00 gave Jackie a bath and washed her hair. Judy here since morning. Jackie took a nap 3:00-5:00. Joe and Angie came at 3:30. 6:00 I took a shower, dressed and had supper. Then went to the movies with Ann & Fan. Saw "Without Love" very good. Joe took the rest of the family out for a ride. (Jackie woke and wanted to kiss daddy goodnight.)

July 1, 1945
<u>Sunday</u>

Hello My Darling:

It's too hot to go to bed so I thought I'd drop you a few lines instead.

Tonight after supper the girls and I went to the Community and saw "Without Love" with Spencer Tracy and Katherine Hepburn. It was swell and I could have sat through it a second time. We got in at 10:30. I put my hair up, took my dress off and now, in my slip, I feel quite comfortable.

Sweetheart, I love you so very much and miss you terribly. How I hope you won't be away very long this time. I think of you always, darling, and want you.

Saturday, I received your letter of June 6th. Look how long it took! I was so happy to get it, dear. Jackie was around while I was reading it and asked if I was reading Daddy's letter. I read her the part where you sent her a kiss and I also put in that you said "Hello" and told her to be a good girl. She was so attentive and thoughtful and when I finished she said, "Daddy went far away on a big boat, on the water." Then she added, "Daddy doesn't want me to put my thumb in my mouth, I have to keep my hands down." She still does it when she sleeps, though. Hon, in your next letter will you write a few lines for her? I know she'll love it.

I went to N.Y. Saturday afternoon. I waited for the 11:45 bus but Martha came out and was going to the post office so she drove me down to the Station. The train left at 12:15 and I met Fan in Hoboken at 1:10. We met Ann at 14th St. This was a shopping trip and we did quite a bit of it. I bought quite a few things, too, Johnnie. Gracie's birthday is July 2nd and your mother's is the 3rd. We, you, Jackie & I, bought a lovely nightgown for your mother. Then I bought myself a pair of play shoes, a set of bedroom scarfs, two gold frames, panties for Jackie and a pop gun for Jackie, like the one Buddy has, you remember, the one with the cork. She was so good about my leaving. I told her I was going to N.Y. and that she had to stay home with Gracie and Grandma. She was quiet for a long time and then said, "Are you going far away?" I guess she was thinking of you. I told her 'no', I was coming right home again and that seemed to satisfy her.

We took the 6:15 train and were home by 7:30. Jackie loved the popgun and wanted to shoot everybody with it.

Last night I fell asleep down here in the chair and woke up 11:30. It was still so hot and muggy so I took a nice cold shower and then went to bed.

I went to the 7:00 mass this morning. Jackie woke at 8:00. After I made her breakfast we went upstairs and I gave our room a good cleaning because I hadn't done it Saturday. I have a pretty summer spread on our bed and the new scarfs look beautiful. I didn't put the rugs down again because it seems to be much cooler without them. Gene brought Mama G and Tadone up and Judy stayed here, too. We had dinner at 12:30, can you imagine! In case you've forgotten, on Sunday, it's usually always 1:30 or 2:00. After dinner I washed Jackie's hair and gave her a bath and then put her to bed. She slept from 3:00 to 5:15. Joe and Angie came 3:30. Fan helped me get supper ready so at 6:00 I took a shower, dressed and after supper we went to the movies. When I came in tonite, Mom said Joe took them all out for a ride. While they were riding Jackie said, "Uncle Joe, I want to eat something." Joe asked her what she wanted and she said ice cream, so they stopped and had some.

Well, I've run myself out again, Sweet. I'm going to say goodnight now and then sit out in the sun porch for awhile. All the breeze seems to be there. Regards from everyone and oceans of love and kisses from your family.

Lou

Monday, July 2, 1945. Grace Petrone's birthday. Woke at 6:30, up at 8:00. Received allotment check, $80 and a letter from Ruth . Express package came. Everything intact. 3:00 took a shower and was dressing to go to New York when it started to rain. Waited for call from Ann. Called cab to go to station. Took 4:52 train. Met Fan in Orange. Ann at 33rd St. Took cab to Stouffers restaurant. Raining. Very good meal. Took cab to Radio City. Good seats. Saw "Valley of Decision." Very good. Out at 11:30. Took cab to 33rd St. subway. Made the 12:30 train home. In by 1:30. Rain had stopped when we came out of R.C.A.

Letter from Ruth Greaves.
252 Leighton Drive
Ventura, Calif.
July 2, 1945
Dear Lou,

As you can readily see I received the box of stationery you sent. Thanks so much for remembering my birthday like you did. It helps a lot to know I have a good friend like you. The stationery is beautiful, too beautiful to use, almost. It's too nice to write on to most people, but nothing is too nice for people I like.

I received your birthday card a couple of days after my birthday, but I can assure you I was very pleased to get it. Your thoughtfulness in remembering me is much appreciated. Thanks, Lou.

I received 12 cards, 8 letters, & 2 boxes from home on my birthday, so I had a much nicer birthday then I ever dreamed of. My mother sent me a beautiful slip, some underwear. A sister-in-law sent me some hand towels. My sister Mary sent me a portrait of her little year old baby. He's adorable. Two other sisters sent me money.

To top it off with, Burton brought the little radio home all repaired and in a new cabinet. It works swell & looks like new. You'll never know how good it is to hear old familiar programs and tunes. We did miss a radio terribly.

While I think of it, Lou, did your two sisters ever receive the pin cushion dolls you sent? Did you get your allotment check from here yet?

Say, you don't happen to have a little bit of sunshine you can spare, have you? Bah! to this so called Calif. Sunshine. It has been foggy here for nearly 3 weeks. The sun rarely shows itself. If it does take a notion to show its face it waits until time to get dark. It makes the days so gloomy. How is the weather there.

We went up to Ojai on Saturday. We heard the sun was shining there. It was! Our trip wasn't in vain.

We had a very good time. We played some tennis, ping pong, and you'll never guess what else I did up there. Burt taught me to shoot pool. They have a pool table at the service men's lodge up there. It's lots of fun! I got in a couple nice shots. In fact, I almost hit the ball once!

We are going to a dance July 4, that is, if the Lord wills and the devil don't interfere. It should be fun. We are hoping there will be some pretty night fireworks here, so Buddy can see them. He never has gotten to see any.

This is Burt's duty week, so he won't be home until Wed. It's the first time he has had duty for 5 weeks. Nice huh!

His mother was to come down this week, but postponed her trip now until he gets his 72-hr pass, which will be in 2 weeks. She wouldn't have gotten to see much of him this week.

Thanks again for the gift and do write soon.

Love, Ruth

P.S. Tell Jackie Buddy surely misses her and give her a kiss from me. How does she like being home?

Tuesday, July 3, 1945. *Received letter of June from Johnnie. Lovely day. Not so hot. 10:30 washed clothes and finished 12:30. Vene came at 1:30 with children. I was going to Estlers to bring the carriage wheel. We all went down in the car. Vene went* into the bank and then we came home again. She went to hospital and the children stayed with me. I baked two lemon merengue pies. Vene came back at 4:30 with quart of ice cream. Rhoda Tufts with her. Vene came down again at 7:30. We went to hospital to visit M.de R. Fran & Eddie there, too. I brought Mother de a lovely nightgown. Said she had a very happy birthday.

Wednesday, July 4, 1945. Ann & Fan home for the 4th. Jackie woke at 6:15 then went back to sleep again until 11:30. Lovely day. Mama G and Tadone came up at 11:00. Joe Petrone came 11:30 with loads of lettuce from their garden. Jackie was having her breakfast. Took her out to buy beers. Had to go back to Bernardsville to work. 2:00 Mike - Jo - Mike Jr. & Mary came. Had dinner 3:00. Birthday cake & hats & gifts for Gracie. 6:30 after kids ate we went to Carnival. Lots of fun. Jackie went on merry-go-round with Fannie, pony ride, Ferris wheel with Ann and Fannie. I went on swings with Gracie & Ann. Came home 8:30. Took 9:30 train. We three went to Newark with Jo & Mike. Girls got tickets on bus to Montreal, Quebec, same bus as Jo. Missed 11:19, took 12:45. Fireworks at Burnham. Michael stayed over. Going to Bernardsville. Joey in California.

July 4, 1945

Hello, My Darling:

I love you, miss you, and want you. I hope you are well and soon that you will be coming home.

I have quite a bit to tell - don't know just quite how to begin.

Monday morning I received the allotment check for $80, a letter from Ruth and that last express package finally came. Although the 2nd was Gracie's birthday, we weren't celebrating it until the 4th, today, because the girls and I had planned to go to New York to see "Valley of Decision" at Radio City. Last time it was playing 3:00. Mon. afternoon, I took a shower, dressed and just before I was finished it started to rain. I was sure the girls wouldn't go anymore so I waited for a call from Ann, but none came. It was raining so heavily that I called a cab to take me to the station. I took the 4:52 P.M. train and met Fan at Orange. We met Ann at 33rd St. We took a cab to Stouffers restaurant. We had a grand meal. Even had a Martini. From the restaurant we took a cab to Radio City. We had swell seats and the picture was very good, altho the book was much, much better. It was quite different from the book, too. Johnnie, darling, the stage show was wonderful! I enjoyed every bit of it! We were out by 11:30 and it had stopped raining. We made the 12:30 train home and were in by 1:30. Now, Tuesday, I received your letter of June 27th and was most happy to hear from you.

I washed the clothes at 10:30 and finished by 12:30. Vene came down at 1:30. She asked me to take care of the kids while she did her shopping. Tuesday was also your Mother's birthday and she loved the nightgown we gave her. She is looking very well and happier than she has in a long time. Did I tell you that Johnnie

Naughton was home last weekend. He couldn't make it this past weekend and Vene was very disappointed. I think I told you that he was stationed at Indian Town Gap, Pennsylvania. Vene told me yesterday that he expects to stay there permanently and if he does, they're going to look for a place to live, and Vene, the kids, and your mother are going up there to live with him. Pretty swell, isn't it! I took care of the kids while Vene and your Mother were together. Vene said she had lots of shopping to do. That afternoon I baked two lemon merengue pies. They turned out very well. Vene came back at 4:30 with a quart of ice cream. Your mother felt hurt because you didn't write to her, Hon. She didn't say so, but I could see.

Today, the 4th of July, Ann and Fan had the day off. Jackie woke at 6:15. I told her it was too early to get up so I put her back in the crib an she fell asleep again until 11:30 A.M. Gene had to work so the man who lives beneath them, their landlord, drove Mama G and Tadone up here at 11:30. Joe Petrone came up with a load of lettuce from his garden. He couldn't stay because he had to go to work. Before he left, he went to the store to buy beer for Mom and he brought Jackie with him. 2:00 Jo, Mike, Michael Jr., and Mary came. We had dinner at 3:00. After dinner we had a large birthday cake for Gracie with candles, party hats, and gifts. Her Godmother, Jo's sister Rose, gave Gracie a Bulova wrist watch. It's beautiful! And Gray loves it. After the kids, Michael and Jackie, had their supper, (6:00), we all, (Jo, Ann, Fan, Gracie, the two kids and I) went to the Carnival at Burnham Park. We had so much fun! Jackie and Michael went on the merry-go-round and then they each had a pony ride. When Jackie saw Michael ride around she wanted to try it - and liked it. Then she and Michael went on the Ferris wheel with Gracie, Ann, and Fannie. Jo didn't want to go up so I stayed down with her. Jackie just loves the Ferris wheel and didn't want to leave it. Ann, Gracie and I had a ride on those swings and we had such fun. After we all had a frozen sherbet, we all came home, 8:30. Jo and Mike took the 9:30 train home. Michael is staying over. Joe is coming for him tomorrow and he'll be in Bernardsville for a week.

Goodnight, dear, I love you very much. Love and kisses from us both.

Lou

Note on flap: *"Darling: I love you and miss you. Here's a special kiss from Jackie. LdR"*

July 5, 1945 - Liberation of the Philippines declared.

[Aboard the U.S.S. Comet.]

Postmarked July 5, 1945, stamp upside down. Still <u>On the Way</u>

My Darling Wife:-

Usually, I begin by telling you of my love and adoration for you, but this time I will save all that for the last. This trip has been pleasant and uneventful so far, and from all indications, it will remain so. The weather is nice, but rather warm. Naturally, we have had a few small showers, but they haven't amounted to very much. The seas have been quite calm, too, so no one is sick. Your adoring husband has been quite well, with not even a trace of a cold.

The chow is good, and I can have all I want. I think I've gained about six or eight pounds since we came aboard, too. This is the best racket I've had in quite awhile, but boy, do I perspire freely while working over that tub of hot water. With the better grub and my laundry done for me, though, I think it is well worth while.

Sorry I can't put the date here, but it's a month less two days since your birthday. I am continually thinking of you and our lovely daughter, though, my dearest one, and how I long to be back there with you. We sure had a swell time together while it lasted, though, didn't we. Gee, why the devil didn't you come out to California sooner, huh? I suppose it is my fault, but I did want you to know what to expect.

Sweetheart, because I didn't receive any mail from you when the others did, I am slightly worried about you and your trip home. Please write as often as you can, sweet, and I'll do the same.

Now, because I am allowed to write on only two sheets of paper, I will have to start my farewells again. I love you, dearest one, with all my heart. Thoughts of you are always with me, and your image is forever locked in my heart. Here's millions of hugs and kisses for you and Jackie, and regards to all. Here's something for Mickey too.

J.De Roxtro EM1/c   Eternally, your loving *Johnny*

Note on flap: Gee, I love you and want you so very much. Here's all my love and adoration.

July 5, 1945 - The USS Comet arrived Ulithi Islands in the Western Carolines Group on the way to Okinawa.

Thursday, July 5, 1945. Fran Kugler's birthday. 6:15 Jackie woke. Michael at 7:30. Had breakfast together. Lovely day. Called Joe up and told him about Michael. Michael and Jackie played together all morning. It started to rain. Joe and Angie came after lunch. Michael didn't want to go any more but Joe managed to get him out to the car. Gave Angie one of Jackie's sweaters and a pair of pyjamas for Michael. At night knitted on a sweater I started before going out to the coast. Jackie stopped saying her prayers and said, "Daddy's nice. He's a nice daddy."

Friday, July 6, 1945. Received letter from Ruth. Allotment check $50. Bill from Glendale. Lovely day, got up at 8:00 Jackie still sleeping. Worked on sweater. After lunch Jackie and I went to town. Cashed checks. Bought pyjamas and ribbons for Jackie.

Came home & started cooking . After supper I worked more on Jackie's sweater and finished it. Turned out well. (Vene came down at 1:00. All went downtown in the car. Came back and took care of her kids. She came back at 4:30 with a qt. of ice cream.) Mrs. De Roxtro coming home tomorrow. Has growth on stomach. Cannot be operated upon.

July 6, 1945

Johnnie Darling:-

I love you with all my heart and miss you loads.

This morning I received another letter from Ruth (I didn't even answer her first) and the $50 allotment check.

I have just yesterday and today to tell you about so I'll begin with July 5th. Jackie woke at 6:15 A.M. and didn't want to sleep any more. What a dirty trick to play on me, huh! Gee, I was so sleepy and she wouldn't let me stay in bed even. She kept saying she wanted to get up and get dressed. So, finally at 7:00 we got up.

I told you in my last letter about Michael staying over. He slept until 7:30. They had their breakfast together and then went out to play. I called Joe up and told him Michael was here and would be ready whenever he came for him. Josephine is going up to Canada for a week with two other girls. When she was here on the 4th she told us about it, and Ann and Fan liked the idea so much that they're going along, too. They are to leave Sunday night. That's why Michael is going to Bernardsville. Joe was always after Jo and Mike to let him have Michael for a while and now he finally is. Jackie and Michael are his favorites and he loves them both.

Right after lunch it started to rain and kept up for a couple of hours. It stopped for a little while and then started again and rained for the rest of the night.

Joe and Angie came for Michael at 2:00. You should have seen Jackie, Hon! She was so hurt because she wasn't going with Uncle Joe. She went up to him and said, "I want to come, too."

Last night I knitted on a sweater I had started for Jackie, before I went out to the Coast.

Oh, you know what! While Jackie was saying her prayers and we came to the part where she says, "God bless daddy," she said it and then stopped and looked at your picture on the chest and said, "Daddy's nice, Mommy, he's a nice daddy." I assured her that you were the nicest daddy in the whole world and she continued on with her prayers.

In her letter today, Ruth thanked me for the writing paper I sent for her birthday. She even used it for my letter. She told me they have a radio in the room now and how much she enjoys listening to it, also that the weather out there has been foggy for three weeks. They spent Saturday up at Ojai at the service men's lodge and had a swell time. They played tennis, ping pong and Burton taught her how to play pool. I haven't played tennis yet and I'm dying to. I miss Ruth, honey, it was swell having a friend to be with. There's no one around here with whom I'd care to pal around.

Ruth said Buddy mentioned Jackie quite often but he has taken it for granted that she won't be back. She said they were riding on the bus one night and while they were passing the mission Buddy said, "That's where Jackie lived but she's in New Jersey now at her Grandmudder's." Ruth said they don't know whether Burton will be transferred or not. All the navy men and "Seabees" are being moved from Port Hueneme. She must mean just Camp Rousseau. That doesn't include Mira Loma, too, does it, honey? The Army is taking over the place this month. But you knew that already. Ruth and Burton both send you their regards.

Jackie and I went downtown this afternoon. I cashed the allotment checks and bought a pair of pyjamas for Jackie. I also bought a yard of pink, blue, white and yellow ribbons. When I came home I cut them up and made twelve pretty bows for Jackie. If I had just bought the bows it would have cost me $1.20. As it was, it only cost me $.38. Right after supper tonight, I worked more on Jackie's sweater and finished it. Oh, Hon, it turned out swell! The nicest one I've made yet!

Paul Camisa is home. He's getting a discharge with 133 pts.

My cousin Joey has landed in California and is expected home very soon. His ship is the USS Evans and his brother, Eugene, said it had been torpedoed and came in for repairs.

I can't think of anything else to tell you, dear. The town is exactly the same except for the addition of a few new stores.

Darling, I love you and miss you so much. I feel so lonely at times. Good night, dearest. Regards from the family especially from Mama G and Tadone and a big kiss and hug from Jackie. All the love I can send, I give you.

Forever yours, Lou

Note on flap: "Hello, Hon, Enclosed are a few pictures. I hope you like them. I love you. Lou"

Saturday, July 7, 1945. Lovely day. Jackie & I up at 8:00. Had breakfast. Broke ESSO bank $17.21. Cleaned drawers and room. Started to knit beret for Jackie. Sent Gracie up to Pete's for suits.

Fan owes me for wool and $.50 for shirt. Loaned Ann $20 for vacation. Girls had their permanents done in Harrison. Very nice.

[Ulithi Islands in the Western Carolines Group, aboard the U.S.S. Comet.]
Postmarked July 8, 1945, stamp upside down.   *Still en route but <u>not moving</u>*
Most precious Darling:

All the love in the world is ours. More than anything else in the world, I desire to be there, making love to you and playing with our Jackie. How I long to take you tenderly in my arms again and tell you how much I miss and want you. You are the only girl in the world for me. All I can possibly do for you would not be satisfactory to me. I won't be completely happy or satisfied until this mess is over and we are once again living a normal life together. How I hope and pray that the end is soon here. I love you, Lou, miss you and want you more than mere words can tell. You are mine and always will be. Here are all the hugs and kisses, which we have missed by being separated and a couple dozen extra for more love. Also give our daughter a few nice hugs and kisses for me, and tell her I'm thinking of her, too.

There isn't much I can tell you because of the censorship regulations, but I will be able to later on, I think. As usual, I am quite well and as happy as I can be, away from the ones I love. Yesterday, some of us went ashore, and I managed to indulge in a few beers. Alas, we were allowed only two each, but four was my limit. I did better than most. Besides the beer, there was nothing of interest, so I couldn't tell you anything even if I were allowed to. It was quite hot though, and those beers certainly tasted good to me.

Give my fond regards to all the folks at home, and tell them I am well. As soon as I reach my destination, I will drop a few lines around, to reestablish my correspondence with the outside world. If you would send Ralph's address, I would appreciate it. So long for this time, my angel. I am thinking of you continually.

J.De Roxtro EM1/c   *Your ever loving,   Johnny*

Sunday, July 8, 1945. *Went to 7:00 mass. Jackie awake when I came home. Lovely day. Gene brought Mama G and Tadone up 10:30. Jackie went to store with Gracie. We had dinner at 2:00. Very good watermelon. Joe & Angie and Michael came at 3:00. I had just put Jackie to bed. Michael had a new suit. Jackie slept until 5:00. Was very glad to see Michael. Played together until supper at 6:30. 7:00 Joe took them all out for a ride. Girls took quarter of nine bus to station. Were going to Jo's to wait until time for us to leave. Mom, Jackie, Gracie, back just before* they left. Gracie went out for ice cream. Gave Jackie a bath and put her to bed.

July 8, 1945
Sun. night

Hello, Johnnie Darling:

How are you? I am anxiously awaiting mail from you. I look for the postman every morning, hoping to hear from you. Can it be that you haven't reached your destination yet?

I love you, dearest, with all my heart and soul and I miss you dreadfully! I am always thinking of you and remembering our two and a half months together in California. Oh, it was just wonderful being with you, darling. If only it had been for a longer time. How sorry I am that I didn't go out there sooner!!

Saturday was a lovely day. Not too hot at all. After breakfast we broke Jackie's Esso bank. I tried putting it in boiling water but it wouldn't come apart so we went downstairs and dropped it on the concrete. Jackie helped me pick the money up and we came back upstairs in the dining room and counted it. Guess how much there was? $17.21! Isn't that disappointing? I had expected it to be much more than that. I'm going to put the rest in and buy her a $25 war bond.

Jackie sure helped me count the money! If you know what I mean. She had the time of her life! She even wanted to help me wrap them in wrappers but I drew the line at that. When we were through we went upstairs to our room and I started to clean out the drawers. Jackie was in her glory here too, but the novelty of it soon wore off and she went out to play.

The girls went to have their permanents done Saturday afternoon, and weren't home until 8:00. Their permanents turned out swell!

I went to the 7:00 mass this morning and when I came home Jackie was awake and in bed with Grandma and Gracie. Gracie said she woke them up by yelling, "Mommy, I have to do wee-wee!" She's just grand about not wetting, now, honey. In all the time we've been home she wet the bed once and that was in her sleep. I happened to be at a movie that night and when she woke up for a drink, Mom didn't put her on the toilet. Else she wouldn't have wet then either. And, honey, she holds it for hours and hours! She only goes about three times during the whole day! Her bowels are a little better although not much. But I don't give her the magnesia tablets at night anymore, so when she does move, she goes naturally. One thing though, she doesn't have the trouble she had in California. Maybe because she's back on her regular diet. She never asks me to hold her hand anymore. In fact, when she has to go she just goes up to the bathroom, does her duty and comes down again. I didn't like that so much because she always flushed the toilet and I never saw just what she did. So now I tell her to call me when she's through and not to flush the toilet. It works out well, and when she gets a drink of water, she always has to throw out what's left in the glass herself. I measured her the other day, honey, and she's 34 inches tall. She's growing so! And how she does talk!

493

Did I tell you about the night last week when she woke up for a drink. She was wide awake as usual when she wakes up, and talks a blue streak. After I had her back in the crib again and kissed her goodnight, she stayed standing there, looked at me and said, "How about kissing my Daddy goodnight?" So I marched over to the chest, brought your picture to her and what does she do but look at it and say, "But _Where's_ Daddy, I want to kiss him." That was the _only_ time she wouldn't accept your picture, hon. I had to explain it all over to her again until she finally consented to kiss you goodnight through your picture.

When Gracie came home from church this morning, she brought Jackie to the store with her. Jackie's been walking everywhere for the past week because I had taken her carriage wheel to Estler's to be fixed. I would have liked to have had a new one but he didn't have any just like it. I'm supposed to pick it up tomorrow. Gee, I hope he does a good job on it.

Gene brought Mama G and Tadone up this morning at 10:30. They asked about you as usual and send their regards. We ate dinner at 2:00 and oh, what a delicious watermelon we had! Joe, Angie and Michael came at 3:00. I had just put Jackie to bed and I had to close the door because I didn't want her to hear Michael. She fell asleep almost immediately. Michael was wearing a new suit which Joe and Angie bought him and he looked adorable. Angie said he likes it in Bernardsville and is having a grand time. He especially likes to help Joe Cirillo in the store.

Jackie slept until 5:00 and she was ever so glad to see Michael and of course, her Uncle Joe. After supper, Joe took them all out for a ride and they came back just before the girls left for their vacation. They left on the 9:15 P.M. train to Newark. They're staying at Jo's until it's time to leave. There's five of them going. They're leaving 12:49 from the Penn Station by Greyhound. 9:00, Mom, Gracie, Jackie & I were left so we had some ice cream and then I brought Jackie up, gave her a bath, and put her to sleep.

It's a lovely night tonight and there's a gentle breeze blowing. Oh, how I miss you darling!! I want you so much! Please take care of yourself, Hon, and I hope and pray that you will be home soon.

When you see Vincent, Fitz, Paul and Hunter, give them my regards. Here's a kiss from Jackie and love from,

Your, Lou

Note on flap: "Darling: I love you."

Monday, July 9, 1945. Eclipse of sun [partial, 60%] 7:10 - 9:15. No mail. Jackie slept until 10:30. Lovely day. Mil called. Talked quite a while. After lunch prepared supper. Then Jackie and I went to get carriage wheel. Cost me $2.00. Came home, fixed it on carriage, then went to Acme. Had supper at 5:15 as soon as Mom came home from work. After supper, Jackie went out in the yard with Mom. At night thunder and lightning shower. Wrote to Ruth, enclosed picture and handkerchief. New town trucks. (got period at night).

July 10, 1945 – 1000 bomber raids against Japan begin.

July 10, 1945 – USS Comet departed Ulithi Island as part of a 29-ship convoy enroute to Okinawa.

Tuesday, July 10, 1945. Jackie woke at 2:30. Had nightmare. Said cow was in crib. Would not sleep in crib again. Brought her into bed with me. We arose at 8:00 had breakfast and Jackie went out front, told me mailman was coming. Nice breezy day. Rained at 4:30-5:00. Wrote letters to Ralph & Mary. Joey Vetere home for 30 days. Made lemon sherbet. Popped corn, a whole bowl full. Jackie ate so much. Cooked supper. Ate at 5:15.

July 10, 1945

Hello, Johnnie darling:

How are you? I'm still waiting to hear from you. It's been so long. I love you, dearest, with every breath that's in me and I miss you so very, very much.

Jackie had a nightmare last night. I was awakened by hearing her say very loudly, "Moooo. Mooooo". I thought she was awake and playing because I heard the "moo" a third time. Then she got up in the crib and screamed, "Mommy, Mommy! The cow is after me. He wants to eat me up!" Of course I was up in a flash and tried to calm her down. She clung to me and said, "It's in my crib, Mommy. The cow's in the crib!" I put the light on so she could see everything was all right. It helped a little but not much. She was still very frightened and shaken so I brought her in bed with me intending to put her back in the crib as soon as she fell asleep. It was 3:00 A.M. by that time. When I awoke again it was a quarter of five. Jackie hadn't moved away from me an inch. I put her back in the crib and went right back to sleep again, myself. Nothing much has happened in the two days I haven't written. It was a lovely day yesterday. Mil called me up in the morning and we talked for quite a while about everything and nothing.

After lunch I prepared the chicken and potatoes and put them in the Frigidaire. I told Gracie to start cooking it at 4:00 and Jackie and I went down to Estlers to get the carriage wheel. He charged me $2.00 for it. We came home again, put the wheel on the stroller and then went to the Acme with Jackie in the stroller. Honey, the front wheel is broken just like the one I had fixed. It hasn't come off yet, but it won't be long now. Oh, dear, the more I want to save money, the more I have to spend it!

Last night we had supper as soon as Mom came home from work. It was swell eating early and nice to have Jackie eating along with us. I tried letting her eat with us when we first came home, but it didn't work out. She'd get hungry about 5:30 and from 5:30 to 6:00 she kept saying she was hungry and wanted to eat. When we finally did eat at 7:00, she probably lost her appetite for she would hardly eat anything at all. I usually have most of the supper prepared by 5:00, so, by the time she's finishing up, we've started eating ourselves. It works out all right but it's much nicer having her eat the same time we do. And she ate so much, Hon;

potatoes, carrots, chicken, milk, and some salad. Then for dessert we had ice cream and you should have seen her dive into that! I can't understand her sudden liking for ice cream. She loves it! We had it for dessert tonight, too. She was so full after eating macaroni, a meatball, salad, and <u>two</u> glasses of milk, but she still had to eat her ice cream.

We had a thunder and lightning storm last night but it was mostly all thunder and little rain.

Last night after I put Jackie to bed I was alone, after Mom and Gracie went out so I wrote a letter to Ruth. I enclosed some pictures for her and a souvenir handkerchief from New York, which I thought she'd like to have.

I also intended to write to Ralph and Mary but my letter to her turned out to be quite long and it was 11:00 before I knew it.

Tonight I put Jackie to bed at 7:30. Mom and Gracie went out at 7:00. It's only 9:30 now so I'll have plenty of time to write Ralph and Mary as soon as I get through with your letter.

Honey, they have new trucks for the water department. Chevys - They're painted the same dark green, only, between the window and the door there's a strip of light green. They look very nice.

After we had breakfast this morning, Jackie went out front to play. I was afraid to let her out there at first but she sits on the steps and watches the cars. She'll either have Cathy with her, or the Lucia Doll. Sometimes she asks me to bring her rocking horse out for her. As long as she was going to be out there I told her to watch for the mailman. Then at 10:00 I heard her yell out, "Mommy, here comes the mailman," only, there wasn't any mail for me.

Joey Vetere came home this afternoon for 30 days.

I popped some corn this afternoon; a large bowlful and poured lots of butter over it and salt, too, of course, and Gracie, Jackie and I ate it all up. Mostly Gracie and Jackie.

I got my period last night and I'm flowing so much. Mil wanted me to go downtown with her but I didn't feel any too good so I didn't go. I wish I had something really of interest to tell you. Well, I love, miss you, and want you too. I long for you so much, my darling. Here's Jackie's good night kiss. I love you so!!

Yours Always, Lou

Note on flap: "How does the situation look, Sweet? Will we be separated for long?

Wednesday, July 11, 1945. Up at 8:30. Cold and windy out. Cold in house. Jackie went out to play after breakfast. Ate pink chalk. Washed her mouth out. Went to lie on sofa and fell asleep 11:15. Slept until 2:30. Had lunch when she woke up. Mama G. came. Jackie and I went downtown. Forgot that stores were closed Wednesdays during July & August. Went to post office. Bought stamps. Stopped in park but no squirrels around. Received card from girls. Came on home. Very cold at night. Used extra blanket.

Thursday, July 12, 1945. Up at 8:00. Cold. Received letter of July 4 from Johnny. Fixed 2 dresses of mine. Ironed a little. Call from Mother de Roxtro. Wanted to know about Johnnie. Said she felt well, but weak. Talked to Vene for a while. Told me about house to move in. M. de R. has cancer of the stomach. Jackie wanted to play with stroller. Brought out old doll carriage. Played with it out in yard. Johnnie Naughton home 2:30. Jackie, Gracie, & I went downtown. Bought shoes for Jackie, pyjamas, sun suit, union suit. After supper went to movies with Mil and Betty. Saw "The Clock." Walker & Garland. Good. Stopped in for a "coc". Home at 10:00. Card from girls.

July, 12, 1945

Dearest Johnnie:

I love you miss you and want you. Yesterday I received your letter of July 4ᵗʰ and was so very glad to hear from you.

The last few days have been pretty cold and windy. It was so cold last night that I had to use an extra blanket.

We received a card from the girls saying they had arrived safely but very tired and that they were having a nice time.

Yesterday morning, Jackie ate some pink chalk! Where she got it I don't know. After I scrubbed her hands and washed out her mouth as best as I could, she went to lie down on the sofa and fell asleep. That was about 11:15 and she slept until 2:30. When she woke up, I fed her and dressed her and then went downtown to buy her shoes. Oh, was I mad! I had forgotten all about the stores being closed Wednesday during July and August! The post office was open so we went there and I bought some stamps which I needed. On the way back we stopped at the park but there wasn't a squirrel in sight so we came on home.

This morning I fixed two dresses of mine and did a little ironing. After lunch, Jackie, Gracie and I went downtown again for Jackie's shoes. Such a time I had finding her a pair! I finally ended up in Lobel's where I always said I'd never buy Jackie a pair of shoes! These are pretty nice though, and fit her very well. She takes a 7C. I also bought her a pair of pyjamas and a sun suit.

Tonight I went to the movies with Mil and Betty Vigilante. We made the first show. We saw "The Clock" at the Community with Robert Walker and Judy Garland. It was a pretty nice picture but I had expected it to be better.

And now, Johnnie, there's something I must tell you and I don't know quite how to begin. Perhaps it would be best if I started from the very beginning.

Friday night, June 22, I received a telephone call from Vene. She told me your mother had an internal hemorrhage and was taken to All Souls Hospital. It shocked me as much as this is shocking you. She told me she was going to the hospital, Sat. so I told her to stop for me and I would go along with her.

Saturday afternoon she came at 2:30. Mother had semi-private accommodations but was placed in the Ward because there were no empty rooms. The hemorrhage had been stopped and she looked pretty well but very pale. We found George already there. He went out to have his blood typed because your mother was going to need a transfusion. After visiting hours we all came back together.

George came in for a few minutes to see Jackie. 6:00 Sat. night Herb called me up from Cutters and said he would be up to see me after he had gone to the hospital. He came as he said he would and then took the last bus to Brookside, to Vene's, where he was staying over until Monday.

Sunday, June 24, Vene came at 3:20P.M. Johnnie Naughton, the two children and Herb were with her and we all went to the hospital. Johnnie and Vene went in first while Herb and I stayed out with the children. When they came out, Herb and I went in. We didn't stay long because mother wasn't feeling very well and didn't feel like talking. Johnnie & Vene went to Mills Street and Herb came home with me. He was here all afternoon and after supper 7:30, Joe drove him to the hospital.

I didn't go to the hospital the next two days. I ordered some flowers from Glendale's and had them sent to her. Wednesday morning Vene called me up and Mother was feeling much better. She had had X-rays taken and another transfusion that Monday, from Herb. Thursday night Vene and I went to visit her and she really did look pretty well. George and Estelle came a little after we did. She was sitting up and talking just like her own self again. (Oh, by the way, she was in a semi-private room, now.) Friday, I took care of Nan and Bonnie while Vene went to the hospital. She came back saying Mother looked and felt very well. I took care of them again Tues. afternoon. Tues. night Vene came down again and I went to the hospital with her. It was your Mother's birthday and Fran and Eddie were there, too. We all had gifts for her and she had a swell time opening them. As we were leaving to go, she told us she had a very happy birthday. I took care of the kids for Vene again on Friday and when she came back, Vene said Mother was coming home Saturday afternoon. She had been in the hospital two weeks. I didn't tell you all this when it happened, darling, because your Mother asked me not to. She said she would tell you about it herself after it was all over.

This morning your mother called me up. After I had inquired about her health, she told me she felt very well but still was a little weak.

I told her about receiving a letter from you and she was happy to hear it. I also told whatever news you wrote me. She spoke to Jackie on the phone and thought it was grand the way she could carry on a conversation. She told me, Johnnie N. came home yesterday and was staying until Friday night. Then I spoke to Vene for a while and after she made sure that your mother had gone outside to sit in the sun, she told me the cause of your mother's sickness. Dr. Mills was her doctor. Without your mother's knowledge, Vene had a private talk with the doctor and he told her that your mother had cancer of the stomach. He told her the growth is situated in such a spot that it can't be operated upon. It's on top of her stomach between the lungs and close to her heart. However, Johnnie, your mother feels no pain or distress at all. You are not supposed to know of this so don't let on that you do. Your *mother doesn't know she has cancer. They're keeping it from her. Vene is moving into a larger house and Nora, George and Herb and helping her with the money. She said she would know definitely about the new place Sunday. It's a few homes down from where she is now, close to the store. That's how things stand now, darling. Please write to your Mother as often as you can but don't let on that you know unless she tells you herself.*

Goodnight, dearest. I love you and wish you were here so very much.

Always yours,   Lou

Note on flap: *"Darling! I love you and miss you!*

Friday, July 13, 1945. *Up at 9:00. Cool day but very nice. After breakfast, cut clippings out of newspapers. Jackie out with Gracie. Mil came over at 8:00, stayed until 9:00. Mom & Gracie out. 6:00 Joe Vetere came. Read magazine until 12:15 A.M.*

July 14, 1945 - The first U. S. Naval bombardment of Japanese home Islands.

July 14, 1945 - The USS Comet arrived Buckner Bay, formerly Nagasuku Bay, Okinawa. The 'cities' of Naha and Shuri were just masses of debris.

[April 1, 1945 - June 22, 1945 -The Battle of Okinawa, codenamed Operation Iceberg, was a major battle of the Pacific War fought by the Allied Marine and Army forces of the United States, United Kingdom, and Australia.]

Saturday, July 14, 1945. *Up at 8:00. Girls came home. Found bags in living room when Jackie and I came down. While I was getting milk, Jackie says, "Daddy came home, Mommy." Girls woke up at 10:30. Brought souvenirs for just the family; picture books, whistle, hangers, medal for Jackie, S & P shakers and nightgown for me. They told me all about their trip. Cleaned house. Jackie ate dirt. Took a shower. Dressed, then cooked supper. 7:00 went downtown with girls & then went to movies. Raining when we came out. Took bus home.*

Sunday July 15, 1945. *Went to 7:00 mass. Raining. 10:30 Mama G & Tadone up. Jackie up at 9:30. Could not get paper. Had dinner at 1:30. Expected Josephine. Came at 2:00. Gave me light oak chest for my dresser and set of garden tools for Jackie. 2:00 gave Jackie a bath & washed hair. After dinner went to Aunt's to visit. Joey was asleep. 6:30 we came home. Joe & Angie came just as we reached Speedwell Place. Jackie & Michael played together and then Judy came & Gene. 8:00 Jo was going to take the train home when Joe decided to drive her to Newark. The girls went to movies. Gene took Mama G & Tadone home. Mom, Gracie, Jackie, Joe & Angie, Jo & Michael & I went along to Newark. Met Mike at Roseville Ave Station. All went to Star pizzeria. Had pizza & beer. Jackie awake & active. Afterwards went to Jo & Mike's house. Stayed until 11:30. Jackie and*

Michael played with toys. Jackie fell asleep on way home. Talked of Johnnie a lot.

July 16, 1945 – First Atomic bomb is successfully tested near Alamagordo, NM.

Monday, July 16, 1945. Up at 8:30. Jackie woke at 9:00. Clear day. After breakfast Jackie went out in the yard to play with her garden tools. Likes them very much. Received letter of July 7, 1945. Ann home from work. After lunch we went downtown. Took 2 pictures of Jackie in blue dress. Lingered in park. Jackie fed the squirrels. Bought Sandbox for Jackie. Stopped in for ice cream. Came home to cook supper. Vene called said they would be down tomorrow. Taught Jackie a new prayer.

July 16, 1945

Dearest Johnnie:

I love you and miss you. I think of you always and wish you were here. Since it's been three days when I last wrote you, a little news has accumulated.

Friday, Joey Vetere came over to visit us but no one was home but me. He and I had a very nice chat just the same. He's changed so much, darling. He's grown taller and has changed in attitude and character. I suppose I shouldn't have said 'changed' because he always was the nicest one of the family. It's only that he seems more serious and acts older. He's seen quite a bit of action, Hon, has eight battle stars and only wears them on his uniform. I think I told you about him being stationed on a destroyer and in the Pacific for fourteen months. The only reason they came home was because his ship was torpedoed and came in for repairs.

That same night, after Mom and Gracie had gone out, who should come over but Mil and Judy. I was just putting Jackie to bed and when she heard Judy's voice she wanted to come downstairs. Never-the-less, it hardly took her five minutes to fall asleep. Mil stayed over an hour so we had quite a talk over our coffee.

Saturday morning, when Jackie and I were coming down for our breakfast, we were very surprised to see two suitcases in the living room. (The girls had come home at 1:20 A.M.) While I was getting breakfast ready, Jackie played around in the living room, very curious about the suit cases, and then came running to me saying, "Daddy came home, Mommy! Daddy came home!" I don't know why she thought that, because I had already told her that Aunt Fannie and Aunt Ann were home. When they got up they told us all about their trip. They had a swell time! Everything was inexpensive and in great abundance. They only spent half of what they brought with them. They brought souvenirs home for Mom, Gracie, Mama G, Tadone, and Jackie and me. They brought Jackie some picture books, a whistle horn, and a medal. For me, a jersey nightgown and salt and pepper shakers in the shape of watering cans. They're darling. There's also a medal for you, bought at St. Joseph's shrine. Will you please put it on the chain with your dog tag? When the meeting was finally adjourned, I started cleaning house. After Fan washed her hair, she helped me. All the time I was so busy, Jackie was very good. She was outside in the back playing with the doll and carriage. I'd take a look at her every once in a while and the last time I saw her, she was feeding dirt to her doll, said it was cereal. Then I had gone upstairs to clean up and take a shower. I was just about ready when I heard Ann yell, "Lou, come down here, quick!" I practically flew down the stairs. There she was choking over some dirt in her mouth. After I fixed her up, Ann told me she had been down in the cellar and hearing a funny noise, went out to investigate and found Jackie gagging. Can you imagine our daughter doing a bright thing like that! After I had my shower, I cooked supper and then at 7:00 we went downtown and then to the movies at the park. At the ticket window, Mrs. Dempsey told me that "Brownie" was home for good, now. Honey, who's "Brownie?" She seemed to take it for granted that I knew him. When we came out of the show, it was raining so hard that we had to wait for the bus. It rained all night long and all day Sunday. We weren't able to get a Sunday paper because of the newspaper strikes in New York. It didn't seem right to be without one. Mama G and Tadone were up as usual.

We expected Josephine up for dinner but it was 1:30 and she hadn't come so we ate and she came at 2:00. Mike was playing golf in the rain qualifying for a tournament. (He didn't make it.) After dinner, I gave Jackie a bath, washed her hair and put her to sleep. Then Jackie, Gracie, Ann, Fannie and I went to my Aunt's to see Joey. He was asleep so we told her not to wake him up. We were home by 6:00 and found Joe and Angie just pulling up to the house. Michael was glad to see his mother but he still wanted to go back to Bernardsville with Uncle Joe. Jackie had just awakened at 5:30 and was so happy to see Michael. While we were having supper, Gene and Judy came over. The three kids were having a swell time playing together. Oh, I forgot to tell you, Jo brought back a set of garden tools for Jackie, (a spade, a rake and a shovel.) For me she brought a light oak chest with the maple leaf imprinted on the top. I have it on my dresser and put all my jewelry in it. I really love it! Josephine and Michael intended taking the 8:15 train to Newark but Joe said he'd drive her down. Gene said he'd take Mama G and Tadone home so Mom, Jackie, Gracie and I went along. The girls had gone to the movies, which I had seen last week. Mike was meeting Joe at the Roseville Avenue Station so we went to pick him up and then we all went to the Star, had Pizza and beer. Golly, Jackie was in such good spirits, laughing and talking all the time. She spoke often of you, that day, dear. When Michael was talking to his father on the phone, Jackie ran to Joe and said, "I want to talk to my daddy." When she was having breakfast in the morning, she said to me, "Mommy, I'm going on a big boat in the water, to see daddy." In the car she said, "We're going to see daddy, mommy!" She seemed to be thinking of you so much. But to get back - The pizza and beer was swell and we had a lot of fun. Afterwards we went up to the house and stayed until 11:30! And Jackie wasn't a bit sleepy! She was so peppy and active. She did sleep on the way home, though, and didn't wake until I was putting her nighties on. I'll have to close now, Hon. It's pretty late and I <u>am</u> a little tired.

I love you, darling, and miss you terribly. You mean so much to me! Regards from the family and a kiss and hug from Jackie. Consider this letter full of them from me. I love you so.

Always, Lou

Tuesday, July 17, 1945. Up at a quarter of eight. Jackie slept until 9:00. Vene, Mother de Roxtro and the children came at 10:30. Raining. Vene went for permanent. MdeR saw yearbook, Neptune Certificate. Had lunch here. Vene came back at 2:00. Sandbox was delivered. They stayed until 3:30. Then went home. Jackie very naughty. Put her to bed at 2:45. Slept until 5:15. I was not feeling well. Had terrific headache. In bed by 10:00.

[Okinawa.]
Postmarked July 18, 1945, stamp upside down.

July, 1945
<u>Another Place</u>

Most Beloved:

Our destination has finally been reached. It was a long trip, but the various interruptions en route made it more bearable. Taken all in all, my latest voyage across the briny blue was entirely satisfactory and completely uneventful with the two trips ashore a most welcome bit of diversion. At each one I managed to indulge in a few beers, which was very tasty, although a bit weak. Later on, when censorship regulations are not quite as strict, I may be able to go into more detail and tell you of the voyage. Right now there isn't much I am allowed to tell, so you will have to be satisfied with the little you can learn from my epistles of love and adoration.

We arrived here a month and eight days after your birthday, which happened to be four days ago. Being quite busy, setting up our temporary residences, I haven't had an opportunity to write previously. I also have my doubts as to whether I'll be able to get down to penning a few lines very often yet, either, but I'll do the best I can. I'm also hoping to hear from you in the next few days. Gosh, but it seems so very long since I kissed you good-bye.

It is rather warm here during the day and my shoulders and back are quite a pretty pink, as is that shelf on my chest. It isn't sore, though, and as I'm taking my sun in small doses, it won't be so very long before I'm browned a little. We've had all nice comfortable, cool nights so far, so sleeping is quite satisfactory. In fact, most of the fellows used blankets last night.

Joe just gave me two pictures which were taken by him in Ventura, and both are very nice. One is of you and I standing together and the other of Jackie in my arms. Both you and our little one turned out swell, so I'm keeping them. I told Joe to tell Marion to send you the negatives and you could have prints made and send the negatives back. If she doesn't, I'll send you these.

Joe and I are in the same tent, along with three other fellows, and I think we'll be comfortable. We all have a lot of work to do yet in order to make this place livable, but that will have to wait awhile. My Company commander informed me, one day aboard ship that I would be in charge of the plumbing shop, so I will be able to arrange to write more comfortably. Our tools haven't arrived as yet, and when they do, I really will be busy, getting things arranged.

Say, Angel, before I forget, there is something I want you to send me. That is a mirror. The one I had got broken while I was back in the states and I haven't been able to acquire another. So if you will be so kind as to purchase me a cheap one and send it, I will love you more than ever, which, of course, is impossible. If you enclose anything else, I will appreciate it, too. But please don't send anything I have to carry around, as I have plenty now.

Darling wife, as I don't want to overburden the censors and as the limit of pages written is two, this will be my last sheet of paper. Send me Ralph's address, will you? I've forgotten it.

I love you, miss you and want you, my sweetheart, and wish I could hold you in my arms again and hold your lovely luscious body close to mine. The pressure of your lips against mine as we fondly embrace would be very lovely. Gee, how I wish we could be together for the rest of our lives. You are the most precious possession I have, and I adore you. Oh, dearest one, I want you so very much. I'm hungry. Best regards to all, and a hug and kiss for our sweet daughter. To you, my beloved, I send my all.

J.De Roxtro EM1/c   Everlastingly, your adoring, *Johnny*

Note on flap: "Here's my love and adoration for you, my darling, with hugs and kisses galore."

Wednesday, July 18, 1945. *Jackie woke at 7:00. Raining heavily. Jackie took a nap 1:00-3:00. Washed hair. Ann and Fan not home for supper. We ate early.*

July 18, 1945
Wed. night

Johnnie Darling:
I wonder if you've reached your destination yet. You've been gone over six weeks now, but it seems so very much longer.

I love you, dearest, with all my heart. You know that, don't you. And you know how much I'm missing you and longing for you. Oh, darling, darling, it just doesn't seem right for us to be separated again! I want you so much!!

Monday, I received your letter of July 7, and was so very glad to hear from you. I look for the mail every morning and am so disappointed when I don't get anything.

Ann stayed home from work yesterday so after lunch, she, Jackie and I went downtown. Before we left I took two pictures of Jackie in that darling blue dress the girls had sent her when we were in California. Remember it? She looked adorable in it. I bought some peanuts while downtown and we went to the park and let Jackie feed the squirrels. She was so happy about it and hated to leave when it was time for us to go. One time after Jackie gave a nut to the squirrel, he scampered up the tree. Jackie was very vexed because he didn't eat it in front of her so she looked up to where he was and said, "Squirrel, come down here, come down here this minute, I said!" It was so cute that Ann and I couldn't help laughing.

I also stopped in Zams to buy Jackie a sandbox because Mom and the girls said they would help me pay for it. It cost $11.95.

We stopped in at Shalits for ice cream and then came on home because I had to get supper ready. Gee, Hon, I sure miss the freedom I had out in California.

While we were eating supper, I received a call from Vene. She said she was going for her permanent tomorrow and your mother and the children would be here at 10:00 to stay with me.

The next day, Tuesday, it was raining again. Vene and your mother were here at 10:15 A.M. Vene left right away. Your mother looks well, Johnnie, but her face is pale. We sat on the sofa and she told me how it first happened. The doctor told her nothing caused it. It's just one of those things that happen. She was told about the growth and the doctor told her it wouldn't grow any larger. She doesn't know the truth yet or even suspect it. I showed her your year book and also the Neptune Certificate. She thought the yearbook was wonderful. Vene came back at 2:00 and ate some lunch that I had saved for her.

The sandbox was also delivered that afternoon. I had to pay for it because Mom and the girls haven't given me the money yet. Your mother and Vene liked it and Vene said she might get one for Nan and Bonnie. Oh, by the way, your mother told me she had received a letter from you and she was so pleased about it. I'm glad you finally managed to write her.

Jackie had become quite cranky during the afternoon so I put her to bed at 2:45 and she fell right to sleep. She had been up since seven that morning. Vene and your mother left at 3:30. Darling, I asked your mother if she would like to spend a few days with me here and she said she might take me up on it. She told me that she wants to spend three weeks in Trenton but she isn't well enough to travel yet. So I guess she's waiting until she feels stronger.

I had a terrific headache myself, last night. I had put Jackie to bed at 8:00 but she wouldn't sleep. She had awakened from her nap at 5:15 and at 10:00 she was still awake. She finally went to sleep when she saw me go to bed. That was at 10:15. I had

504

been lying on the sofa until then but Jackie always kept calling for something or other so I finally decided to go to bed.

Today's another terrible day. It's been raining all day long. Jackie took a nap at 1:00 and slept until three.

I washed my hair while she slept and put it up. Oh yes, Vene said to tell you that Nan and Bonnie kiss your picture every night along with those of their soldier daddy and grampa de Roxtro. I'm teaching Jackie a new prayer, Hon, goes like this. "Now I lay me down to sleep, I pray the Lord my soul to keep, God bless my father and mother dear, and Heavenly Father draw them near. And bless me too, and help me wake, a happy girl for Jesus' sake." Like it? And then afterwards she says the same blesses. Good night dear. A kiss and hug from both of us.

Lou

Note on flap: "Hello Darling, here's Ralph's address: Cpl. R. Petrone, 32760146, 3415 Ord. M.A.M. Co.A.P.O. 718, c/o Postmaster, San Francisco, California

Thursday, July 19, 1945. Raining very hard. Jackie slept until 9:30. Grace went to take care of Sundi's children 10:00. Mil called. Mom received letters from Ralph.

Letter from S/Sgt Mary Lukawitz, postmarked July 21.
Biak, New Guinea

19 July 1945
Dear Lucia,

Yes, I've reached the northern tip of new Guinea, a part of the Netherland East Indies. Our money changes here again. I guess we'll be using Dutch money now. So far I can't say much for the place. Coral everywhere. Can't even go swimming because of the coral and it's as hot as blazes. We're almost on the equator.

Had my first airplane ride, right over the island. It was very thrilling and I had fun all the way. Sat in the co-pilot's seat for the first stretch, then stayed with the radioman, listened to the radio and talked through the microphone to the pilot. Never had so much fun in all my life. The scenery was beautiful. We flew over the clouds most of the way. Passed a live volcano on the way, too, and saw Shangrila off in the distance.

Was lady-of-leisure today. Lay out in the sun for a while then worked on some nylon cards I had. Made a cute pink and white nylon parachute skirt for Jackie. However, I won't be able to send it as we are not permitted to send anything made from parachute material. So she'll have to wait till I bring it to her in person, which will be for some time yet.

They're having a company meeting at the mess hall so I don't know how far I'll get on this letter but I may be able to write a line or two now and then.

Received your sweet letter of July 10th the morning that I was leaving for my present destination. Boy, what a nice send off. Thanks a million.

I should be getting some more pictures from home and as soon as I do I'll send you some. These are much better than the ones I've already sent you. I wish I could lose a little weight. I haven't lost any. It's the outfit that makes me look thin.

Our food here isn't bad at all. For supper we had fresh pork and boiled eggs with mayonnaise (rarity) which I enjoyed immensely.

Oh, yes I hope you'll excuse the holes in the paper but I am out of writing paper. I wanted to write you tonight while I have the time. I'll no doubt have a supply of it in a day or two.

You certainly did receive a lot of lovely gifts for your birthday. Though it's late but may I wish you a Happy Birthday. Hope I can send you something from Manila for your next one.

About a week ago or maybe longer we also saw "Valley of Decision," right out underneath the stars. I thought it was a grand picture. I would like to read the book. Many of the girls said the book was better.

The 4th of July to us was like any other day. We just worked all day. Then I spent the evening writing letters. One night I took a spree and sat up until four in the morning writing letters. Don't remember if you were on the list or not. It's been several weeks ago.

By the way, could you get me a small tube of dark lipstick and some Revlon nail polish? I sure would appreciate it if you would.

They're living in tents here with the coral ground for a floor and nowhere to put our clothes. It's rugged. Sure hope this doesn't last too long. The showers and laundry is outside in separate buildings but one advantage about it is that the shower runs without holding down on a lever and we can drink water right from the faucets; also use it for brushing our teeth which we could not do while at Nugsec. [New Guinea Base Section, controlled the New Guinea Bases.] Whether I'll get to like the place in general remains to be seen. Nugsec was a Garden Spot in comparison to any of the places I've seen of this island including this place.

Well, Lou, give my regards to everyone, to Ann and Fannie, a hug and kiss for Jackie. Loads of luck and happiness to you and Johnnie.

Always, Mary

Friday, July 20, 1945. Jackie up at 9:00. Clear. After breakfast started to wash. Ennis came with sand. Put the sand box up in yard. Jackie played in it all morning. Finished washing at 12:00. After lunch ironed Jackie's starched clothes. Stopped ironing 4:00 to cook supper. After supper went to movies with girls. Double feature at Park. Pretty good.

July 20, 1945
Friday night

Hello, My Darling Husband:

Just got back from the movies and thought I'd drop you a few lines. We saw a double feature at the Park. They were both pretty good. One was a real mystery and the other, light comedy. I enjoyed them both.

We've been having so much rain lately. I'm enclosing a clipping from tonite's paper so that you can see for yourself. It rained heavily all day yesterday. Jackie slept until 9:30. During the night, Jackie woke up and was as wide awake as ever. First she wanted to do wee-wee, then she wanted a drink of water, and then she said she had to go duty (which she didn't.) Anyway she was awake about an hour and oh, I was so sleepy. So it's no wonder I slept so late. 10:15 yesterday morning Gracie went to mind Sundi's kids. She was only supposed to stay there until 2:00 but Sundi didn't come back until 7:00! It's a good thing I didn't need anything at the stores.

Mom received a letter from Ralph yesterday morning. He said his morale was much better at this new place and that he was glad to get out of New Caledonia. He said they're working seven days a week and gets pretty tired. He also sent Mom a "Peso" in Philippine money. Honey, if you ever get a chance to have foreign money, will you send some home to me? I'm making a collection of them and I have a pretty good start already. I have the coins you brought home from New Zealand and then Mary sent me some from New Guinea and Australia. And then I have the dollar stamped Hawaii which I brought home from California. I also have some Canadian coins (which I didn't get from the girls). That's not a bad start, is it?

Today was the first clear day we've had in over a week. Right after breakfast I started to wash the clothes. At 9:30, the sand I had ordered from Ennis (shore sand, by the way) came, so Gracie and I carried the sandbox out to the yard, I fixed the awning onto it and then dumped the sand in it, 100 lbs. Gosh, but it was heavy! It's a good thing I told the fellow to carry it in the back yard for me. Jackie was so happy about it she couldn't wait to get at it. After I had her all settled I went in to finish washing. She stayed out there all morning and wouldn't even leave it to come in for lunch. After lunch she went right back out again.

About 1:30, Angie and Patty Santoro came to ask Gracie to go to their house again but when they saw the sandbox, they stayed here instead and played in it with Jackie. After I had the clothes hung out I starched and ironed Jackie's little blouses and dresses. At 4:00, I stopped to cook supper. Oh, darling, did I feel tired. After I washed, dressed and went to the movies, I felt better.

It looks like it might rain again tonight. Right now it's thundering and lightning out. It's about time I went to bed, now, dear. I love you and miss you so terribly much. I won't be happy again until you are once more by my side. I need you, darling, and I feel lost without you.

Regards from everyone here at home and millions of hugs and kisses from your wife and daughter.

Always, Lou

[Okinawa.]

Postmarked July 21, 1945, stamp upside down.　　　At Destination in Pac.

My Darling Lou:

Once again I find time to put a few lines down on paper, telling you a little of how things are going down here. It has been raining a little and things are slightly muddy, but this is a much better place than the other two were. Our chow hall, or rather the galley, is up and we are eating cooked food which isn't bad at all. The camp is pretty well set up by now, but we all have quite a bit of fixing up to do in order to become more comfortable.

I received quite a few letters from you yesterday, and a Father's Day card. Thanks loads for them all. I won't try to answer them yet because I won't be able to concentrate fully. All the pictures turned out swell, too. That one of Jackie out in those little panties is really tops. How did you ever get her to laugh like that? Those taken in Ventura turned out well too. I was surprised to get the ones from there because I had forgotten all about them. I like the one of Jackie on the cannon, don't you?

I was sorry to hear you had such a messy time going home, though. Things must have become mixed up a little. You do look well, though, in those pictures. I love you, my darling.

I also received the bill from Glendale Florist for the corsages. It came to three dollars, my love. Would you see that it's taken care of, or would you rather I did. It would be more convenient if you did, though. Did I tell you I received the Father's Day card from Jackie while we were on the way? At our first stop some mail came aboard and that was the total for me.

Censorship regulations prohibit my saying very much about this place, but it is nice country, with rolling terrain, trees, bushes and shrubbery. It isn't all wild, either. There are quite a few cultivated places around and some oriental laborers who are the civilian population here. I'm afraid to go more into detail, because I don't want any of my letters removed, causing you to guess about the deleted parts.

Your letters are all long and very interesting, my sweet, and I find myself looking forward to the next one. In a short while, perhaps mine will also become longer and less boring. There isn't much for me to tell you, though I will do my best to be enlightening.

Tell Jackie I always say goodnight sweet to her and ask her not to put her thumb in her mouth. Also that I want her to be a good girl. Let me know what the folks thought of her and you, after being away those few months. I'll bet they were surprised at the change in our daughter, and the way she talks now.

By the way, Angel, I did write to my mother and hadn't known she left Kenneys. I naturally addressed it there, so she will probably receive it later on. As for letting her know when I was leaving the states, I myself didn't know soon enough for her to arrange to come out to California. Did you tell her that? Anyway, I'm quite sure I told her that I expected to leave soon, when I last wrote, didn't I? Regardless, I will make time to write a page or two to her after I finish this, so, she'll be happy again.

I just thought of something else I had forgotten to tell you. I acquired one of those lighters I wanted while we were ashore en route. So you won't have to bother about getting me one. If you already have, though, or still intend to, I will still be able to use it because I'm afraid this one won't last long. My darn pen just ran dry and I was disturbed.

Say, precious one, why not send Marian a print of those pictures in which she and Paul are. You will find the address in the yearbook, as you will Mrs. Phlegar's, in case you decide to write to her. Marion wrote Paul that Blosser had to have another operation. Boy, he's having tough luck.

Your letter of the eighth reached me already, so it should come here in about nine or ten days. Here's hoping mine reach you as rapidly, although you won't have any way of telling, because I am not allowed to date them, yet. As soon as I can, I intend to send a couple of souvenirs to you. I purchased them while on the way over here. Here's hoping you like them.

Tell Jackie I said to drink all her milk and eat lots of potatoes and other vegetables so she will be a really big girl when I get home again. You may also tell her anything else that may induce her to do as you desire.

My adorable darling, this will have to be the last page of this letter because there seems nothing more I have time to say at the moment. I'll try to write again tomorrow.

I love you, miss you and want you more than I ever have, sweet, and I keep hoping and praying that soon we will be able to live and be happy together for the remainder of our lives. Here is all my love and adoration for you and my hug and kiss for Jackie. Regards to all the folks with millions of hugs and kisses to the most wonderful wife and sweetheart in the world.

J. De Roxtro EM1/c   Eternally, your loving *Johnny*

Note on flap: "Tell Mickey I think of her often, and would like to see her soon. Eternal love and all."

Saturday, July 21, 1945. *Jackie woke at 9:30. Clear and sunny out. Jackie couldn't wait to go out in the sandbox. Took 2 pictures of Jackie in sandbox. Turned out to be hot. Cleaned house. Ann & Fan home at 3:00. Stayed home at night. Jackie takes shoes off and stockings.*

Sunday, July 22, 1945. *Went to 7:00 mass. Got up late. Newspaper strike over. Was able to buy Ledger. Jackie slept until 9:00. Rest of family went to 9:30 mass. After Jackie had breakfast I started cooking. Cleaned bedroom, then ironed. Jo & Michael came at 11:00. We had dinner at 12:30. After dinner Jackie out in yard with Michael til 3:00. Gave her a bath and dressed her up. Started to rain at 3:30. Jo decided to stay overnight so after supper we went to the movies. Saw "Counter Attack" with Paul Muni and "Gentle Annie", James Craig and Donna Reed. Both very good. Michael sick while we were gone. Puking all the time. Gene brought carton of Camel's over.*

July 22, 1945
Sunday nite

Dearest Johnnie:

Remember the long curl that always used to form on the back of Jackie's head in the middle of her neck? Well, I cut part of it off and I'm sending it to you. It'll probably be flattened out by the time you get it but if you stretch it out a little it'll from a curl again.

My darling, I love you with all my heart and soul and I miss you more than ever before. Whenever I think of you, which is always, I am filled with eager longing. Johnnie, dear, I want you very much. ----now.----

It's bad for me to think and write like this, especially when I feel the way I do tonite, so I'll switch over to safer channels.

Yesterday was clear and sunny for a change. Later in the day it turned out to be quite hot. All Jackie wore while she played out in the sandbox was a pair of panties.

The girls came home at 3:00 and I didn't get around to cleaning downstairs until 3:30. They wanted to know what I was doing all day just because they didn't find the house already cleaned. Sometimes I get so disgusted, Hon, and feel like letting everything go to the devil.

We stayed in Saturday night. Mom and Gracie went out instead.

Sunday morning, I went to the 7:00 mass but I slept after I shut off the alarm and didn't wake again until five of seven. Of course I was late.

The newspaper strike in New York is over so I was able to buy the Ledger. Jackie was still sleeping when I came home and didn't wake until 9:00. The rest of the family as usual, went to the 9:30 mass.

I felt like having dinner early today so I started cooking right after Jackie and I had breakfast. When Mom came home to look after the sauce and chicken soup, I did some ironing. Jo and Michael came up at 11:00. She had called up last night and said she was coming. Gene brought Mama G and Tadone at 11:30. We were ready to eat dinner at 12:30. As soon as Michael came, he and Jackie played out in the sandbox for the rest of the morning and afternoon. 3:00 I brought Jackie in, gave her a bath and dressed her up. It started to rain at 3:30. Joe and Angie didn't come up because it was raining so hard. Jackie and Michael were waiting for them all afternoon. Jo decided to stay overnight so after supper we went to the movies. We saw Paul Muni in "Counter Attack." It was swell!! The other picture, "Gentle Annie" was good, too. Two good pictures! I won't start another page, darling. It was 11:00 when we came in and now it's after twelve. I'm trying to write every two days, at least, if I possibly can. I wish I could write every day again but I can't seem to get down to it. Maybe later I will.

Goodnight, dear husband. Here are loads of love and kisses from Jackie and me.

Yours, Lou

[Okinawa.]

Postmarked July 23, 1945, stamp upside down.   In the Pacific, N.W.

My Dearest Wife:

Today I received your letter of the twelfth of July and you were absolutely correct. That was more of a shock to me than anything else has been so far. I hadn't the slightest idea that there was the least thing wrong with my mother. As far as I know she never has complained about anything like that, though, as I have very little or practically no faith in Dr. Mills, there is a possibility of an error. I hope so. He is a good surgeon but that's all I can say of him. There is nothing I can do about the situation at home, however. Thanks for letting me know, sweet. But you should have informed me sooner. It is quite alright though because as I said before, there is nothing I can do. If she has a relapse or anything, tell me immediately, will you? Also, if you think it necessary, try and get the Red Cross to get me home. It has been done before, in an emergency, but as long as I have so many brothers and sisters, I have my doubts as to you having any luck. You could try, though, because all they can do is say no. Your letter reached me in very good time, taking only eight days from the time it was postmarked, which was two days after you wrote it. Thanks loads for being so thoughtful of my mother, sweetheart. I love you.

We aren't allowed to date our letters or number them, yet, so you have no way of telling how my letters are coming to you. The postmark probably carries a date stamp, though, so that should assist you a little.

Gosh, angel, I don't know what to say. I received three letters from you today and all those others but I can't do very well tonight in answering them. Please forgive me if this is a short letter, will you? I intend to struggle through one to mom tonight yet, too, and as we don't have lights, it's going to be a tough problem. Maybe I can do better tomorrow. Honey, I think I'll be able to write daily letters now, but don't depend on it too much.

Tell Jackie to be a good girl and that her daddy will be home sometime soon, he hopes. Tell her to eat all her potatoes and vegetables and not to suck her thumb. Here's her hug and kiss from me, too. My darling, I love you, miss you and want so very much to be there with you. You are my one and only, sweet, and I never will be able to do all for you that I would like to. I'm hungry for your love. I want to be there so as to make you and Jackie happy and contented with life. Gee, sweetie, I do love you.

Regards to all, and many hugs, kisses and _____ for you.

J.De Roxtro EM1/c   As ever, your ever-loving hubby, *Johnny*

Note on flap: "Sweetest darling, I love you more now than I ever have. Here's all my love."

Monday, July 23, 1945. *Raining. Jackie and I up at 8:45. We had breakfast and then Michael, Jo & Gracie came down. Received $80 war bond. Staying in all day. Jackie & Michael playing together. Jo & Michael took the 4:15 train home. Wore Jackie's overalls. Heard Jackie say to Michael, "Oh you shut up or I'll hit you!" While putting her to bed she refused to say her prayers. Said to Ann, "I'm not afraid of you!"*

Tuesday, July 24, 1945. *Birthday of Mildred Petrone. Up at a quarter of nine. After breakfast I hung up Mom's clothes to dry. Clear day but sun not shining until afternoon. Girls received letter from Ralph. In 4th Batt. now. Was in 69th. Those not transferred from N.C. [New Caledonia} have furloughs to come home. After lunch Jackie and I went down to the Acme and then stopped in at Mil's. Had cake and coffee. Judy & Jackie blew out candles. Came home. Fixed 2 packages for Johnnie;*

cig. from Mom. After supper, finished beret for Jackie. In pkg, olives, sausage, nuts, nut crackers, 2 pkgs. Charms.

July 24, 1945
Tuesday

Johnnie, Dearest:

"The greatest prayer is Patience." This is the proverb which appears on today's page of my diary. I haven't heard from you in so long, honey. I can't help being a little worried and wondering if you're all right.

This letter will be quite short because I don't have very much to tell you.

Monday it was raining very heavily up until 5:00. Jo and Michael had stayed over from Sunday because of the rain.

Honey, I'm worried about Jackie. She's getting fresh and I don't know how to stop it. It seems that the better she speaks the fresher she gets. Jo and I were in the kitchen talking and Jackie and Michael were in the office playing. Suddenly I heard Jackie say to Michael, "Oh you shut up or I'll hit you!" Just like that! Darling, I was so surprised I lost my breath. Can you imagine Jackie saying that! No, she did not get away with it. I went in and told her she mustn't speak like that to Michael or anyone else, and then I slapped her on the mouth. She doesn't obey like she used to, either. She gets at least one good spanking a day and several little ones. I hate to keep spanking her all the time but what else can I do? How I wish you were here to help me. I don't want her to be a spoiled brat, honey!

At 3:30 it stopped raining for a while so Jo and Michael took the 4:15 train home. It started to rain again after supper and all during the night. It was clear this morning but the sun didn't come out until this afternoon. Mom had washed her clothes Sunday but she couldn't hang them out because of the weather, so after breakfast this morning I hung them out. About 2:00 Jackie and I went to the Acme and on the way back I stopped in at Mil's. Today is her birthday. She had baked a cake so we had coffee and the children had milk. Mil had put two candles on the cake and the kids each had a chance at blowing them out. They even sang "Happy Birthday."

We heard from Ralph today. When he was moved from New Caledonia, he was transferred from the 69th Batt. to the 4th. All the ones of the 69th left on N.C. have furloughs to come home! He sent three negatives home (of himself) and wants prints made of them.

I love you, darling, and miss you and want you. I think of you always and I'm still hoping. Regards from the family and a big hug and kiss from Jackie. She still remembers our days in Calif. with you and speaks of you often.

With every word I write, I send my love,   Yours forever, Lou

Note on flap: "Hi, Sweet, I thought you might be interested in the enclosed article. I love you. Lou"

Wednesday, July 25, 1945. *Anniversary of Joe & Angie. Up at 9:00. Clear day. Jackie just finished her breakfast when Carol and Marilyn Lavada came to play with her. Washed my hair 10:30. 4:30 took shower. Insurance man came. Had to wait five minutes. Gracie & I took 5:45 bus to Olympic Park. Took us one hour. Had to wait 15 minutes for Ann and Fan. We all had tickets. 2 cents to get in. Rode on several rides, chances. Had age guessed. Said I was 21. Asked if I was married. Said "Her husband's got something there" Weight guessed - 123 (127) - won prize. (3 prizes and bought pennant and bird for Jackie. Left 10:15. Home 11:00. Hot night. Jackie wraps up something and says she's sending it to daddy. Sabbath [Bracale] discharged from Army. Mike Sandelli getting discharged. Fred Sandelli being promoted to Captain.*

July 26, 1945 – U.S.S. Indianapolis unloaded components of the Atomic Bomb "Little Boy" at Tinian Island in the South Pacific.

[Okinawa.]

Postmarked July 26, 1945, stamp upside down.   *Same Place*

(probably for duration of stay)

My Darling:

I love you, want you and miss you so very much. I never thought anyone would be missed so very much by me. Gee, sweet, wasn't it swell, being together? If only this darned mess would end so that we could set up house-keeping and make a pleasant home for our family. Gee, that sure will be swell when we can get around the house, doing things as and when we please and doing things without disregard for anyone's feelings except our own and our family's. Why don't you get yourself an apartment or something, sweet? I know darn well the family wouldn't like it but it has to happen sooner or later and they may as well get used to it. But you, being there, know better what to do than I.

I'm not going to send you any money orders unless you ask for it because right now it's a heck of a job to go through. We aren't being paid in American money and we are allowed a maximum of ten dollars a month for our necessities. Our money is not used out here.

I've received more mail from you since I wrote my last letter, but as yet I don't have time to answer them. Sometime soon we will have lights in our tents, I think, so I'll be able to pen daily letters. We are working quite regularly from daylight till dark, so I don't have much time to get down to writing. I will do the best I can, though, my angel, and write whenever I have time. You will just have to get along as well as you can, hearing from me spasmodically, instead of periodically. It is swell of you writing so regularly when you are not receiving any from me. By this time you should have a few.

It has rained practically all day today and there has been quite some wind, but as we have foul-weather gear we can keep dry and even without a shirt, sitting here in the tent it isn't too much of a breeze. This place isn't bad at all, angel, except for a little mud when it rains. Even that dries up in an hour or two after the rain stops. I sure do wish I were allowed to tell you more about this place, but censorship regulations forbid it.

Adorable one, do you remember the picture Joe took of you, Jackie and me walking toward him in the park one day? Well, today he received some prints from Marion and that was in it. Also the one you took of him and Marion sitting on the bench. Both pictures turned out swell. It looks as if we are practically running with Jackie almost running. Honestly, angel, it looks as if we are dragging the poor little girl. You know, maybe we were walking a little too rapidly for her to keep pace with us.

Hunter, Forbes, Fitz, Joe, and several others send their regards to you. Wanda sends hers, through Hunter. He told me that Wanda has written you and also that you had written her. He must be mistaken, though, because you would have told me. I didn't tell him that, though, and gave him your regards.

Your loving hubby is in charge of the plumbing shop, dearest one, so don't worry about him working too hard. Gee, I love you.

Sure pleased to learn that my mother is able to get around, and also that she doesn't know of her actual condition. When I wrote I didn't mention that I knew she was ill at all. I'll do that after I hear directly from her.

Your picture is arranged so that it is the first thing I see in the morning, and the last at night. It's hanging right over my bunk. All night long you are watching over me, my sweetheart. You are my guardian angel.

I smoke my pipe each evening after work now, and that way I save cigarettes. They are quite difficult to get right now, but our ships store will be open soon so we will have plenty of everything. I'll have to borrow stamps until we open the post-office, too. Boy, things are sure messed up for a couple of weeks until we get straightened out and a little organization, but after that, everything runs quite smoothly.

Looks like I'll have to start another page, and I doubt if I will have time to finish it before darkness falls. Gosh but I'm hungry.

I have quite a bit to tell you, my one and only, but it can wait until it is more convenient. I took a little ride on business yesterday and there were quite a few interesting sights. I will have to find out if it is permissible to describe them to you. I would also like to explain a few events which occurred, but I have my doubts as to their passing the censors.

My message to Jackie this evening will be short. Tell her I desire her to be a good girl and to help her mother as much as she can. Tell her also that I love her and kiss her goodnight, nightly for me.

Give my fond regards to all the family and our mutual acquaintances. Thanks for Ralph's address, I'll write him sometime in the future.

All the love in the world is ours, my precious one, and the day of our reunion can't possibly come too soon to suit me. Here are a few hugs and kisses for you, Jackie & Mickey. I miss her too, but not as much as I do you. You certainly are the best wife in the world.

J.De Roxtro EM1/c   As ever, your loving *Johnny*

Note on flap: "All my envelopes are stuck together. I love, miss, and want you. Love forever."

Thursday, July 26, 1945. Up at 8:30. Jackie woke at nine. Dressed and fed her then left at 9:15. Mailed package to Johnnie. Mom mailed cigarettes, too. Met postman on way down. Letter of July 14th from Johnnie. Letter from Mary. 10:30 went to have permanent at Lottys. Feather cut. Turned out very nice. Through at 2:30. Ann home from work. Got home just before it rained.

July 26, 1945
Thurs.

Dearest Johnnie:

Just wait 'til you hear where I went yesterday! As Jackie was finishing her breakfast in the morning, Carol and Marilyn Levada came over to play with her. They wanted to play with the sandbox but it was still very wet from all that rain we had. Yesterday was a beautiful day, though. The sun was shining brightly and it was just warm enough to be comfortable. I washed my hair while Jackie was occupied with the two girls.

While I was taking a shower in the afternoon, the insurance man came. Grace told me that he said he had to see me because he was leaving for his vacation and wouldn't be able to come back. So I told Gray to tell him to wait five minutes. It's the first time he's been here since I've been home so we straightened everything out and I paid up and through August on yours and Jackie's.

At 5:45 Gracie and I took the public Service bus to <u>Olympic Park</u>! We were to meet Ann and Fan there at 7:00. I had never been there by bus before so it was a new experience. Do you know - it took us one hour! Gracie had never been there before and she was so excited. Wed. was Tasty Bread day so we each had a long ticket put out by the Tasty Bread Company. On it were listed all the different rides in the park made into coupons. On each coupon was a reduced rate, which you had to pay along with the coupon. Comprenez-vous? When we got there, Gracie and I had to wait fifteen minutes for the girls. With one of the little coupons we paid two cents admission. Ordinarily it would have been fourteen cents.

You know, honey, I had such a strange feeling as I was going through the gate. You and I used to go down so much with old Esmeralda. Remember?

Oh, what fun we had!! We went on several different rides and there's one that I'm just a little bit afraid of. It's called the "flying scooter." Whew! What a ride! Besides the rides we had tried the different games and we all won a few things. Gracie was very lucky and won the most prizes. And then guess what we did! Fan and I had our ages guessed! You can remember the usual set up. The professor surrounded by a crowd of people. Well, Fan tried and he guessed her to be 19. The limit was within two years before and after. Then I tried and he guessed me to be 21. When I told him I was 26, he was so surprised and asked if I was married. I told him I was and as I went to pick out my prize he yells to the crowd, "Boy, her husband's got something there!" Can you imagine! But, gee, it did feel good to know I only looked 21.

Fan, Gracie and I also had our weights guessed and I won a prize again. Then I bought a pennant with "Olympic Park" on it and a bird on the stick for Jackie. And, oh yes! We all tried archery and gee, Hon, I was punky, out of practice, maybe, huh?

We took the 10:15 bus and were home by 11:00. The night was really quite warm and we had a grand time.

This morning I got up at 8:30 and Jackie woke at nine. After I fed and dressed her, I went to the post office and mailed a package to you. On the way down, I met Willard and he had two letters for me. One from Mary and one from Johnnie, I mean, you, darling! Hon, I was so glad to hear from you! I read your letter as I was walking along the street. I couldn't wait. It certainly took you a long time to get to wherever you are. I thought you were going to let me know!!

It's nice that you and Paul are in the same tent and I'm glad that those pictures he took of us turned out good. I hope Marian does send me the negatives but if she doesn't, you keep the pictures just the same. That's quite a job being in charge of the plumbing shop, isn't it? Let me know how you make out.

I wish I had known about the mirror. I could have enclosed one in the package I sent you this morning. As it is, I'll make up another package and send it out as soon as I can. I have a mirror, here, I can send you but it isn't very large. When I go out I'll buy you a larger one but in the meantime you can be using the small one. Mom is sending you a carton of cigarettes. Let me know in what condition you received them because I'm the one who packed them. After I left the post office I went to the beauty salon. Yes, I finally got around to have a permanent. My appointment was at 10:30. I had it cut very short with curls all around. It's called a "feather cut." It turned out very nice and everyone likes it. P.S. my morale has gone up considerably.

I got in this afternoon just before it rained. Yes, again. Well, Hon, that's all for now. Say "hello" to Paul for Jackie and me and tell him she still speaks of how "Uncle Paul" took her riding in his car!

Goodnight, Johnnie, darling, I love you, miss you and want

517

you. So very much! Loads of love and kisses from your wife and daughter.

Always, Lou

Note on flap: "Darling, I love you. Do you see Fitz and Vincent very much? Lou"

Friday, July 27, 1945. Both of us up at 8:30. Clear and breezy. Jackie out in yard playing with sandbox. Mom came home for lunch. Bought fish from fishman. Talked with Julia quite a while. Told me all about her vacation. Sent Gracie to store. Jackie went too. Cooked supper at 4:30. All ready when girls came home. Had corn for the first time. Very good. Wrote to Mary, Ruth, Ralph.

[Every Friday the fishman would push his cart filled with ice and fish through the Italian neighborhoods calling out, "Pescherie!" or something like that. Being Catholic, we all ate fish on Friday because we didn't eat meat that day.]

[Okinawa.]
Postmarked July 28, 1945. Stamp upside down.

Another day,
<u>Same place</u>

Most Adorable Lucia:

Another page or two to tell you that I love you, miss you and want you more as each moment slowly passes, gradually bringing us closer to the day of our reunion. That day can't possibly come too soon to suit me, either. How I long to hold your sweet lovely body close to mine and press my lips against yours. Honestly, my adorable one, I miss you more now than I ever have. Gee, I want so very much to make a home for you and our family. Wouldn't it be swell if we were happily at home this evening. But perhaps it won't be so very long now, before the Japs surrender. From the scuttlebutt I hear, there are some negotiations by them for a settlement going on now. Let me know if there has been anything in that line going on back there, via the radio. We haven't any yet, so it's strictly scuttlebutt. I love you, Lou.

No mail came from you today, my sweet, but then I don't expect one every day. Those kisses you put on the flaps taste just like your lips, but gosh, what a dead feeling and there isn't any warmth in that envelope, either. I don't care how much lipstick you use, I would certainly enjoy some of it now. And that nice soft bed of ours would be welcome, too. Honey, I sure do want to go home to you.

I'm not in the mood for writing, angel, so this will have to be a short one. Or perhaps I should say, another short one. Last evening I did fairly well, though, didn't I? Give Jackie my daily hug and kiss and tell her I love her and want her to be a good girl.

518

Regards to all the family and our mutual acquaintances. I'll write as soon as I have a little more time and conveniences. You are the only girl in the world for me, my beloved one, and there isn't a minute of the day or night that I'm not thinking of you. Hugs and kisses for you and Mickey.

J.De Roxtro EM1/c   *Eternal love and adoration Johnny*

Note on flap: *"Sweetheart, you are mine and always will be. I love you."*

Postmarked July 30, 1945.
27 July 45
"Somewhere in the Philippines"
Dear Mom,

It's been quite some time since I've heard from you last so I thought I would drop you a few lines just to let you know that I am enjoying good health and I hope to hear the same from you.

As yet, no one has mentioned anything about my watch. I sure hope you received it. It's pretty hard to obtain one over here.

Boy, Mom, I sure spent plenty of dough this month. I guess it was around 30 bucks. It costs me 20 pesos for my laundry a month. That's 10 dollars. Did you receive my last money order yet? I haven't heard about it.

By the way, Mom, will you tell Gene to try to get me a pair of basketball shoes. I think they cost about 10 bucks but it will be worth more than that to me. I've been playing quite a bit because it's the only sort of recreation we have. We were lucky to be camped right by an old tennis court that was made in peace time, and a few of us made it into a basketball court. We have a league going now and it sure eases your mind to play. I was wondering if you would have to obtain a shoe stamp to get the shoes. If so, I think you will be able to receive one if you bring them this letter.

Well, Mom, things are going pretty well with me over here. The time is going fairly well and I do like this place better than N. Cal. I don't think I'll tire of this as soon as I did N. Cal. The weather isn't so good. It rains often and it's hot as hell during the day. They say it gets cold around November. I sure hope so. In N. Cal. It got cold in July or August.

Gee, Mom, I haven't written to Aunt Santa in quite a while and I really feel pretty bad about it. I don't have time to write often and when I do find time I have some old letters to make up. Give her my love and I'll write her soon. Love to grandma, opa & the kids. So long for now.

Your loving son,
Ralph

Saturday, July 28, 1945. Clear day but cool. Fan came home at 1:30. Ann at 3:00. 5:00 we went downtown. Started to rain. Brought dress up to Pete's. Revlon lipstick and nail polish for Mary. Shaving mirror for Johnnie. Came home at 7:00. Had supper. 8:15 went to confession. Raining. Army bomber hits Empire State Building. Set tower of building on fire. (102 stories) 11 floors ablaze. Mike called up.

July 29, 1945 – **After delivering its cargo, components of the atomic bomb, to the island of Tinian, north of Guam, the USS Indianapolis was hit by two torpedoes from a Japanese submarine and sank in just 12 minutes.** The ship sinks before a radio message can be sent out leaving survivors adrift for two days, many of whom were eaten by sharks. Of the 1,197 men aboard, about 900 men survived the initial torpedo attack and were left to survive in the sea. Of the 900 men who went into the water, only 316 survived to be rescued. Under the scorching sun, day after day, without any food or water for days, men were dying from exposure or dehydration, desperate for fresh water. Their lifejackets waterlogged, and many became exhausted and drowned.
https://www.history.com/news/uss-indianapolis-sinking-survivor-stories-sharks.
https://www.history.navy.mil/browse-by-topic/ships/modern-ships/indianapolis.html.
https://www.nationalww2museum.org/war/articles/surviving-sinking-uss-indianapolis.
https://www.bbc.com/news/magazine-23455951
[https://www.bbc.com/news/magazine-23455951]
Nineteen-year-old seaman and survivor, Loel Dean Cox, says in an interview at age 87, "They [the sharks] were continually there, mostly feeding off the dead bodies. Thank goodness, there were lots of dead people floating in the area. But soon they came for the living, too. "We were losing three or four each night and day," says Cox. "You were constantly in fear because you'd see 'em all the time. Every few minutes you'd see their fins - a dozen to two dozen fins in the water. "They would come up and bump you. I was bumped a few times - you never know when they are going to attack you." Some of the men would pound the water, kick and yell when the sharks attacked. Most decided that sticking together in a group was their best defense, but with each attack, the clouds of blood in the water, the screaming, the splashing, more sharks would come. "In that clear water you could see the sharks circling. Then every now and then, like lightning, one would come straight up and take a sailor and take him straight down. One came up and took the sailor next to me. It was just somebody screaming, yelling or getting bit."

Sunday, July 29, 1945. Clear and warm. Went to 7:00 mass. Jackie slept until 10:00. Read paper then started cooking. 11:30 gave Jackie a bath. Gene brought Mama G & Tadone up. Had dinner at 1:00. 2:45 Ann, Fan, Gracie and I took bus to Olympic Park. Were supposed to meet Jo & Michael. Couldn't find them. We all had a ride on the roller coaster, whip. Had my picture taken (came terribly). Went into penny arcade. Lots of fun. 4:30 met Mom, Angie & Joe, Mama G & Tadone. Jackie with Joe. Brought Jackie to kiddie land, 6 rides for $.30 (Ann paid). She rode on merry-go-round (2), cars, boats, airplane, whip, & enjoyed them very much. Left kiddie land. Wanted to go on Carousel. I went with her. Went on Ferris wheel with Fan & Grace. Joe, Jackie, Mom, & Gracie, on old Mill. I brought her to restroom, then to cafeteria to eat supper. She had milk, bread & butter, choc. pudding. We had a record made. I sang sweet dreams, Sweetheart. Girls on other side. Ann had age guessed. 26. We took 8:30 bus and reached home 9:30. Mom, Gracie already home. Jackie sleeping. Had a piece of cold watermelon, then went to bed.

Letter from Wanda Phlegar, postmarked August 1, 1945.

July 29, 1945
Sunday

Dear Lou & Jackie

How are both of you. I got a letter from Hunter last week and he had received some mail from me but he said your hubby didn't get any from you. He was feeling sorry for him. I guess they do look forward to letters more than anything else now.

Say! Did you get home OK? We had a rather easy trip. Lots better than I had even thought of. We rode in the ladies car to Chicago & was it comfortable.

Are you with your mother or where? Jackie are you still as pretty as ever. Make your momma write to me and give her a big kiss to send me and one for Hunter, will you? O.K. Be sure to.

Lou, have you heard very much from Roxy? I heard from Hunter good for a while. Then for 3 weeks I didn't get any mail. Just the other day though I received one letter. Do you remember Chris & Skipper? Well, Skipper wrote to me. I've heard from Julia & Maxine too.

Guess I'll close now. I want to try to write all the girls a line or so. Write to me. Give Jackie my love.

Love, Wanda Mae

July 29, 1945
Sunday night

Dearest Johnnie:

It's pretty late to start this letter but I haven't written you in three days and I didn't want it to be any more than that.

The weather of these last three days has been clear with occasional showers.

Friday was a very dull day. Nothing worth mentioning

happened at all except that we had corn on the cob for the first time and was it good! At night I wrote letters to Ralph, Mary and Ruth.

Mary's been moved up to Biak, New Guinea, almost on the equator. Said she made a pink and white nylon parachute skirt for Jackie but she couldn't send it because they're not permitted to send anything made from parachute material. She asked me to send her a tube of lipstick and some nail polish.

Saturday, I was busy cleaning our room and was through when Fan came home at 1:30. Ann came at 3:00. Five o'clock, the three of us went downtown. I brought a dress of mine up to Pete's to be cleaned and I bought the lipstick and nail polish to send to Mary. I also bought a shaving mirror for you.

Saturday morning, an Army bomber crashed into the Empire State Building. There was a great deal of excitement about it with news flashes coming over the radio at all times.

After supper, it started to rain and the girls and I went to confession. Today was clear and warm.

I went to the 7:00 mass this morning and received communion. Jackie was still asleep when I came home and slept until 10:00. The family went to the 9:30 mass as usual. While Jackie slept, I had my breakfast and read the paper. Then while she was having her breakfast I started cooking.

I gave Jackie a bath at 11:30 and dressed her in her pink overalls and white sweatshirt. Gene brought Mama G and Tadone up and we had dinner at 1:00. A quarter of three, Ann, Fan, Gracie, and I took the bus to Olympic Park again. We were supposed to meet Jo and Michael there but we couldn't find them. No reduction in prices this time. We were all given a pencil upon entering. First ride we had was on the roller coaster and then we rode the whip. We had those 4 for $.25 pictures taken and they came terrible. We spent some time in the Penny Arcade and when we came out who should we see but Joe, Jackie, Mom, Angie and Mama G and Tadone. Joe and Angie had come early so Mom told him where we had gone and asked him to take them, too. We stayed together after we met. We brought Jackie to kiddie land and she rode twice on the merry-go-round, the roto-whip, the little cars, the airplanes and the boats. There are so many rides for children there. Jackie loved them all and was so interested in looking everything over. We left kiddie land and walked around a little. When Jackie saw the Ferris wheel she wanted to go on. No one felt like riding it and since she was holding Fan's hand she kept pulling towards the Ferris wheel until Fan finally gave in and she and Gracie took Jackie up. Hon, that kid loved it! Every time she passed us she waved her hand and was always smiling. Joe marveled because she wasn't afraid of anything. When she saw the big Merry-go-round she wanted to ride on that, too. The girls didn't want to ride on it so I took her. I strapped her in on the horse and stood along side of her. I was afraid to let her go alone on this one because the horse is so big and she always slides over to the side. Then Joe took her on the Old Mill. That was the last ride. She had to do "wee wee" so I brought her over to the ladies room. I had told

522

Mom that if they came down, she was to bring Jackie' potty because the toilets here were filthy. So I had her potty and everything was all right. The girls weren't with us, they had gone for another ride on the roller coaster. I wanted to go too, but I had to take care of Jackie. After she did "wee-wee" I brought her to the cafeteria to get her something to eat. It was 7:00 and she hadn't eaten yet. I didn't care for what they had so I just bought some milk, bread and butter, and a dish of chocolate pudding. She was hungry and ate it all. She was eating when the girls came to find us. I brought her back to Joe and then the girls and I went on ahead. Guess what, honey! We had a small recording made! On one side I sang a song "Good night, Sweet Dreams, Sweetheart" and Ann and Fan sang together on the other side. It didn't come bad at all, darling! We had so much fun making it. We took the 8:30 bus and got home at 9:30. Mom and Gracie were already home and Jackie was sleeping. We all had a cold slice of watermelon and did it taste good! They've all gone to bed and that's just what I'm doing to do now.

I love you, dearest, and miss you and want you. How I wish we were together instead of being so far apart. Regards from everyone and a big hug and kiss from Jackie. I think of you always.

With love, Lou.

Note on flap: "Sweet, I love you very much, but right now I'm tired and sleepy. "nite" Lou

Monday, July 30, 1945. Clear but humid. Jackie slept 'til 10:00. Received letter postmarked July 20. After lunch-3:00 went to Mil's. Stayed until 4:30. Mil gave me some cooked garden beans. Jackie ate some for supper. Read letter to Jackie. Said, "Where's my Daughter" " That's what Daddy says."

[Okinawa.]

Postmarked August 4, 1945, two stamps upside down.   July 30, 1945

A base somewhere in the Pacific.

My Lovable Wife:

Your most welcome letter of ten days ago was received by me today. Thanks loads for writing so often, my darling. You can't have been receiving many, if any at all from me up to this time but you will get a few previous to this one. So far I haven't had time to do much writing, as we have been quite busy. Every once in awhile I think I'll have a little time, but something always comes up to prevent it. Believe it or not, Angel, today was the first time I had a chance to do my laundry. Boy, I had four sets to wash and it certainly was a tough job. But I managed alright, and I think I'll live, after all.

Remember the fellow who visited our place with Porky that day? Well, he was removed from our outfit in the states and he came around to see us the other day. He has been here since April. He is a resident of Caldwell. Pollara is the name.

Ships service opened the other day to sell cigarettes, tobacco, soap and toothpaste, so I managed to acquire some smokes. No beer has been available as yet, but Joe has the reefers [edit. note: refrigerators, refrigerated compartments.] up, so I imagine we will have some before the end of the week. It sure will be a treat to get some, even if it is this special stuff for armed forces overseas.

How do you like the point system the Navy has set up for discharges? According to that, most of us would have to be about forty years old before we could get out, anyway. Oh well, maybe the war will be over in a year or two. According to the news, the Jap opposition is becoming less every day, so maybe it won't be long. I'm tired of being out here, anyway. I want to get home.

As usual, I'm in the best of health and pretty well browned (sort of reddish) from the sun. You should see the blisters on some of these darn fools out here. They must be completely nuts. It's a wonder there hasn't been an order issued compelling us to wear shirts all day. We have to wear them after six in the evening as protection against mosquito bites, which cause malaria.

Gee, wasn't it swell while we were together out in Ventura? Those precious nights with you will be guiding me through these lonely, meatless nights out here, and helping to pass the time in reminders. Ah, such memories. If only I could kiss you goodnight tonight and every night as I did back there. If I could reach over and lay my hands on your sweet lovely body and tell you of my love and adoration and kiss your lips. But it doesn't do me any good to think about such things, so I may as well stop. But I can't stop. The next time we get together, it will be for good, so that is a relief, anyway. Here's hoping it isn't too long before my prayers are answered. I love you so very much, my most precious possession. I'm hungry for your love and miss you more as each day slowly passes. I long for you to be near me again, sweet, and to hear your voice. Darn it, I'm always thinking of you and wanting you. Why the devil did I have to leave you again, when we were so very happy together. I love you so. You are the only girl in the world for me and no one will ever take your place. I adore you.

On the way out here, we stopped at Pearl Harbor, as you guessed, and I had a chance to go ashore. Honolulu is all that it's cracked up to be, as far as I could tell. All I did was go on an excursion around in a bus, but it looked alright to me. It is quite a city, and very modern. The people I saw were quite Americanized and seemed to be quite prosperous. On this tour, I saw quite a few pineapple plantations and acres of sugar cane. After the trip was over, we stopped at a recreation center and had some beer. I managed to acquire eight bottles. It wasn't very cold, but it quenched my thirst for a couple of hours. Those few only made me want more, though, the next day. As we left the rec area, we had to cross a railroad track and would you believe it, a whole trainload, about twenty or thirty freight cars full of nice juicy ripe pineapple stopped. All the fellows were scrambling over it in a second and most of us came away with a couple. Working in the officers' mess, I had access to a refrigerator, so I had nice cold fresh pineapple for a couple days. Boy, what a difference when they are picked ripe.

I'm not quite sure the previous page will pass the censors office, but someone said we were allowed to mention our stop there. Oh yes, that is where I purchased a small souvenir for you, also a small booklet about the peoples of the Pacific in which I though you may be interested. I will send them as soon as it is permissible. At our other stop while en route, all we did was go to a recreation area, which was lousy, so I won't even bother to mention it. I did get four bottles of beer there, though, and saw a native cemetery.

I wish I could tell you more about this place because there are some interesting items, which I may forget when we are together again. It is nothing like the former bases upon which I was imprisoned, and is much larger.

Our food is rather good compared to what I expected and will be much better when we are able to sit down at tables in our new mess hall which is now under construction. Yesterday we had fried chicken and four or five mornings we've had fried eggs (2). Plenty of hot cakes, too.

Hunter and Joe, Fitz and Forbes, and several others (interruption, more later, probably tomorrow) all send their regards to you and Jackie.

Today is the thirty-first and I haven't had breakfast yet. Another fellow and I are brewing a pot of coffee, rather than go to chow. There isn't anything much that I care for. Our coffee will be real good strong stuff anyway and perhaps do us more good.

I feel as if I could have slept at least another hour or two but I'll snap out of it before very long. Darn it, our fire just went out and we don't have anymore gasoline handy. The coffee is just about ready though, so maybe we will be satisfied with it. It doesn't smell so bad.

Give my fond regards to all the folks at home and our mutual friends. Tell Jackie I said to be a good girl until dad comes home. I love you, miss you and want you more as each day slowly passes, bringing us closer to the day of our reunion.

J.De Roxtro EM1/c   Eternally loving you, yours forever, *Johnny*

Tuesday, July 31, 1945. *Jackie slept until 10:30. Received letter postmarked Jul. 23. Went to Mil's. Had lunch there. After*

Chipper had his two o'clock bottle, we all went downtown. Mil had to go to bank. Stopped in park on way back. Judy and Jackie playing with squirrels. Then stopped in new yarn store. Bought 3 hanks of red knitting worsted. $.89 a hank. Started to rain while we were there. Stayed until it let up. Man gave me piece of heavy wrapping paper to cover kids. Got as far as Popular Market. Bought cream and stayed in store next door for ½ hour. Ran out again to Aunt's. Catherine & Carol Ann there. Stayed until 5:00. Razzi drove us home to Mil's. Jackie and I had supper there. 6:00 brought Jackie home. Put her to bed. Mil and I took bus to movies. Saw "The Corn is Green" Bette Davis. Good. Home at 10:30.

July 31, 1945

My Darling Husband:

I have just returned from the movies. Mil and I went to the Community and saw Bette Davis in "The Corn is Green." It was very good. We both enjoyed it.

Yesterday it was clear but very humid. In the morning I received a letter from you postmarked July 21. I was so glad to get it! You said you received quite a few letters from me. I wish you'd tell me the dates so that I could know if you've received them all. I'm glad you liked the pictures. I'll still be able to send you some but not quite as often.

I'll take care of the bill from Glendale's, honey, so you needn't give it another thought. You have me wondering about those souvenirs, now. I hope you'll be able to send them soon.

I read Jackie the parts of your letter, which you wrote to her and she sat so still and listened so attentively. Then as I scanned the pages to find another paragraph, I said, "Now let's see what else Daddy says to you." She comes out with, "Where's my daughter!" "That's what Daddy says!"

Yesterday afternoon, Jackie and I went over to Mil's for a while. Mil gave me some fresh garden beans to take home and Jackie had some for supper. She wouldn't eat them at all before. I hope this will be another vegetable to put down on the list with potatoes and carrots.

Jackie slept until 10:30 this morning. I'm so glad she sleeps late in the morning because she still won't take a nap in the afternoon.

I also received another letter from you postmarked July 23. This letter was in regards to your mother. I'm glad you know about it, darling. I couldn't feel right keeping it from you. If anything else should happen, God forbid, I certainly will let you know.

At 12:30 this noon Jackie and I went to Mil's again. We had lunch there and after Chipper had his bottle, we all went downtown. Jackie and Judy were in the stroller and were they heavy to push! Mil had to go to the bank and afterwards we stopped in the park and Jackie and Judy went hunting for squirrels. On the way home we stopped in at the new yarn store and I bought some red wool. It started to rain while we were in there so we had to wait until it let up a little. The man gave me some heavy wrapping paper, enough to cover the kids entirely and we set out. We got as far as the Popular Market and had to stop because the rain started to come down in torrents. Mil bought a doz. of corn while we were waiting. As soon as it let up again, we went out again and made it to my Aunt's house (Columba St.). She and Catherine were on the porch and they were so surprised to see us. The paper had kept Jackie and Judy dry but Mil and I were soaking wet. Chipper was well covered so the rain didn't bother him, either.

Jackie and Judy played with Carol Ann and my Aunt was holding Chipper. We had to stay there until five o'clock. I didn't worry about the cooking because Gracie can make the sauce and I had told her that if I wasn't back in time, to start everything. When my uncle and the boys came home from work, Razzi drove us to Mil's. Mil's sauce was already done, too, so all she had to do was put the water on for the macaroni. Gene came home at ten after five. Jackie and I stayed there for supper and Jackie sure had an appetite. It stopped raining at 6:00 and 6:30 Jackie and I went home. She had to walk because Mil and I had to leave our carriages at my Aunt's house. Before we left, Mil and I planned to go to the movies. When I came home, I put Jackie to bed and changed my shoes because they were so wet! Then I went out and met Mil at the corner of Speedwell Place and we took the Woodland Ave. bus to the community. It's pretty clear out tonite, so maybe tomorrow will be a nice day.

Jackie still talks about you a lot. Never a day goes by that she doesn't mention you. When ever we talk about you she says <u>she's</u> going on a big boat, too, to see Daddy, and every once in a while she'll wrap up one of her toys and tells me she's sending it to you.

We both miss you very much, darling and I love you with all my heart!

Do you see much of Hunter, Fitz or Vincent? You'd be surprised how Jackie remembers Hunter and Wanda! Lots of times she comes and asks me where Wanda is or where Hunter is. She misses having Buddy to play with, too. And she's getting smart, honey! Saturday, Fan and I were sitting on the sofa talking and Jackie was on the floor listening to us. Every so often she's repeat something Fan said. To fool her, Fan talked in pig Latin. Jackie looked and listened, then said "that isn't nice." Fan said to me, after we had a good laugh, "sometimes she says things to fit even when she doesn't understand what it means." Jackie looked at her and said again, "That isn't nice, to talk like that!" How do you like it!

Love,   Lou

Note on flap: "Darling, I love you, miss you and want you. I long for you so very much. L.DeR."

Wednesday, August 1, 1945. Jackie slept until 10:00. Raining heavily. Received birth announcement from Evelyn Blosser. Paul Franklin. 6 lbs, 14 oz. July 24. Received allotment check for $80. Stopped raining in afternoon. Mama G came up. Girls went shopping in Newark. Soap is limited. One to a customer.

Butter has gone down to 4 points for a quarter of a lb. Soap chips are very hard to get.

Thursday, August 2, 1945. Jackie up at 10:00. Received a letter from Ralph. Said he had hurt his finger and not to tell anyone. Not raining but still damp. Washed my hair. Clear in afternoon. After supper Mom and Gracie went out and the girls went to the movies. Wrote Evelyn Blosser a note of congratulations.

Friday, August 3, 1945. Jackie slept until 9:15. Broken out in hives. Clear and warm. Washed clothes. Mom & Gracie went to Newark to see Doctor. Received letter from Wanda and party invitation from Leslie Ann. After lunch went downtown to bank, post office. Sent money order to Glendale. Bought groceries. Rubber came off. Brought it back to Estler to be fixed. Stopped in at Mil's to give her the vegetables. We all had ice cream. Judy came home with us. Mailed package to Johnnie and Mary. Came home to cook supper. Fish, beets, carrots, corn, salad. Mom and Gracie not home to eat.

August 3, 1945

Dearest Johnnie:

I love you with all my heart and miss you more and more each day. I think of you always and want so much to be with you. I feel lost and lonely without you, dear. It was so wonderful being together and I was so happy! I often think of those days in Calif. The time went by so fast. I wish it would go half as fast, now. Gee, honey, I do miss you terribly!

It's been three days since I last wrote, but nothing much has happened in those three days. Wednesday, Aug.1, all during the night and in the morning it was raining very heavily. Jackie slept until 10:00 and I, myself, didn't get up until 8:30. It was so dreary out. Made you feel like staying in bed.

I received my allotment check for $80 and a birth announcement from Evelyn Blosser! Their son, Paul Franklin, was born July 24th and weighed 6 lbs. 14 oz! I was so pleased because she let me know, that instead of sending her a card, I wrote a short note of congratulations. It's too bad Carl has to be so ill. I feel sorry for them both. Evelyn must be worrying about him a great deal.

It stopped raining about 3:00 in the afternoon and at 3:30 Mama G came up. She brought us a dozen of eggs (which are, by the way, very scarce.) Mayonnaise is even harder to get out here than it was in Calif. I haven't seen any since I've been home. Cleansing tissues aren't very hard to get. I've a good supply in hand. Soap is limited, one to a customer. Butter has gone down in points - 4 points for a quarter of a lb. now. Darling! Are you interested in all this!! O.K.! I won't say anymore.

It wasn't raining Thursday morning but the air was damp. In late afternoon the sun came out. All the mail I received was a letter from Ralph. He said he was very happy to hear from me again. He said he was disappointed because I hadn't written him while I was out in California, but that he enjoyed reading all about my stay out there. When I came home, I wrote him a real long letter telling him quite a bit, and I've been writing every week since. He said he'll try to write you as soon as he can. He hurt the third finger on his right hand in the machine shop and it was pretty bad. At first he thought he was going to lose part of it but the doctor saved all but the nail. He's had it taped up for two weeks and my letter was the first he was able to write. He said I was the only one he told and doesn't want me to tell anyone. He said, if I did, it would be sure to leak out and then Mom would hear about it. He likes it out there in the Philippines much better and said the girls aren't bad either. He wrote me a very nice letter and so far no one even knows that I heard from him. If that's the way he wants it, it's O.K. by me. When the sun came out I washed my hair and my permanent looks so lovely as when I first got it. Honestly, Hon, it's the nicest one I've had yet.

Last night, Mom and Gracie went out and the girls went to the movies. I should have written to you, but I was in a bad mood. I wanted to see the show, too. Jackie slept until a quarter after nine this morning and when I went up to get her, I saw that she was all broken out in hives. How she got them, I don't know.

When I got up this morning it was beautiful, clear and warm. It was such a relief not to see rain! After Jackie had her breakfast I washed the clothes and also the two blue rugs in our room. Jackie received a party invitation from Leslie Ann and I received a letter from Wanda Mae Phlegar! She told me she received a letter from Hunter last week and he told her he had received mail from her but that you hadn't received anything from me and that he felt sorry for you. I'm sorry, too, darling, but you understand, now, why I didn't write you that week. She said she had an easy and comfortable trip back home. That's more than what I can say. She told me she had heard from Hunter and wanted to know if I had heard from you. She also wrote a paragraph to Jackie and Jackie was so thrilled when I read it to her. Wanda wants me to write her and I will, as soon as I can. I like Wanda very much. I wish we had gotten to know her and Hunter better. I like them both.

After lunch, Jackie and I went downtown. It was so warm that I put a sun suit on Jackie. We went to the bank to cash my check and then went to the post office. I sent the money order ($3.00) to Glendale's and I mailed a package to you and one to Mary. While we were downtown, the rubber tire came off the carriage wheel. (the same one I had fixed). I brought it back to him on our way home. He tried to argue with me that he didn't put the tire on and I told him he did and that I paid him two dollars to fix the wheel. Anyway, he put a new tire on and told me after this there was no guarantee on the rubber he uses. My wheels are all breaking, but I hate to go to him (Estler) again. Where else can I go, honey? I had to buy vegetables for us and some for Mil. We went there before coming home and we all had ice cream. Judy came home with us and stayed until Gene came for her at 8:15.

Gracie has to have her appendix out, so today she and Mom went to see Doc Gerard (Newark) about when she should enter the hospital. I'll let you know what develops. I'm running short of space, just room enough to say I love you and miss you. Here's a kiss from Jackie.
Yours, ever Lou
Note on flap: "I'm tired to-nite, sweet. I had quite a day. I love you loads. Lou"

Saturday, August 4, 1945. Both of us up at 8:15. Clear and warm out. Beautiful day. After breakfast Jackie went out to play with swing and sand. Received letter postmarked July 28 from Johnnie. Started in to clean house right away. Fan came home at 1:00 and Ann came home at 2:00. We had dinner at 230. The girls took 4:15 bus to station. Spending one week at Beaver Brook. Gave Jackie a bath and washed her hair.6:oo I took a shower. Mom and Gracie went out. 6:30 Jackie and I went to Mil's. Played with Judy's swing & sand. Mil & I had coffee and cake. Came home at 8:30. Gracie to go to Presbyterian Hospital next week to have appendix out.

Sunday, August 5, 1945. Jackie woke at 6:30. I went to 7:00 mass. Lovely day. Was stopped by the people who work at Kenneys. Said I looked wonderful. Asked about Johnnie. Cooked sauce. Gracie took picture of me & Jackie. Gene brought Mama G & Tadone up. We had dinner at 12:00. 1:00 put Jackie to bed. 2:00 I went to Community. Saw "Thrill of a Romance." Very good. Home at 5:00. Joe and Angie not up. Listened to Radio until 10:00. Then went to bed. Had headache.

August 5, 1945
Sunday night

Dearest Johnnie:
How I miss you!! I think of you so much my darling and long for you terribly. I love you with every beat of my heart and I want you. Oh, darling, I love you so much! This separation is worse than the first time. The days seem to drag! I'm not in a very nice mood, tonight, dear, because I'm so lonesome for you.

Saturday was a beautiful day. Clear and warm. Jackie and I got up at 8:oo. After breakfast, Jackie went out to play with her sandbox and the swing. Did I tell you that Mom took the swing down from the tree because she didn't want her flowers broken? She put it up under the porch, instead. This way Jackie can get in and out of it herself.

I started right in with the cleaning and finished quite early. Fan and Ann came home right after work. They had several last minute things to do before leaving on their vacation. They were taking the quarter of five train to the Poconos. They're going to Beaver Brook again. Since they were leaving so late and wouldn't have ay supper, we had dinner at 2:30. After they left, I gave Jackie a bath and washed her hair. Mom and Gracie went out, so at 6:00 I took a shower, dressed and then Jackie and I went over to Mil's. Jackie and Judy played down in the yard. Judy also has a sandbox and swing. Gene was giving them each turns in the swing. We stayed there until 8:30. Jackie didn't want to leave.

Saturday morning I received a letter from you. It was postmarked July 28. You can't be in Okinawa, honey, because the boys there are allowed to say so. I wish I knew.

According to the newspapers back here, the war with Japan won't be over until next year unless something unforeseen happens. They were given a chance to surrender according to the terms of the Atlantic Charter, but as far as I know nothing ever came of it.

This morning, Jackie woke at 6:30, even before I got up to get ready for church. After I put her on the toilet I told her to go back to sleep again but she said she didn't want to sleep. So before I left I gave her some toys and several books to read. After mass, the women who used to work with your mother at Kenneys, stopped to talk to me. They said I looked wonderful after my trip (are they kiddin'!) and asked about you. They also asked about Jackie. They said they called up your mother last week and she told them they had moved into their new home. I, myself, called Vene's a few times last week and never got any answer. Perhaps I'll call again tomorrow. Although Vene could just as well have called me to let me know. I suppose their telephone number is changed, too. Mama G and Tadone were up as usual, today, and we had dinner at 12:30, because I started cooking early. It was beautiful out.

1:00 I put Jackie to bed for her nap and then I was so restless, I didn't know what to do with myself so at 2:00 I went to the Community. I saw "Thrill of a Romance." It was very good and I enjoyed it a lot. I was home by 5:00.

Joe and Angie didn't come today. I can't imagine why. It was so warm and the riding would have been ideal.

Gene came over at 9:00 and brought Mama G and Tadone home.

I read an article in the paper saying that shoes would cease to be rationed as soon as the Japs surrender. And also that people will be able to purchase radios by Christmas. I'd love to have one for my room but I don't see how I can. I'm trying so hard to save money, Hon, but I can't seem to be able to. I want to start a bank account again. All I had left over from last month's allotment was twenty dollars. I owe the dentist $10 and the doctor $20. I can't start saving until the bills are paid. It's almost like when we first started out. I mean about trying to save money.

Gracie is going to the Presbyterian Hospital, Newark,

531

tomorrow afternoon. She has the same doctor Fan had. He's the one that's such a good friend of Mil and Gene's. Fan swears by him. Said he's a wonderful doctor.

I put Jackie to bed at 8:00 and she went right to sleep. Want to hear something funny! Yesterday morning she was on the toilet and I said to her, "Hurry up, Jackie, I've got to go!" She answered, "I'm coming, too. Where you going?"

She still talks a lot about you and includes you in everything. How I wish you were home with us. Regards from everyone and a big hug and kiss from Jackie and millions more from me. Yours, always and forever, Lou

Note on flap: "Goodnight, Darling, I love you. I'm enclosing some articles you might find interesting. Lou"

August 6, 1945 – First Atomic Bomb is dropped on Hiroshima from a B-29 bomber, the Enola Gay, commanded by Col. Paul Tibbets.

Monday, August 6, 1945. I stayed in bed 'til a quarter of nine. Jackie woke at nine. It was raining. Received check of $50 and letter postmarked Jul. 26, from Johnnie. Gracie and Mom took 2:44 train to Newark. Gracie going to be operated upon tomorrow. Mom staying in Newark until tomorrow nite. 5:00 Gene came for Jackie and me. We stayed overnight at Mils. (hardly slept at all.) Mil and Gene went to movies. Brought ice cream back with them. Went to bed 10:30.

Postmarked August 7, 1945 from Ruth Greaves.

Aug. 6, 1945
Ventura, Calif.

Dear Lou,

I'm really ashamed at the way I have neglected writing you but there have been so many changes since you left. I hardly know where to begin.

I don't take care of Jimmy, the little boy, anymore. Mrs. Taylor's hours were changed so that I didn't have to watch him. I'm rather glad, as I am much freer.

Burton's mother came down on a two-week's visit. What a hectic time. All we did was eat, sleep, talk, & go places. We really enjoyed her visit. Buddy followed her around continuously. We went to Santa Barbara on a shopping trip. Mom bought Buddy 5 whole new outfits and 7 sets of underwear, also 12 pr. Anklets. I got him some new shoes & hat for him. You should see him strut.

His birthday is Sept. 28. He'll be 4 yrs. Old. I guess we will have to plan something special.

It certainly sounds as if you have been having fun.

You certainly have been going places. I want to thank you for the darling lace hankie you sent me from N.Y. I really do love it. It pleased me to know you thought about me while you were having fun. Maybe I can do as much for you sometime. Thanks too for the snapshots. They will always be souvenirs of happy times we had with you kids. I am having several prints made of pictures we have taken since you left. As soon as I get them, I'll send you some. They were taken on the beach.   When you write Johnnie again tell him Port Hueneme is no more. They have done away with all the CB's. They are going to reduce the number of men at Burton's base. We are holding our breath for fear Burton may get transferred. As long as he doesn't get sent to sea I won't care.

The weather here is perfect now. We haven't had any fog for over a month. It gets very hot at times, but there is always a breeze from the ocean, which keeps the heat from becoming unbearable. Of course, the nights are always cool.

I'm glad your permanent turned out so well. I'm getting one in the morning. I have an appointment for 9 o'clock.

Burton still gets me Kleenex at the base. I have about 7 boxes on hand, so I guess I won't run out for a while yet.

We are still in our one room & are pretty much satisfied. We have things pretty much as we want them.

On July 4th we met a new couple. Both 25 yrs. old and they have a 1941 Plymouth De Luxe Sedan!! We went riding & had a very enjoyable 4th. Since then we have become very good friends.

One of the gals (Hazel the one with the little boy) downstairs went back home, leaving a vacant room downstairs. Hazel had the room with cooking facilities. Ellen, the girl who was the new bride & who cooked in with Hazel moved in Hazel's room.

These new kids we met moved in the vacant room. They cook up here with us. It just works out swell. It was okay with Mrs. Taylor too. We go half on everything including points, & cooking. Then Burton rides back & forth to the base with Walt. (the fellow). If you hear me mention Walt & Carol Boguhn, you'll know I'm speaking of our new friends.

Ellen, the other girl downstairs is leaving for home next week so then Walt & Carol are going to take that room. Then we will all be cooking separately. I don't know who will move into the extra room then. It's too bad you and Johnnie aren't here now. We'd all be one big happy family.

Walt & Carol are exactly the type of couple we have been wanting to get in with ever since we first came here. They don't drink, etc, they love to play cards as well as we do. Then, too, they have the car & we are always going someplace. They are really fun to be with.

Carol had a baby girl 4 wks. ago. It was 7 mo. premature. It weighed 2 lbs. 15 oz. It is still in the hospital in an incubator. It is gaining right along but will have to remain in the hospital for at least 2 more months. I saw it & it is just darling but, Lou, it is so tiny!! I can't begin to describe how small it is. I'll be glad when Carol can bring it home.

One Sat. night while Burton's mother was here, Walt, Carol, she, Buddy, Burton, & I went grunion hunting. Grunions are small silvery fish who, at the time of the full moon, lay their eggs in the sand. Hundreds of them come in on one big wave, lay their eggs on the beach, then go back to sea on the next wave. You catch them between waves. We went down about 11:30 P.M. & stayed until 4 a.m. Sunday morning. Did we ever have fun. There were thousands of people on the beach & every one had a bonfire. Fires lined the beach as far as you could see.

Burton's duty has been changed again. He has duty every 4th night. Now I don't have long weeks without him.

I haven't been down to the park since you left.

We go swimming quite often. We are all burnt black. Buddy is worst of all. His back just finished peeling again last week. He's healthy so I never worry about him.

Well, Lou, it's time to start supper. I do hope you'll forgive me for taking so long in answering your two very nice letters, but you can see where and how my time has been taken up. But we think about you & talk of you so often. We'll never forget the good times we all had together.

I hope you'll answer soon again & I'll do better about answering more promptly next time.

All my love, Ruth

534

Tuesday, August 7, 1945. *Judy woke at 7:00 and Jackie at 7:30. We all had breakfast. Then I dressed Jackie and we came home to bring milk in. Clear and warm. Called Vene's. No answer. 10:30 going downtown when phone rings. Mother de Roxtro. Told her I couldn't go to Leslie Ann's party. Very disappointed. Had already told Fran that I would be there. Asked them to stop by for Les' gift. Bought her hankies & soap. Told me she had heard from Johnnie. George had ulcer taken out. Johnnie N. home every eight days. Went to bank. Bought oil for Mil. Went there for lunch and supper. Came home at 6:30. Vene's number 309M.*

August 7, 1945
Tue. Night

Dearest Johnnie:

I love you, miss you and want you. You are never out of my thoughts, darling. I think of you all the time.

Monday morning I awoke to the pitter-patter of the raindrops, loud and heavy ones. Willard brought me a letter from you post marked July 26th, and the other allotment check of $50.

It was a very dismal day! Mom stayed home from work and in the afternoon she and Gracie took the 2:44 train to Newark. They were going to the hospital and Gracie was operated on today. Mom stayed over at Jo and Mike's and is coming home tonite.

Right after lunch Mil called and invited Jackie and me to stay with them so I wouldn't be alone in the house. I accepted, not because I was afraid to stay in the house alone, but because I didn't want to be by myself. It's alright as long as Jackie's awake, but it's pretty lonely after I put her to bed. I packed a little overnight bag, with my pyjamas and Jackie's, and a change of clothing for Jackie. Gene came for us at 5:00, soon as he came home from work.

After we had supper, I told Mil that as long as I was there she and Gene might just as well go to the movies. A good movie was playing and she wanted to see it. She hated to leave me alone, but I finally convinced her to go. Chipper was already asleep in his bassinette. He's no trouble at all. I put Judy and Jackie to bed at 7:30. That's when I had a little trouble. They were always talking to each other. In the room that Gene made for Judy, they have a large size bed. Judy was in her crib and Jackie and I in the bed. To keep them quiet, I went into the room and lay on the bed beside Jackie. Judy fell asleep at 8:15 so I didn't stay in the room anymore. I thought Jackie would fall asleep soon afterward. While I was reading in the living room, I kept hearing noises from the bedroom. I went in, switched on the light and saw Jackie with her eyes closed, apparently sleeping. I stayed there for a while, watching her, then I became suspicious when I saw her lips set in a half smile. I went in closer to the bed and watched her more closely. After a few minutes she opened her eyes, looked at me and burst out laughing. See what a devil she is! It was 9:00 and she was still awake. I told her to be quiet and not wake Judy so I turned out the light and went back to my book.

 Mil and Gene came home at a quarter of ten and they had brought back some ice cream. We divided a pint between the three of us. I stayed up while Mil made the formula and gave Chipper his last bottle and then we all went to bed. I didn't get much sleep, though, because Jackie was all over me.

 Judy woke at 7:00 and started right in to call Jackie. I tried to keep her quiet but Jackie woke at 7:30 and there was no use trying to stay in bed after that. Jackie and Judy ate a very good breakfast. They each had an egg, toast, some cornflakes and milk and a glass of milk. That's very usual for both of them. Oh, yes, and they even had their orange juice first.

 About 9:00 Jackie and I came home because I had to bring the milk in and I wanted to put something lighter on Jackie for it was lovely, today, and later in the morning it turned out to be quite hot. About 10:30, I called up Vene's to let them know that Jackie and I couldn't go to Leslie Ann's party because I had already promised Mil to take care of Chipper. But I couldn't get any answer. Then, just as I was going out the door, Jackie and I were going downtown, the phone rings. It was your mother. We talked for quite a while. She told me she had heard from you and had written you, for the first time, last week. But she didn't say she had been sick. So, honey, please, I hope you didn't let her know that I told you. She said Johnnie Naughton comes home every eight days and the last time he had two whole days. That's how you and I hoped it would be, remember? She also told me that George had been in the hospital and had an ulcer taken out. I asked them to stop by in the morning to bring my gift to Leslie Ann. After Jackie and I came back from town we went back to Mil's and had lunch and supper there. As was to be expected, Judy and Jackie got to fighting, but honey, you should see Jackie defend herself! She does all right! I'm glad! We came home at 6:30 and I put Jackie to bed at 7:00. She was very tired and fell right to sleep. Mom should be home pretty soon so I'll wait up for her.

 Good night, darling. I love you more than ever and miss you terribly! A kiss from Jackie.

Love, Lou

Note on flap: "*Darling, I love you, and love you, and love you. Always, Lou.*"

From S/Sgt. Mary Lukawitz, postmarked August 10, 1945 7 August, 1945

Biak, N.E.I.

Dear Lou,

 Just finished applying a coat of nail polish that I borrowed from one of the girls so if the writing looks a little shaky it's because I'm trying not to smear them. If I succeed, then I'll get two things done at one time. Having to go to work early and less time for lunch, I have to devote most of my evenings to washing, ironing, and writing letters. After supper I went to Mass, then there was sewing to do – had to wash the

536

clothes I wore today and iron two pairs of trousers and a shirt. Then I shampooed my hair and used a little cologne in the rinse water. Well, the water smelled so good that I decided to take down the clothes I hung on the line and rinse them in the scented water. Oh, boy, even my clothes will smell nice. So you see I really have accomplished quite a bit, tonight.

Now to answer your sweet letter of 27 July. Since I've been up on this island my mail reaches me in a week, sometimes less. It's really a grand feeling to get letters in so short a time but most important of all – to get letters. Oh, yes, I've decided to have my letters come to the office so don't get alarmed at the change in address.

We're having rain galore. Sometimes I wonder if the Pacific Ocean is coming in on us. It really pours. We haven't had much hot weather lately for it's the rainy season, and believe me, it does.

So Ann and Fannie went to Canada. I'm glad they had a wonderful trip. Someday I'd like to see Canada and many places that I whizzed by while in the Army. You'd think I'd be contented to stay at home after all the traveling I've done. But not me. I'm ready to go further and look for new thrills and excitement. Which reminds me... I have a roll of film and I better get out and take some pictures of this island for my collection. Before I left Nugsec I took some but as yet I haven't received them. Sure hope they turn out.

Since I've been assigned and doing the kind of work I always wanted and kept busy all day at the office, I really like this place. In fact, I'd be contented to remain here as long as they'd let me. The food has been good, a club across the road where we can get coffee every morning and coke in the afternoon and evening. There are loads of little clubs all over the island. Some are really sweet and the boys really had to work to make them so.

The other night three of us girls from the office went to one at the medical depot –right on top of a steep hill. The inside: a nice small bar, a dance floor (rough but nice), divans, chairs, tables, piano, little curtains. It really was adorable. The orchestra (about five players) were pretty good too. They had ham sandwiches, devil's food cake, ice cream, coke, beer and lemonade. I only ate a huge pint of ice cream, however, I danced and danced. Not a stitch on me was dry when I came home. For the first time I really had a wonderful time at a party here. The girls in my tent asked me to go to one Saturday. Hope I have as nice a time.

Give my regards to Ann, Fannie, Gracie, your mother, Johnnie – a big hug and kiss for Jackie. One Sunday afternoon I went picking shells. I'm going to try making a bracelet for Jackie out of them. If it turns out, I'll let you know. Then I'll mail it. If it turns out alright.

Haven't had cleansing tissues at the post-exchange but I'm well supplied. We can get mirrors. I bought one today making a total of three in my possession. Extras just in case I break one.

Well, Lou, must bring my epistle to an end for this time. My best to you and Johnnie.

Always, Mary

P.S. I have lost weight since I've been here. Feel wonderful.

August 8, 1945 – USSR declares war on Japan, then invades Manchuria.

Wednesday, August 8, 1945. Leslie Ann Kugler's birthday. Jackie and I up at 8:50. Got my period this morning. Vene came at 10:45. Brought my gifts to Leslie. After lunch went over to Mil's. Mailed card to Gracie. Went to Acme. After supper Mom went to Newark to visit Gracie. I knitted on Chipper's stocking. Mom came home at 10:00. At breakfast Jackie said, "Daddy's under the sink, Mommy." I said, "What do you mean, Jack?" She said," Daddy was under there fixing it, that sink." Was referring to Johnnie's last leave home, October 1944.

August 9, 1945 – Second Atomic Bomb is dropped on Nagasaki from a B-29 bomber commanded by Major Charles Sweeney. Emperor Hirohito and Japanese Prime Minister Suzuki then decide to seek an immediate peace with the Allies.

Thursday, August 9, 1945. Jackie up at 8:00. After breakfast Jackie went out and I cleaned around a bit. Then I went out and cut the grass in the yard. Lovely and warm out. Received back letter I wrote to Evelyn. Received letter from Ruth. Stayed home except at 4:00 Jackie and I went to Shalit's to buy the paper. We also bought two Dixie cups. Finished knitting socks for Chipper. Listened to president Truman's speech. Jackie answered telephone by herself.

Aug. 9, 1945
Thurs. night

Hello My Darling:

I love you and miss you more each day. I think of you always and wish you were here. From the looks of things, it won't be long now. Oh, darling, it'll be wonderful having you back again!

I received no mail from you yesterday or today. I hope I get a letter tomorrow.

538

Yesterday, I mailed a card to Gracie and then we went over to Mil's. After supper, Mom went to Newark to visit Gracie and Gene went with her. Mom says Gracie's coming along fine.

While we were having breakfast, yesterday morning, Jackie said, "Daddy's under the sink, Mommy." I looked at her puzzled and said, "What do you mean, Jack?" She answered, "Daddy was under there fixing it-that sink!" Darling! Can it be that she remembered when you cleaned the trap while you were home on leave in Oct.!!

Today was such a lovely day! Jackie woke at eight o'clock. While she was playing out in the yard, I cleaned around the house a bit and then went out and cut the grass in the yard. You should see all there is! The whole yard is covered except the part under the tree around where we keep the garbage can. Remember when I told you about writing to Evelyn? Well, I got the letter back again. Maybe I don't have the right address.

4:00 Jackie and I took a walk to Shalit's to buy the paper. I also bought us each a Dixie cup. The paper was full, about the Russians coming into the war and about the new atomic bomb.

I received a letter from Ruth today. She told me quite a bit. She doesn't take care of her landlady's grandson anymore. Burton's mother was down for a two-week's visit and all they did was "eat, sleep, talk and go places." She said to tell you they have done away with all the C.B's at Port Hueneme. They are also going to reduce the number of men at Mira Loma. The weather out there is perfect, now. She said it gets very hot at times but there is always a breeze from the ocean which keeps the heat from becoming unbearable.

On July 4th they met a new couple, both 25 years old, and they have a 1941 Plymouth De Luxe sedan. They've gone riding with them and since then they've become very good friends. The people who used to live beneath them moved out so this new couple moved in. Burton rides back and forth to the base with the fellow. She said they're having so much fun and wished we were there to get in on some of it. I'm glad she found someone to pal around with. It gets pretty lonely being by yourself.

Since I have nothing else to tell you I'll answer your last letter which I received Monday. Darling: I, too, am looking forward to the day when we will be living in our own place. It's going to be swell. I have thought about getting an apartment, dear, but I don't want to start until I have a little money in reserve.

Honey, I don't remember taking any pictures of Paul and Marion sitting on the bench. Not even the one he took of the three of us. (Any chances of getting it?) By the way, how do you like being boss? How many men under you? The president is speaking tonight. I'd like to listen to him.

Good night, darling; I love you, love you and love you. I want you so much. A big hug and kiss from Jackie.

All my love, Lou

Note on flap: "Dearest: Until I'm once more in your arms, I won't be completely happy. I love you. Lou"

[Okinawa.]

Postmarked August 14, 1945, two stamps upside down. *August 9, 1945*
Same Place

Most precious Darling:

I love you, miss you and want you more as each day passes slowly but surely bringing us more close together. I'm hungry, my sweet, and only being with you will satisfy me. How I long to hold your lovely young body close to me and press my lips to yours in a lingering, loving embrace. Just to be able to sit and look at you would be much more satisfactory than being way out here, with no one to look at excepting these old men. There are a few native women here but they aren't even worth looking at. Even though some of them are fairly well built and nice looking, they are practically covered with some kind of sores. They do have nice straight white teeth and nice eyes, though. None of them are able to speak English though, and are hard workers. They do laundry for the soldiers and work in the fields generally. They never will appeal to me, though, even if I had to remain here the rest of my life, so you needn't worry about that. I'm saving all my love and adoration for you. There are a few Red Cross girls here and some army nurses that I've seen. As for the male population, it's the same here as everywhere. All Army, Navy and Marines. The male natives are very few and from what I hear a very small number of them can speak and understand a small amount of English. There are lots of native children and so far I've seen only one dog. That was probably brought ashore from some ship from the states. I did see a few white cats and a couple of dozen white goats. I adore you, Lou.

Last night I didn't write because I did my laundry, and boy, such a large one it was. Not many pieces, but boy, was it dirty. Not because it was worn very long, either, but because of the mud. There's nothing much to write about anyway, so it makes not much difference. Today I received your letter of the last day of July. It was swell hearing from you again. That's the first letter I received in almost a week. It really helps a lot reading letters from the only girl in the world. Honey, I love you more than ever.

We have interruptions almost every night and sometimes we have more than one. The average so far is about two a night. There never is any damage done, except that my much-needed rest is interrupted.

Say, angel, if you happen to think of it, in your next package, send some garlic. Quite a few pieces because we don't have any for our cooking. I don't care to use this stuff that grows here, on account of the human manure they use as fertilizer. Might cause some illness, you know. Joe just told me to tell you to include some cabossa (spelling incorrect) but he means pepperoni. The aforementioned stuff is polish salami in case you don't know.

Tell Jackie to be a good girl and that her daddy may be home in about a year (I hope it's less). Give her a hug and kiss for me. Regards to all the folks at home. To you my adorable one, I send my all. I love you, sweet, and oh, how I want you. I miss you terribly.

J.De Roxtro EM1/c   Eternally, your loving   *Johnny*

Note on flap: "Scuttlebutt says we will leave here by November first. Here's hoping it's for the States. Here's a kiss for M. JdR."

Friday, August 10, 1945. Up at 8:00. Mil called. Told me to put radio on. Martha called. Japanese surrender according to Potsdam Ultimatum. Not official yet. Jackie woke at 9:00. After breakfast went over to Martha's. Julia Sandelli there, too. Had coffee and cake. Listened to Radio. Stayed until 11:00. Martha took two pictures of me. After lunch washed hair. 2:30 Jackie and I went downtown. Brought film to Sandrian, cards, bought turtle for Jackie. She loves it! Bought veg. on way home. Called Joe to tell him about Gracie being in the hospital.

Letter from Ralph postmarked August 16, 1945.   10 Aug. 45
"Somewhere in the Philippines"

Dear Lou,

I received your letter today and I was glad to hear from you. I wrote you a letter about a week ago so I guess you haven't received it yet. I hope you won't mind this pencil because I don't have a pen available at the moment. You see, Lou, I'm working nights and things are slow right now so I thought I'd drop you a line or two.

Well, Lou, we heard of Japan's offer to surrender last night about 8 o'clock & you should have seen the soldiers. Everyone was so happy and all the bottles of stashed whisky came out of the hiding places and I'll bet 9 out of 10 were

drunk. Yes, Lou, even I was feeling good but boy did I have a big head this morning. The last time was
on New Years Eve in New Cal. Boy, all of us are hoping that they will accept the peace offer because it will mean that we might come home sooner. We heard something about them holding a vote in all the major cities whether to decline or accept the peace offer and the majority didn't want to accept it. Boy, if they only knew all the names we called them. I'll bet they were all the people that don't have anyone overseas in their families. Boy, I sure hope Truman accepts the offer. You know, Lou, when I first heard of it I was so happy that I was shaking like a leaf. I guess I was excited and all that but after all I sweated out quite a bit of time for this. Now at least we have a little chance of coming home.

I had to laugh when I read when you told me about the guy who guessed your age. Gee, you must think your old or something but I guess old women are like that. I'll bet if you told Johnnie about that he would tell all the guys in his outfit.

Well, Lou, there isn't much more I can say right now so I will have to close for this time.

I'm in good health & I hope to hear the same of you, Jackie & the folks. Give my love to all and kiss Jackie for me.

So long for now,   Love, Ralph

August 10, 1945
Friday night

Dearest Johnnie:

Such excitement today! Mil called me up at 8:30 and told me to switch the radio on. I did. And over the air came the news that the Japs had surrendered! Well, you can imagine how I felt! I was happy, yes, but I cried! Listening more carefully, I learned they were willing to surrender under the terms of the Potsdam Declaration as long as Emperor Hiroshito is permitted to remain in power.

Martha called me soon afterward to tell me and asked me to come over. I told her I couldn't because Jackie was still sleeping, that I would, later.

The radio was on from then on. Jackie woke at 9:00. About a quarter after ten Jackie and I went over to Martha's. Julia (Sandelli) Principal was there, too.

Jackie is playing here in the office. She just asked me if I was writing a letter to daddy. We've been having supper at 5:30 this past week and after I get thru with the dishes and cleaning up the kitchen it's still early. I think I'll keep Jackie up until 8:00 tonight. It's still pretty hot out. Today was clear and quite hot. I have the radio on now for the latest news flashes. I wonder if the Allies will accept the Japanese peace proposal!

While we were at Martha's, we listened to the radio and had cake and coffee. However, Jackie became impatient so we left at 11:00. She played in her sandbox for the rest of the morning. I came in and listened to the radio. Then I washed my hair and gave

Jackie her lunch. I'll have to stop and put Jackie to bed, hon. She's bothering me. I'm sitting in the desk chair and she's saying "Move over, Mommy, so I can sit down." You can imagine how much I'd be able to write.

And now to continue! It takes a half hour to put Jackie to bed. I had to wash her, put her pyjamas on, have her brush her teeth and then hear her prayers. Two thirty this afternoon Jackie and I went downtown. I brought a roll of film to Sandrian and bought a card for Jackie to send to Gracie. And guess what! I bought Jackie one of those little turtles with a blue painted shell. When we came home I put it in a bowl and placed it on the dining room table. How she loves it!

Goodnight, my darling: I love you with all my heart and miss you terribly. How I hope we'll be seeing each other again real soon. How soon do you think it'll be, dear?

Love, hugs and kisses from Jackie and me, Lou

Saturday, August 11, 1945. *Susan Jane's birthday. Both up at 8:00. Mom stayed at Jo's last night. No mail. Cleaned whole house alone. Finished at 4:00. Very tired. Mom came home for lunch. They went to see Gracie at the hospital. Gave Jackie a bath and washed her hair. Took a shower myself and dressed. Felt much better. We had supper then went down to buy the record. Ann and Fan came home from their vacation, 7:00. They had a lovely time. Brought paint box home for Jackie and a pin for me. Mil & Dolly and children came at 8:15. Jackie asleep. Talked with girls until 11:00. Mom stayed overnight at Jo and Mike's.*

Sunday, August 12, 1945. *Lovely day. Went to 7:00 mass. Jackie woke at 8:30. Dressed her and fed her breakfast. Went out to play in sandbox. Mama G & Tadone up. Instead of Macs, made steak, mashed potatoes, beet salad, corn, veal cutlets. (girls helped me). 2:45 Joe & Angie came. Brought Mama G & Tadone to Newark. Visited Gracie. Sent Jackie to Silversteins to buy Dixie cup. 7:00 went to movies with Fan. Home at 10:00.*

Aug. 12, 1945

Darling Johnnie:

I love you, miss you and want you more than mere words could ever say. Thoughts of you are with me always. And now, there's the hope that soon you will be home. Somehow I know you will stay out there even after peace is declared, but I don't think it will be for long. I hope you will be home for Christmas. I want you home so much. What a grand feeling it will be-to live with you and know we will never be separated again! Darling, I can hardly wait!! I love you so!

Mom didn't come home Friday night. I was up until 11:30 listening to the news flashes. You probably know as much about it as I do. As yet, there still has been no answer from the Japs in regards to our counter-proposal. Saturday morning, I looked forward to getting a letter from you, eagerly and anxiously, but I received none. I haven't heard from you since last Monday. Right after breakfast I started in cleaning the house and didn't finish until 4:00. Oh, was I tired!

Mom came home from Jo's Sat. morning and went straight to work. She came home for lunch and then went to Newark again, staying over for Sunday.

Gracie is fine and might be home Wednesday. When I was through cleaning house, I gave Jackie a bath and washed her hair. Then I took a shower myself and after I was all dressed I felt much better. Jackie and I had supper, then went down to buy the paper.

Ann and Fan came home from their vacation at seven o'clock. They said they had a lovely time. They brought back a paint box for Jackie and a pin for me. Jackie went to town with her paints and got it over everything, including herself. I put her to bed at 8:00 and at a quarter after, Mil and her sister, Dolly came over with the children. (Anthony and Judy.) They left at 9:30 and the girls and I were up until 11:00, talking and listening to the radio.

Such a lovely day today! I went to the 7:00 mass, as usual, and was all dressed up in my Sunday clothes. I came home, had my breakfast and read the paper before Jackie woke up at eight thirty. She went right out to play after she ate and I started in to cook. Instead of making macaroni, I cooked: steak, mashed potatoes, veal cutlets, beet salad and corn. I thought Tadone would like a change. He loves to have a little of everything and Mama G never cooks like that. When the girls came home from church, I asked them to help me and they did.

Joe and Angie came early in the afternoon. Joe brought a panful of crabs for us but when we went to take them out, they were all dead except for three. What a shame! They cost a dollar a dozen, too! Angie's brother Joe had gone crab fishing, that's how come Joe had them.

Joe and Angie, Mama G and Tadone went to Newark to visit Grace and then went to Jo and Mike's. Joe wanted to take Jackie with them but I wouldn't let her go. She was very cranky and sleepy and I thought it best if she stayed home. You know, she's cutting her two-year molars, now, and they're giving her trouble. I put her to bed but she didn't seep. So I let her rest for an hour and then dressed her up again.

Sat. afternoon while she, mom, and I were eating lunch, she asks Mom, suddenly, "Grandma, do you remember my daddy?" Grandma said she did and Jackie said, "My daddy went overseas on a biiiiiig boat. I'm going on a boat, too." And one night she woke up crying as tho she were heart-broken. After asking her several times what was the matter she answered, with the tears streaming down her face, "I want Chipper!" I told her Chipper belonged to Uncle Gene and Aunt Mil and was Judy's baby brother. She finally stopped crying (she must have been dreaming about Chipper) and was talking away like she always does when she wakes up at night. As I was taking her back into the room from the toilet, she said, "My daddy's going to get _me_ a baby brother, too." I told her yes, daddy would, when he came home.

Good night, darling, I'm so lonely for you and wish you were here. Regards from the family and big hug and kiss from Jackie with millions more from your loving wife.

Always, Lou

Monday, August 13, 1945. *Up at 9:00. Lovely day. Had breakfast and straightened up the house. Mil called 11:15. Chipper, Judy, Jackie & I went downtown. Went to bank, deposited Christmas club, to post office, exchanged war stamps to $25 war bond for Jackie, bought blue wool, oranges and apples. Judy came home with us. Had lunch and put them to bed. Judy slept for an hour but Jackie just rested. When Judy woke, they both went out to play. Mom went to Newark after supper and at 7:00 Jackie and I took Judy home. Gene went out and bought ice cream and at 10 of eight, Jackie & I came home, put Jackie right to bed. Girls went to New York. Wrote to Wanda.*

•

Aug. 13, 1944 *Mon nite*

Dearest Johnnie:

Just a few lines to say "hello" and that I love you and miss you. Mom went to the hospital and the girls are out. Jackie's been sleeping since eight o'clock.

Today was truly bee-yoo-tiful! Imagine! No rain for six days! I felt very lazy this morning and didn't get up until Jackie woke at nine o'clock. We had breakfast and I straightened out the house. Mil called and asked if I wanted to go downtown with her. I intended going in the afternoon, anyway, so I told her I would. Eleven o'clock, Jackie and I were ready so we went to Mil's and had to wait fifteen minutes for her. I carried Chipper down and put him in his carriage (he's a dear, Hon!) and Judy and Jackie in the stroller. (Remember I told you the rubber tire was coming off another of the wheels? Well, I wound that black sticky tape all around the wheel and it's holding pretty good.) Mil stopped in to buy Judy a pair of shoes and Jackie and I went on to the bank. I cashed a check for Mil and deposited some money in my Christmas Club. Then Jackie and I went to the post office. I mailed a package off to you. In it are two cartons of cigarettes. One carton is from Mil and Gene, the rest from me. They're all Camels except one pack. Let me know in what condition you receive them. Then I exchanged a stamp album for a $25 war bond. I took it out in Jackie's name with myself as co-owner. I bought some blue wool on the way home, and some oranges and apples. Mil was waiting for me in front of Shulte's. Judy came home with Jackie and me and had lunch and supper here. Seven o'clock, Jackie and I brought Judy home. We stayed there for a little while. Gene went out to buy ice cream and Jackie and I came home at ten of eight. I put her right to bed and she fell asleep immediately. I'll have to end this now, darling, cause I have nothing else to tell you. I do love you and miss you terribly. I get so lonely for you. Love and kisses from Jackie and me.

Yours Forever, Lou

Note on flap: "*Hello dear, How's everything? Gee, I wish I hear from you soon! Love, Lou*"

[Okinawa.]

Postmarked August 14, 1945, two stamps upside down.　　*August 13, 1945*

<u>*Same Place*</u>

Hello, adorable:

I've been so very busy lately that I haven't had time to write. My last letter was written the ninth of this month. We've been working on the new mess hall and it finally is finished, except for a few minor details, which can be taken care of anytime. We had breakfast there today for the first time, and it tasted swell, even though we've had the same thing before. It must be the atmosphere or something. For dinner we had steak, mashed potatoes, corn, apple pie, raw onions with vinegar on them and iced chocolate. My piece of steak was delicious and tender and I think most of the fellows appreciated it. We worked until twelve last night, eleven the night before, and the preceding one until about ten. And if you don't think I'm tired, you're wrong. I could sleep on a picket fence. But not if you were with me.

In my spare time, during those days of intense labor, I helped put a deck in our tent. That's a relief too, having a wooden floor. I wasn't able to help very much, although the fellows realized I was too busy and didn't complain. One of the fellows even finished the clothes cabinet I had started. Interruption, sorry.

Next day. I've just come in for chow, so though I would try to finish this. I don't know how long the lights were out last night, because I went right to sleep and slept right through until time for breakfast this morning.

The news sounds pretty good, so maybe we will be reunited this Christmas, or before. Boy, I'm still hoping and praying that I'll be home soon, so that we can live together as we should. By Sunday, we should know which way our enemy has decided to operate, and then we will learn more. There will still be a lot of work to do out here, though, so please don't expect too much right away. I love you, my darling.

Joe received a letter from Marion yesterday, and enclosed therein was an announcement of the arrival of the new addition to the Blosser home. His name is Paul Franklin, born July twenty fourth. The first name is Andy's, and the middle is Carl's also. Rather nice of the Blossers don't you think? But Carl always did say he was going to name his first boy Paul, after Andy. You might send our congratulations, if you know the address.

There will be another slight interruption shortly, because a fellow is in here making coffee, and I will have to have some. I likes me coffee. He just poured me a cupful and set it here at my elbow, so I won't have to delay, after all.

Gee, sweet, I can hardly do anything correctly without bawling

546

things up. My thoughts are all of you and the things we will be doing by this time next year. How I long to hold you tenderly in my arms once again and kiss you.

You are the only girl in the world for me and I am proud and happy to be your husband. If only I can be as good to you and our family as I want. At times I am afraid I won't be able to keep you happy and contented with life. Without your help and guidance it would be an impossibility, but even then, I am not quite sure of myself. Perhaps when we are settled in our own little place, things will work out for themselves. I want, more than anything else, to be with you and make and keep you healthy and happy.

Give my fond regards to all the folks at home and especially to Mama G and Tadone. Tell Jackie to be a good girl and that I'll be home soon to spank her and kiss her goodnight and ask "Where's my daughter?"

I love you, dearest one, with all my heart. I miss you more each day and I want you so very much. I'm hungry.

J.De Roxtro EM1/c   Eternally, your   *Johnny*

Note on flap: "Here's my hug and kiss for Jackie and M. Many more for you, but I do wish I could give them all in person. Love, JdR"

Chapter 7
Unconditional Surrender

August 14, 1945- Japanese accept unconditional surrender; General MacArthur is appointed to head the occupation forces in Japan.

Tuesday, August 14, 1945. Jackie woke at 10:45. Mil brought Chipper and Judy over at 11:15. She went downtown. Chipper slept in carriage. No trouble at all. Children played in yard. Hot day. Put Jackie in crib to rest. Judy slept on couch. Mil came for Chipper at 2:00. Had supper when Mom came home. News flashes over radio saying Jap reply had been received. To be told 7:00 P.M. by Pres. Truman. 6:30 washed kids and I brought Judy home. Stayed at Mil's til the news came over. THE JAPS HAVE SURRENDERED! UNCONDITIONALLY!! People went wild! Horns blowing with cars parading around. Some people went to church. Paper all over the streets. When the girls came home we walked up town. Crowds of people standing in the square. Wrote to Ralph.

[Okinawa.]
Postmarked August 16, 1945, stamps upside down.   August 14, 1945
                                                                 <u>Same Place</u>

My Darling:

You are the most adorable wife and sweetheart in all the world. My love and adoration for you increases each day. More than anything else in the world I desire to be there holding your lovely body close to mine and pressing my lips against yours. I long to tell you of my love and how much I've missed you. Darn it, we are about to have another interruption and I thought this mess was about over. You'll have to pardon me again, my sweet. This is none of my doing, cause there is absolutely nothing I can do about it. The generators will be shut off, and we will have no lights for awhile. Our radio went on the bum today, too, so we couldn't listen to that, even if we did have the electricity on. These interruptions are very annoying to me. I love you. Nothing has happened so far so maybe I was mistaken. I will keep writing until the lights go off, anyway.

No mail came from you today, or for a couple of days previous, but

I don't care, because I know they are on the way. I did receive a letter from someone other than you, however. It was from a fellow named Hunter. I'm not quite (there they go) sure whether you met him or not, while we were in California. He was the fellow who had that apartment when he went on his fifteen-day leave and gave it up before I found out about it. He was discharged while we were there, because his wife was quite ill. He asked about all the fellows and even sounds as if he was already dissatisfied with civilian life. He also said his wife is much better, so he is glad of that. Maybe I'll write him.

I have nothing important enough to write about so I don't know what to say. It looks as if I may be spending this Christmas with you but I wouldn't care to wager on it. All I can do is keep hoping and praying that we soon will be happily re-united. It would be our first Xmas together since we've been married and boy, wouldn't it be a happy one. The interruption didn't last very long, so I'm finishing this tonight. At least I hope so. As soon as I learn more about how things are going to happen to us after the peace becomes official, I will let you know. I have an idea that we fellows having over two years of over seas service will be sent home first, leaving the recruits to finish the work. However, I will eventually let you know what to expect. And when I do, you will know it's the truth, to the best of my knowledge. My darling, I love you and want you.

Everyone is expecting the war to be officially over this week and if it isn't I have an idea that it soon will be, by force. Here's hoping the Japs are intelligent enough to surrender, unconditionally, thus saving the lives of many of our boys. I don't care very much about them. In fact, when I was on guard duty I was wishing I saw one. My trigger finger was itchy but I didn't have a chance. Maybe I am just as well off.

Well, I see the bottom of this page coming up so I will close for tonight. Perhaps I will be able to dash off a few lines tomorrow. Give my fond regards to our Annette, also a big hug and kiss. Tell her I said to be a good girl and that I'll be home soon. Regards to all the folks at home too. All my love and adoration to you, my darling. May we soon be together, to remain forever. I love you, miss you and want you.

J.De Roxtro EM1/c   Everlastingly, yours forever, *Johnny*

Note on flap: "That one un-inverted stamp last night was a mistake, so here's an extra kiss. I'm hungry and I love you."

Wednesday, August 15, 1945. *V-J Day! Feast of the Assumption. I went to 7:00 mass. All stores are closed. Ann & Fan home for two days. Joe came at 10:00-11:00. They (Joe, Mom, Jackie) went to get Gracie. I cooked dinner. (no help from girls). Joe, Mom,*

Gracie, Jackie came at 1:30. Dinner ready. Gracie very thin. Pretty well, though. Joe left at 2;30. Gene came at 3:00. Jackie's quite attached to Gene. 6:30 Jackie and I went to Mil's. Had cake and coffee. Home at 10 of 8:00. Family attended special peace services. I put Jackie to bed. After church was over met girls and we went to movies. Saw "Junior Miss." Good. Home at 11:00. No mail deliveries for two days. Received first delivery of Record.

August 16, 1945 - General Wainwright, a POW since May 6, 1942, is released from a POW camp in Manchuria.

Thursday, August 16, 1945. Jackie & I up at 8:30. Lovely day. Cool. Right after breakfast, I washed the clothes. Gene brought Judy over. Stopped to fix lunch for us then, then finished washing. Fan got up at 12:00! Ann got up at 12:20! Mom worked half a day. Aunt Santa and Catherine came in afternoon to see Gracie. Mama G came too. We all had ice cream. Children got along very well. Carol Ann very big for her age. We had supper at six.

August 16, 1945
Thurs.

Dearest John:

I love you, miss you and want you, and maybe soon now you'll be coming home. Think you could make it for Christmas?

These last few days have been just packed with excitement. I'll start from the beginning and tell you everything as it happened.

Tuesday morning, Jackie slept until ten minutes of eleven! She had just finished breakfast when mil came over with Chipper and Judy. She wanted to go downtown and I was to take care of the children. Chipper was no trouble at all. He stayed in his carriage and slept all the time. But you have to watch Judy like a hawk.

After lunch I put Jackie to rest in her crib and Judy slept on the couch. Mil came for Chipper at 2:00. Judy stayed because she didn't want to go home. We had supper as soon as Mom came home. (The girls went to visit Gracie at the hospital.) All afternoon, news flashes were coming over the radio, almost every minute. Then at 4:00 P.M. one came over saying the Jap reply had been received and Pres. Truman would speak at 7:00 P.M. The suspense of waiting was nerve-racking. And then I was so worried because I haven't heard from you in over a week and a half. I was so nervous I couldn't sit still. 6:30 I washed the kids up and Jackie and I brought Judy home. Their radio was on, too, of course and at seven the news came. Pres. Truman declared that the Japs had surrendered unconditionally! Well, for about five minutes everything was so quiet. Then all of a sudden, car horns were blowing, the streets were packed with cars decorated with flags and streamers. Newspapers were torn up and thrown in the air until the sidewalks and streets were practically covered. Kids were riding on car fenders shouting their heads off while others were

551

piled into trucks. The traffic was ten times worse than the old football traffic jams. Everybody rushed out in their cars and paraded around the park. Right after the declaration, the fire alarm blew 21 times and church bells were ringing. That's the picture as best as I can describe it. When I heard the news, I felt a wave of relief pass over me and then I wanted to cry, so I went out on the porch and stayed there for five minutes. Then I went back into the living room where Mil and Gene and the kids were. Jackie and Judy didn't know what to make of all the noise. Jackie would rush from one window to the other watching the people and the cars as they passed the house. The people went wild with joy. Mil and I took a walk down the street but we didn't go down to the park because the kids were in the backyard with Gene. Jackie and I went home at a quarter of eight. We had to wait ten minutes to cross Speedwell Ave. Mom was home looking and feeling very happy. Pres. Truman said that the boys over seas would come home in rotation. Ralph will be one of the first in that case. But what about you, darling. Will you have to be out there for Christmas or will you be sent home. I know I shouldn't expect it but I can't help hoping. When the girls came home at 10:00, we took a walk up to the park. The cars were still going strong and the crowds were as thick as flies, standing around the park.

Wednesday was the Feast of the Assumption, a holy day of obligation. I went to the seven o'clock mass. After the big news was announced, Pres. Truman declared a two day holiday for all the government employees. I don't think many people worked at all these last two days. All the stores were closed and no mail delivery for the two days. Not hearing from you is driving me almost crazy. I know you must have written in all this time!

Joe Petrone came at 10:00 A.M. Wed. morning and at 11:00, he, Mom, and Jackie went to bring Gracie home from the hospital. I cooked dinner while they were gone and they returned just as everything was all ready. Joe ate with us and then left at 2:30. Gracie is fine but a little weak. She lost weight so you can imagine how thin she is. Gene came at 3:00 and stayed until 5:00. You know, Hon, Jackie's become quite attached to Gene. Last Sunday he brought her to the cemetery and the nights we went over there after supper he used to push her and Judy in Judy's swing. Wed. night we were there again. Mil had called and asked me to go over. She had baked a cake so we had coffee and cake while the kids were in the backyard with Gene. We were home by eight o'clock and Mom and the girls attended the special peace services at St. Margaret's. I would have loved to have gone, too. Mom came home at 9:00 and said the girls were waiting for me at the corner of Shalit's, to go to the movies. We went to see "Junior Miss" at the Community. It was very enjoyable. We were home by 11:00. I wanted to write you then, but I felt rather tired so I went straight to bed.

Today was lovely. Nice and cool even with the sun shining. Jackie and I got up at 8:30. I wished she could have slept until 10:00, though. Right after breakfast I sent Jackie out in the yard and I started in to wash the clothes. What a wash! While I was so

552

busy, Gene brought Judy over. I don't have to worry if Jackie's outside alone because I know she'll stay there, but if anyone is with her they have to be watched, especially with Judy. She's all over. I stopped washing to fix some lunch for Jackie, Judy and Gracie. Fan got up at 12:00 and Ann didn't get up until half past. I like to sleep but not that much. Guess they're making the most of this two-day vacation. Can't blame them, tho.

My Aunt and Catherine came over this afternoon to see Gracie. You should see how big Carol Ann is! She'll be three in November. She looks like a child of five! She gets prettier all the time and her blonde hair is lovely. I wonder if any of our children will have blonde hair. You have it on your side of the family and I have it on mine.

The three children played together very nicely. Carol Ann was a little shy at first but after it wore off she didn't want to leave.

Mama G came later on, too. My Aunt said maybe Joey will get a discharge. Oh, Honey, I'm so anxious to hear about you. To know if this will affect you and bring you home sooner. Darling, I want you so much!

I read in the paper that when the war was over, letters aren't supposed to be censored anymore. Is that true? Will all you Seabees be needed out there now, honey? Do you think you'll have to spend six months in the Pacific? Do you hear all the up-to-the-minute news where you are? Gee, I hope I'll hear from you tomorrow.

This will have to be all for now, dear. I love you and miss you terribly! Regards from the family, and a kiss and hug from Jackie.

Yours Always,   Lou

Note on flap: "Hello, Darling, I love you & give my regards to the boys. Lou "

[Okinawa.]
Postmarked August 20, 1945, stamps upside down.   August 16, 1945
Same Place

My Adorable Darling:

I love you, miss you and want you, my precious Angel. Mere words can't possibly convey my feelings to you. You're the most lovely, lovable wife and sweetheart in all the world. Oh, dearest one, if only I could hold you in my arms and kiss you. My one ambition is to get home to you and our Jackie and make a nice pleasant home for us. It can't possibly be long now. A few more months, maybe six or eight, and we should be able to start housekeeping in our own little place. Gosh, won't it be swell, the three of us living together?

At last this mess is over, although there is still quite a lot of work to do. There will be a point system set up by the Navy for discharges, so I imagine I will have enough points to get out. As soon as is practically possible, I will apply for it. Some of the fellows, in fact most of them, seem to think we

553

have a good chance of getting home by Christmas. Boy, that surely would suit me swell. A nice present that would be for me, having you two sweethearts of mine together for the first Xmas since we've been married. But it's a little early to be thinking of that, so don't depend too much on it. Just keep hoping and praying, as I am doing. I will let you know any further progress made in this direction as soon as possible.

I received a card from Ann & Fan, from Montreal, yesterday. It was very sweet of them to think of me, so if you don't mind, my lovely one, please thank them for me. As I haven't heard from any of the family since my return out here, it was greatly appreciated. So far, I haven't even heard from my mother. No one but my darling has found time enough to write. I love you.

Let's see, since I last wrote, I think I received two letters from you. In one, you mentioned a base out here where I couldn't be, because fellows here were allowed to tell where they were. Well, there are also some here that can't, and I am one of them. I'll be home to tell you, in person, soon, so don't worry any more about it. I will have a lot to tell you about this place, it's terrain and peoples etc., when we are reunited so you can look forward to that.

Your pal Mary should be coming home soon, too, shouldn't she. How about Ralph, does he have enough points to get out? I don't remember just how the Army works its point system, so I can't figure it out. I am not sure of his length of service, either, so I couldn't, anyway. I'm glad he is better pleased with his new location, but I doubt if he is deeply interested in the feminine population. He should know better than that. But as I have never been there, they may be a bit of alright. They can't be anything like the ones around this place, though, or the ones that were on Santos. When you next write him, tell him I was asking for him and that I will try to get a line or two off in the near future.

We are getting Sundays off beginning this week, so I may have a chance to write some overdue letters. I will have quite a bit of work to do around here, though, such as help screen the tent, my washing, and several other little things like that, so maybe I won't have much time to write.

This is the end, my lovely one, so give my regards to all the folks at home, and also our friends, if you ever see them. Here's my daily hug and kiss for our darling daughter. Tell her to be a good girl and that I may give her a puppy for Xmas. To you, my adorable angel, I give my all. Millions of hugs and kisses, and all my love.

J.De Roxtro EM1/c   Everlastingly, yours forever *Johnny*

Note on flap: "Here's a little extra love and a few more hugs and kisses. Don't forget to remember me to Mickey. I love you."

Friday, August 17, 1945. Both up at 8:00. Lovely day. Cool. 8:15 Ennis delivered shore sand. Received five letters from Johnnie. A letter from Mary. 3:00 Jackie & I went to Acme to buy vegetables for supper. Bought some for Mil, too. At Shalit's I bought some citronella, Mg. tablets, roll of film. On way back stopped in at Mil's for ½ hour. Came home to cook. After supper, girls & I went to movies. Saw "Nob Hill." George Raft, Peggy Ann Garner. Very good. Home at 11:30. Read book "Earth & High Heaven" until 12:45AM

Saturday, August 18, 1945. Both of us up at 9:00. Lovely day. Cleaned house. For lunch sent Jackie to store for bread. 2 1/2 yrs. old. Mill came at 2:30 with Chipper & Judy. I trimmed her hair. Stayed until four. Judy didn't want to go home. Had supper at 6:00. Gene came for Judy at 7:30. 8:00 Fan & I went downtown. Bought yellow material. Slip and tinker toy. ($7.40). Home at 10:00.

Sunday, August 19, 1945. Lovely day. I went to 7:00 mass. Jackie woke at a quarter of ten. After breakfast I started cooking. 10:00 Mike called up, said they were coming to dinner. They got here at 11:15. We had dinner at 1:00. Mama G and Tadone here as usual. Everybody in living room talking. After supper Mike & Jo left. Took 7:14 train. Gene drove them to station. The girls and I went along. Gene drove us to movies. Saw "Bell for Adano." Good.

8/18/45 Chipper Petrone 3 months old

Aug. 19, 1945
<u>Sunday</u>

Dearest Johnnie:

We've just returned from the movies and since I wasn't sleepy I decided to write you tonite. The picture we saw at the Community, "A Bell for Adano" was pretty good.

My darling, I love you and miss you more and more. How I hope you'll be coming home soon. I want you so much. I need you, too.

Friday morning, I waited and waited for the mailman and when he came I received five letters from you! Oh, I was so glad to get them and so happy! They were dated July 30th, Aug 2,5,6,7. Now I'll see what I can answer in them. Your letter of the 30th was nice and long. Yes, I knew about the Navy point system and was quite disappointed because it couldn't affect us. I could just about see those boys scrambling over for the pineapples. Mmmmmm. I bet they did taste good!

Hon, you said in your letter of Aug 5th that if I checked on your first letter, I'd find that you did just as you've promised. You said, when you went away, that after the salutation, it would be the first letter at the beginning of each sentence in the first paragraph, right? Well, I looked for it when I first received your letter and then I looked again after I received this letter. I still got the same result, "Oitali" and that isn't a word at all! Oh, well, you'll probably be able to tell me outright where you are now.

I don't have trouble with Jackie anymore, not more than usual, anyway. I guess it was just another stage of growing up. She's good and well behaved once again. Her manners are lovely. It was pretty awful for a while, honestly, Hon, not a day passed when she didn't get one or two good spankings. I haven't had to give her a spanking like that in a long time, now.

Darling, you don't bore me when you talk about your work! I love you to tell me and I'm very interested in everything you do. You know that!

I also received a letter from Mary, Friday, and must answer her the first chance I get. I bought another bag of shore sand from Ennis and they delivered it at 8:00 in the morning!

In the afternoon, Jackie and I went to the Acme to buy the vegetables for supper. I always have to go out to do the shopping before I can start cooking. Mom doesn't keep stocked up on anything very much, and it irks me. It's a bother to have to keep going to the stores all the time whenever you need something. Before I left, Mil called up and said she needed some things, too. At Shalit's I bought some citronella for Jackie. She has so many mosquito bites! I was also able to get a roll of film! The first one since I've been home. On the way back we stopped in to bring Mil her vegetables and we stayed for about twenty minutes. I had to come right home to cook. The days are so monotonous-the same thing every day. Saturday, as usual, right after breakfast, I cleaned house. At lunchtime we were out of bread and I wasn't clean enough to go to the store because I hadn't finished with the work yet so I sent Jackie to buy a loaf of bread. I waited out in front of the house for her to come back. Sure enough, when she did she had the bread clutched tightly against her chest. Isn't it wonderful! She's only 2½ yrs. old. Mil came over in the afternoon with Chipper and Judy. She wanted me to trim her hair. Johnnie, Jackie is crazy about Chipper! She loves him. She's always saying, "He's my Chipper," or "He's my little brother." Mil left him out in the carriage to go to sleep, so we all came inside. Jackie wasn't among us so I looked out the window and I saw her standing beside Chipper's carriage rocking him to sleep.

Fan and I went downtown Sat. nite and I bought some material and a slip. Fan sews beautifully. She's made several dresses for Ann and some for herself. Now she's going to make one for me.

Jackie was still sleeping when I came home from church this morning and slept until a quarter of ten. 10:00 Mike called up from Newark saying he, Jo, Michael and their nephew would be up on the next train. They got in at 11:15 and Gene went to pick them up after he brought Mama G and Tadone up. I started the cooking early so we had dinner at 1:00. After dinner we just sat around talking in the living room. Michael, Anthony and Jackie were outside playing and they got along swell together.

They took the 7:14 train home. Gene drove them down and the girls and I went along also. After the train pulled out, Gene drove us to the movies. When we came in, Mom told me that Joe and Angie had come at 8:00. Mom was just putting Jackie to bed. When she heard Joe's voice she had to come down to see him.

I'll have to end this letter, now, dear. Regards from everyone. They all ask about you. Love and kisses from both Jackie and me.

Forever yours, Lou

[Okinawa.]   August 19, 1945
                                                                      Same Place

Hi Angel:

Here it is Sunday and as I haven't had to work. I have all my washing done and some time left over to pen a few lines of love and endearment to you, the most wonderful and gorgeous creature in all the world. I love you, my darling, with all my heart. I miss your lovely sweet

557

smiling face and that beautiful figure of yours. I miss you and want so very much to be there, making love to you and doing those little things with you and for you that only a husband can do. Dearest one, you are mine, to have and to hold, forever. Soon, I hope we will be able to have our own place, and then we can do as we desire and bring up our children as we see fit.

The Navy has adopted a point system, and I am eligible for discharge. All I have to do is apply for it and then await transportation to the states. All this may take several months however, so don't expect me too soon. Naturally the fellows with most points will have the preference, so I may be delayed en route.

There has been nothing official about the discharges for us as yet, except that about the point system. We need forty four points to qualify for discharges, and both Andy and I each have forty six, so we probably will accompany each other as far as Pittsburg, Pa. We are quite certain of going as far as the States together, anyway. I will let you know of any further news concerning the above just as soon as I learn it. There will be less than a hundred fifty of us leaving the outfit, so you can see how lucky I am. At least I can't see any reason for anyone desirous of my attachment to the outfit, any longer. Keep hoping and praying for me to return soon, will you, sweet. Gosh, but it still doesn't seem possible that the war is over and that I am about to be released from military service. It's all like a dream but a very pleasant one it is. You can be almost certain that I will be home for Christmas, though there is a possibility that I won't. Seems to be there are plenty of ships available for transportation, though. I love you.

I wont be able to write anyone else today, with the exception of my mother, as I have only one more sheet of paper and our store doesn't expect to have any until Tuesday. So, my lovely sweetheart, you won't be expecting to hear from me until then, either. Somehow, I can't seem to get in the mood to write, since I've been out this time. I hereby apologize for the brevity and infrequency of my letters, but, gee, sweet, it's so darn tough trying to think of something interesting to tell you. I have an idea that some of my letters have been pretty much cut up, but I tried to let you know a little something of life out here for the natives. When we have time, we will go over them and I will try to re-write the missing parts. It may be possible.

Just think, adorable one, we may be celebrating together this Xmas. We will still be there with your family, though even that will be okay with me. Then next year, the three of us will be all together, celebrating in our own little nest, with maybe a fourth on the way, or already there. That will all be settled later on, though.

Yesterday I received two letters from you, my precious. They were written the ninth and tenth. There was quite a bit of celebrating going on here that night, but also there were a few casualties. It was more beautiful than any fireworks celebration I've ever seen, angel mine. Those in our tent merely took our benches outside and were satisfied just sitting there watching. There was a bit of noise, too, although it wasn't centralized, so wasn't deafening.

More tomorrow, my lovely, if I can locate some paper. I'm quite certain I can, even if I have to borrow it from Joe or one of the other fellows here in the tent, especially if I learn anything of importance.

Give my fond regards to all, Lou darling. Here's my daily hug and kiss for our Jackie. Tell her I'll be home soon, and to be a good little girl. I love you, my darling, and send hugs, kisses, and my all with this note of love. Hope I will see you soon.

J. De Roxtro EM1/c   Eternally, your loving *Johnny*

Note on flap: "Some think we'll be out of here this month. Pray that we'll be together Xmas. I love you. Here's a kiss for M."

Monday, August 20, 1945. Up at 9:00 lovely day. 11:00 man came to fix radio. Had to bring to the shop. Filter. While I was watching, I heard Jackie screaming. I ran down and found that she had been hit on the forehead. She said Richard did it. It was all swollen and bruised. Sent Jackie to store for bread. 3:00 went out to by vegetables. On way back met Mil & Catherine. Took walk to Petrozzo's. Came home and found Mrs. De R here. Looks quite well. Had spent all day in Morristown. Was with Mrs. Parsons. Said Vene, Johnnie & children had gone to N.Y. Came at 5:15. Johnnie comes home every eight days. After supper went to movies with Mil and Catherine. Saw "A Tree Grows in Brooklyn." Very good.

Tuesday, August 21, 1945. Woke at 7:00. Got up at 8:00. Lovely day. 11:00 Martha took 4 pictures of me and I took one of Jackie. After lunch Jackie & I went downtown. Brought film to Sandrian's, patterns, pipe cleaners. Came home at 3:30. Started cooking at 4:00. Estimate to repair radio $11:55. After supper the girls and I went to the movies. Good. Double feature.

Aug. 21, 1945
Tuesday

Dearest Johnnie:

I love you, miss you and want you. I think of you always and wish for you so much.

Our days now are really quite hot although the nights are cool. I sure am glad the "rainy season" is over.

Yesterday morning, the man finally came to service our radio. Jackie was in the backyard playing with Richard, a little boy from the Flats. While I was talking to the radioman, I heard Jackie crying and from the sound I knew something had happened to her. I ran down the stairs so fast I almost flew. I found her alone, with a big bump in the middle of her forehead. It was all swollen and bruised and she was crying painfully. When I quieted her down a little she told me Richard did it. They had been playing with stones and one of them must have hit her in the head. I don't think Richard did it purposely but regardless, it was a pretty nasty bruise and it might have been fatal.

Oh, I've tried keeping all those older kids out of the yard! I've chased them a hundred times but they always come back. Most of them are very dirty and as fresh as can be. I don't know what to do. I asked Gene to make a fence to block the driveway, but how long it's going to take him to make it, I don't know.

Anyway, I brought her upstairs and put some rosebud on the bump. It helped a lot. Then we stayed in the living room with the radio man and she stopped crying to ask, "What's the man doing, Mommy?" She was all right after that so I sent her to the store for a loaf of bread.

Three o'clock we went out to buy the vegetables for supper. We met Mil and Catherine going down so we went as far as Petrozzo's. When we came home, who do you think was here! Your mother! I was so surprised. She had only been waiting fifteen minutes for me so it's a good thing I came straight home. Your mother looks quite well, dear, she's even put on a little weight. She said she had been down in town all day. (Vene, Johnnie and the children went to New York and were coming back at 5:00. Your mother went to the doctor first, did some shopping and then spent the rest of the morning and afternoon with Mrs. Parsons. She came to our place at a quarter of four. We exchanged news about you and a lot of gossip in general. Johnnie and Vene came for her at 5:15. They said they had a lovely time and on the way home they came back by ferry. Johnnie's pretty lucky to come home every eight days, isn't he?

Today was a lovely day, but pretty hot in the afternoon. This morning, Martha took some pictures of me and Jackie. I hope they turn out well.

After lunch, Jackie and I went downtown. I bought you the pipe cleaners but I couldn't find a good penknife. I also looked around for a couple of patterns. It was so hot that we came home as soon as we could.

Did I tell you that as soon as peace was declared, gas rationing was off and so are all the blue points on canned foods. The red points are still going strong. There's going to be a Victory Day Celebration here, on Sept. 8th. There'll be a parade, speeches, band concert and fireworks. The allied occupation of Japan will begin Sunday according to the radio and newspapers. You know, Hon, I bet it won't be easy. I'm glad you're not in an Army of occupation-no telling when you'd be home, then.

The pictures I got back from Sandrian's this afternoon didn't come out too good. As soon as I can have the extra prints made I'll send some to you.

Gracie is recuperating here at home and is coming along fine. Did I ever tell you that besides her appendix she also had a cyst on her ovaries, which was removed at the same time her appendix was taken out.

The radioman took our radio to the shop to be fixed. He said all the filters were bad and new ones had to be put in. We're using the small radio up here, now. It works better here than it does downstairs. Hon, he's charging us $11.55 for the job. Isn't that a lot?

I'll have to say goodnight, now, dear. I love you so much and want you here, terribly. Oh, darling, if only it will be soon!. Regards and best wishes from everyone and love and kisses from Jackie and me.

Yours always,   Lou

Note on flap: "Hello, honey, I love you. Say 'hello' to the boys for Jackie and me. I love my husband. Lou"

Wednesday, August 22, 1945. Jackie woke at 7:30. We didn't get up until 8:30. While I was getting breakfast, Gene and Judy came over. Gene is repairing the roof. Received two letters from Johnnie. Those of Aug. 9, 13. Very hot day. Jackie went for Dixie cup. Gene wanted some lemonade so I sent Jackie to the store. The first time she had a lemon but she still had the money. The second time I sent her back to the store with the money and told her get a big lemon. The third time she comes back with a big lemon but it was rotten. The fourth time I sent her back and told her to get a good lemon. After supper started book "Hotel Berlin."

[Okinawa.]
Postmarked August 23, 1945, stamps upside down.

August 22, 1945
<u>*Wed*</u> *Same Place*

Hello, Beautiful:

Just a short one tonight because I don't have much of anything to tell you. Today I received two letters from my lovely wife. They were written the twelfth and thirteenth of this month and were both postmarked the fourteenth. Eight days to arrive, which isn't bad, I think. I my opinion, the mail service all through this forced separation of ours has been exceptionally well taken care of. You should have gotten at least one letter that week, but perhaps I didn't have a chance to write. I don't think I ever went a week without writing, but I may have, in those first days over here. They were quite tough, so perhaps I didn't.

In one of your sweet letters you mentioned sending cigarettes to me. Please, darling, don't send anymore because as I told you I am able to get them much more easily and cheaper than you. It's swell of you and Mil and Gene to think of me, but it's entirely unnecessary. If you had to send something, you could have sent some pepperoni or whatever you call that hard sausage. Don't send anything now, though, because I don't expect to be here more than a month and a half or two at the most. Anything you have can wait until I return, or you can send it to Ralph if he is staying out awhile.

The latest scuttlebutt today has us leaving here in six days to ten, which may be quite possible, but highly improbable. Personally, I think it will be at least a month before we move, but I'm hoping and praying that it will happen sooner. As you say, it will be heavenly to be together again, knowing that we won't ever have to part. The shores of the good old country will certainly look good to me, and that vision can't possibly come too soon to suit me. A more beautiful and most welcome vision will come later when I cast my eyes longingly on you. And, according to a passage in one of your letters, it looks as if your promise to Jackie suits me fine. I hereby guarantee the utmost in co-operation on my side. I am anxiously awaiting the day when you and I can start fulfilling that promise. In case you've forgotten, your promise was in regards to our darling daughter awakening one night and wanting Chipper.

Speaking of Chipper, he must be a wonderful little one, well behaved, and a model child. I'll bet Jackie does get along swell with him and also that Judy is a little jealous of Jackie's attention to him. Is Judy a little put out because her baby brother gets more attention than she does? Perhaps not, because she is a little older. Gosh, I love you darling.

562

I love you, miss you and want you, my darling. I long to hold you tenderly in my arms and kiss you, that sweet young body of yours as it presses against mine, those lovely luscious lips of yours, as we kiss, and your nice arms encircling my neck. Gee I can actually feel all those things at times and then I come back to normal and there is no you, nothing but this bunch of ugly males around. But those dreams and daydreams are swell while they last and soon they will come true. Then, and only then, will my happiness be complete. Gee, isn't it going to be swell, you and I, working and planning together for the health and happiness of our family. And won't we have fun, just being together. I'm going to make love to you in every way I know, or any new way I hear about, and you will be happy and satisfied with life. Oh, sweetheart, I'm so hungry for your love and hugs and kisses. Soon, dearest one, we will be living together as man and wife should.

Give my regards to all. Here's my daily special hug and kiss for Jackie. Tell her I'll be home soon and that I'll see about getting her a baby brother next year.

J.De Roxtro EM1/c   All my love and adoration, foreve   *Johnny*

Thursday, August 23, 1945. Got up at 8:30. Cool and breezy out. Gene and Judy came over at 9:30 while Jackie was having her breakfast. Gene worked on the roof all day. He went home for lunch. Judy stayed here. 2:00 Jackie and Judy took a nap. Bought crabs from fish man 10:30. Made sauce. I'm not feeling very well. Have head cold. Gene asked me to go over to mind the kids while he and Mil went to the movies. Had supper early. Ann not coming. Fan in at 6:30. Went to Mil's at 6:45. Came home at 11:00. Gene drove me home. Wrote to Ruth.

Aug 23, 1945
Thurs. nite

Dearest Johnnie:
   Well, here I am at Mil's taking care of the kids while she and Gene went to the movies.
   I don't mind doing it because the children aren't any trouble at all when they're sleeping. Chipper sleeps all the time and I put Judy to bed at 7:30.
   Mom is home with Jackie, else I wouldn't have been able to come here to nite.
   What a hot day we had yesterday! Oh, it was terrible. While Jackie was having her breakfast, Gene and Judy came over. Gene is fixing the roof (outside our bedroom window). He's putting on all new shingles because there's a pretty bad leak on the side near the bathroom.
   In the late afternoon I sent Jackie to the store for three Dixie cups, one for herself, Gracie and me. They didn't even put them in a bag for her. What cheapskates!! Then, later in the afternoon, Gene wanted some lemonade. It _was_ terribly hot,

working on the roof but we didn't have any lemons, so I sent Jackie for one. She comes back with a very small lemon _and_ the money. I told her she must bring the money back and as long as she was going I told her to bring the lemon back and get a larger one. She comes running home saying, "Mommy, I got a big one." I was sorry I didn't keep the first one because altho this one _was_ large, it was so rotten that I couldn't use it. I showed it to Jackie and explained why it wasn't any good, so she brought it back again and came home with a good one. I asked her who gave it to her and she said, "Jackie gave it to me!" She must have gotten them herself because the basket is kept right out on the floor. When I told the family about it that night, how they laughed!!

This morning, Jackie and I got up at 8:30. It was cool and breezy out _and_ I woke up with a head cold. Gene and Judy came over at 9:30. They (J & J) played out in the yard until 11:00. I called them in because it had started to rain. Gene kept right on working. The rain stopped after a while. It didn't amount to much. Gene went home for lunch but Judy stayed at our house.

After they ate I put Jackie in the crib to sleep and Judy on the couch. They both fell asleep about the same time. Judy slept for three quarters of an hour and Jackie slept an hour and fifteen minutes. I'm surprised she did, because Gene had come back and was working on the roof. It's a wonder she slept through all that hammering.

Gene asked me to come over here to mind the kids this afternoon. Since Mom was staying home, I said I would. I hope they come right home, though, because I don't feel so good.

Yesterday morning I received two letters from you. Those dated Aug. 9th and 13th. You don't know how glad I was to receive them!

You're not the only one who's hungry, Sweet! I am too, so very much! I certainly do miss your lovemaking! All of it!

Good night, my darling. I love you, miss you and want you. Here's a kiss and hug from Jackie and millions more from "Yours truly." Regards from everyone.

Love always, Lou

Friday, August 24, 1945. Up at nine o'clock. Raining heavily. My cold is worse. I feel miserable. Received letter of Aug. 14th from Johnnie. Mom came home for lunch. 2:00 put Jackie to sleep in crib. Gene & Judy came over. Stayed an hour. I lay on bed until a quarter of five. Started supper. Girls both home at 6:30. After supper Fan cut out my dress. I made a blue beret for Jackie. Read "Hotel Berlin '43"

Saturday, August 25, 1945. Jackie woke at 6:30. Told her to go back to sleep again. Slept until a quarter of ten. Gene and Judy here already. My cold still the same. Cleaned house. Fan and Ann came home early in afternoon. After supper the girls and I went downtown. Bought gift for Fannie - slip. While we were in Woolworth, it rained. Took bus home from bus station. Thunder & lightening.

Sunday, August 26, 1945. Joan Petrone's birthday. Clear. Very cool. Went to 7:00 mass. Came home. Read paper. Jackie woke at 9:00. While Jackie ate breakfast I started to cook. After dinner we all gave Fannie her gifts and sang "Happy Birthday." Mrs. Landi, Mrs. Venezia, Sundi, & Millie came. Fan sewed on my dress all ay. Almost finished it. After supper Gene came over to take Mama G and Tadone home.

[Letter from Lou to Johnnie postmarked August 27 was returned on September 17, 1945]

Aug. 26, 1945
Sunday

Dearest Johnnie:

How are you? I love you, miss you and want you more than I ever have before. I think of you always, darling, and hope with all my heart that you will be home for Christmas.

I received a letter from you Friday and was so glad to hear from you. Yes, I remember about the fellow named Hunter. How could I forget. We were hoping so hard that we could have gotten his apartment. Remember? I'm glad his wife is much better. Have you written him, yet?

Friday was a miserable day. It rained all day long. I didn't do very much at all. While Jackie took her nap, I lay on the bed. I felt so sick with my cold. I lay on the bed until it was time to get up and start supper. I still have my cold but it's much, much, better.

Saturday morning, Gene came over and finished up the roof. Jackie and Judy were together all day and between them and the house cleaning I had quite a day. Those two fight so much that it's not funny. I used to think I'd like to live close to home when we got our own place but now I don't think it would be such a good idea. Gee, Hon, how I wish you were home. Nice places are so hard to find and I'll have to get a place pretty soon because Mama G and Tadone are coming up here to live as soon as it gets too cold. I wouldn't care where I lived as long as you were with me. Gee!!! What a rainstorm we had last night! Thunder, lightning and the whole works! I thought sure we'd have rain again today but it dawned clear and pretty cool. I went to the 7:00 mass, came home, had my breakfast and read the papers. Jackie woke up at 9:00. I started cooking while she ate. Then when Mom came home to take care of things, I gave Jackie a bath and dressed her up. She looked so cute in her red skirt and white blouse.

Today is Fannie's birthday. We had dinner at 1:00 and after we finished eating we all gave her our gifts. She did all-l-l-l right! It was so funny. She exclaimed over everything and we laughed so hard. Our gift to her was a pink slip. Jackie carried the gifts in to her and we all sang "Happy Birthday." The candles on the cake were mostly for Jackie's benefit. She thought it was all so wonderful.

This afternoon Mom had some visitors - members of her old club; Sundi, Millie, Mrs. Landi, Mrs Venezia. They all asked about you and send their regards.

Remember I told you that Fan was going to make me a dress? Well, she worked on it this afternoon and it's coming along swell. The color is yellow. Last night I finished crocheting Jackie a blue beret. It looks darling on her.

Gene just came to take Mama G and Tadone home. Joe and Angie didn't come up today. Gosh! I don't know what else to tell you. How about a joke I just heard recently? 'A father took his small son for a walk in the woods on a nature study. As they were walking along the boy killed a butterfly. "You shouldn't have done that, son. Now you won't get any butter!" said the father. Then pretty soon the boy killed a bee, and the father said, "You shouldn't have done that, son. Now you won't get any honey or anything sweet!" They finished their walk and when they came home they found that the mother had just killed a cockroach. The boy looked at his father and said, "You tell her, Pop!"

I love you, darling. So very, very much. How I miss you. Regards from everyone and a kiss and hug from Jackie.

Yours always and forever, Lou

Note on flap: "Hello Darling. I'm still waiting anxiously for the good news-the day you tell me you're coming home! I love you. Say "hello" to the boys for me and Jackie. Lou"

August 27, 1945 – B-29s drop supplies to Allied POWs in China.

Monday, August 27, 1945. Jackie woke at 7:00 A.M. Nice day but quite cool. After lunch Jackie and I went downtown. Paid radio bill for Mom $11.55. Bought vegetables for myself and Mil. Stopped in at Mil's for ½ hour. Came home to cook. After supper went to the movies with Mil. Saw "Keys of the Kingdom." Very good.

Tuesday, August 28, 1945. I got up 6:00. Had a mass said for Papa at 6:30A.M. No mail. Cool in morning but afternoon very hot. Stayed home all day. Mom worked half a day. 12:30 took bus to station with Gracie. Went to doctor's for check up. Girls home at 6:30P.M. Ate supper. Mom and Gracie home 9:30 P.M. 10:00 I went to bed.

August 29, 1945 – The Soviets shoot down a B-29 dropping supplies to POWs in Korea; U.S. troops land near Tokyo to begin the occupation of Japan.

Wednesday, August 29, 1945. Up at 8:30. 11:30 Jackie and I went downtown. Stopped first at Mil's for Ralph's package. Went to post office. Mailed package to Johnnie (knife), Ralph, and mailed back dresses to Gimbels. Home by one o'clock. We had lunch. Jackie very hungry. 3:00 Jackie, Gracie and I had some ice cream. Very hot out. Had supper at 5:30. Girls went to movies in Newark. 7:30 Mary & her sister came up to visit Gracie. Mom and I crocheted potholders. Went to bed 11:30.

August 30, 1945 – The British reoccupy Hong Kong.

Thursday, August 30, 1945. *Up at 8:30. No mail. Had trouble with Gracie. She couldn't move her bowels. 11:45 called Mom at work. Was home by 12:00. Mom stayed home from work in the afternoon. Mother de called up. Asked if I'd like to go up to Vene's tomorrow. Vene coming at 9:30. I put screen back up in office window. Washed my hair and Jackie's over tub for first time. Went to movies with girls. 2 very good pictures.*

Friday, August 31, 1945. *Arose at 8:00. Had breakfast and dressed. Vene came at 9:45. Waited for postman. No mail. Went up to Vene's new place. We went straight to garden, picked tomatoes, beans, corn, one cucumber. Very nice. Jackie played outside with Nancy and Bonnie. She loved their bikes. Took a walk to store. Bought oranges, canned fruit, vegetable soup. Asked about tricycle. When we came back, lunch was ready. Good meal. Beans, tunafish salad, corn. Jackie ate very well. 2:30 went to Mendham. Had ice cream. Had little ride. Stopped at the woman's house for the tricycle. Asked us in. Stayed an hour. Lovely place. 5:00 we came home. Vene, Nana, and Nan & Bonnie came down too. Found two letters for me, 16-19 of August.*

[Letter from Lou to Johnnie postmarked September 2, 1945, returned on September 17, 1945]

Aug. 31, 1945
Friday

Dearest Johnnie:

What a lovely time Jackie and I had today! And you'll know all about it in just two seconds!

First I'll tell you about yesterday which was just the opposite from today. We had trouble with Gracie! From the time she got up in the morning she tried to move her bowels but she couldn't and it made her actually sick, Hon. She broke out in chills and fever, shaking like a leaf. I gave her an enema and made her try suppositories, but nothing worked. I couldn't stand seeing her suffer any longer so I called Mom up at the shop and told her to come home. That was at a quarter of twelve. She was home by twelve and didn't go back to work in the afternoon. I gave her another enema but it still didn't help. Mom was a nervous wreck. Finally at 7:00 she called the doctor and asked him what she should do. He couldn't do anything but suggest what we had already done - an enema and a physic. By 8:00 everything had calmed down. Gracie had fallen asleep and I had given Jackie a bath and put her to bed, also.

During the afternoon, Mil called up and wanted me to take a walk over but I didn't go because I was busy. I put the screen up in the office. What a time! Then your mother called up and asked if I'd like to go up to Vene's tomorrow (today) and I told her that I'd love to. She told me to be ready at 9:30 and that Vene would come down to pick us up.

Last night after everything had quieted down, the girls and I went to the movies. We saw two very good pictures.

This morning Jackie woke at 8:00 so we had our breakfast and dressed. Mom stayed home from work to be with Gracie else, I couldn't have gone to Vene's.

Vene didn't come until a quarter of ten so I asked her to wait a few minutes until the postman came. When he did, I didn't get a thing. So we left and went straight to her old house. She wanted to pick some vegetables from the garden. She doesn't take care of it anymore and there are weeds all over the place. We picked quite a few beans, some tomatoes, corn, and one cucumber. Jackie was out in the yard playing with Nancy and Bonnie. Only, every once in a while, Nan and Bonnie would leave her and come in the garden. When we finished picking the vegetables we went to the new house. It's a two family house, Hon, but it's enormous! So much that you feel as though you were living in a whole house. They have more ground space than at the old place so you can just imagine how roomy it is. The rooms in the house are very nice, too. Jackie stayed out to play with Nan and Bonnie and she just loved their bikes. They each had one. Jackie was always either on one or the other. She doesn't know how to ride, though. I tried teaching her but it was kind of hard pedaling on the grass.

Your mother looks just fine, Hon. Really wonderful! She feels so good that she wants to go out to work. Johnnie, for heaven's sake! If you ever let it out that you know about her illness, I'll never forgive you!! She said to me again that she hoped I didn't tell you anything about it. That she would tell you when she was good and ready. I told her that I didn't tell you and that you didn't know, so watch yourself!!

We had a grand lunch; tuna fish salad, fixed with lettuce, tomatoes, cucumbers, garden beans and lots of corn. I ate so much. Jackie ate wonderfully <u>and</u> had three helpings of <u>beans!</u> After lunch we took a ride to Mendham for some ice cream, then came back to Brookside and stopped at a woman's house to pick up a tricycle for Jackie. Vene and I and the kids had gone to the store in the morning, and Vene had asked this woman who was also there, if she had any tricycles her children had outgrown. She told us she did have a very small one, but that one pedal was gone and the wheel was broken. We told her we'd take it and have it fixed. I offered to pay her for it but she wouldn't accept it. Outside of the pedal and the wheel it's in pretty good condition, considering that three children had used it. (I hope you're able to read this, Hon, I'm writing so fast.) The woman invited us to stay awhile and we did. I don't remember her name but she lives next to the Pitney property. Her maiden name was mentioned a lot. It was Dean. What a beautiful place they have! She showed us all around the grounds. We had a very nice visit and left there at four o'clock. We went back to Vene's, rested for a while (It was so very hot) and then your Mother made some tea, 4:00 tea. The children were out playing again. They never seem to get too tired to give in. I was so tired myself, I wanted to lie down and go to sleep. Don't know why I felt so exhausted. Must be the country air.

We left for home, a quarter after five and everybody came along. The three kids were up in the back and Vene, Nana and I were on the seat. Vene gave me some beans and a couple of large tomatoes to take home.

Gracie was downstairs lying on the couch. She said she felt better. Mom had given her another enema and it worked. The whole trouble was, Hon, because she couldn't bear down. Her stomach was too tender yet.

To make my day complete, I found two letters from you waiting for me. Oh, how happy I was to hear from you. It had been over a week since I last heard. Your letters were dated the 16th and 19th of Aug.

Darling, you don't know how happy I am to know that you're really coming home! Oh, I can hardly wait. I'm so glad! I hope you'll be able to get home before Christmas. Now if I could only find a place for us to live.

By the way, for your information, none of your letters have been cut up at all. Everything you wrote was intact.

Gee, Hon, to think you'll be coming home to stay for always! I can hardly believe it! I'm so happy!

Goodnight, dearest. I love you and miss you so very much. Regards from everyone and a big hug and kiss from Jackie. That's what Jackie said she's going to give you when you come home.

All my love, always, Lou

August 29, 1945 - Johnny boards a receiving ship as part of those men who were 44-pointers and heads for home.

Postmarked September 2, 1945, stamps upside down.   August 31, 1945
                                                            Okinawa

Most Adorable:

I love you, miss you and want you, sweetheart. More than anything else in the world I desire to be able to take you tenderly in my arms and hold your sweet and lovely body close to me while I smother you with kisses. Words of love and endearment will flow from my lips with sincerity. Your lovely red lips will feel so tender and receptive under mine and they will co-operate so nicely. Your pulse will be beating and I will be able to count it against my chest. Gosh, beloved, it's going to be swell making love to you again. All those nice times we've had before will be relived, but they will be much nicer now that we are sure of being together forever. We will use all the ways we know of and maybe even invent a few more to get the most enjoyment out of our married life. Lou, my most precious wife and sweetheart, I am going to do all in my power to make and keep you and our family more happy and contented with life than ever before. Sweetest wife in all the world, you mean more to me than anything else in the world. There is nothing I wouldn't do to make you happy. Darling, I adore you.

As of yesterday, we fellows with forty-four points and over are transferred to a receiving ship so-and-so. But that doesn't mean a thing because we are still here and haven't the slightest idea where or when we are leaving here. I sure hope we leave here soon. According to the order posted on the board, we are to be transferred into another receiving ship somewhere and from there, we are to be transported to the United States for discharge. So, it will probably be a couple of months before I am home but you can be certain of seeing me before Christmas, this year. After we get to the states, we will have to remain at our port for seventy-two hours. While there, we are to receive instructions on how to become a civilian. Those three days will pass quite rapidly, though, as will my trip across the country. If we are sent to a west coast port, I have made arrangements to ride across in an automobile with several other fellows from the outfit. You never met any of them but they are from New York and are nice guys. It may take longer but at least I'll be in good shape.

I won't bother sending those souvenirs I mentioned before, now that I am practically on the way. I will bring them along with me. I also managed to acquire a couple of native coins and I may have one or two of these occupational bills for you. I don't know what the coins are worth or anything, but at least you will have them. They have either Japanese or Chinese writing on them, so you can be sure they are genuine. They don't mean a thing to me, and won't to you, either, except as a keepsake.

Clere made chief the other day, and Joe and I celebrated with him by helping him drink a case of beer. Several others were in on it two, so we didn't overindulge. Both Joe and I would have made chief too, but we haven't been first class long enough. You see, there is a law or something saying a first class man has to hold his rate for eighteen months before he can become chief. But I would much rather be home with you or on the way, even, than hang around here another three months just to make chief. The two hundred fifty bucks clothing allowance would come in mighty handy, though. I love you, sweet.

Joe managed to get out to take some pictures the other day. He had them developed but not printed and when he has prints made he will send me a set. They turned out quite well. He and I are going to try to get out Sunday to get some more made. I'll let you know how we make out. These natives are hard to photograph.

Mail seems to have just about stopped coming out here. Or rather, it has slowed down greatly. And as I never seem to be in a writing mood, and there is nothing to say, I am not writing very often. Here's hoping you will pardon me, Angel. I'll make up for it when I get home. Say, sweet, I'm thinking of transferring those packages that are on the way to one of the other boys out here instead of having them returned home. Would you mind very much? Naturally if they come while I am still here, I will get them. I'm quite sure Forbes or someone would appreciate them.

570

Give my fond regards to all the family and our friends. Here's my hug and kiss for Jackie, and tell her I'll be home soon. For you, my sweet and lovely wife, I send my all, expecting every moment to begin my long journey to peace and happiness with you.

J.de Roxtro EM1/c   Eternally, yours forever *Johnny*

Note on flap: "Hi Angel! Here's more love and loads of hugs and kisses. As ever, yours."

[Letter from Ruth Greaves.]   August 31, 1945
                                                  Friday 8 P.M.

Dear Lou,

Now that the excitement has died down, I'll tell you all about it. Do you remember the big mountain that is at the end of the street here & extends down to Main Street? Well, due to a careless match it caught fire this afternoon! They finally got it under control when it was a half block from here! We were downright scared! However, nothing burned except the brush on the mountain, but what if it had reached the lemon grove behind the house here? It sure made a lot of smoke. A blanket of smoke lay over all this end of the city. Anyway it was too close for comfort.

It certainly does sound as if Jackie is really growing up fast. I hope she isn't too big when we see her again. Don't you let her forget us! Now that the war is over we may be seeing each other soon. Let us hope so.

Do you know when Johnnie will be getting out of the service? I know he has enough points. I know how happy you must be to know he won't be in any fighting now. At least he's safe.

I don't suppose Burton will get out for a long time yet, darnit! He has only 31 points. Who knows, he may get sent across yet! We are hoping not though.

Walt and Carol are still with us, but I don't imagine they'll be here a whole lot longer. Walt has more than enough points to be discharged. In fact, he has already had his interview, etc. for his discharge & is just waiting for his final papers. Naturally, I am glad he is getting out but we will certainly miss them. You'd like them. They're really a swell couple. They have their baby home now & it's so tiny. It weighs 4 lbs. 12 oz. now & is doing nicely.

Ellen went back to Rochester, N.,Y. & to everyone's surprise Hazel came back! But she is planning on going back home in Sept. You see, they didn't know when she was back home on Ennos' leave that the war was going to end; so reluctantly she came back here. Now Enno is stationed in San Diego & she hasn't

571

seen nor heard from him for 3 wks. She said since she can't see him nor be with him she might as well go home & get things in shape for when he can go home. He has enough points also for a discharge.

Burton will be off all day Sunday & Labor Day so I guess we are going to Santa Barbara. There is a big museum there which we'd like to see. We wanted to go to San Francisco to see the Golden Gate bridge, but it's nearly 800 miles round trip & it would be too tiring for 2 days.

I baked Buddy a gingerbread boy today & my was he tickled! It did turn out swell. I never baked one before. Buddy was so proud that he took it around & showed it to everyone. Buddy is eagerly awaiting his birthday this year. He'll be four Sept 28. I can scarcely believe it! He is growing right away from me. I promised him he could have a little party & the first thing he wanted to know was, "Can Jackie be here too?" Such a time I had explaining why Jackie wouldn't be here.

There was really a lot of celebrating here in Ventura on V.J. day! People actually came to life. There was an awful lot of noise, torn up paper, gayly bedecked cars, etc. A bunch of sailors had a goat out in the middle of Main St. & built fires all around it. They called the goat "Hiro-Hito" & said they would roast Hiro-Hito's goat alive. You should have seen the kick that goat raised.

We didn't get to celebrate much as Burton had the duty. They doubled the guard & it was his luck to get picked. Walt, Carol, & us had planned a picnic for that night. When Walt came home that night without Burton I nearly died! So Walt, Carol, Buddy & I ate our picnic at home. Then Walt drove us all out to Burton's base to see him. Mrs. Taylor loaned me her daughter's guitar so we took it along. Burton came out to the car then played the guitar and we all sang. Naturally there was a gang of sailors around. Most of them were in conditions only to sing "Sweet Adoline." All in all, we did enjoy ourselves. I was so glad to get to see Burton that day because it was truly a happy one for everybody.

Well, Lou, it's time for Buddy's bed, so I had better get him washed up a bit. I was so glad to hear from you. Keep on writing as we do enjoy your letters so much. I don't have the gift of writing the nice, interesting letters you do but perhaps you can endure them.

Always your friend, Ruth

Saturday, September 1, 1945. Up at 9:00. Ann and Fan didn't have to work. Cleaned room and then fixed lunch. Mom had to go back to work. 5:00 went with Gene to bring tricycle to be fixed at Hobby Shop. Will cost $10.50. 6:30 went downtown with *girls. Bought film. Home by 8:00. Heard the signing of the Jap surrender on radio 9:30 P.M. on the USS Missouri.*

September 2, 1945 – Formal Japanese surrender ceremony on board the U.S. Missouri in Tokyo Bay as 1000 Carrier-based planes fly overhead. President Truman declares VJ Day.

Sunday, September 2, 1945. Went to 7:00 mass. Official V-J DAY! Jackie woke at 8:30. Rained during night while I was in church. Jackie still asleep until 8:30. Cooked and read paper. Mama G and Tadone up. 3:00 Joe and Angie came. Jackie so glad to see him. Followed him like a shadow. Took her out riding for an hour. (Big fire during night - Shultes' to Jodo's.) I knitted on Chipper's xmas present. 7:30 Joe took her out again. Mom, Angie, Mama G went too. Looked at the fire. 9:00 all went home.

September 3, 1945 – The Japanese commander in the Philippines, General Yamashita, surrenders to General Wainwright at Baguio.

Monday, September 3, 1945. Labor day. Up at 9:00. Knitted for awhile on Chipper's hat. Gave Jackie a bath and dressed her up in yellow. 11:00 Jo, Mike, Michael Jr & Anthony came up and Mama G and Tadone. Had dinner at 1:30. Big meal. Didn't leave the table until 3:45. 6:00 Jo, Ann, Fan and I went to view the damage of the big fire, Shulte's, United, National Shoe Store completely demolished. Botkin's jewelry store, Jodo's. Margay's dress shop. Great damage. Jo & Mike took 8:30 bus. Gene drove them to station. Jackie went along.

[Letter from Lou to Johnnie postmarked Sept. 5, returned on September 17, 1945 marked 'under orders.']

Sept. 3, 1945
Monday nite

Dearest Johnnie:

Well, here it is, the end of Labor Day, and what a day! Mom and the girls were home, of course, and Gene brought Mama G and Tadone up. Jackie and I got up at 9:00 and after we had our breakfast, I gave Jackie a bath and dressed her up all in yellow. She looked adorable.

At eleven o'clock, Jo and Mike and Michael and little Anthony came to spend the day. The three kids get along very well, no fighting at all.

We had dinner at 1:30 and I ate so much. We had, at first, an antipasto, and I made it. In case you've forgotten, that's the appetizer. Then we had Roast Chicken with potatoes and carrots, beans, corn and chicken soup, cold sliced musk melon for dessert and coffee. We ate and talked and didn't leave the table until a quarter of four!

6:00, Jo, Ann, Fan and I went downtown to view the damage of the big fire we had in town. It started about 1:00 A.M. Sunday morning and wasn't over until 4:30 P.M. Sunday night. I wish I could have seen it! I won't know how it started until we get the paper tomorrow. Anyway, the fire was from Shulte's and ended with Jodo's. Shulte's and the National Shoe Store was completely demolished, so was Botkins jewelry store and the dress chop next to it. Jodo's is practically all gone, too. Honestly, Johnnie, you never saw anything like it. The section is guarded by policemen day and night. I'll send you the clipping from the paper so you'll know all about it.

Jo and Mike took the 8:30 bus home. Gene drove them to the station and then came back and took Mama G and Tadone home. How peaceful and quiet it is now. I put Jackie to bed as soon as our company had left. She gets on very well with Mike, Hon. She's very fond of him.

Saturday afternoon, Gene and I brought the tricycle to the New Hobby Shop on Washington St. to be fixed. All the wheels have to be fixed, a pedal put on, and a good paint job. It's costing me $10.50. That's more than I intended to pay but now it'll be practically new.

After supper, the girls and I went downtown and I was able to get another film.

9:30 P.M. we heard the signing of the Jap surrender broadcast from the U.S.S. Missouri. It only lasted a half hour. Sept. 2 will now be remembered as V.J. Day.

It rained quite hard during the night. I'll bet that's what kept the fire from spreading any more than it did. I went to the 7:00 mass, as usual, and it was drizzling lightly. I couldn't find my umbrella so I had to walk in the rain. While I was in church it really poured. I was afraid I would be stranded for a while but just before mass was over, the rain let up and fell lightly again.

Jackie slept until 8:30. I was able to read the papers and have my breakfast without any interruptions. While Jackie ate her breakfast, I started cooking dinner.

Gene brought Mama G and Tadone up and we ate at 12:30. 3:00 Joe and Angie came. Jackie was so glad to see him and followed him around like a shadow. He brought her out riding for an hour and when they came back she told me all about the ducks, the squirrels and the bi-i-i-i-i-g fire. They must have gone riding too, because they didn't get back until 8:30.

Darling, I love you and miss you so much. This waiting until you come home is going to be the hardest of all. I can hardly wait until I see you again. Oh, I do hope you'll be leaving soon!

Good night, my dearest. Regards from everyone and a kiss and hug from Jackie. All my love, hugs and kisses to you.

Always, Lou

Note on flap: "Darling, I love you with all my heart. Jackie's waiting for you to come home and so am I! Lou."

September 4, 1945 - Japanese troops on Wake Island surrender.

Tuesday, September 4, 1945. Up at 8:30. Lovely day. Mail came at 11:45. Received 2 letters from Johnnie, one letter from Ralph, allotment check for $80. After breakfast cleaned house. 1:30 Mrs. Antonaccio came to see Gracie. Started knitting Judy's sweater. After supper the girls and I went to the movies at the park. Saw "The Song of Bernadette." Came home at 11:30.

September 5, 1945 – British land in Singapore.

Wednesday, September 5, 1945. Up at 8:30. Jackie frightened during night. Slept with me. 11:00 Jackie and I went downtown. Mailed package to Ralph. Cashed check at bank. Bought bell for bicycle. Home at 12:45. Cleaned and prepared meatballs. 3:00 Jackie and I went to Mil's. Stayed for an hour. Came home and cooked. (first day of school and Gracie went.) 6:45 went to Mil's to take care of kids. They went to movies. Came home at 10:00. Brought back ice cream.

Judy & Jackie on Trike. Judy 4,
Jackie 2½, at Sussex Ave house.

Letter from Lou to Johnnie, postmarked September 7, 1945, returned September 20, 1945 marked 'under orders.   ***September 5, 1945***
My Darling:
        I love you, miss you and want you. I'm waiting anxiously for the day when you will be home to stay for always. If it will only be soon!
        I'm writing this letter at Mil's house. Mil and Gene have gone to the movies and I'm here with the children.
        Today is the first day of school and Gracie attended. She's coming along fine, now. Jackie woke up last night very frightened, crying that the big bad wolf was coming. I managed to calm her down but she was afraid to go back to sleep in the crib so I let her sleep with me.
        We went downtown this morning. I mailed a package to Ralph and then cashed my check at the bank. I looked all over for a bell for Jackie's bike and finally found one made of brass and painted black. It'll do for the time being.

575

Yesterday morning I received two letters from you and one from Ralph. Yours were dated the 21ˢᵗ and 22ⁿᵈ of August.

I was sorry to hear that you hurt your toe. I can just imagine how much it did hurt - Poor darling! I hope it's all better, now.

Last night, the girls and I went to see the "Song of Bernadette." This makes the second time that we saw it and I enjoyed it as much as I did the first time. I even cried as much.

I'm enclosing some snaps of Jackie which I think you will like. She's getting so much use out of her sandbox and is still crazy about it. In the other two pictures, she's wearing the blue dress that the girls sent her when we were in California. Remember it?

I can't think of anything else to tell you, Hon, so I'll close sending you regards from all the family and a big hug and kiss from Jackie. To you - all my love -

Always, Lou

Thursday, September 6, 1945. Up at 7:30. Jackie not well. Has little cold. Received letter of Aug. 24 from Johnnie and letter from Ruth. 9:00 washed clothes and finished by twelve. 2:00 Jackie took a nap and slept until 5:00. Her cold not any better. Turned out to be very hot day.

September 7, 1945 - In conformity with the general surrender of September 2, 1945, the Japanese Commanders unconditionally surrender the Ryukyu Islands. [The Ryukyu Islands, also known as the Nansei Islands or the Ryukyu Arc, are a chain of Japanese islands that stretch southwest from Kyushu to Taiwan and includes the islands of Osumi, Tokara, Amami, Okinawa, Sakishima and Yonaguni.]

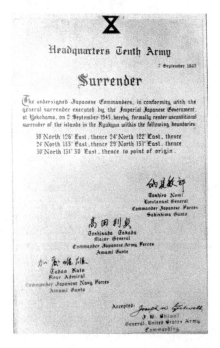

Friday, September 7, 1945. Up at 8:00A.M. Received 2 letters from Johnnie. Those of the 26 & 29 of Aug. Very hot day. Put Jackie to bed at 2:00 but she did not sleep. 3:00 we went out to buy vegetables for supper. Came home and cooked. After supper the girls and I went to the movies. Saw the "Fighting Guardsman" & "I love a Bandleader", both not so good. (I got my period) 5:30 Gene brought me down to get bicycle but it wasn't ready.

September 8, 1945 – General Douglas MacArthur enters Tokyo.

Saturday, September 8, 1945. Up at 9:00 A.M. Mom home because of Jewish Holiday. Most of the stores all closed. No mail. Very hot day. Jackie's cold still the same. Coughed during night. Girls came home 2:00. I knitted on Judy's sweater.

September 9, 1945 – Japanese in Korea surrender.

Sunday, September 9, 1945. Went to 7:00 mass. Cloudy and humid. Jackie awoke when I came home. Girls went to Newark, 10:14. Branchbrook Park to play tennis. Mama G and Tadone up. Hot and humid. Mom and Mama G went to see the dead (Mrs. Bozzi) 5:00. Gracie and Jackie went to Zecca's to buy us some ice cream. 5:30 Aunt Santa and Carol Ann came. Carol Ann wouldn't go home. Stayed here and played with Jackie. Had supper together. Catherine came for her at 7:00. Girls came home at 6:30. 8:00 we went to the movies. Saw "Christmas in Connecticut" B. Stanwick & Dennis Morgan. Pretty good.

Monday, September 10, 1945. Jackie slept until 10:30. Received letter, Aug. 31 from Johnnie. Check from Gimbel's. Scattered showers during morning. Jackie playing in sandbox when it started to rain. Mom came home for lunch. Jackie playing up in the attic with her toys. After supper, the girls and I and Jackie went to church (40 hours devotion). Found Gene here when we came back. He's going to the hospital Friday. Being operated upon for his piles. Joe came to get his chickens.

Tuesday, September 11, 1945. Up at 9:00. Day dark and dreary. Rain. Jackie played up in the attic all morning. I ironed clothes all afternoon. Received skirt outfit from Mary Lukowitz.

Jackie in the "grass skirt" handmade by Mary Lukawitz of parachute nylon.
Letter from Lou to Johnnie postmarked September 13, 1945, returned
September 26, stamped 'under orders.'

Sept. 11, 1945
Wednesday

Dearest Johnnie:

It's been a week since I last wrote. I don't know whether to keep on writing or not. You never said anything about it in your letters, however, I think I'll write at least once a week until I know definitely that you have left.

Oh, darling, isn't it wonderful that you're coming home!! I can hardly wait 'til I can put my arms around you and kiss you until I'm exhausted. I love you so much, my darling, and oh, how I want you.

I can think of nothing else but you and that you're coming home - really and truly coming home. I'm so happy!

Last Thursday I received your letter of Aug. 24ᵗʰ and a letter from Ruth. Do you remember the big mountain at the end of the street where Ruth lives? Well, it caught fire and wasn't under control until it was a half block from her place. It gave them quite

578

a scare. She asked about you and said Burton doesn't have a chance of getting out of Service because he has only 31 points. She said there was a lot of celebrating in Ventura on V-J Day; noise, torn up paper, gayly bedecked cars, etc.

Friday I received two letters from you, those of the 26th and 29th August. Your letter of the 26th was nice and long and both letters contained quite a bit of news. So! You ARE in Okinawa! That's what I had surmised but I wasn't sure.

We've been having very hot weather, again, lately. The weather's been so changeable that now Jackie has a slight cold and I already had one which I haven't gotten rid of entirely. Your last letter, that of Aug. 31st, I received on Monday. I am looking forward to all the things you are. It's going to be wonderful being together again. It's swell about Clere making Chief! Is he leaving the Service, too, honey? I certainly wish you would arrange it so that one of the boys will receive your packages, if you aren't there to receive them yourself, which I hope you won't be. I know Vincent will enjoy all that hard sausage I sent. After supper Monday night the girls and I went to church (40 hours devotion) and we brought Jackie with us. Outside of exclaiming over the Sisters working at the altar and all the lighted candles, she was very good. We were only there fifteen minutes so she didn't have a chance to become restless.

Jackie loves to play up in the attic and I find it very handy for her to be there. Her toys are scattered all over the floor and she really has a good time playing by herself. That also helps from keeping so many of her toys downstairs.

Today was dark, dreary and rainy. Jackie and I didn't get up until nine o'clock. After breakfast, Jackie went up to play in the attic and I was ironing practically all day long. Of course, I had quite a few interruptions, that's why it took me so long.

Gene and I brought Jackie's bike to be fixed and it still isn't ready yet. I almost feel like putting it away for Christmas since she'll only have the use of it for a couple of months.

Mama G and Tadone are definitely coming up as soon as the cold weather sets in. I'm trying to find a place for us to live but so far I haven't had the least bit of luck. I've even called up the different agencies and they have nothing at all. I don't mind staying here at Mom's for a while longer but I'd so much rather we had a place of our own. I even want to have it before you come home.

This afternoon I received a gift that Mary sent to Jackie. It's a pink and white Hawaiian outfit made from parachute nylon. It's adorable!

I have some pictures here but I won't enclose them. You can see them when you come home. I hope you won't be there to receive this letter because I want you here so very much. Good night, my dearest, I love you with all my heart and want you terribly. Here's a kiss from Jackie.

Always, Lou

Wednesday, September 12, 1945. Up at 8:30. Jackie received invitation to Richard's party. 11:00 Jackie and I went to the bank. Bought cards and baby pants for Mil. Bought gift for Judy & Buddy. (overalls & game.) stopped in to see about bike. Home by one o'clock. Took a roll of film of Jackie and myself. Jackie and I brought it down to Shalits. 6:00 went over to Mil's and Gene's to stay with children. Mil and Gene went to Newark to see doc. They came home at 10:30. Brought ice cream. Wrote to Mary, Ralph, Ruth.

September 13, 1945 – Japanese in Burma surrender.

Thursday, September 13, 1945. Up at 7. Lovely day. Called up Hobby Shop. Bicycle not fixed. Cannot fix arm or pedal. 11:00 Jackie took a nap. She doesn't feel very well. She woke up at 4:30P.M. When girls came home from Newark they, Mom and I went to the pizzeria and had pizza and beer.

Friday, September 14, 1945. Judith Ann Petrone's birthday (4 yrs. Old). Anniversary of Mil and Gene. Rain. Received letter of Sept 2, from Johnnie .[this letter wasn't saved] Gene went to hospital. Jackie took a nap 2:30-3:45. Big storm all day.. Jackie climbed in and out of her crib by herself. 2½ yrs. old.

Saturday, September 15, 1945. Richard Kilmer's birthday. Jackie woke at 7:00. Girls home from work. Mom worked half a day. We all cleaned house. Jackie took nap 1:00. 2:30 she went to Richard's party. Her first. Gracie took her. Came home at five with basket pin, etc. Bought spread & drapes and curtains from Star man, paid $5.00 down. Rained off and on during the day. Sent for Kellogg name pin.

Sunday, September 16, 1945. I went to the 7:00 mass as usual. Nice morning. Jackie awoke at 8:30. Girls and I took 12:14 train to Newark. Met Jo at Roseville Ave. Station. All went to Branchbrook Park to play tennis. Played from 2 to 3:00. I haven't played tennis in two years. Became very tired after first hour. We sat out and rested an hour. Anna Mae joined us. Played again from 4:00-5:00. I played a much better game. Won 5 straight games from Ann, 3 from Fan. Changed our clothes in locker room, then went to Parkway Tavern for a sandwich and a glass of beer. 6:30 we took bus to hospital to visit Gene. Met Mil and the Capodeferros there. We got a ride all the way home. We had a very nice day.

Monday, September 17, 1945. Jackie woke at 9:00. Raining. Mom home from work. Took 10:14 train to Newark to shop and to visit Gene. I made a cake but it didn't turn out good. After supper, the girls and I went to the movies. We saw "You Came Along" with Robt. Cummings - Lisabeth Scott. Picture very good.

Tuesday, September 18, 1945. Up at 9:30. Jackie woke at 6:00 and then fell asleep again until 10:30. House very cold and damp. I lit the furnace to warm the house. Rained all day long. I ordered two blankets from Helicks. Mom's and Tadone's birthday. 5:30 Mom and Sundi went down to get Mama G and Tadone. They had supper with us. We had a large mocha cake with candles. All sang Happy Birthday and Jackie blew out the candles. I gave Mom $5.00 and $3.00 to Tadone with card, which he liked very much. 9:30 Sundi brought them home.

Wednesday, September 19, 1945. Up at 8:00. Clear day. Cool. Freddie Sandelli came home early this morning. This morning I washed my hair and Jackie's. Took picture of Jackie (on Mil's film).

Thursday, September 20, 1945. Up at 8:00. Raining. Received slippers for Jackie from Ralph. Also pair for Chipper. Cleaned up after lunch. Mama G dropped in for an hour. I finished Judy's sweater.

Friday, September 21, 1945. Up at 8:00. Hot day. I washed clothes. Took two pictures of Jackie in Hawaiian clothes on Mil's film and two on my own.

Saturday, September 22, 1945. Received letter of Sept. 7 from Johnnie. Ann not working & Fan worked half a day. Cleaned all morning. 5:30 took a shower. Fan and I cooked supper. Went downtown and then to movies. Saw "Out of this World" with Eddie Bracken-Dianna Lynne. "Escape in the Fog." Both features good. P.M. called Mil up in Newark. Gene came home from Hospital. Will be home Monday.

Sunday, September 23, 1945. Went to 7:00 mass as usual. Cold. Later in morning it rained. Vigilante boy drove Mama G and Tadone up. We had dinner at 1:30. I knitted on Michael's sweater all afternoon. Having a lot of trouble with it. 6:00 Joe and Angie came. They stayed until 9:00. Jackie wouldn't go to bed until she knew they were leaving. I listened to the radio until 10:30 and then I went to bed.

Monday, September 24, 1945. Up at 8:30. No mail from Johnnie. Maybe he is on his way home. The day is clear but sun not shining. 1:00 I called up Vene's. Talked to Mother De. Said she was taking a job in Short Hills. Also that Herb and Eleanor were buying a house in Brookside. Jackie took a nap during afternoon. After supper, we all went over to see Gene. He just came home from Newark. Stayed there until a quarter of nine. Betty and Joe there, too.

Tuesday, September 25, 1945. Went to 7:00 mass. Going to try and make Novena of the little flower. Went to confession. Ann home from work because she had her tooth out yesterday. 10:30 Ann, Jackie and I went downtown. Stopped first to see about house on Vail Pl. Already rented. Mailed gift to Buddy. Brought shoes to shoemaker. Ann bought wool for her sweater. Stopped at Foodfair. Then came on home. Jackie took a nap 'til 4:00. We went over to Mil's to read Ralph's letter. First uncensored. After supper Mom and I went to see about another apartment. No luck there either.

Wednesday, September 26, 1945. Ann and I went to 7:00 mass. I received communion. When we came out, it started to rain.

Quite warm. Knitted on Michael's sweater until Jackie woke up. Took picture of Jackie and Patsy in sandbox.

Thursday, September 27, 1945. *Went to 7:00 mass. Nice day. Cool. Gracie brought Jackie to the store to buy meat. After supper Fan and I went to the movies. Saw "A Thousand And One Nights" with Cornel Wilde. Evelyn Keyes and "Boston Blackie Escapes" Both features very good. Took bus down and back. It was raining. Ann angry because Fan and I went to movies without her. She went bowling.*

Friday, September 28, 1945. *Buddy Greaves birthday (4 yrs. Old) Went to 7:00 mass. Damp and cloudy out. Cleared during afternoon. Jackie took a nap 1:30-4:15. I knitted on Michael's sweater in my spare time. When I put Jackie to bed, I cut her hair even. (her first haircut - 2½ yrs.) Big bread strike going on!*

Saturday, September 29, 1945. *Went to 7:30 mass with Ann. Both Ann and Fan not working. They cleaned house. I just cleaned my room thoroughly. In afternoon I washed my hair and Jackie's. Sat. morning received letter I wrote to Johnnie, back. 7:00 Ann, Fan and I went downtown. I bought white buttons. ($.79 a dozen). Baby knit book, 5 hanks green wool. ($4.45).*

Sunday, September 30, 1945. *Went to 7:00 mass. Jackie woke at 6:30A.M. Gene brought Mama G and Tadone up. After dinner, Ann, Fan, Gracie and I took the 2:14 train to Newark. We intended seeing a Victory Parade but got here too late. Took us a long time to get in touch with Jo. She and Michael came with us to the Star for pizza (4.00). Afterwards we went to St. Michael's feast. Bought balloon for Jackie and horn for Michael. 6:00 we went to the Branford. Saw "Lady on a Train." Deana Durbin, David Bruce. & "The Beautiful Cheat" Bonita Granville. Took 9:44 train home.*

Monday, October 1, 1945. *Went to 7:00 mass as usual. Very cold and damp. Split wood all morning. Lit furnace. Received $80 allotment check. Patsy played in the house with Jackie all day long. No bread anywhere.*

Tuesday, October 2, 1945. *Went to 7:00 mass. Raining. Received blanket from Helicks. Paid $1.00 on it. (cost $3.58). Ordered* another and one for the girls. Fan came home at 10:30A.M. Edison on strike! Patsy here playing with Jackie. Gene came over at 3:00.Took me down to get Jackie's tricycle. Was at store a month. We had a little trouble about the job done. Gene did the talking. We were supposed to pay $10.50. Instead paid $8.50. I let Jackie use it right away. Her feet still don't touch the pedals entirely. She doesn't do so bad for the first time, though. A little practice is all she needs.

Wednesday, October 3, 1945. Went to 7:00 mass. Received letter from Wanda. Fan still home from work. Took 2:14 train to Newark. Met Ann 3:20 in Harrison. Shopped until 5:30. Bought black hat, girdle, stockings, slip, and Ann bought me pyjamas for my birthday. We took 6:58 train home. Found Jo, Mike & Mike Jr. here to stay for rest of week. Received lots of my letters written to Johnnie back.

Thursday, October 4, 1945. Went to 7:00 mass. Fan still home. Jo, Fan, the kids and I went downtown. Came home 12:45. M. de R. called while I was out. Mike painted outside window woodwork. Very cold out. I started on Nancy's mittens. Fan started Ralph's sweater.

Friday, October 5, 1945. Went to 7:00 mass. A lovely day. Fan still home. I washed clothes 8:00 finished at 10:15. Mike painting outside woodwork. Jo took Michael and Jackie over to Mil's 11:00. Children play together very nicely. No fighting. After supper we all went to the park and saw "The Strange Affair of Uncle Harry" with George Sanders & Geraldine Fitzgerald. Got my period.

Saturday, October 6, 1945. Up at 8:30. Cleaned room. Rain all day. Parade called off. 4:30 Gene brought the family to Bernardsville to visit Joe and Angie. Only Jackie and I were home. Jackie has caught a cold.

Sunday, October 7, 1945. Went to 7:00 mass. Rainy day. Gene brought Mama G and Tadone up, then he and Mike hooked up our <u>new</u> gas range. We had dinner at 1:00. 5:00 the girls and I went to the movies and saw "State Fair" with Jeanne Crain and Dana Andrews. Very entertaining. Mike and Jo went home 7:00. Joe and Angie came at 7:30 P.M. Jackie sleeping already. Celebrate Jo's birthday. Had Mocha cake with candles. Michael and Jackie blew them out. I started giving Jackie prune juice again for her constipation.

Monday, October 8, 1945. Received letter from Ruth and allotment check of $50. Nice day. After lunch, Fan, Jackie and I went downtown. I bought material for a black skirt and blue material for overalls for Jackie. I also bought corduroy to make M.de R's bag. Came home and cooked supper. Worked on mittens at night.

October 9, 1945 - Typhoon hit Okinawa. The camp was flattened. Quonset huts were tossed about, docks washed away, a seaplane destroyed. Johnnie is on his way home.

Tuesday, October 9, 1945. *Received letter from Ruth thanking me for Buddy's gift. Nice day. Made sauce right after lunch, then Fan and I went over to Mil's. Stayed there until 4:00. Judy came home with us. Ann came home early so we ate supper at 6:00. Mil came over for Judy at 7:00.*

Buddy & his kitten

October 10, 1945 - Johnnie sends telegram from Panama.

Wednesday, October 10, 1945. *Received telegram from Johnnie. He's in Panama. Expects to be home by the 25th of Oct. A very nice day. I started working on corduroy bag for MdeR. I used range oven for first time. Very good!*

Thursday, October 11, 1945. *A lovely day. Brought out Johnnie's clothes to air. Washed my hair.*

Friday, October 12, 1945. *Rain. Cleared later in morning. Fan cleaned room and I gave my bedroom a thorough cleaning. Then I had to cook supper. 8:30 we, Ann, Fan, and I went to the movies. Saw "Mildred Pierce" Joan Crawford, Zackery Scott. Good. I wrote to Ralph.*

Saturday, October 13, 1945. *Received letter from Mary. Letter of Sept. 29th. Mike came up at 10:00A.M. Painted woodwork outside. Ann and Fan helped him. Raw and cold out. 3:00 Jo and Michael came. She brought me the wool for Jackie's suspenders. Sat. night Ann, Fan and Jo went downtown. Got my coat out of cleaners $1.25. Jo and Mike stayed overnight.*

Sunday, October 14, 1945. *Went to 7:00 mass. Joe Petrone came at 11:00. Emptied girls room and began painting. Gene brought Mama G and Tadone up. We had dinner at 1:30. I had to cook. 2:30 we all went to see the Holy Name Parade. The children enjoyed it very much. Jackie was stupefied and so was Michael. Judy was very excited. Saw a sailor carry the flag and* said, "Aunt Lucia, Jackie's got a sailor just like Johnnie." We came home and boys began painting again. Joe went home at 7:30, so did Mike and Jo. Gene brought Mama G and Tadone home at 9:30. Mom and I stayed up until 12:00. We did up my curtains and I ironed my scarfs.

Monday, October 15, 1945. Received letter of Oct. 3 from Ralph. Raw day and cold. Could not get heat up in rooms. I finished stretching curtains and washed my windows. Gracie mailed my package off to Ralph.

Tuesday, October 16, 1945. Mary C. Lukowitz's birthday. Jackie woke at 6:30. Then fell asleep again and slept until 11:30. After lunch she went out and played in the yard. Wore red snowsuit. Took two pictures of her on bike.

Chapter 8
Johnnie's Home!!

October 17, 1945 - Johnny arrives home.

Wednesday, October 17, 1945. A beautiful day! I washed my clothes and Fan washed sun porch windows. Then I gave my room a thorough cleaning. Finished at 4:30. Sent Jackie and Gracie to get telegram for Fan and brought J. shoes to shoemaker. They were back by 4:30. Just beginning to cook supper. 5:15 Johnnie comes home!! I was very, very surprised! Dumbfounded! Jackie was very happy to see him. Began showing off. Called him Dad! She calls me Mom. Johnnie and I were up until 1:00 A.M. (He brought me home from Panama, a blue sport jacket, a genuine alligator wallet, a pillow case, a pocketbook for Jackie.)

October 18, 1945 - Johnny reports to Camp Lido on Long Island, New York.

Thursday, October 18, 1945. Johnnie left for Camp Lido, L.I. on the 5:23A.M. train. A lovely day. Sun shining and warm. Vene came at 11:00. Went to meet MdeR. Back at 11:45. We all had lunch together. MdeR looking very well. Likes her new job very much. Jackie not very intimate with them but played nicely with Nan and Bonnie. I took two pictures of the three. They stayed until three o'clock. Had to take kids to dancing class. Very happy over news about Johnnie being home. Said they would be down Sunday.

Friday, October 19,1945. Johnnie called me up from New York at 8:00A.M. He said he couldn't get home before Sunday afternoon. Vene and kids came here at 11:30. Stayed until 3:00. I ironed my clothes when they left. It was a beautiful day today. Very warm.

Saturday, October 20, 1945. A lovely day. Ann, Fan and I went shopping in New York. I bought a new black dress and a black hat. We were home by 9:00P.M. (Mike and Michael came up in the morning and stayed overnight.)

October 21, 1945 - Johnny calls Lucia from Hoboken. Gene and Lou pick him up at the Morristown train station.

Sunday, October 21, 1945. Went to 7:00 mass as usual. Joe came in the morning to finish painting room. Jo came in time for dinner. Gene brought Mama G and Tadone up. 4:00 Mother de Roxtro came. Johnnie called at 5:30 from Hoboken. 7:00 Gene and I went to the Morristown Station to meet him. (Bob

587

Calihan with him) He was a little potted but very happy about being a discharged veteran. Judy and Michael very happy to see him. Jackie a little shy. Johnnie & I went to station with MdeR. Works in Short Hills. We walked home through town. Johnnie acting very crazy.

Monday, October 22, 1945. I did nothing all day long, just stayed with Johnnie. After supper Johnnie and I went to movies. Saw "Anchors Away" with Frank Sinatra, Gene Kelly, Kathryn Grayson. Very good. After we went to Cutters. Stayed there until 11:30.

Tuesday, October 23, 1945. Damp and raw out. Jackie's cold worse. The three of us went up to Vene's for dinner. We drove up in Vene's car. Nancy & Bonnie were crazy about their Uncle Jack. Vene cooked a very nice meal. We left at 4:00 and were home at 5:00. Raining.

October 24, 1945 – The United Nations is founded.

Wednesday, October 24, 1945. Cold day. Johnnie chopped wood and lit fire. After supper we borrowed car from Gene and went to look at a bungalow for rent. Didn't amount to much. Went back to Mil's and stayed until 10:00. Catherine there too. Gene gave Johnnie two pairs of pants and a pair of shoes. In afternoon Johnnie called up building dept. Would pay him $1900 a year. About $38 a week.

Thursday, October 25, 1945. Rainy and damp out. 11 Johnnie went out to report to draft board to talk to Nelson Butera. Mom didn't come home for lunch. They offered him $1900 a year. After supper we went out for a walk.

Friday, October 26, 1945. Rainy day. Cleared up in afternoon. We all went downtown to buy Jackie a pair of shoes. Nobody had any in her size (7½ C). Johnnie made an appointment at Dr. Reilly's for next Monday (Nov. 5). Bought Johnnie a brown belt in Mintz ($1.50).

Saturday, October 27, 1945. Lovely day. I washed clothes. Johnnie went out at 9:30A.M. and came home 4:30 P.M. !!! When he did come home he brought me a half dozen of roses. He helped Gene move things from Mama G's house. Mama G and Tadone came up here to live. 9:00P.M. Johnnie & I went out for a walk. On way back we bought potato chips and an ice cream cone at Zecca's.

Sunday, October 28, 1945. Johnnie and I went to the 7:00 mass. Joe came in morning to paint bathroom (white). Waited all afternoon for Mother de Roxtro to come. 5:15 took bus to Roselle Park. Eddie and Lesley met us in Springfield. Sharon very sweet. They gave us some of her pictures.

October 29, 1945 – The U.S. Navy 15th Construction Battalion is de-activated.

Monday, October 29, 1945. *A very nice day. After lunch, Johnnie and Jackie and I went downtown to get a pair of shoes for Jackie. Also a coat and legging set. Couldn't find either. After supper, girls went over to Mil's to care for children. Johnnie went out. Joined VFW (Veteran's of Foreign Wars). First meeting at Elks.*

Tuesday, October 30, 1945. *A lovely day. 11:44 Johnnie, Jackie and I took the train into Newark. We went shopping for a winter outfit for Jackie and a pair of black patent leather shoes. We bought the blue outfit, paid $18.50 for it but couldn't find the shoes anywhere. We had a very poor luncheon in Child's Restaurant. Caught 4:28 train home. Jackie behaved very well. But we were all very tired. 8:45 P.M. Johnnie and I went down to the pizzeria. Had beers only. Came home 11:30 P.M.*

Wednesday, October 31, 1945. *Halloween. A lovely warm day. 11:30 Johnnie and I went downtown. Jackie stayed home with Mama G & Tadone. Were home by 1:30. Found nothing good to eat so we brought Jackie with us and we went to the Pizzeria. We had a pizza, antipasto, a sausage sandwich for Johnnie and beer. Came home and took five pictures. Then started the supper. Gene brought Judy over at 7:00. Johnnie and I took Judy and Jackie out to visit the homes. Both children had a very nice time. We dressed Judy up at Mil's then came home with Jackie 9:00 P.M. She was asleep in two minutes after she was put to bed.*

Thursday, November 1, 1945. *Birthday of Bobby Jo de Roxtro. Received allotment check $80. We stayed in all day. In afternoon Mother de Roxtro dropped in. Then Vene and the children, and then Johnnie Naughton. Johnnie gave us several chocolate bars. I wasn't feeling very well. (we went to 9:00 mass). Feast of all Saints. Prune juice working well on Jackie. Moves bowels once a day now.*

Friday, November 2, 1945. *Cold and raw out. Rained a little during day. Kuglers came for us at 8:45P. M. De Roxtro family giving Johnnie a welcome home party. Left here at 9:00. I wore my new black hat, new black dress and Fan's chesterfield coat. Arrived at Vene's 9:30 P.M. All the family present. Party going along very nicely up until 11:30P.M. then trouble started. Johnnie very disgusted and upset over (family feud. Fran started it). We came home with the Leary's at 2:30A.M. Johnnie & I talked until 4:00 A.M. then went to bed. I got my period.*

Saturday, November 3, 1945. *I was still feeling pretty bad. Stomach bothering me. Johnnie helped clean room. In afternoon, Eddie Kugler called up to apologize. Told him we couldn't make it for dinner. Johnnie Naughton brought down eggs. I owe Vene five cents only, paid Johnnie $.50.*

Sunday, November 4, 1945. *Johnnie and I went to 8:00 mass. Had dinner at 2:00P.M. Joe and Angie came at 2:30. Joe gave bathroom another coat of paint. Mike had come up at 1:30. In afternoon Gene and Judy came over. Mike drove Mom to Cemetery. Johnnie very restless all day long. Mother de Roxtro called up at 6:00 P.M.*

Monday, November 5, 1945. *A lovely day. I washed the clothes. Feeling much better. Jackie's cough almost gone. Johnnie went to dentist 9:30. Came home 2:00P.M. Girls had a date with Nick D. and another sailor.*

Tuesday, November 6, 1945. *A lovely day. "Election Day". Fan home from work. After lunch Johnnie and I went downtown, bought a pair of slippers for Jackie and Johnnie bought a pair* of brown tweed trousers. After supper Johnnie and I went to the movies with Mil and Gene. Afterwards, we went to Carbello's for pizza and beer. Jackie's favorite song now is "Bell Bottom Trousers" and "Chickery Chick."

Wednesday, November 7, 1945. *A lovely warm day. I ironed Johnnie's shirts this morning and cleaned my room and the bathroom. 4:00 the Leary's came to visit us. Ginny is very sweet. One month older than Jackie. They stayed until 5:30. Very nice having them. Jackie and Ginny got along very well together. Altho Jackie was very shy before Clemy and Eddie. Took pictures of children and some of Jackie*

Thursday, November 8, 1945. *A lovely day. Jackie played out in the yard with the kids all morning. After lunch, Johnnie, Jackie and I went downtown. We couldn't find any Mary Jane shoes for Jackie. Brought Johnnie's pants to Pete's. Took several pictures of Jackie and Johnnie in the park feeding the squirrels.*

[The photos taken in the park feeding the squirrels were too faded and cloudy to include here.]

Friday, November 9, 1945. *A lovely day. Stayed in all day long. After supper, 9:30 P.M. Johnnie and I went out for a walk. We walked about a mile and a half. Jackie loves to color. Does very nicely and stays within the lines (33 Mos.).*

Saturday, November 10, 1945. *Rainy and damp. Letter from Ralph. Johnnie and I took the 3:44 train to New York. Jackie home with Ann, Mama G and Tadone and Grandma. We reached New York, Gimbles at 5:15 P.M. Went to the Vogue and bought a black bag for me and a pair of black shoes. Also bought wallet for MdeR. Raining lightly all the while. We had dinner at the Brass Rail. Very good. There was too much of a crowd at Radio City so we went to the Rivoli and saw "Love Letters" Jennifer Jones, Joseph Cotton. Very good. Took 2:20A.M. train home. We had a very nice time.*

Sunday, November 11, 1945. *"Armistice Day" Rained all day. Stayed home all day. Johnnie and I went to the 11:00 mass.*

Monday, November 12, 1945. *Foggy and damp. Ann home from work. In afternoon we took Jackie and Judy to movies to see Pinocchio. Jackie was very interested and fascinated. Behaved very well. Judy was restless and a little bored and wanted to go home. After picture, Johnnie took them home. Ann and I stayed for second feature. Out at 5:30. After supper, 7:00 Johnny went to V.F.W. meeting.*

Tuesday, November 13, 1945. *Rain. Letter from the Fitz's. Johnnie went out at 2:00 P.M. and didn't come home until 11:00 P.M.! Drunk!! Am I mad!! Vene dropped in at 2:15P.M. Left children here while she went to the dentist. Children played together very nicely.*

Wednesday, November 14, 1945. *Clear but sun not shining. I'm not speaking to Johnnie. Went downtown after lunch to buy Jackie a pair of shoes. (white). I spoke to John only when necessary. I didn't even ask him to come along. He just came. While we were downtown it started to rain. We came home by bus.*

Thursday, November 15, 1945. *Johnnie went to work for an hour. Searing Ave. Shop. Came home at 11:00. 11:30 Mother de Roxtro came and stayed until 4:30. Vene came at 4:30 with Johnnie N. and the children. After supper I made up with Johnnie. Joe Petrone's birthday.*

Friday, November 16, 1945. *Pretty warm out. In afternoon washed my hair and took a shower. Johnnie did too. After supper we went to the Community and saw Margaret O'Brien and Ed. G. Robinson in "Our Vines Have Tender Grapes." It was very, very, good. We really enjoyed it a great deal.*

Saturday, November 17, 1945. *Carol Ann Russo's birthday (3 yrs. Old). 12:00 Johnnie and I went downtown. 1:30 we had lunch at Cutters. Very good. We were home at 3:15. Dressed Jackie and then went to Carol Ann's birthday party. Johnnie went to barbers. Those present were Judy, Jackie, Mary Grace, Carol Ann, Jimmy, Catherine and Ann, Catherine and myself. Jackie gave Carol a white blouse. Party over at 5:00. After supper Johnnie and I walked downtown. Bought record, "Chickery Chick" for Jackie. Johnnie & I went to Thodes for a banana split and Sundae. Called Vene.*

Sunday, November 18, 1945. *Raining early in morning. Johnnie and I went to 7:00 mass. Called Fran . Joe came to paint kitchen. 2:00 the Kuglers came to take Johnnie, Jackie and me to Nora's. Johnnie bought me a corsage of roses and white chrysanthemums for his mother. Reached Nora's at 3:30. Jackie behaved very well. Nora served buffet supper. Food very good. Grand turkey! Left there at 7:00 P.M. home at 8:30. Jackie fell asleep on way home. Found Jo & Mike here. They were staying overnight at Mil's.*

Monday, November 19, 1945. *Rainy day. Johnnie went to work. Reading meters. Drove No. 8. He came home for lunch at 11:30A.M.(has truck No.8). After lunch I baked two lemon merengue pies. Then cooked supper. 8:00P.M. Johnnie went to V.F.W. meeting. Home at 12:00. Received card from Wanda and Hunter.*

Tuesday, November 20, 1945. *Very windy and cold. Cleaned up in morning and ironed in afternoon. After supper, Johnnie and I gave the kitchen a second coating of paint. We went to bed 12:00.*

Wednesday, November 21, 1945. *A lovely day. Johnnie still reading meters. Brings Mom home from work every day. Gracie home from school.*

Thursday, November 22, 1945. *Thanksgiving Day. Rained heavily in early morning. Cleared about 10:30 A.M. Had dinner at 2:00. 12 lb. turkey. Mother de came at 3:15. Joe and Angie came at 4:00. We took a roll of film. 9:30 Johnnie and I drove Mother de home to short Hills. She gave me a large amount of pie dough.*

Friday, November 23, 1945. *A lovely day. Cold. Ann and I took 9:14 train to New York. Gracie home with Jackie. Ann ordered sleds for all three kids. I bought Jackie two polo shirts, a lumber jacket. A pair of overalls, and a pair of brown gloves for myself. We came home at 5:30. Johnnie met us at the station. Mom went to Newark to stay at Jo and Mike's.*

593

Saturday, November 24, 1945. *A lovely day. In afternoon Jackie and I went around to the pumping stations with Johnnie. Jackie enjoyed the ride very much. When we came in, I made two lemon pies. They turned out very good. After supper, Johnnie and I went downtown. Very cold.*

Sunday, November 25, 1945. *A lovely day. We went to 7:00 mass. Cooked dinner when I came home. Johnnie had to work. In afternoon, Jackie and I went around with Johnnie again. Fan had to work. Mom came home 9:30P.M. from Newark. Gene brought her.*

Lucia, Jackie, Nana (Mrs. de Roxtro)

Lucia, Jackie, Grandma Mary, Mama G

Lucia, Ann, Joan

Jackie, Joe, Angie, Jackie

Monday, November 26, 1945. *A lovely day. I washed clothes. Then ironed while supper was cooking. Feeling very tired!!*

Tuesday, November 27, 1945. *Received slippers and bag from Mary. 11:00 Jackie and I went downtown. Bought several things. After lunch we went around with Johnnie in the truck. Then he left me off downtown while I bought a few more things. He brought us home at 3:00. After supper we went to movies with Mil and Gene. Saw "The Spanish Main" at Community. Good. Afterwards we went to Carbellos for pizza and beer. Took picture of Jackie in coat and legging set.*

Wednesday, November 28, 1945. *Rain all day. I did quite a bit of ironing all afternoon. After supper Johnnie and I went bowling. My highest score was 100. Johnnie's was 192. We bowled five games.*

Thursday, November 29, 1945. *Rain. A very nasty day! Mother de Roxtro came up for a few minutes after lunch. She gave me some dishtowels and washcloths and a fryer broiler as a Christmas present. Do I love it!! Baked two pies for supper. Chocolate and lemon merengue. Very good. Rain turned to snow! Snowing all night long.*

Friday, November 30, 1945. *Snow!! Took 11:14 train to New York. Met Ann in Hoboken. We both went shopping. Did a lot of Christmas shopping. Johnnie met us when we came home. After supper Johnnie and I went to the movies and saw "Her Highness and the Bellboy." Hedy Lamar and Robert Walker. (had period when I came home.).*

Saturday, December 1, 1945. *Received letter from Ruth. Clear and cold. Johnnie working all day. At night I went to confession with girls. Knitting white socks for Gracie's Christmas present.*

Sunday, December 2, 1945. *Johnnie and I went to 7:00 mass. Johnnie working. Jackie went along with him all day. She loves it. Joe and Angie came at 3:00. Gene and Judy came at 5:00. Kids had a lot of fun playing with Jackie's big balloon. Judy is crazy about Johnnie.*

Monday, December 3, 1945. *Raw and cold. In all day. Wrote to Ruth and Ralph.*

Tuesday, December 4, 1945. *After supper Johnnie and I went to the movies. Saw C. Colbert - D. Amici, R. Foran - "Guest Wife." Pretty good. Afterwards we went to Cutters. I had <u>five</u> beers. Johnnie had ale. We met Frank Gannon there. Talked with him. Came home 12:30.*

Wednesday, December 5, 1945. *10:30 Johnnie brought Jackie and me downtown to the post office. Sent off hospitalization and shopped around town. Johnnie met us on the way home 11:30 and gave us a lift. After lunch Jackie took a nap and slept until 1:00 to 3:00. At 1:30 Cat and Carol Ann came. Carol wouldn't go home until she saw Jackie. Both children played very nicely together. They stayed until 4:00. After supper, Johnnie was supposed to go to the VFW meeting but he stayed home with me. We addressed our Christmas cards.*

Thursday, December 6, 1945. *Rain! Cold! Johnnie had trouble at Jockey Hollow with pump. Worked four hours overtime. He has a very bad cold. Jackie can put large puzzles together.*

Friday, December 7, 1945. *11:00 I went to the Acme. Prepared lunch and then later Johnnie drove me downtown. We cancelled the order at Zane's for the doll carriage. I shopped around town until 3:00. Mom sick in bed with a cold. Johnnie* feels much better. After supper Johnnie, Gracie and I brought Jackie to the Park to see the Christmas wonderland. She enjoyed it very much. Was quite awed by it all. She saw Santa Claus and waved back to him. Went to bed at 9:00. I put Ann's sweater together and then Johnnie and I went to bed 10:00 P.M.

Saturday, December 8, 1945. Nice day. Johnnie brought Jackie along with him all morning. Mom feeling worse. Tried to get doctor Wade but he never came. Ann feeling sick, too.

Sunday, December 9, 1945. Johnnie & I went to 7:00 mass. Johnnie had to work. Called Dr. Wade again. Then called Dr. Renna. After lunch Jackie and I went around with Johnnie. 4:00 Dr. Renna came. Said Mom had bronchial pneumonia. Joe & Angie here. 7:00 Dr. Wade came. Diagnosis same. 7:30 Mama G fell down the stairs. Cracked her wrist - bruised her body. Called Dr. Rice. Jo and Mike came at that time to see Mom.

Monday, December 10, 1945. Nancy G. Naughton's birthday. Raw and cloudy. Snow. Gene took Mama G to hospital to x-ray her wrist. 11:45 Johnnie and I took train to New York to do Xmas shopping. Josephine came up to help Fannie. We came home 5:00 P.M. Panties & dress came from Wards. Mom not feeling so good. Vomited at night. Jackie very sick with cold and sore throat. Temp. 103½. Dr. Rice came for Mama G. I applied antiphlegestive on her wrist.

Tuesday, December 11, 1945. Clear day, icy. Jackie received Xmas card from Buddy. Johnnie went to drugstore for Mama G's prescriptions. Mom not feeling better. Jackie's temp. Normal. Mama G feeling very sore. In afternoon I called Dr. Renna for Mom. He came 5:00. She has to sip water every 15 minutes to settle her stomach. Asked him to look at Jackie, too. She was very ill and had temp. He said her tonsils were bad, her throat inflamed, prescribed cough medicine, benzoin inhaler. Johnnie went out to get them. We used inhaler before we went to bed.

Wednesday, December 12, 1945. Jackie slept fairly well during night. Mama G feeling very sore. Mom feeling better. Jackie has bad sore throat and cold. Won't eat anything and coughs a lot. Ann is still sick and not feeling any better. I'm kept very busy running up and down. I changed dressing on Mama G's wrist every 12 hours. 10:00 I washed the clothes. 3 machines full. Very tired. I'm not feeling well myself. I have a cold & my throat hurts. 7:30 Mil and Cat came over and stayed until 10:00 P.M. Jackie very restless, coughing and crying. Used inhaler before going to bed. Our clock broke.

Thursday, December 13, 1945. Received Xmas card from Ruth with Buddy's picture enclosed. Jackie had a very bad night. She kept waking up every hour coughing and crying. Mil sent over some chicken soup at 12:30. Josephine came over at 12:00. Mike has the grips. Jo rubbed Mama G's back and used the inhaler on Jackie and me. While we were under the tent, Mother de Roxtro came. Jo went home at 2:30. M de R took care of Jackie all afternoon. She worked wonders with Jackie. Vene came for her at 5:00. Grace made the sauce for supper. I feel miserable. My back aches me terribly. Johnnie rubbed it for me before going to bed.

Friday, December 14, 1945. Jackie slept pretty well during the night. Mom and Ann feeling much better. I feel better, too. Fan stayed home from work in morning so I could stay in bed. We received Xmas cards from; Betty & Joe Vigilante, R. Ingels. It snowed several inches during the night. Mom felt well enough to get out of bed for a half hour in the afternoon. 4:00 Jackie said she wanted to eat. She hadn't eaten for four days. Dr. Renna called to ask about Jackie. We used inhaler again. Gene and Johnnie put radiator in the attic.

Saturday, December 15, 1945. Received Xmas card from Marge Sebastian with a picture of her daughter enclosed. She's a month older than Jackie. We also received letters from Ralph saying he would be home by Jan. 15. Mom is feeling much better and so is Mama G. She (M.G.) even walks around a little. Jackie still has a very bad cough. I don't feel any better myself. My back still hurts and so does my throat.

Sunday, December 16, 1945. Very cold out. I missed mass. Feeling about the same. Jackie still has her bad cough. Ann went to church. Intends going to work tomorrow. Mrs. De Roxtro came at 3:30. Took charge of Jackie right away. Had her laughing and playing. She stayed until 9:30. Johnnie drove her back to Short Hills in Gene's car. Joe and Angie came at 4:00 and went home 8:00 P.M.

Monday, December 17, 1945. A quiet day. Ann went to work. Mom had to make the soup and take care of the fire. She shouldn't though. She still isn't completely well. My throat and back still hurt me. I've been in bed since Friday. Jackie slept pretty well last night. Only woke once! We brought her down for supper. Mama G Took a turn for the worse. I think she caught cold. Mom's boss and Sylvia Palmieri came to visit her.

Tuesday, December 18, 1945. A lovely day. How I wish I could be out finishing up my Xmas shopping! This morning Jackie received a Xmas card from Carol Ann and Johnnie and I received one from Catherine and Harry. Jackie and I both went down to the kitchen for lunch and supper. Daddy brings our breakfast up to us every morning.

Wednesday, December 19, 1945. Jackie slept all night without waking. More snow during night. Having blizzard. There's about six inches of snow out. This morning I went down for the first time and had breakfast with Johnnie. I feel much better. There's no change in Jackie. Mama G caught cold. Johnnie isn't feeling so good tonite. Gee, I hope he isn't coming down with the grip!!! We received a Xmas card from Joe & Angie and so did Jackie.

Thursday, December 20, 1945. A lovely day. We received Xmas cards from Si Hegman, Vita, Martha, and her mother. 10:00 A.M. I went downtown to finish my Xmas shopping. All the stores were cleaned out!! I couldn't find men's pyjamas anywhere! I bought a belt for Joe and slippers for Johnnie, sachet for Jo. In afternoon we received cards from Nana, Witkowski. After supper Johnnie and I went downtown. We bought game for Richard. Jack-in-the-box for Jackie. Then we went to the movies and saw "That Night With You" S. Foster, F. Towe, D. Bruce.

Friday, December 21, 1945. Received cards from Vene & Johnnie, Nan & Bonnie, the Kuglers. 2:45 Johnnie and I took the bus to Irvington to shop. Reached there 4:00. We walked from Irvington to Springfield Ave., Newark! About six miles. We bought quite a few things along the way. We ate at the "Star" and then went to Jo's but she wasn't home so we took a bus to Newark, shopped around some more, and then took the train home.

Saturday, December 22, 1945. Snowing! Received cards from Mil & Gene & Judy and Chipper. Also a card from Mary with a handkerchief enclosed. Ann and Fan went shopping in New York. After supper, Johnnie and I went downtown to buy a gift for Tommy. Got an alarm clock. And then we went to Summit with the truck to bring the gifts to the Boys. We stayed there until 10:45.

Sunday, December 23, 1945. Johnnie & I went to the 7:00 mass. Johnnie had to work. I wrapped the last of the gifts. Joe came 2:00. 4:30P.M. Johnnie and I went to visit Lui and Frank. We brought Tommy a Xmas present. While we were gone, Fran and Eddie dropped in with a gift for Jackie. So after supper, Johnnie and I had to go to Roselle Park to bring the gifts for Leslie Ann and Sharon Lee. We stayed there until 9:30. Eddie gave us three tree lights.

Monday, December 24, 1945. Received letter from Ruth. A lovely day. Ann not working but Johnnie and Fan are. Ann and I went downtown in afternoon to buy vegetables and other things. Gene and Mil came over with the kids at 5:30P.M. Johnnie came home at 6:00. Then Ann, Johnnie and I went out to buy a Christmas tree, got one for $.35. Joe and Angie came at 7:00 and Jo & Mike came at 7:45. Jackie went to bed at 9:30 and so did Michael, after they hung up their stockings. Mil & Gene went home 10:00. We, Ann, Fan & I, started trimming the tree at 10:30 P.M. We finished by 12:00. 1:00A.M. we woke up Jackie and Michael to come down to see what Santa had brought. They stayed up until 2:00 A.M.

Tuesday, December 25, 1945. After the gifts were all distributed, we all opened the presents up in turn. All the gifts were lovely and everybody was happy. This was Johnnie's first Christmas with me in four years. Jackie was very happy over her toys which were; table & chairs, a mechanical tractor, 2 dolls, pots & pans, dishes, sled, drum, tinker toy, books, pistol. Her stocking was filled to capacity with lots of good things. Mom loved the robe we gave her for Xmas. Johnnie & I received many lovely gifts and so did Jackie. It rained during afternoon. Jo & Mike stayed overnight (We received a telegram from Ralph. Mama G came downstairs for Xmas Eve and Xmas day. Vene & Johnnie dropped in with M. de Roxtro at 11:30. Johnnie drove his mother home. Johnnie gave me a lovely heart chain and I gave him a bathrobe & Jackie gave him slippers.

Wednesday, December 26, 1945. A lovely day. I feel lazy and overstuffed. Gee I did eat a lot! Now I have to go on a diet. I didn't do anything very much all day long. Jackie was as good as gold. She was so busy playing with her toys. She loves the tree and wants the lights on all the time. We're trying to keep the tree up until Ralph comes home. I took some pictures of the Xmas tree.

Thursday, December 27, 1945. A lovely day. 8:30, as soon as Johnnie went to work, I washed the clothes and finished by 12:00. After lunch, Cat, her mother and Carol Ann came to visit us. Carol Ann gave Jackie a pair of hand crocheted slippers that my Aunt had made. Jackie gave Carol a box of soap. 5:00, Mother de came. She just had a permanent. She stayed for supper and left at 10:00. Johnnie drove her home in the truck. I went along, too.

Friday, December 28, 1945. A nice day. Received back the second of the packages I sent to Johnnie overseas. After supper Johnnie and I went to the movies. Saw "Kiss & Tell" with Shirley Temple. Very comical. Johnnie liked it. When we came out it was snowing. We stopped at cutters for a few drinks. Met Eddie Leary there. Left 12:30 A.M.

Saturday, December 29, 1945. Snowing! Johnnie worked half a day. Working for Si now. In afternoon, Johnnie, Jackie and I went over to see Mil's Xmas tree and Judy's toys. Mil wasn't home. Just Gene and Judy were. Snow had turned to rain making a lot of slush. Sat. night, I went to confession with the girls and then we went downtown. Johnnie was asleep when I came home. I woke him up and we had coffee while I ironed him two shirts and some slips for myself. Girls were teaching Mom and Gracie Continental Rummy, a new card game. I haven't learned it yet.

Sunday, December 30, 1945. Johnnie and I went to 8:00 mass. Very slippery out. Johnnie's not feeling well. He has a bad cold. Mama G is still convalescing in bed. Is much better. 2:35 PM we received a telephone call from Ralph. Said he was calling from Pittsburg, Cal. Everyone was so excited. We all talked to him. He had a bad cold, too. Finds the weather freezing. Later Gene came over and all played Continental Rummy.

Monday, December 31, 1945. *Raining. Johnnie feeling pretty badly. Went to work for two hours. Came home and slept until 3:30P.M. 4:30 Johnnie lit the fireplace. We used the Presto Logs. Hard to burn. Had dinner at 6:30. Afterwards we brought the kitchen table into the living room and played Continental Rummy until a quarter of twelve. Ann won the money $.85. Then we played Put'n'take. Johnnie won $.30. Tadone was up with us all. 12:00 we all drank a toast to the New Year. All in all it was a very peaceful New Year's Eve. And I hope 1946 treats us kindly. "So long forever, 1945!"*

Lucia de Roxtro

Johnny's Sea Chest

The Official Emblem of the 15th Naval Construction Battalion

Bibliography

Seabee History: Formation of the Seabees and World War II.

https://www.history.navy.mil/research/library/online-reading-room/title-list-alphabetically/s/seabee-history0/world-war-ii.html

Chronology – World War II, the Pacific War, key events. http://www.ww2pacific.com/chron.html

The History Place – World War Two in the Pacific, Timeline of Events 1941-1945. https://www.historyplace.com/unitedstates/pacificwar/timeline.htm

Encyclopedia Britannica, 1965 edition, Vol. 12, page 876, JAPAN.

Yearbook of the Fifteenth United States Naval Construction Battalion in the Southwest Pacific, Volume 1, "All This and Twenty Per Cent."

Front and back cover, courtesy of pexels-joeypistachio-3159853

Acknowledgments

Thank you to my husband, Michael, ever by my side, my sister Ellen, born after the war, and my son Bryce for their enthusiastic encouragement and suggestions. In addition, Bryce was my editing advisor. I also thank Tziporah Sofare, MA for her assistance in editing portions of the book.

Michael was my computer guru (I am computer challenged) showing me how to use my various apps, restoring it when it crashed because I hit the wrong key, and for putting up with the mess on my side of the kitchen table, which served as my workspace for all the months it took to complete the book. There were also the old movies that both my mother and father saw during those years for which he tirelessly searched and which we were able to watch together.

"Somewhere" is also an emotional journey into my own past since I was born while my father was thousands of miles away. The letters and journals together with the research answered many questions that I had about those war times, and often brought me to tears. I thank my husband for his patience and interest during the ensuing discussions of my family and the workings thereof. If he ever tired of it, I'll never know. Many, many thanks, Michael, for all the support, for listening, and for all your patience.

Many thanks also go to my Aunt Grace, who was a young girl and took such loving care of me and for sharing her memories during that time. Many thanks as well to my dear friend, Wanda Wolosky for sharing her experiences in writing her own book about the Holocaust, and to my long-time friend Virginia Faulkner, knower of many things, who was so generous in sharing information.

Last but not least, I wish to acknowledge the battalion artist who I am sure is responsible for hand drawing the maps and artwork in the Seabee yearbook. From one artist to another, I sincerely thank Berger Fagenstrom (1914-2003), Painter First Class.

"FAGAN"

San Diego, California

Has been Battalion Artist for over two years . . . to those who know him well, he's "out of this world" . . . has finished a series of water colors depicting Seabee activity in the jungles . . . a student of the drama, concert, and ballet . . . Calif. Chamber of Commerce number one booster . . . unmarried.

BERGER FAGENSTROM, Ptr1/c
Art

Movies

Date Seen			Title	Rating
1/25/44	mom		"Girl Crazy"	
2/2/44	mom		"Destination Tokyo"	very good
2/6/44	mom		"His Butler's Sister"	very good
2/15/44	mom		"The North Star"	good
2/22/44	mom		"A Guy Named Joe"	very good
3/7/44	mom		"Madame Curie"	
3/12/44	mom		"The Fighting Sullivans"	very good
3/23/44	mom		"Gung Ho"	very good
3/26/44	mom		"Song of Russia"	very good
3/29/44	mom		"The Uninvited"	good
3/31/44		dad	"Flying Tigers"	
4/1/44		dad	"Tales Of Manhattan"	
4/8/44		dad	"Always a Bridesmaid"	lousy
4/10/44		dad	"Once Upon a Honeymoon"	
4/11/44		dad	"The Major and the Minor"	
4/13/44		dad	"Swing Your Partner"	fair
4/14/44		dad	"Moonlight Masquerade"	
4/15/44	mom		"Ali Baba and the Forty Thieves"	
4/15/44		dad	"Thousands Cheer"	worst
4/16/44		dad	"Journey Into Fear"	bit of alright
4/17/44		dad	"One Dangerous Night"	quite good for a change
4/18/44		dad	"Journey For Margaret"	swell
4/21/44		dad	"Hi Diddle Diddle"	hell of a picture
4/22/44		dad	"Mrs. Miniver"	
4/23/44	mom		"Shine On Harvest Moon"	
4/24/44		dad	"Thank Your Lucky Stars"	Pretty good
4/29/44	mom		"The Desert Song"	
5/6/44	mom		"The Purple Heart"	
5/7/44	mom		"Cover Girl"	very good
5/10/44		dad	"Stand By For Action"	fair
5/12/44		dad	"Crazy House"	fairly good
5/16/44	mom		"The Fighting Seabees"	very good
5/18/44		dad	"Here Comes Elmer"	lousy
5/21/44	mom		"Follow The Boys"	very good
5/23/44		dad	"Bathing Beauty"	lousy
5/23/44		dad	"Whistling In Brooklyn"	lousy
5/24/44	mom		"Lost Angel"	
5/25/44		dad	"A Night To Remember"	poor
5/29/44		dad	"Son Of Dracula"	not so hot
6/1/44		dad	"A Guy Named Joe"	pretty good
6/5/44		dad	"Standing Room Only"	screwy
6/6/44		dad	"Going My Way"	nice
6/7/44	mom		"White Cliffs Of Dover"	very good
6/9/44	mom		"Uncertain Glory"	Fair

Date	Parent	Parent	Title	Comment
6/11/44		Dad	"Girl Trouble"	
6/14/44		dad	"The Falcon's Brother"	
6/15/44		dad	"The Meanest Man In The World"	rained, didn't go
6/18/44	mom		"Tender Comrade"	Sad
6/19/44		dad	"Campus Rhythm"	Fairly decent
6/22/44		dad	"Swing Out The Blues"	Lousy, with a capital L. Stinker. "Preceded by a gal singing nursery rhymes to us."
6/24/44	mom		"Gaslight"	
6/24/44		dad	"Silver Queen"	really pretty good
6/25/44	mom		"Ladies Courageous"	
6/26/44		dad	"Broadway"	pretty fair
6/27/44		dad	"Moonlight In Vermont"	pretty good but nothing to write home about.
6/29/44	mom		"Snow White"	
6/28/44		dad	A Shirley Temple Movie. Dad didn't remember the title.	
6/29/44		dad	"Gung Ho"	
6/30/44		dad	"Captains Courageous"	very good
7/2/44	mom		"See Here, Private Hargrove"	very good
7/4/44		dad	"The Uninvited:	a stinker
7/5/44		dad	"Always In My Heart"	saw it on Santos
7/7/44		dad	"Up In Arms"	pretty good
7/8/44		dad	"Salute To The Marines"	pretty good
7/9/44		dad	"Destination Tokyo"	
7/11/44		dad	"Nine Girls"	lousy
7/11/44	mom		"Cobra Woman"	good
7/12/44		dad	"Crime Doctor"	
7/13/44	mom		"Christmas Holiday"	didn't like it
7/25/44	mom		"Dragon Seed"	good
8/6/44	mom		"Going My Way"	
8/17/44	mom		"Two Girls And A Sailor"	
11/17/44	mom		"Gypsy Wildcat"	
11/26/44	mom		"Together Again"	
12/9/44	mom		"Marriage Is A Private Affair"	good
12/23/44		dad	"Song Of Bernadette"	very good [Actually, Dad RAVED about this movie!!]
12/28/44	mom		"Kismet"	good
1/5/45	mom		"An American Romance"	very good
1/6/45	mom		"The Student Prince" at Papermill Playhouse	very good
1/8/45	mom		"I Love A Soldier"	very good
1/14/45	mom		"Mrs. Parkington"	good
1/17/45	mom		"The Climax"	very good
1/20/45	mom		"Winged Victory"	very good, sad

1/21/45	mom		"Thirty Seconds Over Tokyo"	very good
1/29/45	mom		"Hollywood Canteen"	good
2/18/45	mom		"Frenchman's Creek"	good
2/25/45	mom		"Music For Millions"	very good
2/27/45	mom		"A Song To Remember"	good
3/4/45	mom		"And Now Tomorrow"	
4/1/45	mom	dad	"Sunday Dinner For A Soldier"	both enjoyed it
4/6/45	mom	dad	"Belle Of The Yukon"	
4/6/45	mom	dad	"Keys Of The Kingdom"	
4/7/45	mom	dad	"I'll Be Seeing You"	good
4/11/45	mom	dad	"Can't Help Singing"	pretty good
4/22/45	mom	dad	"Bring On The Girls"	
4/22/45	mom	dad	"Crime Doctor"	
4/22/45	mom	dad	"Eadie Was A Lady"	very good
4/29/45	mom	dad	"Meet Me In St. Louis"	swell
5/6/45	mom	dad	"Naughty Marietta"	very good
5/12/45	mom	dad	"Forever Yours"	good
5/15/45	mom		"Here Come The Waves"	NOT enjoyable
5/20/45	mom	dad	"A Guy, A Gall, and A Pal"	
5/20/45	mom	dad	"The Three Caballeros"	not much good
6/14/45	mom	dad	"Bring On The Girls"	pretty good
6/17/45	mom		"The Affairs Of Susan"	pretty good
June	Mary		"The Corn Is Green" BettyDavis	good one
6/15/45	Mary		"The Picture Of Dorian Grey"	superb acting
6/29/45	mom		"Without Love"	very good
7/4/45	mom		"Valley Of Decision"	very good/not as good as book
7/12/45	mom		"The Clock"	good
7/22/45	mom		"Counter-Attack"	very good
7/22/45	mom		"Gentle Annie"	very good
7/31/45	mom		"The Corn Is Green"	very good
8/5/45	mom		"Thrill Of A Romance"	very good
8/15/45	mom		"Junior Miss"	very enjoyable
8/17/45	mom		"Nob Hill"	very good
8/19/45	mom		"A Bell For Adano"	good
8/20/45	mom		"A Tree Grows In Brooklyn"	very good
8/27/45	mom		"The Keys Of The Kingdom"	very good
9/4/45	mom		"Song Of Bernadette"	
9/7/45	mom		"The Fighting Guardsman"	not so good
9/7/45	mom		"I Love A Bandleader"	not so good
9/9/45	mom		"Christmas In Connecticut"	pretty good
9/17/45	mom		"You Came Along"	very good
9/22/45	mom		"Out Of This World"	good
9/22/45	mom		"Escape In The Fog"	good
9/27/45	mom		"A Thousand And One Nights"	very good
9/27/45	mom		"A Close Call For Boston Blackie"	very good
9/30/45	mom		"Lady On A Train"	
9/30/45	mom		"The Beautiful Cheat"	

10/5/45	mom		"The Strange Affair of UncleHarry"	
10/7/45	mom		"State Fair"	very entertaining
10/12/45	mom		"Mildred Pierce"	good
10/22/45	both		"Anchors Aweigh"	very good
11/10/45	both		"Love Letters"	very good
11/12/45	both		"Pinocchio"	
11/16/45	both		"Our Vines Have Tender Grapes"	very, very good
11/27/45	both		"The Spanish Main"	good
11/30/45	both		"Her Highness And The Bellboy	
12/4/45	both		"Guest Wife"	pretty good
12/20/45	both		"That Night With You"	
12/28/45	both		"Kiss And Tell"	very comical.
				Johnny liked it.

Reviews

The story made me feel like one of the family coping with being separated from the people you love in a world where the best you can hope for is a few handwritten paragraphs of reassurance that everything in the world is somehow okay, even though it is not. It's every family's story of courage, perseverance, and hopefulness at a time when we needed these virtues the most. It's simple and straightforward storytelling that puts the reader right at the mailbox, hoping that there will be another letter from Johnny or Lou reaffirming the normalcy of what were very abnormal   times.

Dominick Mancuso, CPA and attorney, States of New Jersey, New York, and Texas

Within this historical accounting, "Somewhere In The South Pacific" has something of substance to impart. It is a rich mosaic of letters, photos, historical facts, longing, love, fear, and secrecy during a time of total war. Leina'ala Schwartz's book is a gift for all who read it!

Salli Katz, educator, fundraiser Gilda's Club, Civic activist for underserved children

"Somewhere" combines the events of WW2 in the Pacific with the love story of Johnny and Lucia de Roxtro. The author includes the events of Johnny's U.S. Navy service as a Seabee in the 15th U.S. Naval Construction Battalion, and along with the letters and journal entries, provides a snapshot of the stories of hundreds of thousands of the The Greatest Generation who sacrificed so much in order that our present was preserved. The loving manner in which this story is written caused me to feel as if I knew this family.

Arnold S. Lazarow retired mediator, Superior Court of New Jersey, Family Division

About the Author

Leina'ala is a multi-media fine artist concentrating in oils. She holds degrees in Accounting and Taxation from Fairleigh Dickinson and Seton Hall Universities, respectively. She also holds an Associate Degree in Fine Art from County College of Morris, having graduated summa cum laude and she is a member of Phi Theta Kappa. She is ordained as an interfaith minister by the All Faiths Seminary in New York City. She was a certified personal fitness trainer for 20 years, assisting clients with fitness goals as a means of finding their self-truths and personal affirmations. She is a pianist, songwriter, actor, spiritualist, and all around good storyteller.

Leina'ala is passionate about family history and genealogy and knowing who we are and where we come from. She is the family historian and passes down family stories told to her by her grandmother.

She lives in Mendham, New Jersey, with her husband Michael Schwartz, whom she first met in kindergarten.

Somewhere is her first book.

$30.00
ISBN 978-0-578-93692-5
53000>

9 780578 936925

CPSIA information can be obtained
at www.ICGtesting.com
Printed in the USA
BVHW050358060921
616105BV00002B/3